D1544416

Project
Dinosaur

THE PROJECT MAKERS

Steve Parker

WINDMILL
BOOKS ™

Published in 2020 by Windmill Books,
an imprint of Rosen Publishing
29 East 21st Street, New York, NY 10010

Copyright © 2020 Miles Kelly Publishing

Publishing Director: Belinda Gallagher
Creative Director: Jo Cowan
Editorial Director: Rosie Neave
Designers: Joe Jones, Andrea Slane
Projects: Author Gillian Chapman
Indexer: Jane Parker
Image Manager: Liberty Newton
Production: Elizabeth Collins, Caroline Kelly
Reprographics: Stephan Davis, Jennifer Cozens, Thom Allaway
Assets: Lorraine King

Cataloging-in-Publication Data

Names: Parker, Steve.
Title: Project dinosaur / Steve Parker.
Description: New York : Windmill Books, 2020. | Series: The project makers
| Includes index.
Identifiers: ISBN 9781538392294 (pbk.) | ISBN 9781725393042 (library bound)
| ISBN 9781538392300 (6 pack)
Subjects: LCSH: Dinosaurs--Juvenile literature. | Handicraft--Juvenile literature.
Classification: LCC QE861.5 P35 2019 | DDC 567.9--dc23

Manufactured in the United States of America

CPSIA Compliance Information: Batch #BW20WM:
For Further Information contact Rosen Publishing,
New York, New York at 1-800-237-9932

How to use the projects

This book is packed full of amazing facts about dinosaurs. There are also 11 cool projects, designed to make the subject come alive.

Before you start a project:

- Always ask an adult to help you.

- Read the instructions carefully.

- Gather all the supplies you need.

- Clear a surface to work on and cover it with newspaper.

- Wear an apron or old T-shirt to protect your clothing.

Notes for helpers:

- Children will need supervision for the projects, usually because they require the use of scissors, or preparation beforehand.

- Read the instructions together before starting and help to gather the equipment.

IMPORTANT NOTICE
The publisher and author cannot be held responsible for any injuries, damage, or loss resulting from the use or misuse of any of the information in this book.

SAFETY FIRST!
Be careful when using glue or anything sharp, such as scissors.

How to use:
If your project doesn't work the first time, try again – just have fun!

Supplies:
The equipment should be easy to find around the house or from a craft store. Always ask before using materials from home.

Numbered stages:
Some stages of the project are numbered and illustrated. Follow the stages in the order shown to complete the project. If glue or paint is used, make sure it is dry before moving on to the next stage.

T. rex puppet!

Make a *T. rex* snarl and bite to show off his teeth!

SUPPLIES
pencil • white card stock • tracing paper • coloring pencils or felt-tip pens • scissors • three split pins • two wooden dowels about 12 inches (30 cm) long • tape

1. Copy the picture of the *T. rex* adult on this page onto the card stock.

2. Trace the *T. rex* outline without the back legs and lower jaw. Transfer onto card stock, color in and cut out.

3. Trace the outlines of the back legs and lower jaw and transfer them onto the card stock. Add a 1-inch (3 cm) tab where each piece will attach to the body. Color in and cut out.

4. Attach the back legs to the body and the jaw to the neck with split pins, making sure the pieces move freely.

5. Tape the dowels to the back of the body and the lower jaw.

HOW TO USE
T. rex is supported by the dowel attached to the body. The other dowel moves the jaw up and down. The legs will move when you shake the puppet!

CONTENTS

DINOSAURS ARRIVE

Dinosaurs were among the biggest, fiercest animals ever to walk the Earth. Some were giant plant chewers, larger than a house. Others were mini bug munchers, smaller than a pet cat. The first dinosaurs lived over 230 million years ago, and they ruled the land for more than 170 million years.

Dinosaurs had straight legs positioned directly under the body, unlike the bent, sprawling legs of reptiles such as crocodiles. This positioning allowed dinosaurs to run quickly.

Plateosaurus

VICTORINO DINO

One of the first dinosaurs was *Herrerasaurus*, which lived in Argentina, South America, about 231 million years ago. It was about 10 feet (3 m) long including its tail, ran fast on its two back legs, and chased small creatures to eat. *Herrerasaurus* is named after local farmer and part-time fossil hunter Victorino Herrera, who found its remains in 1959.

Silesaurus, a close relative of dinosaurs

Herrerasaurus

The first dinos

Dinosaurs are small but grow, evolve, and spread	Dinosaurs become larger, especially in North America	The biggest-ever dinosaurs live in South America and Africa	Great dinosaurs have died out but some survive – as birds	Birds spread all around the world to every continent	Avian dinosaurs live on – we call them birds
TRIASSIC 252–201 mya	**JURASSIC** 201–145 mya	**CRETACEOUS** 145–66 mya	**PALEOGENE** 66–23 mya	**NEOGENE** 23–2.6 mya	**QUATERNARY** 2.6 mya–now

SMALL AND SPEEDY

About 200 million years ago, *Coelophysis* lived in North America. Around 8 feet (2.5 m) in length, it was slim and speedy, with a long bendy neck and whippy tail. Its small, sharp, curved teeth show that it ate bugs, worms, small reptiles, and similar animals, which it grabbed with its hands and clawed fingers.

Coelophysis had big eyes and could see well. In its mouth were about 50 pointed, back-curved teeth. It may have moved around in groups.

Long tail

Long neck

Long muscular legs

DEATH AT GHOST RANCH

In 1947, over 1,000 fossils of *Coelophysis* were found at a place called Ghost Ranch in New Mexico. It seems they all died together. Maybe they were traveling and feeding in a group that was swept away by a flash flood.

Supercontinent!

HOW TO MAKE

1. Using the map at the back of the book, trace the outlines of North America, South America, Eurasia, Africa, India (which was once a subcontinent), Australia, and Antarctica.

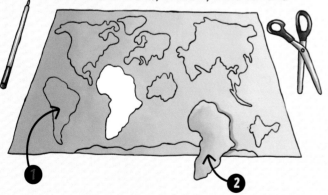

2. Transfer the outlines onto green card stock and carefully cut them out. Use a felt-tip pen to label them with their names and stick a magnet to the back of each.

Over millions of years, Pangaea broke apart into separate landmasses. You can see the rough shapes of today's continents below. India is classed as a subcontinent – today it is part of Asia.

EURASIA
(EUROPE AND ASIA
JOINED TOGETHER)

PANGAEA

NORTH AMERICA

PANTHALASSA OCEAN

AFRICA

SOUTH AMERICA

INDIA

ANTARCTICA

AUSTRALIA

5

GETTING BIGGER

As time passes, all living things change or evolve. Dinosaurs did, too. They spread and evolved into new and different kinds, many much bigger than the early dinosaurs. Some took to eating plants while others became strong, fast, fierce hunters.

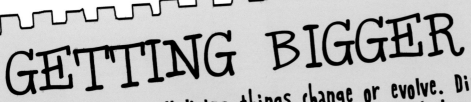

Plateosaurus

Eustreptospondylus

GIANT JAWS

A fearsome carnivore (meat eater), *Eustreptospondylus* prowled England 165 million years ago. Up to 20 feet (6 m) long, it had a large head with strong jaws to attack and tear up victims. Some fossils show it may have hunted along the shore for fish and other water creatures.

LONG NECK

Plateosaurus chewed plants about 210 million years ago in Europe. It was one of the first really big dinosaurs, at 33 feet (10 m) in length and a weight of 4.4 tons (4 t). Its long neck allowed it to reach far around or even up into trees to gather leaves and similar foods.

LUMPY BACK

Around 13 feet (4 m) long and weighing 661 pounds (300 kg), small-headed *Scelidosaurus* was a tough-looking herbivore (plant eater). It plodded around the British Isles 190 million years ago. The ridged bony lumps called scutes along its back, sides, legs, and tail protected it against attacks by predatory dinosaurs.

Scelidosaurus

6

PLATE HEAD

About 192 million years ago, *Dilophosaurus* roamed North America. Up to 23 feet (7 m) long and weighing half a ton, it was one of the biggest meat eaters of its time. Its strange crest of bone looked like two half dinner plates sticking out of its head! No one knows what it was for.

Dilophosaurus

BONY CLUES

One of the best-known dinosaurs, remains of more than 100 *Plateosaurus* have been found in Europe, including all parts of the skeleton. Knowing about dinosaurs such as *Plateosaurus* helps experts to fill in missing parts of similar dinosaurs, for which fewer fossils have been found.

BIRD-HIPPED DINOSAUR

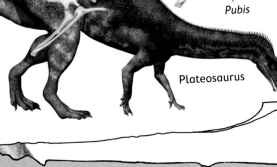

In ornithischians, the pubis part of the hip bone (pelvis) pointed down and backwards.

Pubis

Plateosaurus

Fossil footprints

Make fossil footprints of a giant dino plant eater and a speedy dino predator.

SUPPLIES

plasticine-type modeling material • small (popsicle) sticks • tray of clean, damp sand • plaster mix, water, spoon, bowl

1. Make a pair of *Diplodocus* feet. Shape two lumps of plasticine into the left and right feet of this plodding plant eater, which had four large, round-shaped feet, each with four toes and one big claw.

2. Make a pair of *Allosaurus* feet. Shape two lumps of plasticine into the left and right feet of this fast meat,eater, which ran on two legs with three long, spread-out toes.

3. Push a stick into each plasticine foot to make handles.

4. Press the plasticine feet into the sand to make dinosaur tracks.

5. Then follow the instructions on the pack of plaster mix and mix up some plaster in the bowl. Use it to make casts of the different dinosaur footprints.

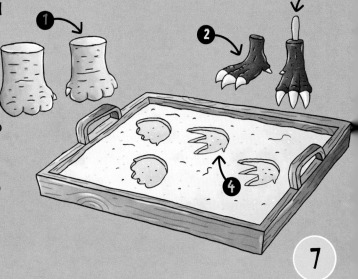

JURASSIC GIANTS

Some of the most enormous dinosaurs lived toward the end of the Jurassic Period, 155–150 million years ago. At this time the Earth was warm and damp, with enormous forests covering much of the land. Dinosaur herbivores had plenty to eat – and they in turn were food for dinosaur carnivores.

ALL NECK AND TAIL

At over 98 feet (30 m), *Diplodocus* was one of the longest dinosaurs. But most of this was extended neck and whip-like tail. Its body wasn't huge, at 11–13 tons (10–12 t) in weight. It probably couldn't lift its head high to feed, so ate low-growing plants.

Upright crest on neck

HEAD OUTSIDE

Like all sauropods, *Brachiosaurus* had a tiny head compared to its body. It would feed for many hours each day, to gather enough plant food. Its nostrils led into a large, bulging chamber on its snout and its eyes were not much bigger than yours!

DINO GIRAFFE

One of the biggest-ever dinosaurs, *Brachiosaurus* weighed a massive 38-plus tons (35 t). Like others in its sauropod group, it had a small head, long neck, and long tail. Unlike other sauropods, its front legs were longer than its back legs, so its back sloped down like a giraffe's.

Cookie monsters!

Sauropods needed to feed for many hours each day to survive! These delicious dinosaur cookies will be eaten up fast by all your friends – so make plenty! This recipe makes about 24 cookies.

SUPPLIES

8 ounces (225g) butter (softened) • 4 ounces (110g) caster sugar • 1 egg yolk • 2 tsp vanilla extract • 9.7 ounces (275g) plain flour • large bowl • wooden spoon • sieve • nonstick baking tray • small plastic dinosaur toys • preheated oven at 340° Fahrenheit (170°C) • cooling rack • Some adult help to use the oven

HOW TO MAKE

1. Cream the butter and sugar together in the bowl using the wooden spoon until light and fluffy. Beat in the egg yolk and the vanilla extract.

2. Sift in the flour and stir well. You may need to work the dough with your hands to give it a really good mix!

3. Roll 1-inch (3 cm) balls of dough and place on the baking tray, flattening them slightly.

4. Press the plastic dinosaurs into each cookie to make different impressions.

5. Bake in the oven for 12–15 minutes or until golden brown. Place them on a rack to cool before eating.

Make sure the plastic dinosaurs are spotlessly clean before pressing them into the cookies! Just use the head or footprints of larger toys to make impressions in the cookies.

The legs of *Diplodocus* were strong and long. These giants often had to travel to find new food.

Spreading out

The second part of the Mesozoic Era is called the Jurassic Period. This lasted from 201–145 million years ago.

Move the continents on your world map (page 5) to their position during the end of the Jurassic Period (above). Most are still close together, allowing land animals to spread easily.

TRIASSIC	JURASSIC	CRETACEOUS	PALEOGENE	NEOGENE	QUATERNARY
252–201 mya	201–145 mya	145–66 mya	66–23 mya	23–2.6 mya	2.6 mya–now

FEATHERS, FLUFF, FUZZ

Fossil hunters have now found many kinds of dinosaurs with coverings of feathers. Some had flight feathers like those on a bird's wings. Some had soft fluff, like a bird's down feathers. Some had fuzzy, hair-like strands. And some dinosaurs had all three kinds!

Filament-like feathers on hips and tail

BIGGEST WITH FEATHERS

Yutyrannus was a huge hunter from China around 124 million years ago. A relative of the great *Tyrannosaurus*, it wasn't much smaller – 30 feet (9 m) long and 1.6 tons (1.5 t) in weight. It is the biggest dinosaur known with feathers, which were up to 8 inches (20 cm) long.

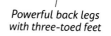
Powerful back legs with three-toed feet

Large toe claws

TWO-LEGGED RUNNER

Microraptor was a small meat eater, just 30 inches (75 cm) long, from China 120 million years ago. It had feathers all over its body, from head to tail – even its back legs. This made running on the ground awkward. But in the air...

Yutyrannus had a narrow bony crest sticking up along the middle of its snout, and a strange outward-pointing, bony horn near each eye.

Long, strand-like feathers on neck

Over 50 sharp teeth

Tiny arms

SMALLEST WITH FEATHERS

One of the smallest feathery dinosaurs was *Mei*, at just 20 inches (50 cm) long. It had feathers on its head, body, legs, and bony tail, and its teeth were small, sharp, and close-set for eating small creatures. It was preserved with its head tucked under one arm – like a sleeping bird.

Feathery timeline

New feathered or fluffy dinosaurs are discovered almost every year.

1861: First fossils of the feathery bird Archaeopteryx

1998: Peacock-like Caudipteryx

1999: Scythe-claw Beipiaosaurus

Micro-glider

SUPPLIES

strips of thick card stock 20 in x 2 in (50 cm x 5 cm), 12 in x 2 in (30 cm x 5 cm), 8 in x 2 in (20 cm x 5 cm) • 4 elastic bands • sheets of colored paper • scissors • glue stick • colored pencils/felt-tip pens

HOW TO MAKE

1. Place the two smaller strips across the longer body strip to make the body and 4 wings. Criss-cross two elastic bands at each junction point to secure the wings, with the longer pair near the head.

2. Cut lots of feather shapes from the colored paper and glue them along the wings, overlapping slightly. Put the same number on each side of each pair of wings for balance. Glue feathers to the tail end.

3. Cut the head of the glider into a point to make the beak. Add the eyes and color the rest of the body.

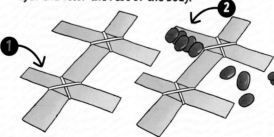

HOW TO USE

Hold the Micro-glider about 3 ft (1 m) off the ground and gently throw it forward. If it nose-dives, move the back wings towards the tail. If it rises and then crashes, move them slightly forwards. If it doesn't glide, turn it into a Micro-mobile!

11

FAMILY LIFE

Most reptiles today breed by laying eggs, which hatch into babies. Dinosaurs, which were also reptiles, did the same. Fossils show that some dinosaurs made nests for their eggs, looked after them as they developed, and even brought food for their babies!

GOOD MOTHERS

Maiasaura was a plant eater about 23 feet (7 m) long that lived 77 million years ago in North America. Its name means "good mother lizard." Fossils of hundreds of adults, nests, eggs, babies, and young show that many Maiasaura raised their families in one area, called a breeding colony.

How old?

Some dinosaur fossils have rings in the bones, like trees have in their trunks. Using these and other clues, experts can estimate their life spans.

Small dinosaurs:
5–7 years

Medium-sized dinosaurs: 10–20 years

Big meat eaters:
30–40 years

Medium-large plant eaters:
20–30 years

Horned and armored dinosaurs:
30–50 years

Giant plant eaters:
70–100 years

Each Maiasaura parent made a nest that was far enough from others in the breeding group, or colony, so the eggs did not get stepped on or stolen.

Each nest was a scoop of earth hollowed out with a raised rim, containing up to 40 eggs

The parent covered the eggs with old plants, which gave off heat as they rotted to keep the eggs warm

Eggs and nest

4. Once dry, paint the eggs. Use any color you like, as no one knows what color dinosaur eggs were.

5. Scrunch up pieces of colored sugar paper to make a nest for the eggs. Cut out paper leaf shapes to cover the eggs.

SUPPLIES

balloons • small plastic dinosaur toys • newspaper • PVA and glue brush • acrylic paints for decoration and paintbrush • sheets of green and brown sugar paper • scissors

HOW TO MAKE

1. Stretch the neck of a balloon open and carefully put a small dinosaur toy inside. Blow up the balloon and knot the end.

2. Tear sheets of newspaper into strips and cover the balloon with two layers using the glue. Make sure you don't cover the knotted end of the balloon. Leave to dry. Make as many eggs as you like!

3. Once dry, holding onto the knot, pop the balloon and pull it out from the inside the egg. Cover over the hole with pieces of glued newspaper. Leave to dry.

HOW TO USE

Listen to the baby dinosaurs moving inside their eggs when you shake them – when you think they are ready to hatch, break open the shells.

WELL-FED BABIES

The newly hatched babies were 16 inches (40 cm) long. Their bones were not strong enough for them to walk or run. However, their teeth had signs of wear from eating. This could mean the parents brought food to them in the nest.

DINO GANG

Psittacosaurus was a small, parrot-beaked, plant-eating dinosaur that lived in East Asia 120 million years ago. One amazing set of fossils shows a group of about 30 young *Psittacosaurus* that died together, perhaps when a cave they were sheltering in collapsed.

The nests were 16-22 ft (5–7 m) apart, enough room for parents to walk between them

SEAS AND SKIES

During the Dinosaur Age, other great creatures flew high in the sky and swam in the sea. Like the dinosaurs, these creatures were reptiles. Some were as huge and fearsome as the dinosaurs themselves.

RHAMPHORHYNCHUS

This long-tailed pterosaur was a winged reptile, and the wings were thin skin stretched between very long finger bones. Its long, thin, sharp teeth probably grabbed fish from the water.

Size: Wingspan 6 feet (1.8 m)
Time: 150 million years ago
Place: British Isles

ELASMOSAURUS

A type of sea reptile called a plesiosaur, *Elasmosaurus* had long, sharp teeth that it probably used to spear fish and squid. Almost half of its total body length was made up by its neck, which probably wasn't particularly flexible.

Length: 46 feet (14 m)
Time: 80 million years ago
Place: North America

LIOPLEURODON

With four big, paddle-shaped limbs, *Liopleurodon* was a fast, sleek swimmer. Its massive mouth and pointed fangs probably tore apart large victims such as ichthyosaurs and big fish.

Length: 23 feet (7 m)
Time: 150 million years ago
Place: Europe

Too cool!

The biggest flying animal of all time was the pterosaur *Quetzalcoatlus* from 70 million years ago. With a nose-to-tail length of 30 feet (9 m), its wings spanned 36 feet (11 m) – three times more than today's longest-winged bird, the albatross.

ARCHAEOPTERYX
The earliest known true bird was Archaeopteryx. Unlike modern birds it had teeth, claws on its wings, and a long, bony tail. But its wings and feathers were designed for proper flight.

Size: Wingspan 24 inches (60 cm)
Time: 150 million years ago
Place: Germany

PTERANODON
Pteranodon was one of the biggest short-tailed pterosaurs. It had a long beak, no teeth, and a tall, pointed bony crest. It probably soared over the sea, snatching fish and similar creatures.

Size: Wingspan 20 feet (6 m)
Time: 85 million years ago
Place: North America

The biggest sea reptile of all time was *Shastasaurus*, from the ichthyosaur group, 210 million years ago. At 66 feet (20 m) long, it was almost as huge as today's great whales. It probably ate small fish and squid.

MOSASAURUS
This huge reptile was a close relative of today's monitor lizards. Its flipper-limbs were quite small, so it probably powered through the ocean by swishing its long tail from side to side, hunting all kinds of prey.

Length: 56 feet (17 m)
Time: 85 million years ago
Place: North America

15

MEGA KILLERS

These dinosaurs from the middle of the Dinosaur Age were some of the the biggest, fiercest, and most cunning predators. They lived around the world and hunted many kinds of victims, both massive and tiny.

SPINOSAURUS
The biggest meat-eating dinosaur, it lived 100 million years ago in North Africa. Its long skull was similar to today's crocodiles and it probably hunted fish in rivers and lakes that existed in North Africa at that time.

Length: 49 feet (15 m)
Weight: 15 tons (14 t)

Not all meat-eating dinosaurs were big, such as *Spinosaurus*. Some, such as *Troodon*, were small, fast killers.

Sharp, piercing teeth, longer around the front of the jaw

SAIL-BACKED SPINO

Spinosaurus had tall rods of bone, some almost 6.5 feet (2 m) long, sticking up from its backbone. The rods may have held up a large "sail" of skin. Perhaps this helped the dinosaur control its body temperature. Or it could have been colored to show off to rivals, enemies, and mates.

Blood vessels spread over bony rods in the sail to carry heat away and regulate body temperature

16

DEINONYCHUS
This medium-sized raptor dinosaur lived 110 million years ago in North America. Some fossils reveal a group that died together - perhaps a pack that was hunting for food.

Length: 11 feet (3.5 m)
Weight: 198 pounds (90 kg)

UTAHRAPTOR
Raptor dinosaurs had ferocious weapons in the form of a sharp, curved claw on the second toe of each foot. *Utahraptor's* claw measured 11 inches (28 cm) around the curve. This was the biggest raptor, and it lived in North America 126 million years ago.

Length: 23 feet (7 m)
Weight: 882 pounds (400 kg)

Long, slim jaws joined at the back of the head to allow the mouth to open wide

Utahraptor probably had feathers on its body and limbs

RAPTOR CLAW
The second toe claw of a raptor was held up off the ground when walking and running. It may have been used to slash larger prey, causing it to bleed to death. A newer idea is that the claw held down small victims as the raptor bit and tore them with its teeth.

17

Large brain in
braincase at the
back of the head

TROODON
A small, slim raptor-type
dinosaur, *Troodon* lived about
70 million years ago in
North America. It had a
large brain for its small size,
which could mean it was one
of the most intelligent and
cunning of all dinosaurs.

Length: 8 feet (2.5 m)
Weight: 88 pounds (40 kg)

Giant curved claw
on second toe

Huge, deep skull and lower jawbone, with powerful muscles

Slim, pointed snout with relatively small teeth, indicating medium-sized prey

BARYONYX
Slim and low-headed, Baryonyx is famous for its enormous thumb claw over 12 inches (30 cm) long. It lurked in swamps in England 120 million years ago, probably using the thumb claw to hook fish from the water into its crocodile-like jaws.

Length: 33 feet (10 m)
Weight: 2.2 tons (2 t)

GIGANOTOSAURUS
Living 100 million years ago in Argentina, *Giganotosaurus* had giant jaws and teeth in its 5.5-foot (1.7 m) head. It could have tackled the biggest dinosaur, *Argentinosaurus*, which lived around the same time and place.

Length: 43 feet (13 m)
Weight: 8.8 tons (8 t)

Biggest killer stats

Land predator:
Spinosaurus

Mouth and teeth:
Giganotosaurus

Thumb claw:
Baryonyx

Raptor dino:
Utahraptor

Pack hunter:
Deinonychus

Brain power:
Troodon

HORNS AND ARMOR

Two groups of dinosaurs were far from being fast and agile. Instead they were big, slow, heavy, and well protected. They were the ceratopsians, or horn-faced dinosaurs, and the armored ankylosaurs – dinosaur versions of today's armadillos and rhinos.

Body and tail covered in lumps and spikes of bone armor

SPIKES AND LUMPS

Edmontonia lived 70 million years ago in North America, and grew to a length of 23 feet (7 m). It had hard lumps of bone on its head, back, and tail, with rows of spikes along its neck and sides. Its low head meant it could eat only plants at ground level.

Scary horn-face mask

Make a *Triceratops* mask and scare your friends!

SUPPLIES

paper and pencil • big board or tray • plasticine-type modeling material • petroleum jelly • newspaper • PVA glue and brush • craft knife • elastic • acrylic paints and paintbrush

1. Look at the pictures of *Triceratops* on page 21. Sketch a mask design on the paper, making it slightly bigger than your face. Draw in the eyes, nose, horns, and wavy neck frill.

2. With the plasticine, create a 3-D head shape on the board, following your sketch.

3. Build up the features on the face, plus the horns and neck frill, using lumps of plasticine, making the mask 3-D.

4. Coat the plasticine mold with petroleum jelly. Tear up the newspaper and cover the mold with four layers of small, glued pieces. Leave to dry.

5. Remove the dried mask from the mold. Wipe off any excess petroleum jelly from the back.

6. Following your design, ask an adult to cut holes for the eyes with the knife (make sure they align with your eyes). Make two small holes in each side of the mask and thread elastic through to hold the mask on your head. Paint your mask.

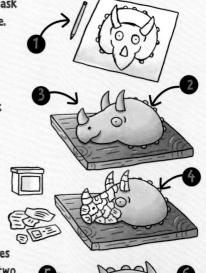

HOW TO USE
Wear your mask and practice scary roars in the mirror. Get your friends to make more masks for a dino-party!

Triceratops may have fought for mates at breeding time

Because of their horns and armor, these dinosaurs were much heavier than others of the same length.

Triceratops
Length: 30 ft (9 m)
Weight: 11 tons (10 t)

Riojasaurus:
Length: 30 ft (9 m)
Weight: 2.2 tons (2 t)

Edmontonia
Length: 23 ft (7 m)
Weight: 4.4 tons (4 t)

Utahraptor
Length: 23 ft (7 m)
Weight: .44 ton (0.4 t)

Minmi:
Length: 6.5 ft (2 m)
Weight: 1,102 lbs (500 kg)

Oviraptor:
Length: 6.5 ft (2 m)
Weight: 66 lbs (30 kg)

FRILLS AND HORNS

Triceratops was the biggest horn-faced dinosaur – 30 feet (9 m) long from its beak-like mouth to the tip of its tail. It had two three-foot-long eyebrow horns, a short nose horn, and a wide frill of bone around its neck. It lived in North America 66 million years ago.

ARMOR OUTSIDE

Euoplocephalus lived 75 million years ago in North America. It was 20 feet (6 m) long, and its body was low and wide. Almost every part of it had a hard covering of bone, including its face. Even the eyelids had tough shields, like bony shutters!

HEAVYWEIGHT CHEWERS

Ceratopsians and ankylosaurs were all plant eaters. They snipped off leaves, buds, and twigs with the beak-like front part of the mouth. It did not matter that they were slow-moving – their food did not run away!

21

HERDS AND HONKS

Ornithopod means bird-foot, and the ornithopod dinosaurs were named after their bird-like feet. Most were medium to large plant eaters that walked on strong back legs. They include some of the best known of all dinosaurs – and the noisiest!

FOSSIL CLUES

Hundreds of fossil *Iguanodon* have been found, especially in Europe, so experts know a lot about this dinosaur. It lived 125 million years ago and grew to 33 feet (10 m) in length and 3.3 tons (3 t) in weight. Some fossils include adults and young of various ages. They were probably a herd on the move when they suffered a disaster, such as a sudden flood or deadly fumes from a volcano.

A big herd of *Iguanodon* would quickly eat all the plants in an area, so they probably moved long distances to find fresh food. This is called migration. Many animals, such as caribou and zebras, migrate today.

Iguanodon could rear up on its back legs to get a better view of its surroundings

Air taken into nostrils to detect scents

PROTECTED BABIES

Fossil footprints show *Iguanodon* could run on two legs or bound along on four. They also show how youngsters remained in the middle of the group, protected from enemies by adults on the outside.

Dino-saurchestra!

Hum, honk, whistle, or roar into these trumpet and didgeridoo mouthpieces to make dino noises!

SUPPLIES

To make the TRUMPET: large piece of colored card stock • tape • scissors

To make the DIDGERIDOO: large cardboard tube (bigger is better) • acrylic paint and paintbrush • colored craft foam • scissors • glue stick

To make the CASTANETS: thick card stock 3 in x 8 in (8 cm x 20 cm) • PVA glue and brush • two large buttons

HOW TO MAKE

1. To make the trumpet, roll the card stock into a funnel shape, with a small hole at one end. Firmly tape the card stock together along the seam. Trim away the excess card stock around the large open end.

2. To make the didgeridoo, paint the large tube and leave to dry. Cut lots of scales from the craft foam. Use the glue stick to glue them all over the didgeridoo for decoration.

3. To make the castanets, fold the piece of card stock in half. Glue a button to the center of each inside half with PVA and leave to dry.

HOW TO USE

Pinch the castanets between your fingers and thumb to get a clacking noise like dinosaurs approaching. Hum and roar into the trumpet and didgeridoo to make dino music!

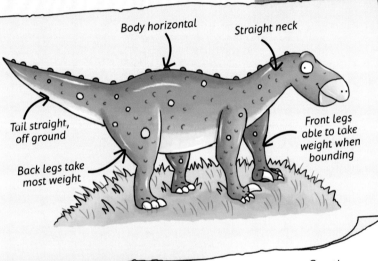

Body horizontal

Straight neck

Tail straight, off ground

Back legs take most weight

Front legs able to take weight when bounding

Parasaurolophus:
Long, curving crest 59 inches (150 cm) high

Corythosaurus:
Tall, helmet-like crest 20 inches (50 cm) high

Lambeosaurus:
Tall, oblong front crest 16 inches (40 cm) high with smaller tube behind

THE DUCKBILLS

The ornithopods called hadrosaurs, or duckbill dinosaurs, had a wide, flat front to the mouth, like a duck's beak. Some also had strange-shaped head crests of hollow bone. Maybe they blew air through these crests to make sounds such as honks, hoots, and bellows at breeding time, or to scare off enemies.

BUILT FOR SPEED

The fastest dinosaurs were slim and light, with a long neck and tail and long, powerful back legs to help them run fast. This body shape is similar to today's biggest bird, the fast-running ostrich, which is why these dinosaurs are called ostrich dinosaurs (ornithomimosaurs).

Beak-shaped mouth

Slim, lightweight body

DINO CHICKEN

Long tail for balance

One of the biggest ostrich-dinosaurs was *Gallimimus*, which lived 70 million years ago in Mongolia. It was 26 feet (8 m) long, stood 10 feet (3 m) high, and weighed over 441 pounds (200 kg). Its name means "chicken mimic" – that's a very big chicken!

Gallimimus's long, clawed fingers could dig up food such as worms and bugs.

Struthiomimus was 6.5 feet (2 m) tall and weighed around 330 pounds (150 kg). About the same as...

The rhea of South America is almost as tall, at 5.6 ft (1.7 m)

Australia's emu is another nonflying, fast-running bird, at 6.2 ft (1.9 m) tall

Powerful leg muscles

The cassowary of Australia and New Guinea is up to 6 ft (1.8 m) tall

EURASIA
N. AMERICA
AFRICA
S. AMERICA
INDIA
ANTARCTICA
AUSTRALIA

Dino world

The third part of the Mesozoic Era is called the Cretaceous Period. It lasted from 145–66 million years ago. During this period, dinosaurs became bigger, faster, and more varied than ever before.

Move the continents on your world map (page 5) to their position at the end of the Cretaceous Period. They are farther apart, meaning dinosaurs evolved separately on huge "islands."

TRIASSIC 252–201 mya	JURASSIC 201–145 mya	CRETACEOUS 145–66 mya	PALEOGENE 66–23 mya	NEOGENE 23–2.6 mya	QUATERNARY 2.6 mya–now

FOOD FOR THOUGHT

The ostrich eats almost any food, from hard seeds to leaves, grass and fruits, as well as bugs, worms, and small animals. *Gallimimus* may have done the same, striding along to nip at plants and peck up creepy-crawlies.

Long, bendy neck

MYSTERY ARMS

In 1965, a pair of huge dinosaur fossil arms and hands, 8 feet (2.4 m) long, were found in Mongolia – but no other body parts were with them. Named *Deinocheirus*, they looked like they belonged to a giant ostrich dinosaur.

Recent finds show *Deinocheirus* was indeed a huge ostrich dinosaur. It had a sail or humpback and was 43 feet (13 m) long, 16 feet (5 m) tall, and weighed several tons – as big as *T. rex*!

Game of survival!

Although *Gallimimus* was built for speed, it might not win the survival game if it encountered too many dangers on the way.

SUPPLIES
20-inch (50 cm) square white card stock • pencil • ruler • colored felt-tip pens • sheet of thin white card stock • 4 plastic bottle lids • sticky tack • dice

HOW TO MAKE
1. Draw a grid on the card stock, with ten columns and ten rows.

2. Design some hazards and rewards into the grid that the dinosaurs might come across in their fight for survival. For example: meet a predator, outrun an enemy, escape up a tree, or get struck down by asteroids.

3. Pencil these onto the grid first to be sure of the positions. Number the squares 1 to 100, then color in the board.

4. Draw some *Gallimimus* onto the thin card stock, copying the ones on page 24. Make one for each player, about 2 inches (5 cm) long. Color and cut out.

5. Stick a lump of sticky tack to each bottle lid and place a dinosaur on each one.

HOW TO USE
Each player must throw a six to start at square one. Take turns to move the dinosaurs around the board. The first dinosaur to reach 100 is the survivor!

SCYTHES AND STONES

Among the last and strangest of all dinosaurs were the therizinosaurs, known as scythe-claws due to their enormous curved hand claws. They were related to fierce meat eaters, such as *Tyrannosaurus*, yet these amazing beasts had feathers and were probably plant eaters. They are a real dino-puzzle!

Big claws!

Most dinosaurs had finger and toe claws, made from the same substance as our fingernails – keratin – but much bigger!

The huge hand claws of therizinosaurs were almost three feet long. They may have been used to pull down or cut leaves from trees, which the dinosaur then ate with its spoon-shaped teeth.

Utahraptor second toe claw: 11 in (28 cm)

Baryonyx thumb claw: 12 in (30 cm)

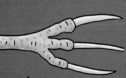

Therizinosaurus finger claw: 37 in (95 cm)

SUPER SCYTHE

Scythe-claws appeared about 125 million years ago. The last and biggest was *Therizinosaurus*, which lived 70 million years ago in East Asia. At 33 feet (10 m) long and 5.5 tons (5 t) in weight, it was almost as big as *Tyrannosaurus rex*.

Fossil hunt

SUPPLIES

pack of self-hardening modeling clay • large mixing bowl • salt dough mix: 10.5 oz (300g) plain flour, 10.5 oz (300g) salt, 7 oz (200 ml) water • spoon • old tray • sand/grit • microwave oven • poster paints and paintbrush • toothpicks • some adult help

HARD TO EAT

Tough, fibrous leaves; thick, woody stems; twigs; and similar plant parts are very difficult to chew thoroughly so they can be digested properly. So many plant-eating dinosaurs used a secret weapon – they swallowed stones!

FEATHERS

Most scythe-claw dinosaurs had a covering of fluffy feathers, but these were not designed for flight. Maybe the feathers kept in body warmth or had bright colors to impress mates.

TO MAKE THE FOSSILS

1. Use the modeling clay to make some fossil shapes, such as the claws shown on page 26. You could also make teeth and bone shapes.

2. Follow the instructions on the pack and leave the fossils to dry.

TO MAKE THE ROCKS (from the salt dough mix)

3. Place the salt and flour in the bowl and slowly stir in the water, a little bit at a time – you may not need it all.

4. Knead the mixture with your hands until smooth. If the dough is too wet, add more flour. If it is too dry, add a little more water.

5. Take a handful of dough and shape it into a rock around a fossil. Make sure the fossil is completely covered and hidden inside.

6. Sprinkle the sand/grit into the tray. Press the rocks in the sand so they pick up a rough, sandy texture all over.

7. To harden the rocks, ask an adult to zap them in a microwave. The exact cooking time will depend on the type of microwave, but start with 3 minutes. If they are still wet, then put them back for 20 seconds and repeat until dry.

8. Now the rocks are ready to paint. Choose colors to make them look really rocky. Use toothpicks to chip away the rock to find the fossils hidden inside!

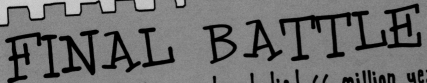

FINAL BATTLE

One dinosaur that lived and died 66 million years ago is more famous, and more studied, than almost any animal today. It was the global superstar *Tyrannosaurus*, or *T. rex*. One of the last dinosaurs, it was also one of the biggest meat eaters, and left amazing fossils for us to study.

KING OF THE MEAT-EATERS

At 39 feet (12 m) long and 6.6 tons (6 t), *T. rex* was the biggest land carnivore of its day. Its long, strong teeth were not particularly sharp – they were more suited to gristle-tearing and bone-crunching than slicing through flesh.

Some fossils of *Triceratops* have tooth marks that match *T. rex* teeth. But *Triceratops* was a big, tough dinosaur to tackle. Probably *T. rex* attacked only the old, young, sick, or injured, or scavenged on dead bodies.

BIG BONES, MIGHTY MUSCLES

Tyrannosaurus was certainly not lightweight in build. From its head, jaws, and neck to its hips, legs, and toes, it had thick, sturdy bones moved by powerful muscles.

Muscle

SMILE PLEASE!

Fossils show that dinosaurs, like many reptiles today, continually grew new teeth to replace old ones that wore down or broke. So along the jaws were a mix of small new teeth and older big ones.

T. rex puppet!

Make a *T. rex* snarl and bite to show off his teeth!

SUPPLIES

pencil • white card stock • tracing paper • coloring pencils or felt-tip pens • scissors • three split pins • two wooden dowels about 12 inches (30 cm) long • tape

1. Copy the picture of the *T. rex* adult on this page onto the card stock.

2. Trace the *T. rex* outline without the back legs and lower jaw. Transfer onto card stock, color in, and cut out.

3. Trace the outlines of the back legs and lower jaw and transfer them onto the card stock. Add a 1-inch (3 cm) tab where each piece will attach to the body. Color in and cut out.

4. Attach the back legs to the body and the jaw to the neck with split pins, making sure the pieces move freely.

5. Tape the dowels to the back of the body and the lower jaw.

HOW TO USE

T. rex is supported by the dowel attached to the body. The other dowel moves the jaw up and down. The legs will move when you shake the puppet!

Tyrannosaurus had tiny arms, probably hardly larger than yours, each with two mini-fingers. No one knows what they were for.

GROWTH SPURT

A baby *Tyrannosaurus* hatched from its egg was about 27.5 inches (70 cm) long. By 20 years, it was a huge, 39-foot (12 m) monster.

Most growth was during its teens, from ages 14–18.

T. rex hatching

T. rex *adult*

What's in a name?

The first *T. rex* fossils discovered in 1895 were thought to be of *Ornithomimus*.

Tyrannosaurus was officially named in 1905.

In 2000, the biggest *T. rex* skeleton, Sue, went on display in Chicago.

NOT DEAD AT ALL

About 66 million years ago, disaster struck. Probably a massive space object – an asteroid or comet – crashed into Earth. The effects killed more than three-quarters of all plants and animals around the globe, including the great dinosaurs.

Hundreds of volcanoes poured poison gases and suffocating ash into the air.

So many names

Dinosaurs have some weird names. Which one is your favorite?

First in alphabet list – Aardonyx

Shortest names – Mei, Kol, Zby

Longest name – Micropachycephalosaurus

Most difficult to say – Piatnitzkysaurus

Last in alphabet list – Zupaysaurus

BEFORE THE STRIKE

For a million years before the space rock hit, the world was already changing fast. Vast areas of volcanoes erupted in what is now India. Drifting continents reshaped seas. The climate altered rapidly.

Dead and dying dinosaurs were food for scavengers, but only for a short time.

ASTEROID WINTER

The space strike happened in the Gulf of Mexico, off the coast of Yucatán. It caused worldwide earthquakes, floods, and more eruptions. Dust and fumes from volcanoes darkened the skies for years.

AFTER THE DISASTER

With the sun blotted out, plants died in the gloom. With their food gone, so did plant-eating animals, followed by the meat eaters that preyed on them. The mass extinction affected land and sea.

The baby hoatzin, or stinkbird, uses its wing claws to clamber around its nest and in nearby branches.

DINOSAURS LIVE ON

The modern view is that not all dinosaurs died out. Some small ones had already changed or evolved into birds, and many birds survived the great disaster. Today's birds are, in effect, living dinosaurs!

Tyrannosaurus was one of the very last of the big dinosaurs.

Dino asteroid mobile

An asteroid strike meant disaster to all the great dinosaurs on Earth. Hang up this mobile to remember some of their amazing names!

SUPPLIES

this book • sheets of thin cardstock • pencil and tracing paper • coloring pencils or felt-tip pens • scissors • sheet of thick cardstock • small hole punch • string

HOW TO MAKE

1. Choose five favorite dinosaurs from this book. Draw or trace them onto the thin card stock. Color them as you like and cut them out. Write the correct name of each dinosaur on the back. Make sure you get the spelling right!

2. Draw a large asteroid shape onto the thick card stock. Color both sides; cut out. Punch five holes around the edge of the asteroid, plus one hole in the center. If the hole punch doesn't reach, make this hole with a sharp pencil.

3. Punch a hole in the top of each dinosaur. Tie different lengths of string through each hole .

4. Now tie the other ends of the string to the asteroid.

5. Tie string through the center of the asteroid and hang your mobile.

INDEX

ACKNOWLEDGEMENTS

The publishers would like to thank the following artists who have contributed to this book:

Cover Peter Bull Art Studio

Insides Peter Bull Art Studio, Stuart Jackson-Carter, and Chris Jevons (The Bright Agency)

All other artwork is from the Miles Kelly Artwork Bank

The publishers would like to thank the following sources for the use of their photographs:
t = top, c = center, b = bottom, l = left, r = right, m = main
Alamy 30–31(m) Stocktrek Images, Inc.,

Corbis 4 Mohamad Haghani/Stocktrek Images; 25(tr) Louie Psihoyos Rex Features 13(br) Jinyuan Liu Shutterstock.com 7(r) Jean-Michel Girard; 10(bl) Michael Rosskothen, Michael Rosskothen; 14(bl) Andreas Meyer, (tr) Michael Rosskothen; 14–15(bg) Sergey Nivens, (t) Michael Rosskothen; 15(t) Catmando; 23(descending from cr) Jean-Michel Girard, Linda Bucklin; phugunfire, pandapaw, Eric Isselee; 28–29(m) Elenarts Science Photo Library; 26–27 Jose Antonio Peñas

Every effort has been made to acknowledge the source and copyright holder of each picture. Miles Kelly Publishing apologizes for any unintentional errors or omissions.

ARCHITECTURAL
AND INTERIOR MODELS

A SIMPLE MODEL WITH DRAFTED-ON DETAIL.

PROJECT: Yale Rare Book Library.
DESIGNED BY: Skidmore, Owings and Merrill.
MODELBUILDERS: members of the architect's staff.
PHOTOGRAPHER: Louis Checkman.
SCALE: $1/8'' = 1'$.

This extremely effective design and client presentation model was built from cardboard. Building facades were drafted and the drawing photostated and cemented to the model. People were cast in metal; trees were steel wool on wire armatures. The plaza pattern was made from tape.

The final presentation model constructed for this project, interestingly enough, used slabs of real onyx as a wall material.

This photograph was taken with a Sinar $4'' \times 5''$ view camera, $6\frac{3}{8}''$ lens and Super Panchro Press film. 1 750-watt spotlight, its beam directed by gates to shine mainly on the library and its plaza, was the main source of illumination. Light from a flood lamp was bounced into shadows, created by the spotlight, to pick up details in these areas.

Sanford Hohauser **ARCHITECTURAL AND INTERIOR MODELS**
Design and Construction

Architects · Students · Landscape Architects · Town Planners · Modelmakers
Stage-Set Designers · Interior Designers · Space Planners · Structural Engineers

VNR VAN NOSTRAND REINHOLD COMPANY
NEW YORK CINCINNATI TORONTO LONDON MELBOURNE

ACKNOWLEDGMENTS

Thanks are due to all those who assisted me in the preparation of this book—especially Louis Checkman, architectural photographer; Theodore Conrad, model builder and architect; Hugh Hardy, architect; Richard Kelly, lighting consultant; Robert Mark, engineer; I. M. Pei and Associates, architects; Joseph Santeramo, model builder; Warren Skidmore of Davis, Dorland and Company, Insurance consultants; Smith, Smith, Haines, Lundberg and Waehler, architects; and Lev Zetlin, engineer.

Van Nostrand Reinhold Company Regional Offices:
New York, Cincinnati, Chicago, Millbrae, Dallas

Van Nostrand Reinhold Company International Offices:
London, Toronto, Melbourne

Copyright © 1970 by Litton Educational Publishing, Inc.

Library of Congress Catalog Card Number: 68-16029

ISBN 0-442-11301-3

Published in the United States of America
by Van Nostrand Reinhold Company,
450 West 33rd Street, New York, N.Y. 10001.

Published simultaneously in Canada by
Van Nostrand Reinhold Ltd.

16 15 14 13 12 11 10 9 8 7 6 5 4

CONTENTS

A NOTE ON PRODUCTS AND EQUIPMENT

All brand names, addresses, and prices mentioned in this book are as accurate as I could make them at the time of writing. Some of the brand names will doubtless become obsolete, some of the manufacturers will change their addresses, and many of the prices will fluctuate, probably upward in the general direction of our economy.

Mention of products or equipment by trademark or by name of manufacturer does not imply my unqualified recommendation ; there may be other products or equipment that are as good or better for the purpose.

I have recommended various techniques and procedures to use with specific tools and materials. These are, to the best of my knowledge, efficient and safe if the model builder is reasonably cautious. However, I assume no liability for any personal injury, wastage of material, breakage of tools, or imperfection of result that may be attributed to my recommendations.

1 INTRODUCTION

WHY MAKE A MODEL?

Why spend a day, a week, a month of your time, or $50,000 of a design fee on a miniature model—tedious to construct and hard to store—when easily prepared thumbnail sketches could serve as adequate presentations of your design? Why design a three-dimensional creation in a two-dimensional study medium? Can you visualize complex spatial relationships without resorting to studying actual mock-ups of them? Why can't your clients, their associates and bankers understand and visualize plans, elevations and perspectives?

The answers to these questions are self-evident: a day, a week, a month of your time, or occasionally even $50,000, is small enough outlay for the study and presentation of your creative ideas to best advantage; a set of two-dimensional sketches does not thoroughly depict so complex a creation as a town, a building, a factory layout or a stage set. And clients and people with whom a designer comes in contact usually have trouble grasping and analyzing elevations, plans and even renderings.

Design models have been in existence since the beginning of design, and comparing current architectural and interior design publications with those of 1900, 1930, 1950 or even 1960, the use of models seems to be increasing dramatically.

Some of the reasons for the importance of models are the following:

1. MODELS AID IN DESIGN

They show the design more effectively than pictures; they allow the designer to study three-dimensional problems in all three dimensions. Often, when certain details or complicated parts of designs are reached, even repeated sketching doesn't aid in better visualization of the problem. A rough model will more often than not bridge this impasse and sometimes uncover possibilities the sketches do not show. Particular aspects of design—massing, shadows and intersections—usually can be studied in model form with greater time efficiency; so many two-dimensional drawings of each condition would be required that, if accurately executed, the time expenditure would be prohibitive. For all these reasons, a designer should make sure that his fee provides sufficient funds for the construction of design models, or he should request that the owner himself pay for a

1-1

THE MODEL AS A CONSTRUCTION DOCUMENT.
Project: The American National Exhibition, Moscow, Russia.
Designed by: George Nelson.
Modelbuilders and photographers: members of the architect's staff.
Scale: 1″ = 1′.
The model pictured was constructed by the designer as a study aid and project presentation for the client. When the final design was completed, the model was rebuilt in brass and sent to Russia along with details, but without plan or elevations, as the contract documents. This model was made from strip basswood. Graphics were representative and not actual reproductions of what would be displayed. Furniture forms were carved in balsa and then covered with fabric.

model that first could be used as a design aid and then refurbished and used for presentation or project promotion.

2. MODELS ARE THE MOST EASILY UNDERSTOOD PRESENTATION TECHNIQUE

This is true for lay people, professional consultants and designers as well. Also, since models represent a simplicity of communication as opposed to technical drawings and renderings, people spend more time analyzing them. Drawings, no matter how highly rendered or simplified, often tend to confuse the layman.

3. MODELS ARE ACCURATE

An inferior design can be detected faster on a model than in a rendering. A sketch artist's virtuosity can camouflage a poor design until it has been completely built. Students and young practitioners are especially vulnerable to this trap. A model can be a final check on design and on many design sketches.

No sculpture design goes from drawings into the final three-dimensional form without one or more small scale mock-ups. How can an architect or a decorator afford such a dangerous shortcut?

4. MODELS ARE NECESSARY FOR HARD-TO-VISUALIZE DESIGN FORMS

Many forms (space frames, hyperbolic paraboloids, designs in the style of Louis Kahn, freeform shell structures, stage-sets using extensive lighting effects, etc.) are hard to draw technically and are too elaborate to be accurately shown in a few renderings. Important commissions using these forms have sometimes required hundreds of design models; one can only guess how many thousands of sketches would have been needed to achieve the same results.

5. MODELS ARE NECESSITATED BY NEW DESIGN FORMS

New, unusual, highly personal design forms and materials often can only be presented adequately by models.

6. MODELS "SELL" PROJECTS

It would be encouraging to say that, with two designs of equal quality, a good model will sell a project faster than a set of good renderings. Although this is not always the case, a good model

1-2

TWA AIRLINE TERMINAL, KENNEDY AIRPORT, NEW YORK CITY—BUILDING THAT COULD BE DESIGNED ONLY THROUGH EXTENSIVE USE OF MODELS.

DESIGNED BY: Eero Saarinen and Associates. Engineers: Ammann and Whitney. MODELBUILDERS: members of the architect's staff. PHOTOGRAPHER: Baltazar Korab.

Models were employed in all design phases of this complexly shaped building. The over-all shape of the shell roof was studied on small cardboard models. These were torn apart and rebuilt as aesthetic and engineering considerations were amalgamated until 3 basic designs were educed. The 3 were then modeled in detail and studied, and from them came the final design.

The interior was first studied on cardboard models; see illustration 1-3. Then 3/4″ = 1′ interior presentation models were built with a wood core; and the curved ceiling was cast, in Fiberglas, on plaster molds. Illustration 1-3 shows a design model of one of the massive supports of the roof. Illustration 1-4 is of the final 1/8″ = 1′ model. All 3 photographs were taken with a Graphic view camera and either a 150 mm Schneider Xenar or 90 mm Schneider–Angulon lens.

1-3→

TWA PROJECT.

Rough study model of the interior.

This is one of many cardboard models made of the interior of this building. Similarly constructed exterior models were also studied. With a model of this (3/4″ = 1′) scale, it was possible to analyze the many subtleties of interrelationship of the many shapes of this building.

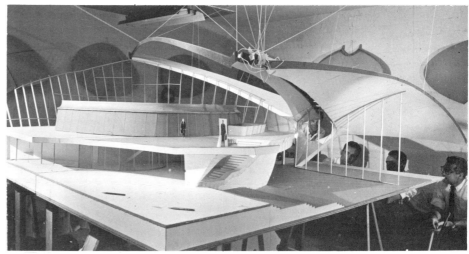

←1-4

TWA PROJECT—3/4″ = 1′ SCALE MODEL AIDED IN THE DESIGN OF A FREE-FORM CONCRETE COLUMN.

After the basic shape of the shell roof was decided upon, its thrust reactions were computed. Heavy wire representing these thrust lines was set into a baseboard. After a study of the required concrete volume and reinforcement placement of the column, light wire was used to outline its facets. A cardboard skin was then set on top of this wire skeleton.

7

will often assure the successful reception of a mediocre design, while a set of good renderings may not achieve success for a better design. Projects depicted in model form seem more feasible, appear less fanciful and communicate a greater air of actuality than those presented by perspective. This has been attested to by designers from the level of students to leading professional practitioners in all the fields covered by this book.

7. MODELS HAVE THE MAGIC OF ALL MINIATURES

Fascination for models is universal. The delight a viewer experiences with a model goes beyond that evoked by a technical drawing or photograph. This may be related to his psychological desire to be physically greater and more important than objects which are ordinarily larger than he is.

These arguments, however, should not imply that models can replace sketching and rendering. All techniques must be intelligently used together to produce creative design. Modelmaking, however, is more than a presentation aid; it is a way to study simultaneously all aspects of design, an efficient way to express ideas and, at the same time, a way to study materials and their detailing.

1-6

A 4,000-YEAR-OLD MODEL.

Funerary model of a residence taken from the XI Dynasty tomb of Mehenkwetre, Thebes, Egypt.
SCALE: about 1:20. The model measures 84 by 42.5 cm by 39.5 cm in height.
The entire model was made of coniferous wood covered with gesso. The base block originally had the same length and width as the outside walls, but it has shrunk with age. Walls were mortised and tenoned to the base and mitered to one another. Doors, windows and columns were carved. The pool (in the center of the courtyard) was lined with copper sheet evidently to allow it to be filled with water. Trees were wood covered with gesso; branches, leaves and fruit were carved separately and doweled together. Cracks were filled with gesso.

1-5

***Project:* A FACTORY FOR MASPETH, NEW YORK.**
DESIGNED AND MODELED by students of Pratt Institute School of Architecture, Brooklyn, New York.
SCALE: $1/16'' = 1'$.
Walls and roof of this presentation model were made of illustration board. Mullions and roof trusses were of stripwood. People were cut from 3-ply Bristolboard. Plaza pattern was Zip-a-Tone overlay. Trees were dried baby's-breath.

MODEL USE IN THE PAST

Past civilizations evolved numerous uses for models. The ancient Egyptians placed house models (1–6) intended to provide symbolic living accommodations in the tombs of their dead. Models of granaries, stables, craft shops and other types of buildings have been found in the tombs of the wealthy. In dedicatory rites, other ancient civilizations placed models of buildings on the altars of their gods.

Before the discovery of photographic reproduction, master builders, engineers and craftsmen carried models of structures and their details from patron to patron and town to town. Use of models increased with the expansion of trade and the accompanying development of new materials and systems of engineering. Because of the crudity of drafting, difficulty of fast reproduction of drawings and widespread illiteracy, many structures were built by taking measurements directly from detailed models.

By the twentieth century, modern drafting systems, inexpensive photocopying and blueprinting had lessened this use for models; however, the growing number of new forms and materials, construction systems and shapes has now reversed this trend.

Methods of using models are also undergoing changes. Not only have they come into use in many new design fields, but models are being modified and complexified as well, usually from the high value placed on them as a tool in presentation and design study. Before World War II, engineers used piping models as presentation devices only in the design of refineries and chemical plants. After the war, models were used for presentation, construction estimating, training of plant workers and as a means to checking the working drawings from which they were constructed. Then came a period when the design itself was evolved directly on the model which still performed all the other functions. Now some designers submit elevation and plan view photographs of the model, dispensing with much of the necessity for drawings. Models are often shipped to construction sites and used for reference by contractors.

WHOM THIS BOOK IS FOR

Besides being a reference for practicing architects; engineering consultants; landscape architects; interior, stage-set and display designers; and space planners, this book is also geared toward the needs of the students in these fields. It is for practitioners who make or supervise construction of their own models.

In addition, this book has been designed to reduce the time expended on learning techniques and acquiring product information for those who are required only occasionally to construct a model. It will relieve the designer in whose office the model is being constructed of much of the burden of teaching modelbuilding to employees. Practitioners who usually give out their model work to professional builders can learn about the problems of the modelbuilder and how the model can better be used. A study of the many photographic examples of simplified models in this book ought to enable the designer to understand construction and its relation to the sacrifice of detail and thereby to specify less expensive, more effective models from his builder.

This book is also for fledgling professional modelmakers—students working part-time or the beginning professional.

This book presents basically two types of information:

1. What it is possible to achieve with models, as reviewed in the text and illustrated by pictures of finished models.

2. How to build models, as outlined in step-by-step instructions, construction drawings and pictures of available products. This book may also be used as a reference to the various techniques recommended to solve construction problems. Look up what you desire to know in the Index. See the first page of it for instructions.

TALENTS OF THE MODELMAKER

The fundamental talents in successful modelmaking are ingenuity and the ability to perform manual operations with precision. With these skills a reasonably intelligent person can almost immediately fabricate successful, simple models. Through practice, exposure to other examples of modelmaking and a well-rounded collection of reference materials, a neophyte can evolve into a craftsman capable of constructing varying, complex models. Secondary talents that can be nurtured are: (1) the ability to plan thoroughly each construction step before undertaking it, and (2) a knowledge of tools, materials and shortcuts.

Once the modelbuilder has reached the point

where he can model anything with professional results, he will probably have attained one of two plateaus of skill : He will be either a master craftsman capable of translating a specified design into model form or a creative designer in his own right, capable, through his command of design and aesthetics, of developing and improving design. Attempts along these latter lines, however, may lead to conflicts between the modelmaker and the designer who is not interested in design comments from this source. If, however, there has been a long relationship between the two, or if the modelmaker's design abilities are recognized and he knows the aesthetic objectives of the designer, he can render great assistance. Professional modelmakers, with architectural or design training, have won the confidence of clients to such an extent that criticism, suggestions and recommendations are welcomed and often eagerly sought. These men have left their own mark on

the design of many buildings and structures. If the modelmaker is an employee of the designer and has worked in a design capacity for him, his suggestions will also more likely be influential.

The craftsman-modelmaker must understand precisely what the designer is trying to achieve. He must be true to the materials of the prototype design and not mitigate the effect of the design by substituting materials merely for the sake of expediency. Ideally, he should be able to draft and read technical drawings, to speak the technical language of the designer and to be knowledgeable about model photography. And, of course, the modelmaker must have the true craftsman's pride in achievement. But he must realize that his craftsmanship is not always appreciated by the designer, who, of course, has different problems to worry about.

DESIGNER-PRODUCED MODELS

Most architects and designers make simple models in their own offices. With the purchase of a few power tools and the training of personnel, many offices could undertake the building of most types of models with the exception of those constructed of materials needing elaborate machining. A small percentage of offices now employ one or more professional modelmakers who, alone or with several assistants and a large supply of tools, can produce any kind of model. Though there are small architectural offices that employ a full-time modelmaker, " captive " model shops are generally practical only for the architect or designer who employs a total staff of forty or more.

A survey of ten architectural firms noted for the quality of their design indicates that about 5 per cent of their man-hours are spent on modelmaking. This includes time spent by outside professional shops and draftsmen's time for making and modifying design models.

Offices that use design personnel to make models encounter the following problems : (1) A designer, simultaneously designing and making study models of a structure, may influence his design by his inability to simulate parts of his project in the way he desires. This may cause needless modification of design. (2) Designers are not necessarily as proficient with their hands as they are with their heads. Slow modelmaking may push the cost of the model above practical limits. (3) Employing a part-time modelmaker involves extensive and careful supervision. It is not unusual to have to supervise a part-time modelbuilder as he undertakes each portion of his project, and to follow this with a walk past his workbench when each portion is partially finished. Close control of this nature is often required even with experienced modelbuilders.

The problems of performing actual modelwork in a design office are manifold : Dust and noise can be considerable. Spray paint and many types of glue and brush-on paint can cause olfactory discomfort. Care must be exercised with the many tools necessary for modelbuilding ; tools that are

not being used must be locked away until they are needed. A model being constructed in part of a drafting room is a distraction to the rest of the staff. If a separate room is obtainable, however, most of these problems can be reduced to workable levels.

Advantages of making models in a design office are : (1) Modelmaking can be used as a design aid by having a member of the design team construct the model. (2) The model can be checked more often by other members of the team who, in the process, can improve and modify it at each stage of its development.

To make the advantages outweigh the disadvantages, the correct type of personnel must be chosen for modelbuilding. One or more of them must have adequate experience. The office must have the proper tools. Someone must know what materials are commercially available and one of the objectives of this book is to provide a list of the latter.

Many insurance policies (fire and workmen's compensation) must be redrawn to include modelbuilding, especially when power tools and spray painting are employed. The new policies will naturally be at higher rates for the modelbuilders and sometimes for the entire staff. Spray painting may increase the fire rates for an *entire* office building and may make a designer liable to a legal claim by his landlord for the insurance. An insurance broker should be consulted.

MODELMAKING IN SCHOOLS

Despite the fact that most professional schools have courses in architectural rendering and drawing modelmaking is very seldom presented as a

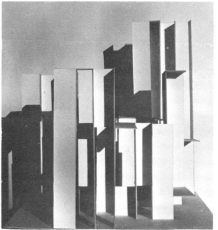

1-8/1-9

USE OF ARCHITECTURAL MODELS TO CREATE A FEELING FOR ARCHITECTURAL FORM.

Projects by students of the Cooper Union School of Art and Architecture, New York City.
In this architectonics course, clay, paper, illustration board and wood were used by students to study architectural form and detailing.

1-7

USE OF A MODEL TO VISUALIZE THE FINAL APPEARANCE OF AN ADDITION JUXTAPOSED TO THE EXISTING STRUCTURE.

PROJECT: a church tower, Berlin, Germany.
DESIGNED BY: Frei Otto and Ewald Bubner.
MODELBUILDERS: members of the architect's staff.
SCALE: 1:20.
A design model was made of the tower and photographed; a print was superimposed on a photograph of the existing church.

formal course. Most schools require a percentage of design problems to be presented in model form; students are allowed to draw upon their previous hobby experience, if any, or their exposure to what is done by their more experienced classmates. This reduces modelbuilding to an appendage of two-dimensional presentation techniques; not only presentation but design concepts suffer as a result. Study of projects in three-dimensional form would greatly contribute to a total understanding of design.

Some schools have three-dimensional design courses that serve as an introduction to model-building techniques. However, these courses were basically meant to teach spatial relations and to help provide a feeling for detailing and materials (1–8). While an extensive modelbuilding course is probably not needed in the curriculum of most schools, I have found that several lectures with strong emphasis on sources of materials and model photography is a definite aid in the study of design.

To minimize the amount of work that must be done by each class member, the purchasing of basic materials for a model presentation can be divided among individual students: tree materials, automobiles and people, baseboards and material for laminated contours, paint and glue, cardboard and wood strips—each category of items could be located and bought by a single student. One or more students could assemble and paint trees; two students could photograph models (with assistance from the model's owner); and one could act as treasurer and take orders for the materials. This procedure is especially efficient in schools where sources of supply are not easily accessible.

THE PROFESSIONAL MODELMAKING SHOP

Many professional modelmaking shops can be found throughout the country. These range from one-man operations to large shops equipped with a hundred or more machine tools and provisions for precision large-scale casting and sufficient space for big models and even full-size mock-ups of parts of buildings. To compete with students and draftsmen who inexpensively free-lance modelbuilding, the professional must make use of power tools and produce highly detailed models that are unobtainable with the techniques of part-time modelmakers. By contrast, the part-time modeler will use materials requiring a few simple tools. This will often restrict him to working in paper, cardboard and soft woods—less durable materials that require laborious handwork.

Many shops also make industrial design models and full-size mock-ups or working models of new industrially designed products. Some shops can complete a large model in a matter of days by concentrating their entire labor force on its fabrication. Employees of the highly mechanized shops usually start their careers as patternmakers, cabinetmakers, sculptors, toolmakers, architectural draftsmen or graduates of trade schools. The shopowner must therefore train these men very nearly from scratch.

Because labor costs vary between 80% of total costs (on simplified models) to 95% (on highly detailed models), the professional must carefully plan and supervise his labor use. Without constant supervision, time and cost estimates and research to find new tools and materials, a shop may find itself priced out of competition. This is why there is an upper limit to the number of employees that can be controlled by one proprietor.

To produce durable, precise models and lower the cost of surface finishing, large shops almost exclusively use acrylic plastic for buildings and metal castings for repetitive parts. These materials require fairly intricate tooling and die-making. The highly mechanized professional, unlike the part-time modeler, does not search for ready-made materials that are almost to scale. He precisely machines what he needs himself—and even if he may simplify tiny objects by omitting impossible-to-model, unimportant facets, he does not build them with even slight inaccuracies in size.

Average salaries for these professionals run between $3 and $4 per hour. The owners of the shops sometimes have architectural or industrial design training; others have training which is similar to that of their employees. During slack periods some shops have been known to do cabinet and machine shop work; others take the opportunity to make and stockpile miniature autos, trees, figures and other details.

In recent years the trend toward giving model work to Danish, German, Japanese and other foreign shops has grown because of their lower labor costs. This is especially true with bridge, dam and plant models.

Joseph Santeramo, the head of Philip Johnson's captive model shop and builder of several of the models shown in this book, has outlined some of the requirements for launching a professional modelmaking business. In his opinion, an ideal starting point would be a staff consisting of the shopowner and two employees, and a capitalization of $20,000, enough to sustain the business for at least a year while its reputation was being developed. Clientele would be built on the new business' reputation for quality work and its ability to keep deadlines, and only secondarily on low bids. At first the new firm would rent a minimum of 500 sq. ft. of loft space at a rate of $2 to $3 per sq. ft. per year and the space would be close to the offices of a majority of potential clients. Employees would be paid from $2 per hour for a helper with minimal experience who must be constantly watched to $4 per hour for a craftsman who would require little or no supervision by the shopowner. A man worth over $4 per hour would know how to work skillfully with many different materials and would be capable of taking over complete management of jobs. Although their presence is necessary to allow the shopowner to expand beyond about a half-dozen employees, such skillful craftsmen present a problem to their employer, because they tend to quit and set up their own businesses when they discover the value of their skills. Thus a highly talented employee must be made a partner at a certain point in his career or perhaps be lost. With him as a partner and with another very highly skilled modelmaker, a total staff of perhaps 10 could be utilized to maximum capacity. Such a business, having good clients, should net (before taxes) $20,000 for each of the principals.

To cut overhead and to accomplish as much as possible with the men who have been thoroughly trained, a shop should arrange for as much overtime as possible. Mr. Santeramo suggests an average of about 15 hours per week. Overtime should be paid at a $1\frac{1}{2}$ rate.

A complete set of precise hand and machine tools would eliminate outside shop fabrication with the exception of sand blasting, plating and the vacuum molding of large objects. As new materials appeared, they would be purchased for experimentation.

Job getting and public relations would be brought about through introductions to architects arranged by mutual friends, attendance at meetings of local architectural societies, by the sending of brochures to architects and advertising in the Yellow Pages. Article writing as a publicity medium could sometimes be attempted by some of the larger shop owners.

Only a minimum of supervision would be required from the architect once the design of the building had been frozen. A visit to the shop when the model parts were ready to be painted and assembled would frequently be all that would be necessary. At this stage size could be checked and colors selected.

Some shops could lease out modelbuilders to work in the offices of the architect or designer where they could work closely with the design team. Some shops could sell castings of people, cars, furniture, grills, etc. to their clients.

Modelbuilding fees are usually cost plus profit; customarily, a rough preliminary estimate of the total is given. Since changes are often made while a model is being constructed, a preliminary fixed fee is usually unfeasible. If a deadline, stipulated in a letter or contract, cannot be met, the model-builder is penalized a percentage of his fee for each week or month of lateness. The contract specifies the degree of detail expected on the model.

The designer or architect customarily orders the model, though sometimes this is done directly by the client. Some designers have their favorite shop and do not solicit competitive bids, but most designers get a handful of bids before awarding the contract. The finished model will usually belong to the client.

2 PLANNING THE MODEL

Many models inadequately fulfill their function because the builder did not take time to analyze the precise purposes for the model. The following questions must be asked before starting construction:

USE

What will this model be used for—massing, semidetailed or superdetailed study? Will it be photographed? Will it be displayed? How long should the model last?

DETAIL

What is the minimum detail that must be shown? If time and money permit, how far should this minimum be exceeded to fulfill the "use" considerations?

BUDGET

How much time and expense should be allotted for the model? If the budget were raised, could the model be put to greater use?

TECHNIQUES

What construction techniques could do the job economically? What materials and tools would be needed? Could they be purchased in time?

Approximate time and cost estimates should be made for a minimum model and also for more elaborate versions. These estimates should be reviewed with the designer and one approved. All reference material from the designer and from the modelmaker's reference file should be assembled.

A list of photographs to be taken should also be secured because of its bearing on the technique eventually to be chosen.

Prior to starting the model, prepare a painting and assembling schedule. Because abutting parts cannot be painted different colors neatly once they have been assembled, much of the painting has to be done before assembling.

Assemble the plans and drawings from which you will work. It is simplest to work from drawings that are the same scale as the model will be. Check all prints to make sure that they have not been distorted by atmospheric conditions or aging. Draft the important parts of the model on the drawings. Accurately show the thickness of all the materials used for walls and floors. Also indicate internal bracing.

A trip to the construction site may be needed to collect information: shape and color of adjacent buildings or rooms; size and type of surrounding flora; color of adjacent roads and sidewalks; ground texture; amount of pedestrian and vehicular traffic; and, in the case of space-planning models, details of existing conditions. A camera is indispensable in recording most of this information. On this first trip you may want to take background photos that can be superimposed on model pictures to form an effective photographic composite (8-13).

COST AND DETAIL

The amount of detail shown on a model will determine the model's price to a far greater extent than will its scale or materials. An almost endless variety of model types is encompassed, from the simplest massing study model to the most detailed display model.

1—Massing study solid block model made of roughly cut clay or balsa (2-1).

2—A more refined version, with the material cut precisely and some important textures worked into the clay or drawn on the balsa (2-3).

3—Solid block massing model made of precisely cut wood with only major parts shown; the model painted in one or more colors.

4—Solid block model with detail either drawn on it or on paper that is pasted to the block (14-20). This type of model may be used for study of details and textures as well as basic massing.

5—Solid block model with some major details (moldings, parapets, overhangs, exterior columns, etc.) built on the block.

6—Built-up or hollow model made of cardboard, paper, wood or acrylic with cutout windows perhaps glazed; all major details shown and the model fully painted (15-9).

7—Built-up model showing all details (11-21).

8—Built-up model with all visible interiors furnished and perhaps the model internally lit.

Interior design models can be built on all but the eighth level.

The type of detail shown on a model must be logical. You cannot show 2″ mullions and leave out parapet walls 3′6″ high × 8″ thick. It is best to establish the size of the minimum detail that will be shown. If, for instance, you decide to show everything that measures over 2″, you will have to simplify complex molding by eliminating any part that projects less than 2″; also, exposed 4×4″ H-columns will be shown as square strips without flange representation since each area between flanges and web measures only about $1\frac{7}{8}″ \times 3\frac{1}{2}″$; small furniture knobs can be omitted, etc.

SCALE SELECTION

By the time you have reviewed "Planning the Model," you may have developed some definite feelings about the scale that will best satisfy your needs. Besides the factors already enumerated, the degree of realism that the model and the photographs must convey and the amount of detail to be shown have to be considered. Then a

2-1/2-2/2-3/2-4/2-5

EXTENSIVE USE OF THE STUDY MODEL TO AID IN THE DESIGNING OF A LARGE PROJECT.

PROJECT: Metropolitan Opera House, Lincoln Center, New York City.
DESIGNED BY: Harrison and Abramovitz. Consulting engineer: Ammann and Whitney.
MODELBUILDERS: members of the architect's staff except for the final model. This was built by Thomas Salmon, a professional modelbuilder.
PHOTOGRAPHERS: the architect's staff except for the photo of the final model (2-5). This was taken by Ezra Stoller.
SCALE: earliest 2 models (2-1 and 2-2): 1/32″ = 1′. Illustration 2-3: 1/16″ = 1′. Illustration 2-4: 1/32″ = 1′. Final model (2-5): 1/16″ = 1′.

Many rough plasticine massing models of early ideas were sculpted and subjected to close study. When several design trends were educed, the crude masses of these models were replaced by carefully cut plasticine blocks on which major detail was simulated: glass was represented by a rough comb scraped finish; important panel lines were scribed or projected by inserting thin stripwood in the plasticine; arches were pressed from sheets of plasticine on rough carved wood forms; columns were made from balsa strips. These models were mounted on rough plywood bases.

As the final solution evolved, more detail was added to the model: its masses were further plumbed; textures were developed with serrated clay modeling tools, stairs were cut into the plasticine; simple trees were made from dried weeds; and people were added to lend scale. By this phase of planning, a model of the surrounding buildings, made from illustration board covered with plasticine, had been constructed. Various plasticine models were placed on it for juxtaposition study. The final design had now been selected and the rough model was replaced by a cardboard and plaster one. Because of the importance to the design of the tranparent front glass wall, it may have proven advantageous to use a sheet acrylic insert as early as the third model pictured. The vaults could have been held up and kept in shape with 1 or more plastic walls, each running parallel to the front of the building. In this way the full depth massing of the front lobby could have been studied on the early plasticine model.

The final model, used for presentation, was built by a professional modelbuilder. Walls, roofs and windows were of acrylic; columns were cardboard; vaults were carved from hydro-stone; elevated walks were sheet metal; railings and figures were cast metal; trees were steel wool on metal armatures.

2-1

2-2

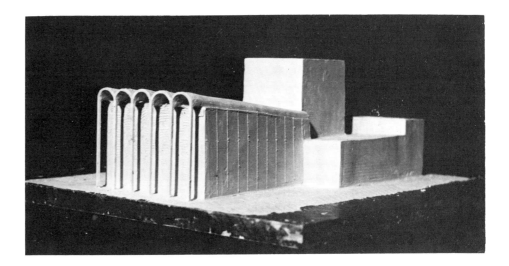

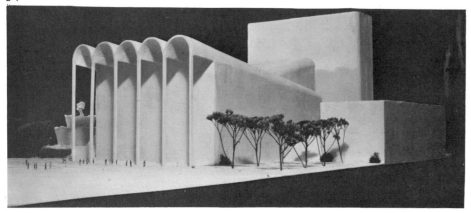

2-3
2-4

2-5

minimum and maximum scale range can be formulated.

Large-scale models allow you to show more detail, look more realistic in pictures (even if they are only as detailed as a smaller model), are more impressive, and can be used to study the appearance of smaller intersections and parts of the design.

Smaller scale models take less time to construct (if details are simplified or omitted) and are easier to ship and to protect from breakage.

Check the scales at which ready-made parts (simulated building materials, structural shapes, etc.) can be obtained.

Usually, models are built at the following scales:

TOWN PLANNING MODELS

These can be built at 1 : 2000 to 1 : 1000 scale if only a block model is required. If some indication ot fenestration, balconies, parapets and other building parts is required, then 1 : 500 (about 1″ = 40′) is a better scale.

ARCHITECTURAL MODELS

These are used for massing studies and can be made at 1″ = 40′ (about 1 : 500). For modeling very small buildings, you may want to increase the scale to $\frac{1}{16}$″ = 1′ (about 1 : 200). Detailed models of large buildings may be done at $\frac{1}{32}$″ = 1′ (about 1 : 400), $\frac{1}{16}$″ = 1′ or larger. At these scales, complete fenestration and columns can be shown satisfactorily. If superdetailing is required, and you must show small mullions, grillwork, stairs, etc., your scale may have to be as large as $\frac{1}{8}$″ = 1′ (for large buildings) and up to $\frac{1}{4}$″ = 1′ for small buildings.

FACTORY AND OFFICE LAYOUT MODELS

Most available castings are $\frac{1}{4}$″ = 1′, but, if you intend to make your own castings, $\frac{1}{8}$″ = 1′ may prove to be an acceptable scale if little detail is required.

LANDSCAPE MODELS

These can be as small as 1 : 500, if only a rough layout of trees and bushes is needed, to as large as $\frac{1}{16}$″ = 1′ (1 : 200) for a fairly accurate rendition of plant size, shape and texture.

REAL ESTATE AGENTS' MODELS OF APARTMENTS AND HOUSES

These are acceptable at $\frac{1}{4}$″ = 1′, but more useful at a $\frac{1}{2}$″ = 1′ scale.

INTERIOR DESIGN MODELS

These may range from $\frac{1}{4}$″ = 1′ for rough models to $\frac{1}{2}$″ = 1′ and 1″ = 1′ to show greater detail.

STAGE-SET MODELS

These may also be $\frac{1}{2}$″ to 1″ = 1′.

USUAL SCALES ENCOUNTERED IN MODEL WORK

Scale	Proportion
	1 : 2000
1″ = 100′	1 : 1200
	1 : 1000
1″ = 60′	1 : 720
1″ = 50′	1 : 600
	1 : 500
1″ = 40′	1 : 480
1/32″ = 1′	1 : 384
1″ = 30′	1 : 360
1″ = 20′	1 : 240
1/16″ = 1′	1 : 192
000 or N model-train gauge	1 : 152
3/32″ = 1′	1 : 128
1″ = 10′ (TT model-train gauge)	1 : 120
	1 : 100
1/8″ = 1′	1 : 96
HO model-train gauge	1 : 87
OO model-train gauge	1 : 76
3/16″ = 1′ (S model-train gauge)	1 : 64
1/4″ = 1′ (O model-train gauge)	1 : 48
3/8″ = 1′	1 : 32
1/2″ = 1′	1 : 24
3/4″ = 1′	1 : 16
1″ = 1′	1 : 12
	1 : 10

PLANNING CONSTRUCTION TECHNIQUES

More mistakes in craftsmanship are due to lack of planning than to lack of skill. The technique used on each object must be planned before starting work. Each new object that is to be modeled can be compared to similar past modeled objects. Ask yourself the simplest ways to make it. After two or three techniques have come to mind, analyze them and see if they can achieve a satisfactory model: Do these techniques require trips to different, hard-to-locate suppliers? Do they require additional tools? Do they require greater craftsmanship than you possess? These kinds of questions can probably eliminate all but the most practical system.

A designer working on a model of a display had to model three 2″ outside diameter, washer-shaped pieces of decorative trim. These objects were to be about $\frac{1}{32}$″ thick and have a cross-sectional shape similar to that of a bowl with a large hole cut in the bottom. Forming the curved concave surface posed the greatest problem. The designer brought drawings of the objects to me, and my first response was to consult a nearby supplier of parts for handbag manufacturing in order to buy brass or copper collars of approximately the needed dimensions. This was a typical first thought—full of superficial cleverness but impractical for two reasons: (1) it might take much time and legwork to secure such parts; (2) the acquired parts would probably not exactly duplicate the outside and inside diameters and the curve contours. My second thought was to obtain polystyrene sheet material of the necessary thickness and, by pivoting an X-Acto blade around a center point, to scrape out the concavity. The outside diameters could be cut on an electric jigsaw and the center holes drilled and then the objects sanded. This technique, requiring a time-consuming shopping trip and the pivoting of an X-Acto blade, on further consideration seemed complicated, even if feasible. My third thought was to form a shallow cone from 3-ply Bristol board. The point could then be cut off leaving a washer-shaped object that could be reinforced and made thicker with additional layers of 3-ply. This technique came to mind while I was thinking about ways I had made curved objects before. On comparing the three techniques, it seemed obvious that the third was the most reasonable for modeling accuracy and time expenditure. The entire thought process took a few moments. When I suggested the last technique to the modelbuilder, he appeared unimpressed and favored the second technique instead. It seemed that he had experienced past difficulty with paper construction warping (due probably to improper bracing or waterproofing). After reflection, and no little coercion on my part, he undertook to use the paper technique which required only a few minutes of construction time. Our efforts resulted in an accurate, and so far, durable model.

This illustration demonstrates three psychological factors in the selection of techniques: the handbag idea represented a desire to be ingenious; the scraping of *polystyrene* was an attempt to locate a new, perhaps magical technique that would replace the need for manual skill; and the modelmaker's initial refusal to consider paper construction represented his distrust of a technique that had not previously worked (due mostly to lack of knowledge and improper handling).

As modelmaking experience increases, impractical ideas and prejudices decrease, and basic truths about techniques can be recognized:

1—First try to find some place where you can buy the object already fabricated.

2—If a technique has been used by others successfully, it can in all probability be perfected by you with adequate tools and instruction.

3—If the use of a particular technique has never been heard of before (in modelmaking or any other handicraft), thorough investigation must be undertaken before attempting it.

4—Assembly of tools and references takes much longer with new techniques than with familiar ones.

5—Obtaining new materials almost always takes more time than anticipated.

6—An unsuccessful technique should be analyzed to discover what went wrong.

Throughout the text I have noted the *approximate* price of various tools and materials. This is to aid in making rough preliminary cost estimates and to give additional facts upon which to base analyses of comparative building techniques.

Faced with the problem of construction, one should select the techniques with which one has had prior experience and which require tools that one has on hand. Some of the construction techniques discussed will often not be suitable. However, it is well to know about alternate construction techniques and sometimes to experiment with new ones. Before starting a model, try to ascertain whether or not less widely used systems could save time and expense and/or increase the quality of your model.

It is important to determine the intended longevity of your model. Its construction can be simplified if it is only going to be photographed, shown for a short time and then stored away for possible (but not probable) future reference. On the other hand, a 10 or 20% increase in model cost will sometimes assure that a model will last for decades.

VISUAL BALANCE

Successful models, like artistic creations, should have: (1) color balance; (2) a balance of light and dark colors (this is important for black-and-white photography); (3) a well-proportioned baseboard outline; (4) surroundings complementing the model; (5) no viewing distractions.

Color hue and chroma and color value are usually dictated by the designer, but there are creative areas for the modelmaker, too: the edges of the baseboard, the nameplate, the display case and the reverse wall sides of an interior design (if they are not part of the design), etc. The yearly changes in foliage and other vegetation allow the modelmaker to choose among a wide variety of colors and shapes and still be true to nature.

The baseboard should complement the planned shape of the model. Enough border has to be left around the building or interior to avoid a feeling of visual cramping. Complex baseboard shapes should be avoided in favor of simple square or rectangular ones. The thickness of the baseboard and its edge molding can aid the overall appearance of the model.

Entourage (cars, people, boats, etc.) may be treated in several ways. They can be greatly detailed and in natural color (this representational accuracy tends to compete with the design for the viewer's attention). They can be detailed but painted in muted colors (or even solid gray). They can be simple, undetailed block forms painted naturally or in restrained colors. If an architectural model must show surrounding buildings, these buildings should be block models, with or without detail (2-4), and should be painted white or gray. Existing construction on a model of an alteration or addition may be treated in a similar way.

Do not allow individual parts of the model to be distracting: title blocks should not be oversized or garish; signs on the model (street and building names, etc.) should be unobtrusive; model covers should be attractively, but simply, shaped and should not obscure parts of the model or be glaring.

3 THE WORK SPACE

Most work areas are a compromise in space. Care must be taken that economizing does not result in cramped or dangerous working conditions or in a work space that could detrimentally affect the rest of the office. Modelmaking creates problems: fire hazards, noise, dust, smells, distractions; dangers result from the use of tools, and there is tool loss. A separate room for extensive modeling activities eliminates most of these problems. Small cardboard and paper models are often successfully made in drafting rooms, but power tool and spray painting operations have no place there. Because of the relatively large floor area needed per modelbuilder and because of the complications of insurance, large design firms often prefer to locate model shops in separate quarters.

SMALL SHOPS

If modeling activities require that one or more models be in the process of construction at the same time, it would probably be wise to have a separate shop. A minimal 2-man 100′ square shop is shown in 3-1. Its freestanding model table affords access to all sides of the models being constructed. The workbenches are sufficient to hold mounted power tools (circular saws, jigsaws, etc.). All photographs can be taken in the shop. A portable spray painting booth may be made from a 2′ sq. (or larger) corrugated cardboard carton, set up when needed on a workbench and stored the rest of the time under the model table. Since shop equipment must be periodically supplemented, projections of future needs must be carefully estimated to keep a shop from becoming crowded and inefficient.

LARGER SHOPS

If the modelmaker intends to make many solid wood block or machined Plexiglas models or wood model bases, he will need heavy power tools permanently mounted on stands. Such tools require sufficient work space around them both for safety and to accommodate the large sizes of materials that are sold in lumberyards. The following table shows space requirements and suggested tool locations.

Tool	Workspace required	Location in room
Drill press	Front, sides	Wall, corner
Jig saw	Front, sides	Wall, corner
Band saw	Front, sides	Wall
Table circular saw	Front, rear, sides	Center
Radial arm saw	Front, sides	Wall
Disc sander	Front	Center, wall
Belt sander	Sides	Center, wall
Grinder	Front	Center, wall, corner
Lathe	Front	Wall, corner
Jointer	Front, rear	Center, wall
Shaper	Front, sides	Wall

A SMALL SHOP

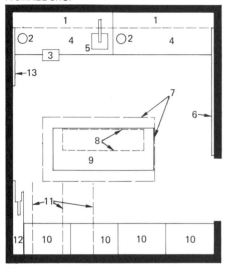

3-1

A 2-MAN WORK SHOP THAT HAS A MINIMAL NUMBER OF POWER TOOLS

1—12″ deep shelf at 5′ 6″, 6′, 7′ and 8′ levels. Keep plastic small parts cabinets on the lowest shelf and infrequently used materials and tools on the top shelves.
2—Table lamp.
3—Vise.
4—24″ × 60″ workbench with a single full length 3″ deep drawer and two 18″ wide, 12″ high drawers. 1 bench is for rough, messy work; the other for drafting and paper and board cutting.
5—Portable electric jig saw (store it in workbench drawers with other portable power tools).
6—Tackboard or Homosote board to which drawings and pictures can be pinned.
7—Border of maximum size model that can be comfortably fabricated in shope (3′ × 5¼′).
8—Ceiling light.
9—24″ × 60″ model table with low shelf. Store clay, plaster and other heavy supplies on the shelf.
10—Steel, small drawer cabinets 38″ high and 12″ to 18″ deep. Drawers measure 3½″ high × 18″ deep × 24″ wide, 3½″ × 16″ × 9″, and 5″ × 24″ × 11″. Store tools, paint and materials in drawers. Finished models may be stored in a vertical position on top of the cabinets.
11—Rack made of 1″ diameter pipe (1½′ oc) connected by elbows to vertical pipes which are screwed to the ceiling. Bottom of rack should be about 6½′ above the floor. Store sheet material, dowels, stripwood and rolled plans or racks.
12—Board storage.
13—Perforated Masonite hand tool storage board.

3-2

Project: HOUSE IN NEW CANAAN, CONNECTICUT.

DESIGNED BY: Ulrich Franzen and Associates.
MODELBUILDERS: members of the architect's staff.
PHOTOGRAPHER: Maris-Ezra Stoller Associates.
SCALE: 1/8″ = 1′.
This presentation model was built of paper-covered acrylic.
CONSTRUCTION TIME: about 80 hours.

Before room planning, you must decide what types of operations will be performed on each machine. Cutting baseboards out of 4×8′ plywood sheet will probably be the most space consuming operation, but regular work on the jigsaw, band saw, radial arm saw, drill press, sander and jointer will also require considerable space: a 2-man shop containing 5 heavy power tools and the same amount of workbench and storage space as shown in 3-1 will require 150 to 200 sq. ′.

To conserve space:

1—Mount the tool stands on casters and move them to the center of the shop when they are required to hold large materials.

2—Substitute a Lazy Susan revolving table (called a tool turret) for individual tool stands. The turret can be made from sheet metal and mounted on a 2 to 4″ diameter pipe pedestal attached to a workbench. Two or three tools can be kept on this table which requires the wall space of only one conventional tool.

3—Buy multipurpose tools, such as radial arm saws, that perform several operations and reduce the number of individual tools required.

If one intends to spray paint with lacquers, it will probably be required by his insurance company that he work in a separate room and store his paints in steel cabinets. Certain insurance policies will not allow the storage of lacquers on the premises under any circumstances. See page 184, for other insurance problems. Incidentally, keeping painting activities away from the dust of other working areas facilitates good finishes. Larger shops may require areas for hot casting, photo taking, clothing lockers, water supply, slop sink and model storage.

WORKBENCHES

There are several types of furniture that may efficiently be used as workbenches: old drafting tables, commercially made woodshop benches or flush doors set on sawhorses. Benches should be about 36″ high, contain one or more drawers (for tool and flat material storage) and perhaps a lower open storage shelf. Tops of benches should be covered with a sheet of material that could be replaced when badly mutilated. Use ⅛″ Masonite or plywood held in place by countersunk screws on a rough workbench, and an inexpensive illustration board stapled or tacked on a workbench

where delicate work is performed. If the bench is located against a wall, the table should have a low rear wall to prevent small parts from falling off. Bench tops should overhang in front to facilitate fastening vises and clamps.

Commercial benches are made in several styles: the machine and layout bench without a built-in vise or drawers has a low, open storage shelf; the elementary workbench has a built-in wood vise, drawers and a storage shelf; the woodshop bench has a built-in wood vise, drawers and holes in its top for tool storage. Sears & Roebuck has a 60×24″ steel bench that costs about $70. From time to time, sales of benches can be located in the illustrated classified section of major newspapers. It is possible to obtain a 2×4′ steel bench (without a vise) for as little as $30 or a 2×6′ bench for about $35.

Sawhorse legs for benches can be made by using 5 pieces of 2×4″ lumber plus prefabricated Dalton brackets costing $5 for 2, or they can be bought for $7 from the same company as prefabricated bipods and completed with a crossmember made out of 2″ lumber. Steel worktable legs can also be bought from Qualcraft for $7. Flush wood doors, 1 or 2″ thick, may be used to make workbenches of almost any length. Silvo Hardware Co. carries most of the above table components.

STORAGE

To keep a workshop uncluttered and efficient and to preserve tools, adequate storage space must be provided. An almost universal tendency is to underestimate the number of tools and material samples that will collect, and not to prepare for storage expansion. Storage space must be provided for many basic types of materials:

1—Large (30×40″ to 4×8′) sheets of board and plywood. These are best stored flat in shallow plan drawers. Vertical storing may result in warping unless the boards are stored exactly vertical. Overhead pipe racks (3-1) are also a possibility. A sheet of Mylar plastic will keep the boards dust free.

2—Heavy bulk material—plaster, clay, etc.—should be stored near floor level in drawers or cabinets.

3—Portable power tools and light but bulky materials can be stored on wall shelves or in cabinets. If shelves are used, they should be adjustable ones with wall-mounted, slotted metal strips into which shelf brackets can be fitted. Save small corrugated cardboard cartons or shipping boxes: tools and materials kept in them are protected from dust.

4—Hand tools should be kept on pegs or wire brackets on wall-hung, perforated Masonite sheets. Each tool should have its permanent location on the board shown by a painted outline. To prevent blade damage, cutting tools should never be piled into drawers.

5—Blocks of wood and other materials. Small drawer, steel cabinets 38″ high, with 4½″ high, 24″ deep, 10½″ wide drawers, will be suitable for all but the largest blocks which can be stored on

3-3

Project: **ATTWOOD RESIDENCE.**
DESIGNED BY: Oppenheimer, Brady and Lehrecke.
MODELBUILDERS: members of the architect's staff.
PHOTOGRAPHER: Louis Checkman.
SCALE: $1/4'' = 1'$.
Walls and roof of the presentation model were made from illustration board internally braced with carboard and strip balsa. The block texture was a black on white print; concrete texture was achieved by a very dry paint spray. Siding: stained, scribed basswood. Mullions: basswood.
CONSTRUCTION TIME: about 250 hours.

open shelves. Steel cabinets are obtainable at office supply stores.

6—Sheets of balsa and Plexiglas may be stored in the long low drawers of workbenches or in a plain storage cabinet.

7—Strip wood, structural shapes, dowels and wire are stored inside 1 to 2″ diameter cardboard tubes near the balsa and Plexiglas sheets.

8—Small material and assemblies—trees, cars, people, furniture, electrical equipment, camera supplies, etc.—should be stored categorically in individual drawers or bins. A system of storage should be organized as early as possible and room made to store boxes or small compartment chests as they begin to pile up. A shallow-drawer, steel cabinet 38″ high, with $3\frac{1}{2}\times16\times9''$ drawers, is a good system.

My system for storing materials of this type has been to build compartments $2\times2''$ (or of whatever dimensions are required) out of $\frac{3}{8}''$ thick cardboard. The cardboard is glued in an egg crate pattern on cardboard bases which have been set into the drawers of steel cabinets. The advantage of making one's own compartments for all shapes and quantities of materials is that $\frac{3}{8}''$ material wastes less space than does fitting various size plastic chests and bins into the drawers. Valuable equipment can be safeguarded with a locking bar.

9—Small bottles and tubes of paint and glue can also be stored in narrow-drawer, steel cabinets.

10—Small tools—those that cannot practically be pegged onto Masonite racks—may also be kept in steel cabinets.

11—Very small tools and fasteners (nails, screws, drills, knife blades, etc.) should be kept in small plastic drawers, purchasable at hobby and hardware stores. These are available in small metal or plastic cabinets each containing from four to about twenty drawers. They can be stored on a low shelf or on top of large steel cabinets. A $7\frac{1}{2}\times7''$ cabinet made by Nifty containing ten drawers costs about $3 and is one of the most economical to be found. Extremely small things can be kept in divided plastic boxes; these come with compartments as small as $1\times1''$, and can also be stored in steel cabinets. Another system is to use terry clipped rows of baby food bottles hung on a horizontal wall-hung wood runner, or to buy the plastic mounting clips, sold by Wickliffe Industries for $1 a dozen, that allow one to clip baby food bottles to a pegboard. No matter what system is used, it is necessary to buy enough small drawers and boxes so that one compartment can be allotted practically every size of screw, nail, washer, etc. Drills, knife blades, burrs and other small sharp tools should be kept in some sort of protective rack or stand.

12—Catalogs of tool and material suppliers as well as articles on tools and modelbuilding can be kept in one or more filing cabinet drawers.

Even if one contemplates making only an occasional model in a drafting room, and wishes to keep the materials of categories 1, 2, 3, 6, 7 and 12 with his office supplies, he should purchase at least one small-drawer, steel cabinet for his other storage. Cabinets $30\frac{1}{2}''$ wide, 37″ high, 13″ deep containing $27—3\frac{1}{2}\times9\times12''$ drawers are usually called letter-sized cabinets and are sold for about $50. Cabinets $23\frac{1}{2}''$ wide, 37″ high, 25″ deep containing $14—10\frac{1}{2}\times4\frac{1}{2}\times24''$ drawers are called canceled check or microfilm files and cost over $85. Cabinets $25\frac{1}{2}''$ wide, $37\frac{1}{2}''$ high, $18\frac{1}{4}''$ deep containing $10—23\times3\times17\frac{1}{2}''$ drawers are called sample cabinets and retail for over $80.

ELECTRICITY AND LIGHT

All power tools made for the hobbyist and home craftsman run on 110 volt, 60 cycle alternating current. It is a good policy to provide two outlets per workbench. Some shops have continuous plug-in strips located a foot above the top of their workbench and these have outlets every 18 inches. If there are a number of power tools, 2 or more electrical circuits should be used to separate the energy supply for the shop's lighting from that for its tools. Thus, if a tool causes an overload and blows a fuse, the lights will remain on.

Note the rated amperage of tools and provide the proper fusing for them:

FUSES FOR VARIOUSLY RATED TOOLS

Tool rating (amperes)	Fuse (amperes)
1–5	15
6	20
7–8	25
9–10	30

Use 3-prong plugs with power tools. If receptacles in the shop will only take 2-prong plugs, buy an adapter equipped with a pigtail (Drumcliff Co. sells them for $1). To ensure that the tool is safely grounded, the pigtail should be screwed to the receptacle's coverplate. Since overloading can occur much more easily with shop tools than with home appliances, don't use adapters that allow more than one tool or lamp on an outlet. Use heavy-duty extension cords; the longer the cord, the heavier gauge its wire must be. If photographs are to be taken in the shop, make sure that the circuits have sufficient capacity for floodlights—a minimum of 1,000 to 1,500 watts.

A lighting level equal to that maintained in drafting areas is desirable. This may be provided by a combination of ceiling fixtures (to provide over-all lighting) and individual lamps (adjustable drafting lamps may be used) located at each workbench and power tool stand. Many bench-mounted power tools have accessory lamps. Movable lamps can be directed at the work from different angles to reveal defects. Table fixture

lights must be angled so that one's body will never block light from the work.

VENTILATION, WATER, HUMIDITY

Take care to ventilate shop and paint area properly. Forced ventilation will probably be needed to clear rapidly the fumes produced by some paints. Ideally, air should be evacuated from the area where the workers stand, across the workbench and directly out of the building.

Running water is not indispensable in small shops. A sufficient supply collected in plastic bottles can be kept easily. Such a supply will be adequate for occasional plaster casting and tempera painting.

Humidity and temperature levels must be reasonably stable. Extreme variations in temperature can cause warping of models made from a combination of several materials, and can also make it difficult to machine parts to exact size. Excess humidity can cause problems in wood and paper construction and painting. Air conditioners, humidifiers and dehumidifiers help maintain an even shop environment.

SOUND AND DUST CONTROL

Some cutting operations will create acoustical disturbances no matter what sound control measures have been taken. Mounting acoustic tile on the ceiling and using perforated Masonite on walls (from which tools may be hung), however, will appreciably deaden shop noises. Also, placing power tools on rubber casters cuts vibration noise.

Dust caused by sanding and cutting is a persistent problem. Some power sanders are equipped with built-in vacuum cleaners allowing little dust to escape. However, any shop will benefit from the acquisition of a small electric vacuum cleaner that could also provide suction for vacuum sheet forming. Metropolitan makes a small hand vacuum cleaner called a DeLuxe Goodyear Vac-ette that sells for under $15 including eight attachments.

Dust is especially troublesome during painting, the slightest amount in the air can ruin a model's finish. A separate paint room or paint booth can solve this problem.

SHOP SAFETY

It is wise to review basic shop safety rules. Following them and being alert to the dangers inherent in working with tools can prevent many accidents.

1—Keep your shop uncluttered; put away tools and materials as soon as you have finished with them.

2—Use sharp tools; this will alleviate the need

15

to apply excessive pressure in order to make dull ones cut.

3—Do not store rags that are wet with paint.

4—Concentrate on the cutting surfaces of the hand tool in use and on the direction in which it is moving. Make sure that you are not in the line of its path or the path it may take if it is somehow deflected.

5—Have on hand a well-supplied first-aid kit. When using power tools:

6—Do not wear loose clothing; remove ties or other encumbrances and roll up sleeves.

7—Wear goggles whenever working with a machine that throws out sparks, chips, or sawdust.

8—Analyze blind cuts; make sure that your hand is not in the way of the cutting blade.

9—Do not overload your electrical supply.

10—Make sure your work is firmly held in place while you are working.

11—Cover all motor belts.

12—Use blade guards.

13—Do not allow tools to overheat.

Since continuous inhalation of the fumes of certain paints, solvents and cements is dangerous, adequate shop and paint room ventilation should exist. Always read and respect the warnings that are printed on the labels of products. Use applicators when working with injurious cements and Polyethylene throwaway gloves if there is any likelihood of contact. Ben Walters has some which cost about 10¢ a pair and are impervious to most chemicals and paints.

A dust mask is needed for those sensitive to the huge amount of dust produced by hand sanding of balsa as well as the power sanding and cutting of other materials. These cost about 25¢ and can be obtained from tool supply companies. $1.30 Paintmasters Safety Respirators with replaceable filters can filter out most nontoxic paint fumes. Other more expensive devices, obtainable from spray equipment manufacturers, will render harmless any type of fumes that could conceivably be encountered.

Fire Fighting

Fire extinguishers are indicated by simple prudence and required by insurance companies. Small CO_2 or CO_2 powdered dry chemical (sodium bicarbonate) extinguishers are effective in fighting all types of fires (including those in electrical equipment.) Test them yearly by reading the gauges or indicators (if available) or by weighing the CO_2 cartridge. A loss of weight of $\frac{1}{4}$ of an ounce or more suggests that a recharge is necessary. Extinguishers cost $8 and up.

OTHER TYPES OF EXTINGUISHERS

Foam extinguishers are of marginal use since they do not work on all types of electrical fires. Soda acid extinguishers will not work on electrical fires or on inflammable liquids. Vaporizing liquid (Carbona, etc.) extinguishers and small Aerosol units can even cause noxious fumes.

4 HAND TOOLS AND THEIR USE

The greatest investment made in model-building, after paying the rent, will be in tools. While one can economize on rent by utilizing unused drafting space, for example, it is best to purchase tools of quality and adequacy, disregarding the cost. Unless one comtemplates a *very* limited amount of use, cheap tools will be more expensive because of frequent replacement, sharpening and adjustment. Inadequate tools can prove a liability on even the first model undertaken: wasted time and spoiled materials derived through lack of equipment and involving just one part of a model can add up to the price of an expensive tool.

High quality tools are, surprisingly enough, more essential to the beginner than to the expert, since the easily discouraged neophyte does not have the skill to compensate for malfunctioning tools. Models have been successfully built using only a straight edge, a razor blade, sandpaper and a pencil. But despite what some purists may claim, there is something inconsistent about having a trained draftsman or designer in the mid-twentieth century work with primitive tools. If models are to be constructed periodically, it is a reasonable procedure to purchase tools whose time savings, effected on even the first model, will equal as much as one third of the tool's price.

In the case of power tools, there is always the possibility of renting. Rental fees can be kept low through careful scheduling of work procedure. Most rental contracts now allow a deduction of the rent from the price of any tool subsequently purchased. However, most available rentable tools are intended for home craftsmen and construction workers and tend to be too heavy and overpowered. Their use is therefore unfeasible except for the construction of baseboards, cases and block models.

I have listed throughout the text the names of suppliers or manufacturers of many well-made tools. Many have proven themselves to be of special use to the modelmaker and are competitively priced. Other tools may also be satisfactory. One or more varieties of each type of tool may be purchased in any large hardware store. The prices that I have noted are intended as a rough guide; they are either prices from the manufacturer's list or the discount prices of major mail-order companies (not local stores). Thus it may be possible to locate some discount prices that are substantially below the ones I have quoted. Check local large discount houses for bargains. Catalogs of one or more large mail-order companies should be obtained before extensive purchasing of tools. The company that I have dealt with in the past is Silvo Hardware, 107 Walnut Street, Philadelphia 6, Pennsylvania; their catalog contains listings of many hundreds of tools. Local large hardware stores will also be able to supply many of the tools mentioned. Magazines like *Popular Science* contain extensive reviews of new tools as well as articles on the use of tools.

All metalworking tools are listed and discussed in Chapter 8.

TOOL CARE

Tools should be kept in good condition, free from rust that can so easily build up. After a tool is used, it should be wiped and restored to its position on the tool pegboard. Heavy accumulations of grease and dirt may be removed only by dipping the tool in cleaning fluids or solvents. Hard-to-remove gum deposits found on saw blades or router and shaper cutters can be removed with solvents, called gum and pitch removers, that are best applied with a toothbrush. If the shop is humid, all metal tools have to be wiped with a light machine oil or paste wax. There are also convenient anti-rust oils in spray cans. Jars of silica gel or magnesium chloride may be used to dry out the air inside of cabinets and drawers. If rust does form, it can be removed with fine steel wool or abrasive paper. If these are found to be too abrasive, rust can be cleaned off with a prepared rust remover. From time to time all moving parts should be oiled. Stanley's slide lubricant comes in a spray can which facilitates its application.

Sharpening of Tools

It is extremely important to keep tools sharp. Dull tools make for sloppy models, wasted time and materials and create safety hazards. It is probably more expedient to have dull saws reshaped and ground professionally, but it is also possible to grind and whet knives, planes, chisels and scrapers oneself. Procedures for each type of tool are outlined in individual sections of the book. In general, one needs a grinder, a honing stone, a slip stone and a strop to do this work.

Grinding Wheels are for grinding. A motor-driven circular Carborundum or emery grinding wheel equipped with a tool rest can be used. A special motor or stand may be bought to convert portable electric drills into grinders. General sells a $6 conversion kit that fits $\frac{1}{4}$" portable electric drills; it includes a stand, wheel guard, grinding wheel and a drill sharpening attachment. One may also purchase a horizontal shaft that can be turned by the motor of other power tools. Arco has a $3 kit that fits $\frac{1}{4}$" drills; it includes a 3" wheel, drill stand and tool rest. Multi-use power tools and radial arm saws can be fitted with grinding wheels, and belt sanders may also be used to sharpen tools.

In an improvised grinder, the wheel should not be turned too fast. If the manufacturer's recommended speed is exceeded, the wheel may burst. Always wear goggles when grinding, even if the tool rest is equipped with an eye shield. When possible, purchase jigs to hold blades against the wheel at the correct angle. If jigs are unobtainable, they can be made (4-1). When the wheel becomes

4-1

SHARPENING PLANE BLADES

Board
Rest for straight edge grinding
Grinding wheel
1" x 1"
Rest for 60° grinding, board can be elevated by placing other boards on it if necessary

worn, it can be dressed with a Carborundum stick. The grinder may also be converted into a buffer and sander, further defraying its cost.

Honing Stones are for tool sharpening. You will need a honing stone, best made artificially of Carborundum or aloxite. Stones must be kept wet with oil (3-in-1 or Pike oil) or their pores will clog with metal particles. Carborundum stones may be used dry, with water or with oil; the latter works the best. Most hones have both a coarse and a fine side. To prevent stones from becoming gummy, they should be stored in a piece of cloth

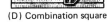
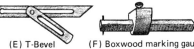

(A) Zigzag rule   (B) Micrometer   (C) Caliper   (D) Combination square   (E) T-Bevel   (F) Boxwood marking gauge   (G) Contour marker

moistened with oil. If gum does form, place the stone on nails in the bottom of a shallow pan. Slowly heat the pan until the oil runs out, but be careful not to allow it to evaporate. Wipe the stone dry while it is still hot. If the stone is worn, its surface may be resmoothed by rubbing it with a piece of metal covered with a creamy mixture of water and aluminum oxide powder whose grit is somewhat coarser than that of the stones. The Carborundum Company makes silicon carbide hones in 3 grades; these measure $4 \times \frac{3}{4} \times \frac{3}{8}''$ and cost 65¢ each. Lectro-Hone makes an electrically powered horizontal stone that comes complete with tool rest and costs $13.50.

Slip Stones are used to sharpen gouges. The Carborundum Company has a line of aluminum oxide stones (sometimes called tool room sticks) that come in 3 grades and with square, triangular, half-round and round cross sections. These cost between 50¢ and $1 each.

To bring honed tools to razor sharpness, strops are used. They can be formed with a strip of leather glued to a hard wood block.

MEASURING AND LAYOUT TOOLS

An Architect's or Engineer's Scale may be used to lay out dimensions precisely on modeling materials.

A 6" Zigzag Rule (4-2A) is for large layout work on baseboards, tables and cases. This comes in several models with maximum extended lengths from 2 to 8'. Stanley's 6' long model with brass 6" slide-out extensions on both ends (a very useful feature) costs $3. Stanley's 6' rule without extensions costs $1.50. A metal tape rule can be used instead of a zigzag.

A Metal Ruler is for measuring and is also used as a knife guide in cutting sheet material.

Stanley sells a 24" steel calibrated square for $4.25. Fairgate sells hard aluminum rulers that cost from 25¢ for 6" specimens up to $1.25 for 24" models. All sizes may be obtained from artist supply stores.

A Divider and Compass is for circle drafting or for transferring dimensions from the drawing to the model material. Old drafting tools may be used or, for large work, a wing divider may be purchased. Millers Falls makes a 7" long, $2 model that comes equipped with 2 steel points (1 may be replaced with a pencil).

A Beam Compass is for the drafting of large circles. An old drafting tool may be used or trammel heads may be purchased and mounted on a wood beam. Stanley makes a pair for $7.

A Micrometer (4-2B) comes in a wide range of cost and accuracy. In general, it is calibrated down to 1/1,000 or 1/10,000 of an inch and has a 1" capacity (0 to 1", 1 to 2", etc.). For not too exacting work a $3 tool will suffice, but for the

fine machining of Plexiglas a better model, costing $10 to $20, is needed.

A Vernier Caliper (4-2C) is used for inside and outside measurements and the transfer of dimensions from one object to another. Stanley's $1.50 model with a capacity of $3\frac{1}{4}''$ for outside measuring and with the capacity to measure inside openings of between $\frac{3}{16}$ and $\frac{3}{4}''$ is graduated by 32nds of an inch. International Models has an outside measuring tool that is calibrated down to 1/1000th of an inch, costing under $13.

A Combination Square (4-2D) multipurpose tool with 9 or 12" blades combines the functions of an inside and outside try square, 45° miter square, level, depth gauge, marking gauge, scribe and straightedge with calibrations down to $\frac{1}{32}$ nd of an inch. Stanley makes them for under $3.

A Sliding T-Bevel (4-2E) lays out and tests bevels of any angle. It is useful in baseboard construction. Stanley makes one with a 6" blade for $1.50.

A Marking Gauge (4-2F) makes lines parallel to an edge of a sheet of material. The sliding head resting on the material's edge is fastened by a thumbscrew. This tool is useful in the making of baseboards and other pieces of heavy carpentry. Stanley sells them for $2.50.

A Contour Marker (4-2G) transfers complex contours from drawing to material or from material to material. Lay it against the curve to be copied and push its sliding slats into position, then snap the lock to capture the curve. Scott Mitchell House has a 10" long marker having 19 slats per inch that costs $6. This tool also makes a very useful variable template.

A Magnifier is a great aid in working with small parts. Swift makes a complete line of pocket magnifiers selling for 50¢ to $1. Magnifiers on stands or magnifiers with handles cost $1 to $3, and magnifiers with built-in battery operated lights sell for $4.

GRIPPING TOOLS

Vises

Odd shaped objects may be held in a vise if precast into a block of low melting point metal (Cerrosafe, Cerrobend, etc.). After the object has been worked on, the metal, whose melting point is lower than the flash or melting point of the object, can easily be melted off.

TYPES OF VISES

A Bench, Workshop or Utility Vise (4-3A) is the most useful all-around vise, even though it is basically intended for metal and its unprotected jaws might scar wood. Its jaws have either serrated faces for firm gripping or smooth faces for use with finished work. Sharp pointed jaws facilitating metal bending are also available. More

expensive vises have interchangeable jaws. Jaws softer than one's work should always be used. Bench vises have stationary bases, swivel bases, or swiveling bases and swiveling rear jaws. The latter vise aids in holding tapered work. Vises can either be clamped on the workbench—providing greater flexibility of use but less rigidity—or screwed into place. The machinist vise is a heavier version of the bench vise. Sig makes a small one for modelmakers (with 1" jaw capacity) for $1. Stanley has a 2" jaw capacity model with or without anvil and with interchangeable jaws for $8.50. The same company also has a $5.50, $2\frac{1}{2}''$ model, with interchangeable jaws, that can be rotated around its vertical axis. Millers Falls has a $2\frac{1}{4}''$ model with a swivel base ($4.50) and with a stationary base ($3.50)

A Woodworker's Vise (4-3B) has long jaws faced with replaceable wood facings. Some have metal "dogs" on their outer jaws that can be raised and used for clamping long work against a bench stop. Some also have quick acting jaws which can be slid open and closed without the usual handle turning. Craftsman has a 3" jaw capacity model selling for a bit over $3.

A Machine or Drill Press Vise (4-3C) is used to position precisely small work that is being machined. It is meant to be bolted to a drill press table. It can be bought as a stationary model, with a swivel base, with a tilting (up and down) base, with a swiveling and tilting base (called an angle vise), or with a sideways sliding and swiveling base. Stanley has a $2\frac{1}{4}''$ jaw capacity model for $11.50.

A Gyro-Vise is a $15 vise for woodworking or metalworking made by The Columbian Vise and Manufacturing Co. It swivels and tilts and can be mounted upright or on its side.

An Instrument Vise (4-3D) holds small work in position. Eclipse has a model costing $14.

A Hand Vise (4-3E) is for the handgripping of small work. Sig has a $1\frac{1}{4}''$ jaw capacity $1 model.

Clamps

Clamps must be properly positioned before work can be started. Test this position to make sure that the pieces being held are not pulled out of line. Pieces of Bristol or cardboard placed between the clamp and the work will usually prevent marring the surface of soft materials. Figure 4-4 shows devices that facilitate the clamping of various types of joints.

TYPES OF CLAMPS

Improvised Clamps are paper clips, bulldog letter clips, binder clips, clothespins and rubber bands. Drops of sealing wax can be used to clamp small oddly shaped joints together.

Magnetic Holders hold metal parts together while they are being soldered or hold parts of non-

4-3

VISES AND CLAMPS

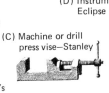
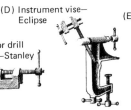
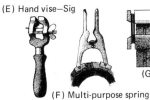

(A) Bench vise—Stanley   (B) Woodworker's vise—Craftsman   (C) Machine or drill press vise—Stanley   (D) Instrument vise—Eclipse   (E) Hand vise—Sig   (F) Multi-purpose spring clamp—Craftsman   (G) C-Clamp—Miniclamp   (H) C-Clamp—X-Acto   (I) Common wood hand screw

CLAMPS

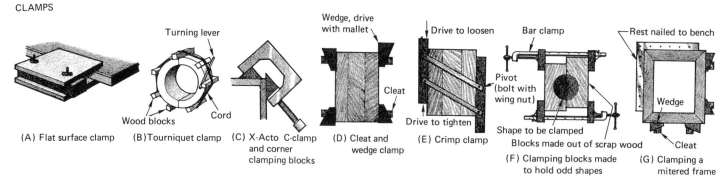

(A) Flat surface clamp   (B) Tourniquet clamp   (C) X-Acto C-clamp and corner clamping blocks   (D) Cleat and wedge clamp   (E) Crimp clamp   (F) Clamping blocks made to hold odd shapes   (G) Clamping a mitered frame

magnetic material in position on a metal work surface. Magnets can be obtained that will hold parts in a perfect 90° (or any other) angle intersection. Eclipse makes a very extensive line of magnetic holders.

Magnetized Rubber is a product with many uses from clamping small parts to holding together sections of take apart models. The rubber comes in sheets that can be bent or cut. Creative Playthings sells 20 sq. " of it for $2.

Multipurpose Spring Clamps (4-3F) have pivoting jaws allowing surfaces to be gripped at practically any angle. Craftsman sells them for $3 each.

Carriage Makers or C-clamps (4-3H) are the most important clamps encountered in model work. Small clamps are made of nylon, malleable iron and magnesium with jaw sizes ranging from $\frac{3}{8}$ to $1\frac{1}{2}$". Nylon clamps with $\frac{3}{8}$ to $\frac{3}{4}$" jaw sizes, costing 35¢ each, are made by Miniclamps. Malleable iron ones with $\frac{3}{4}$, 1 and 2" throat depths are obtainable from Model Shipways for from 30¢ to 50¢ each. X-Acto has a line of magnesium clamps with a throat depth of 1 and $1\frac{1}{2}$" that have a 1 and $1\frac{1}{2}$" jaw size (4-3G). These cost $2.50 for a 4 clamp set. Larger clamps made of malleable iron can be bought with a 2×3" to a 4×8" opening at any hardware store.

Clamps for Large Flat Surfaces can be made out of scrap wood (4-4A) or one can use a pile of heavy books. For curved surfaces use small sandbags.

Workbench-Mounted Holddown Clamps are permanent clamps that secure work to a table. The clamp slides into a bolt projecting from the bench. When not in use, the clamp is removed and the bolt drops into a counter-bored hole leaving the bench surface clear. Drumcliff Co. sells one for $3.

Tourniquet Clamps (4-4B) can be string tightly wound and used on moderate size jobs. Place wood blocks between the object and the cord to prevent damage to the surface of the work.

Common Wood Hand-Screws (4-3I) are heavy clamping tools for making glued baseboards. They cost from $1.50 for those with a $1\frac{1}{4}$" opening to $2.25 for those whose opening is $2\frac{3}{4}$".

Substitutes for Bar Clamps are clamps pictured in 4-4D and E. They are easily made substitutes for commercial bar clamps which are used to butt glue planks into wide boards. These substitute clamps may be made in a variety of sizes to facilitate the gluing of baseboards or model assemblies.

OTHER GRIPPING TOOLS

Tweezers by X-Acto are sturdy and pointed and cost 50¢; they also have a cross-action lock model (it is normally in a closed position, and must be squeezed to be opened) for under 75¢. These come with pointed or blunt ends.

Forceps by X-Acto have a scissor action for 75¢.

Pliers and Nippers

Pliers and nippers should be made of hammer-forged, tempered steel. They have to be tested to make sure that their jaws fit closely. Some have built-in wire cutters that can be made in three basic styles: (1) squared sections on each jaw that cut with a shearing action; this type of cutter has a tendency to loosen up; (2) side cutters consisting of short chisel-like blades on each jaw; these are more reliable than the squared style; (3) button cutters with wire-size notches on each jaw; these shift past one another as the pliers close and cut the wire.

TYPES OF PLIERS

Round Nose Pliers (4—5A) are for making curved bends and for holding wire and strips. X-Acto has a model that costs under $4.

Chain Nose Pliers (4-5C) make sharp bends in wire and strips. They are for holding small parts and are used as small wrenches. Pliers come in long nose and needle nose lengths. X-Acto sells both types for under $4 each; Channellock has several that are about as expensive.

Flat Nose Pliers (4-5E) perform identically with chain nose pliers. X-Acto has a model that sells for under $4; Channellock has a $3 model.

Combination Nose Pliers (4-5B) have a nose rounded on one side and flat on the other. X-Acto has a model that sells for under $4.

Slip Joint or Combination Pliers (4-5F) have a slip joint which allows the jaws to be opened extra wide. These pliers are used for gripping rods and small pipes or for bending wire and sheet metal; because of possible marring, they should not be used on nuts and bolts.

Bernard Side Cutting Pliers (4-5G) have compound leverage giving great holding and cutting power. Jaws are parallel, allowing this tool to be used as a wrench. International Models has a model which sells for a little over $3.

Diagonal Cutting Pliers or Sharp Nippers (4-5D) are used to cut small wire, nails, screws.

They have the ability to cut close to the surface from which the nail projects. X-Acto has a model that sells for under $4. Channellock has several that sell for $3 to $3.50.

End Cutting Nippers (4-5H) have long handles. Compound leverage makes these tools more powerful than diagonal cutting pliers. They may also be used to pull nails. Good end cutters cost between $2.50 and $3.

Lineman's Side Cutter Pliers or Side Cutters (4-5I) are for the cutting and splicing of all but piano wire and tempered steel wire. Good ones cost about $3.50.

Sets of pliers of the types most useful to the modelmaker are sold by various companies. International Models has a good 7-plier set selling for $9. The set includes: round nose, flat nose, diagonal cutting, end cutting, snipe nose, one side round—one side flat, and combination pliers.

Wrenches

Adjustable Wrenches (4-6A) are for turning nuts and bolts. They come in various sizes ranging in maximum jaw capacity from $\frac{1}{2}$ to $1\frac{3}{4}$", and in cost from $2.50 to $4. Sig sells a small locking adjustable wrench for $1.

Open End Wrenches (4-6B) are also for turning nuts and bolts. A wrench must fit exactly the object being turned or it will damage it. Open end wrenches come with their openings at various angles to their handles to facilitate turning hard-to-reach nuts. Cost ranges from 50¢ (4" handle) to $1.25 (12" handle).

Box Wrenches (4-6D) are for use on nuts and bolts unreachable with an open end wrench. Costs range from 60¢ (8" handle) to $1 (12" handle).

6-Sided Socket Wrenches are for use on small nuts and bolts, and are fitted to a screwdriver-like handle.

HAMMERS

Hammers come with hickory, tubular steel, solid steel (the strongest) and Fiberglas handles. Striking faces are: plain (flat), bell (slightly convex), ball-peen (very convex), checkered, and soft (plastic-faced). A plain face is easiest to use, but a bell face can drive a nail flush without leaving marks on the wood. A ball-peen head is for spreading rivets. A checkered face is for rough fast work such as crating. A soft face is used with

PLIERS AND CUTTERS

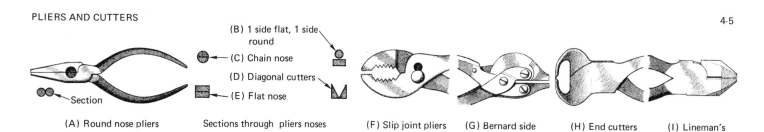

(A) Round nose pliers   Sections through pliers noses   (B) 1 side flat, 1 side round   (C) Chain nose   (D) Diagonal cutters   (E) Flat nose   (F) Slip joint pliers   (G) Bernard side cutting pliers   (H) End cutters   (I) Lineman's side cutters

WRENCHES, HAMMERS AND SCREWDRIVERS

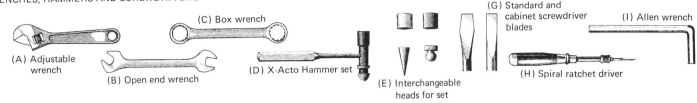

(A) Adjustable wrench
(B) Open end wrench
(C) Box wrench
(D) X-Acto Hammer set
(E) Interchangeable heads for set
(G) Standard and cabinet screwdriver blades
(H) Spiral ratchet driver
(I) Allen wrench

wood handled chisels. Hammers are graded by the weight of the head, 10 ounces being the size most often found in the household toolbox. A hammer that is too light will bend nails as will the imperfectly made heads of cheap hammers. Hammerheads should be of drop-forged steel with a hardened striking surface. Claws come in two styles: curved, best for nail pulling; and ripping (straight), usable for nail pulling or prying nailed joints apart. When pulling nails, place a block of wood between the hammer's head and the work to prevent damage to the latter.

In hammering, the nail should be held near its point until a few light blows from the hammer have started embedding it. Then hold the hammer near the handle's end for best leverage. The head should be brought down squarely on the nail. If the nail should bend, retract it and start again with a new one.

The price of good light hammers is about $3.50, as, for example, Stanley's 10 oz. wood handle hammer and Eastwing's 12 oz. solid steel hammer.

X-Acto makes a hammer set (4-6C and E) that contains a 7″ metal handle and 6 interchangeable heads: 2 ball, 3 flat (including a plastic soft face head) and a tinner's (conical) head. While this set is a bit elaborate for simple modeling, at $2.25, it is a good investment for more complicated future projects.

SCREWDRIVERS

The tip of a screwdriver must be square; if use has rounded it, restore it to its original shape on a grinding wheel. Long handles transmit more power to the screw. Short drivers (stubbies) are used to reach otherwise inaccessible screws. Use insulated drivers when working on electrical hookups. 6″ long drivers cost about 50¢ each.

BLADE STYLES

Standard Blades (4-6F) are for normal work.

Cabinet Blades (4-6G) are for use on deeply set screws.

Phillips Screwdrivers have blades that fit into the cross shaped slots of Phillips screws. Because of their greater driver-to-screw-bearing surface, Phillips screws seldom cause driver slip. They are used extensively where screws are visible and where driver slippage could mar a finished surface. Phillips screwdrivers cost about $1 each.

TYPES OF SCREW-DRIVERS

Spiral Ratchet Screwdrivers (4-6H) have blades which turn when the handle is pushed down. Some come with interchangeable bits permitting the drilling or countersinking of holes. Ratchet drivers cost $3.50 to $6.50 depending on size.

Jeweler's Screwdrivers have small interchangeable blades locked into a handle. General has a set of 6 blades (sizes No. 0 to No. 5) that costs $3. Moody has sets of miniature hex socket wrenches, Phillips drivers, Allen drivers and regular drivers that cost from $1.50 for a set of regular blades to $4 for a set of hex and regular drivers.

Screwdriver Bits are used with standard bit

braces to create the necessary amount of driving thrust for large screws.

Screw-Holding Screwdrivers are useful in starting screws in hard-to-reach places. They are made for standard and Phillips-type screws. These drivers cost 50¢ and up.

Nut Drivers have a hexagonal opening on the blade which fits standard nuts. They cost about $1.

Allen Wrenches (4-6I) have hexagonal heads that fit Allen cap screws.

Set Screw Wrenches are metal bars fitting into the head groove of set screws.

CUTTING TOOLS

Knives

All cutting should be done on a sheet of Masonite or heavy cardboard attached to the workbench. When the cutting surface has become badly marred, it should be replaced. Use a metal straightedge to guide the blade in straight cuts. Put a strip of masking tape along the underside of the metal to prevent its sliding under the pressure of the knife. Straightedges of varying lengths will facilitate the making of long cuts and short cuts without unnecessary maneuvering. An 18″ metal rule will suffice for most long cuts, and the ruler part of a combination square is good for short work. The square may be used as a guide for cutting perfect 45° or 90° angles.

When cutting all but the thinnest of materials, make several light runs over the cut line rather than attempting to sever the material at once. A sharp single cut can result in beveled cuts, deviation from the intended line and possible stab wounds.

TYPES OF KNIVES AND CUTTERS

A Mat Cutter and Beveler by X-Acto comes in the form of a 30″ straightedge. This can be used to guide the knife when making perpendicular or beveled cuts. It costs $9 (including a knife).

A Balsa Stripper by X-Acto has a $1.25 knife-holding guide that can be used to cut perfect strips ($\frac{1}{16}$ to $\frac{1}{2}$″ wide) from a $\frac{1}{32}$ to $\frac{3}{16}$″ thick balsa sheet. This tool permits the cutting of odd size strips that are unobtainable ready-made.

Razor Blades are cutting tools and the

handiest is the common single-edge razor blade. The thin, sharp blade allows the cutting of thin, fragile material without damage. Some people find it difficult to get the proper leverage with a blade and some fear them; however, with practice a razor blade can be made to perform most of the cutting required on paper, cardboard and balsa models and will cause, at least in my experience, fewer accidents. When the point dulls, it can be broken off, and the newly formed end serves as the point.

Throw-Away Razor Blade Knives are now being sold by the Edmund Scientific Company which has 5″ long knives with 2″ long razor sharp, steel blades. The low cost (3¢ each) allows them to be thrown away as freely as razor blades.

X-Acto Knives come in a very complete line of knife handles (4-8B, C, D and E) and interchangeable blades (4-8A and 4-10G) that can be used for cutting, carving, chiseling, routing, punching and sawing.

Following are knives that fit X-Acto's No. 1 (lightest, costing 60¢) handle: blade No. 10 is for small, fine cutting and carving; No. 11 is for fine, angle cutting, deep cuts and cutting in narrow spots; No. 16 is for making small holes and friskets; No. 17 has a $\frac{1}{4}$″ wide chisel blade for narrow, flat cutting.

Knives that fit their No. 2 (for medium work, 75¢) handle, their No. 5 (for heavy work, $1.20) and their No. 6 (all metal for heavy work, $1.80)

4-7

Project: **BANKERS TRUST COMPANY BUILDING, LINCOLN CENTER BRANCH, NEW YORK CITY.**

DESIGNED BY: Oppenheimer, Brady and Lehrecke.
MODELBUILDER: Joseph Santeramo.
PHOTOGRAPHER: Louis Checkman.
SCALE: 1/4″ = 1′.
This entire presentation model was made from acrylic. The lettering on the sign was cut from printers' type slugs. Trees were of steel wool.
The photograph was taken with a 4″ × 5″ Sinar view camera and 90 mm Angulon lens. 2 floodlights illuminated the spray painted backdrop, 1 750-watt spot was used on the model and bounced light from 1 flood picked up detail in the shadow area.
CONSTRUCTION TIME: about 120 hours.

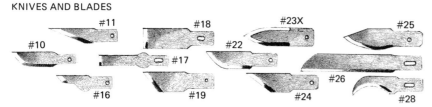

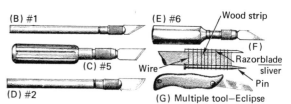

(A) X-ACTO BLADES (drawn to half size)   **X-ACTO AND OTHER KNIVES (not drawn to scale)**

handles: blade No. 18 has a ½″ wide chisel blade for flat cuts; No. 19 is for deep scoring and cross cutting; No. 22 is for making long cuts and for whittling; No. 23X is for fine work in close quarters; No. 24 is for cutting mats out of cardboard or wood; No. 25 is for general carving and whittling; No. 26 is a large whittling blade; No. 28 is for the carving of hard materials. Small blades cost about 12¢ each and the large whittling blade costs 15¢.

X-Acto blades should be kept sharp by being honed on a pocket-size dry Carborundum stone.

Mat Knives are very handy for cutting the heavy cardboard used for laminated contours, cardboard baseboards and templates.

Stanley's Quick-Point Knives are similar in appearance to mat knives. The blade, however, can be broken in ten places to present a series of unused cutting points.

The Multiple Tool (4-8G) by Eclipse is a mat knife with a handle that accepts various types of blades: saw blade (32 teeth per inch), slotting blade, cutting blade and scribing blade. The entire set costs $2.25.

Paper Cutters are very useful for rapidly cutting out a large number of objects. Their built-in squaring edges allow cutting of perfect 90° corners. Econo-Cutters (sold by artist supply stores) cost $7 (for a 10″ cutter) to $40 (for a 24″ cutter).

Circle Cutters

For Small Radial Cuts one can fabricate the instrument shown in 4-8F or buy an artist's cutting blade that is made to fit into the lead slot of standard compasses. X-Acto makes ¼ and ½″ diameter punches that fit their No. 5 and No. 6 handles. These cost about 30¢ each.

X-Acto Beam Compass and Circle Cutters costing $3 a piece can be used for cutting circles with 1½ to 15½″ diameters.

Large Circle Cutters can be easily fabricated in the shop: at the end of a strip of wood cut a groove perpendicular to the length of the strip. Clamp a mat knife into the groove. Drive a long sharply pointed nail through the other end of the wood strip parallel to the knife with the nail point on the same side as the blade of the knife. The distance between the nail and the blade determines the radius of the desired circle.

Scribers

Awls, such as scratch awls or engineer's scribers, can be used. Eclipse makes several lines of scribers; their general needle point scriber

costing 60¢ has several extra points stored in its handle.

Improvised Tools, such as hat pins, nails, ballpoint pen cartridges and the like, can also be used.

Multiple Line Scriber (4-9A) can be shop fabricated to make an endless variety of line patterns.

Scissors

Several sizes with 2″ and longer blades are available. Wiss makes an extensive line that includes 6 and 8″ trimmer shears costing $3 and $3.50.

Saws

Since saws are very prone to rust, a light oil should be applied as a preventative. If rust does form, emery cloth will remove it.

Material being sawed should be held in a vise or, if too large or oddly shaped, placed on a saw horse and held steady with the left hand or knee. A saw cut should be started by cutting a kerf. Position the blade with the thumb and then draw it over the material in the direction opposite to the cutting stroke if cutting wood, or in the direction of the cutting stroke if cutting metal. Once the kerf is deep enough to support the blade, start the actual cut. While the actual cut is being made, check the position of the saw to be sure the material is being cut squarely. Test by using a try square or by developing a practiced eye.

Sawing should be accomplished with long easy strokes, and pressure should be applied only when the blade is moving in the cutting direction. Let the blade lift slightly on the return stroke. If the blade starts to wander from its intended path, twist the saw slightly to move it back into line.

When the crosscut, rip or back saw becomes dull, sharpening, blade reshaping and the restoration of the saw's set should be professionally performed.

The coarseness of a saw blade is measured by the number of tooth points per inch. The more and finer the teeth, the cleaner the cut.

Saw teeth are alternately bent to the left and right of the plane of the blade. This is called set, and its amount determines the width of the cut. Set comes in various patterns: wavy set, on finer metal cutting blades, has one unbent tooth, then three that are bent in one direction (the first bent tooth is slightly bent, the next has maximum set, the third is slightly bent), the fifth tooth is unbent, then come three bent in the other direction. This pattern then repeats. Raker set has an unbent tooth flanked on both sides by teeth bent in

opposite directions. This pattern is found on wood and coarser metal cutting blades.

Spiral saw blades (used on piercing, coping and fret saws) can be used to cut plaster, plastic and other materials that clog regular saw blades.

Saws with thin blades: coping saws, hacksaws and others, easily break. If the blade twists and then breaks, the frame is not holding it with enough tension. If it breaks without twisting first or breaks near an end, it is held with too much tension. Blades may also break because they are too coarse for the stock being sawed, because the blade was twisted during sawing or because it was pushed with too much pressure.

If a cut turns out crooked despite the use of reasonable skill in following the guideline, it may be due to a dull blade, not enough tension on the blade or unalignment of the saw's frame.

SAWS FOR MAKING STRAIGHT OR GENTLY CURVED CUTS IN WOOD AND PLASTIC

Eclipse Multiple Tool Saws have 32 teeth per inch and replaceable blades. They come as part of a multiple tool set.

Keyhole Saws (4-9B) cut square or curved holes in the centers of panels. They can be used after being inserted into holes drilled through the material. Their blades, 10 to 18 teeth per inch, cut well both with or against the grain. Strombecker sells one for 70¢.

Compass Saws are large versions of the keyhole saw.

SAWS FOR MAKING STRAIGHT CUTS IN WOOD

Back Saws (4-9C) are used to make fine straight wood cuts that are not too long. Their crosscut-like blades come with 18 to 32 teeth per inch. Sig has one with a 10″ long blade costing $1.

Dovetail Saws are small back saws used for very fine cutting and miter cutting. Their blades come with 32 to 60 teeth per inch and cost about $1.50.

SAWS WITH REPLACEABLE BLADES THAT ARE USED FOR MAKING STRAIGHT OR CURVED CUTS IN THIN WOOD AND PLASTIC

(Some blades will also cut thin metal.)

Coping Saws (4-9E) have blades with 14 teeth per inch. They are used for cutting intricate curves

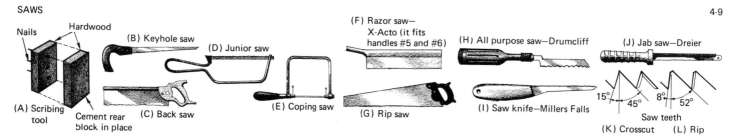

PLANES, CHISELS AND ROUTERS

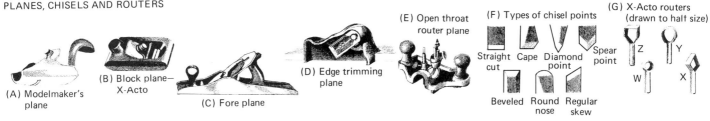

(A) Modelmaker's plane

(B) Block plane—X-Acto

(C) Fore plane

(D) Edge trimming plane

(E) Open throat router plane

(F) Types of chisel points

Straight cut Cape Diamond point Spear point

Beveled Round nose Regular skew

(G) X-Acto routers (drawn to half size)

Z Y

W X

in thin (up to about 1″ thick) wood and plastic. Since the blade may be turned in the frame, the depth of cut is unlimited. The teeth should point toward the handle so that the saw cuts on its back stroke. Spiral blades cut in any direction without having to be turned in the frame. Coping saws are obtainable at all hardware and hobby stores and cost $1 and up. X-Acto makes one (called a Hobbycraft saw) that comes with 3 spiral and 1 regular blade and costs about $1.75.

Piercing or Jeweler's Saws are like coping saws but have less clearance between their blades and the rear of the frame. Their blades have 32 to 80 teeth per inch. They cost about $2.

Junior Saws (4-9D) are small versions of the coping saw. They have 32 teeth per inch on their replaceable blade.

Fret Saws are like coping saws but have more clearance between the blade and the rear of the frame. Their blades have 16 to 32 teeth per inch.

SAWS FOR MAKING STRAIGHT AND, SOME-TIMES, GENTLY CURVED CUTS IN WOOD, PLASTIC OR METAL

Razor Saws (4-9F) are among the finest cut saws obtainable, having about 40 teeth per inch on their replaceable blade. They are used for making delicate cuts in cardboard, wood and metal and may be used in small miter boxes. They are not able to make curved cuts. X-Acto makes 2 for 40¢ and 45¢ each (fitting their Nos. 5 and 6 handles) and Strombecker makes 1 for 70¢.

Saw Knives (4-9I) from Millers Falls come in a set, costing $1.50, that includes 5 replaceable blades and a handle.

Jab Saws (4-9J) have hacksaw blades that may be extended out from the handle and flexed to lie flat against a surface. This facilitates the making of flush cuts. Dreier Brothers makes a good model of this saw.

All-Purpose Saws (4-9H), sold by Drumcliff Company, can be used to cut holes in the centers of panels and to cut curves.

Pad Saws use hacksaw, keyhole saw or pad saw blades that have a 10 to 32 teeth per inch range; with a hacksaw blade they may be used for cutting metal. Eclipse makes a pad saw for $1.

Eclipse General Purpose Saws have 10 teeth per inch and can cut wood or metal. The saw's replaceable blade pivots into 9 different positions.

SAWS FOR MAKING STRAIGHT CUTS IN HEAVY WOOD

Rip Saws (4-9G and L) have 5 to 7 teeth per inch and a small amount of set. They are used to cut with the wood's grain. The saw should be held at a 60° angle between the blade and the work. When ripping a long board, a screwdriver inserted into the cut will prevent the board from binding the saw blade.

Crosscut Saws (4-9K) have 8 to 12 teeth per inch and a great amount of set. Their blades are between 16 and 26″ long. The saw should be held at a 45° angle between blade and work. If

the crosscut blade is polished, the reflection of the board will be mirrored in it and this will help to make perfect 90° cuts. If the saw is being held exactly perpendicular to the edge, the reflection of the wood's edge will appear to run continuous with the actual edge. Make a perfect 45° miter cut, by placing the blade in the correct position so that the reflection of the board's edge is perpendicular to the front (the edge that the saw will first enter) of the wood.

Miter Boxes are box-like devices in which strip wood to be crosscut is placed. The saw fits into slots in the box which position it to make exact 90° or 45° (miter) cuts. Miter boxes come in various sizes. Small wood ones, costing under $1 and obtainable at hobby stores, are used with razor or dovetail saws. Larger boxes are sometimes made of metal and some can be adjusted to make cuts of all angles. These boxes are used with back saws. Millers Falls makes a $10.50 box that can be set at any angle.

Planes

After wood has been cut, it is necessary to plane it down to its approximate dimensions before sanding to a smooth finish. The proper adjustment of a plane is necessary for accurate performance. The blade must project evenly slightly below the bottom of the plane. Shavings are deflected by the cap iron (the plate that rests on top of the blade). So that shavings are not caught between the cap iron and the blade, the cap iron should be secured slightly back from the cutting edge of the blade. The throat of the plane (the slot through which the shavings feed) can be adjusted—wide for deep cuts in soft wood and narrow for cuts in hard or cross-grained woods. From time to time clear the throat of the plane from shavings with a wooden stick.

In making a cut of constant thickness, press down slightly on the front of the plane at the start of a planing stroke; at the end of the stroke (as you approach the end of the wood) press down on the rear of the plane. If the cut is even, the shaving will be of constant thickness. The plane must always be held perpendicular to the work; never tilt the plane from this position when removing a high spot. Planing must be done with the grain, not against it (4-11A and B).

To avoid splitting the corners of a board when planing its end, you must either: (1) plane from both edges to the center; or (2) plane from one edge to the other, first clamping a scrap board to the work so that the plane will finish its stroke on the scrap. When planing the thin edge of a board, clamp a scrap board along the edge to give the

USING THE CHISEL

4-11

(A) CORRECT—Cutting away from the grain

(B) INCORRECT—Cutting into the grain

(C) Direction chisel should move

Work

plane enough surface to rest on. If planing produces a rough or torn finish, reverse the direction of planing. Wide boards should be planed by a series of diagonal cuts.

Fasten planing work in a vise or, if planing the top of a plank, use a bench stop to keep the wood in position on the worktable. A long plane will cut a flat surface; a short plane will ride curves in the wood. Thus a shorter plane should be used only on level wood, or to plane curved surfaces.

SHARPENING THE PLANE

Plane irons must be kept sharp. Dullness may be removed by whetting the edge on an oilstone. When nicks develop or bevels are no longer the correct shape because of repeated whetting, blades must be reground, either in the shop or by a knife grinder.

Whetting: clamp an oilstone in a vise. Move the blade's cutting edge back and forth at a 30° to 35° angle to the stone. Be careful to move the blade without rocking it; when the cutting edge is sharp, rub the blade on its flat side until the burr caused by the first rubbing is removed. Be careful not to taper the flat side of the blade because it won't refit against the cap iron. After whetting, strop the cutting edge on a piece of leather or on a smooth wood block.

Grinding: use a circular grinding wheel. Place the blade as shown in 4-12A. The bevel must be cut at a 25° to 30° angle to the flat side of the blade; it must be straight and at a perfect 90° angle to the thin edges of the blade. Hold the blade on a tool rest and move it from side to side across the wheel's edge. If the 90° angle is lost, it should be restored by rubbing the blade on a perfectly flat, medium fine oilstone. Use a try square to test the 90° side angles.

TYPES OF PLANES

Razor Planes come in a model by Willoughby that uses double edged razor blades. The cost of this tool, which can be used on balsa and other soft materials, is $1.75.

Modelmaker or Violin Planes (4-10A) have a curved bottom and a conforming curved blade. They are used for planing flat, concave or convex (down to a 12″ radius) surfaces. These planes are 3 to 4″ long. Model Shipways has a 3½″ cast-iron long modelmaker's plane with a 1″ wide blade for $2.75.

Block Planes (4-10B) are for smoothing the end grain of large boards, shaping small boards, making chamfers, etc. The blade fits into the plane with its bevel side up. Model Shipways has a $1.25 model. Millers Falls has 5½ to 7″ long planes that cost $4 to $5.

Jack Planes—(11½ to 15″ long), *Fore Planes*—(18″ long) (4-10C) and *Jointer Planes*—(22 to 24″ long) are basically the same tool with different lengths. The longer planes eliminate peaks and the shorter planes smooth level work. Blades are set with their bevel side down. The cap iron should be placed about $\frac{1}{16}$″ behind the blade's cutting edge when cutting with the grain and as near the edge as possible for cross-grained cutting or with curly wood. Millers Falls and Stanley have many sizes of the above planes ranging in cost from $8 for a jack plane to over $20 for larger jointer planes.

Smoothing Planes are small ($5\frac{1}{2}$ to 10" long) versions of the jack plane. They are used for finishing. The blade is set into the plane with its bevel side up. Millers Falls has several 8 to 9" long planes (called bench planes) that cost $7.50.

Low Angle Planes have their blades set at a low angle to give a smooth cut cross grain. This type of plane is used on work too heavy for a block plane.

Open Throat Router Planes (4-10E) are used to make grooves, dadoes, etc. Millers Falls and Stanley have models costing about $8.

Rabbit Planes

These have one side of their frame omitted. The blade extending to the side edge of the plane will cut extremely close to a vertical obstruction; thus, the plane may be used to smooth out the insides of boxes, cut rabbits, etc.

Cabinetmaker's Rabbit Planes are 4 to $5\frac{1}{2}$" long. Stanley has several costing $9 to $11.

Bull Nosed Rabbit Planes can cut into corners because the blades are at the very front of the plane. Millers Falls has a 5" long model for $1.50.

Edge Trimming Block Planes (4-10D) are used to trim and square off the edges of boards of up to 1" thicknesses. They are a great aid in squarely planing edges. When used for beveling, a wood block (cut to the desired bevel) can be attached to the bottom of the plane to tilt the plane to the desired angle.

Chisels

Secure work so that it cannot move before cutting with a chisel. Cuts are accomplished by a series of light passes; cutting too deep may split the work. Cut with the grain (4-11A and B) or directly across it, holding the chisel at a slight angle towards the cut (4-11C). For heavy cutting the chisel's bevel should face down; it should face up for lighter shaving. Cut from a penciled guide-line into the waste area so that a slip will not carry you into good wood. Push the chisel with the palm of the right hand, guiding the top of the blade with the left. Make the first, outlining cuts with a parting tool.

To maintain razor-sharp edges, frequently whet blades. Secure an oilstone to the bench, rub the chisel's bevel on the stone's rough side, maintaining a 25° to 30° bevel edge. Then whet the bevel on the fine side of the stone, smoothing the rough bevel to a 30° to 35° angle. Remove any burr that may have formed by rubbing the flat side of the chisel on the fine side of the oilstone. Finally, whet the edge on a piece of leather. It takes skill to rub the blade at a constant angle across the stone; a poor job will cause a rounded bevel. When the edge becomes badly nicked or when the bevel has become rounded or distorted, the chisel will have to be reground by either the modelmaker or at a hardware shop. An emery or Carborundum wheel with an adjustable tool rest is necessary if grinding is done in the shop. To keep the blade from overheating and losing its temper and hardness, the wheel should be kept wet with a constant application of water or kerosene. If the wheel is not smooth or true, it can be dressed with a Carborundum stick. The chisel is moved from side to side across the wheel that is turning toward it. After grinding has been com-

pleted, the chisel should be whetted. Hollow ground or V-point edges may be produced by grinding the chisel on the wheel's edge.

TYPES OF CHISELS

Chisels come in three handle constructions: (1) tang chisels for hand pushing or light mallet driving, (2) socket chisels which can be driven by a heavy mallet and (3) everlasting chisels which are strong enough to be driven by a steel hammer. Chisels also come in various blade shapes: paring chisels have thin blades which are meant to be hand driven. Firmer chisels have long strong blades that may be mallet driven to perform heavy cutting. Butt chisels have short blades allowing them to be used in places inaccessible to longer blades. Chisel blades range in widths from $\frac{1}{8}$ to 2".

Cutting edges come in: straight cut, beveled edge, cape, round nose, diamond point, regular skew and spear points (4-10F and G). Stanley sells a complete line of the above. They cost 50¢ to 80¢ each for $\frac{1}{4}$" blades (without handles), and about $2 for blades mounted in wood handles. X-Acto sells light-duty (suitable for use on softwood) $\frac{3}{16}$ and $\frac{1}{4}$" chisel blades that fit their Nos. 5 and 6 handles.

X-Acto also makes four light-duty routers costing 25¢ each that fit their Nos. 5 and 6 handles (4-10G).

Gouges

A gouge is a chisel with a concave blade. The bevel can be on the inside or outside of the blade. Gouges are held in the same fashion as chisels. Unlike chisels, cutting across the grain allows better control.

To whet a gouge, use a wedge-shaped slip stone that is kept wet with oil. First whet the bevel, then the flat side of the gouge, to remove any burr that may have formed. In whetting a concave surface, move the gouge with a slight rotary motion. To regrind an outside bevel gouge, use a wet grindstone and move the gouge across the wheel's perimeter with a rolling motion. An inside bevel gouge is ground on a cone-shaped grinding wheel. In general, follow the instructions for grinding chisels.

Carving Tools

Carving tools or lino cutting tools are chisels and gouges used for fine carving. Their blades taper toward the tang (the tapered end fitting into the handle) instead of being parallel to it. Cutting edges may be square or oblique to the long axis of the tool; blades may be straight or bent.

Blade cross sections are: V-shaped, and called parting tools (they come with obtuse, medium and acute angles); U-shaped, and called veiners if they are deep and narrow or fluters if they are large; flat and curved and called quicks if their curve is almost U-shaped, or called medium if their curve is about the shape of a quarter moon, or called flats if they are almost flat. There are, also, perfectly flat blades called firmer or corner chisels.

All these shapes can be procured at art supply stores. Lino tool blades cost 10¢ each, handles cost about 25¢. Millers Falls has a $4.50 set of 6 assorted carving tools. X-Acto has light-duty $\frac{3}{16}$

and $\frac{3}{8}$" V-gouges, $\frac{3}{8}$" U-gouges, and a $\frac{3}{32}$" U veiner that fit their Nos. 5 and 6 handles. Hand forged carving tools with high carbon steel blades and hardwood handles can cost as much as $2 to $4.50 each. These are available at art supply stores. Extremely minute carving, gouging and scribing can be done with dental picks. Greenland Studio sells a 4-piece set for $2.

Spoke Shaves

Make chamfers and curved edges with spoke shaves by holding them with both hands and pulling them forward. Stanley makes a $1.30, 9" long spoke shave and X-Acto has a miniature one that sells for 55¢.

Scrapers

These are employed to remove small amounts of material—wood, plaster, acrylic or polystyrene. Scrapers are used after planing and before sanding. Some scrapers have beveled cutting edges and are used for paint scraping. Others have square edges and are used for smoothing the surface of wood. Scrapers should be gripped with both hands; they may be pulled or pushed but always must be inclined at a 75° angle toward the direction of travel. Unlike the plane, the chisel or the gouge, the scraper's blade edge does not do the cutting. Cutting is done by hook edges that are adjacent to the blade (4-12D and E). When the blade loses its hook or becomes damaged, it must be sharpened.

TYPES OF SCRAPERS

Hand Scrapers (4-12F) have flat, concave or convex overall shapes. Their cutting edges may be square or beveled.

Cabinet Scrapers resemble a spoke shave. Their beveled blade will produce a smooth cross-grain cut but will not cut soft wood well. If the blade produces dust instead of shavings, it is dull and must be burnished.

To sharpen a square edge scraper: (1) clamp the blade in a vise and square file the cutting edge with a smooth mill file. (2) Whet the edge on an oil stone. (3) Lay the scraper flat on its side on the stone and remove any burrs that may have formed. (4) Lay the scraper flat on the workbench and draw the edge with a few strokes from a burnisher (4-12C). (5) Clamp the scraper in a vise and turn the edge with a few strokes of the burnisher. Hold the burnisher at a 90° angle to the side of the blade for the first stroke and slowly decrease the angle until it is 85° at the last stroke (4-12D). Oil the scraper during burnishing. A bevel edge scraper is sharpened in the same general way, except that (4) is omitted and, in (5), the burnisher is held for its first run at an angle slightly more than the angle of the bevel. This angle is increased to 75° by the last burnishing (4-12E). A cabinet scraper is sharpened in the same general way.

Files

The thousands of files available are identified by their cross section (4-12H), tooth cut type (4-12G) and coarseness. Single cut files—like mill files—are used to achieve a final finish and are

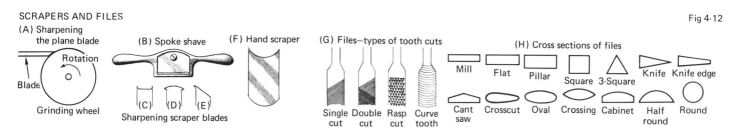

SCRAPERS AND FILES   Fig 4-12

(A) Sharpening the plane blade   (B) Spoke shave   (F) Hand scraper   (G) Files—types of tooth cuts   (H) Cross sections of files

Rotation   Blade   Grinding wheel

(C) (D) (E) Sharpening scraper blades

Single cut   Double cut   Rasp cut   Curve tooth

Mill   Flat   Pillar   Square   3-Square   Knife   Knife edge

Cant saw   Crosscut   Oval   Crossing   Cabinet   Half round   Round employed on lathe work. Double cut files are used for the removal of large amounts of material. Rasp cut files are used on wood and other soft materials. Curved tooth files are used on sheet metal.

The different degrees of coarseness are: dead smooth, smooth, second cut, bastard, coarse and rough. Small files are numbered 8 (finest) to 00 (coarsest). Some files have edges without teeth which are called safe edges.

To file, clamp the work in a vise. Have one's eye level with the surface of the work that is to be cut. Hold the file in the right palm with the other hand holding its tip. The file must be held level throughout the stroke; it should be kept in firm contact with the work on the cutting stroke, or it will be worn out quickly. Filing is done on the forward stroke only. The file should be lifted on the back stroke to prevent excessive wear. When filing soft metal, rub the work on the back stroke to clear the teeth of the file. Fine filing should be done perpendicular to the grain, rough filing at a 30° angle to the grain.

To apply a smooth finish to metal, use a smooth file, but not one with a short-angle cut. Hold the file at a 90° angle and draw it back and forth along the long axis of the surface being filed.

Files should be cleaned with a stiff wire brush (file card). Very clogged teeth may be cleaned with the point of a scriber. Covering the file with chalk or turpentine before filing helps to prevent clogging, and removes oil.

Storing files on a rack will protect their teeth from damage. Never store them with their teeth in contact with other files or with metal.

FILES FOR VARIOUS MATERIALS

Material	File
Plaster	Rasp cut
Wood	Rasp cut
Aluminum	Special-purpose aluminum rasp for heavy removal; a special-purpose aluminum file for smooth-finish filing
Copper and brass	Special-purpose brass file
Soft steel	Double-cut file for heavy removal; a single-cut mill file for smooth-finish filing
Die castings	Special-purpose die-cast file

A good selection of files to start with would include a 6 or 8″ wood rasp and some 6″ metal files having flat, round and triangular cross sections and fine and coarse cuts. Hardware stores carry a large supply of files costing from 50¢ (for 6″ long tools) to $2 (for 12″ models).

Small Jeweler's Files or Swiss Pattern Files cost 35¢ each and are obtainable from Model Shipways. They have single and double cut teeth, come in most cross sections, and may be used on metal and acrylic plastic.

Abrasives

The most commonly used abrasive papers are the following:

Flint (Buff Colored) is an inexpensive sandpaper found in most stores. While not effective for sanding wood or metal, flint may be used advantageously to sand plaster and paint which, because of their tendency to clog the abrasive, cannot be abraded with more expensive substances.

Garnet (Orange or Red) is obtainable in a wide variety of grit sizes, grit spacings, and in wet or dry types. It performs well on wood. Its longer life offsets its higher cost.

Aluminum Oxide (Reddish Brown) is used mostly on metal but it also performs well on wood. Carborundum Company's Aloxite sandpaper is of this type.

Silicon Carbide (Blueish Black) is a very hard grit of silicon carbide and is good for the fine sanding of paint finishes and acrylic plastic. Silicon paper is sold under the following trade names: Resinized Speed Grits, Durite, Crystalon and Tri-m-ite.

Emery is made with a natural abrasive. It has been superseded by some of the more effective synthetic abrasives.

Crocus uses iron oxide as the abrasive. It is a good abrasive for fine sanding and metal polishing.

Steel wool can be used to polish metal and finish the edges of acrylic sheets and blocks.

BACKING

The backing sheet on which the abrasive is fixed can be made from: paper—most commonly used for hand sanding chores; Mylar or cloth—for flexibility and strength; combinations—for heavy grinding jobs; and open cloth mesh backing—that allows sanding residue to flow through. Open mesh prevents clogging and extends the working life of the abrasive. The Carborundum Company makes a version of this backing and markets it under the name of Sandscreen.

Thickness of paper is designated by A (the thinnest) to E (the thickest). Thickness of cloth is designated by J for lightweight, X for heavyweight and EX for extra heavy.

COARSENESS OF ABRASIVES

There are two systems for grading the size (thus, the coarseness) of abrasives. The system used for flint and emery paper runs from 8/0 (the finest) up through 7/0, 6/0, 5/0, 4/0, 3/0, 2/0, 0, $\frac{1}{2}$, 1, $1\frac{1}{2}$, 2, $2\frac{1}{2}$, 3, $3\frac{1}{2}$ (the coarsest). There are, however, some slight variations in the actual coarseness of the different papers of the same number put out by different manufacturers.

Aluminum oxide and silicon carbide papers have a different system; their designation is roughly keyed to the number system for flint and emery papers presented in parentheses: 600—the finest, 500, 400 (10/0), 360, 320 (9/0), 280 (8/0), 240 (7/0), 220 (6/0), 180 (5/0), 150 (4/0), 120 (3/0), 100 (2/0), 80(0), 60 ($\frac{1}{2}$), 50 (1), 40 ($1\frac{1}{2}$), 36 (2), 30 ($2\frac{1}{2}$), 24 (3), 20 ($3\frac{1}{2}$), 16 (4), 12 ($4\frac{1}{2}$)—the coarsest. This system is based on the number of openings per inch in the smallest screen through which the grit used on the paper will pass. Garnet paper is graded with both systems. Experimentation will determine the grit size producing the best finishes on various materials.

PLACING OF ABRASIVES

The abrasive is positioned on its backing sheet in the following ways:

On closed-coat paper, or cloth, the abrasive particles are spaced close together, producing a smooth finish. However, the paper will rapidly clog with sanding dust.

On open-coat paper, or cloth, particles are spaced farther apart causing a rougher finish but less paper clogging.

ABRASIVES FOR VARIOUS MATERIALS

Abrasive	Material
Aluminum oxide	Hardwoods, aluminum, copper, steel, plastics
Garnet	Hardwoods, softwoods, composition boards, plastics, paper
Silicon carbide	Glass, finely finished paint, acrylic
Flint	Plaster, paint removal
Emery	Acrylic, soldered joints

For a sharper cutting surface, the abrasive is sometimes fixed to its backing with the long axis of the grits pointing up. Trade names of these products are Electro-Coated, Lightning and Elec-Tro-Cut.

SANDING

Sanding should be done only after planing and scraping because the abrasive particles left behind after sanding will dull blades. For smooth finishing, sand with the grain. For maximum material removal, sand at a 90° angle to the grain. See 4-12A for the correct sanding of the edge of a small object.

Clear the abrasive of sanding dust by slapping it against a hard surface.

Before the final sanding of wood, its surface should be rubbed with a damp cloth. This will raise the grain, which, after it has dried, can be sanded smooth.

Use a constant application of soap and water as a lubricant for wet sandpaper. Keep the surface being sanded free of residue by sponging it clean.

For extremely fine finishes, Flex-I-Grit abrasive-coated Mylar should be used. It comes in 5-sheet, 50¢ sets, of 8/0 to 10/0 coarseness. The plastic backing allows cleaning of the paper by flexing.

Sanders

Abrasive paper should be mounted when possible on a block backing that will hold it in the shape to be imparted to the work. Block shapes used for sanding can be flat, slightly concave, convex (in varying degrees), and, also, in the form of dowels ranging in diameter from $1\frac{1}{2}$″ down. If a large flat surface is being sanded, place the paper on top of the workbench to create a flat contour.

Contour Sanders come in a set by X-Acto of 5 differently shaped abrasive paperholders mounted on a handle (4-12B). The set costs $4 and includes Flex-I-Grit abrasive paper.

For heavier work one can make one's own block or buy a ready-made block sander. X-Acto makes them in 1 and 2″ widths, costing 50¢ and 75¢. Carborundum and Millers Falls make blocks that measure 2 to 3″ by 6″. To make one, use a hardwood block and attach the abrasive paper with thumbtacks, or hold the abrasive in place by hand. When sanding flat surfaces, avoid blocks that are made from flexible materials because they will deflect under pressure. Sandpaper can be mounted on a rubber block for use on slightly curved surfaces.

4-13

SANDERS

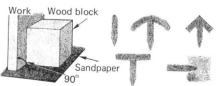

(A) Sanding guide
(B) End views of X-Acto contour sanders (note only one holder is shown)

Cutters, for fast material removal, are made by a few companies. They are sanding block-shaped tools whose faces are covered with steel teeth somewhat similar to those found on a food grater. Arco makes a Plane Form for $1, and a 10″ long sander that costs 75¢. Stanley makes the Surform line, which includes a file and a plane-shaped sanding block.

Project: THE UNITED STATES EMBASSY IN NEW DELHI, INDIA.

DESIGNED BY: Edward Durell Stone.
MODELBUILDER: Theodore Conrad (a professional modelbuilder).
PHOTOGRAPHER: Louis Checkman.
SCALE: $1/8'' = 1'$.
This magnificent presentation model was built mainly from acrylic. The exterior columns were cast in metal then spray painted gold color. The grill was sent out to be punched in vinyl. Water: a sheet of acrylic painted on its lower side. Trees: sawdust on wire armature. Lily pads: paper.
The photograph was taken with a $4'' \times 5''$ Linnhof view camera, 90 mm Angulon lens and Super Panchro Press "B" film. 1 750-watt spot was used for general illumination; 4 floods illuminated the spray painted background in a way that emphasized the horizon. 1 flood light was used to pick up detail in the areas put in shadow by the spot.

DRILLING TOOLS

Starting the Hole

To start a hole in wood, draw intersecting lines and punch the center of the intersection. In metal, repeat the process and then, using an inking compass and layout ink, draw a circle the size of the diameter of the drill. Use the punched depression as the center of the circle. If the drill starts to drift off center, retract it and punch a center hole opposite to the drift. This should reposition the drill and compensate for the inaccuracy. If holes are to be drilled in a great number of similar pieces, make a template with the hole cut into it. Clamp the template over the work and use the hole as a guide.

Centering Tools

Prick or Dot Punches have 60° points. They are the best instrument for locating small holes. After applying the dot indentation, increase it in size with a 90° punch. Stanley has several models of punches selling for 50¢ each.
Automatic Center Punches are good for precise punching. They have a spring that pushes the point into the surface to be marked. Eclipse makes one for $3.
Bell Punches or Self-Centering Punches precisely locate the center of the end of a bar.

Drilling

Gripping the fluted portion of a drill in a chuck may cause it to snap. Before starting to make a hole, test the drill for straightness. Small work must be clamped down or the drill will cause it to rotate. Thin sheets, when drilled, will climb, so they too must be clamped down.

When drilling without the aid of a drill press, make sure that the drill is going into the work at a 90° angle. Test with a try square or sight by eye from 2 positions: at a point when the drill rests on the material and at a point after it has cut a short distance. Make a cardboard guide when drilling at a slight-to-moderate angle. When the angle is considerable, bore a similar sized hole into a wood guide block, saw off the bottom of

the block at the proper angle and clamp it to the work. Then make the final hole through the guide into the work. Use a power tool for holes smaller than $\frac{1}{16}''$ because hand drilling tends to bend or break the bits.

If the drill squeaks, it may be clogged, have been fed too fast or simply dull. Overheating causes fast dulling and may even cause the tool to lose its temper. In general, small drills should be turned and fed faster than large ones.

DRILL AND WIRE SIZES

Drill no.	Diameter (inches)	Wire no.	Escutcheon pin no.	Pin[1]	Drill no.	Diameter (inches)	Wire no.	Escutcheon pin no.	Pin[1]
80	0.013	28			38	0.102	10		
79	0.015				37	0.104			
78 (1/16")	0.016	26			36	0.107			
77	0.018				7/64"	0.109		12	
76	0.020	24			35	0.110			
75	0.021			B, S	34	0.111			
74	0.023		24		33	0.113			
73	0.024				32	0.116			
72	0.025	22			31	0.120		11	
71	0.026			S	1/8"	0.125			
70	0.028		22		30	0.129	8		
69	0.029			B		0.134		10	
68 (1/32")	0.031			D	29	0.136			
67	0.032	20	21		28 (9/64")	0.141			
66	0.033			B	27	0.144			
65	0.035		20		26	0.147			
64	0.036			D, B	25	0.150			
63	0.037				24	0.152			
62	0.038				23	0.154			
61	0.039				5/32"	0.156			
60	0.040	18			22	0.157			
59	0.041				21	0.159			
58	0.042		19		20	0.161	6		
57	0.043				19	0.166			
	0.046			B	18	0.170			
56 (3/64")	0.047				11/64"	0.172			
	0.050	16	18		17	0.173			
55	0.052				16	0.177			
54	0.055				15	0.180			
	0.058		17		14	0.182			
53	0.060				13	0.185			
1/16"	0.063				3/16"	0.188			
52	0.064	14			12	0.189			
	0.065		16		11	0.191			
51	0.067				10	0.194			
	0.070				9	0.196			
50	0.072		15		8	0.199			
49	0.073				7	0.201			
48	0.076				13/64"	0.203			
5/64"	0.078				6	0.204	4		
47	0.079				5	0.206			
	0.080	12			4	0.209			
46	0.081				3	0.213			
45	0.082				7/32"	0.219			
	0.083		14		2	0.221			
44	0.086				1	0.228			
43	0.089				A (15/64")	0.234			
42 (3/32")	0.094				B	0.238			
	0.095		13		C	0.242			
41	0.096				D	0.246			
40	0.098				E (1/4")	0.250			
39	0.100								

[1] Pins described are: B = bank pins; D = dressmaker's pins; S = satin pins. All are obtainable at dressmakers' supply stores.

DRILLS AND BITS

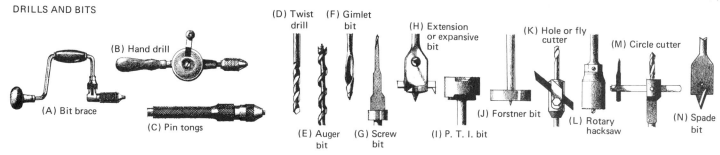

(A) Bit brace   (B) Hand drill   (C) Pin tongs   (D) Twist drill   (E) Auger bit   (F) Gimlet bit   (G) Screw bit   (H) Extension or expansive bit   (I) P. T. I. bit   (J) Forstner bit   (K) Hole or fly cutter   (L) Rotary hacksaw   (M) Circle cutter   (N) Spade bit

DRILLING VARIOUS MATERIALS

When woodworking, cut large holes from both sides to prevent the drill from splitting the wood around the exit hole. This can easily be done by waiting for the first hole to puncture slightly the exit side of the wood; this hole should be used to start the drill from the other side.

When drilling plaster, frequently withdraw the drill to clear it of chips. Wet plaster should be removed from the drill with a piece of wood.

Drill a pilot hole first when drilling through rough metal, or when working with wood whose grain pulls the drill off center or when using large twist drills.

Lubricate your drill bit when drilling metal: kerosene for steel; white paraffin for aluminum or brass.

For extremely deep holes, drill from both sides of the work or buy an extension drill. Both techniques enable the drilling of holes about twice the length of any given drill.

Holes may be drilled into the sides of dowels by inserting the dowel into a wooden block pierced by a hole that will position the drill on its pass through the dowel.

Drill Holders

Bit Braces (4-15A) allow a great amount of pressure to be exerted in the making of $\frac{1}{8}$ to $\frac{1}{2}$" holes. Their ratchet device allows the brace to be worked in confined spaces where it would be impossible to turn the tool a full 360°. The brace holds taper or round shank bits. Small ones cost about $5. Large ones cost $12 or so.

Hand Drills or Wheel Braces (4-15B) are for small hole drilling. Twist drills up to $\frac{1}{4}$" diameters can be used. The breast drill, a larger version of the hand drill, takes twist drills up to $\frac{1}{2}$" diameters. A large amount of thrust can be directed through the drill by leaning on the end plate. X-Acto sells a good $2.75 hand drill.

Automatic Push Drills have sliding sleeves that, when pushed back and forth, turn the drill. Stanley has a model costing $3.50.

Pin Tongs (4-15C) are chuck-type instruments for holding small round tools and work. Eclipse makes one costing $1.50.

Pin Vises are similar to, but larger than, pin tongs. Eclipse makes several costing $1.25 to $1.75. X-Acto also has 3 sizes costing $1.25 to $1.50 each. They are capable of taking drills from No. 44 to No. 80.

Drill Bits

Twist Drills (4-15D) are for drilling small holes in metal, plastic and wood. They usually come in $\frac{1}{32}$" increments from $\frac{1}{16}$ to $\frac{3}{4}$" and in many smaller sizes. Twist drills may be used in both hand and power drills. Twist drills must be used slowly or they will not be cleared of chips and will, therefore, become hot. Some have square shanks for use in bit braces. Special taper shank drills have tangs that fit into drill press spindles. Carbon tool steel drills can be used for hand and low speed power drilling.

Tempered drills can be used to drill soft metals. High speed steel drills used for high speed drilling have the longest life expectancy. Never use twist drills on hardened steel. When drilling hard material or using very small drills, withdraw the drill periodically to clear it. If the drill squeaks, it must be withdrawn and cleared.

Larger drills have number designations stamped on them; smaller drills must be identified by measuring them in a drill gauge; extremely small drills have to be measured by micrometers. To eliminate constant measuring, keep your drills in a numbered drill stand.

The factory-made point angle of a twist drill is usually 59°, a compromise angle that works truly well only in brass. Anyone contemplating extensive drilling of other materials may want to have some specially modified drills.

BEST DRILL-POINT ANGLES FOR VARIOUS MATERIALS

Material	Best angle
Wood, fiberboard	30°
Plastic	30°–45°
Soft cast iron	45°
Copper	50°
Heat-treated steel	62°

Carbon steel drills, Nos. 1 to 80, are obtainable at most hobby stores. They cost 25¢ to 50¢ each. Chrome vanadium drills, $\frac{1}{2}$" to No. 60, can be obtained from Scott Mitchell House, which has a set of Nos. 1 through 60 drills that sells for under $6.

Auger Bits (4-15E) are used in bit braces and electric drills for drilling medium and large size holes in wood. They come in $\frac{1}{16}$" increments from $\frac{1}{4}$ to 2". Their identification numbering system is based on $\frac{1}{16}$ of an inch: a No. 1 bit has a $\frac{1}{16}$" diameter, so a No. 2 bit has a $\frac{1}{8}$" diameter, etc. Augers have a screw on their end which makes contact with the wood first, then draws the bit into it. Screws are designated by their pitch: fast (for end hole drilling and for use in resinous wood), medium, and slow (for the smoothest hole). Spurs (nibs) at the front of the bit score the circumference of the hole, cutting a cleaner hole than is possible with a twist drill. Single twist or straight core (solid center) auger bits are used for hard or gummy woods, and double twist auger bits for soft woods. Augers were not designed for end grain drilling.

Gimlet Bits (4-15F) are used in bit braces for boring screw holes into wood. They come in $\frac{1}{32}$" increments from $\frac{1}{16}$ to $\frac{3}{8}$".

Screw Bits (4-15G) are used in hand and electric drills for simultaneously cutting the pilot, clearing and countersinking holes for screws.

Stanley sells them for 75¢ each and also sells bits that cut these holes, plus a hole for a plug, for $1.25 each.

LARGE HOLE DRILLS

The following large hole drills are used in electric drills:

Extension or Expansive Bits (4-15H) are adjustable in size, one bit being able to cut holes of from $\frac{1}{2}$ to 3" in diameter.

PTI Bits (4-15I) come in $\frac{5}{8}$ to 2" diameters and are for drilling holes in wood. This type of bit requires no pilot hole.

Forstner Bits (4-15J) come in 1 to 2" sizes and are also used for drilling holes in wood. They produce very smooth holes and are especially good for boring end wood and thin wood. They may be used to drill overlapping holes and to rout out wood and plaster objects.

Hole or Fly Cutters (4-15K) are used to drill holes in wood and metal. They are adjustable so that the smallest model cuts holes from $\frac{5}{8}$ to $2\frac{1}{2}$" in diameter and the largest cuts holes from $1\frac{1}{4}$ to 8" in diameter.

Rotary Hacksaws (4-15L) are for drilling up to 3" diameter holes in thin wood and metal. Smaller rotary hacksaws may be used in a breast drill. Some can be adjusted to cut a variety of hole sizes. Arco makes one costing $8 that cuts seven hole sizes from 1 to $2\frac{1}{2}$".

Circle Cutters (4-15M) for drilling holes in wood or steel are adjustable. Small circles may be cut out with a breast drill. Some brands can be obtained for under $1.50 in hardware stores.

Spade Bits (4-15N) are for drilling holes up to $1\frac{1}{4}$" in diameter.

Bit Gauges limit the amount of penetration of a drill or bit.

CLAY WORKING TOOLS

For cutting heavy blocks of clay, a carving knife can be used, as can any of the knives made for the trowel trades. Hyde makes flexible high carbon steel joint knives with 4 to 6" wide spade-shaped blades that sell for $1 to $1.50. For lighter cutting and smoothing, a stiff high carbon steel putty knife may be used. One with a $1\frac{1}{2}$" wide square end blade costs 70¢.

Wire-End Modeling Tools are about 8" long and come with square, pointed, round, asymmetric and oval ends. Square ones can be employed to square off small surfaces and pointed ones, to clean up intersections. These tools are obtainable from artists' supply stores for about 80¢ each. Thin line tools are smaller versions (5" long) of the wire-end tools. They cost about 95¢ each and are available from the same source.

Boxwood or Duron Modeling Tools are used to impart textures and to cut clay. Boxwood modeling tools cost from 20¢ (for 6" long tools) to 35¢ (for 8" tools). They come with serrated, plain, curved and flat edges.

Polyethylene Film and Wax Paper are good wrappings in which to store clay and scraps.

5-1

***Project*: TEAMSTERS, CHAUFFEURS AND HELPERS UNION OFFICE BUILDING, NEW HAVEN, CONNECTICUT.**
DESIGNED BY: William Mileto.
MODELBUILDER: Henry Bayer.
SCALE: 1/4″ = 1′.
This design and presentation model was constructed entirely out of unpainted basswood assembled with white polyvinyl glue. The basewood was made of 1/4″ plywood edged with pine and braced with plywood gussets. People were carved from balsa; trees were formed from natural twigs.

A good supply of power tools, while not indispensable in the making of precise models, is a great saving in muscle and time. Recent price reductions and savings gained by shopping in discount stores can reduce the cost of many power tools to the point where they can be used economically on even a single model. Sears, and Montgomery Ward, for example, have extensive lines of well-constructed, inexpensive tools. Tools are rentable, and some may be used in commercial shops. Tool rentals per diem vary between 2 and 10% of their cost, amounting to about $3 to $6 for bench-mounted tools and $2 to $4 for powered hand tools. Most stores have a minimal daily rental of approximately a dollar. Incidentally, non-powered tools can also be rented for a few cents per day. Before purchasing a power tool: (1) Make a list of the types of operations to be performed. Take into account any conceivable future jobs. (2) List the tools that can perform these operations either with or without special attachments. (3) Obtain and carefully consider information about all the tools contemplated for purchase. Since there is overlapping in the functions of power tools, a comparison of the two lists may reveal that many operations can be accomplished with a basic tool and its attachments.

FUNCTIONS OF POWER TOOLS

The following chart lists the operations that can be undertaken with various tools:

Key:

A—The tool will perform this operation if the proper cutter is used. Note: Some manufacturers' versions of this tool may not perform all the operations that I have noted. B—The tool will undertake this operation if an adapter is purchased. Note: Not all available adapters will fit all tools. C—This hand held tool will function if it has the proper cutter, or it will perform the operation as a bench-mounted tool if a stand is obtained.

Naturally, multi-use tools will each perform many of the listed operations.

Tool power or capacity must also be considered; roughly, there are two basic sizes of tools with which the modelmaker must concern himself: (1) Tools needed to make baseboards, carrying boxes, hardwood and Plexi-glas block models, as well as highly machined Plexiglas models. (2) Tools that cut thin sheet material and stripwood used in hollow models and tools used in the fabrication of furniture and other small assemblies. The former category requires bench-mounted or portable power tools usually found in the average home craftsman's workshop. The latter requires small, powered hand tools and tools that come with small stands that can be set up on a worktable; these are designed for the amateur modelmaker, and may be obtained from hobby shops.

The tools mentioned in this book tend to be the least expensive models available. They represent sensible beginning purchases. Sometimes, how-

ABILITIES OF VARIOUS TOOLS

Key:
A = tool adequate with proper cutter; however, some models may not be adequate for all operations.
B = tool adequate with adapter.
C = tool adequate as hand-held tool with proper cutter, or as bench-mounted tool if stand is obtained.

Tool	Drilling, light	Drilling, heavy or light	Shaping and cutting, light	Shaping and cutting, heavy	Disc sanding, light	Disc sanding, heavy	Belt sanding	Orbital or reciprocating sanding	Drum sanding	Buffing and polishing	Grinding, light	Grinding, heavy	Jig sawing	Band sawing	Saber sawing	Circular sawing, light	Circular sawing, heavy	Lathe turning, light	Lathe turning, heavy	Planing	Routing	Engraving	Paint mixing
Small portable hand motor tool	C	C	C					A	C	C						C		C			C	A	C
Portable electric drill		C	C		C		B	A	C		C				B	B		C	B			C	C
Drill press (bench-mounted)	A	A	A	A	A			A	A		A						A	A	A				A
Jig saw (bench-mounted)			A	A				A					A										
Scroll saw (portable)													A										
Band saw (bench-mounted)														A									
Portable saber saw														B	A								
Cut-off saw (portable)																C							
Circular saw (bench-mounted)						A							A	B	B	A					A		
Radial arm saw (bench-mounted)	A	A	A		A								A	A		A	A				A		A
Orbital sander (portable)								A	A														
Portable belt sander							A	A			A												
Bench-mounted disc sander					A			A															
Bench-mounted belt sander							A	A			A												
Grinder (bench-mounted)												A											
Lathe (bench-mounted)			A			A					A	A						A	A				
Jointer planer (bench-mounted)																				A	A		
Router shaper (bench-mounted)									A												A	A	
Portable router									A												A	A	

ever, they lack the precision and the accessories that a highly mechanized professional model shop would require. Some fabricators of acrylic models, incidentally, have rebuilt even highly expensive tools to achieve the 1/10,000″ tolerances that they require.

ACCESSORIES

The Miter Gauge

Two of the most useful (even indispensable) accessories are the miter gauge and rip fence. The best miter gauge is shaped like an adjustable protractor mounted on a long arm running in a track on the table with the power tool. Material held against the protractor may be squarely pushed into the blade for an exact cutting angle. The stock must be held firmly against the gauge to prevent pivoting created by the thrust of the blade. Facing the gauge with sandpaper will increase traction. Miter gauges are found on good circular, cut-off, band and radial arm saws; bench-mounted disc and belt sanders.

The Rip Fence

The rip fence or rip guide is an adjustable stop on a tool table placed parallel to the cutting direction of the blade. It is adjustable to any distance from the blade so that material pressed against the fence will be cut to the desired width. This allows multiple cutting of exact measurements. Rip fences can be found on good circular, band, portable saber, cut-off and radial arm saws; router shapers and jointer planers. A fence may be improvised by clamping a strip of wood to the table.

Other Accessories

Useful accessory features include a tilting table for bevel cuts and tool bench casters for mobility when working on unusually large material. Tools (screwdrivers, wrenches, etc.) will be needed to disassemble and maintain power tools.

Motor Speed Control

Wood is drilled and cut at higher speeds than the speeds that should be used on metal or plastic; large holes are drilled better at slower speeds; paint mixing must be done at slow speeds to reduce splashing; soldering temperatures differ according to metal used; incandescent light intensity for photography should be controlled. Since most inexpensive power tools have only one speed, some sort of speed controlling device is probably needed. Illustration 5-2 shows a minimal control that can be fabricated quickly. By changing the wattage of the bulb, the tool's speed can be altered. More sophisticated devices, one, for example, manufactured for $20 by Lutron Electronics Company, will vary tool speed from 0 rpm to the maximum factory-rated speed. Electronic variable speed controls also automatically feed more voltage when a motor starts to slow down under load. These controls only work with the small motors of portable power tools and with resistance soldering irons.

If overheating occurs at low speeds, disengage the tool and turn the speed up to maximum; the tool's fan will increase to its maximum speed and quickly cool the tool. The capacity of speed controls is rated by amperes: a $7\frac{1}{2}$ ampere model is sufficient for use with portable tools; if three 500 watt photo bulbs are used, a 15 ampere capacity control is necessary.

POWER TOOL CARE

All bench-mounted tools should be checked periodically to adjust the relationship between the blade, table level, rip fence and miter gauge. Miter gauges and table tilting apparatus must be tight and not vibrate out of position during operation. The greasing schedule suggested by tool manufacturers should be posted in the shop and followed.

Do not overload tools by feeding the work too rapidly. If a tool is stalled, back it off from the work until its motor resumes full speed. On the other hand, if not enough pressure is applied to the tool, it will skim across the work, eventually dulling the blade.

Record the width of the cut of each blade. This will reveal how much material wastage to expect.

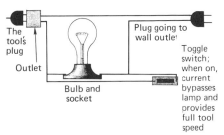

A MOTOR TOOL SPEED CONTROL DEVICE

The tool's plug
Outlet
Bulb and socket
Plug going to wall outlet
Toggle switch; when on, current bypasses lamp and provides full tool speed

POWER DRILLS

Portable Hand Motor

This tool and the jig saw are the two most useful power tools needed for the construction of simple models. The motor tool is capable of drilling, circular sawing, sanding, buffing, polishing, paint mixing, grinding, engraving, turning, shaping and routing. Some of these operations can be facilitated by the use of an accessory table to position the work accurately. But, in general, the operations require only the insertion of a different cutting tool into the motor's chuck. Dremel makes three extremely good motor tools: their No. 1 (see Illustration 5-4A) turns at 25,000 rpm and costs $17 (without blades); No. 2 has a 27,000 rpm speed and costs $20; No. 3 also is 27,000 rpm and costs $30. These tools have oilless bearings that require no lubrication unless the tool is heavily used. Strombecker makes a $4 battery-operated tool that runs up to 10,000 rpm.

Cutting and Sanding Tools Made by Dremel for Their Motor Tool

Buy cutting and sanding tools as needed because large sets often include tools that are rarely if ever used. All of the following cutting and sanding tools are made by Dremel.

DRILL POINTS, CUTTERS, GRINDING WHEELS, POLISHING TIPS AND BRUSHES
FOR THE DREMEL HAND MOTOR TOOL (shown at one half full size)

(B) Regular cutters ⟶ (C) Speed drill (come in 5 sizes)

(A) Small engraving cutters ⟶ (D) Silicon grinding points ⟶

(E) Emery polishing wheels (F) Steel brush (G) Saw (comes in 2 thicknesses) (H) Bristle brushes

189 193
190 194
191 196   197
109 100 121 131 141 192 115 116 117 178 118 198
107 112 114 124 134 144 125 199

83322 83702 84642 85342   85602
83142 83642 84382 84922 85422 85562 85622

425 427   428   403 404 405

Each also comes in 2 other sizes

941 943 945 952 953 954 962 964 971 973 974 981 984 997 914 921 903 904 911 932 8236 and 8143 101 103 104 94 95 96 97 98 422
963 992 913 915 922 from the 8000 414 and 429 423
923 series
924

(I) Emery wheels ⟶

(J) Routing cutters (K) Carbide cutters (L) Felt polishing tips

Cutters (5-3B) cost between 80¢ and $1, and are used for cutting grooves, shaping, inlaying and for concave routing. Small ones costing 30¢ (5-3A) can be used for engraving and scribing. Other companies sometimes refer to cutters as rotary files or rasps. Large ones may be used on wood, plastic and metal; smaller ones are not strong enough to be used on hard metal. Tungsten carbide cutters may be used on hard steel as well as on softer materials.

Routing Cutters (5-3J) are used for the routing, inlaying and mortising of metals. They cost $1.25 each.

Emery Wheels (5-3I) cost 50¢ and are used for shaping and sanding. In grinding soft materials, a little candlewax on the wheel can prevent its pores from being filled. Wheels may be cleaned and reshaped on a dressing stone.

Silicon Grinding Points (5-3D) shape and grind steel and other hard materials, and cost about 40¢ apiece.

Emery Cutting Wheels, made of thin stone, are for the cutting and grooving of metal and wood. Dremel makes them in diameters up to 1½", and charges 50¢ per dozen.

Cloth-Backed Abrasive Discs remove flash from castings, and are used for cutting. The non-rigid disc depends on centrifugal force to stiffen it for cutting. Dremel makes these in ⅝, ¾ and ⅞" diameters, and charges 40¢ per 100.

Abrasive Drums are drum-shaped mandrels over which abrasive coated cloth skirts are slipped. They are used for sanding (wood, metal and plastic) and come in ¼ and ¾" diameters. They cost 75¢ each.

Felt Polishing Tips and Wheels (5-3L) screwed into mandrels are used for polishing metal and plastic. Dremel makes 4 which cost 25 to 30¢ each and also supplies the polishing compound used with them.

Polishing Wheels and Points (5-3E) impregnated with fine emery are used to polish metal. Dremel's cost 30¢ each.

Bristle Brushes (5-3H) clean and polish metal and cost 25¢.

Wire Brushes (5-3F), costing 50¢ ,remove rust and excess solder, and produce a wire-brushed finish on metal.

Saws (5-3G), costing 75¢, cut thin plastic, soft metal, wood or cardboard; they are also used for grooving and dovetailing.

Accessories for Dremel Motor Tools

Collets come in various sizes and cost from 55¢ to $1.50. They allow for the use of a wide variety of tool shaft diameters in a motor.

Mandrels are shafts which hold emery impregnated polishing wheels, sanding discs, felt polishing tips and wheels and saws in the motor's chuck.

Flexible Shafts allow for working in tight places. Dremel makes a motor with an attached flexible shaft for $35.

Rheostats can be used to lessen a tool's speed when working on plastic or drum sanding wood; the tool's high speed might, otherwise, melt or burn these materials. Dremel makes a speed rheostat for $7.50.

Tables and Stands for Dremel's Motor Tool No. 2

A *Universal Stand* (5-4A) holds the motor, freeing both hands for work. It may be adjusted up or down, and sells for $5.

A *Shaping Table* (5-4B) may be raised or lowered to regulate the depth of cut. It costs $7.50.

A *Drill Press Stand* (5-4C) has a table that can be raised and lowered. It costs under $15.

Portable Electric Drill

This is a larger version of the small, hand motor tool. A motor's power is rated by the largest drill that it can efficiently drive into a steel plate. Motors come with ¼, ⅜ and ½" ratings. The ¼" size, of which the maximum speed is between 1500 and 2500 rpm, is of most use to the model-maker. More expensive models have variable speeds. There are three common types of electric drill chucks: hand chucks (tightened by hand) will easily loosen up under the bending loads imposed by certain accessories; hex-key tightened chucks are stronger; geared chucks, however, are the most highly recommended.

Sears & Roebuck's 9G799 ¼" drill costing $8 is a good 1-speed tool. Others cost up to $65. Thor makes a variable speed ¼" drill (D72-SC) costing $22.

Cutting and Sanding Attachments for the Portable Electric Drill

Drills and Large Hole Cutters—See page 25 .

Rotary Files and Burrs (5-4H) are used for cutting grooves, shaping and routing. Costal makes these for 70¢ each and Arco for $1 each.

Rotary Rasps (5-4I) shape and rout. The Drumcliff Company makes the illustrated line, each rasp costing $1.

Rubber Discs hold sheets of sandpaper and polishing bonnets. Arco makes a $1 set composed of a 5" disc, a lamb's wool polishing bonnet, sanding discs and an arbor.

Sandpaper Discs are mounted on rubber discs. The Carborundum Company sells them for between $1 and $3.50 per 10.

Carborundum Wheels (5-4J) are used for shaping and sanding. The Carborundum Company and Costal make complete lines. Carborundum's wheels cost from 55¢ to $2 each.

Air Inflated Pads are used to hold buffing bonnets. Their flexible surface will not burn or leave rings or whirl marks on a fine finish.

Polishing Bonnets are attached over air inflated or rubber pads and are used for buffing. Arco makes 6" muslin buffs that sell for $1 a dozen.

Grindstones by Arco are 3", include a buffing wheel and arbor, and cost $1. Carborundum sells a 5" wheel for $1.75.

Ball-Jointed Disc Sanders sand flat surfaces without the necessity of holding the drive shaft of the drill perpendicular to the surfaces.

Compass Cutters cut large circles if one end of the beam is pinned to the center of the desired circle and the drill is fitted on the other end. John Surrey sells one for $4.

Roto-Forms (5-4E) are used for heavy shaping. Arco makes a line of these ranging in diameter from ¾ to 1⅞" and costing between $1 and $2.

Router-Drills or *Hole Saws* (5-4G), if moved laterally, rout away material after a hole is cut. Arco makes one for $1.50.

Portable Electric Drill Accessories

A *Speed Reducer* mechanically lowers a tool's speed and increases its torque. This often becomes a necessity in drilling hard materials. Babco sells a 5 : 1 reducer for $9.50.

A *Flexible Shaft* allows greater maneuverability, enabling cutters to reach otherwise inaccessible places. Sunset House sells a 36" shaft for $3.

A *Drill Guide* steadies a drill for perpendicular cutting. Scott Mitchell House sells one for $5.

A *Horizontal Bench Stand*, which converts a drill into a grinder or sander, is sold by Millers Falls for $2.50.

A *Drill Press Stand* (5-4D) changes a drill into a drill press. It is made by Millers Falls and costs $12. Other models are made by Babco and Porter Cable.

A *Cut-Off Saw Attachment* made by Arco and Millers Falls is an excellent attachment that converts a ¼" portable electric drill into a cut-off saw. The attachment includes a tilting shoe and rip guides, and is adjustable for depth of cut. Arco's model has a dado cutter which cuts up to ½" in width and 1" in depth in one pass of the saw. The Millers Falls tool costs $11; Arco's costs $13.

A *Saber Saw or Jig-saw Attachment* (5-4F) Millers Falls and Arco make models of these, which cost around $8.

An *Electric Hand Plane* is an attachment made by Millers Falls, costing $16, that converts a drill into a plane.

5-4

DREMEL MOTOR TOOL ACCESSORIES

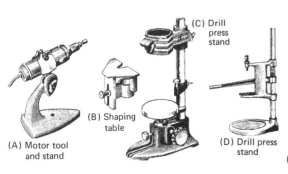

(C) Drill press stand

(B) Shaping table

(A) Motor tool and stand

(D) Drill press stand

ACCESSORIES FOR THE ¼" DRILL

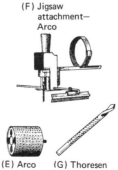

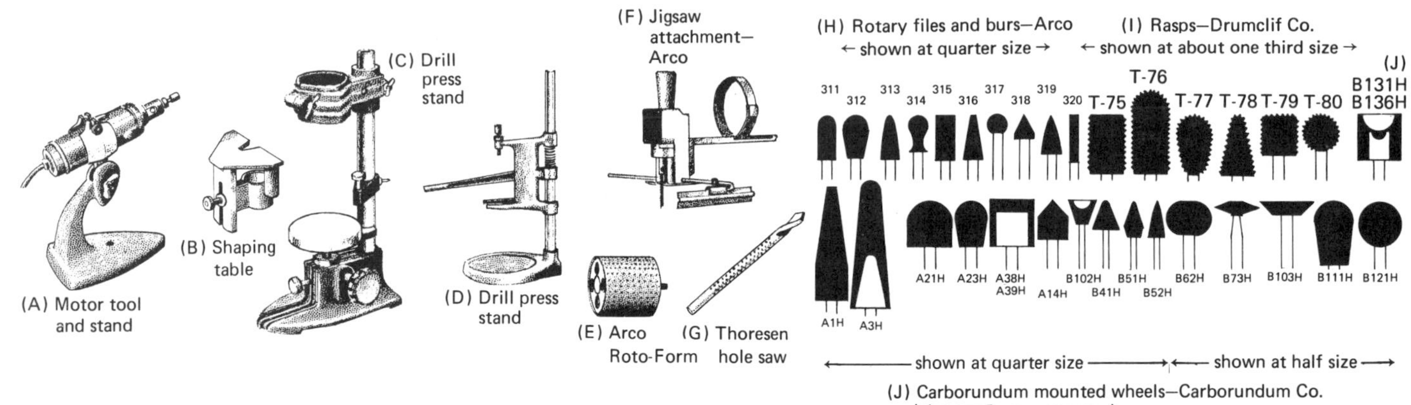

(F) Jigsaw attachment—Arco

(E) Arco Roto-Form   (G) Thoresen hole saw

(H) Rotary files and burs—Arco
← shown at quarter size →

311 312 313 314 315 316 317 318 319 320

T-75 T-76 T-77 T-78 T-79 T-80

A21H A23H A38H A39H A14H B102H B51H B41H B52H B62H B73H B103H B111H B121H

A1H A3H

(I) Rasps—Drumclif Co.
← shown at about one third size →

(J) B131H B136H

←——— shown at quarter size ———→ ←— shown at half size —→

(J) Carborundum mounted wheels—Carborundum Co.
(also see 2 on upper row)

5-5

Project: **A MOTOR CAR SHOWROOM.**

DESIGN AND MODEL BY: Sanford Hohauser and John Fisher.

PHOTOGRAPHER: Sanford Hohauser.

SCALE: $1'' = 20'$.

Floors, walls and roof of this presentation model were made of illustration board. The floors were clamped together and column holes were simultaneously drilled. Dowels became columns, acting as internal bracing. Cars were made from casting rubber cast in a female plaster mold. Glazing and stair enclosure (left end of building) were formed from acetate.

The photograph was taken with a $4'' \times 5''$ press camera, 90 mm Wollensak Raptar wide angle lens and Super XX film.

CONSTRUCTION TIME: about 40 hours.

A Portable Router Shaper Stand, made by Comp-Tool Inc., sells for $7.

Bench-Mounted Drill Press

This tool combines highly accurate drilling, routing, carving, shaping, grinding, polishing, buffing, mortising, rabbeting, tenon cutting, milling, paint mixing, rotary planing and disc sanding. Its capacity is rated by its throat depth (the distance from chuck center to support column).

Many bench-mounted drill presses are equipped with tilting tables allowing angle drilling and the raising and lowering of tables. Another important feature is adjustable speed. This allows proper drilling and routing of all types of material. Many presses have a speed range of from 400 to 5400 rpm.

When the drilling speed can not be adjusted, use a high speed steel twist drill that will resist excessive speeds.

Bits with threaded tips should not be used unless the press is slowed down enough to match rotation and to feed speeds to the screw's thread. With large tools the work must be clamped to the drill press table. Use a special chuck to hold those cutting tools that develop side thrust.

Drill presses cost from $30 (made by the

DRILL SPEEDS FOR WOOD AND METAL

Operation	Speed
Wood	
Drilling holes up to 1/4" in diameter	3800 rpm
Drilling 1/4" to 1/2" holes	3100 rpm
Drilling 1/2" to 3/4" holes	2300 rpm
Drilling 3/4" to 1" holes	2000 rpm
Drilling holes of over 1" in diameter with twist drills and large hole drills	Slowest speed
Routing	Highest speed
Carving	4000–5000 rpm
Mortising hardwood	2200 rpm
Mortising softwood	3300 rpm
Metal	
Grinding	3000 rpm
Fine wire brushing (use a slower speed for coarse brushing)	3300 rpm
Buffing soft metal with a cloth wheel (use a slower speed for hard metal)	3800 rpm
Drilling large holes using hole or circle cutters	Slowest speed

American Tool and Machine Company) to $150, not including motor.

Accessory Cutters

Mortising Cutters have a drill inside a square chisel. The drill removes most of the wood and the chisel squares off the edges of the cut. Long mortises are made by a series of cuts. Mortising cutters may also be used to cut open side mortises.

Tenons and rabbets may be formed with a rotary planer disc.

POWER SAWS

Bench-Mounted Jig Saws

These saws make intricate cuts in sheet material (wood, cardboard, metal and plastic), and cut lengths from thin strip material. The cut depth capacity of a saw is limited by the distance be-

tween the blade and arm support; some machines, however, have swiveling blades that can be set sideways to give an unlimited depth. Try to buy a saw with a tilting table. Some jig saws will accept files and sanding drums placed in their lower jaws, and perform as saber saws. Many saws have a removable arm. By detaching it and fixing a saber saw blade in the lower chuck, the machine's capacity to cut bulky material can be increased.

The blade of a saw should be kept tangent to the line of curved cuts without forcing the cut or twisting the blade. Internal cuts can be made by drilling a hole in the material, passing the unseated saw blade into the hole and reattaching it into the saw's chucks. This procedure is called piercing.

When cutting metal, use beeswax as a lubricant.

Sandwich very thin sheets of material between two sheets of scrap wood to prevent fluttering by the blade.

Too much blade tension will cause the blade to snap.

Dremel makes a good light saw with an 8" throat and a $7 \times 7''$ table for $25. See Illustration 5-6A for another jig saw that they manufacture. Sears & Roebuck's Model 99G2072N is a good medium-weight tool having a $12 \times 12''$ table and an 18" throat. It costs $48 (less motor). Other saws cost up to $300.

BLADES

Blades come in many thicknesses (0.01 to 0.03"), many widths (0.025 to 0.25") and with many teeth per inch counts. In general, the thicker the material being sawed, the heavier the blade and the slower the saw's speed; the narrower the blade, the tighter the curve it is possible to cut; and the greater number of teeth per inch there are, the smoother the cut. Use a wide blade when making straight cuts.

Portable Scroll Saws

These saws are used for the cutting of intricate curves in thin (up to $\frac{3}{4}''$) material (5-6B). Being portable, they may be taken right to the model to cut out windows, area ways, etc. It is fairly difficult to make long straight cuts with this tool. The scroll's function is similar to that of the jig saw. Therefore, it is not indispensable to the modelmaker. Dremel makes a $7 model.

POWER SAWS

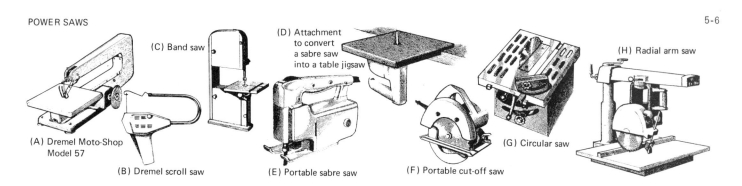

(A) Dremel Moto-Shop Model 57
(B) Dremel scroll saw
(C) Band saw
(D) Attachment to convert a sabre saw into a table jigsaw
(E) Portable sabre saw
(F) Portable cut-off saw
(G) Circular saw
(H) Radial arm saw

5-6

JIG SAW BLADES FOR VARIOUS MATERIALS

Material and thickness	Quality of cut	Teeth per inch: blade type	Speed (rpm)
Wood, up to 1/16″	Very smooth	20; thin, fairly narrow blade	1600
Wood, up to 1/8″	Very smooth	18; thin, fairly narrow blade	1600
Wood, 1/8″ to 1/2″	Very smooth	14; thin, fairly narrow blade	1500
Wood, 1/8″ and up	Medium	15; medium-thick, medium-wide blade	1200
Wood, 1/4″ and up (up to 2″ with most saws)	Rough	7; thick, wide blade	750
Fiberboard, 1/8″ and up	Medium	15; medium-thick, medium-wide blade	1200
Plastic, up to 1/16″	Very smooth	20; thin, fairly narrow blade	1600
Plastic, 1/16″ to 1/8″	Very smooth	18; thin, fairly narrow blade	1600
Plastic, 1/8″ to 1/2″	Very smooth	14; thin, fairly narrow blade	1500
Metal (nonferrous and mild steel), up to 1/16″	Smooth	30; thin, medium-wide blade	1200
Metal (nonferrous and mild steel), 1/16″ to 1/8″	Medium	20; medium-thick, medium-wide blade	950
Metal (nonferrous), 1/8″ to 1/2″; mild steel, 1/8″ to 1/4″	Medium	15; medium-thick, medium-wide blade	1200

Bench-Mounted Band Saws

Used to make curved and straight cuts in heavy material, some bench-mounted band saws will even cut 8″ thick stock (5-6C). Band saws are very useful in cutting the large blocks of wood and acrylic that are used in solid block models. The saw's throat depth determines the depth of maximum cuts. Since the blade is in the form of a continuous loop, piercing is impossible.

To cut a tightly curved object with a wider blade, a series of radial or tangential cuts must be made (5-7A and B). Compound cuts are shown in 5-7C. To make sharp interior corners, holes at the corners have to be cut by drilling. Then the modelmaker must saw up to these holes and use them to maneuver the saw around to cut the next side (5-7D).

Blade width determines the tightness of the minimum radius cut. A $\frac{1}{8}$″ blade will cut a $\frac{1}{4}$″ radius; a $\frac{1}{2}$″ blade, a $1\frac{1}{4}$″ radius, etc. Band saws run at speeds of 2000 to 4000 ft. per min.; this speed must be slowed down to 250 or 350 ft. per min. for nonferrous metal and to 75 or 150 ft. per min. for ferrous metal. The best purchase would be a saw that has a tilting table (for bevel cutting), a rip fence and a miter gauge. In general, faster speeds produce smoother cuts; slower speeds are for heavier work; coarser blades should be used on thick material; and finer tooth blades on thinner material. Blades with the smallest amount of set give the smoothest cuts but are harder to maneuver through curved cuts.

BANDSAW BLADES FOR VARIOUS MATERIALS

Material	Tooth Style; teeth per inch	Speed (ft. per min.)
Softwood	Hook or skip; 3–6	4000–5000
Hardwood	Hook or skip; 3–6	3000–4000
Paper and cardboard	Hook or skip; 3–4	2500–5000
Fiberboard	Raker or wavy; 6–8	500–1000
Plywood	Hook or skip; 4–6	3500–4500
Masonite	Hook or skip; 3–6	1000–2000
Acrylic	Hook or skip; 3–6	3000–4500
Polystyrene	Hook or skip; 4–6	3000–4000
Copper tubing	Wavy; 14–18	250–500
Steel tubing	Wavy; 18–32	125–200

The Nicholson Company makes raker set blades in from $\frac{1}{16}$ to 1″ widths with 6 to 24 teeth per inch. These can be used on thick ferrous material. They also make wavy set blades of from $\frac{1}{16}$ to 1″ widths with 8 to 32 teeth, hook tooth blades from $\frac{1}{4}$ to 1″ widths with 2 to 6 teeth, and skip tooth blades from $\frac{3}{16}$ to 1″ widths with 2 to 6 teeth. The 2-tooth rule should be observed when cutting thin material.

Forcing the work will cause the blade to bow, producing a cut that is not perpendicular to the table. A special all-purpose blade may be used on plastic, nonferrous metal and on wood.

Montgomery Ward makes a $55 1-speed saw; others cost up to $200.

Portable Saber Saws

Saber saws are used to make straight and curved cuts in fairly heavy material (5-6E). One with a rip fence can be substituted for a cut-off saw to make baseboards and model cases. If possible, purchase a saw that has a tilting base (for bevel cutting), a rip guide and the ability to cut wood at least up to 2″ thick.

Because saber saw blades may cause splintering along the cut, cover the cut line with transparent tape before cutting; also, keep the good

SABER SAW BLADES FOR VARIOUS MATERIALS

Material	Teeth per inch
Softwood up to 2″ thick	7
Softwood over 2″ thick	7; extra-long teeth
Hardwood and composition board	10
Plywood	10; taper-ground
Nonferrous metals	14

side of the material facing down. Blade ends are pointed to allow the piercing of sheet stock without having to drill an insertion hole. Saber saws cost from $13 (Montgomery Ward Model 84C8986) to $135.

SABER SAW ACCESSORIES

A *Jig-saw Conversion* converts a saber saw into a table jig saw; they are made by Skil ($5) and Wren ($11). Tables must be used with their saber saws and these cost $35 and $45 respectively.

A *Saber Saw Conversion* (5-6D) is a table that converts a portable saw into a bench-mounted saber saw. Ram sells one for $15.

Portable Cut-Off Saw (5-6F)

This is used to make straight cuts in heavy wood and other materials which cannot be worked on a table circular saw. It can also make rabbet and dado cuts. Its use to the modelmaker is generally limited to construction of baseboards and carrying boxes. Saws are rated by the diameter of their circular blade, usually running between 4 and 8″ for shop saws. A $6\frac{1}{4}$″ blade is sufficient for making a 45° cut through 2″ material. The depth of cut of the saw can be adjusted by raising or lowering the shoe of the tool. Buy a tool that has a shoe that may be tilted (for bevel cutting), a miter gauge and a rip guide. Some saws have a safety clutch that stops the blade from turning when it kicks back from the work. Another good safety feature to look for is the telescoping blade guard. Cut-off saws run from $20 (for the Ram F-7 Model with a 7″ blade and tilting shoe) to as high as $145.

CUT-OFF SAW BLADES FOR VARIOUS MATERIALS

Material	Blade type
Wood, cross-cutting	Cross-cut
Wood, cutting with the grain	Rip
Plywood	Plywood
Soft composition board	Fine-tooth
Plastic, 1/16″ or less	Fine-tooth (8 to 14 teeth per inch), blade 1/16″ to 3/32″ thick
Plastic, 1/4″	3 to 3 1/2 teeth per inch, blade 1/8″ to 5/32″ thick
Metal	Cut-off wheel (an abrasive disc)
Miscellaneous	Combination (the blade usually supplied with a new saw)

The smoothest cuts are made by hollow ground blades, but these may burn your stock if not projected at least $\frac{3}{4}$″ beyond the other side of the cut. When cutting, always keep the good face of the material facing down. Piercing cuts can be made by resting the front of the saw's shoe on the work and by lowering the spinning blade until it cuts through.

To make a perfectly straight, long cut in places where the rip guide cannot be used, clamp a stick to the work and use it as a guide for the saw. Due to the shape of the cut made by the circular

CUTTING WOOD BLOCKS

Cutting curves

(A) Make radial cuts first then cut off segments to form final shape

(B) Cut the form to shape with a series of tangential cuts

Cutting three dimensional shapes

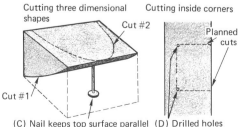

(C) Nail keeps top surface parallel to the saw's table while cut #2 is being made

Cutting inside corners

(D) Drilled holes

blade, interior corners must be finished with a hand saw. Rabbet cuts may be accomplished by two passes of the saw. To cut into a narrow edge, clamp a piece of scrap wood along the edge to give a wider surface on which to rest the saw's shoe. Dado cuts may be made by running the saw several times across the cut until the required material has been removed or by buying a dado cut attachment for the blade.

CUT-OFF SAW ACCESSORIES

A Table Which Converts a Cut-Off Saw to a Table Saw is made by Black & Decker.

A Saw Guide by the Drumcliff Company is a $3, 18" steel straightedge with an adjustable T-square head mounted on one end. By placing this guide on the work and running a cut-off or portable saber saw along it, straight cuts at any angle to the edge can be made.

Bench-Mounted Circular Saws

These saws are used to make straight cuts in heavy wood and other materials (5-6G). Useful in fabricating baseboards and model cases, they can also be used to cut out pieces for wood and plastic solid block models. Some saws have tilting tables or blades that can make bevel and chamfer cuts. All may be used to make dado cuts. Saws are rated by blade diameter, usually running between 7 and 12". The table size also is an indication of the tool's capacity; some machines have extender arms that increase the holding capacity of the table. Purchase a saw with a miter gauge, a rip fence and, if possible, a hood guard (to go over the blade). A circular saw may be converted into a disc sander by mounting a sander disc in place of the saw. Saws cost from $20 (for American Tool and Machine Company Model 21651 with an 8" blade and a $10\frac{1}{2} \times 13$" table) to almost $400. Prices do not include motors.

For the various blades that may be used on this saw, see the chart for portable cut-off saws, page 30. Saws usually come from the factory equipped with a combination blade.

Keep the good side of the material facing up when cutting. Make sure that the stock has good support and do not let it bind the blade. Use a pushing stick to feed the work through the saw whenever you are making a narrow cut. When crosscutting do not stand in line with the cut.

CIRCULAR SAW ACCESSORIES

Dado Blades are a sandwich-like grouping of three blades; the inside and outside are cutting blades with the center blade acting as a chipper to remove the material between the two cutters. Rabbet cuts may be made with dado blades. Two passes of the saw are required—one with the stock on its edge. Warren sells a variable dado blade for $3.50.

Molding Heads are held in the arbor of the saw in place of the saw blade. They are used to cut grooves and other shapes for moldings. Vermont sells molding heads for $3.50.

Jig-Saw Attachments by the Drumcliff Company cost $12, and will cut stock up to $2\frac{3}{4}$" thick.

Radial Arm Saws

These are combination tools that will saber and circular saw; cut miters; rout coves; shape; disc and drum sand; grind; buff; drill; and make tenon, dado and rabbet cuts. The tool's motor and cutter, movable in all directions, is mounted on an overhead arm. The saw is useful in making baseboards, carrying boxes and large block models. Some models have lathe attachments and variable speed controls. Prices run from $150 (for Sears' Model 99G2931N that comes with a 20 × 32" table, 9" blade and 1-speed motor) to $440.

SANDERS

These are useful for finishing baseboards, model cases and solid block models. Bench-mounted disc sanders may also be used to perform various shaping and finishing operations on hollow built-up models.

Portable Orbital Sanders (5-8A)

These are for the removal of a moderate amount of material and for sanding to a finish. The sander has a sandpaper pad that moves with a slight orbital motion. This sander is constructed to sand right up to obstructions. It is important to apply the correct amount of pressure to this tool; too little will result in no sanding action. Some models have a built-in vacuum action and dust collecting bag. The size of this sander is usually measured by the area of its sanding pad. Prices run from $14 (for Sears' Model 9G762) to $65.

Portable Reciprocating Sanders

These are similar to orbital sanders except that the pad moves back and forth and produces a finish smoother than does the orbital machine. Some sanders move both in an orbiting and reciprocating motion. Orbital sanders are priced from $12 (for Montgomery Ward's Model 84C8514) to $38. Machines performing both orbital and reciprocating actions cost from $32 (for Sears' Model 9G2246) to $55.

Portable Belt Sanders (5-8B)

These are for the fast removal of material from large surfaces. The size of this machine is specified in terms of its belt width, running between $2\frac{1}{2}$ and 4". Since a great deal of wood dust is produced, a dust collector is always a useful accessory. Most good models have provision for mounting one.

When starting to sand, contact the work with the rear of the belt, then bring the rest of the belt down onto the work. The sander must be kept

constantly moving or a depression will be sanded into the object. Too fast a belt speed will burn the material. For smooth, satin finishes use a canvas belt covered with a mixture of powdered pumice and paraffin oil. The surface to be sanded should be painted with a 1 : 2 mixture of paraffin oil and kerosene. Some portable sanders come with stands to convert them into bench-mounted belt sanders. Portable sanders cost from $18 (Montgomery Ward's least expensive model) to $110.

Bench-Mounted Disc Sanders

These can be used by the modelmaker to sand flat surfaces and to square corners on large and medium sized objects (5-8C). They are especially useful in the squaring of partitions, walls and floors. Since a disc sander is best for use on end grain, a belt sander should be used for surface sanding.

A disc sander with a tilting table (for bevel sanding) and miter gauge should be acquired. Because the disc sands more rapidly at its edges, the work must be moved across the disc's face. Hold the work on the down rotation side of the disc or it will be flung off the table. Perfect circles may be sanded by drilling a hole in the center of the piece, attaching it with a bolt to a piece of scrap wood and clamping the scrap in the proper location to the sander's table. To sand a number of objects to the same width, clamp a guide stick to the table (5-8D). Abrasive discs are attached to the sander's disc with rubber cement. Disc sanders cost from $22 (Delta-Rockwell Model 31-200, which has an $8\frac{1}{2}$" disc and 4" × 10" table but no motor) to over $70.

Bench-Mounted Belt Sanders

Belt sanders are used for grinding and for the fast removal of stock. They give fine 1-directional sanding not possible with the rotary action of the disc sander (5-8E). Some machines come with a vertical table that may be tilted, and a miter gauge; others do not have a table, only a stop to prevent the work from being carried off the belt. The sanding belt of most machines may be positioned in a vertical (for edge and end sanding) or horizontal position (for surface sanding). Inside curves may be sanded if the material is placed over the sander's idler drum (the drum that is not powered). Irregular shapes may be sanded on the back of the belt where it is not supported and has enough slack to gently sand convex objects. Belt sanders cost from $19 (Sears & Roebuck Model 99G2236C or Montgomery Ward's Model 84C2705M; both have a 4" belt) to over $130.

Bench-Mounted Combination Disc and Belt Sander

The price range for these sanders starts at $25, not including motor (for the American Tool and Machine Company's model that has a 4" belt and 5" disc) and runs to $145.

ABRASIVE DISCS AND BELTS FOR VARIOUS MATERIALS

Material	Abrasive	Grits for rough to fine sanding
Softwood	Garnet	40–100
Hardwood	Aluminum oxide	50–180
Nonferrous metals	Aluminum oxide or silicon carbide	36–220
Plastics	Silicon carbide	80–400

5-8

POWER SANDERS

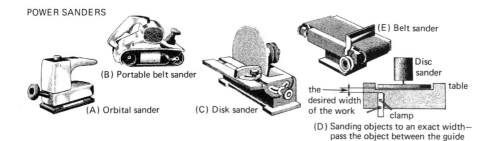

(B) Portable belt sander

(A) Orbital sander   (C) Disk sander

(E) Belt sander

Disc sander

table

the desired width of the work   clamp

(D) Sanding objects to an exact width— pass the object between the guide stick and the sanding disc

Project: **BARCARDI OFFICE BUILDING, SANTIAGO, CUBA.**
DESIGNED BY: Mies van der Rohe.
MODELBUILDERS: members of the architect's staff.
PHOTOGRAPHER: Hedrich-Blessing.
SCALE: 1/8″ = 1′.
This model was made for original presentation and to demonstrate to the client the flexible interior of the building. The model was constructed from acrylic. Columns were screw fastened to the roof. Ground contours were made from cardboard textured with paint into which sawdust had been mixed. People were rolled from fabric.
The photograph was taken with an 8″ × 10″ Deardorff camera, 165 mm lens and Kodak Royal Pan film.
CONSTRUCTION TIME: about 700 hours.

Grinders—see page 16

LATHES

Lathes can be used for turning, boring, drilling and sanding. Lathe capacity is measured by the maximum size stock that can be turned on it and expressed by the length (center-to-center distance) and diameter (swing) of the work.

There are two ways to turn work on the lathe: (1) Spindle Turning is achieved by attaching the stock between the two centers of the lathe; (2) Faceplate Turning has the work attached to a faceplate that in turn is attached to the head stock spindle of the lathe. Because most small objects needed by the modelmaker can be turned on a drill press, with a portable electric drill or even with a small hand motor tool, the lathe is superfluous to all but the best equipped shop.

Spindle Turning of Long Objects

First locate the center of both ends of the stock. Push the spur center (on the lathe's head stock spindle) into one center; make a seat with an awl in the other end of the stock and attach it to dead center of the lathe. Adjust the pressure of the center and oil it to allow the stock to turn freely. Draw the position of various details on the stock and cut them roughly with a parting tool. Finish the object by using cardboard templates to check its shape.

Faceplate Turning of Flat Saucer-Shaped Objects

Center the stock and mount it on a faceplate with screws, or so as not to mar the object, paste it to the faceplate. Attach the faceplate to the lathe's headstock spindle. If the work is small, it may be screwed into a device called a screw center that attaches into the lathe's spindle.
Lathe Chisels come in the following shapes: skew (for general smoothing, detail cutting, forming tapers, trimming ends and shoulders, forming beads and making V-cuts); round nose (for forming long curves and coves and forming concave grooves in faceplate-mounted stock); gouges (for rough cutting and heavy stock removal, for forming coves and smoothing); parting tools (for forming small V's, shoulders and tapers, for sizing cuts and cutting off end stock); square nose (for fast removal of material, cutting square shoulders, forming tapers as well as recesses and bands, for making V-cuts and smoothing convex forms). Blades should be slowly and steadily fed into the work. They should be held by placing the left hand on the blade (directly behind the lathe rest) and the right on the handle.

Tools that are carbide tipped may be used on nonferrous metals. Jeweler's files and small carving tools are used when turning small objects mounted in a hand motor tool or in other small improvised lathes.

In general, the larger the work the slower the turning speed. Rough abrasive paper should be used at a slow speed; fine paper at a high speed.

LATHE SPEEDS FOR VARIOUS MATERIALS

| Material | Speed (rpm) for | | |
	sanding	shaping	finishing
Wood, to 2″ diameter	900	2500	4200
Wood, 2″ to 4″ diameter	800	2100	3500
Nonferrous metals, to 3″ diameter	600	1300	3000

Wood Lathes have a range of speeds that run as low as 200 rpm, in some models to as high as 6,400 rpm. Most tools, though, have a much narrower range of speeds. Metals and plastics may also be turned on wood lathes. The cost, not including motor, runs from $10 (American Tool and Machine Company model that has a 6″ swing and a 23″ center-to-center length) to over $200.
Metal Lathes have speeds which range from a low of 20 rpm on some tools to a high of 7,200 rpm. Metal lathes can also be used to mill and cut threads. Costs (not including motor) run from $99 (Sears & Roebuck Model F99G2128N, with a 6″ swing and an 18″ center-to-center length) to over $500.

BENCH-MOUNTED JOINTER PLANER

These jointers are able to surface wood and to make rabbet, bevel, chamfer, recessing and taper cuts. They are of extremely limited use to the modelmaker since they are needed only in the construction of baseboards, model boxes and solid block models—functions satisfactorily performed by other tools. Jointers are rated by the width of the material that they can plane and also by the length of their table. Jointer planers start from $20 (without motor) for American Tool and Machine Company's model.

ROUTERS
Bench-Mounted Router Shapers

Router shapers are used to rabbet, dovetail, groove, plane, and to make coves, chamfers, dadoes and round edges in wood (5-10A). Their adjustable cutting blade, mounted on a vertical spindle projecting through a table, turns at about 20,000 rpm, producing smoothly machined surfaces. Straight surfaces are shaped with the aid of the tool's fence; curved material requires a guide of scrap wood (5-10D). Shapers also may be converted into a drum sander. Costs range from $15 (for the American Tool and Machine Company's model, without table and motor, or $76 for Sears' Model 99G2394N, which has a table but no motor) to $320. These tools are for working wood of the size that would be used in baseboards, model boxes and larger plastic and solid wood block models.

A light router (sufficient to shape the thin pieces of plastic and wood used in hollow built-up models) may be improvised from a small portable motor tool. See Illustration 5-10C for the possible construction of such a tool. A Dremel shaping table may also be used for light routing.

Portable Routers

These tools can perform the same operations on heavy wood as can bench-mounted routers (5-10B). Blades, adjustable for various cut depths, must be held perfectly flat on the surface of the work or the cut will be ruined. A guide used in making grooves or dadoes will keep the line of cut parallel to the edge of the material. If the cut is too far in from the edge to allow using the guide, clamp a straight board to the work to run the router along it. Circular grooves can be cut by building a pivot into the router. A portable plane attachment can be purchased to convert the router into a power plane.

MULTI-USE POWER TOOLS

These tools combine many functions without duplicating basic components (motor, table, etc.), conserving shop floor space as well as cost. To convert from one tool to another usually takes a

ROUTERS   5-10

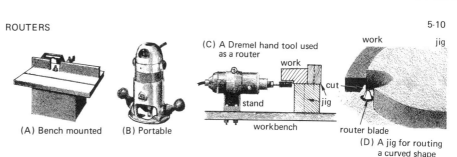

(A) Bench mounted   (B) Portable   (C) A Dremel hand tool used as a router   work / jig / cut / jig / stand / workbench / router blade   (D) A jig for routing a curved shape

matter of a few minutes. Some of these tools are sold without motors.

Multi-Use Bench-Mounted Tools for Heavy Work

These can be used to construct baseboards and model boxes, to cut heavy, solid block models and to perform operations on hollow built-up models.

The Dewalt Power Shop Model 1250 is a 9" circular saw, an 8" disc sander, grinder and polisher, all in one. Its basic price, including a 1-speed 1.8 hp motor, is about $200. Additional accessories can make the tool into a jointer ($25), 36" lathe (a motorless lathe is needed), horizontal drill, saber saw ($20) and drum sander ($6).

The MultiMatic 8 (sold by American Edelstaal) is an 8" circular saw, 7" disc sander, 2" belt sander, band saw (with a 6" throat depth), lathe (36" center-to-center length), jig saw (with an 8½" throat depth), saber saw and molder; its motor turns at 1,700 or 3,500 rpm. Additional accessories will make the tool into a 6" grinder ($14) and horizontal drill ($10).

The Shop Smith is a 9" circular saw, drill press, 34" lathe, 12" disc sander, horizontal drill, shaper, and has a built-in vacuum cleaner. Its variable speed motor runs from 700 to 5,200 rpm. It is priced under $300.

Multi-Use Portable Tools for Heavy Work

A Multi-Use Tool Based on the ¼" Portable Drill may be had by purchasing the many accessories available for this tool. It can then be made to perform the functions of a portable drill, portable router shaper, drill press, bench-mounted grinder, portable cut-off saw, portable saber saw and portable orbital sander. All this may be had for a price as low as $60 (with a 1-speed motor) and $75 (with a variable speed motor). Thor has a $30, ⅜" portable drill that comes with drill press, bench saw (4½" blade), grinder, portable cut-off saw and miter gauge. General Electric sells a hand held, multiple tool with a ⅓ hp motor (costs $19, includes a ¼" drill); attachments consist of a saber saw ($14), orbital sander ($14), and ⅜" drill ($10).

Multi-Use Bench-Mounted Tools for Light Work

The Unimat (sold by American Edelstaal) is for light, highly accurate plastic, wood and metal machining. It combines the features of a lathe (with 7" center-to-center length), grinder, drill press and portable drill. Its motor has 11 speeds up to 3,500 rpm. Basic cost is $140. Accessory

attachments allow milling, jig sawing and circular sawing (with 2½ to 3½" blades).

The Dremel Combination Tool is basically a jig saw with flexible shaft, grinder and shaper attachments. Motor speed is 3,500 rpm, and cost is just over $50.

A Multi-Use Tool Based on a Dremel Motor Tool can be built with the various accessories for Dremel's No. 2 motor. This tool will perform the functions of a hand drill, drill press, grinder and shaper. It has 7 speeds and costs about $60.

MOTORS

Since some bench-mounted power tools are sold without motors, it is a good idea to be familiar with various facts about electric motors.

Motor sizes required by various tools are as follows: grinder and jig saw, ¼ hp; small jointer, drill press and lathe, ⅓ hp; band saw, table saw, belt sander, disc sander and shaper, ½ hp. Motors come in 2 types: (1) the split-phase motor used in tools that do not draw a great starting load (sanders, grinders, drill presses) and (2) the capacitor-type motor, used where a heavy starting load is encountered (saws, shapers, jointers). Tool speeds are determined by the motor speed and the pulleys used both on the motor and on the machine. The formula for computing this is: Diameter of motor pulley times motor speed divided by diameter of machine pulley equals the machine speed. Efficient ½ hp motors cost $20 and more.

6 THE MINIMAL TOOL BOX

There are eight areas of basic modelmaking techniques. Thus, eight minimal tool boxes have been drawn up, each containing the *basic* tools needed for efficient construction of models.

As a purchasing and inventory guide, the following minimal tool box inventories have been arranged. Using these forms, jot down purchases and their probable cost. New tools, as they appear on the market, can be written up in the blank spaces.

Minimal Tool Box No. 1 provides the tools needed to construct rough clay or plasticine massing models, which can be mounted on un-

finished pieces of composition board or heavy cardboard.

Minimal Tool Box No. 2 contains the tools necessary for the construction of rough hollow models made of cardboard, stripwood and balsa wood supported on light wood carcasses. Thin sheets of Plexiglas may also be used for this type of model. The models can be mounted on unfinished pieces of composition board or heavy cardboard.

Minimal Tool Box No. 3 lists the tools used to construct finely finished models made of the above materials and also from plaster and vacuum-formed sheet plastic.

Minimal Tool Box No. 4 shows the tools needed to construct heavy wood and plywood bases and carrying boxes.

Minimal Tool Box No. 5 has the tools for making precise hardwood or Plexiglas solid block models.

Minimal Tool Box No. 6 indicates the tools needed to cast assemblies from rubber, plastic and plaster molds.

Minimal Tool Box No. 7 lists the tools for metal forming and soldering.

Minimal Tool Box No. 8 provides tools for producing highly detailed models built from acrylic plastic.

Estimated costs are for tools of fair to excellent quality with a reasonable life expectancy to initial cost ratio. To make all types of models properly would require a minimum expense of between $500 and $700 unless one were willing to rough it.

6-1

A RATHER HIGHLY DETAILED MODEL.

PROJECT: Bryn Athyn School, Bryn Athyn, Pennsylvania.
DESIGNED BY: Vincent G. Kling and Associates.
MODELBUILDERS: members of the architect's staff.
PHOTOGRAPHER: Lawrence S. Williams.
SCALE: 1/4" = 1'.
Columns were made from balsa, siding from scribed balsa, stone walls from hand-painted cardboard, windows from acetate and roofing from scribed cardboard. The baseboard was constructed from plywood on a lumber frame. Contours were made from flocked cardboard. Trees: lichen on natural twigs. This model was used for study and presentation.
The photograph was taken with a 4" × 5" Graphic view camera, 135 mm lens and Tri-X film.

MINIMAL TOOL BOXES FOR VARIOUS MODELING TECHNIQUES

Key:
Tool Box No. 1 (clay-massing models) : $35
Tool Box No. 2 (rough, built-up models) : $125–150
Tool Box No. 3 (fine, built-up models) : $215
Tool Box No. 4 (baseboards, carrying boxes) : $215
Tool Box No. 5 (solid block models) : $250–275
Tool Box No. 6 (cast parts) : $100–125
Tool Box No. 7 (metal-forming and soldering) : $150
Tool Box No. 8 (machined acrylic models) : $550–625

Tools	Tool Box Numbers
MARKING TOOLS:	
Pencils (HB, 3H, and 6H)	1–8
Drafting set (including inking pen and compass)	2, 3, 5, 8
MEASURING TOOLS:	
Architect's (or engineer's) scale	1–3, 5–8
18" metal ruler	2–8
Zigzag ruler (6' long with slide-out extensions)	4
Divider	1–3, 6–8
Beam compass	2–4, 8
1" micrometer	7, 8
Caliper or caliper rule	3, 5, 6, 8
Combination square	1–8
Sliding T-bevel	8
Marking gauge	8
Contour marker	3, 8
Magnifier	3, 6, 8
Burnisher (for overlays)	2, 3, 5, 8
VISES:	
Bench vise	2, 3, 5–8
Woodworking vise	4, 5, 8
Mechanics vise	8
Instrument vise	8
Hand vise	3
CLAMPS:	
Improvise clamps (several)	1, 2, 5–8
Magnetic holders (2 or more)	3, 7, 8
Multipurpose spring clamps (2 or more)	4, 5, 8
C-clamps (4 or more)	1–8
Clamps for large flat surfaces (can be books for 1–3, 5)	1, 2, 3, 4, 5, 8
Workbench-mounted hold-down clamps (2 or more)	3, 8
Common wood hand screws	4
Tourniquet clamps	3, 8
OTHER GRIPPING TOOLS:	
Tweezers	1–8
Forceps	6, 7
PLIERS:	
Round-nose	2, 3, 5–8
Flat-nose	2, 3, 5–8
Combination	1, 3, 6–8
Diagonal-cutters or side-cutters	2, 3, 5, 6, 8
End-cutting nippers	7
Bernard side-cutters	8
WIRE BENDERS:	
Bending jig	3, 7, 8
Wire-bending die	2, 3, 5–8
Sheet-metal bending tool (homemade)	7
HAMMERS:	
10 oz. bell-face, curved claw	1–3, 5–8
16 oz. bell-face, curved claw	4
10 oz. soft-face	3, 5, 8
SCREWDRIVERS:	
Standard-blade (2 or more sizes, preferably a driver with a hollow handle that contains 3 other drivers of diminishing size)	3–8
Phillips driver	4
Jeweler's screwdriver set	3, 7, 8
KNIVES AND ACCESSORIES:	
Plywood or Masonite cutting surface	1–8
Mat-cutter and beveler	3, 8
Balsa stripper	3, 5
Razor blades (single-edge) or throwaway razor-blade knives	1–3, 5–8

Tools	Tool box Numbers
X-Acto knives (a lightweight and a heavyweight handle, and a selection of at least 4 different blades)	2, 3, 5, 6, 8
Mat knife	1–5, 7, 8
Paper cutter	3, 8
CIRCLE CUTTERS:	
X-Acto beam compass and circle cutters	3
Artist's cutting blade	2, 4, 5
SCRIBERS:	
Improvised tools	1–3, 5, 6, 8
Awl	3, 5, 7, 8
Multiple-line scriber	1–3, 5, 6, 8
SCISSORS:	
2 1/2" and 6"	1–3, 5–8
Snips (combination)	2, 3, 5–8
SAWS:	
Razor saw or dovetail saw (with blade having 50 or more teeth per inch)	2, 3, 5–8
Multiple-tool saw, saw knife, back saw, or dovetail saw (with blade having 32 teeth per inch)	1–3, 5–8
Keyhole saw, all-purpose saw, or general-purpose saw	4
Jeweler's saw or fine coping saw	1, 3, 5, 6, 8
Fret saw	4
Hacksaw	4, 7
Jab saw	4
Ripsaw	4
Crosscut saw	4
Miter box, small	2, 3
Miter box, large	4, 5, 8
PLANES:	
Modelmaker's plane	3, 5
Block plane	2–5
Smoothing plane	5
Fore plane	4
Cabinetmaker's rabbet plane	4
Chisel (heavy-duty)	4
CARVING TOOLS:	
X-Acto, small-size blades (5 or more)	2, 3, 6, 7
Heavier set (5 or more)	3, 5, 8
Spokeshave, standard	6
Spokeshave, miniature	3, 4
Scraper—hand scraper	4
FILES:	
Jeweler's files (5 or more)	2, 3, 5–8
Full-size files (several)	3–5, 8
Abrasive paper (a selection of 10 coarsenesses)	1–8
Sanding block (homemade or commercially made)	1–8
PUNCHES:	
Dot punch	2–8
90° punch	4, 7, 8
DRILLS:	
Wheel brace	1–8
Pin vise or pin tong	1–3, 5–8
TWIST DRILLS:	
10 to 15 selected sizes	1–7
Complete set	8
Screw bits (several sizes)	4, 8
Large hole drill	4, 8
Countersink bits	4, 8
TOOL-CARE EQUIPMENT:	
Grinder (see power tools)	
Honing stone	1–8
Strop	2–8
Oil	1–8

Tool	Tool Box Numbers
CLAY-WORKING TOOLS:	
Joint knife	1
Putty knife	1
Wire-end modeling tools (3 or 4)	1, 6
Boxwood modeling tools (3 or 4)	1, 6
Sheet of polyethylene film or wax paper	1, 6
PLASTER-WORKING TOOLS:	
Woodwork surface	3
Mixing bowl	3
Mixing spoon	3
Metal scrapers (2 or 3)	3
Steel rasps (perforated or unperforated, 2 or 3)	3
Miscellaneous running outriggers and slipper-board assemblies	3
Brushes (to apply separators and to dust sanded surfaces)	3
CASTING TOOLS:	
Melting ladle (stainless steel or iron)	6, 8
Glass, slate, or marble work surface	3, 6, 8
Electric heater or bunsen burner	6, 8
PAINTING EQUIPMENT:	
Selection of paint brushes	1–6, 8
Air gun or airbrush, air compressor or compressed air tank, hose paint cups	3–5, 8
Masking tape or other masking material	2–5, 8
Rags	2–5, 8
Spray booth with turntable	3–5, 8
Flock applicator	3–5, 8
PLASTIC-FORMING TOOLS:	
Infrared lamps or electric heating elements (2 or more; lamps may also be used to speed the drying of paint, resin, and some cements)	3, 8
Thermometer	3, 8
Electric oven	3, 8
Homemade or toy pressure chamber for vacuum forming	3, 8
SOLDERING TOOLS:	
Start with a 50-watt soldering iron or gun and get a pencil iron or torch when the need arises	2, 3, 5–8
Asbestos sheet (table protector)	2, 3, 5–8
CEMENTING TOOLS:	
Hypodermic glue gun	2, 3, 5, 6, 8
Porcelain enamel solvent trays (several)	3, 8
Mixing cups	3–5, 7, 8
Annealing oven	8
POWER TOOLS TO PERFORM:	
High-speed turning of small drills, cutters, emery wheels, cut-off discs, cloth-backed abrasive discs, polishing wheels, etc. (tool boxes 3 and 5 will need a rheostat and shaping table)	2, 3, 5–8
Accurate heavy drilling	3–5, 8
Light-duty jig sawing	2, 3, 5, 7, 8
Band sawing	5, 8
Portable saber sawing	4
Circular sawing	4
Dadoing and molding	4, 8
Portable orbital or reciprocating sanding	4
Bench-mounted disc sanding	3–5, 8
Bench-mounted belt sanding	5
Light lathe turning	2, 3, 5, 8
Heavy lathe turning	8
Grinding	3–5, 8

6-2

Project: ZION EVANGELICAL LUTHERAN
CHURCH.
DESIGNED BY: Tasso Katselas.
MODELBUILDERS: members of the architect's staff.
PHOTOGRAPHER: Jay-Bee Photographic Studio.
SCALE: $1/8'' = 1'$.
Columns and beams of this presentation model
were made from balsa; brick textures were drafted
on colored paper. Building was internally braced
with balsa strips. People were bought. Trees were
made of steel wool on wire armatures.
CONSTRUCTION TIME: about 250 hours.

CONCLUSIONS REGARDING POWER TOOLS

Tool Box No. 1 does not require power tools.

Tool Box No. 2 includes the rental or buying of
some power tools if many rough, hollow built-up
models are to be made. This tool box chart and
the one on page 26 indicate that the best starting
tools would be either (1) a small portable hand
motor tool with stand and a light bench-mounted
jig saw, or (2) a Dremel combination tool. Either
way, power tools will cost under $60 (including a
good assortment of blades, cutters and sanders).

Tool Box No. 3 probably requires the buying or
rental of several tools if several elaborate built-up
models are to be made. There are quite a few
possible combinations of tools that will encompass
all the required operations. The least expensive
combination is probably a Dremel combination
tool, a $\frac{1}{4}''$ portable drill with drill press stand and
horizontal bench stand and a grinding tool rest.
These and a good assortment of blades, cutters
and sanders should cost about $85.

Tool Box No. 4 definitely requires the rental
or purchase of power tools unless one does not
mind hard work and less than perfect results.

There are a great number of possible combinations
of tools available. The least expensive of these is
probably a $\frac{1}{4}''$ portable drill with accessory drill
press stand, horizontal bench stand, saber saw
attachment, orbital sander attachment, rubber
disc, a bench-mounted table saw with dado blade
and a bench-mounted belt sander. This should
cost about $120 including blades, sanding discs
and molding heads.

Tool Box No. 5 also requires some power tool
rental or purchase unless balsa is substituted for
harder woods and the extra work involved in
finishing is allowed for. Again, there are a great
number of possible tool combinations, the least
expensive of which is a small portable hand motor
tool with rheostat and shaping table, a bench-
mounted band saw, and a $\frac{1}{4}''$ portable drill with
drill press stand, horizontal stand and rubber disc.
Total cost with an assortment of blades, cutters
and sanders should be under $140.

Tool Box No. 6 does not require power tools
unless objects are to be cast. Then a small portable
hand motor tool with miscellaneous cutters and
sanders should cost under $35.

Tool Box No. 7 also does not require power
tools unless there will be much metal work. Then
either (1) a small portable hand power tool and a
light bench-mounted jig saw, or (2) a Dremel combination tool will probably suffice. The minimum
cost, including miscellaneous cutters and sanders,
should be under $60.

Tool Box No. 8 requires a shop full of tools.
This is one of the reasons why the types of models
made with these tools should be given out to the
professional modelmaking shop. A makeshift tool
collection that could produce moderately well-
machined acrylic or similar types of models
would cost over $200, and a moderately well-
equipped 2-man shop would require $400 to
$600 worth of power tools and their accessories.
Even this array of equipment would equip one to a
far lesser degree than several professional modelbuilders whose shops contain over $10,000 worth
of power tools.

Before starting the first model, a survey should
be made of home or office tool box. Any employee
or associate should also take an inventory of his
stock. Add to these tools only as the need arises,
but keep in mind that completion of the first of
each type of model built will probably mean
completion of the minimal tool box required.

As more models are made, so will the supply of
additional types and sizes of tools grow. Since
some that are not mentioned in this book may be
acquired, the final cost may grow far in excess of
what has been suggested.

7 CEMENTS AND FASTENERS

CEMENTS

Cements are, by definition, substances capable
of holding material together by surface attachment.
They must wet the surfaces of a joint, and come
into molecular contact with as great an area as
possible. To accomplish this, cements must be in a
liquid form when they are applied. Cements are
liquified by being (1) dissolved in water or solvent,
(2) heated, or (3) mixed with a catalyst that
solidifies by chemical action.

Cements that harden by evaporation usually
have little filling capacity. When this type of
cement contracts, the objects being glued must
be free to move together, or a crack will develop.
To prevent cracking, the pieces constituting the
joint must fit together tightly, and must be clamped
so that they constantly will be pushed toward the
cement line.

Porous surfaces must be penetrated by the
cement or the bond will be poor. Quick drying
cements often harden before they have a chance

to infiltrate pores deeply. End grain wood, foam
plastics and porous plaster are materials that often
cause trouble.

Cements having an animal, fish or casein base
are sometimes called glue. Cements made of
flour or other vegetable base are called pastes.

To aid in the mixing of cement, use paper medi-
cine cups with gradations printed on the inside.

Adhesives should be used as soon after they are
purchased as possible.

MAKING STRONG JOINTS

Butt joints are not sufficiently strong for use
in baseboard and model carcass construction.
Some interpenetration of material is needed. See
the Appendix, p. 200, for illustrations of various
ways to construct strong joints. Do not attach too
many parts to an assembly at one time. Let the
cement on earlier parts set before attempting to
attach new pieces.

Applying Cement

Apply enough cement to both surfaces so that,
when clamped, only a small excess will be squeezed out of the joint. To prevent too much excess
from being squeezed on the surrounding material,
do not spread the cement to the edges of the
pieces being joined. With a cement that requires
clamping, care must be taken to apply pressure
evenly along the pieces.

Masks of tape may be used to prevent cement
from flowing onto parts of objects that should
remain uncoated. Make certain, however, that the
solvent in the cement will not eat through the
tape.

Applicators must be picked with care. They
must not spread cement beyond the desired area.
Brush applicators are generally best for rubber
cement and plastic solvents; syringes for cellulose
cements; and metal ladles and spreaders for
heavy wood glues. A toothpick can be used to
apply cement to a very small area.

7-1/7-2

A SIMPLE ACRYLIC PRESENTATION MODEL.
PROJECT: Roosevelt Field Shopping Center, Long Island, New York.
DESIGNED BY: I. M. Pei and Associates.
MODELBUILDER: Thomas Salmon (a professional modelbuilder).
PHOTOGRAPHER: a member of the architect's staff.
SCALE: 3/16″ = 1′.
Buildings were first framed in Masonite and wood; acrylic walls and roofs were then added. People were made of nails with lead dripped onto them. Trees were steel wool on cast metal or twisted wire trunks. Cars were carved from wood, cast metal ones not being available when this model was constructed. The umbrella-like shelter was made from acrylic struts assembled on a jig and the covering of dip-dyed acrylic sheer was then added. Awnings (see street level view right-hand building) were made from bent and painted sheet brass.

TYPES OF BONDING AGENTS

Bonding agents that are commonly used for making models and furniture are listed in the Tables. Types of cement used on furniture can also be employed on baseboards, carrying boxes and special situations. Any instructions I have given should be superseded by the suggestions of the manufacturer of the specific brand purchased. Because of frequent innovations in adhesives, be alert for the appearance of new products in hardware stores and hobby shops.

Materials that may be bonded, by various adhesives, with fair to excellent success are as shown in the table below.

The Franklin Glue Company, Columbus, Ohio, assisted in the preparation of parts of this table.

Cellulose Cement is a quick drying, clear, waterproof, flexible cement in liquid form which is packaged in tubes. Its solvent is acetone. It may be used on most porous, and on nonporous,

material (if the solvent is able to evaporate). Both model airplane cement and slower drying household cement are cellulose cements. Cellulose cement shrinks on drying, and can distort thin objects. Its rapid drying speed often prevents it from thoroughly penetrating the surface of porous objects. When cementing porous objects, coat each side of the joint, allow the cement to dry partially, then put on a second coat and press the joint together by hand, or clamp, until dry. Nonporous objects need be coated with only 1 coat. Cellulose cement lasts indefinitely in the tube. Model airplane cements are made by Testors (Types A and B), Ambroid, Comet, Lepages, etc. Household cements are made by Lepages, DuPont (Duco), Franklin, Woodhill, etc.

Contact Cement is a quick drying, water resistant, thin liquid made of neoprene and naphtha or toluol. Contact cement also comes in a non-inflammable water-based type. A joint covered with contact cement will adhere on contact without clamping. This cement is of rather low strength (household cellulose cement is just

Syringes (glue guns) are sold in hobby stores: Austin-Craft makes a $1.50 gun with interchangeable screw-on tips. E-Z Flo nozzles, costing 20¢, can be attached to the nozzles of glue tubes.

Clamps

See page 17 for a listing of the various clamps commercially available and of the additional clamps that you may fabricate to solve special problems.

If it is impossible to clamp the work, a cement that does not require clamping should be used. Contact cement, rubber cement and Epoxy cement are such adhesives. When making complicated joints, impossible to hold together with clamps, all joints except those that require maximum strength should be cemented with fast drying cellulose cement and hand held until they set.

Small work should be cemented on a sheet of glass. A double-edged razor blade that has been broken lengthwise can be worked under the joint easily to cut it loose. Place large work (baseboards, etc.) over sheets of wax paper while the joints dry.

Cleaning Joints

Use a clean, dry rag or one dipped in the solvent of the adhesive to remove any excess cement dripping out of the joint while it is still wet. Rubber cement is easiest to remove when it has dried. Areas covered with plastic solvents are another exception since they should not be touched while wet.

ADHESIVES FOR VARIOUS MATERIALS

Adhesive	Paper	Cardboard	Light wood	Heavy wood	Metal	Foam plastics¹	Plastics¹	Plaster	Fabric
Solder					×				
Liquid solder					×				
The solvent of the various plastics							×		
The solvent of the various plastics and chips of the plastics							×		
The resin of the various plastics							×		
Cellulose cement (model airplane and household)	×	×	×		×		×²	×	×
Contact cement (neoprene base)	some ×	×	×		×	×	×	×	×
Rubber cement	×	×	×		×	×		×	×
Rubber adhesive (nitrile base)	×	×	×		×		×	×	×
Casein glue			×	×				×	
White glue (polyvinyl acetate resin)	×	×	×	×		×	×	×	×
Epoxy cement			×	×	×	×	×	×	
Resorcinol resin glue	×	×	×	×			×	×	×
Plastic resin glue (urea base)				×			×	×	
Acrylic resin glue			×	×	×		×		
Aliphatic resin glue	×	×	×	×				×	×
Hide glue	×	×	×	×				×	×

¹ Test a scrap of the plastic with the cement or glue before using.
² Use when cementing celluloid and acetate to other materials.

about 7 times as strong). Some cements come in cans, others in spray bombs. Apply a coat to both surfaces, allow it to dry, apply a second coat, allow this to dry thoroughly (30 to 40 minutes), and join the objects within 3 hours. If the second coat is not allowed to dry thoroughly, the joint will open when heated (by sunlight, etc.). Contact cement is made by Weldweld, Elmer's, Barge, Franklin, Krylon, Woodhill, 3M (Fast Bond), etc.

Rubber Cement comes in tubes and cans, is flexible, and can be used on anything; it bonds with low strength, and loses strength when applied under conditions of high humidity. When making a temporary bond, coat 1 surface and join the pieces while the cement is still wet. On nonporous materials the cement should be allowed to dry, and then heated before joining. For joints of greatest strength, apply cement to both pieces, allow to dry, then join. The solvent is methylethylketone.

Rubber cement is especially good for use on paper, fabric and on materials having dissimilar expansion rates. Attach moldings and other thin parts to models with it. Excess dry cement may be removed by rubbing it off the work when it has dried. It does not wrinkle paper, fabric or other thin materials.

A special type of rubber cement, called 1-coat rubber cement, remains tacky indefinitely. With it one can make pressure sensitive materials that can be pressed into place many days after coating. Rubber cement is made by Woodhill, Best Test, Sanfords, Columbia, etc.

Synthetic Rubber Adhesive (nitrile base) is a waterproof, flexible adhesive. Coat both parts to be joined with adhesive, allow them to dry for 2 minutes, then press the assembly together. This adhesive drys in 5 minutes. Any excess must be removed with acetone solvent. Joints may be heat cured for additional strength. Made by Walthers (Goo).

Casein Glue is water resistant and a good gap filler. It has a shelf life of over 2 years. It should be mixed, applied and cured at a temperature of 70°F. Casein is best used to glue heavy wood assemblies and most other porous and nonporous materials to wood. When gluing oily woods (yellow pine, etc.), wash the wood first with a strong solution of alkaline household cleaner. Casein in powder form should be mixed 1 part (by weight) glue to 1 part water that is at 50° to 70°F. Stir until the mix becomes pasty, let stand for 10 to 15 minutes, then stir again until mixture becomes smooth. Apply an ample amount with a stiff bristle brush. Clamp the joint and with a damp cloth wipe off any excess. Set starts in 10 to 15 minutes. Retain clamps on softwood for 2 or more hours and on hardwood for 5 or more hours. Some woods are stained by regular casein glue; these should be cemented only with nonstaining casein.

Casein is made by Casco, Lepages (Sure Grip), Weldwood (Presto Set), Franklin (Ever-Tite), Elmer's, etc.

White Glue (polyvinyl acetate resin) is water soluble, dries clear, and is fast drying. It comes in ready-to-use liquid form in bottle or plastic containers. White Glue is not compatible with lacquer solvents. Use it on wood, paper and cloth, but not on metal. Clamp until it has set, in about 30 minutes; it attains full strength in 3 days. Clean off the excess with a damp cloth before it sets. The shiny residue, which sometimes remains, is hard to sand off. Mix the glue with an equal part of water to make a transparent joint.

White Glue is made by Ambroid, Franklin (polyvinyl emulsion), Woodhill, Lepages (acetate glue), Weldwood (Presto), DuPont, Freeman Suppy Co. (white polyvinyl emulsion), Sobo, Elmer's (Glue All), etc.

Epoxy Cement comes in 2 parts and sets by chemical action, not by solvent evaporation. Epoxy will bond almost any material, and can also be used on all plastics as a body cement. Excess must be removed with denatured alcohol

before it sets. Epoxy must be used within about 2 hours after it has been mixed. It dries in 3 hours and completely cures in 18 hours. Infrared heating will shorten this time to 1½ hours. Shelf life is about a year. Epoxy does not shrink on setting, and is waterproof. Contrary to popular belief, it is not as strong as household cellulose cement. Mix on a piece of glass or other disposable surface. Apply to both surfaces which are to be joined, after first roughening nonporous surfaces; press the parts together (no clamps are necessary); clean hands with nail polish remover or denatured alcohol immediately to prevent dermatitis.

There is also an instant Epoxy, available in a hypodermic-like applicator, that hardens in a minute. Another type of Epoxy is Eastman 910. Already prepared, it is very expensive and bonds most materials. It sets almost immediately after the joint is pressed together, but not before. Its shelf life is only 90 days.

Epoxy is made by Franklin, Woodhill, Lepages, Elmer's, etc.

Resorcinol Resin Glue comes in 2 parts, liquid resin and powdered catalyst, and is used on wood and paper. Apply at 70°F or over, keep clamped for 10 hours or longer. It sets in 8 hours and attains full strength in 6 weeks. It is waterproof and it will keep indefinitely on the shelf.

Resorcinol is made by Franklin (waterproof glue), Elmer's (waterproof glue), Weldwood, etc.

Plastic Resin Glue (urea base) bonds wood. It comes in powder, and is water resistant when dry. The powder is mixed in cold water; 2 parts (by volume) powder to 1 part water, or, if you desire the glue to set rapidly, use only half as much water. Apply glue to 1 surface only and clamp 5 to 6 hours; joints must fit perfectly.

Plastic resin glue is made by Casco (Cascamite), Franklin, Weldwood, Elmer's, etc.

Acrylic Resin Glue comes in 2 parts. Setting time can be varied depending on the proportions of the mix. It is usable on almost anything and is a good gap filler. It is made by Franklin.

Aliphatic Resin Glue comes in a powder (which may be pre-colored with water-soluble dyes) or in liquid form. It is a good gap filler and is water resistant. It has a shelf life of up to 1 year. Light work requires 2 minutes clamping; heavy work, 45 minutes.

Aliphatic resin glue is made by Franklin (Tite Bond), etc.

FASTENERS

Pins

Pins serve several purposes in modelmaking: they may be used to pin together balsa, stripwood and other materials that are being glued; they may be inserted into joints (in small assemblies) to act as miniature nails. Modelmaking pins come in sizes of from ½″ (No. 8) to 1⅞″ (No. 32) long. Lil pins which are ⅜″ to ½″ long can also be obtained in hobby stores. Escutcheon pins are available in hardware and dressmaker's stores; bank and satin pins are available at dressmakers' supply stores. See page 24 for a chart showing the diameters of available pins.

Nails

Among the over 100 existing varieties of nails, several are useful in modelmaking.

Finishing Nails have brad heads that can be driven 1/16″ into the wood with a nail set and then concealed with putty, plastic wood or sawdust mixed with glue. They are often used on baseboard and carrying boxes or wherever an exposed nail head would be objectionable.

Nail Sets, Taps or *Brad Awls* may be used with finishing nails or to drive nails into places a hammer cannot reach. Stanley makes them in several diameters for 35¢ each.

Brads are small versions of finishing nails; they are used for the same purposes and, also, to hold the carcasses of built-up models together. They can be obtained in lengths as short as ⅜″.

Common Nails have flat heads and diamond-shaped points. They are used whenever a nail head's presence would not be visually objectionable.

Wire Nails are small versions of common nails. Fiberboard nails have about the thinnest shafts of all.

The Holding power of nails may be increased by using nails that have barbs, screw threads or rings along the shafts or nails coated with adhesive cement. The latter can be applied to nails as short as 1″; the other devices appear on nails 2″ and longer. The holding power for any given nail is greater in hardwood and side grain than in softwood and end grain. Splitting in wood is caused by the shape of the nail's point and by its diameter in relation to the thickness and type of the wood. It can be prevented by using thinner or oval cross-sectioned nails. Sharp nails tend to split hardwood.

Corrugated Fasteners are for holding 2 pieces of wood together side by side. Use saw edge fasteners on softwoods and plain edge fasteners on hardwood.

Wood Screws

They are identified according to their head style, length and diameter. Length is measured from the tip to where, fully driven, they intersect the top of the wood. To prevent the wood from splitting and to create greater holding capacity, holes must be drilled to start wood screws. First drill a "lead" or "pilot" hole to direct the screw and to hold its threaded part, then drill a "body" hole for the shank of the screw and, if the screw is to be countersunk or counterbored, a third hole to take its head. In hardwood the pilot hole should be the full length of the screw; in softwood it should be half the length of the screw.

SCREW HOLES

Screw holes should be as follows:

DRILLS FOR VARIOUS SCREW SIZES

Screw size	Drill for lead hole	Drill for body hole
0		53
1		49
2	56[1]	44
3	52[1]	40
4	51[1]	33
5	49	1/8″
6	47	28
7	46	24
8	42	19
9	41	15
10	38	10
11	37	5
12	36	7/32″

[1] Lead hole required only in hardwood.

Countersink Bits by Arco cost $1.50. They are for use on electric drills, and are adjustable to any depth.

When fastening 2 pieces of wood together, the screw threads should grip only the lower piece. The top piece should be drilled entirely through with the body hole. Wood screws are easier to drive if soap has been rubbed into the threads. When a part is to be held by several screws, first drive all of them snugly into place, then go back and tighten them up.

Screws may be concealed by wooden plugs obtainable in many diameters at boat supply, and some hardware stores. You may also make your own, using a plug cutter. Match the wood of the object and cut so that the grain runs across the end of the plug, not lengthwise through it. Glue the plug into place and trim off any excess to make it flush with the top.

Walthers has a good selection of Nos. 00 to 20 wood screws in $\frac{1}{8}$ to $\frac{1}{2}$" lengths. These come with both round and flat heads.

Machine Screws

These are used for working in metal. They come in a variety of head styles including flat, round and oval. They are specified in terms of their material, type of head, outside diameter, length and the number of threads per inch. Follow standard tables for the recommended tap drill to use with each size of screw. Tap drills run a bit larger in diameter than the diameter of the central shaft of

MACHINE SCREWS

     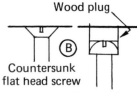

Flat Round Oval Full Hex Countersunk flat head screw Wood plug Counter bore

the screw. The tap hole must then have screw threads cut into it (tapped). This is done by screwing taps into the hole. Taps may be obtained in hardware stores, small ones in hobby shops. Also obtainable are dies (or thread chasers) that are used to cut threads into rods. A drop of oil or a little graphite on the threads will simplify the driving of machine screws.

Walthers sells a line of brass machine screws (and nuts to fit), whose sizes run from Nos. 00—90 to 2–56, with lengths of $\frac{1}{8}$ to $\frac{1}{2}$". Head styles are hex, round, flat and full.

---

8 MATERIALS AND HOW TO WORK WITH THEM

A professional modelmaker, noted for the speed at which he worked and the quality of his models, commented, "I'm not a fast worker. I construct models rapidly because my shop is well organized and I know most of the materials that exist and how to work with them. This allows me to select those which can save me huge amounts of time." Personal experience, as well, also leads me to believe that a complete knowledge of available materials and techniques can greatly help the beginner.

The choice of the materials to be used is governed by: (1) the object being modeled; (2) the handling given the model and its desired life expectancy; (3) the modelmaker's skill in working with various materials; (4) the tools that are available; and (5) the availability of the material. It is generally the rule, also, to limit the number of different materials attached together, since the more that are used the greater the chance of uneven expansion and warpage.

File current catalogs of material suppliers and always refer to them as the need arises. If the modelmaker is located in a small town, he will have to obtain some material by mail. Thus extra time is needed to complete models or, in some cases, a stockpile of hard-to-locate materials should be established.

When purchasing new material, lay aside a sample with its manufacturer's name and address written on it. I paste flat samples into a loose-leaf book, some pages of which are reproduced in this volume. Ads for interesting new materials may also be kept. When shopping for materials, carry an architect's scale to measure the exact scale dimensions of the materials. Materials meant for model railroad construction are often out of scale and must be checked carefully.

Another source of potential model material is the throwaway office, also, household things that can sometimes be improvised into model parts. These include architectural samples, broken toys and jewelry, scraps of cardboard and paper, etc. Some modelers save all the odds and ends that cross their path, but I have found, after years of junk collecting, that precious few of these things are ever used. I have been able, though, to use certain architectural samples (especially fabric, wall coverings and other flat materials). I mount samples of these in my scrapbook along with the name of local suppliers who do not mind selling (or sometimes giving) a square foot or two of the product to a modelmaker.

Because many models are built on a rush basis and on weekends, it is better to start their construction with an oversupply of materials to compensate for material that will be wasted through cutting, making mistakes and experimentation.

An occasional copy of *Model Railroader* will provide the names and addresses of suppliers of structural shapes, simulated building materials, vegetation, etc.

The brands of materials that I have mentioned in this book are those that I have had success with. There are other good brands available worth experimenting with from time to time. Some of the techniques described here are also outlined on the instruction sheets that come with the materials. I have reviewed them so that they may be analyzed without once having to buy a sample batch of the materials.

The professional modelmaker will at some time encounter a section of the work that requires a technique for which he lacks either tools or experience. He can usually subcontract this work to another modelbuilder or to a fabricator. Truly difficult techniques not meant for eleventh hour experimentation are metal casting, milling vacuum forming, electroplating, engraving and photoprinting. It is good for the occasional modelbuilder to know and make use of outside services.

Use of Real Materials

A modelmaker is sometimes overtaken by an uncontrollable urge to construct a model or part of a model out of real materials. In college I decided to make the ground slab of a $\frac{1}{4}$"=1 ft. scale house out of concrete and reinforcing bars. After taking inventory of available materials, I compromised somewhat and used plaster of Paris with 2 sizes of sand as the concrete and aggregates, and piano wire for the reinforcement. The results, while rather good for this type of exotic experiment, took a long time to achieve. The error of my undertaking was impressed on me when I was complimented by several classmates for the cardboard slab which, while it did not resemble concrete, did have a look to it that was unlike anything that they had ever seen.

Once, a client of a leading professional model-maker insisted that the plaza in front of his building be modeled in real stone. After it was machined, at great cost, the stone mason announced that its 1,000 lb. weight did not allow it to be placed into the model in any but an exactly

vertical position. Since he wanted a plaza, not a monolith headstone, the client had to abandon the slab.

PAPER AND CARD-BOARD FABRICATION

Paper and cardboard are the most useful, versatile and inexpensive of all easy-to-work materials. Complete models can be made from these materials using only a razor or knife, clamps, a straightedge and glue. There is no limit to what can be constructed. Walls, floors, roofs and partitions can be made as can laminated ground contours and lightweight baseboards. Curved surfaces can be wet-formed from some types of cardboards or laminated from multi-plys of thin Bristolboard. Extremely intricate objects may be built, as well as strong and durable models, some of which have outlasted the buildings they depicted. Illustration 8-1 shows a cardboard and paper model that is in perfect condition after almost half a century. Illustrations 8-4 and 9-3 show some of the complex shapes that may be constructed from paper. Industrial designers even use cardboard for the construction of full-size mock-ups of objects as large as computers and gasoline pumps. Many boards come with surfaces requiring no further finishing. With a little ingenuity any type of opaque material may be simulated with paper and board. To keep paper and board free from fingerprints, keep your fingers covered with French chalk (obtainable from art supply stores) while you are working. Heat and sunlight can cause most boards and paper to crack, warp or become brittle; cold has no effect on these materials.

Cutting Paper and Board

Use a razor or thin-bladed knife. The shearing action of scissors will cause curling cuts in thin strips of paper and in medium and heavyweight board. Knives with thick blades create wedge-shaped cuts. A paper cutter guarantees long straight cuts. By setting the material against the top cutting guide, perfect 90° corners can be made. When cutting with a blade or knife, place the material on a hard (plywood or Masonite) cutting surface. A soft cutting surface may produce a ragged cut on the bottom face of the paper or board or cause a fin to be depressed along the

HOW LONG CAN A CARDBOARD AND PAPER MODEL LAST?

Model of Delphi as it appeared in about 160 A.D. This photo shows the temple of Apollo and surrounding buildings.
MODELBUILDER: Hans Schlief.
SCALE: 1:200.
This model, which is on display at The Metropolitan Museum of Art, New York City, remains neat and unwarped after over a 1/3 century. Walls, roofs and stadium seats were made from illustration board; columns from wood dowels; small statues from paper, large ones from clay. Windows and decorative details were inked on the board. Ground contours were constructed of plaster.

8-2

A ROUGH CARDBOARD MODEL.

DESIGN AND MODEL BY: students of the Cooper Union School of Art and Architecture, New York City.
SCALE: 3/32″ = 1′.
This rough but useful study model was made from cardboard except for balsa columns and window walls. Baseboard was constructed of homosote.

length of the cut. Cut material heavier than 3-ply Bristolboard with several strokes. Use a metal straightedge to guide the blade when making straight cuts. To cut outside curves, use scissors on thin material. Cut thicker board with a blade and then sand with abrasive paper mounted on a sanding block or with a manicurist's emery board. For inside curves, cut with a razor blade and then sand with abrasive paper mounted on a dowel or wood strip.

To cut clean inside corners (when cutting out windows, doors, etc.), pierce the corners with a pin. Cut from the pin prick toward the center of the cut to avoid overcutting the corner.

All identically shaped objects should be cut out together (one over the other) with the sheets temporarily clamped or tack-cemented together. If the pile of boards is too thick to cut out in one operation, use the first object cut (not subsequent ones) as a die to lay out the remaining ones. Place it on the stock and transfer its corner with a series of pin pricks.

To drill clean holes, sandwich the board between sheets of plywood. Holes may be punched with X-Acto punches, or wad punches may be used to execute 1/10 to 1″ diameter holes.

Bending and Sheet Forming Paper and Board

To bend thin board and paper, score halfway through with a scriber and bend. Thicker board should be partially cut through on the outside of the bend, and then bent. In both cases use a straightedge to guide the bend. Many types of pulp and strawboards cannot be bent to neat 90° angles.

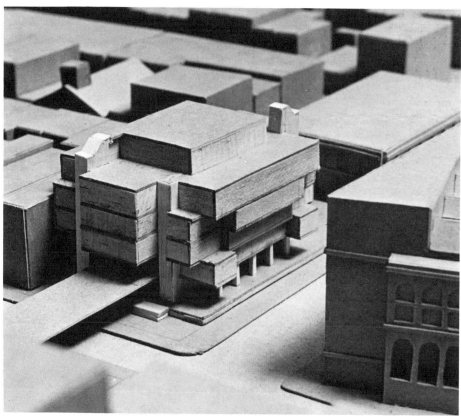

Cylindrical shapes can be made by rolling paper or thin board around a dowel, beveling its edges with a 30° bevel cut and then lap gluing the seam.

Cones, coned discs and bullet shapes may also be made. Accurate patterns for these shapes can be perfected through experimentation.

Extruded shapes can be formed by using dowels and stripwood for the male molds. Build up the extrusion with several plys of Bristolboard. For best results, steam the paper over a kettle of boiling water. Tight or intricate bends may require both a female and a male mold. Put the steamed paper into the female mold and press it into shape with the male mold.

To form complex curved shapes, use gumstrip

(parcel tape) or paper placed over a male mold, or wet strawboard (cardboard) pressed into a female mold. Press the strawboard into the mold with a ball or file handle. Even tightly curved articles can be fabricated in this fashion. After the board has dried, remove it from the mold and waterproof it.

To laminate medium and large objects with paper, construct a male mold out of plaster or wood. Apply 5 or more coats of shellac to the mold; sand each coat so that the last coat will have a glossy finish. Wax the mold and cover it with a layer of wax paper. If gumstrip is used, a layer of wet rag-tissue may be substituted for the wax paper. Apply the paper strips—gumstrip, strips of 2-ply Bristolboard or bond paper held on by liberal amounts of cement—and slightly overlap adjacent ones. At least 3-plys of paper should be used on the smallest objects; up to 10-ply on objects measuring several feet. Apply the first 4 layers at angles of 45° to the preceding ply. The final layers may all run in the same direction. To prevent warping, allow the assembly to dry out thoroughly after a few layers have been applied. Care should be taken to prevent air bubbles from forming between plys. When the object has dried thoroughly, pry it off its mold. The shape may be sanded smooth, and have its inside and outside surfaces sealed with paint or sanding sealer. Handled properly, gumstrip may be bent into curves with as small a radius as $\frac{1}{32}''$. The more intricate the shape, the narrower must be the gumstrip or paper.

Molding Details on Board

After gesso, or Barbola paste applied to cardboard, has dried, details may be carved out. Test the board to make sure that the mix is not so wet as to cause damage.

Internal Bracing

The secret of strong and long-lasting paper and cardboard models is internal bracing. Walls, floors and roof will mutually brace each other, but additional bracing is needed for the large unsupported areas between these intersections. Brace joints with either (1) a fillet of cement (test the adhesive for warpage as it dries on scrap), or (2) a piece of wood strip laid along the joint. See 8-2A for some of the many ways possible to brace typical surfaces. Brace cardboard models across the grain. The grain can be found by bending the cardboard in both directions; the grain runs parallel to the direction of the more flexible bend.

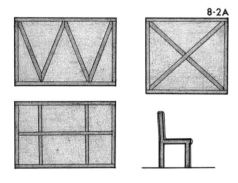

8-2A

Bonding Paper and Cardboard

Prior to bonding the parts, assemble them and check all corners with a square.

Butt joints may be used with thicker boards. Thinner materials must have flap joints; on flap joints that are not visible, staples may be used for added strength. Pressure-sensitive tape may be used on rough models to strengthen butt joints.

CARDBOARD-TO-CARDBOARD BONDING

Use a slow-drying cellulose cement; quick-drying cement will harden before it penetrates the material's surface. Water-based cements must be avoided, though white glue can be used. Rubber cement or white glue, while not producing a hard joint, may be used where excess cement must be easily removed. Cellulose cement may cause joint warpage in some instances. Place the

cellulose cement as quickly as possible. See illustration 8-3 for 2 placement diagrams. If properly located, the cement will spread out to cover most of the board when clamping pressure is exerted. Learn by experience how close to the edges and corners to place the cement and how thick a bead of cement may be used. Press flat assemblies under books for about $\frac{1}{2}$ hour, or roll them with a photographic roller and spot clamp. Exert fairly even pressure throughout the entire length of the assembly.

PAPER-TO-PAPER AND PAPER-TO-CARDBOARD BONDING

Use rubber cement to cement a paper ply to a sheet of cardboard or to another paper: (1) Coat the 2 surfaces to be joined with an even layer of rubber cement and use a 1 × 6″ scrap of illustration board as a cement spreader. (2) Inspect both surfaces and level any thick concentrations of cement. Let the cement dry. (3) Lay the heavier material on your workbench with the cemented side up. (4) Cover the cemented surface with a sheet of tracing paper, allowing a $\frac{1}{8}''$ wide strip of cement-coated material to protrude from under the paper. (5) Have an assistant hold the second sheet that is to be joined above the first sheet with the 2 cement-covered surfaces facing one another. (6) Carefully lower the top sheet so that it contacts the $\frac{1}{8}''$ strip of exposed cement in the exact position in which it is to be attached. If a mistake in positioning has been made, pull apart the narrow cement line and start all over again. (7) If the sheets are positioned correctly, press down the top sheet with a clean cloth. (8) Pull the tracing paper back from between the 2 sheets with 1 hand and have an assistant drop more of the top sheet on the bottom sheet. With the other hand, press the already attached part of the sheets with a photographic roller or with a roll of tracing paper. (9) When the 2 pieces are completely mounted, inspect their surfaces and roll out any minor blemishes that may have appeared. (10) Give the entire surface a final hard roll.

DRY MOUNTING

Dry mounting is of use to modelers who make a number of built-up models. Dry mounting allows rapid and perfect adherence of printed simulated building materials and colored paper to the cardboard sides of models. Embossed papers must be tested to see if the embossing is compressed by the mounting pressure. Often, while it is somewhat flattened, the embossing is still presentable. Some embossed or flat plastic sheets may be dry mounted, but this will depend on the temperature of the press and on the melting point of the plastic. To test, place 2 plys of brown wrapping paper on either side of the plastic and cardboard assembly and put it in the press for 2 seconds. Remove and note the amount of plastic melting that has taken place and how well the dry-mounting tissue has adhered the plastic to the cardboard (in 2 seconds the tissue probably has not melted). Then gradually increase the time in the press.

When mounting a new type of paper or board, perform a test on scrap material to determine the degree of the warps that are caused.

To dry mount: (1) Preheat the backing board and the overlay material to remove any moisture. (2) Tack mount (using a small heated tacking iron)

a sheet of dry-mounting tissue to the overlay material. Trim the tissue to the outline of the overlay. (3) Place the overlay tissue-sandwich on the backing board and insert the entire assembly into the dry-mounting press. Put a protective sheet of brown wrapping paper on top of the assembly. (4) Close the press for the amount of time recommended in the instructions for that thickness. Try to heat the work as little as possible and yet achieve a good bond. Too much heat, or prolonged heat, may cause blisters to form in the work. (5) Remove the work from the press. Before cutting it into small pieces, or cutting out windows or assembling the materials, allow it to reabsorb a normal amount of humidity. This will take 1 or 2 days. This step, while obviously a nuisance, will help prevent warping.

A dry-mounting press is quite expensive; one that can mount material up to 24″ wide by any length costs about $70. Dry-mounting tissue costs about 2 to 3¢ per 8 × 10″ sheet; it also comes in larger sheets as well as in rolls.

A dry-mounting sheet called Instant Mount with pressure-sensitive adhesive on both sides is commercially available. These sheets require no heat and cost about 50¢ per sq. ft.

STAPLING

Rough study models can be stapled together, but each part must have tabs that can be bent under and stapled to adjacent parts. If possible, use a small, low stapling gun to facilitate use in tight places.

Sealing and Waterproofing

Remove all blobs of cement with a razor; this is especially important if oil paint will eventually be used. Seal the material with sanding sealer; 1 coat is enough for average finishes, with up to 3 coats for a fine finish. Sand each coat of dried sealer with No. 600 abrasive paper. The ends of boards must be given special attention either in the form of extra coats of sealer or an application of Ditzler's Rip Rap primer. Most boards can be waterproofed with one or more sprayed coats of French polish, cellulose varnish or cellulose lacquer. These substances render the board resistant to water or poster paints. In addition, French polish will stain the board yellow. If a water-based paint must be used, first paint the board, then apply one of the cellulose-based chemicals.

Available Papers and Boards

The following chart shows many of the papers and boards that are commonly used. Listed are materials in a complete range of thicknesses (from 3/1000 to 1/8″), colors and shades of gray, textures and finishes. An extensive knowledge of what is available will aid you in constructing faster and more realistic cardboard models. Suppliers and manufacturers listed are those with whom I have had personal contact, but others throughout the country have similar products. Some manufacturers channel their papers and boards to supply houses and retail outlets which then stamp their own brand name on the material. Many papers of potential use to the modelmaker can be obtained from artist supply outlets, from gift wrapping and

APPLYING CEMENT TO SHEET LAMINATIONS

8-3

Cement

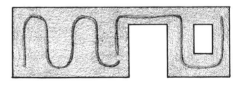

8-4/8-5

CURVED STRUCTURES MADE FROM PAPER.

PROJECT: Monastery and Church of the Priory of St. Mary and St. Louis, St. Louis, Missouri.
DESIGNED BY: Hellmuth, Obata and Kassabaum, Inc.
MODELBUILDERS: members of the architect's staff.
PHOTOGRAPHER: Mac Mizuki.
SCALE: 1/16" = 1'.
Concrete shells were modeled in bent paper and fastened 1 tier upon the next without internal columns. The grills of the church were made from acrylic covered with a Zip-a-Tone pattern. The other grills were stamped brass obtained at hardware stores. Baseboard was heavy cardboard. Trees were baby's-breath. The model was used for presentation and limited study.
The photograph was taken with a Rolleiflex camera and Panatomic X film.
CONSTRUCTION TIME: about 100 hours.

wholesale paper suppliers. Boards are carried by artist supply stores. To learn who, in a given city, carries a paper or board, it may be necessary to write the manufacturer.

Try to obtain papers and boards from local distributors. If this is impossible, send a letter to the manufacturer telling him what his product is intended for, and enclose 50¢, or $1, for each sheet (most run 18 × 24" to 24 × 36"). In all probability, this will break down his resistance to doing business on such a small lot basis.

Very smooth finish: is like plaster at ¼" scale or smaller.

Smooth finish: is like concrete at 1/16 to ¼" scale.

Rough finish: somewhat rougher.

The rear surface of many illustration and other boards listed as colored is covered in part by printing.

AVAILABLE PAPER AND BOARD

Key:
A = Distributed by Art Brown & Bro., Inc.
B = Bienfang Paper Company
BA = Bainbridge
BU = Butler
C = Craftint Paper (can be obtained from art supply store)
CR = Crescent Cardboard Company
F = Fasson self-adhesive paper; comes with a pressure-sensitive adhesive backing
H = Hamilton Gainsborough Paper
L = Liberty
LE = Lehigh (distributed by Bienfang)
N = National Card and Mat Board Company
R = Royal Crest
S = Strathmore
W = Whatman

Name	Mfg. or supplier	Thickness (inches)	Shades & colors available						Texture	Finish	Reverse sides
			White	Gray	Black	Colors	Gold	Silver			
Bond, layout & ledger paper	B	3/1000	3						Smooth or *very* slightly textured (pebbled or lined)	Mat	Prime
		4/1000	4								
		5/1000	2								
Signwriter's postal paper	B	3/1000	1		1	5			Smooth	Mat	Prime
		5/1000	1								
		7/1000	1								
Fasson self-adhesive paper	F	4/1000	1			1	3	3	Smooth	Mat (some S & G are glossy)	Adhesive
		5/1000	1								
		6/1000				3					
		8/1000	1								
		9/1000	1								
Patent Office board	S	4, 8 & 12/1000	3						Smooth; thinnest is slightly transparent	Mat	Prime
Display & banner paper	B	5 or 6/1000	1	1	1	20	1	1	Smooth, except G & S, which have an extremely fine pebble	Mat	Off-white

(continued on next page)

Name	Mfg. or supplier	Thickness (inches)	White	Gray	Black	Colors	Gold	Silver	Texture	Finish	Reverse sides
Text & cover "Gainsborough"	H	5, 7, 9 & 11/1000	4						Highly textured finish like pastel paper	Mat	Prime
		10/1000		1							
		6 to 10/1000				4					
Text cover Bristol "Starwhite"	H	5, 6, 7, 8, 10 & 15/1000	5						Smooth	Mat	Prime
		6, 8, 10 & 12/1000	5						Fairly smooth		
		5 & 8/1000	2						Light stipple		
Charcoal drawing paper	S B	6/1000	1	1	1	8			A parallel-line texture, lines 1/32" O.C.	Mat	Prime
True-Tone papers	A	6/1000	1	12	1	223			Smooth	Mat	White
Aluminum foil board, "bright finish"	B	7–8/1000				8	1	1	Fairly smooth	Glossy	White
Aluminum foil board, "dull finish"	B	7–8/1000				5	2	1	Very smooth	Semi-glossy	White
Watercolor paper	S	7, 8 & 9/1000	3						Fairly smooth, slightly, & very crinkly	Mat	Prime
Text paper, "Carousel"	H	7 or 9/1000	3	1		5			Highly textured finish like pastel paper	Mat	Prime
Text & cover paper "Carousel"	H C S	7, 10 & 13/1000	3						Crinkly	Mat	Prime
		7/1000		1		3					
		10/1000				2					
Tag & postcard "Husky"	H	7, 9, 11, 13, & 15/1000 (=100, 125, 150, 175, & 200 lb.)	5			5[1]			Very smooth	Mat	Prime
Drawing Bristol- paper & -board	B S BA	7, 17, 20, & 24/1000 (=1, 2, 3, & 4 ply)	8		1[2]				2 Textures: "Vellum," "Medium" or "Kid" are fairly smooth; "Plate," "High" or "Smooth" are very smooth	Mat	Prime
Drawing paper	B	9/1000	1			1			Smooth	Mat	Prime
		5, 7, 8, & 14/1000	5						Smooth to Blotter and Banknote-like texture		
		10/1000		1							
		7 & 8/1000				4					
Pastel paper	B	9/1000	1	1	1	5			Very crinkly	Mat	Prime
Construction paper	B	9 to 10/1000	1	2	1	24			Blotterlike texture	Mat	Prime
Folding Bristol, "Rollstone Folding Bristol"	H	9, 11, 13 & 15/1000	4						Smooth	Mat	Prime
		9/1000		1							
		9, 10 & 11/1000				9					
Velour paper	B	10/1000	1	1	1	13			Fine flocked finish	Mat	Various pastel colors
Sunfast paper	BU	10/1000	3	3	1	44	1		Fine texture, like blotting paper or smooth	Mat	Prime
Watercolor paper	B	10, 18, 20 & 31/1000	4						Very crinkly	Mat	Prime
		20/1000	1						Slightly crinkly		
		8/1000	1						Smooth		
T. V. Bristol	CR	11/1000		1					Smooth	Mat	Gray

[1] Manilas.
[2] Available from Bienfang only.
[3] Light tan.
[4] Bronze.

Name	Mfg. or supplier	Thickness (inches)	Shades & colors available						Texture	Finish	Reverse sides
			White	Gray	Black	Colors	Gold	Silver			
Coquille Bristol	BA	14/1000	2						Fine & coarser stipple	Mat	Prime
Watercolor paper	S	14, 15 or 16/1000	4						Various degrees of crinkle finish—from slightly to extremely	Mat	Prime
Coated display board	H	14, & 20/1000	3						Smooth, except G & S, which have a very slight texture	Mat	Various card-boardlike finishes
		19/1000				1					
		27/1000						1			
		24/1000					1				
Coated blanks	H	15, 18, 21, 24 & 32/1000 (= 3, 4, 5, 6 & 8 ply)	5						Smooth	Semimat	Prime
Railroad board	LE	16 & 25/1000 (= 4 & 6 ply)	1		1	12			Smooth	Semimat	Prime
Posterboard	LE	24/1000 (= 6 ply)	1		1	5			Smooth	Semimat	Cardboard color
Illustration board No. 60	N	30/1000	1						Smooth	Mat	Off-white
Posterboard	LE	32/1000 (= 8 ply)	1						Smooth	Semimat	Cardboard color
Display cardboards	N	32/1000 (= 8 ply)	1		1	4			Smooth or pebbled is obtainable in each	Semimat to mat	Gray
		54/1000 (= 14 ply)	2	3	1	29	1	1			
		84/1000 (= 22 ply)	1		1						
Illustration board No. 108	CR	36/1000	1						Fairly smooth	Mat	Prime
Pulp board	N	36/1000		1		1[3]			Smooth	Mat	Prime
Mount board	N	44 to 49/1000	2	5	1	6			Smooth	Mat	Gray
Illustration board	CR (No. 202) BA (No. 905)	46/1000	1						Very smooth	Mat	Gray
Mat board	BA	47 to 52/1000	6	8	1	16	1		Smooth	Mat, golds are semi-glossy	White
				3		1	1		Pebbled		
			1			17			Linen		
				6	6	5			Parallel-line texture		
Show cardboard	BA	48/1000	2	2	1	23	1	1	Smooth	Mat, G & S are semiglossy	Ochre
Show cardboard	B	48/1000	1	2	1	18	1	1	Smooth	Semimat	Blue
Colored board	B	48 to 51/1000				7			Very smooth	Semi-glossy	Blue
Illustration board No. 99	CR	49/1000	1						Smooth	Mat	Gray
Mat board	N	49/1000	1		1	2	1[4]		Linenlike texture	Mat, except for G & bronze, which are semiglossy	White
Mat board	N	49/1000	1	1		1	1[4]		Stippled texture	Mat, except for G & bronze, which are glossy	Most are white
		91/1000	1			1					
Corrugated backing board	N	50/1000				1[3]			Smooth	Mat	Prime
Display cardboards	N	54/1000	1				1	1	Pebbled	Semi-gloss, except white is mat	Prime

(continued on next page)

Name	Mfg. or supplier	Thickness (inches)	Shades & colors available						Texture	Finish	Reverse sides
			White	Gray	Black	Colors	Gold	Silver			
Illustration board No. 48	N	50/1000	1						Smooth	Mat	Gray
Natural veneer mat board	N	50/1000				1			Looks like balsa wood	Mat	White
Mounting board No. 5030	N	51/1000	1						Smooth	Mat	Prime
Illustration board No. 59	N	52/1000	1						Smooth	Mat	Gray
Mat board	N	52/1000 except 1 gold	4	6	1	10		2[4]	Smooth	Mat; 1 G is glossy	White
"Art" board	N	52 to 57/1000			1	2			Smooth	Mat	White
			1			5			1/32" parallel-line texture		
				2		17			Misc. other textures		
Illustration board No. 172	BA	Single weight= 53/1000	1						Very smooth	Mat	Ochre
Illustration board No. 27	N	53/1000	1						Very smooth	Semimat	Gray
Charko board	CR	54/1000	1	1		1			A parallel-line texture; lines are 1/16" O.C.	Mat	White
Mounting board	N	54, 82 & 91/1000 (=14, 24 & 30 ply)	3						Smooth	Mat	Gray
Mounting board	BA	54, 92 & 103/1000 (=14, 24 & 28 ply)	3						Smooth	Mat	Gray
Illustration board No. 3	N	55/1000	1						Smooth	Mat	Gray
Illustration board No. 351	CR	55/1000	1						Smooth	Mat	Gray
Mounting board No. 1899	N	56/1000	1						Very smooth	Mat	Gray
Mounting board No. 550	N	56/1000	1						Smooth	Mat	Prime
Illustration board No. 52	N	56/1000	1						Very smooth	Mat	Gray
Illustration board No. 61	N	56/1000	1						Smooth	Mat	Gray
Illustration board No. 350	CR	56/1000	1						Smooth	Mat	Prime
Illustration board No. 80	BA	Single weight= 57/1000	1						Fairly smooth (mfg. calls it "rough")	Mat	Ochre
Illustration board No. 201	CR	57/1000	1						Very smooth	Semimat	Gray
Illustration board No. 69	N	58/1000	1						Smooth	Mat	Gray
Colored drawing board	CR	59/1000				1			Heavy parallel-line texture	Mat	White
			1	3	1	12			Rough		
			1			12			Fairly smooth		
Illustration board No. 201	CR	59/1000	1						Hot press smooth	Mat	Gray
Illustration board No. 310	CR	59/1000	1						Fairly smooth	Mat	Gray
Illustration board No. 169	BA	59/1000	1						Crinkly	Mat	Ochre
Illustration board No. 108	CR	Single weight= about 60/1000	1						Fairly smooth	Mat	Prime
Illustration board	S	61/1000	1						Very smooth	Mat	Prime
Illustration board No. 300	CR	62/1000	1						Fairly smooth	Mat	Gray

Name	Mfg. or supplier	Thickness (inches)	Shades & colors available						Finish	Texture	Reverse sides
			White	Gray	Black	Colors	Gold	Silver			
Illustration board	S	78/1000	1						Smooth	Mat	Prime
Mounting board No. 20c	CR	80 pt.= 80/1000		1					Smooth	Mat	Prime
Illustration board No. 26	N	87/1000	1						Very smooth	Semimat	Gray
Coated 2 sides	CR	90 pt.= 90/1000	1						Smooth	Mat	Prime
Illustration board	CR (≠110) & N (≠79)	92/1000	1						Fairly smooth	Mat	Gray
Cardboard	N	92/1000	1						Smooth	Mat	Prime
Illustration board No. 200	CR	95/1000	1						Smooth	Mat	Gray
Illustration board	N (No. 5) N (No. 74)	98/1000	1						Smooth	Mat	Gray
Illustration board No. 172	BA	Double weight= 101/1000	1						Very smooth	Mat	Ochre
Illustration board No. 90–s	BA	Double weight	1						Smooth (mfg. calls it "medium")	Semimat	Gray
Illustration board No. 169	BA	Double weight= 104/1000	1						Crinkly	Mat	Ochre
Illustration board No. 80	BA	Double weight= 104/1000	1						Fairly smooth	Mat	Ochre
Canvas mat board	N	114/1000	1						Canvaslike	Mat	White
Watercolor board No. 112	CR	125/1000	1						Rough, crinkly	Mat	Tan
Illustration board No. 1	CR	126/1000	1						Fairly smooth	Mat	Gray
Watercolor board No. 115	CR	129/1000	1						Smooth	Mat	Tan
Cardboard	N	130/1000	1						Smooth	Mat	Prime
Watercolor board No. 114	CR	134/1000	1						Rough	Mat	Tan
Colored board No. 89	N	135/1000	1						Rough	Mat	Gray
Colored board No. 88	N	135/1000	1						Fairly smooth	Mat	Gray
Colored board No. 87	N	135/1000	1						Smooth	Mat	Gray

[1] Manilas.
[2] Available from Bienfang only.
[3] Light tan.
[4] Bronze.

Other Boards and Notes

Strawboard, also known as cardboard, cannot be folded or bent; its extreme absorbency makes it swell when many adhesives are applied. Thus it is no good for the building of surfaces that are exposed to view, but it may be used as reinforcement. Shellacking makes it waterproof and increases its strength.

Playing-Card Board is extremely strong because of its high linen content. Salvage old decks of playing cards to obtain small quantities.

Corrugated Paper is useful for forming curved, fairly thick surfaces.

Composition Board includes: Masonite, Presswood, Roddiscraft and Fomecor (an extremely light, easily cut sandwich of expanded polystyrene plastic, and Kraft Paper board). These come in $\frac{1}{8}$" thicknesses.

Bristolboard allows some of its ply to be stripped down to form recessed areas. The strength and the ease with which it bends makes it the best thin board.

Transparentizer may be used to make Bristolboard or heavy paper transparent.

PRESSURE-SENSITIVE OVERLAYS AND DRY-TRANSFER OVERLAYS

Several applications for pressure-sensitive textures and colors have been enumerated throughout this book. If textures must be modeled that are not obtainable in embossed papers, then catalogs of various manufacturers should be reviewed for the overlay most closely representing the desired texture. If a single overlay does not approximate the texture, try to visualize what combination of overlays might meet the requirements. Color can be imparted to texture by placing the overlay on colored board. Plan the construction of the model so that colored board is substituted for white board where this is required.

Pressure-sensitive overlays are removed from their sheet of backing paper and are placed over the surface to be covered. They can then be burnished down lightly with a bone or plastic burnishing tool. The desired border of the overlay is cut with a pinpoint and the excess material

CORK AS A MODEL MATERIAL.

PROJECT: Hotel at Machu Picchu, Peru.
DESIGNED BY: Schweiker and Elting.
MODELBUILDERS: members of the architect's staff.
PHOTOGRAPHER: Hedrich-Blessing.

Walls, roofs and balconies of this presentation model were made from board covered with gray and white paper. Ground contours and retaining walls were respectively cut from sheets of coarse and fine cork.

The photograph was taken with an 8″ × 10″ Deardorff view camera, 165 mm lens and Super Panchro Press type B film.

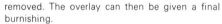

removed. The overlay can then be given a final burnishing.

Dry-transfer overlays, on the other hand, are removed from their sheet of backing paper, positioned and burnished. The image comes away from the disposable plastic carrying sheet.

Names of some of the lines of pressure-sensitive overlay textures are: Zip-a-Tone (mat or gloss finish), Blue-Zip (mat or gloss, heat resistant), Artype, Paratone, Transograph, Craftone, Graphic Products Corp's Format line (mat finish and heat resistant), Chart Pak, Inc. (Contak color tint line, comes mat or glossy and heat resistant).

Dry-transfer overlay textures are made by Chart Pak, Inc. (Contak shading film line, mat or glossy and heat resistant).

AVAILABLE PRESSURE-SENSITIVE OVERLAY PAPERS

Product	Shades Black to white	Colors	Opacity	Finish
Craft-Color by Craftint	5	30	Transparent, translucent, opaque	Glossy or mat
Bourges Colotone and Cutocolor[1]	9	65	Transparent	Semimat
Zip-a-Tone	14	66	Transparent, white, black; also opaque	Glossy or mat
Cello Tak color film	4	36[2]	Transparent	Mat
Contak color tints by Chart-Pak Inc.	6	21	Transparent except for 2 whites	Glossy or mat
Blue-Zip[3]	15	65	Transparent	Glossy or mat
Presto-Colors (heat-resistant)	3	15	Transparent, except for black	Mat
Lettraset Instant dry colors	7	33	Transparent, except for black gold, silver	"Brilliant"

[1] Colotone's color may be scraped off; the line also comes with overlay sheets without adhesive backing; matching liquid colors and colored pencils are available. Cutocolor is heat-resistant and may be drawn on with pencil, ink, or watercolors. Both come in 100%, 70%, 50%, 30%, and 10% values of 11 colors, plus a single value each of 10 other colors, plus 100%, 70%, 60%, 50%, 40%, 30%, 20%, 10%, and 5% values of gray.
[2] 36 shades in 15%, 30%, 45%, 60%, and 100% tones.
[3] Heat-resistant version of Zip-a-Tone.

TAPES

Tapes may be employed to represent plaza patterns, mullions, moldings and similar prototype parts.

Key:
G = glossy, M = mat.
Names of Suppliers:
A = Applied Graphics Co.; AC = ACS; C = Craftint; CE = Cello Tak; CH = Chart-Pak, Inc.; P = Prestape; X = All of These.
Note—colors of one manufacturer do not always match those of another

AVAILABLE PRESSURE-SENSITIVE TAPES[1]

Width (inch)	Black G	Black M	White G	White M	Gray G	Gray M	Red G	Red M	Dark orange G	Dark orange M	Orange G	Orange M	Yellow orange G	Yellow orange M	Yellow G	Yellow M	Dark green G	Dark green M	Light green G	Light green M	Green G
1/64	X	X	X	X	AC, C, CH, P	C	X	X	CH, P	CH, P	X	A, AC, C, CE	A, AC, C, CE	A, C, CE	X	X	A, AC, CE, CH, P	X, CE	X	X	X
1/32	X	X	X	X	AC, C, CH, P	C	X	X	CH, P	CH, P	X	A, AC, C, CE	A, AC, C, CE	A, C, CE	X	X	A, AC, CE, CH	A, CE	X	X	X
1/16	X	X	X	X	AC, C, CH, P	C	X	X	CH, P	CH, P	X	A, AC, C, CE	A, AC, C, CE	A, C, CE	X	X	A, AC, CE, CH, P	A, CE	X	X	X
3/32	A, AC, CE, CH, P	A, AC, CE, CH, P	A, AC, CE, CH, P	A, AC, CE, CH, P	AC, CH, P		A, AC, CE, CH, P	A, AC, CE, CH, P	CH, P	CH, P	A, AC, CE, CH, P	A, AC, CE	A, AC, CE	A, CE	A, AC, CE, CH, P	A, AC, CE, CH, P	A, AC, CE, CH, P	A, CE	A, AC, CE, CH, P	A, AC, CE, CH, P	A, AC, CE, CH, P

	Opaque																				
Width (inch)	Black		White		Gray		Red		Dark orange		Orange		Yellow orange		Yellow		Dark green		Light green		Green
	G	M	G	M	G	M	G	M	G	M	G	M	G	M	G	M	G	M	G	M	G
1/8	X	X	X	X	AC, C, CH, P	C	X	X	CH, P	CH, P	X	A, AC, C, CE	A, C, C, CE	A, C, CE	X	X	A, AC, CE, CH, P	A, CE	X	X	X
3/16	A, AC, CE, CH, P	A, AC, CE, CH, P	A, AC, CE, CH, P	A, AC, CE, CH, P	A, AC, CH		A, AC, CE, CH, P	A, CE, CH, P	CH, P	CH, P	A, AC, CE, CH, P	A, AC, CE	A, AC, CE	A, CE	A, AC, CE, CH, P	A, AC, CE, CH, P	A, AC, CE, CH, P	A, CE	A, AC, CE, CH, P	A, AC, CE, CH, P	A, AC, CE, CH, P
1/4	X	X	X	X	AC, C, CH, P	C	X	X	CH, P	CH, P	X	A, AC, C, CE	A, AC, C, CE	A, C, CE	X	X	A, AC, CE, CH, P	A, CE	X	X	X
3/8	A, AC, CE, P	A, AC, CE, P	A, AC, CE, P	A, AC, CE, P	AC, P		A, AC, CE, P	A, AC, CE, P	P	P	A, AC, CE, P	A, AC, CE	A, AC, CE	A, CE	A, AC, CE, P	A, AC, CE, P	A, AC, CE, P	A, CE	A, AC, CE, P	A, AC, CE, P	A, AC, CE, P
1/2	X	X	X	X	AC, C, CH, P	C	X	X	CH, P	CH, P	X	A, AC, C, CE	A, AC, C, CE	A, C, CE	X	X,	A, AC, CE, CH, P	A, CE	X	X	X
5/8																					
3/4	A, AC, CE, CH, P	A, AC, CE, CH, P	A, AC, CE, CH, P	A, AC, CE, CH, P	AC, CH, P		A, AC, CE, CH, P	A, AC, CE, CH, P	CH, P	CH, P	A, AC, CE, CH, P	A, AC, CE	A, AC, CE	A, CE	A, AC, CE, CH, P	A, AC, CE, CH, P	A, AC, CE, CH, P	A, CE	A, AC, CE, CH, P	A, AC, CE, CH, P	A, AC, CE, CH, P
7/8																					
1	X	X	X	X	AC, C, CH, P	C	X	X	CH, P	CH, P	X	A, AC, C, CE	A, AC, C, CE	A, C, CE	X	X	A, AC, CE, CH, P	A, CE	X	X	X
2	A, C, CE, CH, P	A, CE, CH, P	A, C, CE, CH, P	A, CE, CH, P	C, CH, P		A, C, CE, CH, P	A, CE, CH, P	CH, P	CH, P	A, C, CE, CH, P	A, CE	A, C, CE	A, CE	A, C, CE, CH, P	A, CE, CH, P	A, CE, CH, P	A, CE	AC, CE, CH, P	A, CE, CH, P	AC, CE, CH, P

	Opaque																Fluorescent				
Width (inch)	Green	Light blue	Blue	Violet	Purple		Brown		Beige	Lavender		Cerise	Salmon	Chrome	Gold		Silver		Pink		Green
	M	G	M	G	M	G	M	G	G	M	G	G	G	G	G	M	G	M	G	M	M
1/64	X	X	X	X	X	CE	CE	AC, CH, P	X	X	AC	AC	AC	AC	CE, CH, P	AC, CE, CH, P	A, C, CE	X	A, C, CE	CH, P	CH, P
1/32	X	X	X	X	X	CE	CE	AC, CH, P	X	X	AC	AC	AC	AC	CE, CH, P	A, C, CE, CH, P	A, C, CE	X	A, C, CE	CH, P	CH, P
1/16	X	X	X	X	X	CE	CE	AC, CH, P	X	X	AC	AC	AC	AC	CE, CH, P	A, C, CE, CH, P	A, C, CE	X	A, C, CE	CH, P	CH, P

(continued on next page)

Width (inch)	Green M	Green G	Light blue M	Light blue G	Blue M	Blue G	Violet G	Purple G	Brown G	Brown M	Beige G	Lavender G	Cerise G	Salmon G	Chrome G	Gold G	Gold M	Silver G	Silver M	Pink M	Green G
3/32	A, AC, CE, CH, P	A, AC, CE, CH, P	A, AC, CE, CH, P	A, AC, CE, CH, P	A, AC, CE, CH, P	CE	CE	AC, CH, P	A, AC, CE, CH, P	A, AC, CE, CH, P	AC	AC	AC	AC		A, CE, CH, P	A, CE	A, AC, CE, CH, P	A, CE	CH, P	CH, P
1/8	X	X	X	X	X	CE	CE	AC, CH, P	X	X	AC	AC	AC	AC	CE, CH, P	A., C, CE, CH, P	A, C, CE	X	A, CE	CH, P	CH, P
3/16	A, AC, CE, CH, P	A, AC, CE, CH, P	A, AC, CE, CH, P	A, AC, CE, CH, P	A, AC, CE, CH, P	CE	CE	AC, CH, P	A, AC, CE, CH, P	A, AC, CE, CH, P	AC	AC	AC	AC		A, CE, CH, P	A, CE	A, AC, CE, CH, P	A, CE	CH, P	CH, P
1/4	X	X	X	X	X	CE	CE	AC, CH, P	X	X	AC	AC	AC	AC	CE, CH, P	A, C, CE, CH, P	A, C, CE	X	A, CE	CH, P	CH, P
3/8	A, AC, CE, P	A, AC, CE, P	A, AC, CE, P	A, C, E, P	A, AC, CE, P	CE	CE	AC, P	A, AC, CE, P	A, AC, CE, P	AC	AC	AC	AC		A, CE, P	A, CE	A, AC, CE, P	A, CE	P	P
1/2	X	X	X	X	X	CE	CE	AC, CH, P	X	X	AC	AC	AC	AC	CE, CH, P	A, C, CE, CH, P	A, C, CE	X	A, CE	CH, P	CH, P
5/8																					
3/4	A, AC, CE, CH, P	A, AC, CE, CH, P	A, AC, CE, CH, P	A, AC, CE, CH, P	A, AC, CE, CH, P	CE	CE	AC, CH, P	A, AC, CE, CH, P	A, AC, CE, CH, P	AC	AC	AC	AC		A, CE, CH, P	A, CE	A, AC, CE, CH, P	A, CE	CH, P	CH, P
7/8																					
1	X	X	X	X	X	CE	CE	AC, CH, P	X	X	AC	AC	AC	AC	CE, CH, P	A, C, CE, CH, P	A, CE, C	X	A, CE, C	CH, P	CH, P
2	A, CE, CH, P	A, CE, CH, P	A, CE, CH, P	A, C, CE, CH, P	A, C, CE, CH, P	CE	CE	CH, P	A, C, CE, CH, P	A, CE, CH, P						A, C, CE, CH, P	A, CE	A, C, CE, CH, P	A, CE	CH, P	CH, P

Transparent (brilliant colors unless otherwise noted)																					
Width (inch)	Yellow	Red	Gray	Red	Red orange	Orange	Yellow	Light green	Green	Dark green	Light blue	Blue	Violet	Purple	Brown	Pink G	Pink M	Peach G	Peach M	Others² G	Others² M
1/64	CH, P	CH, P	P	P	P	P	P	P		P	P	P		P	P	P					
1/32	CH, P	CH, P	CH, P	C, CE, CH, P	P	C, CE, CH, P	A, C, CE, CH, P	CH, P	A, C, CE, CH	P	CH, P	A, C, CE, CH, P	CE	CH, P	CH, P	AC, CH, P	AC	AC, CH, P	AC	AC	AC

Width (inch)	Yellow	Red	Gray	Red	Red orange	Orange	Yellow	Light green	Green	Dark green	Light blue	Blue	Violet	Purple	Brown	Pink G	Pink M	Peach G	Peach M	Others[2] G	Others[2] M
																Transparent (brilliant colors unless otherwise noted)					
1/16	CH, P	CH, P	CH, P	A, C, CE, CH, P	P	C, CE, CH, P	A, C, CE, CH, P	CH, P	A, C, CE, CH	P	CH, P	A, C, CE, CH, P	CE	CH, P	CH, P	AC, CH, P	AC	AC, P	AC	AC	AC
3/32	CH, P	CH, P														AC	AC	AC	AC	AC	AC
1/8	CH, P	CH, P	CH, P	A, C, CE, CH, P	P	A, C, CE, CH, P	A, C, CE, CH, P	CH, P	A, C, CE, CH	P	CH, P	A, C, CE, CH, P	CE	CH, P	CH, P	AC, CH, P	AC	AC, P	AC	AC	AC
3/16	CH, P	CH, P															AC	AC	AC	AC	
1/4	CH, P	CH, P	CH, P	A, C, CH, P	P	C, CE, CH, P	A, C, CE, CH, P	CH, P	A, C	P	CH, P	A, C, CE, CH, P	CE	CH, P	CH, P	AC, CH, P	AC	AC, P	AC	AC	AC
3/8	P	P														AC	AC	AC	AC	AC	AC
1/2	CH, P	CH, P	CH, P	A, C, CE, CH, P	P	C, CE, CH, P	A, C, CE, CH, P	CH, P	A, C, CE, CH	P, CE, CH	CH, P	A, C, CE, CH, P	CE	CH, P	CH, P	AC, CH, P	AC	AC, P	AC	AC	AC
5/8																AC	AC	AC	AC	AC	AC
3/4	CH, P	CH, P														AC	AC	AC	AC	AC	AC
7/8																AC	AC	AC	AC	AC	AC
1	CH, P	CH, P	CH, P	A, C, CE, CH, P	P	C, CE, CH, P	A, C, CE, CH, P	CH, P	A, C, CE, CH	P	CH, P	A, C, CE, CH, P	CE	CH, P	CH, P	AC, CH, P	AC	AC, P	AC	AC	AC
2	CH, P	CH. P	C			C	C		C			C									

Key: G = glossy, M = mat
Names of Suppliers: A = Applied Graphics Co.; AC = ACS; C = Craftint; CE = Cello-Tak; CH = Chart-Pak Inc.; P = Prestape; X = all of these.
[1] Colors of one manufacturer do not always match those of another.
[2] Lemon, maize, tangerine, cherry, magenta, wine, plum, indigo, turquoise, emerald, mint, lime, azure, lilac, charcoal, smoke, caramel, sand.

Graphic Products Corp. makes pressure-sensitive overlay sheets that have lines from hairline to $\frac{1}{2}''$ widths.

Tape may be conveniently applied with a tape pen guided along a straightedge, thinner tape can be drawn along a French curve so that the tape will lie in any desired curved pattern. Chart-Pak, Inc. sells a pen for about $7.

Striping may also be achieved by applying thinned paint with a ruling pen or with a striping tool. The latter applies the paint by means of a wheel receiving a continuous flow of paint from a small reservoir. Wheels may be obtained in various widths from artist supply stores.

SIMULATED BUILDING MATERIALS

These represent various building materials (brick, siding, shingles, etc.) printed, embossed or milled on paper, wood or plastic. They are used primarily by the railroad modeler, and usually come in $\frac{1}{8}$ or $\frac{1}{4}'' = 1'$ scales. Chapter 15 contains a complete listing of these materials. Since less detail is required at scales under $\frac{1}{8}'' = 1'$, it is fairly easy to draw or scribe individual patterns at small scales. At this size, for instance, brick need only be a pattern of horizontal lines; other building materials may similarly be simplified. A good poché draftsman can easily turn out building paper rapidly and economically. At larger scales ($\frac{1}{2}'' = 1'$ and up) the problem of making one's own paper is much more complicated. It is often easier to have a metal die cut by a local producer of embossed stamps and to use this die in an inexpensive hand press for thin Bristolboard or polystyrene sheet. At $\frac{1}{8}$ or $\frac{1}{4}'' = 1'$ scales, building paper can be drawn that compares favorably in cost (but not quality) with commercially obtainable embossed paper (about 2¢ per sq. ″ commercially printed paper, however, costs about 1/5¢ per sq.″). Some of the suppliers of simulated building materials are listed in the following tables. The prototype building materials these products represent are listed in the sections devoted to these materials. In addition, some manufacturers, Holgate & Reynolds among them, will custom emboss patterns to your order.

DRAFTING AND EMBOSSING MATERIALS

All materials may be drawn on thin Bristol, or other, boards. If color is desired, use colored board or paper, or color a pattern drawn on white material with watercolors, transparent photographic oil paints (Marshall's Photo-Oil Colors is one brand) or with dusted-on pastel colors. The harder one presses when drafting, the more 3 dimensional the pattern will be.

Time can be saved by drawing the texture on drafting paper and reproducing it by either the black-, blue- or brown-on-white process. The resulting prints can then be mounted, or colored and mounted.

The scribing of board or polystyrene may also be employed. Choosing a board the texture of which matches the prototype material will equal all but the most realistic ready-made product. Spray painted sandpaper can be scribed to make realistic brick, block, stone or roofing. A multi-line scribing tool can be improvised, or use devices like a heavy comb (to emboss corrugated metal pattern on foil).

Large patterns with pronounced 3-dimensionality, should be vacuum-formed against a pattern.

Applying Simulated Building Materials

If possible, lay out the desired shape on the back of the material, since pencil marks are difficult to remove. Because of the danger of splintering, cut with a single-edge razor, using extremely light runs in embossed and milled woods.

Bond simulated materials with regular paper, plastic or wood cements. Orange shellac may be used to hold thin paper on cardboard, but the paper must be quickly applied to the brushed-on shellac. Dry mounting may also be used if it will not ruin the embossing or melt the plastic. Embossed plastic should be glued with a filler cement that will not attack the plastic. Apply cement to the simulated material, not to the understructure. Use tweezers to position small pieces. Be careful to parallel the courses of brick, siding, etc. to the bottom of the building and to line them up between adjacent sheets.

8-7

COVERING WITH OVERLAY MATERIAL

Possible locations of seams

(A) Wall elevation

(B) Covering small objects—plan

Note double ply

Embossed simulated building materials (and all embossed papers) should be tested to see if they will withstand an application of cement without wrinkling. Brush on several thin layers of adhesive to strengthen the material, allowing each coat to dry before applying the next. When the embossed paper has achieved sufficient rigidity, it may be cemented in the usual way.

ART SUPPLIES THAT CAN BE USED AS SIMULATED BUILDING MATERIALS

Supplier	Embossed or printed	Colored or uncolored	Thickness (inches)
Pressure-sensitive overlays			
Artype Format (made by the Graphic Products Corp.) Zip-a-Tone Blue-Zip Contak Shading Film Presto-Colors	Printed	Black line on transparent backing	1–2/1000
Dry-transfer overlays			
Instantex (made by the makers of Instant Lettering)	Printed	Black line	about 1/1000
Boards			
Ross Board	Embossed	Unpainted (white)	13–15/1000

SHEET SIMULATED BUILDING MATERIALS SOLD AT MODEL RAILROAD HOBBY SHOPS

Supplier	Embossed or printed	Colored or uncolored	Thickness (inch)	Base
All Nations	Embossed	Colored	9/1000	Coated board
Aristo Craft distributed products:				
Herpa	Embossed	Colored	17/1000	Cardboard
Herpa	Printed	Colored	4/1000	Paper
Rivarossi	Printed	Colored	3–5/1000	Paper
Unnamed (same as Model Hobbies line)	Printed	Colored	7/1000 (unless noted)	Paper
Dyna Models	Embossed	Colored	22/1000	Plastic
Faller	Embossed	Colored	11/1000	Cardboard
Kemtron	Engraved	Colored	21/1000	Brass
Holgate & Reynolds	Printed	Colored	5/1000	Paper
	Embossed	White	18–25/1000	Polystyrene
Model Hobbies	Printed	Colored	7/1000	Paper
Northeastern	Printed	Colored	60–70/1000	Basswood
	Milled	Uncolored (basswood)	0.04, 3/64, 1/16, or 3/32	Basswood
Real Like	Printed	Colored	4/1000	Paper
Superquick	Printed	Colored	3/1000	Paper
Suydam	Embossed or printed	Colored or uncolored	Various	Various
Vollmer	Embossed	Colored	34–70/1000	Plastic
Walthers	Printed	Colored	8.9/1000	Paper

SEAMS

Small objects (chimneys, columns, etc.) should be completely covered, with paper overlapping 1 side (8-7B). To turn corners, first cement 1 side in place, leaving a $\frac{1}{8}$" excess; then bevel cut the paper with a razor guided by a bevel-edged steel straightedge. Bevel cut the paper that will cover the second side before it is cemented in place. Cement this piece, making sure that the beveled joint is tight, without a visible seam. If a crack is visible, carefully fill it with sanding sealer, or balsa dust and cement. Sand it smooth to alleviate any shadow caused by the crack, and touch up the joint with paint. Bevel cutting is difficult to master, but it will produce better results than lap or butt joints.

Attempt to cover a surface with a single piece of simulated building material, even if it means a certain amount of wastage. If the material to be used is not large enough, carefully plan where the seams will fall. See 8-7A for the best location of seams on a wall with windows, doors and other openings. If possible, run all seams along a natural line in the paper (the horizontal mortar line of brick, the line between two pieces of siding, etc.). This is usually easy to accomplish with horizontal seams. Vertical seams require a delicate matching of material. Brick, tile and similar material may be laboriously matched by cutting out individual members along the two sides of the seam and by fitting the resulting crenelated pattern together.

Window and door returns should be covered with material. This can be done by folding the material back into the opening if it is paper or by making a miter joint in plastic or wood. Sills and frames can be made from stripwood. If the scale of the model is too small to allow for covering the returns, they may be painted the color of their prototype material. Paint them first and then cover that side of the model with the simulated building material.

Painting Simulated Building Materials

If the embossed material requires a mortar line, paint the material the basic color first. Use lacquer or oil paint, first test a scrap of the material to judge if that paint will have detrimental effect. When the basic coat has dried, apply a water-based paint the same color as the mortar lines. Wipe the still wet coat from the top surface of the embossing, allowing it to remain in the mortar lines. Mortar lines can also be produced with white pencil. Embossed wood must first be carefully sealed with thin coats of wood sanding sealer. Before the sealer dries, brush as much of the liquid from the embossed joints as possible so as to prevent filling them.

Printed paper sometimes has a rather pristine look. To add a bit of irregularity, apply a thin transparent coating with artist's oils thinned with turpentine, or with thinned watercolors or poster paints. Apply the paint with a large wad of cotton, making sure that enough cotton lies between fingers and work surface to prevent streaking with finger pressure. Paint with a circular motion. Sometimes the effect of the paper can be improved if individual bricks, stones or slates are selectively brush painted.

BALSA WOOD

Balsa is probably the wood of greatest use to the architectural modelmaker. Its credits are many but so are its shortcomings. Balsa is the easiest wood to cut and shape, to bend and to cement. But it is relatively hard to give balsa a good grain-free finish, and the wood scars easily upon impact. To offset its faults, buy as hard a balsa as can be found, especially if it is to be used for carving. Avoid using even hard balsa in prominent places and on models that must have a hard glossy finish. The density of balsa ranges from 3 to 50 lbs. per cubic ft. Often a small plank will be a given density at one end and up to 3 times that density at the other. If bought from a mail-order firm that grades the wood (such as Sig Manufacturing Company), samples of the wood can be marked with these weights and kept for reference. Use samples of weights that have worked well in the past and try to match them when buying new supplies. Balsa may be used to make entire models, to construct walls, floors, roofs, partitions or internal bracings. Blocks of balsa may be carved to form furniture, people, cars, molds and solid models, and sheet material may be bent into such curved objects as vaults, etc.

Cuts of Balsa

The three common ways to cut balsa are:

1—Tangential to the growth rings (8-8, 1): planks and sheets cut in this way have a broad grain pattern, and are flexible across the grain; they are appropriate for making objects that involve cross-grain curves (tubes, curved walls, etc.). These parts must be reinforced across the grain, or the balsa may eventually split along the grain.

2—Between the tangential and the radial cuts (or quartersawed) (8-8, 2): this is the strongest of the planks; its grain has tiny golden flake or curl markings.

3—Radial to the grain (8-8, 3): these planks and sheets have narrow, closely spaced grain, and are very stiff. Since this cut of wood is prone to splitting if it is curved, it should be used only for flat objects. When reinforced across the grain, this cut becomes quite strong.

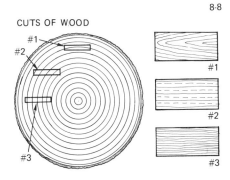

8-8

CUTS OF WOOD

Cutting Balsa

Using a razor or sharp knife, cut a series of light strokes rather than a heavy one that might tear the wood if the cut is across the grain. A very fine-tooth saw without set may also be used.

Incidentally, strips of exactly the same length should not be cut from stripwood, because this often results in some length variation. Instead, cut a sheet with a width equal to the length of the strips and then cut the strips from this sheet.

SIZES OF AVAILABLE BALSA STRIPS, SHEETS AND PLANKS (INCHES)

	1/16	3/32	1/8	3/16	1/4	5/16	3/8	1/2	5/8	3/4	1	2	3	4	6	8
1/64													X			
1/32												X	X	X	X	X
1/20													X			
1/16	X		X	X	X		X	X		X	X	X	X	X	X	X
3/32		X		X	X		X	X		X	X	X	X	X	X	X
1/8			X	X			X	X		X	X	X	X	X	X	X
3/16				X	X		X	X		X	X	X	X	X	X	X
1/4				X	X		X	X		X	X	X	X	X	X	X
5/16					X	X	X	X		X			X			
3/8							X	X		X	X	X	X	X	X	X
1/2								X		X	X	X	X	X	X	X
5/8									X	X						
3/4										X		X	X	X	X	X
1												X	X	X	X	X
1 1/2												X	X	X	X	X
2												X	X	X	X	X
3													X	X	X	X

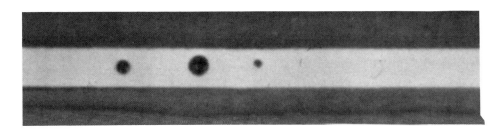

8-7A
SOME AVAILABLE TYPES OF STRIPWOOD:

Top row: ebonized marble.
Middle row: boxwood on which has been mounted

(from left to right): Kemtron medium hex nut, Kemtron large nut, bolt and washer, Kemtron very small hex nut.
Bottom row: rosewood.

Bending Balsa

Only thin sheets may be bent. First try to bend the wood when it is dry, if this does not work, soak it in hot water or steam it over a kettle. Pin and clamp the wood in place on a bending die or male mold. Allow it to dry, then cement it to the rest of the model. To build up very tight curves, use lamination of thin sheet rather than trying to bend a single thicker plank. These suggestions can also be used with basswood and other woods.

Painting Balsa

When painting balsa, take special care to fill and to even out the grain. For the first coat, use sanding sealer that also acts as a prime coat. Allow it to dry thoroughly, then lightly sand with O grade emery paper, working up to OOO. 1 coat of sealer is usually enough for mat paint or small intricate objects; elsewhere use 2 or 3 coats.

Use sanding sealer if intending to paint with a cellulose-base paint. Use shellac as a filler for enamel painting. Sand the shellac with wet abrasive paper.

These sizes can be obtained from the Sig Manufacturing Company in 36" lengths. Some sizes can also be purchased in 3, 6, 12, 18, 24 and 48" lengths. Often, when large blocks or planks of balsa are needed, it is more economical to buy at a lumberyard, where they will sometimes cut large planks into thinner sheets ($\frac{1}{2}$" thick and up) at no extra cost. Such lumberyard balsa costs only $\frac{1}{4}$ as much as the well-finished balsa found in hobby stores, but it is often *very* roughly cut.

OTHER WOODS

Other woods besides balsa should be considered for model construction. Basswood, lime, satin walnut, sycamore, white chestnut and obechi have excellent properties for the construction of walls, roofs and other flat objects. They can be easily finished, are warp-free (if they are properly sealed), and require only slightly more sophisticated tools than balsa. Thin strips may be cut from dry selected pine, birch, spruce, mahogany, beech, basswood and obechi.

Carved objects may best be made out of obechi; yellow pine, beech and lime are almost as good. Small, highly detailed, carved objects can be made from beech or sycamore. Most of these woods can be obtained from lumberyards that specialize in uncommon wood and in stores that sell veneers and inlaying wood. Basswood, spruce and mahogany are obtainable from mail-order model supply houses. Basswood, the easiest wood (after balsa) to obtain, is soft and easy to carve because of its uniform texture, and it will cut in any direction. Its greater density and strength make it superior to balsa for the construction of beams, columns, mullions, space frames and furniture legs. Many fairly rough models have been beautifully constructed from unpainted basswood (15-19).

It is possible to obtain a selection of stripwood

Key:
B = kiln-dried basswood, stripwood and sheet
S = spruce
A = American holly
M = black walnut and mahogany

Inches	1/32	0.04	3/64	1/16	5/64	3/32	1/8	5/32	3/16	0.20	1/4	5/16	3/8	0.40	1/2	3/4	1	2	3	4	6
0.012	B, A	B, A	B, A	B, A	B, A	B, A	B, A														
0.020	B, A	B, A	B, A / M	B, A / M	B, A / M	B, A / M	B, A														
1/32	B, A	B, A	B, A	B, A / M	B, A / M	B, A / M	B, A / M	B, A / M	B, A / M	B, A / M	B, A / M	B, A / M	B, A / M	B, A / M	B, A / M	B, A / M	B, A / M	B, A / M	B	B	
0.040		B, A	B, A / M	B, A	B, A		B, A	B, A / M			B, A	B, A	B, A / M		B, A		B, A	B, A / M	B	B	
3/64			B, A / M	B, A / M	B, A / M	B, A / M	B, A / M	B, A / M	B, A / M	B, A / M	B, A / M	B, A	B, A		B, A / M	B, A / M					
1/16				B, A / M	B, A / M	B, A / M	B, A / M, S	B, A / M	B, A / M, S	B, A / M	B, A / M, S	B, A / M	B, A / M	B, A / M	B, A / M	B, A / M	B, A / M	B, A / M	B	B	
5/64					B, A / M	B, A / M	B, A / M	B, A / M	B, A / M	B, A / M	B, A / M	B, A / M	B, A / M		B, A / M	B, A / M	B, A				
3/32						B, A / M, S	B, A / M, S	B, A / M	B, A / M, S	B, A / M	B, A / M, S	B, A / M	B, A / M		B, A / M	B, A / M	B, A / M	B, A / M	B, A / M	B	
1/8							B, A / M, S	B, A / M	B, A / M, S	B, A / M	B, A / M, S	B, A / M	B, A / M, S	B, A / M	B, A / M, S	B, A / M, S	B, A / M	B, A / M	B, A	B	
5/32								B, A / M	B, A / M	B, A / M	B, A / M	B, A / M	B, A / M		B, A / M	B, A / M	B, A / M	B, A / M	B, A	B	
3/16									B, A / M, S	B, A / M	B, A / M	B, A / M	B, A / M, S		B, A / M, S	B, A / M	B, A / M	B, A / M	B	B	
0.20										B, A / M	B, A / M	B, A / M	B, A / M								
1/4											B, A / M, S	B, A / M	B, A / M, S	B, A / M	B, A / M, S	B, A / M	B, A / M	B, A / M	B, A / M	B, A / M	B
5/16												B, A / M	B, A / M	B, A / M	B, A / M	B, A / M	B, A / M	B, A / M	B, A / M	B, A / M	B
3/8													B, A / M, S		B, A / M	B, A / M	B, A / M	B, A / M	B, A / M	B, A / M	B
0.40														B, A / M							
1/2															B, A / M	B, A / M	B, A / M	B, A / M	B, A / M	B, A / M	B, A / M
3/4																B, A / M	B, A / M	B, A / M	B, A / M	B, A / M	B, A / M
1																	B, A / M	B, A / M	B, A / M	B, A / M	B, A / M
2																		B, A / M	B, A / M	B, A / M	B, A / M

8.9

CUTTING STRIPWOOD TO EVEN LENGTHS

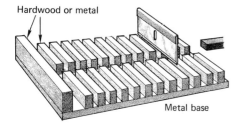

Hardwood or metal

Metal base

in many colors and shades. Shops selling to cabinetmakers and inlayers carry wood in colors from white (white maple) to black (ebonized maple). Very interesting models can be made with unpainted wood of various colors. Cut stripwood in a small miter box using a razor saw (8-9).

Basswood, American holly, black walnut and mahogany can be obtained from Northeastern in 24″ lengths. Spruce can be obtained from the Sig Manufacturing Company in 36″ lengths and some sizes in 48″ lengths. Basswood and spruce cost about twice as much as balsa; holly, mahogany and walnut about 3 times as much.

Unsupported stripwood, including balsa, will often warp when subjected to varying temperatures; that is why strip acrylic is used.

SCALE LUMBER

The Camino Scale Model Company makes precisely milled 24″ long basswood stripwood that duplicates major lumber sizes in $\frac{1}{8}″=1′$ and $\frac{1}{4}″=1′$ scales. This is a great help in making wood framing models at all scales. Prices run from 3¢ for 2×4″ and 4¢ for 2×10″ to 11¢ for 24×24″.

The Miniature Model Lumber Company makes

PROTOTYPE SIZES OF LUMBER REPRODUCED IN VARIOUS SCALES BY SUPPLIERS

Inches	1	2	3	4	6	8	10	12	14	16	18	20	22	24
1	X	O X	X	O X	O X	O X	O X	O X	X	X	X	X	X	X
2	X	O X	O X	O X	O X	O X	O X	O X	X	X	X	X	X	X
3			X	X	X	X	X	X	X	X	X	X	X	X
4				O X	O X	O X	O X	O X	X	X	X	X	X	X
6					O X	O X	O X	O X	X	X	X	X	X	X
8						O X	O X	O X	X	X	X	X	X	X
10							O X	O X	X	X	X	X	X	X
12								O X	X	X	X	X	X	X
14									X	X	X	X	X	X
16										X	X	X	X	X
18											X	X	X	X
20												X	X	X
22													X	X
24														X

X = Sizes made by the Camino Scale Models Company, in 1/8″ = 1′ and 1/4″ = 1′ scales.
O = Sizes made by the Miniature Model Lumber Company, in 1″ = 1′ scale.

saw-cut smooth lumber 24″ long that duplicates many lumber sizes in a 1″=1′ scale.

Examples of what can be done with stripwood can be seen in 15-19.

PLYWOOD

The warp-resistant quality of plywood makes it useful in 2 aspects of modelbuilding. Model bases

and carrying boxes can be made from $\frac{1}{8}$ to $\frac{1}{2}″$ material. Wood with an outer ply of pine is usually satisfactory; for natural wood finish, see what the local lumberyard offers.

Walls, roofs and other flat members of the actual model may also be made from plywood. For these parts material may be obtained with thicknesses of $\frac{1}{4}$, $\frac{3}{16}$, $\frac{1}{8}$, $\frac{3}{32}$, $\frac{1}{16}$ and $\frac{1}{32}″$. Sig sells birch plywood in these sizes in sheets 6 and 12″ wide by 12″

long and 12″ wide by 24 and 48″ long. America's Hobby Center sells $\frac{1}{16}$, $\frac{1}{8}$ and $\frac{1}{4}$″ mahogany plywood in sheets 6 and 12″ wide by 12″ long.

For modelbuilding, avoid using other species of plywood, inferior plywood and plywood with unequal laminations that will warp and come apart at the edges, especially along cut lines.

Bending Plywood

Curves may be bent into up to $\frac{1}{8}$″ plywood, but in only 1 plane. When making tight curves, see that the outside grain of the wood runs perpendicular to the bend. If the grain runs in any other direction, the minimum radius of the bend will be about double that shown in the table. Wetting or steaming will allow a tighter bend.

	Plywood thickness			
	1/32″	1/16″	1/8″	1/4″
Minimum radius	1″	2″	6″	15″

Cutting Plywood

Cut 3/64″ and thinner plywood with a knife, thicker material with a fret saw or some equivalent tool. It is not advisable to work the edges of plywood more than is necessary. Try, therefore, to make a fine, accurate cut requiring the least possible finishing. It is difficult to cut strips narrower than $\frac{1}{4}$″ wide in $\frac{1}{32}$″ plywood, $\frac{3}{4}$″ wide in $\frac{3}{8}$″ plywood, etc., because the plys may separate.

Finishing Plywood

Plywood panels of any appreciable size should be supported by frames to prevent warpage. Nails should be located a distance from the edges of at least 4 times the thickness of the sheet to prevent splitting. Since it is hard to finish plywood smoothly, many coats of sanding sealer are required to close the grain. Panel ends must be filled with plastic wood and sanded smooth. Pine or birch plywood is generally the easiest to finish.

BONDING LIGHT WOOD CONSTRUCTION

Balsa wood and small parts made of other woods are best cemented with quick- or slow-drying cellulose cement; white glue may also be used. Use the double-coat technique with cellulose cement to increase the joint's strength up to eightfold (with balsa) over the strength of a single coat. Parts may easily be pinned together until dry. The pinholes can be filled and sanded smooth as part of the sealing and finishing step.

Dowels may be glued into holes by first rounding their ends and by cutting a small air vent groove along the length of the dowel that will be buried in the assembly.

Thin plywood should be cemented with a slow-drying cellulose cement.

STRUCTURAL AND TRIM SHAPES

Commercially available are many formed wood, plastic or brass shapes that are extremely helpful in the construction of detailed models. In addition to these, the modeler may fabricate his own shapes out of laminated basswood, bent brass, bent or laminated Bristolboard, and bent or laminated polystyrene sheet. Forming jigs (8-11) can build up almost all shapes from moldings and angles to double-latticed girders. Almost any shape may be ordered custom-fabricated out of brass by the Special Shapes Company and by Milled Shapes, Inc. But these are quite expensive. In general, non-custom-made brass shapes cost 5 to 8 times as much as basswood shapes. If local hobby stores do not carry the material, see the table for manufacturers.

Working with Structural Shapes

Cut shapes by inserting pieces of stripwood between the webs and flanges to prevent the shape from crumpling under the pressure of the saw or knife. Always use moderate pressure to achieve a cut. Use a zona saw to cut metal shapes and razors or fine-toothed saws to cut plastic and wood shapes. Wood shapes must often be sanded, preferably with sanding blocks.

8-11

FORMING STRUCTURAL SECTIONS FROM BOARD

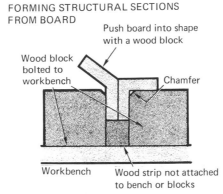

Wood block bolted to workbench

Push board into shape with a wood block

Chamfer

Workbench

Wood strip not attached to bench or blocks

8-10

A HIGHLY DETAILED PRESENTATION MODEL WITH STRUCTURAL SHAPES MADE FROM METAL.

PROJECT: Theater for Mannheim, Germany.
DESIGNED BY: Mies van der Rohe.
MODELBUILDERS: members of the architect's staff.
PHOTOGRAPHER: Hedrich-Blessing.
SCALE: $1/8″ = 1'$.
Roof trusses, mullions and columns were made from milled brass sections assembled on wood jigs, soldered together and then nickelplated to represent stainless steel. Glass walls were represented by gray acrylic.
The photograph was taken with an $8″ \times 10″$ Deardorff view camera, 165 mm lens and Kodak Royal Pan film.
CONSTRUCTION TIME: about 500 hours.
Models with exposed structural shapes may also be constructed out of cemented milled basswood. The results, while probably not as superb as this model, will take much less time.

Fabricate shapes out of bent Bristolboard or metal by using bending dies (8-11). Shapes can also be built from strips of polystyrene. Most structural shapes are built up from combinations of cemented or soldered angles and flat plates. T's and Z's are made from 2 angles; channels from 2 angles and a plate; I- and H-beams from 4 angles and a plate.

Moldings, cornices and other trims are fabricated from quarter-rounds and from strips of basswood or sheets of Bristolboard or polystyrene cut into strips.

AVAILABLE STRUCTURAL SHAPES AND TRIM SHAPES

Shape	Material	Sizes available[1] (inches except when indicated)	Manufacturer or distributor
Slotted round bar	Brass	1/8 diameter with 1/32 slot, 3/16 diameter with 3/64 slot, 1/4 diameter with 1/16 slot	Milled Shapes Inc.
Half-round	Extruded Acrylic	1/2, 5/8, 3/4 diameter by 4' long, clear	Plastic supply houses, such as Commercial Plastics Co.
Quarter-round	Basswood	3/64, 1/16, 3/32, 1/8 height & width; Northeastern also carries them in American holly, black walnut and mahogany	Northeastern and Model Hobbies
Square bar	Brass	1/32, (3/64), (1/16), 3/32, (1/8), (3/16), (1/4), (5/16) square (Walthers supplies those in parentheses plus 5/32 and 3/8)	Special Shapes Co. Engineering Model Associates Inc. & Milled Shapes Inc.
	Acrylic	1/4, 3/8, 1/2, 5/8 square by 4' long, clear	Plastic Supply Houses, such as Commercial Plastics Co.
Square tube	Brass	(0.03 wall): 1/4, 5/16, 3/8, 7/16, 1/2, 9/16, 5/8 square	Special Shapes Co.

(continued on next page)

Shape	Material	Sizes available (inches except when indicated)	Manufacturer or distributor
Square tube	Styrene	1/2 square	Industrial Model Supplies
	Plastic	3/16, 1/4, 5/16, 3/8, 7/16, 1/2, 9/16, 5/8, 3/4 square	Engineering Model Associates Inc.
Flat bar	Brass	0.005 × 3/4, 0.01 × 5/16, 3/8, 1/2, 5/8, 0.02 × 3/16, 1/4, 0.025 × 1/4, 1/2, 0.05 × 1/4, 1/2, 1/8 × 3/16, 3/4	Wm. K. Walthers
		1/64 × 1/32, 1/32 × 1/64, (1/16), (3/32), (1/8), (5/32), (3/16), (1/4), 5/16, 3/8, 1/2	Milled Shapes Inc., (Special Shapes Co. & Engineering Model Associates Inc. carry only sizes in parentheses)
	Bronze	0.005 × 5/8, 0.015 × 1/4, 0.016 × 5/8	Wm. K. Walthers
Rectangular tube	Brass	(1/8 wall): 7/8 × 1 1/4	Wm. K. Walthers
	Plastic	1/4 × 3/16, 5/16, 3/8, 7/16, 1/2, 9/16 3/8 × 1 1/8, 5/8 × 1 1/4, 3/4, 7/8, 1	Engineering Model Associates Inc.
Door track	Basswood	3/32 × 3/4, 1/8 × 1/16, 3/16 × 1/16; Northeastern also carries them in American holly, black walnut and mahogany	Model Hobbies & Northeastern
Corner post	Basswood	1/16 × 3/32	Northeastern
Deep fish belly	Basswood	1/64 × 13/64, 3/16 × 5/16, 7/32 × 7/16, 9/32 × 7/32	Northeastern
Slotted T	Brass	3/16 × 3/16 with 1/16 slot, 1/4 × 1/4 with 3/32 slot, 5/16 × 5/16 with 1/8 slot	Milled Shapes Inc.
Case or box corner	Brass	3/16 × 3/16 with 1/16 slot, 1/4 × 1/4 with 3/32 slot, 5/16 × 5/16 with 1/8 slot	Special Shapes Co. & Milled Shapes Inc.
Case or box divider	Brass	3/16 × 3/16 with 1/16 slot, 1/4 × 1/4 with 3/32 slot, 5/16 × 5/16 with 1/8 slot	Special Shapes Co. & Milled Shapes Inc.
Square channel	Brass	(1/16), (3/32), (1/8), (3/16), (1/4), 5/16, 3/8, 1/2, 5/8 square	Milled Shapes Inc. (Special Shapes Co. makes only sizes in parentheses)
Window & door frame stock	Wood	Various	Miniature Model Lumber Co.
Window molding	Basswood	3/64 × 1/16	Northeastern
Anticlimber strips	Brass	1/8 × 0.039, 3 grooves; 1/4 × 1/16, 4 grooves	Milled Shapes Inc.
Threshold	Basswood	5/64 × 1/8	Northeastern
Belt rail	Basswood	3/64 × 1/16	Northeastern
Hat section	Basswood	1/16, 3/32, 1/8 square; Northeastern also carries them in American holly	America's Hobby Center, Model Hobbies & Northeastern
Flange	Basswood	3/32 × 1/64, 1/8 × 1/32, 3/16 × 1/32, 1/4 × 1/32, 3/8 × 3/64; Northeastern also carries them in American holly	Model Hobbies & Northeastern
Equal leg angles	Basswood	5/32 (3/64), (1/16), (3/32), (1/8), 5/32, (3/16), 7/32, (1/4), 9/32, 5/16, 3/8, 7/16, 1/2, 9/16, 5/8, 11/16, 3/4 square	Camino Scale Models Co. (Model Hobbies carries only sizes in parentheses)
		3/64, 1/16, 5/64, (3/32), (1/8), 5/32, (3/16), 5 mm, 1/4, 5/16, 3/8, 10 mm square; Northeastern also carries sizes from 3/32 up in American holly, black, walnut and mahogany; & 3/64 to 5/64 also in American holly	Northeastern (Engineering Model Associates carries only sizes in parentheses)
	Brass	(1/32), (1/16), (3/32), (1/8), (3/16), (1/4), 5/16, 3/8, 1/2, 5/8 square; Max Gray carries 1/8 square	Milled Shapes Inc. (Engineering Model Associates Inc. & Special Shapes Co. carry only sizes in parentheses)
	Gray impact styrene	1/8, 3/16, 1/4 square; legs have rake	Industrial Model Supplies & Con Cor Models
	Plastic	3/32, 1/8, 3/16, 1/4	Engineering Model Associates Inc.
Unequal leg angle	Basswood	Long leg equals: 3/16, 1/8, 1/4, 5/16, 3/8, 1/2; short leg is about 1/2 the length of long leg	Camino Scale Models Co.
T	Basswood	(3/64), (1/16), (3/32), (1/8), 5/32, (3/16), 7/32, (1/4), 9/32, 5/16, (3/8), 7/16, 1/2, 9/16, 5/8, 11/16, 3/4 square. Engineering Model Associates Inc. carries only 3/32, 1/8, 3/16, 1/4 square	Camino Scale Models Co. (Model Hobbies & America's Hobby Center carry only sizes in parentheses)
		3/64, 1/16, 5/64, 3/32, 1/8, 5/32, 3/16, 5 mm, 1/4, 5/16, 3/8, 10 mm square; Northeastern also carries sizes from 3/32 up in American holly, black walnut & mahogany; 3/64 to 5/64 also in American holly	Northeastern
	Brass	(1/16), (3/32), (1/8), (3/16), 1/4, 5/16, 3/8, 1/2, 5/8 square (Special Shapes Co. carries only those in parentheses plus 1/4 & 5/16)	Milled Shapes Inc. (Engineering Model Associates Inc. carries only sizes in parentheses)

Shape	Material	Sizes available (inches except when indicated)	Manufacturer or distributor	
T	Gray impact styrene	1/8, 3/16 square; legs have rake	Industrial Model Supplies & Con Cor Models	$\top$
	Plastic	3/32, 1/8, 3/16, 1/4 square	Engineering Model Associates Inc.	
Z	Basswood	(3/64), (1/16), (3/32), 1/8, 5/32, 3/16, 7/32, 1/4, 9/32, 5/16, 3/8, 7/16, 1/2, 9/16, 5/8, 11/16, 3/4 square; Northeastern also carries 3 sizes in American holly	Camino Scale Models Co. (Model Hobbies, America's Hobby Center and Northeastern carry only sizes in parentheses)	L
	Brass	(1/16), (3/32), (1/8), (3/16), (1/4), (5/16), 3/8, 1/2, 5/8 square	Milled Shapes Inc. (Special Shapes Co. carries only sizes in parentheses)	
Channel	Basswood	1/16, (5/64), (3/32), (1/8), 5/32, (3/16), 7/32, (1/4), 5/16, (3/8), 7/16, (1/2), 9/16, 5/8, 11/16, 3/4 height; width is about half of height; flanges have rake, except those shapes carried by Engineering Model Associates Inc.	Camino Scale Models Co. (Model Hobbies and Engineering Model Associates Inc. carry only sizes in parentheses)	C
		5/64, 3/32, 1/8, 5/32, 3/16, 5 mm, 1/4, 5/16, 3/8, 10 mm, 1/2 height; width is about half of height; flanges have rake; Northeastern also carries the 5/64 size in American holly & all the other sizes also in American holly, black walnut & mahogany	Northeastern	
	Brass	(1/16), (3/32), (1/8), (3/16), (1/4), (5/16), (3/8), 1/2, 5/8 height; width is about half the height	Special Shapes Co. (Engineering Model Associates Inc. carries only sizes in parentheses)	
		1/8 × 1/16, 5/16 × 1/16, 3/8 × 1/8	Max Gray	
	Gray impact styrene	3/16 × 1/16, 1/4 × 3/32, 5/16 × 3/32, 3/8 × 3/32, 7/16 × 1/8, 1/2 × 1/8, 9/16 × 1/8, 5/8 × 5/32; flanges have rake	Industrial Model Supplies & Con Cor Models	
	Plastic	1/8 × 0.05, 3/16 × 1/16, 1/4 × 0.07, 5/16 × 0.08, 3/8 × 3/32, 7/16 × 1/8, 1/2 × 1/8, 9/16 × 1/8, 5/8 × 3/16, 3/4 × 3/16	Engineering Model Associates Inc.	
I-beam	Basswood	(3/32), (1/8), 5/32, (3/16), (1/4), 5/16, (3/8), 7/16, (1/2), 9/16, 5/8, 11/16, 3/4 height; flanges have rake, except those shapes carried by Engineering Model Associates Inc.	Camino Scale Models Co. (Model Hobbies & Engineering Model Associates Inc. carry only sizes in parentheses)	I
		5/64, 3/32, 1/8, 5/32, 3/16, 5 mm, 1/4, 5/16, 3/8, 10 mm, 1/2 height; flanges have rake; Northeastern also carries them in American holly	Northeastern	
	Brass	(1/16), (3/32), (1/8), (3/16), (1/4), (5/16), (3/8), 1/2, 5/8 height; width is half the height	Milled Shapes Inc. (Engineering Model Associates Inc. & Special Shapes Co. carry only sizes in parentheses)	
Wide flange	Gray impact styrene	3/16 × 3/32, 4/16 × 5/32, 5/16 × 3/16, 3/8 × 3/16, 7/16 × 3/16, 1/2 × 7/32, 9/16 × 1/4, 5/8 × 1/4, 11/16 × 9/32, 3/4 × 9/32, 7/8 × 5/16, 1 × 3/8, 1 1/8 × 1/2; flanges have rake	Industrial Model Supplies & Con Cor Models	I
	Plastic	1/8 × 0.075, 3/16 × 3/32, 1/4 × 1/8, 5/16 × 5/32, 3/8 × 3/16, 7/16 × 7/32, 1/2 × 1/4, 9/16 × 1/4, 5/8 × 1/4, 3/4 × 5/16, 7/8 × 3/8, 1 × 3/8, 1 1/8 × 1/2	Engineering Model Associates Inc.	
H-beam or columns	Basswood	1/16, (3/32), (1/8), 5/32, (3/16), 7/32, (1/4), 9/32, 5/16, (3/8), 7/16, (1/2), 9/16, 5/8, 11/16, 3/4 square	Camino Scale Models Co. (Model Hobbies & Engineering Model Associates Inc. carry only sizes in parentheses)	I
		5/64, 3/32, 1/8, 5/32, 3/16, 5 mm, 1/4, 5/16, 3/8, 10 mm, 1/2 square; Northeastern also carries them in American holly	Northeastern	
	Brass	(1/16), (3/32), (1/8), (3/16), (1/4), (5/16), (3/8), 1/2, 5/8 square	Milled Shapes Inc. (Special Shapes Co. & Engineering Model Associates Inc. carry only sizes in parentheses)	
	Gray impact styrene	1/8, 3/8, 1/2, 5/8, 3/4 square; flanges have rake	Industrial Model Supplies & Con Cor Models	
	Plastic	1/8, 3/16, 1/4, 5/16, 3/8, 7/16, 1/2, 9/16, 5/8, 3/4 square	Engineering Model Associates Inc.	

[1] Shapes come in the following lengths: Engineering Model Associates Inc., Model Hobbies, Northeastern, Camino Scale Models Co., basswood shapes, 24″ long; Engineering Model Associates Inc., Special Shapes Co. (except their tubing, which can be purchased by the foot), Milled Shapes Inc., Industrial Model Supplies, brass shapes, 30″ long; Engineering Model Associates Inc., plastic shapes, most are 30″, some are 24″ or 15″ long; Walther's brass bar and tubes, 24″ long. Approximate wall thickness of the shapes made by Milled Shapes Inc. and Special Shapes Co., unless otherwise noted, are: shape size 1/32″, approximate wall thickness 0.010–0.015″; 1/16″, 0.015″; 3/32″, 0.020″; 1/8″, 0.024″; 3/16″, 0.026″; 1/4″, 0.030″; 5/16″, 0.032″; 3/8″, 0.050″; 1/2″, 0.060″; 5/8″, 0.062″.

SPECIAL LATTICED OR RIVETED BRASS SHAPES

manufactured by Max Gray in 7 7/8" lengths

Shape	Size (inches)
Latticed box girder	3/16 × 1/16
Diagonal latticed channel	5/16 × 1/8
Latticed H-column or post	3/8 × 5/16
Solid H-column or post	3/8 × 5/16
Cover plate strip	5/16 × 1/32
Deck girder rib	5/16 × 1/32
Deck girder interior brace	3/8 × 1/8
Large gusset plate	1 × 1
Anchor bracket	5/16 × 3/16 × 3/16
Small flanged gusset	7/32 × 7/32
Large flanged gusset	1 1/16 × 15/32

METAL

Sheet metal is not used often in model construction. In simple models the use of metal is usually relegated to the modeling of railing and furniture legs. But from time to time the need may arise for the high strength-to-thickness ratio that only metal provides for the construction of mullions, space frames, plaster and plastic scrapers, light baffles, hammer-formed domes, vaults and other complexly curved thin-wall objects. Metal is sometimes etched with acid to form small scale facades and larger scale railing, as well as wall and floor textures.

AVAILABLE THREAD, WIRE, CHAIN, ROD, DOWEL, AND TUBING

Type	Material	Size (inches)	Manufacturer or Distributor
Invisible thread	Monofilament nylon		Spencer Gifts
Music wire	Flexible spring steel	1/32, 3/64, 1/16, 3/32, 1/8, 5/32, 3/16 diameter	Sig Manufacturing Co.
		0.013 diameter	James Bliss & Co.
Aircraft wire	Tinned steel	1/32 diameter	James Bliss & Co.
Chain	Brass	Links per inch : 7, 9, 12, 14, 16, 18, 20, 22, 32	Selley
Dowel	White birch	1/8, 3/16, 1/4, 5/16, 3/8, 1/2 diameters by 12 & 36	Sig Manufacturing Co.
Round bar or rod	Polystyrene	0.5 and 1 diameters, transparent	Walthers
		Natural finish : 1/8, 3/16 ; Annealed : 1/4, 5/16, 3/8, 7/16, 1/2, 5/8, 3/4, 7"8, 1, 1 1/8, 1 1/4, 1 3/8, 1 1/2, 1 5/8, 1 3/4, 2, 2 1/4, 2 3/4, 3, 3 1/4, 3 1/2, 3 3/4, 4, 4 1/8, 5, 5 1/2, 6, 6 1/2, 7, 7 1/2, 8 × 6' long	Plastic supply houses such as Commercial Plastics Co.
	Cellulose acetate	1/8, 3/16, 1/4, 5/16, 3/8, 7/16, 1/2, 9/16, 5/8, 3/4, 7/8, 1, 1 1/8, 1 1/4 diameter, crystal clear	Plastic supply houses such as Commercial Plastics Co.
	Acrylic	0.25, 0.312, 0.375, 0.500, 0.625, 0.750, 0.875, 1, 1 1/8, 1 1/4, 1 3/8, 1 1/2, 1 5/8, 1 3/4, 1 7/8, 2, 2 1/4, 2 1/2, 2 3/4, 3, 1/2 increments up to 11 diameter ; cast, clear	Plastic supply houses such as Commercial Plastics Co.
		Extruded acrylic : 1/16, 1/8, 3/16, 1/4, 5/16, 3/8, 7/16, 1/2, 9/16, 5/8, 3/4, 7/8, 1, 1 1/8, 1 1/4, 1 3/8, 1 1/2, 1 5/8, 1 3/4, 2, 2 1/2 diameter by 6' long, polished and clear	Plastic supply houses such as Commercial Plastics Co.
	Soft steel	0.016, 0.029 diameter	Walthers
	Brass	0.020, 0.025, 0.030, 0.035, 0.040 diameter	Kemtron
		0.016, 0.02, 0.025, 0.032, 0.045 diameter and the first 4 below	Special Shapes Co. & Milled Shapes Inc.
	Aluminum	1/16, 3/32, 1/8, 3/16, 1/4, 5/16, 3/8 diameter	America's Hobby Center
Tube	Brass	(0.014 wall thickness) : 1/16 to 13/32 diameter (by 1/32 increments) telescoping	Special Shapes Co.
		(0.03 wall) : 1/8 to 2 1/2 diameter (by 1/16 increments)	Special Shapes Co.
	Copper	1/16, 1/8, 3/16 diameter	America's Hobby Center
	Aluminum	1/16, 3/32, 1/8, 5/32 ,3/16, 7/32 diameter, telescoping	America's Hobby Center & Sig Mfg. Co.
	Acrylic[1]	1/4, 5/16, 3/8, 1/2, 5/8, 3/4, 7/8, 1, 1 1/4, 1 1/2, 1 3/4, 2, 2 1/4, 2 1/2, 2 3/4, 3, o.d. × 6' long wall thickness : 1/16 on all sizes up through 1 1/4 o.d., 1/8 on all sizes over 3/8 o.d., 5/32 on 1/2 o.d. size only ; clear. 1.5, 1.625, 1.75, 2, 2.25, 2.5, 2.75, 2.875, 3, 3.125, 3.25, 3.5, 3.625, 3.75, 3.875, 4, 4.125, 4.25, 4.5, 4.625, 4.75, 5, 5.5, 5.75, 6, 7, 8, 8.75, 9, 10, 11, 12, o.d. diameter. Wall thickness : 0.25, 0.187 & 0.125 (available with all size tubes) ; 0.375 is available with all stock of 4 & larger ; 0.5 is available with all stock of 5 & larger.	Plastic supply houses such as Commercial Plastics Co.
	Polystyrene	1/4, 3/8, 1/2, 5/8, 3/4, 7/8, 1, 1 1/4, 1 1/2, 1 3/4, 2 o.d. × 6' long ; wall thickness is 1/16 on tubes under 1 1/4 o.d., 1/8 on rest ; clear	Plastic supply houses such as Commercial Plastics Co.

[1] Tubes come with inside polished or with inside and outside polished. They also come in the following transparent colors : 2 greens, red, 4 blues, amber, fluorescent red, violet. Translucent colors : green, red, 4 blues, 2 ambers, 8 whites, 2 ivories, pink, yellow, orange. Opaque colors : white, black, "pearl," 3 greens, 2 reds, 6 blues, white, pink, yellow, orange, 2 blacks, 2 browns, beige, lavender, purple, silver, bronze, copper, gold.

Layout

When it becomes difficult to see penciled layout lines on metal, use blue layout dope. This chemical, available in hardware stores, should be sprayed on the metal and lines scribed into it. When the work is finished, the dope may be removed with alcohol.

Cutting Metal

Reducing stock sheet metal to the desired shape requires either sawing or cutting with snips.

SNIPS

These are used for the cutting of thin sheet metal. The top blade of the snip should be placed on the line of the planned cut to insure accuracy. Insert the metal as far back between the blades as possible. Blades must be held perpendicular to the metal to prevent a beveled cut. Blades should not be bolted together too tightly or they will chew the metal as well as worsen the distortion caused by the shearing action of the cut. Oil the pivot occasionally. If a cut requires a great amount of pressure, clamp one of the snip's handles in a vise, and use both hands on the other handle.

Types of Snips

Regular Pattern Snips have a straight blade for making straight cuts and for making curved cuts of large radius. Wiss has an extensive line of these with 11½ to 14½" long, crucible steel blades costing between $4 and $5.25, and a line of solid steel snips with 8 to 12¼" blades costing $2 to $2.75.

Combination Snips are for straight or curved cuts.

Duck Bill and Hawk's Bill Snips are combination snips. Wiss has 12½ and 14½" crucible steel combination snips for $5 to $6, and a line of 7 to 13" solid steel snips costing $1.75 to $3.25.

Aviation Snips are for straight or curved cuts ; they have a compound lever action that can cut thicker metal.

TYPES OF METAL CUTTING SAWS

Jeweler's, Coping and Fret Saws are reviewed on page 20 . When using them to cut metal, be sure to select a blade hard enough to perform the task. A blade meant for wood will also cut aluminum. Never use these saws on hardened steel.

Hack Saws can cut plastics and metal. Their replaceable blades have 14 to 32 teeth per inch.

Use high-speed steel blades on hard steel ; low-tungsten steel blades for mild steel, brass, copper, aluminum, etc. Hard blades are more prone to break than flexible ones. Coarse blades have standard alternate set to their teeth. Fine-tooth blades have undulating set.

The saw's frame can be adjusted to take blades 8, 10, or 12" long. Blades can be adjusted to pointing down or sideways. Teeth should point away from the handle.

The 3-Tooth Rule—When cutting thin material, make sure that the blade is fine enough so that at least 3 teeth come in contact with the work so as to prevent the blade from being damaged. If the

METAL FORMING

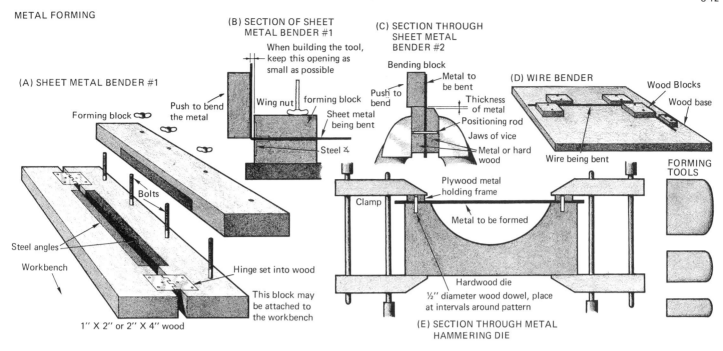

(A) SHEET METAL BENDER #1

Forming block
Push to bend the metal
Bolts
Steel angles
Workbench
Hinge set into wood
This block may be attached to the workbench
1" X 2" or 2" X 4" wood

(B) SECTION OF SHEET METAL BENDER #1
When building the tool, keep this opening as small as possible
Wing nut
forming block
Sheet metal being bent
Steel ∡

(C) SECTION THROUGH SHEET METAL BENDER #2
Bending block
Metal to be bent
Push to bend
Thickness of metal
Positioning rod
Jaws of vice
Metal or hard wood

(D) WIRE BENDER
Wood Blocks
Wood base
Wire being bent
FORMING TOOLS

Plywood metal holding frame
Clamp
Metal to be formed
Hardwood die
½" diameter wood dowel, place at intervals around pattern
(E) SECTION THROUGH METAL HAMMERING DIE

STRUCTURAL SECTIONS AVAILABLE FROM MAX GRAY

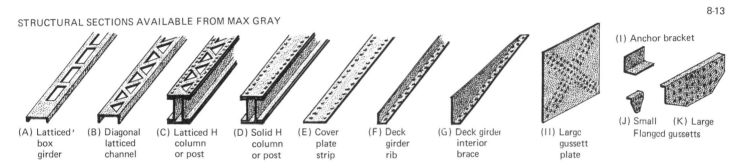

(A) Latticed box girder
(B) Diagonal latticed channel
(C) Latticed H column or post
(D) Solid H column or post
(E) Cover plate strip
(F) Deck girder rib
(G) Deck girder interior brace
(H) Large gussett plate
(I) Anchor bracket
(J) Small (K) Large Flanged gussetts

TOOLS TO CUT SHEET METAL OF VARIOUS THICKNESSES

Tool	Brass & copper	Aluminum	Steel
Snips	Up to 1/16"	Up to 1/16"	Up to 1/32"
Jeweler's, coping, or fret saw	Up to 1/8"	Up to 3/16"	Up to 1/16"
Hacksaw	Any thickness	Any thickness	Any thickness

BLADES FOR VARIOUS MATERIALS

type; teeth per inch	For cutting
Flexible; 32	Thin (1/16" and under) sheet metal or tubing
Flexible; 24	Sections 1/16" to 1/4" thick; wire tubing with walls over 1/16" thick
Hard; 18	Tool steel, brass, or bronze sheet, sections 1/4" to 1" thick
Hard; 14	Solid over 1" thick pieces of aluminum, soft steel or copper, asbestos, fiber

thickness of the metal is less than the distance between teeth, the saw will bounce in the cut, tear the metal and possibly damage the blade. When starting a cut at a sharp corner, hold the saw at a small enough angle to a flat side so that at least 3 teeth come in contact with the work.

Clamp thin sheet metal to be cut between 2 pieces of wood to give it rigidity. Mount metal in a vise with jaws close to the cutting line to eliminate sawing vibration. While being cut, the metal should be frequently repositioned to keep the cut line close to the jaws. Start cuts in tubes in a filed notch.

While in use, the saw should be held parallel to the ground or with its handle slightly elevated. If a blade snaps and the new one, not being worn down, does not fit into the cut, start a new cut on the opposite side of the work and try to make it run into the first. Millers Falls makes a $3 hack saw.

Other Metal Saws. See page 21 for a description of pad, its general purpose, and jab saws, and for a review of the causes of blade breakage.

To cut an opening in sheet metal, drill away as much of the material as possible, then enlarge the hole with a triangular file and finish the corners with a file that has a knife cross section. Saw from corner hole to corner hole.

Drilling Metal

Locate the drill hole with a fine center punch. Use a sharp drill and work on a hard surface to prevent a raised rim on the hole. See page 24 for general drilling instructions and descriptions of the drills to use in metal. See page 25 for the best drill-point angles to be used on various metals.

Wire Bending

When a specific radius is required, bend cold or heated wire on a properly sized wooden dowel. When a number of identical pieces must be bent, a bending jig may be warranted. A tube may be bent kink free if a snugly fitting wire is first placed inside.

A Bending Jig (8-12D) should have its base made out of a plywood sheet. Bends must be made a few degrees more than the intended final angle because of the wire's tendency to spring back slightly when it is removed from the blocks.

A Wire Bending Die is sold by Drumcliff Company. This $1 tool is held in a vise or screwed to the workbench. It can bend wire of up to $\frac{5}{32}$" in diameter.

Sheet Metal Bending

Pliers and Nippers and various tools that may be used to grip, bend and nip thin metal objects have their descriptions on page 18.

To accomplish long bends in sheet metal, some sort of bending tool is needed. To bend medium lengths of lightweight stock, the tool in 8-12C may be used. When bending with hand pressure, use a pushing block the full length of the material. When hammering a bend, move the block from one end of the material to the other and gradually hammer it into shape with light blows.

For really long bends and bends in heavy metal, construct the tool in 8-12A and B. To compensate for the tendency of the metal to spring back after pressure is released, bend it slightly more than the desired angle; the forming block should be slightly beveled.

Sheet Benders make 90° bends in metal of up to 16 gauge. They are sold by Silvo Hardware Company for $14.

Sheet Metal Forming

Metal is easily hammered into almost any curved form. Construct a hardwood female mold and a clamping frame for the metal (8-12E). Carve a set of hardwood (oak or maple) bumping tools in the shapes shown in the illustration. Use annealed (soft) aluminum sheet of 0.01 to 0.02″ thickness; it is about the easiest metal to hammer form. Clamp it over the mold and tap it gently into shape. Hammer the bumping tools with a light cellulose-faced mallet; use light blows to depress the metal gradually down into the mold. Make several circuits around the perimeter of the mold and gradually work the bumper towards the center, moving the bumper in circles of ever-decreasing diameter. Be careful not to allow the metal to wrinkle too deeply. Use the largest bumper to smooth out the wrinkles that will inevitably form. Use the smallest bumper to shape the tightest curves. When the material has been worked to the bottom of the mold and smoothed out, remove it from the mold. If there are wrinkles on the outside of the shape, return it to the mold and continue hammering. When the shape is finally smooth, trim off the excess metal with shears.

Metal Etching

Etching is employed by professional model-makers to cut entire facades (8-13A) or minor details, such as metal railings, safety treads, etc., or to make molds into which objects like railings may be cast. Metal may be etched in low relief (to a depth of about 15/1000″) from one side, or it may be etched from both sides, and cut through completely. The latter technique can produce such items as railings, or the store front shown in illustration 8-13A, done by Kemtron, a company that does custom etching. Etching is accomplished by covering the metal sheet with a thin layer of acid-resisting wax and then by scribing the desired pattern through the wax with an etching needle. The plate is then etched with acid to the required depth.

Metal Finishing

See page 23 for a table showing the types of files to use on various metal, and for general instructions on filing.

Sand metal with aluminum-oxide paper and roughly polish it with crocus paper.

Painting Metal

A microscopic film of oil, greasy fingerprints, soldering flux, metal shavings or dust on metal can prevent paint from sticking. Painting thus must be prefaced by a thorough cleaning. First, sand off any rust or corrosion. Then cleanse with any of the following cleaning agents: naphtha; benzine; carbon tetrachloride; a bath in a warm solution of water and synthetic detergents followed by an application of lacquer thinner that is then wiped from the metal; boiling in a strong solution of soda water followed by a rinse in hot water, and then a rinse in acetone or lacquer thinner; household vinegar (if the grime is not too tenacious). Diluted hydrochloric acid, etc. can also be used. Certain commercially prepared cleaners may also be used: Metal Prep can be employed on iron and steel (it not only removes grime and rust, but also etches); Alumi Prep and Galva Prep are usable on aluminum or zinc. These

8-13A

PHOTOENGRAVED FACADE DETAIL.

PROJECT: Seagram office building, Chicago, Illinois.
DESIGNED BY: Mies van der Rohe.
MODELBUILDERS: members of the architect's staff.
PHOTOGRAPHER: Hedrich-Blessing.
SCALE: 1/8″ = 1′.
The facades of the building were photoengraved zinc plates. Window areas were burnished with charcoal and then lacquered. Plates were then mounted on a wood block that was cut to the outline of the building.
The photograph was taken with an 8″ × 10″ Deardorff view camera, 165 mm lens and Kodak Royal Pan film. The photo composite was achieved by first taking a picture of the site, developing it and then making a sketch of it on a sheet of plastic. The sheet was next mounted on the viewing glass of the camera and used as a guide in matching the angle at which the model photo was taken.
CONSTRUCTION TIME: about 80 hours.

three products are made by the Neilson Chemical Company of Detroit. Floquil's metal conditioner may be used to clean and etch many types of metal. Use a brush to loosen grime.

Once the metal is clean, it should be etched so as to convert its smooth surface into one that will hold paint. Etching is most needed on brass, aluminum or die-cast metals. The etching solution may be white vinegar mixed into water to the ratio of 1:10 or 1:20, crystalline etcher (purchasable in many hobby stores) mixed with water, or the commercial preparations made by the Neilson Chemical Company.

To clean soldered assemblies, use a white vinegar bath; or boil them in soapy water followed with a scrubbing and then a washing in hot water; or clean them with either alcohol, lighter fluid, carbon tetrachloride or printer's naphtha.

Priming is also very important, especially if one intends to paint by brush: use lacquer thinner as the prime coat if lacquer is to be used. For oil paints, use a regular metal primer (obtainable in paint stores). To make a water-base paint adhere to metal, mix a little glycerin into it. Since this will slow the drying of the paint, bake the painted object at about 225°F.

Sharp corners and edges are hard to paint and even when the paint has finally been placed, it is easily worn off. Use several coats to prevent this.

Natural Metal Finishes

The natural luster of brass, copper or aluminum may be retained if a coat of clear lacquer or paste wax is regularly applied. Metal that has become dull must first be cleaned with a commercial metal polish or cleaner before lacquer or wax is applied; wipe off all traces of polish or cleaner with a solvent.

Bonding Metal

Epoxy is the best adhesive besides solder; cellulose cement may also be used. Prior to applying the adhesive, make sure that the surface of the metal is free of grease, and slightly sanded.

SOLDERING

Soldering can be one of the most frustrating of construction techniques. To solder successfully, it is absolutely necessary that the soldering iron, flux and solder be of high quality, and meant for the job at hand. Unlike many other techniques, soldering will not allow the substitution of skill and perseverance for incorrect tools and materials.

Soldering, by definition, is the holding together of metals using the surface adhesion of the solder as the binder. Unlike welding, where the metals to be joined are fused together, the soldered pieces are not melted—only the solder becomes molten. The strength of solder, which is low, diminishes as it ages in a joint that is under stress. Solder comes in two basic types: soft and hard. Soft solder may be melted by the use of matches, electrically heated irons or blow torches; hard solder usually requires a torch.

Soldering Irons

The proper selection of a soldering iron (or irons) is extremely important. An inexpensive iron will soon wear out; an iron of the wrong size can overheat, damage the work and unsolder adjacent joints, or it may not be able to create sufficient heat.

An iron must be matched in size to the work undertaken. The iron should be able to produce a temperature of about 100°F, above the flow point of the solder. The following table will give an indication of the type of work that may be undertaken with some available irons.

Irons come with fixed or interchangeable tips; the latter naturally provide greater flexibility. Some irons come with an on-off switch, eliminating the need to disconnect the plug after finishing a job.

AVAILABLE SHEET METAL

Material	Size (inches)	Distributor
Brass	0.001, 0.002, 0.003, 0.005, 0.010, 0.015 thick by 6 × 12 or 2 1/2 × 8	Sig Manufacturing Co.
	0.006, 0.008, 0.01, 0.012, 0.016, 0.02, 0.025, 0.032, 0.04, 0.05, 0.064 thick by 6 × 12	Special Shapes Co. & Milled Shapes Inc.
Copper	0.005, 0.010, 0.016, 0.032 thick by 4 × 12 or 12 × 12	America's Hobby Center
Aluminum	0.012, 0.020, 0.032 thick by 4 × 12, 12 × 12, or 12 × 24 and 0.064 thick by 4 × 12	Sig Manufacturing Co.

Type of iron	Type of work
Pencil Iron: 6 to 20 watts	Miniature parts, very small bulbs
Iron or Gun: 50 watts	Small parts, electrical connections
60 watts	Medium-sized parts
100 watts	Medium-sized parts (speed)

Rest soldering irons in a holder when they are not in use.

Oryx has a very complete line of pencil-size irons costing from $6 for a 6 watt iron (capable of 540°F) to $8 for a 25 watt iron that can reach 1000°F. Oryx also makes a small soldering tweezer for $15.

Stanley makes a 50 watt iron for $4, and a 115 watt iron with replaceable tips for $12.

Weller has a 25 watt soldering gun for $5. The company also has a line of "dual heat" soldering guns that permit an instant switch from high to low heat. Guns come in 100/140 watt, 145/210 watt and 240/325 watt sizes costing $7, $10 and $11, respectively.

Blixt makes an iron that automatically feeds flux-core wire solder to the iron's tip. The iron costs $12, includes 2 replaceable tips and a stand.

TINNING THE SOLDERING IRON means the tip of the soldering iron must be tinned (covered with a thin coat of solder) or oxidation will form, and prevent the iron from transmitting its full heat. To tin an iron: (1) sandpaper all oxidation from the tip; (2) heat it until it starts to darken; (3) rub it with solder covered with flux or with a flux-core solder. An easy way to do this is to melt a little solder in a tin can and dip the iron into it; (4) wipe off the excess.

If the iron overheats, black scale, or a bluish color, will form on the tip. This must be sanded off and the iron retinned. Hooking a thermostat to the iron will prevent this from becoming a frequent occurrence. This device will cut off the electricity when the iron reaches its optimum temperature. Some more expensive irons are constructed with a built-in thermostat.

Solder

SOFT SOLDER is compounded of tin and lead. It melts at low temperatures (under 700°F) and adheres well to copper, brass, tin and steel. The more tin in the solder, the more easily it melts and the less brittle it will be. The more lead that the solder contains, the longer it will remain in its melted state. The ratio of solder metals commonly used in modelmaking ranges from 40 parts tin/60 parts lead to 70/30. Solder comes in bars (for heavy work), ribbon or wire form. Ribbon or wire solder comes in a solid state or cored with flux.

For the best solder to use on various metals see page 60.

There are several solders on the market especially prepared for the soldering of small parts: Kemtron Solder Paint contains solder and noncorrosive flux in a paste form. Swif solder (obtainable at hobby or hardware stores) is a 50/50 tin-lead paste solder (containing flux). Its squeeze tube container makes it possible to dispense extremely small amounts.

HARD (SILVER) SOLDER, often called braze or filler metal, is an alloy that can contain lead, tin, bismuth, copper, gold or silver. It has a higher melting temperature (1600°F for the Victor No. 1 brand and 1175°F for Easy Flo) than soft solder, and greater strength. Hard solder comes in rod or wire form; some solders are flux covered. A torch must usually be employed to reach the hard solder's melting temperature. Following are some of the torches that are available and their maximum temperatures: alcohol lamps (2100°F) and bunsen burners (1400°F), both usable only on small joints; propane torches (3600°F), good for small and medium-size work; acetylene (5500°F) and oxy-acetylene (6300°F), torches required for heavy and very heavy work. Those silver solders that contain cadmium should be used only in a well-ventilated area, or by a worker wearing a respirator. Prolonged exposure to cadmium fumes can cause illness or death.

LIQUID OR COLD SOLDERS do a reasonably good job of adhering to metal. They are applied like cement, and require no heat. Their disadvantages are shrinking and the long time they take to dry. Apply them to a clean surface and compensate for their contraction. Apply the first coat, let it dry 5 minutes, then apply the second coat and press the joint together. Allow the solder to dry before loading the joint. Cold solder should be used only where the heat from an iron would damage the work or on assemblies that do not have to be overly strong.

Chapter 7 details several all-purpose adhesives that will bond metal.

Flux

Flux forms an oxidation-preventing film over the joint to be soldered. This is necessary because heated metal rapidly oxdizes and this interferes with the holding ability of the solder.

Flux is usually a rosin or acid compound in paste form. It can be purchased in cans or cored into ribbon or wire solder. Corrosive flux should not be used on electrical connections or on fine parts. For the best flux to use on various metals see page 60.

Rosin Flux is noncorrosive and nonconductive. It comes in lump or powdered form. It may be applied as a powder, or dissolved in alcohol and brushed on. Rosin works best on tinned metals, electrical connections, brass, copper, lead and small parts. Rosin, after being applied to the parts to be soldered, must be heated until it vaporizes into smoke. For fine soldering, dissolve the rosin in alcohol and brush it onto the work. Rosin core wire solder may be used on tinned metals, brass or copper.

Zinc Chloride Flux is corrosive. It must be washed off the finished joint with a solution of soap, washing soda and water. It must be stored in a container that, along with its stopper, is made of plastic or glass. Apply it with a special rubber bristle brush. Zinc chloride should be used on copper, brass, bronze, zinc and steel.

Soldering salts are a crystalline form of zinc chloride; they must be dissolved in water before using.

Soldering Paste Flux usually is zinc chloride mixed with vaseline, palm oil or ceresine wax. It

is corrosive, and used on the same metals as zinc chloride.

Tallow and Stearine Flux is noncorrosive, and may be used on copper and lead. It comes in the form of a candle which must be scraped into shavings, and applied to the joint.

Muriatic Acid Flux is extremely corrosive. It must be washed off hands and clothing. Use at full strength on zinc, steel, stainless steel, brass, copper and tin.

Stainless Steel Flux is extremely corrosive, and also must be washed off hands and clothing.

Preparation of the Joint and Soldering

Metal must be free of rust, paint, dirt, grease and oxides for solder to adhere. Clean the joint thoroughly with emery cloth or steel wool. Do not polish the metal, since minute scratches will give the solder a better grip. Clean oily fingerprints from the joint with a weak solution of sulfuric acid, then rinse in water.

Do not rely on the solder alone to make the joint strong. Where possible, let the metal do some of the holding work: employ interlocking joints and, when joining electrical wires, first wind them together. Joints must not move while soldering is in progress. Hold pieces in position with wire, clamps or magnets. If clamps or magnets tend to conduct heat away from the joint, they must be insulated with newspaper. Allow the iron to heat for about a minute before starting to work.

Apply a thin, uniform coat of flux with a piece of scrap wood or brush. Never dip the soldering iron into the flux can. To solder a large area (with an iron), tin the surfaces to be joined in the same manner in which the iron was tinned. This is necessary because it is impossible to run the solder under large pieces, as one can under small objects.

Solder tends to flow into fluxed and heated areas. Thus, by the proper application of flux and heat, molten solder can be led to where it is needed. If the solder line is too broad, too much flux was applied or it was spread over too wide an area. Only experience will show how much to use. Large objects may have to be preheated with a torch.

When molten solder stands on the work in balls, it means: (1) the metal may not take that type of solder; (2) the wrong type of flux is being used; (3) the work is not sufficiently clean.

A sheet of asbestos tacked to a piece of $\frac{1}{4}$" plywood makes a good work surface and will protect the workbench from heat.

Mass production of many similar joints may be facilitated by the construction of hardwood positioning jigs. Metal jigs should be avoided because they conduct heat away from the objects being soldered.

X-Acto makes a $2 soldering aid kit that contains cleaning tools and flux applicators.

Soft Soldering

When soldering small and long, narrow joints, hold the iron so that it contacts and heats both pieces. Put some solder on the joint, melt it and draw the iron across the joint so that the solder flows between the two members. If very small pieces are to be soldered, it may be possible to

Solder	Ratio of tin to lead	Melting temperature
Slicker solder (the tin-lead solder with the lowest melting point)	66/34	356°F.
Standard soft solders	48/52	360°F.
	25/75	545°F.

SOLDERING

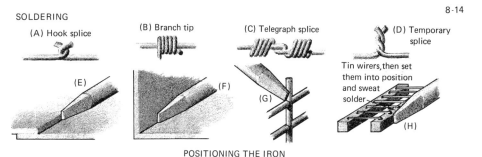

(A) Hook splice
(B) Branch tip
(C) Telegraph splice
(D) Temporary splice

(E)
(F)
(G)

Tin wirers, then set them into position and sweat solder

(H)

POSITIONING THE IRON

run the iron along the sturdier of the pieces a fraction of an inch from the joint. Thus heat can be conducted to the joint without danger of the iron's pressure pushing the pieces out of alignment (8-14H). The procedure is called sweat soldering. It is accomplished when the solder is melted by heat conduction rather than by direct contact by the iron on solder.

Do not carry the solder to the work on the iron. Heat the work with a flat side of the iron's tip, and place the solder on it so that the solder is melted into the joint rather than just being deposited on it in a melted state. After completing the joint, wash it clean of flux. Use water on most metals; a solution of soapy water and washing soda is best on bronze and brass.

Silver, or Hard, Soldering

(1) Clean and flux the joints. (2) Clamp together the pieces to be soldered. Since brazing metals melt into a thin liquid that will not fill gaps, the parts that form the joint must fit together tightly. (3) Place a length of solder on each joint. (4) Heat the solder slowly in the torch's flame. When the flux starts to melt, increase the heat until the solder melts and flows into the joint. If the brazing metal does not flow evenly after the joint has been heated to pink-white, it may be because the joint is dirty. Once the solder starts to melt, remove the flame immediately. Too much heat will adversely affect the metal. (5) Clean off the flux. If the object is bronze, brass or copper, immerse the joint in a 1 : 50 solution of sulfuric acid and water. Then wash it in water. Flux should be removed from steel with a bath of plain water. (6) Smooth off the joint with emery cloth and a metal file.

Soldering Many Joints Simultaneously

Use the following technique if many joints are to be soldered simultaneously, either on a single piece of work or on several, or when soldering a joint so extensive that it would be impossible to heat it all at once with the iron (situations encountered when fabricating a complex metal grill, several metal furniture legs, railings, etc.: (1) Obtain a frying pan (an aluminum pan will do for soft soldering, otherwise one of steel or stainless steel. (2) To prevent the pan from being ruined, line it with a sheet of aluminum (stainless steel if hard soldering is being performed). When this sheet becomes marred, it can be sanded clean. (3) Clean and flux all joints. (4) Apply solder in 1 of 3 ways: (A) Heat each part individually and tin its joint with solder, then join the entire assembly together in the pan and reheat it. This will cause the joints to sweat together. (B) Place all parts in the pan, put bits of solder on each joint and then heat the pan. This will cause the solder to melt. (C) Assemble all parts in the pan, heat it and then touch each joint with a length of wire solder.

The pan may be heated with an electric hot plate. 6″ diameter hot plates with one heating element can be obtained at drug stores for under $2. Try to limit, both in duration and intensity, the amount of heat that is used. To do this, the entire object must be evenly heated. A tin can with an end removed and placed over the work will concentrate and more evenly distribute the heat.

Soldering Joints That Are Close to Other, Already Soldered Joints

USING SOFT SOLDER is an alternative if, when making several soldered connections on 1 object, the technique outlined in the preceding paragraph is impossible to use. (1) Position a large piece of metal against the object being soldered. Place it between the new joint and the finished connection. The metal will draw the heat from the object so that it does not attack the old connection. Beryllium-copper clips, called heat sinks, can be purchased to perform this chore. (2) Keep finished connections wrapped in wet rags. (3) Use a blowtorch; its high temperature, but low Btu. output, may not affect nearby finished joints.

USING SILVER SOLDER allows objects to be reheated without the first joint coming apart (this cannot be done with soft soldered objects). Thus complicated jobs can be silver soldered one joint at a time.

Soldering Various Metals

SOLDERING COPPER is easy. Its melting point is 2000°F. Any solder or flux may be used. Most convenient are acid core solder or all purpose rosin core electrical solder. When hard soldering, use Easy Flo braze metal and borax flux.

SOLDERING BRONZE AND BRASS is easy. Their melting points are over 2000°F. Use any tin-lead solder and rosin or zinc chloride flux. If using a flame, be careful not to overheat the metal. After soldering, wash off the flux with soapy water and washing soda. For hard soldering, use Easy Flo braze metal and borax flux.

SOLDERING TIN is difficult because of the metal's extremely low melting point (450°F). Use a special tin-lead-bismuth solder (alloy of wood) and muriatic acid flux. Tin cans and other tinned iron and steel objects can be soldered with tin-lead solder and rosin flux. Brazing is not recommended.

SOLDERING LEAD is easy, but its low melting point (621°F) dictates that a cool iron be kept in motion over the joint. Use a solder with a low melting point. Ordinary tallow is the best flux, though rosin may also be used. Hard soldering may be done with lead solder without a flux.

SOLDERING IRON AND STEEL requires tin-lead solder, aluminum solder, silver solder or stainless steel solder, and aluminum, zinc chloride or muriatic acid flux. When hard soldering, use Victor No. 1 braze metal and Victor No. 3 flux.

SOLDERING ALUMINUM is hard. It has a 1200°F melting point. Use aluminum brazing alloy (solder) and special aluminum flux. Carefully clean the joint and scrape all aluminum oxide from it. Immediately cover it with flux (aluminum oxidizes extremely rapidly and failure to remove the subsequent deposit will make soldering impossible). Since a temperature of at least 500°F must be reached, an ordinary iron will not work. Place the iron on the joint. When the flux starts to smoke, apply solder to the iron, and let it run into the joint. The same procedure can be followed with a torch. When soldering aluminum to another metal, use aluminum solder and flux.

SOLDERING STAINLESS STEEL requires stainless steel solder and flux. Apply the solder when the flux flows freely from the heat of the iron. Or use silver solder and flux. Apply the solder when the heat turns the flux to a clear red liquid.

Soldering Dissimilar Metals

A solder and flux must be selected that will work on both metals. This is why it is only satisfactory to solder iron or steel to copper or bronze.

Soldering Rods and Wires

Joints in rods or wires will be strong only if a large overlap is provided (8-14A, B, C, & D). The soldering procedure is : (1) Clean the material that is to be joined. (2) Apply solder to each piece. (3) Place pieces together. (4) Sweat the joint.

Soldering Electrical Connections

(1) Remove all insulation and clean the exposed wire. (2) Wind the wire ends together (8-14A, B, C & D) and bend them back. (3) Hold a length of rosin core wire solder to the top of the joint. Apply a moderate amount of heat from a small iron held below the joint. Too much heat will destroy the flux or weaken the wire. Use a 60:40 (tin-lead) solder.

Soldering Sheet Metal

Extensive joints in sheet metal can be strong only if : (1) A large lap is provided and the joint is tinned. (2) A lock joint is constructed.

Torches

When a very high temperature is needed, as in silver soldering or brazing, or when a large area must be heated, a torch is better than an iron. Small work must be held in position during torch soldering or it may be blown out of line by the flame. Torches may also be used for spot welding of various metals.

If the area to be soldered is extensive, combine techniques: Preheat with a torch or Bunsen burner and then apply the solder with an iron.

Torches, fueled by various chemicals, are listed for model work:

The Small Lenk Alcohol Torch costs $3, and is available from James Bliss & Co.

The Birk Super Jet Solid Fuel Blowtorch costs $2 and includes a 2 hour fuel supply. Its 2000°F flame is created by the operator's blowing into the torch. Each solid fuel pellet lasts for 10 minutes.

The Kidde-Jet King Butane Torch costs $2, includes a half-hour fuel supply, and can reach 3500°F. It is powered by small cylinders of compressed butane, each lasting about half an hour.

The Craftsman Propane Torch, sold by Sears & Roebuck, comes with 5 interchangeable tips, and costs $10.

Bernz-O-Matic makes propane torches whose tips are interchangeable. Some tips produce open flames; others use the burning propane to heat a soldering-iron-like tip. Model TX 10, equipped with a pencil tip, costs a bit over $5 and produces a 2300°F flame. Replacement cylinders, lasting 15 hours, cost $1.20 each. Model TX 610, costing $9.50, is equipped with a pencil tip that is joined to the propane tank by a 4 foot flexible shaft that provides greater maneuverability.

Microflame Oxy-Butane Torch costs $20 (including 2 refill tanks and 3 flame tips), and can reach 5000°F. This instrument is powered by small cylinders of butane; its extremely hot flame can be used to weld small pieces of iron and steel wire (up to $\frac{1}{32}$″ in diameter).

Welders are on the market in several very inexpensive ($15) outfits containing: a power source (operating from a 115 volt wall outlet), an eye-protecting hood, flux and welding rods. Operations that can be performed by these light-duty (11,000°F) welders include: brazing (up to $\frac{3}{16}$″ thick metal), soldering, metal cutting (up to $\frac{3}{32}$″ thick metal), metal softening (for bending), arch or fusion welding (up to $\frac{1}{16}$″ thick metal) and tempering. Thicker metal may be worked, but it takes great skill and effort. Companies that sell these units include Four Way Welder Company, Midway Welder and National Electric.

Soldering With a Torch

(1) Clean the joint. (2) Apply flux. (3) Heat the joint until it is hot enough to melt the solder. (4) Apply more flux. (5) Heat again. (6) Remove flame and apply solder to the joint. The metal must be hot enough to cause the solder to flow freely into the joint.

Match Soldering

Soldering by match is an improvised technique that should be resorted to only when soft soldering electrical connections, or other joints, which are not to be too closely scrutinized. Place a spliced wire joint on a small sheet of aluminum foil, with a piece of tape or wire solder resting on it. Hold a match below the joint and hope that the solder will run into the joint.

CHARACTERISTICS OF COMMON PLASTICS

Characteristic	Acrylic	Nylon	Polystyrene	Acetate
Tensile strength (psi)	8,000–11,000	10,000	5,500–7,000	4,500–8,000
Impact strength (120 D) ft. lbs./in. notch	0.4–0.05	1.0	0.26–0.6	1.0–3.0
Flexural strength (psi)	12,000–17,000	13,800	8,000–19,000	6,000–10,000
Compressive strength (psi)	11,000–19,000	4,900	11,500–15,200	18,000–25,000
Heat distortion temp. (degrees F.)	150–210	300–360	176–194	130–160

PLASTICS— MISCELLANEOUS

Selecting plastics for use in models becomes more difficult as new materials become available. Often a modelbuilder will use a type of plastic simply because he likes 1 or 2 of its characteristics and because he is accustomed to it. A more scientific analysis of plastics would benefit him as would obtaining, for testing, a few scrap pieces of each new type as it is marketed. As new plastics are invented, obtain information about them directly from their manufacturer.

Certain general instructions should be followed when any type of plastic is used:

Purchasing Plastics

When buying a piece of material smaller than a full size sheet, rod or strip, it is usual to pay a 15 to 20% price premium. This may be eliminated if suppliers can find remnants.

Machining Plastic

Follow general instructions pertaining to the power cutting of acrylic (see page 64) and to attaching plastic with screws (see page 66). Thermosetting plastics: acrylic, acetate, polystyrene, etc., should be cooled during machining. Water, soapy water or a solution of water and water-soluble oil may be used. Subjecting plastic to excessive heat can cause color change, distortion or fusing together of the cut. Be careful when lubricating plastic with water or a water-and-oil solution. The lubricant must not be allowed to drip into the motor or electrical wiring of the tool. If it does, a dangerous shock can occur. This is an especially serious problem when working with portable electric drills or small hand motor tools. The problem can be alleviated by holding the tool above the work or by using a flexible shaft attachment.

Special Shapes

Model Makers and other companies custom-injection-mold many types of plastics. They make all sorts of extrusions, patterned sheets and castings to specifications.

Correcting Warps in Plastic Sheets

If sheets of thermosetting plastic warp, they may be straightened by being placed on a flat surface and heated until they soften and flatten.

Sheet Forming Plastics

Sheet thermosetting plastics may be heated and formed into complexly curved shapes. Acrylic plastic is easily molded; regular acetate is difficult to mold into deep shapes, and will become white if the temperature is not high enough while it is being stretched. Special acetates made for pressure molding and polystyrene are workable. Each desired shape presents its own problems in determining the forming system to be used. Possible systems are: (1) vacuum forming on male or female molds; (2) forming in a tight fitting male and female mold; (3) forming on a precise male mold using a loosely fitting female mold; and (4) forming on a precise male mold using manual pressure to press the plastic into shape.

Male molds give greater sharpness of detail on the inside surface of the object, and are simpler to build than female molds which create sharpness of detail on the outside surface.

Molds may be made of cardboard, hard balsa, patternmaker's wood (mahogany, sugar pine, etc.), or plaster (Hydrocal or Ultracal). Balsa will suffice only if one is molding thin plastic. To save material build large hollow molds, and reinforce them with internal partitions. If they are made of plaster, they should also be reinforced with hemp fiber. Small details may be added to the mold by using wire or

Bristolboard. If detail is to be scribed into the plastic, it should be done before the plastic sheet is formed. Finish the mold as smooth as possible. Use synthetic resin, high-temperature varnish or casein paint to close the grain. Shellac, or ordinary paints and varnishes, will not be able to withstand the heat of the molding process. Covering the mold with a sheet of soft (billiard table) felt, imitation chamois or suede-covered rubber will also help to impart a smooth finish to the plastic.

When determining the dimensions of the male mold, take into consideration the thickness of the plastic. The dimensions of the mold plus the thickness of the plastic should equal the desired size of the object.

When forming objects that have curves in 2 directions, the plastic will have to be stretched. This will result in the final object having a wall thickness less than the thickness of the original sheet.

HEATING PLASTIC

Plastic sheets may be heated with 1 or more infrared lamps held about 18″ above the material. A thermometer should be used to gauge the temperature being created. An air oven can be constructed by building 1 or more electric heaters inside a box and hanging the plastic through a slit in the top of the box. A fan placed inside will circulate the heat.

Illustration 8-16A shows an electric heater used without a surrounding box. Electric heating elements can be purchased in large drugstores or hardware stores. 2 or more elements providing the necessary area of heat should be hooked up in series. An electric kitchen oven may also be used if it is equipped with a heat control. Infrared radiant ovens can be made hot enough to soften plastic up to $\frac{1}{4}''$ thickness.

Whatever type of heater is used, it is most important that it heat the plastic uniformly. Allow the heater to warm up before placing the plastic under it. Experiment with a scrap of the plastic to determine how long a heating period is necessary. If the plastic is too rigid to form or if it tears on the mold, it has not been heated enough. If the formed plastic shape cools with a rough or bubbly surface, it has been overheated.

Since plastic, especially thin material, cools rapidly, it must be worked upon quickly after removal from the heater. If the work does not progress quickly enough, it may be necessary to heat the mold also. First, test any material covering the mold to make sure that it will withstand this heating.

To avoid leaving fingerprints on heated plastic, handle it with clean, soft, cotton gloves. Double-

8-15

PRESSURE-FORMED ACRYLIC.

PROJECT: Eric Boissonnas House, Cape Benat, France.
DESIGNED BY: Philip Johnson Associates.
MODELBUILDER: Joseph Santeramo of the architect's captive model shop.
PHOTOGRAPHER: Louis Checkman.
SCALE: 1/8″ = 1′.
This presentation model was built entirely from acrylic. The curved roof was formed between male and female plaster molds from heated acrylic. The columns were fluted on a small routing machine. People: aluminum foil; bushes; steel wool.
The photograph was taken with a 4″ × 5″ Sinar view camera, 90 mm Angulon lens and Super Panchro Press "B" film. 2 spotlights were used to illuminate the spray painted backdrop. 1 750-watt flood illuminated the model. 2 additional small floodlights were used to illuminate the ceilings.
CONSTRUCTION TIME: about 80 hours.

THE SHEET FORMING OF PLASTIC

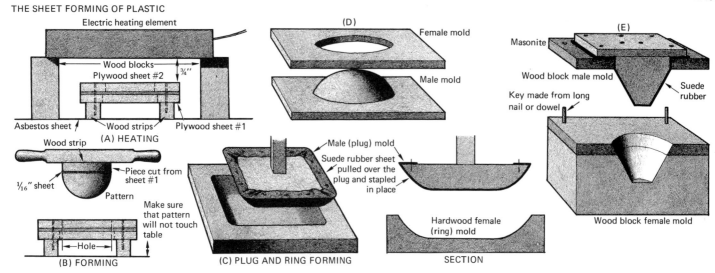

(A) HEATING

(B) FORMING

(C) PLUG AND RING FORMING

(D)

SECTION

(E)

thickness (for heat insulation) cotton gloves can be bought in many novelty or hardware stores.

Hot plastic may be cut to shape with shears.

Once formed, plastic must be allowed to cool evenly or internal strains will develop that can cause crazing or splitting. A fan may be used to hasten cooling, but should not blow directly on the plastic.

FORMING BETWEEN 2 MOLDS

Sheet plastic may be formed between 2 closely fitting molds (8-16C & E). The male mold should be made from plaster or wood, then the female mold constructed. To allow for the thickness of the plastic, cover the male mold with a sheet of self-adhesive or regular pattern maker's wax, the thickness of which equals the plastic. If using pattern maker's wax, lacquer the male mold and, while the lacquer is still wet, apply the wax. To cover complicated surfaces, make the wax pliable by softening it for a few minutes in hot water. Cast the female mold in plaster. The molds must be brought into contact with the plastic at a steady speed. If forming is attempted too quickly, the material will tear ; if too slowly, the plastic will cool before it is shaped. An example of the results obtainable from this technique can be seen in 8-15.

FORMING ON 1 MOLD

There are several ways to avoid making 2 molds. The heated plastic may be drawn down manually onto a male mold, or the mold may be pressed into plastic held in a frame. Both processes draw the plastic out to roughly half its original thickness. The procedure for forming a shape by pressing the mold into the plastic is :

1—Make a male mold out of balsa or hardwood. (8-16A).

2—Out of $\frac{3}{8}$", or thicker, plywood cut out 2 sheets the size of the base of the object with a 1 to 2" addition in all directions. Trace the outline of the base of the object onto these sheets.

3—On the first sheet, measure a distance from the outline (traced in step 2) equal to the thickness of the plastic. Draw a new outline that represents the base of the object plus the thickness of the plastic, and then cut the plywood according to this line.

4—On the second sheet of plywood, measure a small distance from the outline (traced in step 2). Draw a new outline that represents the base of the object plus this small dimension, and then cut the plywood along this line.

5—Set the 2 plywood sheets one above the other and drill 2 or 4 (if the sheets are large) dowel holes through the sheets. Cement dowels into the first sheet and, when the cement has dried, place the second sheet on the dowels, testing the fit and alignment of the system.

6—Cement the piece of wood cut from the second plywood sheet to the base of the male mold. Trim the plywood piece flush with the sides of the mold.

7—Cement a strip of pine to the underside of the mold assembly. The strip should be of sufficient strength to withstand the pressure of the plastic forming operation ; it should be sufficiently long to provide a good handgrip.

8—Heat and form the plastic (8-16B). The plastic is ready to form when it starts to sag in the heating frame. This will require approximately 2 seconds of heat for every 1/1000" thickness of plastic. If the plastic seems hot enough but re-

quires great pressure to form the hole, the first plywood sheet may not be large enough.

If the mold has a complex pattern with several facets, drill small venting holes through each facet up, through and out of the plywood mold backing.

See illustration 8-16D for another setup that requires only 1 mold. It is not as reliable as the assembly used in illustration 8-16A & B but it is much easier to make.

To form shapes by manually drawing the plastic down onto a male mold, the following procedure should be observed : (1) Heat the plastic. (2) With the aid of an assistant (if necessary), grip all 4 corners of the plastic and stretch it over the mold. Hold it in place until the material cools. An alternate technique is to use a soft cloth or thin metal sheet to press the plastic against the pattern. (3) Trim the edges with a hack saw and file smooth.

VACUUM FORMING

Vacuum forming is a molding system that uses air pressure to force plastic sheet against a mold or to blow it through a frame. The latter technique limits the variety of shapes (hemispheres, etc.) and the preciseness of their dimensions. Vacuum suction can be obtained from an ordinary vacuum cleaner, an air compressor or a water-tap-activated aspirator. See 19-7 for a typical shape that may be vacuum formed.

Vacuum forming against a mold may be done in several ways : Snap-Back forming utilizes the tendency of plastic when heated to return to its original form. The steps in this technique are : (1) Blow the sheet into a dome. (2) Introduce a male mold under the blown plastic. (3) Reheat the plastic, and it will try to drop back to its original

VACUUM FORMING PLASTIC

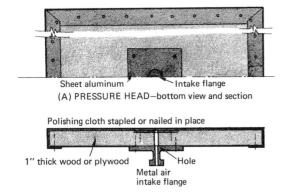

(A) PRESSURE HEAD—bottom view and section

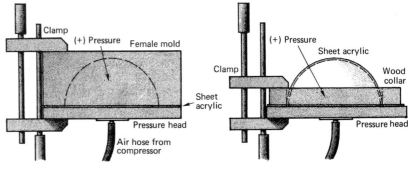

(B) A DOME FORMED IN A MOLD-SIDE VIEW

(C) A FREE BLOWN DOME-SIDE VIEW

sheet form. It will press against the mold assuming its shape.

A pressure chamber can be constructed that can accomplish various techniques of vacuum forming. Make the pressure head (8-17A) at least 4″ wider in both dimensions than the size of the largest object to be formed. Molds are clamped securely at all corners of the head and along all the sides (8-17B, C & D). Use a sufficient number of clamps to prevent a pressure leak. This may require as many as 4 large wood clamps (or twice as many C-clamps) if your pressure head measures about 1 × 1 foot. To form the object: (1) Heat the plastic and quickly insert it between the pressure head and the female mold. The plastic must be evenly heated or it will blow into an uneven shape. (2) Start the compressor. As air is forced behind the plastic, it will be blown against the mold. (3) When the form is fully blown, idle the compressor so that the air pressure behind the plastic is kept constant. (4) After a few minutes, open the compressor to full pressure for a minute or so. This will compensate for any shrinkage that the plastic may have undergone. (5) When the material has cooled, remove it from the mold, cut off the rim of excess material and finish its edges.

Another, and more versatile pressure chamber that may easily be fabricated is shown in 8-18. The first section (8-18C) shows a female mold (metal in this case) in place. Note that the vacuum hole cut into the mold is at the lowest point of the mold. The second section (8-18D) shows a process called Drape Forming that produces an object the wall thickness of which is more constant than that produced by the other system illustrated. Note that the mold has 4 air holes (2 show in the section), each one at a low point in the form. If the object being formed were to have many low points, a vacuum hole below each point would be required.

Another version of vacuum molding useful in the forming of shallow objects is Blowup Vacuum Reverse Forming. A sheet of hot plastic is draped over the pressure chamber and the compressor is turned on to create positive pressure, billowing the plastic up into a dome. A heated male mold is pressed into the hot plastic dome from its outside, and is held there until the plastic cools. Use auxiliary infrared lamps to heat the molds and

to keep the plastic soft when using pressure chambers.

Bonding Plastics

Plastic may be bonded to itself in 3 ways: (1) Resin from the plastic (mixed with a hardener) may be used as a cement. (2) Solvents that dissolve a thin layer of the plastic may be used. They weld the joint together when they evaporate. (3) "Body" cements (also used to bond plastics to other materials) bind objects together by flowing into the irregularities of each surface. Epoxy makes a good body cement for most plastics.

Thick filler cements, with the ability to fill cracks in joints as well as to bond, may be made by mixing chips of a plastic with its solvent. The mixture may then be applied like glue.

Since solvent will mar the finish of the plastic, it must be deposited only where the pieces will be joined together. Opaque plastic may be easily refinished, but transparent or translucent plastic will often have to be replaced, since refinishing clear material is extremely difficult.

Painting Plastics

Be careful to use paint the solvent of which will not craze or dissolve the plastic. If in doubt, experiment with a small piece of scrap.

ACRYLIC PLASTIC (PLEXIGLAS, LUCITE, ETC.)

Acrylic was initially used by modelmakers to represent transparent materials. In recent years there has been an almost universal trend among professional modelbuilders to construct most solid block and hollow built-up models entirely out of this type of plastic. This trend away from plywood and hardwood is easily explained when the magnificent and often unique properties of acrylic are studied. The favorable qualities of acrylic are:

1—It is strong and fairly lightweight.

2—It is almost as workable as wood and, with the correct power tools, it is less costly to fabricate.

3—It may be machined with standard metal or woodworking tools.

4—It may be readily machined to close tolerances (some modelmakers hold to a 0.001″ tolerance).

5—Since it has no grain, it does not require the laborious filing and finishing of wood.

6—It does not warp with changes in humidity.

7—An extremely fine finish can easily be achieved.

8—It may be formed into 3-dimensional shapes by the hot forming of sheet material or by injection-compression molding of its powder.

9—Clear acrylic has light-transmission characteristics comparable to those of optical glass.

10—It can be obtained in transparent or opaque stock.

11—The great versatility of acrylic allows it to be used in the making of complete models; in the modeling of columns, mullions, roofs, floors, walls and partitions; in glazing; in the carving of furniture, lighting fixtures, glassware and other furnishings; in the making of covers for display cases; in such heat- and pressure-formed objects as domes, vaults and skylights; and in many other applications.

The only unfavorable qualities of acrylic are that:

1—Proper machining requires a shop with extensive power tools.

2—Its soft surface is easily scratched.

3—At extremely low temperatures acrylic models become fragile. Many have shattered when handled roughly in shipping. To prevent this, hollow built-up models must be constructed on a wood core.

The Brand Names of Acrylic are Lucite (made by DuPont), Plexiglas (Rohm & Haas), Acrilan (American Viscose), Midlon (Plastex Corporation), Mothaflex (Plax Corporation).

SHEET ACRYLIC (Plexiglas)

This is available from such plastic supply houses as Commercial Plastics.

AVAILABLE SHEET ACRYLIC

Color	Shades in each thickness (inch)			
	0.060 (1/16)	0.125 (1/8)	0.187 (3/16)	0.250 (1/4)
Clear[1]	1	1	1	1
Black opaque[2]	1	1	1	1
White opaque[3]				
Fluorescent				
Red	1	1	1	1
Yellow	1	1	1	1
Translucent				
Blue	3	6	6	6
Coral		1	1	1
Green	3	5	5	5
Ivory	1	1	1	1
Orange	1	1	1	1
Peach		1	1	1
Red	5	6	6	6*
Turquoise	1	1	1	1
Violet	1	1	1	1
Yellow	2	4	4	5
Transparent				
Amber	1	1	1	1
Blue	2	2	2	2
Gray	2	2	2	2
Green	3	3	3	3
Red	1	1	1	1
Yellow	1	1	1	1

[1] Also available in thicknesses of 0.03″ (1/32″), 0.04″, 0.05″, 0.08″ (5/64″), 0.1″, 0.15″ (5/32″), 0.312″ (5/16″), 0.375″ (3/8″), 0.5–1.0″ (in 1/8″ increments), and 1.25–4.0″ (in 1/4″ increments).
[2] Also available in thicknesses of 0.375″ (3/8″) and 0.5–1.0″ (in 1/8″ increments).
[3] Available only in thickness of 0.375″ (3/8″).

BLOCKS

Clear acrylic blocks can be obtained in (inches): 5, 6, 7, 8, 9, 10, and 11 by 6 × 24, 12 × 24, 18 × 24, 12 × 12, 18 × 18 and 24 × 24. Special sizes are available on request.

8-18

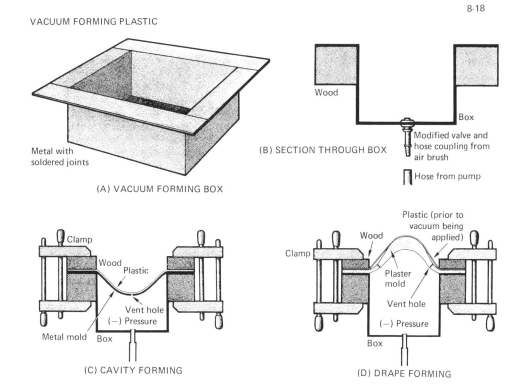

VACUUM FORMING PLASTIC

Metal with soldered joints

(A) VACUUM FORMING BOX

Wood

Box

Modified valve and hose coupling from air brush

Hose from pump

(B) SECTION THROUGH BOX

Clamp
Wood
Plastic
Vent hole
(−) Pressure
Metal mold
Box

(C) CAVITY FORMING

Plastic (prior to vacuum being applied)
Wood
Clamp
Plaster mold
Vent hole
(−) Pressure
Box

(D) DRAPE FORMING

RODS AND TUBES

Available acrylic round, half-round, and square rods and round tubes are listed on page 53.

SHEET MATERIAL

Care must be taken when purchasing sheet material because fabrication techniques can result in variations of thickness between 1 end of a sheet and the other. Manufacturers state that their sheet material may possibly be as far off from nominal as 30% (on 0.03" thick sheets) to 6% (on 4" sheets). The above tolerances are for class A commercial grade acrylic. Classes B and C commercial grade acrylic are even worse. Premium grade class A sheets run from 20% off (on 0.06" sheets) to 5% off (on 1" sheets). Classes B and C premium grade sheets are between premium and commercial grades in accuracy. Not all colors can be obtained in premium sheets.

Sheet acrylic comes with a protective paper cover that should be kept on the material as long as possible and certainly until all shaping and end finishing operations have been completed. The paper can facilitate the laying out of parts by pencil on the sheet, an operation difficult to do on the smooth surface of the uncovered plastic. If the paper is hard to remove, dissolve it with kerosene or hexane; do not use other solvents or cleaning fluids that might affect the surface of the acrylic. Protective paper that has become wet should be removed from the acrylic before it dries to prevent a residue from forming. Store exposed acrylic on a felt-covered board kept scrupulously clean of shavings, grit and other objects that might mar the finish of the plastic.

Acrylic, even with its protective paper, must be protected when held in a vise. Make pinewood inserts for the jaws of the vise. Uncovered acrylic must be held in a vise the jaws of which are covered with pinewood plates that have, in turn, been covered with illustration board.

Bending and Sheet Forming Acrylic

Acrylic is a thermoplastic substance the forming temperature of which (temperature at which the material becomes soft and pliable) is between 275° and 320°F. Heated acrylic may be bent or sheet formed over dies made of wood, plaster or other materials. If a mistake is made in heat forming, the plastic may be reheated and placed to cool on a flat surface. This will restore it to its original flat state. Straight bends may be made by heating the plastic over a strip heater (obtainable at many plastic distributors) that applies a line of heat. The plastic may then be bent along this line. Simple shallow shapes, such as ceiling vaults or hyperbolic paraboloids, may be formed by placing a heated plastic sheet over a form, pulling it down manually and holding it until the sheet has cooled. Deeply formed shapes, such as domes, are made by stretching the hot plastic over a form and clamping the sheet at its edges until it has cooled. Some shapes are best fabricated by 1 of the vacuum forming processes. Cold forming may be used only when the radius of curvature is over 180 times the thickness of the plastic sheet. Cold forming is accomplished by building the plastic into a frame that permanently holds it in the desired curvature.

In general, follow the instructions for the sheet forming of miscellaneous plastics. Remove the protective paper and heat the plastic to 250° to 300°F (Plexiglas I-A) or 340° to 360°F (Plexiglas II) for 15 minutes. Keep the plastic on a clean, flat, metal surface while it is being heat softened. The plastic should be heated to the upper limit of the heat ranges because it cools rapidly when removed from the oven. Overheating, though, should be avoided since it will mar the high gloss finish. Material under $\frac{1}{4}$" thick may be bent by hand over a male mold or by the other systems listed on page 61. Acrylic shrinks upon cooling.

If the model must be accurate, make the mold compensate for this. Shrinkage runs about $\frac{1}{16}$" per foot (in Plexiglas I-A) and $\frac{3}{32}$" per foot (in Plexiglas II). Use $\frac{1}{16}$" thick acrylic for molding objects that are the size of a fist. Experiment with molds (and vacuum equipment if using this system) to ascertain the proper thickness of material for each object.

Vacuum Forming Acrylic

Use a compressor capable of producing at least 50 pounds of pressure (a good paint spray compressor will do). See page 63 for drawings of various pressure chambers that may be constructed for vacuum forming and 10-5 for an example of what can be produced with this technique.

Scribing and Inlaying into Acrylic

Intricate scribing can be done in acrylic. Well-tooled modelmakers can cut such patterns as sidings, horizontal brick courses, etc. with a milling machine or by mounting several circular saw blades (separated by spacers) in circular or radial arm saws. Without this equipment, use the scribing techniques for cardboard. Regular acrylic will warp when scored on one side. To prevent this, anneal it (after it has been scored) or use "normalized" acrylic.

8-20

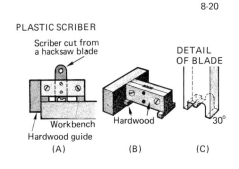

PLASTIC SCRIBER

Scriber cut from a hacksaw blade

DETAIL OF BLADE

Workbench
Hardwood guide
(A)

Hardwood
(B)

30°
(C)

Many types of details (such as mullions and projected brick courses) must be built up from the side of the model. Cut grooves into the acrylic and inlay strips of material in these grooves. Simply bonding a noninlayed strip in the underlay material will not produce a neat bonding line. The strips should usually be acrylic, but if material under $\frac{1}{16}$" in thickness must be used, it is advisable to work with metal.

Engraving may be done with a hand motor tool or with drill press mounting cutters.

Cutting Acrylic

To execute straight cuts by hand, in thin material, score halfway through the acrylic with several passes of a knife, put the scored line over the edge of the workbench and snap the material off along the line. To make curved cuts or straight cuts in thicker material, use a fret saw with a fine blade.

Power cutting presents some problems. Vibration shocks may be eliminated by clamping the acrylic to a plywood backing. Saw blades must be occasionally cleaned with acetone or trichloroethylene to remove plastic deposits. When cutting several sheets of thin material at once, insert an occasional sheet of oiled paper into the stack to aid in lubrication.

Take into account how much material will be lost because of the saw kerf and sanding. Be careful not to cut acrylic pieces too small, since

it is difficult to build up this material to the desired dimension once a mistake has been made. Pieces cut too small must be thrown away. Keep saw blades sharp and free from nicks and burrs. Cutting edges should scrape rather than cut, and have no rake to chip the plastic.

If the rate of feed and the speed of the blade is correct, coolants may not be needed. But when using single speed power tools, or cutting thick material or attempting a smooth cut, some provision must be made to lubricate the blade. A solution of detergent in water or a 10% solution of soluble oil in water may be used. Accurate machining should be attempted only under temperature conditions approximating those that will be encountered by the assembled model.

After a part is machined, it is advisable to anneal it if it will be subjected to stress. This reduces the internal stress that has built up during the cutting, and increases the dimensional stability of the part. It also prevents crazing when the part is cemented. See page 66 for annealing instructions.

Circular Sawing of Acrylic

Straight cuts may be made on a 3,400 rpm powered circular saw mounting an 8 to 10" blade that has alternately set, radially filed teeth. See the table on page 30 (under Plastic) for the number of teeth and the blade thicknesses to use on various sizes of acrylic. To find blade specifications to use on material of any thickness, interpolate the 2 surrounding material sizes given. Carbide tip blades work better than steel ones. To prevent overheating during sawing, lubricate thick materials with a 10% solution of soluble oil in water and keep it constantly running onto the blade. Lubricate the blade with oil, tallow or white soap when cutting all thicknesses of material to prevent the protective paper from sticking to, and dulling, the blade.

Band Sawing Acrylic

To make large radial cuts in acrylic sheets or to trim blocks, use a band saw. Blade speed should be between 3,000 and 4,500 feet per minute if a 3 to 6 tooth per inch blade is employed. If an 8 to 22 tooth blade is used, its speed should be 1,000 to 1,500 feet per minute.

Jig-sawing Acrylic

The short stroke of the jig-saw blade often does not allow the plastic chips a chance to clear the blade. They fall back into the cut, and are melted by the continuous friction, causing the plastic behind the blade to weld together. To prevent this, use a skip-tooth blade. See the table on page 30 for the type of blade to use on acrylic.

Drilling Acrylic

Standard twist drills, with slow spirals and wide polished flutes, may be used, but the best results are obtained with repointed standard twist drills. The factory-obtained drill should be reground to a cutting edge with a zero rake angle and an inclined point angle of 55° to 60°. This modification will cause the drill to scrape, rather than to cut, the plastic, allowing the drill to emerge from the acrylic without fracturing it. Larger holes can be cut with hole saws or fly cutters with zero rake angle.

Drill at moderate speeds and with light pressure to avoid fusing the acrylic. Lubricate with mineral oil. The correct combination of drill shape and speed will produce a continuous, equal width, spiral of waste material. When drilling, place a sheet of plywood back up material under the hole. When drilling holes that are not intended to go through the material, use a drill with a 90° point angle. If the hole is over 3 times as deep as it is wide (but is not meant to go through the material), use a drill with a 120° angle.

Transparent holes may be made by drilling a pilot hole, filling it with wax and then redrilling the hole to its final diameter.

Routing Acrylic

Acrylic may be routed at a speed of 10,000 to 22,000 rpm (when using $1\frac{1}{2}''$ diameter, 2- or 3-fluted cutters). If router speed is lower than 10,000 rpm, use a cutter with more flutes, or with a larger diameter, to arrive at the optimum surface speed. Cutters should have a positive rake angle of up to 15°.

Turning Acrylic on a Lathe

Work with up to $2\frac{1}{2}''$ diameters should be turned at about 700 to 800 rpm. Maintain a surface speed of 500' per minute on large work. Feed should be about 0.004 to 0.005" per revolution. Use water as a coolant.

Lathe tools should be held at or below the center line of the part being turned. Cutting tools should have a zero or slightly negative rake.

Internal Carving of Acrylic

The internal carving of acrylic is sometimes used in the preparation of modeled grills. Carve with a hand tool mounted on a metal cutter. Insert the cutter into the acrylic sheet and then, if required by the pattern, move it sideways, thereby, enlarging the hole into the desired shape. The resulting internal patterns may be painted, left clear or filled with plaster of Paris.

Laminating Acrylic

Lamination is sometimes required in the preparation of thick sheet formed shapes if a single thicker sheet is unable to be molded. A laminating cement is compounded out of 25% (by weight) Plexiglas VS-100 clear molding powder, or acrylic sawdust, and 75% ethylene dichloride cement. Dissolve the powder (or sawdust) in the cement until a syrup-like liquid forms; apply this to the surfaces being joined and clamp them evenly together until dry. Allow 1 to 2 days to elapse before attempting to sand the edges.

Filing, Sanding and Polishing Acrylic

To smooth acrylic edges, use a file or scraper to remove rough cut marks. Finish with several grades of silicon carbide or emery paper or fine steel wool. Start with wet grade 320 paper mounted on a hard felt or rubber block. Sand with a circular motion, then use, in progression, Nos. 360A, 400A, 500 and 600A paper; wash the acrylic between sandings. If a large surface must be sanded, use ashing compounds on a powered buffing wheel. Use wet pumice to remove any sandpaper scratches that may be left.

Polish by hand or with a powered wheel. For hand polishing use a piece of flannel that has been rubbed with buffing tallow; follow with applications of white emery compound to the flannel; rub; and finally wipe the plastic with a clean piece of flannel. Before polishing, peel the protective backing paper of the acrylic away from the edge to be polished. Wheel polishing is accomplished with a powered muslin wheel dressed with tallow and revolving at 1,800 to 2,000' per minute. The wheel should be continually moved to prevent melting the plastic. Final buffing is done with a clean, soft imitation chamois or flannel buff. The finished edge will be transparent. If a mat finish is desired, omit the buffing step. Powered belt and disc sanders may also be used for sanding. Start with Nos. 60 to 80 paper to remove cut marks, then follow with finer grades of paper. Polishing wax may be removed with alcohol.

Small acrylic parts and edges may be polished with a few drops of ethylene dichloride solvent. Depositing too much solvent will eat too deeply into the surface, and roughen it.

If unpainted acrylic becomes severely scratched, it must be repolished. Hand polishing will suffice if the surface is small, but if it is extensive, power polishing is more practical.

Bonding Acrylic

For strong, clear joints, bond acrylic by welding it with a solvent. Solvent cements that may be used are: Rohm and Haas Cement I-A for very strong joints in Plexiglas I-A; Cement II for very strong joints in Plexiglas II or in cementing Plexiglas I-A to II; Cement I-C for joints of somewhat less strength in Plexiglas I-A; and ethylene dichloride for moderately strong, quick-drying joints in Plexiglas I-A. The first 2 cements require the addition of benzol peroxide (a catalyst) and a stabilizer before use. Due to the ease with which it can be employed, its quick-drying properties and its strength, ethylene dichloride is the most convenient solvent to use. It sets in $\frac{1}{2}$ a minute, dries in 1 hour, and is obtainable at all Plexiglas dealers.

It is a good idea to keep solvent bottles in safety stands made from wood blocks, in which holes the diameter of the bottles are drilled. This can prevent disasters caused by spilled solvent.

A filler cement for acrylic can be made out of dichloride and acrylic chips. It takes 2 minutes to set and 2 hours to dry. High-strength fillers can be made with Rohm and Haas PS-18 (a cement that comes in 3 parts).

Lap and dado joints can be made in acrylic. The combination produces the strongest joints possible.

PREPARING THE JOINT

The acrylic to be joined should be smooth but not polished. Low-viscosity solvent cements cannot fill cracks, so the pieces of the joint must fit tightly together. Masking may be used to confine the solvent to the joint area; this is especially important in the dip application of solvent. Cellophane tape may be used provided it is burnished down so that the solvent has no opportunity to run under it. Plasticized gelatin solution may also be used. It is made from 7 parts (by weight) of water, $8\frac{1}{2}$ parts of dry hide glue and $7\frac{1}{2}$ parts of diethylene glycol or glycerin. Heat the mixture and coat the surfaces to be masked with a thick film. When dry, cut and strip the film from the areas that should be exposed to the solvent.

APPLYING THE SOLVENT (ethylene dichloride)

The solvent may be brushed onto small areas with a brush, pipe cleaner or eye dropper. Apply a light coat to each part, let it dry, apply another coat and then press the parts together. This produces a low-strength joint.

If, in the process of dissolving the material around the joint, the solvent runs over the good surface, try dip applying the solvent. Place a felt strip in a porcelain enamel tray containing a little solvent. After the felt has blotted the solvent, touch the plastic to the felt.

For the strongest bonding of joints, soak both surfaces to be joined directly in solvent for 2 to 3 minutes if ethylene dichloride is to be used (8-19A). The tray should be filled with just enough solvent to contact the lower edge of the object. Remove the object after 2 to 3 minutes (if objects are small, and will not be under stress, they may be soaked as little as $\frac{1}{2}$ to 1 minute), and allow the excess solvent to run off. Join the joint and clamp it together for 5 minutes. If extensive acrylic gluing is to be performed, have several sizes of trays so as to conserve solvent. See 8-19B for a cementing jig that will help make perfect 90° intersections. Position the 2 guides so that they exert a downward pressure on the joint. For joints not of maximum strength soak only 1 piece. Then lightly hold the joint together for about 30 seconds. This allows the solvent to attack the unsoaked piece. Finally, apply full clamping pressure. Pieces may be butt cemented on the jig shown in 8-19C. When truing a 90° corner, use a square the point of which is beveled so that it will not come in contact with the solvent line.

CLAMPING

Pressure should be applied evenly and with about a 10 pound per square inch force. Too much pressure may cause the softened material around the joint to balloon out. Use clamps—weights, rubberbands and spring clips—that will move the pieces together as the joint dries and shrinks. If the parts are allowed to shrink apart, the material around the joint will be drawn out, and slight concavities will form. Heat lamps will hasten the drying of the solvent. Parts may be unclamped and handled in a few minutes if they are small and subjected to little load. Allow up to 4 hours to go by before handling large and heavily loaded parts.

CEMENTING ACRYLIC AND OTHER PLASTICS

8-19

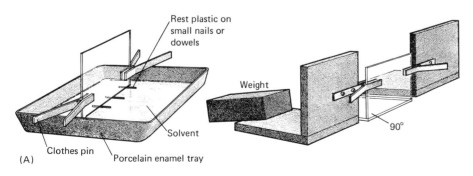

Rest plastic on small nails or dowels

(A) Clothes pin / Solvent / Porcelain enamel tray

Weight / 90°

(B) Wood jig

(C) Slot stops solvent from running onto wood and then spreading over back of plastic

CRAZING

Acrylic has the tendency to craze when it is exposed to solvent cements. If the piece is to be painted, crazing does not necessarily have to be prevented, but if the joint is to be left transparent, and it is in a prominent place on the model, crazing must be precluded by annealing. Besides preventing crazing, annealing strengthens cement joints and increases the dimensional stability of the plastic. Cemented Plexiglas I should be annealed for 24 hours at 122°F after machining and immediately before cementing. Plexiglas II should be annealed for 24 hours at 158°F. Higher temperatures (up to 230°F) reduce the annealing time. To prevent crazing from appearing after cementing, Plexiglas must again be annealed for the same amount of time. Annealing should be done in a forced circulation air oven. After removing the plastic, allow it to cool slowly.

BONDING VARIOUS MATERIALS TO ACRYLIC
Bonding Metal to Acrylic

Metal can be joined to acrylic if it is heated and fused to the plastic or if Rohm and Haas Acryloid B-7 is used.

Bonding Wood to Acrylic

Acrylic can be cemented to wood by using Rohm and Haas Acryloid B-7, ethylene dichloride, Rohm and Haas Acryloid PS-18, methylene chloride, vinyl trichloride, or Rohm and Haas Cement II.

Bonding Other Plastics to Acrylic

For bonding cellulose to acrylic, use Rohm and Haas Acryloid B-7. For bonding polystyrene to acrylic use Rohm and Haas Cement I-C.

Attaching Acrylic with Screws

Use screws with American standard coarse threads, not the ones with sharp V threads. Cut threads into the plastic with the standard tapping tools used on brass and copper. Cut threads with rounded grooves to prevent cracking.

When joining plastic to wood or metal, allow for the difference in lateral thermal expansion by elongating the holes in the part directly below the head of the screw. For any given temperature change, acrylic expands and contracts about 10 times as much as wood or metal. When attaching acrylic, do not tighten screws and bolts excessively or damage will occur to the threads of the plastic.

Painting Acrylic

Lacquer may cause machined or formed plastic to craze as a result of the solvent of the paint acting on the plastic. Use special acrylic-based lacquers, anneal the plastic, or use a protective primer (such as Logo Treatment CJ-1150) to prevent this.

Translucent lacquers are also obtainable. They should be spray painted on the reverse side of the plastic. Slow drying enamels may also be used, though they are less satisfactory than lacquers.

Sanding wood sealer or shellac may be used as a prime coat for many paints.

Acrylic may be colored with special dyes. A light transparent tint may be made by diluting the dye with water.

Cleaning Unpainted Acrylic

Acrylic must be freed from an accumulation of static electricity before it can be cleaned. Spray it with antistatic aerosol spray made by the Simco Company, or dab the surface with a facial tissue dipped in refined kerosene or hexane. Then remove the kerosene with dry tissues. Dust with a soft cloth or featherduster. If the plastic needs cleaning, use a soft cloth of chamois dipped in water or rubbing alcohol. The plastic may also be cleaned with a weak solution of any household detergent. Since this counteracts static electricity, the need for antistatic spray or kerosene is eliminated. All these static combatant treatments last for a few months. Dry the cleaned acrylic with a clean, damp chamois that does not build up a static electrical charge.

Waxing acrylic with commercial automobile paste wax will simplify future cleaning, fill in minor scratches, and help prevent new ones from forming. Rub the wax in with a dry, soft, cotton flannel cloth. Deeper scratches must be removed by repolishing the surface, either by hand or by power tool.

CELLULOSE ACETATE

Acetate is useful in representing glass and other transparent prototype sheet materials. It may also be used for sheet forming of fairly complex objects, such as domes, vaults and curved furniture. Brand names of acetate are Lumarith (made by the Celanese Corporation), Plasticele (DuPont), Tenite Acetate (Eastman Chemical Products).

Wet-media acetate is used for making windows with inked mullions. A similar material is micromat vinyl.

RODS AVAILABLE

Round rods are listed on page 56 .

Bending and Sheet Forming

Acetate may be softened in a solvent, and then molded over a smooth mold. Or it may be softened in a pan of hot water and drape formed over a male mold.

Cutting and Drilling

Follow the instructions given for the cutting and drilling of polystyrene.

Bonding Cellulose Acetate

A solvent will most strongly bond acetate to itself. These solvents include acetone (the fastest acting), methyl cellusolve, and methyl cellusolve acetate. All are obtainable at plastic supply stores.

Acetone sets in $\frac{1}{2}$ a minute and thoroughly dries in 15 minutes. Clear model dope may also be used as a solvent. Its setting and drying time is similar to that of acetone. Because of their toxicity, all solvents should be used with care. A filler cement for use on acetate-to-acetate joints may be made from acetone and acetate chips.

Cellulose cement can produce a fairly strong joint when it bonds acetate to other materials. Setting time for fairly quick drying cement is 1 minute and drying time is $\frac{1}{2}$ hour. Extremely strong joints may be made with the very expensive Eastman 910 that can be used between acetate and polystyrene, wood or metal.

Painting Acetate

Use a cellulose acetate-base lacquer. Apply only by spray.

POLYSTYRENE

Polystyrene is a material that has gained recent popularity in model construction. Its attributes are: low cost; the ease with which it can be cut, drilled, scribed and finished; its lack of grain and the facility with which it can be bonded and painted. It also is not affected by changes in temperature and humidity. It is considered by some to be a replacement for paper and cardboard in the construction of walls, floors and roofs; strips of it may be used for mullions or combined into structural shapes; it may be bent in one direction into vaults or curved walls; it can be vacuum draped or die formed into domes, complexly curved structures or curved furniture; complexly detailed moldings and mullions may be run from it; or it may be hot cast. Thus it is a material of almost unlimited potential.

Polystyrene comes in 2 types: (1) general purpose—crystal clear and rigid but brittle. General purpose polystyrene should not be cut into sections with widths under 0.01". It is often used for window glazing. This type of polystyrene starts to distort at temperatures above 160°F. Heat resistant polystyrene, though, is able to endure high tem-

AVAILABLE SHEET ACETATE

Key:
A = art supply stores
B = Bienfang Paper Company
Bo = Bourges
S = plastic supply houses such as Commercial Plastics Supply Corp.

Thickness (inch)	Transparent[1]	Colored	Wet media or prefixed[2]	Mat acetate[3]
0.00088	B			
0.0015	B			
0.003	B, S, A		B	A, B
0.005	B, S, A		B, Bo	A, B
0.0075	B, S, A	A[4]		A, B
0.01	B, S, A	A[5]		A, B
0.015	B, S, A	A[5]		A
0.02	B, S, A			A
0.025	S, A			
0.03	B, S, A			A
0.04	B, S, A			
0.05	B, S, A			
0.06	B, S, A			A
0.08	B, S, A			
0.1	S, A			
0.125	B, S, A			A
0.187	S, A			
0.25	S, A			

[1] Available in plastic supply houses in AA grade high-polish finish and in GG vacuum-forming grade; available in art supply stores in AA grade only.
[2] Will take all wet media including inks and watercolors without crawling, flaking or cracking.
[3] May be drawn on.
[4] Green, red, blue, and orange.
[5] White opaque.

peratures. (2) High-impact polystyrene has 3 to 5 times the impact strength of the general purpose variety. This allows it to be cut into much thinner sections. High-impact polystyrene comes in opaque semigloss colors only. It is more heat resistant than the general purpose material. Use it for walls and roofs.

Brand names for polystyrene are Ampacet (American Molding Powder and Chemical), Lustrex (Rohm & Haas), and Styron (Dow Chemical).

AVAILABLE SHEET POLYSTYRENE

Key:
W = Walthers (in 6 1/2" by 10" sheets)
K = Kemtron (in 6 1/2" by 10" sheets)
HR = Holgate & Reynolds (in 3 1/2" by 8" sheets)
S = plastic supply houses such as Commercial Plastics Supply Corp.

Thickness (inches)	General purpose (clear)	High impact (white opaque[1])
0.01		W, K, HR
0.015	W	W, K
0.02		W, K, HR, S
0.031 (1/32)	S	S
0.04		W, K, HR, S
0.063 (1/16)	S	W, K, HR, S
0.08		W, K, S
0.094 (3/32)	S	
0.10		W, K
0.125 (1/8)	S	S
0.188 (3/16)	S	
0.250 (1/4)	S	
0.313 (5/16)	S	
0.375 (3/8)	S	
0.438 (7/16)	S	
0.500 (1/2)	S	
0.563 (9/16)	S	
0.625 (5/8)	S	
0.750 (3/4)	S	
0.875 (7/8)	S	
1.0–2.0[2]	S	

[1] Some manufacturers, including Commercial Plastics Supply Corp., also make in white translucent.
[2] In 1/8" increments.

AVAILABLE POLYSTYRENE STRIPS

Arvid L. Anderson sells polystyrene strips that measure 2, 4, 6, and 8" in HO and $\frac{1}{4}$"=1' in scale. The HO material is cut from 0.01" sheet, the $\frac{1}{4}$" scale material from 0.015" sheet. The cost is $2 for 120 strips (in either HO or $\frac{1}{4}$" scale) plus 1—$6\frac{1}{2}\times10$" sheet of each of the following inch thicknesses: 0.010, 0.015, 0.020, 0.030, 0.040 and 0.060.

Bending Polystyrene

Cold bending may be employed to form styrene into objects gently bent in one direction. Bend the plastic on a form that gives it a slightly tighter bend than is desired so as to allow for spring back. When bonding bent shapes, use as little solvent as possible; too much applied at the site of the bend will cause splitting.

To make sharp bends, evenly heat the styrene with a soldering iron or strip heater, being careful not to form blisters. Then bend with hand pressure, using a wood block to impart the desired angles to the material. Polystyrene, a thermosetting plas-

tic, will return to its original shape if reheated. All sorts of shapes may be made out of thin sheet in the same way as they are made out of Bristol-board, except that, when made of styrene, shapes are less susceptible to warping, and do not require the finishing that paper demands.

Sheet Forming Polystyrene

Polystyrene may be heated until it becomes soft (at about 200°F), and then pressed by a vacuum against a metal die. The same instructions for the vacuum forming of acrylic can be followed, except that a pressure of only 20 to 25 pounds is required. There is a $16 toy vacuum forming set on the market called Vac-U-Form. It has a capacity to form shapes of up to $3\times3\frac{1}{2}$", thus it is useful in making such diverse objects as patterned spandrel panels, bucket chairs, lighting globes, etc. in most scales. The vacuum is created by a hand operated pump.

DIE FORMING

Carve a male pattern, cover it with the same thickness of patternmaker's sheet wax as the plastic sheet to be used. This will build up the correct separation between the 2 molds. Cast a female mold on this assembly. Place a sheet of heated plastic between the molds and bring them together.

DRAPE FORMING

Stretch a heated sheet of plastic over a male pattern. The sheet should be hand held or tacked to a frame and kept in place until the plastic cools.

Thin polystyrene shapes may tend to distort under their own weight. In certain instances, they may be stiffened by being filled with clay.

Casting Polystyrene

Small (up to 2×2") objects that are not too deep may be "cast" in carved metal or cast Epoxy female molds. Squeeze the heated styrene into the mold, use a metal back-up plate and a vise, or press, to hold it firmly in place until it has cooled. True casting of styrene is sometimes employed by professionals to make complexly shaped mullions; many of them farm out this type of work to plastic fabricators.

Scribing and Hand Routing Polystyrene

Polystyrene is one of the easiest of all materials to scribe. Textures as fine as the grain of wood may be imparted at scales as small as $\frac{1}{4}$"=1'. All sorts of wall, floor and roof textures may be scribed as well as trim patterns, bas-reliefs and cornices. Rivets and similar details may be embossed on thin material. Scribers can be made from nails, old drills or dental picks. File their points to conform with 8-20C.

Cutting Polystyrene

Cut thin (0.01") material with shears or a paper cutter. On heavier material, use a knife or a single-edge razor and a metal straightedge. Heavy sheets should be scored, then broken along the score line. This produces better results than trying to cut all the way through. Sawing may be done with a fine-toothed blade. Use a razor saw on all but the thickest material; there a hacksaw can be used. Power tool blades must be continually cooled with oil to prevent their fusing the plastic. If the cut is rough, scrape it smooth with a knife blade or scraper. Clean plastic deposits from blades with solvents. Styrene is quite abrasive, and will rapidly dull tools.

CIRCULAR SAWING

Use a hollow-ground combination-type blade. Set the blade so that its top emerges slightly above

the surface of the plastic. Feed the material at a rapid rate to prevent fusion by prolonged contact with the hot blade.

BAND SAWING

Use fine-toothed blades at low speeds only; skip-tooth blades should be used on heavy stock.

Drilling Polystyrene

Drilling should be done at a low tool speed. Frequently remove the drill from the hole and clear it of plastic fragments. Keep the drill well lubricated with water or oil.

Carving Polystyrene

Polystyrene may be carved with a knife, chisel or motor-powered burrs and shapers. Burrs and shapers should be frequently cleaned by immersion in gasoline.

Lathe Turning Polystyrene

Turn styrene at slow speeds. Employ tools without back rake; run them along the center line of the work. Improvised tools may be made from knives.

Laminating Polystyrene

Spread the solvent on one sheet with an eye dropper. Put the other ply in place and clamp both pieces together with weights evenly distributed over the entire surface. The speed at which the solvent will dry is determined by the width of the coated surface.

Filling and Filing Polystyrene

Surface irregularities may be filled with automobile metal filler (Duratite) or polystyrene body putty (obtainable in hobby stores). Both are putty-like substances that are easily worked. Use ketone to clean automobile filler from the applicator. Slightly roughen the surface of the styrene with No. 400 abrasive paper before applying fillers. When building up large areas, apply several coats, allowing each coat to dry before putting on the next. Final sanding can be done with No. 500 or 600 wet abrasive paper. To file, use a fairly coarse bastard-cut file. Clean it frequently on a file card.

Bonding Polystyrene

Polystyrene can be bonded to itself with one of several solvents. The three most common ones are: mek (methyl-ethyl-ketone, fastest drying); perchlorethylene toluene; or amyl benzene (slowest drying). These are sold in hobby stores in squeeze tubes; amyl benzene comes in bottles with brush applicators. Tubes do not work well because of the low viscosity of the solvent; the slightest squeeze will send the solvent cascading over the work. Assemble the parts, then apply the solvent; it will be drawn into the joint by capillary action. Take care that fingers, clamps or jigs are not in contact with the joint line or they will divert the solvent out of the joint and over the plastic. Apply just enough solvent to do the job; too much will extend the drying time and will warp thin stock; if the solvent partially eats through the stock, the dried area will shrink and form a concavity on the outside surface of the plastic. Properly executed joints fuse together rapidly, but full strength is not reached for some time. Use the gluing jigs illustrated in the section on acrylic plastics.

Since solvents are toxic, avoid prolonged skin contact and breathing their fumes. Revel, A.M.T., Monogram, Ambroid, Testors and Lepages all package polystyrene solvents, which they call polystyrene cement.

To bond polystyrene to metal, use Epoxy resin; Eastman 910 works well if both surfaces are first roughened. To bond polystyrene to paper, use contact cement. To bond it to wood, metal and other materials use high-viscosity styrene cement

clamping the joint until it dries. If styrene must be fastened with screws, use a 2-flute tap to cut the hole, lubricating it with light machine oil. Use only screws with coarse threads to minimize stripping. Wire parts can be fixed to styrene if the wire is held against the plastic and its other end is heated with a soldering iron. As the plastic starts to soften, press the wire into it.

Painting Polystyrene

In general, use the plastic paints available in hobby stores. These are made by Aero Gloss Pactra, Comet, A.M.T., and 410 M. Spray apply these paints, thinning them with ketone to make them stick more readily to the plastic.

Lacquer may be used on top of a prime coat (A.M.T. makes one). After the primer dries, lightly sand it down and rub it with a clean, soft cloth. "Dry" spray the lacquer since a wet spray or a brush application may detrimentally affect the plastic.

Enamel (such as Pactra Namel) may be used also. Spray it on, allowing $\frac{1}{2}$ hour drying time between coats. Dry rub with a rubbing compound (Aero Gloss, etc.) to remove dust, hair and other minor imperfections. The final coat may be waxed to a high-gloss finish with Pactra Aero Gloss wax.

Casein and oil-base paints may also be used. Water-base paints should be mixed with a small amount of acetone to make them adhere to the plastic.

Cleaning Polystyrene

Polystyrene may be cleaned with a 2% solution of a household detergent (liquid Joy, etc.) in water. This will also help eliminate some of the electric charge that attracts dust to this material.

FOAM PLASTIC

This superlight, easy-to-cut material has a few applications in modelmaking. Rough massing models may be quickly made from it, as may rough- and fine-ground contours. Foam may also be used in the carving of female patterns used in casting. This material comes in planks measuring up to 4 × 8' with thicknesses of $\frac{1}{2}$ to 17". Trade names are Dylite, Styrofoam, Pelaspan and Uni-Crest. Cost runs about 24¢ per board foot.

Cutting Foam Plastic

A band saw with a fine-tooth or scalloped edge blade may be used, though it leaves a rough finish. A special electric powered hot wire cutting machine leaves a semi-rough cut the surface air spaces of which are fused closed. A wire cutter can be made by stretching a 0.004" chromolux wire on a wood bow. The heat of the wire is governed with a rheostat. Accurate cuts are made with the aid of a plywood template.

Hand sawing may be performed with a coping or any fine-toothed saw. Foam plastics may be milled (on high-speed routers, drill presses or milling machines) and may be lathe turned (if a sharp thin tool is used with a slicing, not a cutting, action). Rough contours may be cut by using a soldering iron to melt the plastic. The resulting rough surface may be finished smooth with an application of plaster. Carving can be accomplished with an electric pin. Foam may be sanded on power sanders or by hand. Its surface can be made more durable with a coat of sprayed paint or an application of plaster or Epoxy; it may be surfaced with sheets of Celastic if the surface of the foam is protected from the solvent of the Celastic with Ben Walters softener.

Bonding Foam Plastics

Bond foam plastic to itself and to other materials with white or contact cement or with Fuse-N-Grip glue obtainable from the Illinois Bronze Powder and Paint Company. Common adhesives tend to dissolve the foam immediately or over a period of time. Many of the jointing details of woodworking

are usable on foam plastic construction. Planks may be dovetailed, rabbeted and joined by plugs.

OTHER PLASTICS

Almost every year, new plastics become popular in modeling. In addition to the ones mentioned in detail, the following plastics have been used to a small degree. Vinyl plastic has been used for vacuum forming (8-22 and 8-23). Its ability to conform to highly detailed small molds makes it valuable. It has also been used for the construction of walls, floors and other flat assemblies. Nylon is very easy to cut, machine, punch and cement. Perhaps its best characteristic is that, unlike acrylic, it may be cold punched.

FILLET AND OTHER CARVABLE MATERIAL

Often large fillets, too large to be constructed with a heavy application of filler cement, must be built. Since the fillet must usually be sanded into final shape, it is important that it be made with a material easier to sand than its surrounding construction. If it is not, a tendency to cut into the surrounding areas, while attempting to sand the fillet, will develop. Fillet material may also be used to fill cracks and holes in material.

FILLET MATERIAL FOR VARIOUS MATERIALS

Material	Fillet	Notes
Cardboard	Plastic balsa wood, gesso or barbola paste	Test the board first to see if it will be warped by the fillet material. Barbola paste and gesso may be colored with artist's drawing inks or watercolors.
Balsa and softwoods	Plastic balsa wood	Obtainable from Sig (Supermold), Aero Gloss, etc.
Harder woods	Plastic wood, or cement and fine sawdust (to fill very shallow cracks)	Thin plastic wood with acetone or lacquer thinner. Franklin Mendwood is nonshrinking plastic wood
Polystyrene	Automobile metal filler or polystyrene body putty	
Acrylic	Dichloride and acrylic chips or Rohm & Haas PS-18 (cement)	
Metal	Sculpt metal or solder	Franklin Mendwood also may be used.
Plaster	Plastic wood, French putty or crack filler	Crack filler is sold under various trade names. French putty is a mixture of oil paint or lacquer and plaster.
Miscellaneous	Hard wax	

8-21

FOAM PLASTIC AS A MODELBUILDING MATERIAL.

PROJECT: an entry to the Lawrence Hall of Science (University of California) competition.
DESIGNED BY: Skidmore, Owings and Merrill.
MODELBUILDER: Architectural Models, Inc. (a professional modelbuilder).
PHOTOGRAPHER: Dwain Faubion.
SCALE: 1/32" = 1'.
This model, made entirely from foam polyurethane, was milled by Architectural Models, Inc., on a patented machine of their design. They call this process Conturfoam. This presentation model was built to show the massing of the design and its relation to the site.
The photograph was taken with a Linhof camera, 350 mm Protar lens and Gevaert Panchromosa film.

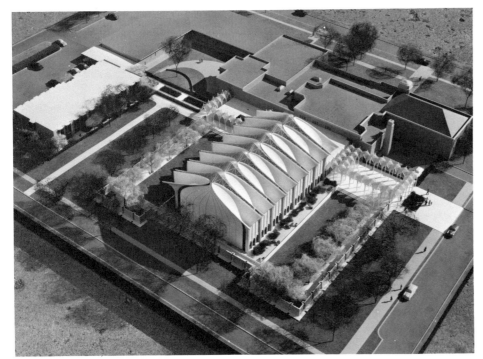

8-22/8-23

VINYL CONSTRUCTION.

PROJECT: North Shore Congregation Israel, Glencoe Illinois.
DESIGNED BY: Minoru Yamasaki and Associates.
MODELBUILDERS: members of the architect's staff.
PHOTOGRAPHER: Baltazar Korab.
SCALE: over-all model—1/8″ = 1′.
       interior model—3/8″ = 1′.
The over-all model: existing buildings were made from hardwood. Ceiling vaults, Sidewalk covering vaults. and Clear skylights of the new building were vacuum-formed from opaque and clear vinyl. Walls were made of acrylic with vinyl overlays to represent opaque areas. The wall around the site was also constructed of vinyl as were columns and pilasters. Trees: steel wool on wire armatures. Cars were purchased at a hobby store.
The interior model: columns and vaults were made of Fiberglas. Skylights and windows were constructed of acrylic with mullions of tape. Walls: vinyl. Pews: painted wood.
CONSTRUCTION TIME: over-all model—500 hours
           interior model—200 hours

Apply fillet material to a surface that has been cleaned and roughened. Some fillet materials may be applied to surfaces painted with only certain paints. Check the instructions of the product to find out on what paint it may be used.

Plastic Wood

Since some plastic woods shrink, put wood plugs in large holes and use plastic material around them

Plaster as a Fillet Material

Huge fillets that have been molded and carved from plaster are shown in 8-24. The basic shapes of the columns were cut from Masonite.

Gesso

Liquitex makes an acrylic emulsion-base gesso. Sand or other aggregates may be mixed in to create various textures. Gesso should not be used to build up thick shapes.

8-24

LARGE-SCALE MODELING OF CURVED SURFACES.

PROJECT: Lincoln Center Ballet Theater, New York City.
DESIGNED BY: Philip Johnson.
MODELBUILDER: Joseph Santeramo of the architect's captive model ship.
PHOTOGRAPHER: Louis Checkman.
SCALE: ½″ = 1′.
Columns, arches, floors and ceilings of this study model were made from cemented Masonite. Curved areas were built up from plaster. People: twisted tin foil.
The photograph was taken with a 5″ × 7″ view camera. 1 750-watt spot, illuminating the model from a low angle, achieved a late afternoon effect. 1 flood lamp was used to light the painted backdrop.

Liquitex Modeling Paste

This is an acrylic putty pigmented with finely ground marble. It may be used to build all sorts of shapes and, if Liquitex Gel medium is added, the objects can remain flexible permanently. Modeling paste takes a day or longer to dry and harden. Once dry, it can be carved, sanded and delicately tooled. The addition of gel improves the modeling characteristics of the paste but complicates sanding of the dried mix. The addition of gel will also prevent shrinkage. To prevent excessive shrinkage and cracking, the paste should be applied in a series of $\frac{1}{8}''$ thick layers. Modeling paste can be applied to any non-oily surface. It can be painted with oil, enamel, casein or tempera paints.

Epoxy Paste (Ren Shape)

This is a paste that can be carved with woodworking tools. It comes in cans and tubes and once mixed, has to be applied within 15 to 30 minutes. It can be machined at the end of about 45 minutes. It will adhere to many materials and is used by patternmakers to repair molds and construct fillets. Another Epoxy paste is Epoxical Pattern Putty made by U.S. Gypsum. It is mixed from 2 parts and lasts between 15 and 50 minutes (depending on whether the fast or slow set type is used). When dry, it can be machined like soft pine. It will adhere to most clean surfaces.

Epoxy Metal Compound

This is a very hard filler—like cold solder in appearance—and its preparation is similar to Epoxy cement. Large shapes made from Epoxy metal may be built on a wire armature. Deep fillets should be built up from several layers. Many Epoxy metals will adhere to wood, metal and plaster. While it is still wet, Epoxy metal can be worked with clay-modeling tools. Once hardened, it must be cut, or ground, with power tools; filed or sanded. Denatured alcohol or acetone should be used to clean Epoxy off tools before it hardens. Once dry, this material may be painted with enamels, lacquers or waterpaints; its natural metal finish may be burnished to a high luster.

Materials of this and similar types include: Duro Liquid Steel (an atomized steel powder in a vinyl resin), Duro Epoxy Steel, Duro Plastic Aluminum (aluminum powder in vinyl resin), Duro Plastic Chrome and Elmer's Epoxy Metal Compound.

Sculpt Stone

Sculpt stone is an easy-to-carve natural stone widely used by artists. Modelmakers can sometimes use it to carve large curvilinear shapes. The material can be cut, drilled, turned, filed, scraped, sanded and polished. It comes in many colors, some translucent. Its cost runs about 45¢ per pound. A relatively thin-walled object carved from sculpt stone is shown in 2-5.

Sculpt Metal

This is an air-hardening, putty-like aluminum compound that adheres to metal, wood and plaster. It may be used by modelbuilders to form curvilinear shapes. Worked like clay, thick masses should be built up of $\frac{1}{8}''$ layers. Permit each layer to start to dry before applying the next. After the entire object is completed, it must be allowed to dry from 6 hours (for $\frac{1}{4}''$ thick objects) to 2 to 3 days (for massive pieces). Infrared heat will speed hardening. Build up domes and similar objects on $\frac{1}{8}''$ metal screening. Hardened material may be cut, sawed, carved, filed, sanded, buffed or burnished to a high luster. Sculpt metal may be painted with lacquers, synthetic enamels and oil-base paints. This material costs about $5 for 3 pounds.

NONHARDENING PLASTICINE AND AIR-DRYING CLAY

There are many uses for these materials in modelmaking. Patterns for casting may be made from them as can rough massing models and even highly detailed plastic shapes. The complete versatility of clay and plasticine can be seen in 2-1, 8-25, 8-26 and 19-17.

Nonhardening plasticine is obtainable from artist supply stores in 9 colors and costs about $22.50 for 100 pounds. Other more expensive plasticines are sold under the trade names of Plasticum, Italian Plastilina and Venus Plastic Modeling Clay. Plasticine is made from kaolin, gypsum and oil. If it should dry out, it can be made pliable again with the addition of glycerin. Plasticine may be painted with oil paints, Krylon spray or acrylic lacquers, but not with water-base colors.

Clay can be obtained in a wide variety of firing temperatures. Della Robbia Miracle Clay may be fired in an ordinary kitchen oven at 250°F for $\frac{1}{2}$ to 1 hour. It costs $4 for $12\frac{1}{2}$ pounds. Other modeling clays require up to and over 2,000°F firing temperatures. Clay comes in 1, 2, 5 and 50 pound blocks; cost runs from 30¢ to $1 per pound. Firing transforms the chalky dry clay into a hard material. Other hard clays, called industrial clays (used by industrial designers in making full-size mock-ups of autos, etc.), are first heated or mechanically kneaded into plasticity; they are then modeled into rough shape. Precise detailing and final surface finishing are done after the clay has cooled and hardened. They harden sufficiently so as not to require firing. This type of clay may be machined and extruded to extremely close tolerances, and finished to a polished surface. Amaco Mock-up Clay (heat to 130° to 150°F before working) and Harbrix Industrial Plastine HBX 362 are examples of industrial modeling products. They are both sold by the American Art Clay Company, and cost 80¢ per pound.

Clay shapes may be build solid, or on armature wire or wood forms. Unsupported clay cannot be fabricated into thin shapes, but, if it is partially cut down to its final dimension while wet and allowed to dry, it may be carefully sanded and scraped to the desired dimension. Cover clay with a wet cloth to keep it from drying out between work sessions.

PLASTER

Plaster is a material that can be permanently avoided if desired. The fact that it is a wet material,

8-25

COMPLEXLY CURVED THIN WALLS.

PROJECT: a beach house.
DESIGN, MODEL AND PHOTOGRAPHS BY: Sanford Hohauser.
SCALE: $1/2'' = 1'$.
This design and presentation model was constructed in a rather unusual way. Since the exact final shape of the building was to be created only after the model had been studied and modified, it was decided not to make the model from mesh and plaster. A high firing temperature clay was used instead. The rough exterior shape of the building was modeled in the clay, which was studied and modified. The shape was then partially hollowed out; wood props prevented it from collapsing. When it became difficult to remove any more material without causing the external contour to sag, the clay was allowed to dry. Additional material was then removed with a scraper. When it became obvious that further thinning would cause the model to crumble, it was fired at around 2000°F. The resulting hard, porcelain-like material was then scraped and sanded to its final thin wall dimensions. The room divider was carved from balsa and filleted to the fired clay wall with plastic balsa. Rocks were cast by placing lumps of clay into a gunny sack, flexing the sack, allowing the clay to dry and, prior to its removal, breaking it into suitable sized pieces with a hammer.
The baseboard was 1/2" plywood on a 1" × 2" pine strip frame.
The photograph was taken with a 4" × 5" Press camera, 90 mm wide-angle Wollensak Raptar lens and Panatomic X film. The photograph of the sky was taken separately; to this the photo of the model was dry mounted and the resulting composite was photocopied.
CONSTRUCTION TIME: about 50 hours.

8-26

A DETAILED MODEL MADE FROM CLAY.

PROJECT: house for Mr. and Mrs. James H. P. Hamilton.
DESIGN, MODEL AND PHOTOGRAPH BY: Louis Sauer.
SCALE: 1/8″ = 1′.
This design and presentation model is a good example of the precision that can be achieved with clay. The material was cut and smoothed into place with a 4″ kitchen paring knife. Corners were cleaned up with a wire and clay modeling tool. Shingle texture was achieved with a wood clay modeling tool. The texture of the paving block was scribed.
The photograph was taken with an Exacta single lens reflex camera, Zeiss Biotar 58 mm lens and Tri-X film.

8-27

A MODEL MADE FROM PLASTER SLABS.

PROJECT: The Alcoa building.
DESIGNED BY: Harrison and Abramovitz.
MODELBUILDER: René Chamberlin.
SCALE: 1/16″ = 1′.
This facade texture study model was made from cast plaster slabs assembled on a wood frame.

requiring mixing and a certain amount of dexterity to apply, discourages people from using it. In most applications, it can be replaced with other materials. Thus, it is often totally excluded from the repertoire of modelmakers. In the past, plaster was a major modelbuilding material used almost as universally as wood was a generation ago or as acrylic today. Highly detailed baroque and renaissance buildings were modeled, in all their detail, exclusively from plaster. Slabs, with end dimensions as small as 1/100″, were cast on linen and other reinforcements. Roof tiles, friezes and other surfaces in relief were also cast. Illustration 8-27 shows a modern facade with a repetitive pattern that was cast entirely in plaster. Plaster may be used in the making of open molds if the object to be duplicated has no undercuts; it may be used for 2 or more pieces, in closed molds that cast certain types of undercuts. It is useful in the making of curved structures, such as domes and large fillets in casts and ground contours.

Plaster can be finished smoother than most types of clay. Its homogeneous texture makes it easier to carve than wood. Plaster comes in a large variety of hardnesses, strengths and workability characteristics.

Plasters to Use

Any plaster selected should reflect the use to which it will be put. In general, soft plasters (those with low strength) are easiest to carve, although finer detail may be cut into slightly harder material. Plasters used for wet modeling or running of shapes should have a long period of plasticity. All plasters will cast into intricate shapes, so, for casting, one should select a plaster for its strength or expansion qualities. For carving, running or extruding, Bestwall Sunflower molding plaster is often used.

Gypsum plaster can be divided into the following types: plaster of Paris, fast setting, soft and brittle; molding plaster, a finely ground grade of plaster of Paris, is used for fine molding work; Gypsum wall plaster and patching plaster are both crude grades of plaster of Paris, and have retarder added. Wood-fiber plaster is comparable to gypsum wall plaster with wood fibers added to reduce cracking. Keene's Cement and Hydrocal are dense and finely ground; they harden into alabaster, and do not expand upon setting.

Mixing Plaster

Mix plaster in a flexible bowl. When cleaning, knead it so that hardened plaster residue pops loose. Or use a Pyrex bowl that will not cake the plaster, and is readily cleaned. Slowly pour the powdered plaster into a bowl filled with water (never the reverse). Stir with a rubber cake-mixing spatula until the mixture assumes the consistency of thick cream, and is completely free of lumps. Too thin a mixture will result in weak plaster; too thick a mixture is hard to pour, and may not fill all the extremities of a mold. If the plaster does not readily combine with the water, a wetting agent may be added. 2 or 3 drops of liquid household detergent or $\frac{1}{2}$ an ounce of Kodak Photo Flo per quart of water will do the job. Commercial plaster containing retarder has a wetting agent already mixed into it. Besides hastening mixing, wetting agents will reduce lumping and bubbles and help the plaster to bond with adjacent dry plaster. Violent stirring is to be avoided, since it will force air into the mixture. When the stirring is finished, do not add more plaster to the mix. Continuing to stir the plaster after it starts to harden will result in soft, powdery material.

To maintain a supply of plaster for an extended

CHARACTERISTICS OF BESTWALL PLASTERS[1]

Name	From first wetting to		Setting expansion (percent)	Compressive strength when dry (lbs. per sq. inch)
	Initial set (minutes)	Final set (minutes)		
Brakeway	40–50	50–60	0.09–0.11	250– 350
Sunflower Low Expansion	25–35	35–45	0.09–0.11	2100–2400
Sunflower	25–35	35–45	0.17–0.19	2100–2400
Pottery K-55	38–50	50–65	0.17–0.19	2100–2400
Densite K-20	30–40	40–50	1.00–1.20	2200–2700
Pottery K-60	38–50	50–65	0.08–0.12	2500–2900
Pottery K-58, K-59 & K-61	38–50	50–65	0.18–0.20	2500–2900
Pottery K-62	38–50	50–65	0.19–0.21	3300–3700
Densite K-32	35–45	45–60	0.05–0.065	4200–4800
Densite K-36	25–35	35–45	0.21–0.23	4300–4700
Densite K-25	30–40	40–50	0.04–0.05	4800–5800
Densite K-31	24–30	27–33	0.04–0.055	5000–5600
Densite K-17	20–30	30–40	0.06–0.07	5000–6000
Densite K-12	25–35	35–45	0.035–0.045	5600–6300
Densite K-33	25–35	35–45	0.035–0.050	5600–6300
Tooling Densite	25–35	35–45	0.045–0.060	5600–6300
Bestrock		30–45	0.12–0.14	6500–7500
Densite K-40	25–35	35–45	0.07–0.10	8000–10,000
Densite K-34	20–25	25–30	0.11–0.13	9500–11,500

[1] All Bestwall plasters are also available mixed with glass fibers.

CHARACTERISTICS OF U.S. GYPSUM PLASTERS[1]

Name	From first wetting to initial set (minutes)	Setting expansion (per cent)	Compressive strength when dry (lbs. per sq. inch)
High Expansion Hydrocal	25–35	2.08–3.04	1700
Industrial White Molding Plaster (plaster of Paris)	25–30	0.18	2000
Medium High Expansion Hydrocal	25–35	1.04–1.56	2100
Pattern Shop Hydrocal	20–25	0.15	3200
Hydrocal B-11 (slow set)	45–55	0.04	3800
Hydrocal B-11	20–25	0.05	3800
Hydrocal A-11	20–25	0.05	4500
Industrial White Hydrocal	20–30	0.3	5500
Ultracal 30	25–35	0.03	7300
Ultracal 60	75–90	0.02	7300
Hydro-Stone	20–25	0.2	11,000

[1] Some of these plasters may be purchased at local hobby craft or hardware stores.

plastering operation: (1) Fill a shallow pan with water, (2) Pour a mound of plaster into the center of the pan. The top of the mound should be well above the top of the water. (3) The water will be slowly drawn up into the mound by capillary action. Use plaster that has mixed itself to the correct consistency. In time the bottom of the mound will set. Despite this, the system will provide a supply of fresh plaster for a much longer period than if prepared in the standard way.

The exact proportion of water to plaster will vary with the type of plaster used and the use to which the mix will be put. For example, 100 parts (by weight) of Pattern Shop Hydrocal should be mixed with 55 parts of water for a "normal" mix. If a plaster is wanted that can be used for smooth finishing coats, the mix should contain 10% more water. For a stiff plaster to be used as the first coat in bulk applications, use a mix with 10% less water. As layers of normally mixed plaster are added, the bulk coat will absorb some of the water from the subsequent coats, creating a stronger interlayer bond.

If mixing by eye rather than by exact weight, mix the plaster to the ideal thick cream consistency; then, if making a thin mix, add 10% more water. If making a thick plaster, add 10% more dry plaster.

Plaster may be applied by pouring, troweling or even by spraying. The latter requires a special spray gun (which may also be used to spray mold-making rubber and plastic resins) that eliminates the possibility of pinholes and air bubbles forming. Vibrating the plaster as it is being poured will also lessen the possibility of pinholes. Remove hardened plaster from tools by soaking them until the plaster dissolves.

Drying Plaster

Most types of plaster take about $\frac{1}{2}$ hour from wetting time to initial set. It generally takes another 10 minutes to reach final set. About an hour after setting, it achieves about 45% of its final strength. Drying parts must be supported for some time because their own weight may warp them. Slabs should be placed on a level surface, and other shapes propped up as well as possible.

Accelerators for Plaster

If it is desired that the plaster set faster, it may be stirred faster or longer, mixed with warm water (160° to 180°F) or used with an accelerator. Potassium sulfate, or pulverized set plaster, added to the mixing water may be used as an accelerator. An accelerator can also be made by mixing a

pound of plaster with a gallon of water and by continuing to mix it through its set ($\frac{1}{2}$ hour). This will prevent it from hardening. 1 cup of this mix added during the mixing of 50 pounds of plaster will accelerate set from 5 to 10 minutes. Accelerators used in excessive amounts can cause efflorescence. If plaster seems to set slower than usual, it may be because it is getting old.

Retarders for Plaster

To slow the setting action of the plaster, mix size, vinegar, or cream of tartar (obtainable at paint supply stores) into the powdered plaster. Cold water (50° to 60°F) added to the mixing water will also extend the setting time.

Hardeners for Plaster

To create a harder plaster, immerse the cured object into a strong solution of borax, and gradually heat it. This treatment will result in plaster that will be hard enough to polish. Commercially packaged hardeners are sold by Jay Hawk, Mold-craft, Rubbertex and other suppliers of molding products. Bone emulsion may also be used.

Plaster Reinforcement

Plaster may be reinforced by placing a layer of plaster-impregnated scrim (an open canvas mesh) over a layer of poured plaster. A final thin layer of plaster is then poured onto the scrim. Another way to reinforce is to mix sisal or hemp fiber into the wet material before it is placed. Make fiber by cutting hemp rope into short lengths. Then twist the fiber apart. Edges of thin slabs may be reinforced with brass or aluminum rods (steel or iron ones are not used because they may rust). If these rods are projected from the slab, they may be used to anchor the finished slab in place against adjacent material.

MESH

Reinforcing mesh, tied inside of molds with thread, may also be used. Run the thread out of the mold and tie it to the workbench. Complexly curved thin-walled shapes may be built up on a wire armature covered with galvanized screen mesh, copper mesh, buckram or similar reinforcement materials. A low-expansion plaster (0.005" per ' or less) should be used with mesh reinforcement. For constructing large curved surfaces, such as topographical contours, $\frac{3}{4}$" lace wire may be used. A refined version of chicken wire, very soft and malleable, it is easy to work with. It comes in 36" wide, 50' long rolls from Ben Walters Incorporated, and costs $15 per roll.

Defects in Plaster

Perhaps the rejection of plaster by some model-makers is due to the many types of defects that can occur, including:

PINHOLES, which occur if the plaster was not soaked long enough in the mix water, or the mixing was too vigorous. If the plaster has voids, it may be due to these factors or because it was too stiff when poured or because an air pocket was trapped during pouring.

HARD SPOTS, which occur if the plaster was not soaked long enough in the mix or the object was not dried properly.

EFFLORESCENCE occurs if the plaster was contaminated, or it was not dried properly (evaporation should be through the back of the object).

ROUGH FINISH occurs if the plaster mix was not creamy enough or if the plaster was of too coarse a grade.

DETERIORATING PLASTER occurs if the plaster was of a low quality, or contaminated. Possibly the mixing procedure was not carefully followed, the plaster was not soaked long enough in the mix water, or it was mixed too vigorously, or not dried properly.

Constructing Plaster Slabs

The easiest procedure to follow in building up a slab or strip of plaster is to: (1) Cut four pieces of stripwood that are as thick as the intended slab or strip. (2) Assemble the strips in a frame the inside dimensions and thickness of which corresponds with the dimensions of the desired plaster shape. (3) Cut several canals from the inside to the outside surface of the wood frame. The excess plaster will flow through these apertures. (4) Lay a sheet of glass on the workbench. Put the wood frame on the glass. (5) Place a mound of mixed plaster in the center of the frame. Allow the plaster to thicken enough so that it will not run too freely when a second piece of glass is put in place. (6) Press a second sheet of glass down on the plaster hill. Squeeze down the glass until it comes in contact with the wood frame. (7) After the plaster has set, remove the top piece of glass and fill any voids.

Plaster Extrusions

Parts may be extruded from wet or dry plaster. Circular dish and cylindrical shapes may also be run in plaster. Complexly shaped assemblies may be built up with parts made from several types of extruding or running operations. Join the parts

8-28

RUNNING PLASTER

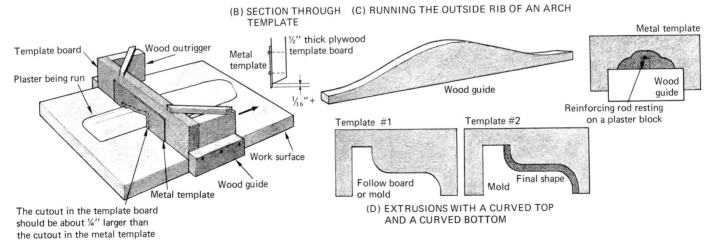

(B) SECTION THROUGH TEMPLATE   (C) RUNNING THE OUTSIDE RIB OF AN ARCH

Template board
Wood outrigger
Plaster being run
Metal template
½" thick plywood template board
Work surface
Wood guide
Metal template
Wood guide
$\frac{1}{16}$" +
Metal template
Wood guide
Reinforcing rod resting on a plaster block
Template #1
Follow board or mold
Template #2
Mold
Final shape

The cutout in the template board should be about ¼" larger than the cutout in the metal template

(A) RUNNING A LONG EXTRUSION

(D) EXTRUSIONS WITH A CURVED TOP AND A CURVED BOTTOM

with fresh plaster, using clay to mask and protect surfaces that have already been finished.

PLASTER EXTRUSIONS WITH DETAIL ON ONE SIDE

Plaster may be extruded into many shapes. For instance, a long strip may be run, the cross section of which resembles the end view of a small home with a sloping roof. Cut the strip into small blocks, each one representing a house for a model of a residential development. The same procedure may be followed with large moldings and cornices, odd shaped columns, etc. Thus, for certain shapes, plaster running can be an efficient substitute for plaster casting.

The extruding of plaster is basically the running of a metal template through a mound of wet, stiffish plaster. The template should be made of 16 gauge steel or 27 gauge half-hard brass or zinc, if the object to be run measures $6 \times 3''$ or larger. Use thinner metals on smaller extrusions. File the scraping surface of the template to a bevel (8-28B). After cutting the template with snips or a jeweler's saw mounting on a spiral blade, attach the template to the template board with nails. The cutout in the board should be about $\frac{1}{4}''$ larger than the cutout in the template. The running assembly should be made from hard stripwood or lumber of adequate thickness so as to be rack free (8-28A).

Work on a surface made of a fairly thick piece of wood. Protect it from absorbing water, and warping, by cementing aluminum foil to it or by giving it several coats of shellac. Anchor the wet plaster to the wood with small lumps of clay or half-driven brads. Grease the wood under the template board, outrigger and slipper board, but not the surface on which the plaster will rest. The plaster must be of a consistency that is thick enough to hold the shape and yet be moldable. Run the template over the plaster, keeping it in a straight course by pressing it firmly against the guideboard. Add more plaster to any voids that form on the extrusion; make additional runs only in 1 direction. Frequently remove the plaster which has collected on the template, or it will scuff and damage the extrusion.

If the plaster hardens before it can be precisely shaped, and the template starts to pit and tear it, apply another batch of plaster of a normal mix consistency. If the first layer of plaster has hardened into glaze, the second coat will not adhere unless the surface of the first layer is scraped off.

To finish an extrusion, pour a thin mix of plaster over the roughly shaped object and immediately run the template. After the extrusion has dried, give it another pass of the template.

PLASTER EXTRUSIONS WITH DETAIL ON 2 SIDES

In addition to running extrusions that have detail only on 1 side, objects may be run that are shaped on both sides. Accomplish this by running a plaster follow board or mold, which will impart the shape, to 1 side of the extrusion, and then run the final extrusion on top of the follow board (8-28D). After running the follow board, give it several coats of cut shellac to seal it, and a coat of parting agent. Take the template used to run the follow board and retrim it to the dimensions of the top surface of the extrusion.

PLASTER EXTRUSIONS WITH FINISHED ENDS

Square or rectangular objects may be extruded, and their ends also run. The wet plaster is mounted on a baseboard that conforms in shape to the plan view of the object. The template or templates are then run from all sides of the baseboard.

PLASTER EXTRUSIONS WITH AN ARCH

To run an extrusion with an arched underside,

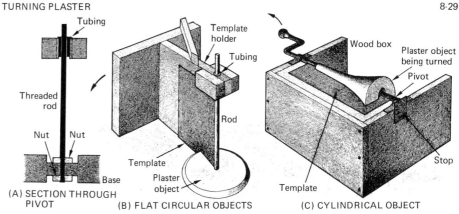

(A) SECTION THROUGH PIVOT   (B) FLAT CIRCULAR OBJECTS   (C) CYLINDRICAL OBJECT

make a wood guide ramp with the intended curve of the arch. Shellac the ramp and grease all the surfaces that the template must slide over.

RUNNING PLASTER PATTERNS WITH AN UNDULATING SURFACE

Setups for running patterns with repetitive lateral or vertical undulation may also be created.

TURNING CIRCULAR OBJECTS FROM PLASTER

Domes and other flat circular objects may be turned on the device shown in illustration 8-29A and B. Columns and other cylindrical objects may be turned on a homemade lathe (8-29C).

Dry Forming of Plaster

Plaster can be turned or run when dry as well as wet. The complete procedure for making a part such as a saucer dome is: (1) Cut out of cardboard a plan-view template of the dome. (2) Cement it to the side of a block of plaster thicker and larger than the desired object. (3) Cut the plaster block to the desired plan shape. (4) Make a running template out of metal, sharpen its cutting surface and attach it to a back-up sheet of wood. (5) Run the curve holding the template at a 90° angle to the edge of the disc. If the angle is not held throughout the scraping, the section run will not be even.

Plaster may also be dry turned on a lathe. Wood-turning tools, files and scraping templates may be used. A drill press mounted homemade scraper may also be used to rout various shapes into plaster. Solder this scraping template in a slot cut into a brass or steel rod and hold the rod in the chuck of the drill.

Plaster Modeling Tools

Italian Rasps are used for filing hardened plaster. They come in beavertail and knife shapes that cost about $2 for $7\frac{1}{2}''$ long tools and under $3 for 10" tools.

Hand Forged Steel Tools are for modeling and retouching. They come in chisel, spear, hook, pointed and beavertail shapes, some with serrated edges. Cost ranges from slightly under $2 to over $2 for 7 and 9" tools. These tools and rasps may be obtained from Sculpture House.

Other Tools and Accessories for Plaster Working

To facilitate working with plaster, a ready supply of water is needed. Less extensive plaster work may be accomplished with bottled water, but the repeated use of plaster requires running water. Sinks should have a plaster trap or strainer to prevent plaster from stuffing the drain. Other

provisions needed for extensive plaster work are: a glass, marble or slate work surface; mixing bowl; mixing spoon; scoop (which can be made out of cardboard); trowels and putty knives (to clean up bowls and work surfaces and to apply small quantities of plaster); file cards; brushes (to apply separator and to dust off sawdust). Plaster will rust tools if it is not removed quickly, and the tool kept clean and well oiled. Plaster also quickly dulls cutting tools.

Sawing Plaster

Saw plaster immediately after it has cooled, but while it is still wet. If it has dried, soak it in water before sawing.

Scraping Plaster

Use either a sanding block, or saw-toothed or smooth edged steel scrapers to finish flat surfaces. Concave surfaces should be finished with an aluminum, or zinc, scraper.

Patching and Filling Plaster

The pores of plaster parts must be closed before the object can be cemented or have parting agent applied. This is accomplished by painting with 1 or more thin coats of cut flake-orange shellac diluted in grain alcohol. The mixture must be thin enough to sink into the surface of the material.

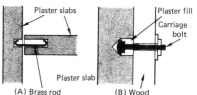

(A) Brass rod   (B) Wood

Joining Plaster Parts

Wet plaster pieces may be cemented together with cut shellac. (1) Mix 1 pound of flake-orange shellac with 1 gallon of grain alcohol. (2) Fill a dish with 1" of the mixture and set it on fire. (3) Stir while it burns and, when bubbles cover half of the surface of the liquid, snuff out the fire. (4) Let the mix cool and remove the surface skin. (5) Paint the burnt shellac on the plaster joint that has been primed with several coats of cut shellac. Press the joint together and let it dry 1 day or longer.

Dry plaster parts may be cemented with white glue, casein, cellulose or contact cements, or they may be welded by wetting the area around the joint and filleting the parts together with fresh plaster.

Plaster may be nailed by first drilling a pilot hole that is $\frac{1}{16}$" smaller than the diameter of the nail. Screws do not work as well as nails in plaster. Use nails which will not rust. The plaster is less likely to crack if the nails are driven into wet plaster. A line of nails will provide a stronger joint if they are driven in a staggered, not a straight, row.

Large plaster parts may be doweled together for added strength. Use brass or aluminum, not wood, dowels, since the moisture in plaster will make the latter swell. Nails with cutoff heads may also be used. To make the dowels invisible, sink them below the plaster surface and fill the ends of the holes with plaster.

To form a right angle intersection with plaster slabs, use the doweling technique or use brass reinforcement rods (8-30A). First, cut the edge of the slab, which is horizontal (in this case), so that there will be a $\frac{1}{16}$" crack between it and the vertical slab. Drill or gouge holes in the slabs into which the reinforcements will be inserted. Roughen the plaster around the joint. Assemble the parts and dampen the joint. Fill the crack and reinforcement holes with a wet mix of plaster. When dry, sand the joint smooth.

JOINING PLASTER TO WOOD

When joining wet plaster to wood, take into account the expansion properties of the materials. If the plaster is even slightly wet when it is joined to the wood, it will cause the wood to expand. When dry, the wood will shrink away from the plaster causing a crack to form. To prevent this, when pouring plaster on wood: (1) Shellac the wood so as partially to prevent it from absorbing moisture. (2) Drill holes into the wood and moisten it before pouring the plaster. The plaster will infiltrate the holes, and be less likely to separate from the wood .(3) Rubber cement a layer of aluminum foil to the wood and partially drive flathead nails into the wood before pouring on the plaster. The nails will help anchor the plaster, and the foil will tend to prevent the transfer of moisture from the poured plaster

To anchor half-dried plaster parts to wood, first drive nails, which have had gauze flaps placed under their heads, through the plaster and into the wood part. Roughen the plaster area under and around the flap and apply a thin layer of fresh plaster over the flap and nailhead.

Heavy plaster and wood parts may also be attached with bolts (8-30B). First drill a hole into

the plaster and set in the bolt. Fill the hole with wet plaster and attach the part to the wood.

JOINING PLASTER TO METAL

Drill holes in the metal, allowing the poured plaster to infiltrate, or insert screws or bolts in the metal and pour the plaster around the projecting shanks.

Painting Plaster

Color pigments (Alpha Color dry tempera or Free-Ex powder) may be added to the mixing water of the plaster before the plaster powder is introduced. These pigments create a dull finish. They are obtainable from craft hobby stores. See page 131 for the procedures employed with dry color powders.

Painting plaster with fluid dye is described on page 131.

Plaster is sometimes difficult to paint because of its porosity and tendency toward small surface cracks. The prime and sealer coat must cover these irregularities as well as bond together any loose surface particles. The prime coat should be shellac thinned with denatured alcohol (use 1:1 or 1:2 mix); wood sanding sealer; or the plaster can also be soaked in boiled linseed oil to which a little turpentine and dryer have been added. Sand the prime coat with Nos. 220 to 280 calcium carbide or garnet paper, using water as the sanding lubricant. Before priming, release agents must be removed with alcohol from plaster casts.

8-31/8-32

A MODEL OF A THIN WALL COMPLEXLY CURVED STRUCTURE.

PROJECT: a shell concrete house designed for the Universal Atlas Cement Company.
DESIGNED BY: John M. Johansen.
MODELBUILDER: Cappabianca Displays.
PHOTOGRAPHER: Robert Damora. Photo courtesy of the Universal Atlas Cement Division of the United States Steel Corporation.
SCALE: $1/2'' = 1'$.
Curved wall and roof surfaces were made of wire mesh on which several plys of maché were applied. When dry, a heavy coat of adhesive was added onto which marble dust was sifted. Chairs and sofa were bent from lead sheet. Upholstery was made of sponge rubber. Water: a sheet of texture glass; rocks: real. People were carved from plaster that was applied to wire armatures and painted with Japan colors. The trees: natural plants mounted on twigs. Ground cover: sand and soil. The photograph was taken with an $8'' \times 10''$ Deardorff view camera, Schneider Angulon wide-angle lens and type B pan film. Note the effect achieved by creating a hot spot of light on the water and the depth created in the close-up shot by illuminating the rear wall of the model.
CONSTRUCTION TIME: about 400 hours.

74

Paint plaster with tempera. A glossy finish may be obtained with a finish coat of white shellac, clear glaze, clear lacquer or varnish. Porelize will give plaster a china-like surface.

Storing Plaster

Store plaster powder in a dry, warm place. It will get lumpy if water gets into it.

SMALL SHAPES

It is useful and time saving for the modeler to know where he can obtain finished shapes of various types. Often he will require a large number of shapes when making furniture tops, skylights, etc.

Hemispheres in the form of plastic buttons are obtainable with $\frac{1}{4}$ to $\frac{3}{4}$" diameters. Wood beads with $\frac{1}{4}$ to $\frac{1}{2}$" diameters are obtainable at craft hobby stores. Compressed cork shapes with $\frac{1}{2}$ to $1\frac{1}{2}$" diameters are available from bead craft suppliers. $\frac{5}{16}$" to $1\frac{1}{2}$" clear plastic hemispheres can be procured from novelty companies that make parts for greeting cards. 2 to 18" diameter clear plastic hemispheres can be ordered from Plaxall, Incorporated.

Spheres as plastic beads come in $\frac{1}{16}$ to $\frac{1}{4}$" diameters, as wood beads in $\frac{1}{8}$ to $\frac{3}{4}$" diameters, as cork balls in $\frac{1}{2}$ to $1\frac{1}{2}$" diameters. Ball bearings, marbles and plastic balls range in sizes from $\frac{1}{32}$" up.

Oval Shapes can be had in the form of beads made from compressed cork that measure $\frac{1}{4}$ to $\frac{1}{2}$", and 1 to $1\frac{1}{4}$".

Cylinders as plastic and wood beads are available in $\frac{1}{4}$ to $\frac{1}{2}$" sizes. Expandable polystyrene foam cylinders are obtainable from Industrial Model Supplies in $\frac{3}{4}$ to $4\frac{5}{16}$" diameters.

Cubes as transparent plastic boxes of 1" and up or compressed cork cubes $\frac{3}{4}$ to $1\frac{1}{4}$" can be bought.

Flat Circular Discs as spangles are obtainable in $\frac{1}{16}$ to $1\frac{1}{2}$" diameters. Wood beads come in $\frac{1}{4}$ to $1\frac{1}{2}$" diameters. Wood beads come in $\frac{1}{4}$ to $\frac{1}{2}$" diameters. Flat discs and flat ovals can be had in brass from millinery ornament supply houses.

Flat Domes With Dished or Elliptical Heads are obtainable from Industrial Model Supplies. They are made of clear acrylic and come in $\frac{9}{16}$ to 8" diameters.

Squares and rectangles with a shallow 3-dimensionality can be procured in brass from millinery ornament supply houses.

Imprints in the form of parallel lines (12 to 64 to the inch), crosshatching (8 to 16 lines to the inch), squares (black or white, $\frac{1}{16}$ to $\frac{7}{32}$"), circles (black or white, $\frac{1}{16}$ to $\frac{3}{8}$"), triangles (black or white, $\frac{1}{16}$ to $\frac{5}{8}$") can be bought with pressure-sensitive adhesive backing from Artype.

Beads and buttons can be obtained at sewing supply stores or costume jewelry wholesale outlets; sometimes a large assortment can be found in large novelty stores. The largest assortment of plastic boxes and spheres is found at wholesalers. A list should be kept of other sources as they are encountered.

PHOTOPRINTING

It is possible to reproduce any pattern or image on wood, metal, plastics or fabric with the photoprinting technique, or to transfer a 1- or 2-color image to acetate with the Ozachrome technique. Both of these types of work must be sent out.

MAKING SCALE DRAWINGS OF EXISTING BUILDINGS AND INTERIORS

It may frequently be necessary to model existing buildings and rooms that are adjacent to those being designed. Sometimes the client or designer will be unable to supply drawings of these existing constructions. To measure them directly would be extremely time consuming and often (in the case of building facades) impossible. The simplest way to find the dimensions is through the use of photography. Photograph each wall and facade from its center line. If possible, elevate the camera so that it is halfway between the floor and the top of the wall or facade. Take the horizontal and vertical measurements of one easy-to-measure

detail at the center and at the edge of each picture. If a detail recurs throughout the wall or facade (such as a brick course, window, molding, etc.), so much the better. After developing and enlarging the photos, pencil a grid of lines a scale 1' apart on them. Use the known dimensions of the details measured to start the grid. Interpolate between the known objects to finish the grid. Because of perspective distortion, these grid lines will be closer together at the sides of the picture than at its center.

From these grid photographs, the approximate dimensions of the object can be told at a glance.

LAYING OUT SHAPES ON MODELING MATERIALS

The outline of objects that must be cut from flat modeling materials may be laid out in one of two ways. (1) Place the drawing of the part over the sheet modeling material and transfer its outline by a series of pin pricks, or by running a sign painter's pounce wheel (a wheel with many points radiating from it) over the outline. The points of the wheel will cut a series of holes through the drawing. These are covered with powdered charcoal, marking the sheet below. (2) Transfer the outline by means of a sheet of carbon paper.

An outline may be transferred to any metal that does not take carbon lines by spraying the material with a light coat of casein paint and by then using carbon paper on it. Or the metal may be coated with layout ink and the outline scribed into it.

If drawings are not to be saved, they may be cut and rubber cemented to the material. To reproduce the shape of a 2-dimensional part many dozens of times, cut the outline of the object into a linoleum block and, with carving or lino tools, remove the linoleum on the outside of the outline. Stamp the block on an ink pad and transfer the image to the material as often as needed.

Often it is easiest to assemble parts of a model directly on top of a drawing. To protect the drawing from cement, cover it with a sheet of wax paper or rub it with a block of paraffin until a thin layer is distributed on top.

9 CONSTRUCTION SYSTEMS

SOLID BLOCK CONSTRUCTION

Many objects, from as small as parts of furniture measuring a fraction of an inch to entire buildings, may be carved from solid blocks of wood or plastic. The elevations and plan of the object can be pasted or tacked off on the block as a guide for making the first 3 outlining cuts. These cuts are made on a band saw or, if the material is thinner than 2", on a bench-mounted jig saw.

After the elevations and plan have been recorded on the block: (1) Cut the outline of 1 elevation (9-1A). (2) Pin or lightly cement the 2 resulting pieces together, inserting a piece of Bristolboard between the 2. The thickness of the board should be equal to the kerf thickness of the saw. If pins are used to fasten the pieces, make sure they are not in line with the second cut. (3) Make the second cut. (4) Remove the surplus material from the first cut. (5) Make the third cut. (6) Using templates made from available sections as a guide, finish carving the object.

ACCURATE CUTTING WITH HAND TOOLS

Cut #3

Cut #1   Cut #2

(A)

Clamp holds 3 guide blocks to stock

Bolt guide blocks together

(B)   Stock

Saw, using this edge as a guide   Shim

9-1

Cut No. 1: Clamp 90° guides to both sides and bottom of block or put the block in a mitre box.
Cut No. 2: Clamp a 90° guide to end of block and a beveled guide to the side of the block or put the block in a mitre box.
Cut No. 3: Use the same arrangement as with No. 2.

Carving

Wood is carved to its rough outside shape with a knife, spokeshave, or plane; smoothed with a Stanley Surform plane or file; and finished with abrasive paper. An electric drill or small hand motor tool-mounted abrasive paper discs may be used in place of the hand tools. Acrylic objects should be hand filed down or cut away with an electric drill-mounted rotary rasp, Stanley Surform drum or Arco-Rotoformer. To prevent fusing of the plastic, constantly move the cutter and use oil as a lubricant. Acrylic objects may then be finished with files and abrasive paper.

Internal carving or hollowing of wood should be done with a spoon gouge or an electric drill-mounted rotary rasp or Arco Roto-former. Small objects may be hollowed out with an X-Acto gouge or a small hand motor tool mounted shaper. Acrylic objects can be hollowed with the above power tools.

Measure carving progress and the resulting wall thickness with calipers. If possible, hollowed out shapes with thin walls should be permanently braced internally. If this is not practical, temporarily brace them (a woodstrip or 2 is all that may be needed) while they are being painted. This will prevent them from being distorted by the drying paint. To prevent the object from distorting with age, seal and paint both its inside and outside with the same number of coats.

Objects should be held securely during carving. Small shapes can be temporarily glue-mounted on wood scrap to ensure a better manual or vise grip. Large objects should be clamped down to the workbench. One of several possible clamping devices is illustrated in 9-2A. It allows the clamping of many shapes of blocks to the workbench.

Solid Block Construction with Limited Tools

If a band saw or jig saw of sufficient power to make the initial 3 cuts in thick block material is lacking, objects may still be made by the block technique: (1) Make them out of soft balsa and cut them out with a fret saw. (2) Make them out of harder wood and laboriously cut them out with a fret saw, using a homemade hardwood guide to keep the blade cutting perpendicular to the surface of the wood. (3) Build them out of several plys of harder wood (see paragraph below on bread-and-butter construction). Cut each ply separately on a power jig saw or with a fret saw.

BREAD-AND-BUTTER CONSTRUCTION

Because of the unavailability or expensiveness of thick blocks or planks of wood or plastic, objects must often be built up out of thinner sheets. This type of lamination is known as bread-and-butter construction. For instance, if a 2' long model of a hanger shaped like a barrel vault, is being carved, considerable material can be saved by progressively laminating narrower plys from the base to the top of the vault. Plan the laminations on the drawing of the object and account for the thickness of the glue line. Cement the material together and securely clamp it until

dry. Since many objects are too large for the clamping devices already described in the book, a clamp of one's own may have to be devised (9-2B). Since the sides of a bread-and-butter lamination are rough, the elevations of the object can not be pinned or transferred on to it. Carve them instead by using templates of the elevations as guides.

PLANKED CONSTRUCTION

When constructing large complexly curved objects, (roofs, entire buildings, etc.) the wall or ceiling thickness of which will be visible, use the planked construction technique when unable to hollow out sufficiently a carved solid block (9-2C). First locate the positions of the formers that will support the planking. Formers should be located where they will not block window, or other intended, openings. If the actual building has internal trusses or partitions, make the formers correspond to their location. Cut formers out of wood sheet or make them of segments of attached pieces of stripwood. Provide formers with sufficient strength to hold the bent planking. Formers should be held in position on the workbench with pins while they are being cemented together. When all formers are in position and dry, flex the frame by hand to be sure that it is strong enough to hold the planking. If it seems weak, add additional formers or stringers where needed. Stringers should bed into notches cut into the formers. Then apply balsa or basswood planking of about 1/64 to $\frac{1}{8}$" thickness, depending on how tight a bend must be negotiated. Run the grain of the planks parallel to the curve that has the least curvature. Often the planks have to be cut into a pattern before they can be applied to the formers. In the dome in 9-2C, the planks must be in the form of a triangle so that they may close. It is not necessary to plot geometrically the shape of the planks with great accuracy; it is much simpler to take a small representative area of the work and temporarily cover it with 2 or 3 roughly cut oversize planks held in place with pins, and then trim them to exact shape. These planks may then be removed from the frame and used as cutting templates for the rest of the planking. When all the planks are cut, cement them onto the frame and pin them in place until they have set. See the instructions for wood bending on page 51 . Areas of extreme curvature should be carved out of solid blocks of wood. If possible, these blocks should be notched to take the planks

(9-2D). Set the blocks permanently into the planking only after all the planks have been cemented in place. A complexly curved object may have to be built up of several areas of different planking patterns.

Planked Construction Without Formers

If the object is to be completely hollow and have no formers, first build the frame as previously described. Then cover the frame with overlapping strips of wax paper. Cut the planks as suggested above, but bevel their edges so that they can be bevel-joined for additional strength. Cement the planks to one another and temporarily pin them to the formers. When the cement has dried, remove the planked skin (it should come free of the wax paper without too much trouble) and give it several coats of sanding sealer on both sides.

In many cases, it will be necessary to build the planked skin out of several plys of thin sheet to be able to form tight curves. Several plys will also be stronger if the joints of each layer are staggered so that no joint runs through all the plys. For even greater strength, run the grain of the second layer of planks at as near to a 90° angle to the grain of the first layer as is possible given the curvature of the object. Another way to strengthen this type of construction is to cover the outside or the inside of the object with gauze impregnated in cement. A gauze-covered surface may be smoothly finished with several coats of sanding sealer or plastic balsa wood filler, each followed by a light sanding.

PLASTER ON EGG CRATE CONSTRUCTION

Large shapes may be built up of plaster on a skeleton of formers. Practiced by a modelmaker with some experience, solid or nearly solid objects can be constructed in this technique faster than with the 3 all-wood construction systems. Steps in this construction technique are: (1) Using section drawings of the object as guides, cut enough cardboard or wood formers to create an egg crate pattern (12-2E). (2) Assemble them on a wood base. (3) Partly fill the area between the formers with crumpled paper or wood scrap. (4) Apply plaster slightly above the level of the tops of the formers. (5) Carve the hardened plaster to the accurate shape. (6) Fill the plaster with shellac and sand it to a satin finish.

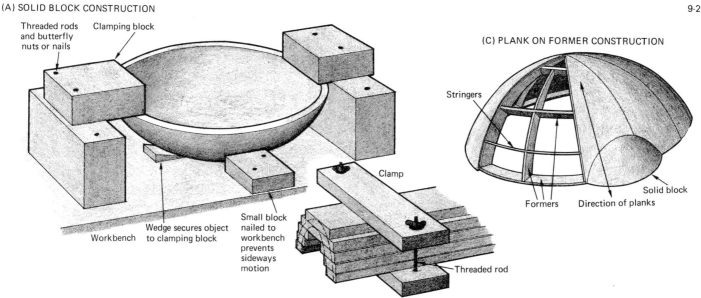

(A) SOLID BLOCK CONSTRUCTION

9-2

Threaded rods and butterfly nuts or nails
Clamping block
Wedge secures object to clamping block
Workbench
Clamp
Small block nailed to workbench prevents sideways motion
Threaded rod

(B) BREAD AND BUTTER CONSTRUCTION

(C) PLANK ON FORMER CONSTRUCTION
Stringers
Solid block
Formers
Direction of planks

FORMING COMPLEXLY CURVED OBJECTS WITH SHEET MATERIAL

Almost every sheet material mentioned in this book may be bent into objects curved in 1 or more planes. The following materials may be curved on a mold (male or female): Sculpt-o-Glas, Celastic, plaster-impregnated paper or cloth. Such plastic materials as sculpt metal, sculpt stone, clay and plasticine may be applied to buckram, copper mesh or galvanized metal wire held in shape on wood formers.

Through the use of 1 of the casting systems outlined in Chapter 10, it is possible simultaneously to form curved objects and to impart sharp details and textures to 1 or both of their surfaces.

Of the materials listed on the chart, all but wood, plywood and acrylic may have details impressed upon them during their forming. These details, however, will be less sharp than those derived through casting. See page 82 for a review of patternmaking or male moldmaking and see the entire chapter on molds for female moldmaking techniques.

FORMING OBJECTS OUT OF CELASTIC

Celastic is a relatively new product used in the display industry as a replacement for papier-mâché, buckram and paper soaked in plaster. This celloid-treated fabric is normally stiff. When soaked in a softener for 5 seconds, it becomes limp, and can be molded on a male or female mold. When it dries, it regains its rigidity, forming a strong, lightweight, thin-walled object. To mold,

9-3

MODEL OF FOLDED PLATE CONSTRUCTION MADE FROM PAPER.

PROJECT: a memorial.
DESIGNED BY: Sanford Hohauser and Joseph D'Amelio.
MODELBUILDER AND PHOTOGRAPHER: Sanford Hohauser.
SCALE: $1/4'' = 1'$.
The structure was made from 6 pieces of 3-ply Bristolboard that were carefully plotted, scribed and bent into shape. 3 pieces of board were placed in the top half of the shape and the other 3 formed the lower shell. The sections were assembled over a 5″ diameter, 3″ long section of cardboard tubing which provided stiffness for the structure and acted as an assembly jig. An alternate way to construct such a shape would be to cut the rough form of the structure in styrofoam. The Bristolboard plates could be pinned in place over the form which would then be pressed into final shape. The board sections could then be butt cemented together. In this case, the Bristolboard was shellacked on both inside and outside and the exterior spray painted with Krylon spray paint. The baseboard was formed in $1'' \times 2''$ pine. The shape of the pool was made of buckram wired to the frame. Waterproof plaster was applied to the buckram and, when it dried, was shellacked.
Because we desired to photograph the design against a background of water having several ripple patterns, we decided, against our better judgment, to use real water. Some difficulty was encountered in leakage, but the water patterns and the foreshortening of objects under the water were fairly effective and worth the experiment.
Name markers were acrylic blocks set on copper rods that had been cast into the plaster. Pool side paving was shellacked cardboard (it should have been acrylic).
The photograph was taken with a $4'' \times 5''$ view camera, 90 mm Wollensak Raptar wide-angle lens and Super XX film. This photograph and most of the others were taken by natural light. This seemed to complement the subtle reflections and ripples in the water better than any devised combination of artificial lights.
CONSTRUCTION TIME: about 40 hours.

SUITABILITY OF VARIOUS SHEET MATERIALS FOR COMPLEX CURVES

Material	Mold requirement	Strength of finished object	Opacity	Required for a smooth surface	Notes
Paper—Bristolboard for curves in 1 direction, gum strip for complex curves (page 38)	Male or female	Satisfactory	Opaque	Sealing and sanding	Simplest to make if tools are limited; walls can be of varying thickness
Wood (page 51)	Male or female	Satisfactory	Opaque	Sealing and sanding	Simple to make but curves cannot be too tight in second direction; walls can easily be carved into varying thickness
Plywood (page 52)	Male or female	Fairly high	Opaque	Sealing and sanding	Can only be curved in 1 direction
Metal (page 56)	Female	High	Opaque	Smooth hammering and buffing	Highest strength and thinnest wall; a female mold is needed; requires special skills to hammer out a good finish
Acrylic (page 63)	Male or female or both	Fairly high	Opaque, translucent, or transparent	None	Requires special tools, heater, and possibly a pressure chamber; a female mold may be needed; many integral colors can be obtained
Polystyrene (page 66)	Male or female or both	Satisfactory	Opaque	None	Requires special tools, like acrylic; a female mold may be needed
Sculpt-O-Glas (page 78)	Male or female	Satisfactory	Transparent	None	Fairly simple to use; walls can be of varying thickness
Celastic (page 77)	Male or female	Fairly high	Opaque	Sealing and sanding	Fairly simple to use; walls can be of varying thickness
Fiberglas (page 78)	Male or female	High	Opaque, translucent, or transparent	Grinding and sanding if material is made with one rough side; otherwise only sanding	More complicated to prepare than Sculpt-O-Glas or Celastic; color is integral; walls can be of varying thickness
Plaster-impregnated paper or cloth (page 70)	Male or female	Satisfactory	Opaque	Sealing and sanding	Fairly simple to use; walls can be of varying thickness

9-4

COMPLEXLY CURVED SURFACES LAMINATED IN FIBERGLAS.

PROJECT: the Monsanto plastic house.
DESIGNED BY: The M.I.T. School of Architecture and Planning and Hamilton, Goody and Clancy.
MODELBUILDER AND PHOTOGRAPHER: Marvin Goody.

SCALE: 3/4″ = 1′.

Walls, floor and roof were made in 16 sections from laminated Fiberglas. Top sections dowel into lower sections to allow for removal. Each section was made from 2 sheets of formed Fiberglas that, when dry, were cemented together to create the desired thickness of the structure. The Fiberglas was formed on wood molds. Partitions, built-ins, cabinets, beds and tables were made from hard-

wood and acrylic. Steps were made from bronze. Trees from natural twigs. Ground contours from laminated cardboard. The model originally was used for study, and then for presentation. When the full-size building was constructed, the curves of the sections were translated directly from the model and its molds to the form work of the building.

CONSTRUCTION TIME: about 500 hours.

first cover the pattern with the separator. Tear small swatches or strips of Celastic, dip these in solvent and completely cover the mold. Celastic may be repeatedly softened. Methyl ethyl ketone and acetone may also be used as its softener. If an object that has undercuts must be molded, follow the instructions; when the Celastic has dried, cut it in half to remove it from the mold. Reassemble the 2 halves and temporarily join them together with masking tape. Permanently tape up the underside of the cut with a strip of Celastic dipped in softener. The resulting seams may be smoothed over with Celastic patching compound. After the object has thoroughly dried, about $\frac{1}{2}$ hour, it may be painted.

Celastic is sold by Ben Walters, Inc. The fabric comes in light, medium, heavy and extra heavy weights, in 43 to 50″ width rolls. It costs from 20¢ to 35¢ per square foot. Ben Walters also supplies softener (called activator), separator and patching cement. Sig carries 9 × 8″ sheets of the material for 85¢ or $1, depending on its thickness. The company suggests using model airplane dope thinner as the softener.

FORMING OBJECTS OUT OF SCULPT-O-GLAS

Sculpt-O-Glas is another product sold by Ben Walters, Inc. It is a crystal clear plastic film that, after being treated with its solvent, can be used for laminating, embedding or sheet forming. Its solvent will bond it to acrylic, wood, plaster, etc. if these materials are first painted with Sculpt-O-Glas stain. The stain, which comes in 8 colors, can also be used to color the plastic.

To embed, place the objects on a thin sheet of acrylic. Dip a sheet of Sculpt-O-Glas in solvent for a second and place it over the acrylic. If the intention is to make a very thin assembly, embed the objects between 2 sheets of Sculpt-O-Glas. Work on a piece of glass and allow the work to dry for an hour before removing. To sheet form, spray the male or female mold with Sculpt-O-Glas separator. Apply the first layer of film by the dip method. Build additional layers as needed.

The plastic costs about 7¢ per square foot, and solvent needed to cover this area costs a similar amount.

FIBERGLAS AND CASTING RESINS

If a complexly curved thin wall object of maximum strength is desired, such as a large dome or shell structure, the decision may be to make it out of Fiberglas. This technique requires 4 materials: glass cloth, resin, catalyst and hardener. The resin (with its catalyst and hardener) may also be used alone to form strong transparent, translucent, opaque or colored casts, furniture, lamps, skylights, stained glass or screens. Illustrations 8-23, 9-4 and 9-5 show the types of objects that may be made with reinforced Fiberglas.

Cloth

Fiberglas cloth is composed of drawn filaments of glass. Various manufacturers sell several types of cloth and fiber in their line. U.S. Gypsum supplies the following:

Plain Weave has its thread alternately crossed, making it the least pliable but dimensionally the

most stable cloth. It comes in 0.013″ thickness (called Epoxical E-13), 0.022″ (E-22) and 0.055″ (E-55) thicknesses. Gypsum also supplies 0.013″ thick tape in $1\frac{1}{2}$, 3, 6, and 12″ widths.

Leno Weave has its threads locked together to prevent shifting.

Mock Leno Weave is what its name implies. It comes in 0.029″ thickness called Epoxical E-29.

Most cloth comes in 38 or $44\frac{1}{2}$″ widths. Cloth may have different types of surface finishes to improve adherence to the resin or its draping characteristics. Cloth with a silane finish should never be used with polyester resins.

Other companies make cloth that is as thin as 0.002″, as well as a thin cloth called surfacing mat, used where a high finish is required.

Milled fibers are used to make a putty-like mix to fill sharp corners of a mold.

Resins

Resins are available with several bases: Polyester resin is probably of greatest use to the modelmaker. The vaults in the model shown in 9-6 were cast from this resin. Since resins have great toxicity, it is important that the work area be properly ventilated and that prolonged contact between resins and skin are avoided. Never allow them to come in contact with eyes. Wash hands and tools with hot water and borax or household detergent. Wear protective gloves or use hand creams whenever possible. The different types of polyester resin are: (1) Artist resin, which is usually used with Fiberglas; it cures rapidly, is of medium viscosity, and becomes clear and rigid upon curing. (2) Flexible resin, which is for laminating objects with Fiberglas; it has medium-fast curing, a medium viscosity, and becomes clear and flexible upon curing.

Some form of catalyst is usually already mixed into the resin. Thus, only the addition of the hardener is required to produce a workable mix. Overmixing will result in a shortened pot life.

Apply resin by brush or squeegee. Setting time, running about 1 to 2 hours, is determined by the percent of hardener in the mix and by room temperature. It is usually good practice, no matter what type of resin is being used, to try for a lamination that is about half resin and half cloth.

After attaining its initial set, the object may be removed from the mold and allowed to cure fully at room temperature for several days. Curing time is affected by temperature and humidity. The higher the temperature, the faster the cure. Resin that comes in contact with the mold (or work surface) will harden, but the side that is exposed to the air may not. To insure hardening, wax may be added to the mix. Many brands of resin are manufactured that already include wax. If a surface is still tacky when it has cured, sand it down to solid material.

Resins have shelf lives ranging from a few months to about a year. Refrigerating them will increase this 2 or 3 times.

Dyes are made that may be mixed into the resin to impart an integral color. Filler mixed into the resin will turn the usually translucent Fiberglas opaque. Some companies make their coloring agents in the form of powders. These should be mixed into the resin before the hardener is applied.

Separators

THE FOLLOWING SEPARATORS MAY BE USED BETWEEN POLYESTER RESIN AND MOLDS, OR PATTERNS, MADE FROM:

Wood or Plaster : (first seal the pattern)
A separator may not be needed.
Separators are available from Crystal Craft and the Castolite Company.
Wax polish.
Moldcraft 3G oil spray.
One coat of Johnson's Glocoat followed by a coat of silicone mold release agent or Lunn Lease.

THE FOLLOWING SEPARATORS MAY BE USED BETWEEN POLYESTER RESIN MOLDS AND CASTS MADE FROM:

Polyester Resin :
Separators are available from Crystal Craft and the Castolite Company.

Low Melting Point Metal :
A separator may not be needed.
Oil or graphite.

Possible Pitfalls

If moisture gets into the hardener or resin, the plastic will be cloudy on hardening. Do not cast objects to thicknesses over $\frac{3}{4}''$; heat caused by the chemical action may ruin them. Delamination of a Fiberglas object is usually due to poor cloth wetting, air entrapment, interruption of the laminating process or use of only partially gelled resin.

A MODEL CONSTRUCTED FROM LAMINATED FIBERGLAS.
MODELING ONLY 1/2 OF A SYMMETRIC BUILDING SAVES TIME.

PROJECT: Assembly Hall for the University of Illinois.
DESIGNED BY: Harrison and Abramovitz. Consulting Engineers: Ammann and Whitney.
MODELBUILDER: Leon A. Rosenthal. Model with roof: Alexander and Jones.
SCALE: model with roof, 1/4″ = 1′; model without roof, 1/16″ = 1′.
Model with roof: segments of the dome were built of Fiberglas on an acrylic pattern that was made of 1/16 of the dome. First, a female Fiberglas mold was made and then the final, male mold was cast into it. Ramps, columns, windows and buttresses were made from acrylic. Mullions were drawn on. The model was built of only 1/2 the building; it was then placed against a mirror to be photographed. Model was used for presentation. *Model without roof:* seats and ramps were made from acrylic. People were cut from paper; cars made from wood, mullions from tape. Baseboard and contours were constructed of illustration board, filled and given 6 coats of lacquer. This model was used for design and presentation.
CONSTRUCTION TIME OF THE MODEL WITHOUT A ROOF: about 150 hours.

Applying a Fiberglas and Polyester Resin Lamination to a Mold or Pattern

1—Make the mold or pattern out of hard balsa, hardwood or plaster. Sand the mold to a satin finish using shellac to fill its grain.

2—Treat the mold with wax polish or with one of the separators previously listed.

Porosity is caused by the beating of resin during mixing, the use of porous molds or patterns, the use of chilled materials or the presence of moisture.

The side of the Fiberglas or resin that touches the mold will have a smooth finish provided the mold is extremely smooth. The other side will have to be power sanded for a good finish. Thus one may decide to mold a dome or other similar shape in a female mold to get the finished side on the outside.

LAMINATING A VARIABLE THICKNESS OBJECT FROM FIBERGLASS

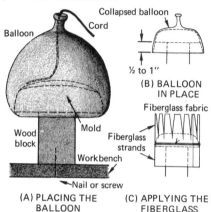

Fiberglass and resin laminations

Pattern

(A) SECTION

Mylar or release agent | Mylar | Metal rod

Pattern

Fiberglass and resin

(B) DETAIL

fitting rubber will form a smooth outer side to the Fiberglas and will press it firmly against the mold. (J) After the resin has hardened for about 3 hours, remove the balloon and work the Fiberglas off the mold. (K) Cut the excess fiber off the bottom of the object, file and sand it smooth.

Embedding Objects in a Fiberglas and Resin Lamination

Embedding may be used to make weak sheet materials rigid. It may also be used to construct models or screens, stained glass, fused glass murals and similar objects. A Fiberglas cloth that can be made transparent, such as Crystal Craft's Glassmat, should be used. Work on a flat surface that has been covered with glass, Mylar or Saran Wrap. The procedure is as follows: (1) Coat a sufficiently large area of the covered surface with a layer of Crystal Cast or other transparent resin. (2) Place a layer of Fiberglas on the resin. (3) Apply a second layer of resin, carefully working out all air bubbles from the lamination. (4) Position the object that is to be embedded, taking care that no air is trapped under it. (5) Lay down a second piece of Fiberglas on the object and soak it with more resin. (6) Place another sheet of Saran Wrap on top of the sandwich and squeegee out all trapped air. (7) While the panel is still tacky, trim its edges. (8) When it has dried, remove the pieces of Saran Wrap.

If flat objects are to be laminated (such as a stained glass photo transparency or delicate grill), or if the sandwich is not required to have 2 smooth sides, it will only be necessary to: (1) Place a layer of transparentizable Fiberglas on a sheet of Saran Wrap. (2) Fix the objects to be laminated. (3) Use 1 coat of transparent resin to hold them in place, and transparentize the mat.

3—Brush a coat of resin on the mold and allow it to gel.

4—Brush on a second coat of resin and, while it is still wet, place the first layer of glass cloth, coated with resin, on it and press down. To eliminate wrinkles on cloth that is curved in 2 directions, cut slits into the cloth. Make sure that no air bubbles are trapped and that no wrinkles are allowed to form. Avoid bubbles by wetting all materials—cloth, mat and any embeded material—with resin prior to placing them. Work out any trapped bubbles by stippling them with the resin applicating brush. If the object must be uniformly thick, the pieces of cloth making up 1 ply must be laid with butt joints. If greater strength is desired, and the object can have a varying thickness, use lap joints.

5—Apply strips of chopped strand mats along the edges of the object to strengthen them. In general, only 1 layer of glass cloth will be needed on objects up to 2' large, especially if edges and other potentially weak points are bolstered with strand mat.

6—When the resin has set, the object may be removed from the mold. Trim the edges of the Fiberglas into shape with shears.

7—If the object has been made on a female mold, examine its outside surface for air bubble holes and fill them with resin.

8—sandpaper the surface.

Note: Detail may be cast into the side of the object that faces the mold.

Illustration 9-7 shows a system that I have used to form Fiberglas objects the walls of which are not of constant thickness. To determine how much any part of the object must be built up, insert metal rods coated with release agent into the pattern, allowing them to protrude a distance equal to the desired thickness at any given point. Then build up the thinner portions of the object with additional plys of cloth or mat. After the resin starts to harden, the rods are retracted through the bottom of the mold. The same general system may be used with Celastic and plaster-impregnated cloth.

Laminating with Epoxy Resin and Fiberglas (description of Epoxy Resin can be found on page 87)

1—Apply a surface coat of resin to the mold with a paint brush. Do not brush it on—let it flow on freely. Dab it on those areas whose fine detail must be reproduced. The coat should be $\frac{1}{32}$ to $\frac{1}{16}$" thick. Allow it to become tacky.

2—Fill sharp corners and projections with a mix of the laminating resin and its hardener; then add glass fibers.

3—Apply the glass cloth plys. Either 3 or 4 layers of lightweight cloth or 1 layer of heavyweight cloth will be needed to make a $\frac{1}{16}$" thick lamination.

Forming Objects with 2 Smooth Sides Out of Laminations of Fiberglas and Resin

Forming Fiberglas objects with 2 smooth sides may be accomplished in 1 of 2 ways: (1) A female

CASTING FIBERGLASS OBJECTS WITH TWO SMOOTH SIDES

Balloon | Cord | Collapsed balloon

½ to 1"

(B) BALLOON IN PLACE

Wood block | Mold

Workbench

Fiberglass fabric

Fiberglass strands

Nail or screw

(A) PLACING THE BALLOON

(C) APPLYING THE FIBERGLASS

mold may be made and pressed down upon a lamination that has been placed on a male mold. The pressure created will also facilitate the forming of tighter curves. (2) Medium-size objects with 2 smooth sides may be formed if these steps are followed: (A) Make a smoothly finished male mold and cover it with release agent. (B) Screw the mold to the workbench with its smallest end facing up. (C) Cut enough thin Fiberglas cloth to go around the mold 2 or 3 times. Attach it to the mold as shown in 9-8C. Use strands of Fiberglas to tie the cloth in place. (D) Cut tabs in the top of the Fiberglas, trim them so that when they are folded over the mold they will cover the end without overlap. (E) Brush on a sufficient quantity of resin so that it soaks through all the layers of Fiberglas. (F) Partially inflate a toy balloon; turn it upside down over the mold. (G) Press it down on the mold as far as possible, then slowly let it deflate while continuing to push it down (9-8A). It is important that the balloon be of the correct size and that it be made of thick, high quality rubber. (H) By the time all the air has escaped, the balloon should be in the position shown in 9-8B. (I) Cut the neck off the balloon and turn the balloon inside out on the mold. Do not worry if the rubber tears a bit around the cut. The tightly

CAST POLYESTER RESIN.

PROJECT: David Lloyd Kreeger House, Washington, D.C.

DESIGNED BY: Philip Johnson Associates.

MODELBUILDER: Joseph Santeramo of the architect's captive model shop.

PHOTOGRAPHER: Louis Checkman.

SCALE: 1/8" = 1'.

The vaults of this presentation model were cast in polyester resin. Walls, flat roofs, screens, and columns were machined from acrylic. Contours from 1/8" Masonite, People from tin foil.

CONSTRUCTION TIME: about 250 hours.

Casting Transparent Thin-Walled Objects in Resin

(1) Make the pattern. Hollow it out to the desired wall thickness. (2) Coat both sides with parting agent and allow them to dry. (3) Obtain a paper cup or other disposable container. Cut the container down so that it is about $\frac{1}{2}''$ higher than the pattern. Position the pattern upside down in the container so that its bottom is even with the top of the container. (4) Pour a moldmaking resin such as Crystal Craft's Crystal Mold around the object. (5) After this female mold has dried, fill the inside of the pattern with casting resin. (6) After the interior "plug" mold has dried, remove it, allow it to cure and coat it with release agent. (7) Remove the pattern from the female mold, allow the mold to cure and coat it with release agent. (8) Reposition the plug mold in the female mold. (9) Fill the cavity with a clear casting resin (such as Crystal Craft's Crystal Cast). When dry, remove it from its mold and cure. Do not remove it too soon or it will warp.

Filleting and Cementing Fiberglas and Resin Objects

Fillet one Fiberglas object to another by using strips of cloth or Fiberglas soaked in resin.

Resin objects can be glued to other materials with Amboroid or Epoxy cement. They may be joined to other resin objects by first roughening the surfaces to be joined and by then cementing these with an application of resin.

Machining and Finishing Fiberglas and Resin Objects

To avoid chipping objects, first heat them in 180°F water for $\frac{1}{4}$ hour (small objects) to $\frac{1}{2}$ hour (large objects). Saw with a hand jig or hacksaw, or use a hollow-ground blade with no set on a power saw. Use lard oil, paraffin oil or soap as a lubricant.

Drill with a standard drill. Use soap for the lubricant and withdraw and clear the drill frequently.

To remove the soft film that sometimes forms on top of the plastic, sand with No. 80 paper. Use No. 220 paper to remove the scratches left by the rougher paper and No. 400 paper to finish. All papers should be of the wet variety. Polish with wax and a soft cloth.

Suppliers of Fiberglas and Resin

SIG

This company sells a $2.75 Fiberglas kit composed of 7 square feet of glass cloth, resin and hardener. Sig also sells a release agent. Their resin has wax in it which rises to the surface of the coat and creates a hard smooth finish.

THE CASTOLITE COMPANY

This company sells 2 weights of Fiberglas mat and Fiberglas cloth in 38" wide rolls costing $1.50

per yard; 3" wide Fiberglas tape that costs 25¢ per yard; and Castoglas, a pink casting or laminating resin that hardens in $\frac{1}{2}$ hour to a fairly clear (slightly pink) consistency. The company also has clear resin, which cures to a water clear plastic; China Clay, a filler that is used with Castoglas to reduce cost and shrinkage; Castosil, a thixotropic agent that prevents Castoglas from running when it is applied to vertical surfaces; dyes that come in 12 colors as well as white and black; and thinner for both of their resins.

CRYSTAL CRAFT

This company sells: Crystal Cast, a clear casting resin; Crystal Mold, a pink flexible resin that can be used to make flexible molds or casts; Glas Mat, an almost transparent (when used with Crystal Mold) Fiberglas that comes in 2 thicknesses (costing 10¢ and 35¢ per square foot); Glascloth and Glastape, which (both costing about 15¢ per square foot) can be bent into compound curves without wrinkling; Crystal Fluff, a transparent filler that permits resin to be painted on vertical surfaces without sagging or running; Crystal Talc, a white filler; Crystal Glass, a filler composed of fibers of glass used to give extra strength to resin; Crystal Tints, dyes that come in 4 transparent colors to be mixed into Crystal Cast; Crystal Tones, dyes that come in 5 opaque colors also to be used with Crystal Cast; and Crystal Tempers, which come in 3 metallic colors. Crystal Craft also makes releasing agent and solvent, cleaner and mold release.

U.S. GYPSUM

See page 87.

---

10 CASTING

From time to time it will be necessary to produce many copies of an object. Furniture, cars, people, cast-concrete columns and moldings are some of the almost endless items that must be reproduced in great numbers. When making repetitive parts (whether casting them or not), carefully estimate the construction time. Since a repetitive part may have to be reproduced 1,000 or 10,000 times, all attempts should be made to refine its construction, no matter how small the resulting saving in time per unit or step may be, since the saving will be multiplied by a large factor.

Before deciding to cast, determine what the effort incurred in moldmaking plus casting will be in comparison to making each item individually. If it will be easier to make each item, the decision may still be to cast because (1) the molds may be needed for future use; (2) the objects must be identical in the smallest detail; or (3) because the object must be produced in a material unworkable with the available tools.

Professional modelmakers often carve the pattern of an object in brass, or a similar durable material, and send it to a professional caster who makes the mold and does the casting. Even though this entire process costs in the neighborhood of $100 for a fairly elaborate small object (grills, patterned facades, etc.), professional modelmaker Theodore Conrad estimates that this is more economical even for a run of as little as 6 objects. Beginner craftsmen, whose time costs less than what Conrad pays his staff, will probably need a run of 10 to 15 objects to justify this procedure.

If objects must be cast to close tolerances, choose moldmaking and casting materials whose expansion and contraction relate to one another. If, for instance, a female mold is made out of a plaster that expands 2% on hardening, the plastic or metal used for the casts should also contract 2% on curing so as to produce casts equal in dimension to the pattern. Casting materials can (1) contract as they solidify and cure; (2) contract as they solidify, then expand as they cure; or (3) expand as they solidify and cure. Shrinkage and expansion are not simple problems. Parts of an object which have different thicknesses will shrink different amounts, thus causing distortion. As a hot casting cools, stresses are created that might result in cracking. Since inside corners are especially prone to this, always use filleted corners to avoid failures.

When casting the repetitive pattern of an exterior embossed metal panel wall or other texture finish, it is especially important to predetermine expansion and shrinkage. If this is not done, the number of panels intended for casting will not cover the correct wall area.

If a cast must be duplicated over and over, make several molds that can be poured simultaneously to save time.

If the object has deep slender parts, make provision for the casting material to flow into the mold to the end of these parts without being blocked by trapped air. See 10-2C for a typical air vent constructed to allow air to exit from the end of a chair pedestal.

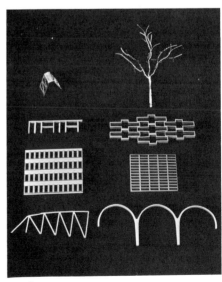

10-1A

EXAMPLES OF CASTING THAT CAN BE OBTAINED FROM PROFESSIONAL MODELMAKERS.

These castings made by Tolo Industries represent the type of precise part that is often better and more economically obtained from a modelmaker who has considerable experience in casting. Other objects that can be "farmed out" are: cars, people and furniture.

10-1

A SEMI-SEETHROUGH MODEL.

PROJECT: Huntington National Bank, Columbus, Ohio.
DESIGNED BY: Skidmore, Owings and Merrill.
MODELBUILDER: Theodore Conrad (a professional modelbuilder).
PHOTOGRAPHER: Louis Checkman.
SCALE: 1/8″ = 1′.

This presentation model was built entirely of acrylic. Mullions and spandrels were milled, and window walls tinted acrylic, thereby providing the feeling of a hollow model without requiring the interior to be detailed. Cars and people were cast in metal. Trees were made from wood chips and sawdust from wire armatures.

The photograph was taken with a 5″ × 7″ Deardorff camera, 90 mm Angulon lens and Super Panchro Press "B" film. The model was illuminated by 1 750-watt spot. A floodlight bounced from the walls of the studio picked up detail in the areas put into shadow by the spot. 2 floods were used to illuminate the sprayed background.

GLOSSARY OF TERMS USED IN CASTING

Blanket Mold is a mold made of a flat object, such as wall or ceiling texture.

Cast or Casting is a duplication of the original object.

Closed Mold is a female mold that is entirely closed. Casting material is poured into it through a pouring channel.

Flash is casting material that leaks out between multi-part molds. When dry, flash resembles a thin fin.

Key is the female or male indentation built into the parts or multi-piece molds to make the assembled parts fit together in perfect alignment.

Mold is the shape in or on which casts are made.

Open Mold is a female mold that is open on one side; casting material is poured into the mold through the opening. If the object to be cast has detail on both sides, it may be made in two open molds; the two resulting casts are then joined together.

Parting, Release or Separating Agent is a substance that is placed on a pattern to facilitate the removal of the mold or a substance placed on the mold to facilitate the removal of the casts.

Pattern or Master Model is the original of the object that is to be duplicated.

Sprue is a channel, through which the casting material is poured, that runs from the outside of a closed mold into its cavity.

PATTERN MAKING

Patterns may be made out of almost any material. Highly detailed objects may be carved out of hardwood or acrylic blocks. Medium and large undetailed shapes may be made from hard balsa, other woods, plaster (Hydrocal or Ultracal are good), Sculpt stone, rapidly hardening clay, etc. Large wood shapes may be built up by the bread-and-butter or solid block carving tech-

niques, large plaster objects by the plaster on egg-crate method.

Any surface air holes in plaster patterns should be filled with wet plaster and smoothly sanded before molding is attempted.

Wax or hard clay may be used to make patterns with extensive and fine detail. Excessive handling of the finished pattern may deform it.

Wax

Wax comes in consistencies ranging from that of grease to that of plaster. Melting points range from 100° to 300°F. Moldcraft sells hard red pattern wax that can be carved into intricate forms. It costs $1.50 per pound. Other softer patternmaker's waxes cost as little as 25¢ per pound. Wax may also be obtained in sheets of from 1/64 to $\frac{3}{8}$″ thickness (Kindt-Collins Co. Master HT-260). Wax in sheet form saves time when building up objects that have parallel sides.

Clay

Clay may also be used for patterns. See page 70 for data on it.

Wood

Special woods, upon which materials may be sheet formed as well as cast, may be obtained for the making of patterns. The desirable properties of such woods are (1) lack of grain; (2) dimensional stability (when exposed to temperature and humidity changes); and (3) ease in carving. Mahogany meets these requirements as does Stabilite (a resin-impregnated wood laminate).

Patternmaker's Mahogany may be obtained from the Kindt-Collins Co. Stabilite is obtainable from the Georgia-Pacific Co.

Ren Wood (despite its name) is a carvable plastic. It costs between $4 and $5.50 per board foot depending on purchase quantity. This grain-

10-2
MOLDS

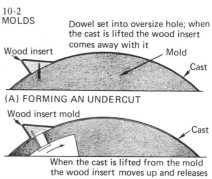

Dowel set into oversize hole; when the cast is lifted the wood insert comes away with it

Wood insert — Mold

— Cast

(A) FORMING AN UNDERCUT

Wood insert mold

— Cast

When the cast is lifted from the mold the wood insert moves up and releases

(B) FORMING AN UNDERCUT

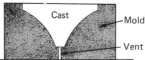

Cast — Mold

— Vent

(C) VENTING A MOLD SO THAT AN AIR BUBBLE WILL NOT FORM IN ITS LOWER EXTREMITY

less material produces unbelievably good carving results. Molds and solid block models are among the things that may be made from it.

U. S. Gypsum's Epoxical Pattern Putty is also a good patternmaking material.

When making a mold from a pattern made of light materials, anchor the pattern to the work surface to prevent its floating up through the mold material.

Undercuts

Undercuts may be cast in several ways: (1) Flexible molds may be used. They may be removed by being stretched past all but the deepest undercuts. (2) Rigid molds with undercut insertions may also be used. Illustration 10-2A shows an undercut form that is attached to a male mold by means of a dowel in an oversize hole. When the cast is removed, the form comes away with it. Female molds may have similar detachable inserts. Illustration 10-2B shows a form that stays with the mold. As the cast is lifted, the undercut form rides up the surface of the mold, and is released from the cast. When a large portion of the object is undercut, a male pattern may be made that can be collapsed and withdrawn from the cast. In general, planning for undercuts is a custom thing; each object presents its own problem.

SEALERS

All patterns or molds made from porous materials must be fully sealed to prevent the casting material from being locked in place when dry. One sealing procedure recommended for use on porous objects coming in contact with casting Epoxy is as follows: (1) Seal with 2 coats of lacquer. (2) Apply 2 coats of polyvinyl alcohol. (3) Apply a generous coat of Epoxical Mold Sealer in a heavy paste (it may be thinned with white gasoline or kerosene). (4) After 5 minutes, remove any excess with a soft cloth. The surface will be sealed and it will, without further treatment, separate from the Epoxy. Casting must take place within $\frac{1}{2}$ to $\frac{3}{4}$ of an hour to prevent a repetition of the entire procedure.

There are other sealers which require less effort to use; they include sanding sealers and varnish. Some brands of sanding sealers will be attacked by the casting material, and so must be tested prior to using.

SEPARATORS OR RELEASE AGENTS

Under each casting and moldmaking material mentioned in this book is a section that lists the release agents to be used with that material. If any combination of materials is not listed, an agent suggested for another combination may work. Keep in mind that very hot materials will cause some agents to boil off, and some agents and materials chemically attack one another.

Separators that will not mar delicate detail may be obtained from dental suppliers. These separators may be applied to plaster (and other) patterns that have not been sealed. Sanderac Varnish is one such agent.

REMOVING MOLDS AND CASTS

Remove rigid molds from patterns and rigid casts from rigid molds by: (1) gently blowing them apart with compressed air; (2) evenly wedging the parting line with a sharp tool; (3) suspending one of the objects so that its weight, aided by light tapping, results in a separation; (4) soaking them for a short time in warm water; (5) using knock-out pins. (See illustration 10-4 and page 86 for additional instructions.)

FLEXIBLE MOLDMAKING MATERIALS

Mold material	Relative cost	Shrinkage during storage	Resistance to tearing	Materials to be cast in mold
Rubber (black or white)	Low	Medium[1]	High	Wax, plaster, metals with melting temperature below 300°F.
Silicone rubber	High	Low	Medium	Wax, plaster, metals with melting temperature below 500°F.

[1] Store in a sealed container containing a teaspoon of water.

FLEXIBLE MOLDS

Flexible molds make possible the casting of objects that have undercuts. Ordinary flexible molds may be removed from patterns and casts that have slight to moderate undercuts. To make a mold with undercuts so deep that the rubber could not be stretched enough to release it, build release slits in the mold. Flexible molds may be made from several materials. The following table lists the 2 most common materials and some of their properties.

In addition to the materials in the table there are 3 others that are now almost obsolete.

Molding Gum

This is only good for 1 or 2 castings and it must be used immediately after it has been molded. During storage it shrinks rapidly and extensively, is weak and is no good for use with hot casting materials.

Moulage

This must be melted over a fire; molds made from it also shrink rapidly and extensively, and it cannot be used with metal.

10-3

CASTING FIGURES

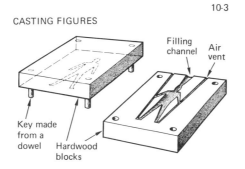

Key made from a dowel — Hardwood blocks — Filling channel — Air vent

Gelatin

This must be soaked for 8 hours and then melted. It, too, shrinks rapidly and extensively, and cannot be used with metal.

Latex Rubber Molds

Molding rubber comes in 2 colors—black and white. The black is a bit tougher and lays up better on vertical surfaces. Both materials have a limited shelf life, so buy only enough to meet immediate needs.

MAKING OPEN MOLDS FROM RUBBER

1—Cement the pattern to a sheet of wood or plastic larger than the base of the pattern. Make sure that the base of the pattern is sanded absolutely flat.

2—Apply the appropriate release agent (see page 84).

3—Use a soft brush to paint several thin coats of liquid rubber over the pattern. Let each coat dry about $\frac{1}{2}$ hour or, when using Rubbertex, wait for each coat to turn a deep red before applying the next coat. Build up a total rubber thickness of about $\frac{1}{8}$". This should entail approximately 10 coats. Objects as small as 1 to 2" in height may only require 8 coats.

4—Blow off or prick with a pin any air bubbles that may form on the rubber. If they are allowed to remain, they will break and mar the surface of the mold.

Rubber has a tendency to shrink and pull away from large patterns. To prevent this, apply the first coat in the standard way and the second coat in a checkerboard pattern. The third coat is applied as the first, and the fourth coat is checkerboarded on the areas not covered by the second. Repeat this procedure for the full 10 coats. Between painting coats of rubber, keep the brush in soapy water to prevent the rubber remnants on it from hardening.

CASTING IN PLASTER
10-4

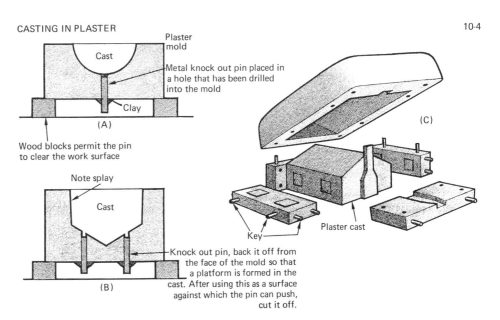

Plaster mold — Cast — Metal knock out pin placed in a hole that has been drilled into the mold — Clay — (A)

Wood blocks permit the pin to clear the work surface

Note splay — Cast — (B)

Knock out pin, back it off from the face of the mold so that a platform is formed in the cast. After using this as a surface against which the pin can push, cut it off.

(C) — Key — Plaster cast

Before using the brush again, shake it out. Apply rubber to small patterns by dipping them into a vessel filled with the liquid. Rubber may also be spray applied.

5—When at least 5 coats of rubber have been applied, reinforce the base of the mold with 1 or more layers of gauze. A flange, from which the finished mold may be hung, can be constructed from gauze or extra layers of rubber and also placed around the base.

6—Additional support to the rubber around undercuts and other areas may be given by building up these places with cotton flock filler mixed with liquid rubber (1 part of each). Do not attempt to apply a coat of much over $\frac{1}{4}$" in 1 application. The filler, which may be applied with a palette knife, is a sponge-rubber-like substance. It is obtainable from most of the companies that sell liquid rubber.

7—Allow the mold to dry. Remove it from the pattern.

8—To cure the mold, place it in a warm place for 2 or more days, or place it 3" away from a 40-watt bulb for 24 hours. (This will maintain about a 110°F curing temperature.)

BACKUP MOLDS

Backup molds or overmolds are sometimes required to stiffen large rubber molds that would collapse or become distorted under the weight of the cast making material.

1—Place a topless and bottomless cardboard box around the completed rubber mold that has been filled with sand or some other light granular material. If the mold is small, a paper cup may be used. The container should be an inch (or more) larger than the mold in all directions.

2—Fill all undercuts (on the outside of the rubber mold) with clay or flock filler mixed with liquid rubber.

3—Coat the rubber mold with soap or an appropriate release agent.

4—Slowly pour a plaster mix into the box, being careful not to allow it to distort the shape of the mold.

5—Remove the rubber mold from the back-up just as heat of crystallization starts.

MAKING 2-PART MOLDS FROM RUBBER

When objects have no flat side, a 2-part mold must be constructed.

1—Place the pattern into a block of modeling clay. Push it down until the top of the clay is at the level desired for the parting line of the mold halves. Make sure that the clay is tightly packed against the sides of the pattern.

2—Build a sprue by running a wood dowel from the pattern to the outside of the clay.

3—With another dowel, press cylindrical indentations into the corners of the clay block. The holes of the dowel must be absolutely perpendicular to the surface of the clay. Keys will be cast into these recesses. Molds for keys may also be made by making a series of dents in the clay with a modeling tool.

4—Apply the liquid rubber coats to the exposed half of the pattern.

5—Make a plaster of Paris overmold. When it has dried, turn the assembly over and remove the clay from the bottom half of the pattern.

6—Make the second half of the rubber mold and the plaster overmold.

7—Pull the plaster overmold halves apart. Notice that it has keys cast into it.

8—Remove the rubber mold halves from the pattern.

9—Reassemble each rubber half in its overmold. Prepare to make castings. When pouring, hold the mold halves together with rubber bands.

MOLDS WITH RELEASE SLITS (10-4A)

If the pattern has deep undercuts, casting it in a mold that has release slits may be possible:

1—Rubber cement a sheet aluminum fin along the side of the pattern running perpendicular to the base of the pattern. The fin may also be attached by cutting a slot into the pattern and inserting an aluminum sheet.

2—Apply the liquid rubber to the pattern and to the fin. The release slit will be formed by the fin.

Fins may also be constructed with a clay wall perpendicular to the side of the pattern:

1—Paint 1 side of this wall with several coats of pearl essence lacquer. Allow each coat to dry before apply the next. Let the last coat dry overnight.

2—Pull the clay away from the lacquer, which has dried into a fin. Be careful not to rip the fin away from the pattern.

When casting with a slit mold, first clamp the closed slit to prevent casting material from entering it. A back-up mold or a clamping frame are other possible ways of closing the slit.

MATERIALS THAT MAY BE CAST IN RUBBER MOLDS

These include art plaster, Hydrocal, Red Top Molding Plaster, Keen's Cement, artificial stone, Hydro-Stone, hot wax, liquid marble, low melting point metals (below 300°F, such as Wood's Metal, Cerro Bend, Cerro Safe, etc.), plastic aluminum and Epoxy metal compound.

WHEN CASTING IN A RUBBER MOLD

1—Grease the mold with unsalted shortening, glycerin or other appropriate release agent (see the separators listed below).

2—Pour the plaster. Let it dry for about $\frac{1}{2}$ hour before removing it from the mold. Apply soap-suds to the outside of the mold, before attempting to lift it from the cast. Remove the rubber as if peeling off a glove.

3—Before storing the mold, wash it in a mild detergent and rinse it in clean water. Rubber molds should be kept away from direct sunlight and from temperatures of over 125°F.

SEPARATORS

The Following Separators May Be Used between Latex Molding Materials and Patterns Made from:

WOOD (first seal the pattern)
2 coats of varnish.
WAX
Shellac or lacquer.
Moldcraft 4H.
PLASTER HYDRO-STONE, SCULPT STONE
(first seal the pattern)
If latex is vulcanized, no separator is needed.
2 coats of varnish.
Moldcraft 4H.
Shellac, lacquer or banana oil.
CLAY OR PLASTICINE
2 coats of shellac.

The Following Separators May Be Used between Latex Molds and Casts Made from:

PLASTER
Moldcraft 4H.
Liquid soap, glycerin and water.
Zinc stearate and alcohol.
CASTING RUBBER
Equal parts of water, liquid soap and Epsom salts.
LOW MELTING POINT METAL
A separator may not be needed.
Moldcraft 2D (allow mold to dry before pouring the metal.
Oil or graphite.

BRAND NAMES OF RUBBERS USED IN MOLDMAKING

These include: Griffin Craft Liquid Rubber, Rubbertex Liquid Rubber, Flexmold, Rubamold, Jay Hawk Liquid Rubber, Pliatex Mold Rubber. Most casting rubbers may be obtained from art supply stores. Costs range from $2 to $3 per pint.

Silicone Rubber Molds

The advantages of silicone rubber over latex in the making of flexible models is that it will allow the casting of hot materials (of up to 500°F melting point), and the mold will last for a much longer time in storage. The instructions contained in this section should be used with Dow Corning Silastic. They are, however, fairly typical of those used with other makes of silicone.

1—Follow the instructions listed under rubber molds in the setting up of the pattern.

2—Mix the silicone rubber and its catalysts in a disposable vessel (paper cup, etc.) and follow the manufacturer's instructions. Stir gently to avoid the formation of air bubbles.

RUBBER MOLDS

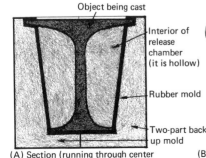

Object being cast
Interior of release chamber (it is hollow)
Rubber mold
Two-part back up mold

(A) Section (running through center line of release chamber)

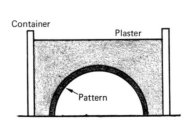

THIN WALL CASTS

Release chamber

(B) Perspective of rubber mold

Container
Plaster
Pattern

(C) Making the female mold

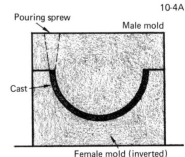

10-4A

Pouring sprew
Male mold
Cast
Female mold (inverted)

(D) Making the cast

3—Pour the mix over the pattern to a depth of $\frac{1}{8}''$ or less. The formula of the chemicals will determine their working and setting (curing) times. With Silastic these can run from 10 minutes to 3 hours and $\frac{1}{2}$ hour to 1 day, respectively. Silicone cures at room temperature, but moderate heating will accelerate the process.

Build up the base of the mold, and other areas that will be subjected to constant flexing, with an open-weave fabric of 20 to 25 mesh. If the mold will be exposed to temperatures over 350°F, use glass fiber for the reinforcement. Place the fabric on the wet rubber and pour an additional layer of rubber over it.

2-part molds may be constructed according to the instructions for latex rubber molds.

THIN-WALLED OBJECTS MAY BE CAST IN THE FOLLOWING WAY (10-4C and D):

1—Construct the exterior mold by pouring the rubber into a container placed around the pattern. Carefully pour the mix into the corners of the container to prevent air pockets from forming.

2—When the rubber has set, remove the container and cut keys into the bottom of the mold.

3—Coat the inside of the pattern and the bottom of the mold with parting agent.

4—Turn the first half of the mold upside down and return it, with the pattern still attached, to the container; fill the inside of the pattern with rubber.

5—After the rubber has set, disassemble the molds, remove the pattern and cut a sprue and the needed vent holes into the mold. Reassemble the 2 mold halves and begin casting.

CASTING IN A SILICONE MOLD

Heat the mold to a temperature of from 25° to 50°F higher than the casting material and pour the cast.

MATERIALS THAT MAY BE CAST IN SILICONE RUBBER MOLDS

These include: plaster of Paris, modeling plaster, Hydrocal, low melting point metals (including lead, Wood's Metal, linotype metal), Polyurethane foam, plastic resins and wax.

SEPARATORS

The Following Separators May Be Used between Silicone Rubber Molding Materials and Patterns Made from:

WOOD (first seal the pattern)
2 coats of varnish.
A 5% solution of household detergent in water. (This can be used on all except very complex, undercut patterns.)
WAX
A separator may not be needed.
Moldcraft 7S.
The 5% detergent solution (see Wood above).
PLASTER (first seal the pattern)
A separator may not be needed.
2 coats of varnish.
Moldcraft 7S.
The 5% detergent solution (see Wood above).
HYDRO-STONE, SCULPT STONE OR SCULPT METAL (first seal the pattern)
The 5% detergent solution (see Wood above).
CLAY OR PLASTICINE
2 coats of shellac.
The 5% detergent solution (see Wood above).
ACRYLIC PLASTIC
The 5% detergent solution (see Wood above).

The Following Separators May Be Used between Silicone Rubber Molds and Casts Made from:

PLASTER
A separator may not be needed.
Moldcraft 7S.
Liquid soap, glycerin and water.
Zinc stearate and alcohol.
LOW MELTING POINT METAL
A separator may not be needed.
Oil or graphite.
Moldcraft 7S.

BRAND NAMES OF SILICONE CASTING RUBBERS

Acralite Silicone Impression Rubber is obtainable from dental supply houses. It is the most flexible casting rubber. It comes in 2 parts and sets in 3 minutes. Silastic RTV is manufactured by the Dow Corning Company. It costs $5 per pound, and may be obtained from local Dow Corning regional offices. General Electric RTV is another silicone casting rubber.

Synthetic Rubber Molds

The Smooth-On Manufacturing Company makes several polysulfide rubber moldmaking materials. Their formula FMC No. 100 is a 2-component chemical which comes in 3 drying speeds. It produces molds that have a tendency to shrink slightly with age and with repeated usage; these molds withstand prolonged 170°F temperatures.

Set up the pattern as for a latex rubber mold. Carefully blend and stir the components of the rubber and brush these onto the pattern. Depending on the curative used, pouring life runs from 10 to 40 minutes, setting time from 1 to 3 hours and curing time from 4 to 28 hours. At the end of the curing period, the mold can be stripped from the pattern. High room temperature and humidity hasten the curing. Because of this, a slower curative chemical can be used in the summer. When applying rubber to the pattern, pour it slowly and in a thin stream. This will cause air bubbles to break as they pass over the lip of the pouring container. A stream of warm air against the poured, but still wet, rubber will cause any bubbles to rise to the surface. If the pattern is intricate, paint the rubber on.

LARGE BLANKET MOLDS

To make large blanket molds that require a long and dimensionally stable life, use Smooth-On FMC No. 300.

1—Set up the pattern and cover it with release agent (if such is needed).

2—Brush on a thin coat of FMC No. 100. When it becomes tacky, brush or trowel on a $\frac{1}{4}''$ thick coat of FMC No. 300. Allow it to set.

3—If the mold is small and slight shrinkage is permissible, reinforcing is not necessary. Next, make the plaster overmold by brushing a film of Smooth-On Sonite release agent on the rubber. Then pour or trowel on a layer of stiff plaster. Sisal or hemp fiber may be incorporated into the plaster for added strength. A lifting frame may be made from wood furring. Use the fiber to tie the plaster to the furring. The plaster may be permanently attached to the rubber by setting copper wool or chopped hemp into the still liquid rubber. The plaster will grip the exposed strands and anchor itself to the rubber.

4—If all shrinkage must be avoided, apply a layer of burlap mesh to the wet FMC No. 300, making sure that no air is trapped beneath the fabric and that it is thoroughly saturated by the rubber.

5—Apply a second coat of FMC No. 300 after the first one has set.

6—If desired, make an overmold as described in step 3. Store the rubber mold in a cool, dark place.

If intending to make castings from Epoxy or polyester resins in a blanket mold, use FMC No. 302 for a first ($\frac{1}{8}''$ thick) coat and apply a layer of FMC No. 300 when the first coat has partially set.

MATERIALS THAT MAY BE CAST IN SYNTHETIC RUBBER MOLDS

These include: plaster, polyester thermosetting resins (which can be cured at low temperatures) and Epoxy resins.

Before each casting of Epoxy in a synthetic rubber mold, protect the mold by (1) sponging it with a warm 1% to 2% solution of household detergent and water. (2) After this has dried, brush or spray the mold with a film of polyvinyl alcohol (purchasable from the Ferro Corporation). (3) Allow the alcohol to dry and, taking care not to crack its film, spray the mold with 1 or 2 layers of fluorocarbon telomer dispersion (this may be purchased from the Ram Chemical Company).

SEPARATORS

The Following Separators May Be Used between Synthetic (Polysulfide) Rubber Molding Material and Patterns Made from:

WOOD, WAX, PLASTER, HYDRO-STONE, SCULPT STONE, SCULPT METAL, CARDBOARD, CLAY, PLASTICINE AND ACRYLIC PLASTIC (first seal porous patterns).
Smooth-On Manufacturing Company's Sonite.
Vaseline thinned with kerosene.

The Following Separators May Be Used between Synthetic Rubber Molds and Casts Made from:

PLASTER
Equal parts of vaseline and kerosene.
POLYESTER RESIN
Smooth-On Manufacturing Company's Sonite.

BRAND NAMES OF SYNTHETIC CASTING RUBBERS

These include: Smooth-On Manufacturing Company's FMC No. 100, FMC No. 300 and FMC No. 302. These cost $3 to $4 per pint.

Quick Setting Flexible Molds

Adco-Mold makes a powder moldmaking compound that, when mixed with water, will set in 5 to 10 minutes. When mixed, the material must be applied to the pattern immediately. It may be removed from the pattern in 2 to 3 minutes (while it is still soft) if care is taken not to distort it. Casts may be made by filling the mold with alternate layers of solvent and plastic powder. When the mold is filled, allow the cast to dry for 20 minutes before removing.

RIGID MOLDS

Casting in Plaster

PLASTER PATTERNS

Plaster patterns should be sealed with gum shellac thinned with alcohol (1 part of each). Finely detailed patterns should be sealed with applications of numerous coats of soap dissolved in water; a surface finished in this fashion does not require a separator.

PLASTERS TO USE

See page 71 for a list of available plasters and their properties.

OPEN MOLDS MADE OF PLASTER

Molds must have splayed parts to permit removal of the casts. A splay is usually referred to as draft (10-4B). To make a female mold: (1) seal the pattern and apply the separator to it and to the surrounding work surface. (2) Pour the plaster over the pattern. If intending to cut down on the weight of a large mold, reinforce the first layer of plaster applied to the pattern with cloth; as the plaster hardens, gradually build it up to a 1" thickness. (3) Allow newly made molds to dry before using. 1" thick molds require about a day's drying time. 4" thick molds require 3 day's time. Prorate for other mold thicknesses. When the plaster is dry, remove the mold, allow it to cure, fill any air bubbles or flaws, shellac and sand to a satin finish.

To make plaster casts in a plaster mold: (1) Hold the bottom of the mold level, if it is not flat, on the work surface with lumps of clay. (2) Before casting, immerse the mold in water for about 10 minutes. The liquid will fill tiny air holes, and prevent air bubbles from later working their way into the casting plaster. (3) To avoid getting air bubbles trapped in the mold, pour the plaster into the mold. (4) Immediately pour it out. Many of the air bubbles will be swept out with the plaster. (5) Refill the mold a little at a time, jarring or vibrating the mold while pouring.

Never pour plaster across a pattern or mold; the turbulence may cause streak or flow marks to form and remain on the hardened plaster.

It is better to cast large objects with a wall that is the same thickness everywhere. Such an object will dry evenly with less chance of cracking. Pour the plaster to a $\frac{3}{4}$" thickness along the bottom of the mold; then build up a layer of stiff plaster to the desired even thickness along the sides of the mold.

To make a plaster mold for casting shallow metal objects, such as screens, fences or wall textures, try the following procedure:

1—Make a wood frame to enclose the mold. Pin it to a woodworking surface.

2—Oil the frame and work surface.

3—Pour the plaster into the frame. When it has almost set, draw a straightedge across it, leveling it with the top of the frame.

4—When dry, remove the slab from its frame.

5—Turn the slab over and trace the elevation of the object that is to be molded.

6—Carve the outline with a pointed instrument and gouge out the depth of the object. To get an idea of the progress being made, periodically press plasticine or clay into the depression, remove it and study the detail and depth that has been carved.

7—Drill holes for keys in each corner of the slab.

8—When the female pattern has been completed, melt 1 part of soft soap into 5 parts of water and brush many layers of the liquid mix into the plaster.

9—Wash off any surplus soap and allow the plaster to dry.

10—Oil the plaster, then immerse it in water for about 10 minutes.

11—Make a new wood frame. This one should be the same size as the plaster slab but twice as deep.

12—Put the slab into the frame pattern side up, and oil the slab and frame.

13—Pour plaster into the frame, and when the plaster is almost set, strike off the top of the slab as before.

14—After the plaster has set, remove the frame and separate the 2 slabs. You will now have a positive impression of the object and 4 keys cast into the second slab.

15—Remove the positive impression of the object with a scraper and a pointed instrument, and incise the other side of the object into the second slab.

16—Cut air vents and a sprue into 1 mold half.

17—Place and clamp the 2 finished mold halves together.

18—Pour metal into the mold (10-3).

CLOSED MOLDS MADE OF PLASTER

If undercuts or details on the sides of an object make 1-piece open mold casting impossible, cast in a closed mold (10-4C) of 2 or more pieces. The procedure is to:

1—Determine how many mold pieces are required to clear all undercuts.

2—Make the biggest part of the mold first. Build fences to contain the plaster of the first mold piece. Fences can be made out of clay, with the exception of those fences that touch clay patterns. These must be made from sheet metal inserted into the pattern.

3—Cut keys into the fences.

4—Coat the pattern and fences with separator.

5—Pour the plaster. Remove the fence when dry.

6—Coat the other side of the pattern and the edge of the first part of the mold with separator and cast the second mold part. Repeat the procedure with the other mold parts.

To hold multi-piece molds together for casting, cement the cracks with plaster. Chip this plaster off when disassembling the mold.

1-SHOT MOLDS FOR CASTING OBJECTS WITH UNDERCUTS

If sheet forming or casting an object that has undercuts, make the mold from Bestwall Brakeaway Plaster. This restricts the mold to being used once; also, the material used for the cast must be able to withstand a temperature of 170°F.

Carve the mold out of plaster. To facilitate removal, make its walls as thin as possible. After casting or sheet forming the object, soak it and the attached mold in 170°F water until the plaster dissolves. It may then be removed with a spatula. Male molds can be carved into a mass of plaster that has been cast onto a wood plug. The plug is withdrawn before disintegration of the plaster.

SEPARATORS

The Following Separators May Be Used between Plaster Molding Material and Patterns Made from:

WOOD (first seal the pattern)
Oil.
Wax polish.
WAX
Moldcraft 4H.
PLASTER (first seal the pattern)
Wax polish may be used on plaster molds when casting with most materials (if the pattern is large and without detail). Apply in a thin coat and polish with a soft cloth until a glass-like surface is obtained.

Olive, raw linseed, light lubricating or white mineral oil (used in moderation).

1 part melted soft soap in 5 parts of water. Apply several brushed-on coats to the pattern, wash off any excess, let dry and oil.

Russian tallow and olive oil.

Suet and paraffin melted to the consistency of cream.

1 part beeswax, 3 parts paraffin and 16 parts kerosene.

$\frac{1}{4}$ pound of stearic acid (stearin) cut into fine shavings and mixed with 1 part kerosene. Boil to dissolve (overheating will cause it to burst into flame).

Potters or neutral potash soap. Rub several applications into the pattern and wipe off excess with a clean sponge.

Spirits of camphor (good on finely detailed patterns).

1 part Vaseline and 2 parts kerosene. Heat, mix and brush on.

Moldcraft 6Q.

Wet the mold with water until it stands on the surface of the plaster.

METAL
Spray on a mixture of: 10% S.A.E. No. 10 mineral oil, $2\frac{3}{4}$% bayberry wax, $\frac{1}{4}$% Aerosol O.T. and 87% water.

CLAY OR PLASTICINE
Powdered talc.
Soap jelly made from a solution of soap and water.

The Following Separators May Be Used between Plaster Molds and Casts Made from:

PLASTER (first seal the mold)
Use any of the separators listed in the plaster patterns and plaster molding materials section.

POLYESTER RESIN (first seal the mold)
Wax polish.
Separators are available from Crystal Craft and the Castolite Company.
Moldcraft 3G oil spray.

EPOXY RESIN (first seal the mold)
Smooth-On Manufacturing Company's Sonite.
U.S.G. Epoxical Release-All. Apply 3 coats and buff; then apply 3 more coats.

LOW MELTING POINT METAL (first seal the mold)
A separator may not be needed.
Moldcraft 2D (allow mold to dry before pouring the metal).
Oil or graphite.

EXPANSION

Plaster expands as it sets. When making a plaster mold or cast, remove it from its mate while it is still hot. Final expansion runs from about 3% (with High Expansion Hydrocal) to as little as 1/500 of 1% (Ultracal 60). See table on page 71 for the expansion rates of various plasters. If slabs and other objects are not allowed to expand freely, they will warp. Female molds must have walls of sufficient thickness to resist the expansion of the casting material.

REMOVING CASTS AND MOLDS

Remove plaster molds from their patterns and casts from the plaster molds by gently prying and tapping; if intending to make more than a handful of casts, avoid this procedure since in time it will damage the mold. In these instances, use heavy ($\frac{1}{8}$" diameter or more) brass or steel knock-out pins. Set them into a hole drilled in the center of the base of the mold (10-4A). If, because of its size, the mold requires more than one pin, allow them to protrude an even amount from the mold so that, when the mold is pressed against the

COURTESY OF THE UNIVERSAL ATLAS CEMENT DIVISION, U.S. STEEL CORP.

MODELING A COMPLEXLY CURVED THIN WALL STRUCTURE.

PROJECT: La Concha Supper Club, Santurce, Puerto Rico.

DESIGNED BY: Osvaldo L. Toro, Miguel Ferrer and Charles H. Warner Jr.

MODELBUILDER: Theodore Conrad (a professional modelbuilder).

PHOTOGRAPHER: Robert Damora.

SCALE: 1/4″ = 1′.

The roof of this presentation model was vacuum-formed from acrylic over a male mold. The reflecting pool was made from sheet acrylic. Furniture and people were cast in metal, railing was made from soldered wire and rod, lily pads and plants from paper.

The photograph was taken with an 8″ × 10″ Deardorff view camera and a Schneider Angulon wide-angle lens. The ocean photograph was placed behind the model when the photograph was taken.

---

workbench, the pressure against the several pins will evenly push the cast out (10-4B).

The first cast is always the hardest to remove. The more the mold is used, the easier becomes removal. Suction may make it difficult to remove a large plaster cast from its mold. To break this adhesion, place the mold under water and gently pry the cast from it. Dry the mold before using it again.

CLEANING UP CASTS

If a cast is removed from its mold with damaged corners or pits, patch it while it is still wet.

Apply plaster to pits with a pointed tool. Fill larger voids by applying the plaster with a wet palette knife. Broken corners should be roughly built up first, and partially allowed to set. While the plaster is still wet, file and sand the corner to its final shape.

Remove flash with a flatface file while the plaster is still wet. Since fine detail on plaster casts will not stand up as well under handling as will fine detail on casts made from metal or plastic, the material must be carefully worked.

TROUBLES ENCOUNTERED WITH PLASTER MOLDS

CRACKED OR WARPING IN MOLDS can be caused by curing the mold at too high a temperature or for too long a time. Molds may warp if the plaster is of low quality or if too much parting compound has been applied.

CHALKINESS IN MOLDS is caused by curing at excessive temperatures.

SOFTNESS IN MOLDS may be caused by too much water in the plaster or by curing the mold at too high a temperature. If the mold softens after being used, it probably has not been sufficiently dried between castings.

HARDNESS IN MOLDS may be caused by an insufficient amount of water in the plaster mix.

RAPID DETERIORATION IN MOLDS may be brought on by the same factors which cause plaster to deteriorate (see page 72), or because the mold was not dried before using.

MOLDS THAT DEVELOP MILDEW must be thoroughly washed and dried.

Epoxy Molds and Casts

Epoxy resin has been used increasingly in recent years to make both molds and casts. Its high strength and dimensional stability make it, in many instances, a more attractive material than plaster. Shrinkage of Epoxy resin is low. U.S. Gypsum's surface coat resins shrink only 0.0001 to 0.0007″ per foot. Their Fiberglas laminating resins shrink 0.0001 to 0.0005″ per foot. Compressive strengths of Epoxy run from 10,000 to 22,000 pounds per square inch. The use of Epoxy resin and Fiberglas in the lamination of thin-wall objects is detailed on page 80 .

RESIN

Many companies have extensive lines of Epoxy resins. U.S. Gypsum's line includes surface coat, laminating, and thick section casting resins. Each should only be used in the application suggested by its name.

Surface Coat Resins

Some of those sold by U.S. Gypsum are:

Epoxical Surface Coat S-404 is a machinable, black, iron-filled gel coat resin used with Fiberglas laminations or for casts and molds. It has good wear characteristics. It will not run off vertical surfaces, and can be applied in thicknesses up to ½″. Its pot life is 25 minutes, and it becomes firm in 50 minutes.

Epoxical Surface Coat 405 is a thixotropic resin used for surfacing plaster molds or for applying Fiberglas laminations. It will not run off vertical surfaces and will harden even if in contact with wet plaster. Epoxical Surface Coat 406 is a faster setting version of No. 405. Its pot life is 9 to 13 minutes.

Resins have a storage life of about 1 year. Surface coat resins should be brushed on to eliminate the possibility of air bubbles. Resin comes in pint, quart and larger containers; it must be mixed with a hardener.

HARDENER

Both U.S. Gypsum's Regular Epoxical Hardener or its Low Irritant Potential Hardener (it is practically nontoxic) may be used. Both have a pot life of between 25 and 30 minutes.

USES OF EPOXY

The following uses of Epoxy are of interest to the modelmaker. Instructions quoted and products named come from the various catalogs of the U.S. Gypsum Company. Many other firms also make useful Epoxy resins. Many of the techniques for molds and casts outlined in the plaster casting section may also be used with Epoxy.

Using Epoxy to Face Plaster Molds

Sometimes a plaster mold is prone to breakage, surface marring or chipping because of its size, shape or use. If the plaster molds are lined with Epoxy, they will be greatly strengthened and their casting life will be extended. The procedure is:

1—Place the pattern in a box the dimensions of which will determine the size of the outside of the mold. Patterns (and molds) that may be used with Epoxy include: plaster, wood, metal, vulcanized rubber and plastic. Seal plaster and wood with quick drying automotive-type Duco Lacquer No. 1907, Tygon or Epoxical Polyvinyl Alcohol Liquid Mold Release. The latter agent should be applied only after the pattern has been coated with lacquer; let it dry and wax it.

Wood with a really open grain should first be sealed with DuPont Paste Wood Filler diluted with Dulux thinner or naphtha. Brush on the filler, let it dry, and wipe off any excess by rubbing the pattern across its grain and let it dry overnight. Apply a coat of DuPont No. 1991 Duco Clear Sealer, let it dry and sand it. Apply several coats of Duco No. 1907 Clear Lacquer, let it dry, wax with Simonize or paste wax and polish it. Apply 2 spray coats of polyvinyl alcohol and 1 coat of Epoxical Mold Sealer Separator. Open-grain wood should be avoided as pattern material when used against Epoxy or with other casting materials.

2—Spray the pattern with Epoxical Mold Sealer Separator.

3—Brush on a face coat of Epoxical surface coat resin.

4—For extra strength (needed mostly in large molds), spray or flock on a $\frac{1}{32}$ to $\frac{1}{16}$″ layer of copper, steel or aluminum reinforcing slivers. Do not allow a build-up of metal in the corners of the mold. If the mold is not too prone to breakage, omit the metal.

No type of Epoxy, except that made from thick section casting resins, must be cast in thicknesses over ½ to ¾″. Thicker sections would be damaged by the excessive heat generated during setting. This heat would break down the parting agent, warp the plastic and form air voids and bubbles in the surface.

5—After the Epoxy has hardened, brush on a coat of Ultracal plaster.

Greater bonding between plastic and plaster can be achieved by allowing the plastic coat to become tacky, by then brushing on a second coat of plastic, and by, immediately after, pressing wads of hemp into it. Fiberglas tape can also be pressed into the still-wet resin, and the form undulated like a multilooped serpent, with loops projecting ½″ or more from the surface of the plastic.

6—While the plaster is still wet, pour on additional plaster to fill the box completely.

7—Remove the pattern and box just prior to the drying of the plaster (3 to 4 hours from the start of its mixing).

Laminations of Epoxy and Fiberglas can also be backed up with gypsum plaster. This is sometimes done to provide additional strength in huge molds. Another way to back up Epoxy and Fiberglas lamination is to add U.S. Gypsum Epoxical Core Fill to it. Core Fill (5 or 6 parts) is mixed with laminating resin (1 part) and is applied after the last layer of cloth is in place. The hardened fill has a compressive strength of 2,000 to 4,000 psi, depending on the hardener used.

CASTING THICK SECTIONS IN EPOXY

Molds and casts that are $\frac{1}{2}$ to $4\frac{1}{2}$" thick may be cast from Epoxical thick section casting resins. 8" thick sections can be cast by adding aluminum granules to the resin; this also improves the dimensional stability of the Epoxy. Additional thicknesses can always be added with a backing of plaster or a wood core insert. The intended thickness of the section should be estimated and the correct formula of thick section resin and 2 types of hardener then computed from U.S. Gypsum's tables. Pouring sprues made from tubing should be used with all but the smallest objects. Fill the tubes to the top with resin after the object has been cast. This will create hydrostatic pressure to keep the mold or cast filled with resin as the resin sets and shrinks. Without this pressure, square corners may contract and become rounded. Cast objects should be allowed to dry overnight, and then removed from their pattern or mold by wooden wedges, ejector pins or air pressure.

SEPARATORS

The Following Separators May Be Used between Epoxy Resin Molding Material and Patterns Made from:

PLASTER OR WOOD (first seal the pattern)
Smooth-On Manufacturing Company's Sonite.
General Electric Company No. 9700 Bake On Varnish (cure it for 16 to 20 hours at 260°F).
U.S. Gypsum Expoxical Release-All. Apply 3 coats and buff; apply 3 more coats.
Tygon.
Automotive-type Duco Lacquer No. 1907.
Coat with lacquer, wax and then apply polyvinyl alcohol (Partall No. 10 film).

The Following Separators May Be Used between Epoxy Resin Molds and Casts Made from:

LOW MELTING POINT METAL
A separator may not be needed.
Oil or graphite.

CASTS

High Melting Point Metal Casts

Industrially produced, finely detailed castings are cast in metal with a melting point above that found in the Cerro alloys. Because of the relatively complex foundry equipment that is required for such casting, it is only used in the more elaborate professional model shops. The smaller shop and the designer who makes his own models, however, may buy small foundry kits from such suppliers as the Kansas City Specialties Company. Their $35 kit includes a 2,400°F furnace ($\frac{3}{4} \times 4$" capacity), blower, mixing vessel and melting crucible. Smaller, lower temperature furnaces are sold by the Home Foundry Manufacturing Company. These cost between $5 and $15 for sets that include a heater and metal ladle.

One interesting industrial metal casting process that may be worth reviewing is lost-wax casting. This system is used to produce complicated objects with numerous undercuts in one cast. The alternatives to this system are the tedious several part casting and assembling of such objects or else casting in a less precise, flexible mold. The latter system also limits the melting point and therefore the metal that can be used. The steps in lost-wax casting are: (1) Make a wax pattern. (2) Make a female mold from refractory plaster. (3) Melt out the wax. (4) Fill the mold with casting metal. (5) Break away the plaster.

Variations on this technique allow one to make the pattern in a material other than wax and then to reproduce it in many wax pattern copies. These copies are assembled on a wax tree (which also creates the pouring sprue). For dense castings free of surface flaws, the molten metal is often injected into the plaster mold in a vacuum chamber; or the mold and its still hot cast are swung on a centrifuge.

These systems, and the others possible with high melting point metals, are further complicated by the danger inherent in working with molten metal. If the mold contains moisture, the hot metal may cause it to explode. Metal casting problems may be solved by allocating them to a local jewelry-casting firm. Some professional modelbuilders such as Tolo Industries or Devpro will also make custom metal casting to specifications.

Low Melting Point Metal Casts

The major inconveniences of casting in hot metals can be eliminated by using low melting point metals. Molds that would be destroyed by high temperatures may be employed. Boiling water can be used to replace a more elaborate furnace and the danger of the molds exploding will be eliminated. Objects that may be cast include: people, tree armatures, furniture, railings and grill work.

The Cerro De Paso Corporation manufactures an extensive line of such metals. They include Cerrobend (melting point, 158°F) and Cerrosafe (1 component melts at 160°F; all others melt by 190°F). These metals can be obtained in some model train hobby stores in 1 and 2 pound pigs or in smaller ingots (4 to the $1 package). Cerrobend expands $3\frac{1}{3}$% as it cools, making a sharp casting equal to those produced with high-pressure Zamac metal. Cerrosafe contracts on cooling.

Molds may be made of the usual mold materials (including rubber) and of cardboard or wood as well. A mold of a complex cornice made out of cardboard is illustrated in 10-6C, D and E.

CASTING WITH LOW MELTING POINT METAL

1—Melt small quantities of the metal in an iron or stainless steel (not brass or aluminum) ladle suspended in a pot of boiling water. Melt large quantities in a pot. Take care not to overheat the metal or, when cooling, it will revert to a brittle crystalline form.

2—Pour into a cool mold. To fill a deep mold, pour the metal through a tube inserted into the bottom of the mold. Withdraw the tube while pouring.

3—Remove the casting from the mold immediately after it has cooled. If Cerrobend is allowed to stand too long in the mold, it will expand and tightly grip the mold.

Long objects cast in low melting point metal must be supported in the model, or they may sag in time.

"BOLOGNA" CASTING WITH LOW MELTING POINT METAL

To cast very delicate repetitive objects (such as trusses, joists or fences) that are needed in great numbers, a technique called bologna casting may be used (10-6A and B).

1—After precisely constructing the mold, preheat it by encasing it in aluminum foil and hold it over an electric heating element or in an oven.

2—When the mold is heated above the melting point of the metal, slowly pour in the molten metal. Hold the mold at a slant; if any air bubbles are forming, they will be visible through the acrylic mold top. If they do form, tap the mold to work them out.

3—If a substantial number of air bubbles refuse to be worked out of the mold, wrap it in foil and reheat it, then resume the agitation.

4—After the entire mold has been satisfactorily poured and cooled, remove the acrylic and slice the metal and wood sandwich on a band or circular saw equipped with a fine-tooth metal cutting blade. Sections as thin as 1/50" can be made with these tools.

5—To remove the pieces of wood from the metal cast, position each wood piece over a hole cut in a sheet of wood and carefully push it out of the fragile metal frame.

If it is impossible to saw sections thin enough, sand crudely cut sections to the desired thickness

CASTING WITH LOW MELTING POINT METAL

(A) CASTING A TRUSS

(B) SECTION OF TRUSS

(C) CASTING A MOLDING SECTION

(D) THE FINISHED MOLDING

(E) PLAN VIEW OF THE MOLDING IN ITS MOLD

by first cementing them to a sheet of wood. Then cement strips of cardboard (thickness equal to the desired thickness of the section) to the periphery of the sanding block. These strips will limit the amount that can be sanded off the metal section. Remove the sanded section from the wood sheet by pouring cement thinner over it.

SEPARATORS

The Following Separators May Be Used between Low Melting Point Metal Molding Material and Patterns Made from:

WOOD, HYDRO-STONE, SCULPT STONE, SCULPT METAL, CARDBOARD, CLAY, PLAS-TICINE OR ACRYLIC PLASTIC (first seal the pattern)
A separator may not be needed.
Oil or graphite.
PLASTER (first seal the pattern)
A separator may not be needed.
Oil or graphite.
Moldcraft 2D (allow the pattern to dry before pouring the metal).

The Following Separators May Be Used between Low Melting Point Metal Molds and Casts Made from:

PLASTER
Spray on a mixture of 10% S.A.E. No. 10 mineral oil, $2\frac{3}{4}$% bayberry wax, $\frac{1}{4}$% aerosol O.T. and 87% water.

Cold Metal Casts

Two "short cut" casting materials are plastic aluminum (Sculpt metal) and Epoxy metal compound which may be cast into latex rubber molds.

Plastic aluminum comes in tubes sold under the brand names of Duro, Magic and Hercules. It may be formed into casts with fine detail. This material shrinks and warps badly, especially in castings that measure $\frac{1}{4}$" or more in dimension. Larger castings may be made in several pieces to lessen the warpage. Pack the liquid aluminum into the rubber mold with a palette knife.

Elmer's Epoxy Metal Compound is a filler and sealer material which comes in 2 parts that are mixed in the same way as Epoxy cement. It may be cast in a well-oiled latex rubber mold.

Rubber Casts

Certain types of rubber may be used to make casts as well as molds. Pliatex Casting Rubber, available from Sculpture House, may be made into flexible or rigid, hollow casts. It is formed in female plaster molds. The casting rubber is mixed with Pliatex Filler. The amount of filler determines the rigidity of the cast. The mix is poured into the mold and allowed to stand for 15 to 30 minutes. The excess liquid is then poured out. Parting agents are not required. Cured rigid casts may be painted with oil, watercolors, lacquer or enamel, Flexible casts must be painted with Pliatex Flexible Rubber Paints, which come in only 3 colors.

Plastic Casts

See page 78 for descriptions of the resins that may be used with or without Fiberglas reinforcement in the making of casts.

Casting Foaming Plastic

Foaming plastic may be cast in most types of molds. Sig sells a product called Polyurethane Superfoam that expands up to 25 times its original volume when its 2 ingredients are mixed.

---

11 FINISHING

An extremely critical operation in modelmaking and other crafts is painting. After spending laborious hours on a model one is often prone to rush the final painting. One's schedule may demand it or one may just desire to see work finished and on display. This is an impellent to hurry and not plan carefully. A rushed paint job will always look just that, and can easily ruin the skilled craftsmanship that is underneath. On the other hand, a good paint job can successfully complete the model, and even improve it, though paint should never be expected to cover sloppy construction or fully make up for lack of detail.

Painting takes more time than most people realize; many builders of all-acrylic models estimate that painting and finishing take up to $\frac{1}{3}$ of the total construction time.

PLANNING

Two secrets of a good paint job are the use of good tools and materials and thoroughness in planning. Before starting construction of the model, study all its parts to determine which must be painted before being permanently attached to the model. Visible parts placed inside others must be painted before being assembled, as must parts painted a different color from surrounding areas. The only exceptions should be those parts the paint lines of which are easily masked. When possible, try to obtain materials that are manufactured in the desired color, as is often the case with paper, cardboard, simulated building materials, acrylic, flock, etc. When flat material in the desired color cannot be obtained, paint the uncut stock before reducing it to its final shape. This will help to prevent warping.

Painting should not be the final construction operation, but should be done in phases throughout the construction of the model. When painting small intricate objects, such as people or furniture, apply the largest areas of color first, then the smaller touches.

Paint thickness must be relative to scale. Too thick a finish can destroy detail and cause the model to look like a toy, not like a miniature structure. To preserve detail, it is best to select a paint that will cover with 1 moderately thin coat; if this is impossible, apply the paint in 2 thin coats rather than in 1 thick one. Sand lightly between the coats if possible. The problem of atmospheric dust marring the finish can be overcome by the use of a spray booth and quick drying paint.

THE COMPONENTS OF PAINT

Paint is composed of pigment, which gives color and opacity; it is also comprised of vehicle, the liquid in which the pigment is suspended; when dry, vehicle bonds the pigment together. Thinner or reducer is sometimes added to paint to make it flow easily. Being more volatile than the vehicle, it evaporates first. Thinner may also be used to rejuvenate some types of dried paint.

Paint may be applied in several coats. The first or primer coat forms a bond between the material and the paint. Because the primer possesses a greater clinging tendency than most paint, it helps ensure that the paint will not peel or flake. Primer also helps to prevent paint from being peeled off when tape masking is used. Primers used on porous materials also seal the surface, and are often called sealers.

After the primer, surfacer coats containing pigment are applied. These coats fill pores or grain, impart some color and produce an even surface for the final or top coat. Well-primed materials and materials with a smooth surface do not require surfacer coats. Some paints are self-leveling—they have a tendency to flow into a level finish, eliminating brush marks and other irregularities.

COLOR COMPENSATION

Models are usually displayed under artificial lighting, which provides less light intensity than the actual building would receive from natural light. This may be compensated for by painting the model in slightly lighter colors than would be used on the actual building.

Some models have painted-in shadows so that they will not have to rely on display lighting to provide these accents. Of course, do not shadow-paint models that eventually will be photographed under varied lighting conditions.

Large town-planning models, which will be primarily viewed from one side, and dioramas should be painted with some degree of aerial perspective. Colors farthest from the viewer should be muted and misty; those closer to the viewer more chromatic and contrasting.

PREPARATION FOR PAINTING

Inspect the surface of the object. Fill all cracks, holes and end grain with filler. Sand it smooth, making sure that all saw marks, whiskers or flash are also removed.

Protect work surfaces from dripping paint and spray by covering with newspaper. Keep a nearby supply of clean, lint-free cloths or soft paper in case of an emergency.

Thoroughly mix all paints before starting to paint. A wire rod with a hoop end can be inserted into an electric drill and used as a power mixer. If there are lumps or other particles in the paint, strain it through gauze, or through a discarded nylon stocking stretched over the mouth of a paint jar and held in place by a rubber band; or cut the tip from a cone-shaped paper cup and plug the resulting hole with a pad of lint-free

11-1/11-2

A FULLY DETAILED ACRYLIC MODEL.

Project: Chase Manhattan Building, New York City.

Designed by: Skidmore, Owings and Merrill.

Modelbuilder: Theodore Conrad (a professional modelbuilder).

Photographer: Ezra Stoller.

Scale: $1/16'' = 1'$.

Walls, windows and floors were made from acrylic. Mullions and columns were metal extrusions inlayed into the walls. Due to the height of the building, care had to be taken in calculating whether or not the scale columns would support the weight of the model. The model could be lifted for transportation by 2 eye bolts attached to the roof, which was then reinforced to distribute the suspended weight of the model down through the columns. Interior columns and floors contributed internal bracing. The plaza was made from scribed wood, exterior walls of existing buildings from wood and windows from tinted acrylic. Trees were formed from sawdust cemented to wire armatures.

This model was used for presentation and to study the relationship of the new building to existing surroundings.

The model cost the client $15,000 (in the mid 1950's).

cheesecloth and use as a strainer. Commercially made strainers are also obtainable from hardware stores. From time to time stir the paint. Keep 2 containers of paint remover on hand: 1 to be used for the first dipping of brushes. After they have been wiped clean of the majority of the paint, swish them through the second container.

Mix small test amounts of paint by the drop. Paint a test strip and allow it to dry before judging its color. Glossy paints usually become darker as they dry; flat paints become lighter. Some pigments (red, Prussian blue, etc.) become more vivid. To facilitate matching of colors, an exact record should be kept of all the ingredients mixed in a batch. When mixing larger quantities, convert the drop count into larger quantities ($\frac{1}{2}$ ounces, ounces, etc.). 1,200 drops equal 1 U.S. fluid ounce.

Test each new type of paint on the material to be painted to discover whether or not the paint will adhere, and not warp it. If slight warps do occur, eliminate them by bracing the material internally or by using the paint in a drier state. If a test on a flat piece of material is inconclusive as to the degree of warpage, build up a rough mock-up of the assembly and test for the amount of bracing required to prevent this condition.

Clean caps and paint bottle tops before closing them. Paint bottles should be stored upside down to allow the paint to seal up the cap and prevent evaporation.

Paint may usually be removed with a cloth dipped in thinner. Since cardboard and paper models may warp from this procedure, lightly sand or scrape off misplaced paint on these materials. Removing paint from metal parts can be facilitated by immersing them in thinner and by brushing the paint off with a toothbrush; in more severe cases, remove paint by giving the metal object a bath in caustic lye and water solution. Some plastics will be attacked by certain thinners. To prevent such an accident, first try the thinner on a piece of scrap.

MASKING

There are several masking agents that are of use to the modelbuilder. In general, masks can be divided into 2 categories—those that are hand held and those that are temporarily attached to the surface being painted.

Hand Held Masks

These are commonly used when painting 1 surface of the inside of a corner or a 90° intersection. These masks may be cut from acetate, stencil paper, cardboard or other thin stiff sheet. Only simple borders (straight lines, etc.) should be attempted with a hand held mask.

Masks Attached to Painted Surfaces

These can be made from:

1—Pressure-sensitive tape and paper. Tape must be carefully selected and a scrap must be tested before use. Try drafting tape, Scotch Decorator's Tape, or Permacel Home Craft Tape. Many spray painted mat paints cannot be masked with tape without being damaged; some painted surfaces (lacquer, etc.) must be allowed to dry several hours before being masked. Scotch Electrical Black Tape can be stretched to mask curve lines neatly, but it usually proves hard to remove. Never use transparent, or other tape, the sticking tenacity of which makes it impossible to remove without damaging the surface of the work. If a recommended tape is hard to remove, its holding power can be lessened by pressing it onto, and then removing it from, window glass a sufficient number of times to kill some of its adhesive quality. After the paint has dried, remove tape by pulling it back from the surface at a 30° angle; make sure that it is pulled straight back and not

slightly sideways so as to prevent raising the surface of the underlying material.

2—Extremely thin lines should be masked with striping tape, available at the model car counter of hobby shops.

3—Flat surfaces that require an irregular masking line should be masked with a frisket. (1) Transparent frisket paper can be obtained at art supply stores; cover it with a thin coat of rubber cement. (2) After this coat has dried, apply another thin coat, and while it is still slightly wet, lay the paper (cement side down) on the object to be masked. (3) Smooth the paper down with a straightedge, working from the center to the edges. (4) Cut the paper to the desired outline, being careful not to cut into the object. (5) Remove the unwanted part of the frisket and check its edges to make sure that they are down tight. (6) If any rubber cement has remained on the surface to be painted, allow it to dry; then carefully remove it with the sticky side of a piece of drafting tape or with a rubber cement pick-up (also available at art supply stores). (7) After applying the paint, remove the frisket and clean any cement from the object.

4—Gum strip can also be used for masking some hard, waterproof surfaces. It can be removed by being soaked in water.

5—Liquid frisket (Art Maskoid, Frisketine, E-Z Mask, etc.) can be painted on flat or irregular surfaces. Surplus frisket can be removed by rolling it off with fingers or with a bit of art gum or by picking it up with a piece of masking tape.

When painting 2 colors up to a masked line, either mask twice and apply the 2 colors so that they butt up against another, or (if the added thickness of paint is not objectionable), paint the entire object with the lighter color, mask the line and then apply the second color.

Paint thickness along a mask barrier will generally relate to the thickness of the mask. To achieve a thin coat at this point, either use a thin mask (frisket) or spray the paint with a dry spray. Be careful, however, not to build up a paint ridge against the mask.

BRUSH PAINTING

Brush painting demands patience and skill to avoid visible brush strokes, a deposit of hair on the model or a loss of detail. The difficulty of brush painting is proportionate to the size of the surface that must be painted. Whenever possible, spray the finish. The extra equipment cost will be amortized quickly by the savings in time, temper and model.

Dip the brush only halfway into the paint. Avoid getting paint into the roots of the bristles. Do not accumulate too much paint on the brush. Brush paint with long, even (in thickness and width) strokes applied in 1 direction. Try to achieve even coverage. If irregularities or runs occur, go back over them and smooth out high and low spots. Specks of dust or hairs should be removed immediately with a pin.

After painting, clean brushes by: (1) wiping off as much paint as possible; (2) washing the brush in oil-paint reducer (if painting with an oil paint), lacquer thinner (if using lacquer), or alcohol (after using shellac); (3) washing the brush in soap and water. Liquid brush cleaners, obtainable at hardware stores, may be substituted in step 2. Next time the brush is used, inspect it, especially the roots of its bristles, to be sure that it is clean. The brush may be returned to its original shape by moistening and molding with the fingers.

Brushes

Sable is the most durable (and expensive) brush. White bristle comes next in cost, but is much harder. Camel hair is soft, and costs only $\frac{1}{4}$ as much as sable. Buy the best of each type to avoid the problem of falling bristles.

The shape of the brush is important. See 11-3 for the various shapes of small and medium-sized brushes that are available. Use thin pointed shapes for detail work; flat shapes for painting extensive flat surfaces and straight borders of large areas, and round brushes for painting moderately small objects and for reaching into corners. Brushes must carry enough (but not too much) paint to the work. Since fast drying lacquers may dry on a very small brush before they can be deposited on the work, use a larger brush for this type of paint.

SPRAY PAINTING

Spray painting produces the best finish, and is the easiest technique to master. Certain multi-faceted objects (trusses, trees) can be practically painted only by spraying. Spray paint also dries faster, is less liable to obscure detail, and creates a more uniform coat. A compressor or air cylinder system also permits the dusting of models and work surfaces with a jet of air. On the other hand, very small touches of paint cannot be sprayed easily unless complicated masking is undertaken; the time it takes to clean the equipment may make it more practical to brush paint these small areas. Masking is often required when spray painting.

There are spray instruments at almost every price level, but do not be overly economical, and sacrifice results. If only the finest finishes will be acceptable, consider an artist's air brush (for painting fine and medium-size objects), or an air gun (for large area application); both are powered by an air compressor or a compressed gas cylinder.

Sprayers Providing an Uneven Supply of Air

FIXATIVE SPRAYING TUBES

Lung-powered spray tubes, costing under 50¢, will suffice for the spraying of fixative, and even thin ink and watercolor paint, if a highly spackled texture is acceptable. Sometimes this is just the effect desired for rough model ground contours.

11-3

PAINT BRUSH SHAPES

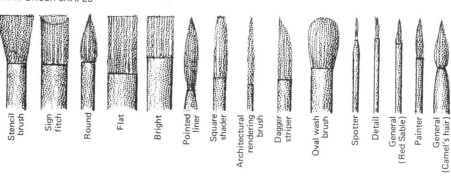

Stencil brush | Sign fitch | Round | Flat | Bright | Pointed liner | Square shader | Architectural rendering brush | Dagger striper | Oval wash brush | Spotter | Detail | General (Red Sable) | Painter | General (Camel's hair)

PERFUME AND THROAT ATOMIZERS AND FLIT GUNS

These household sprayers can also be used to apply thin paints in a spackled finish. Another disadvantage is that pumping requires quite a bit of work.

PUMP ACTION SPRAYS

Sunset House sells a $1.50 pump-action sprayer that has more finesse than a flit can. It is held by and pumped with the same hand.

ELECTRIC VIBRO SPRAYERS

These are run by inexpensive vibrators but their usefulness is diminished by the roughness of their spray.

Sprayers Supplying Air Under a Constant Pressure

PAINT BOMBS

These come in 2 types: that with the paint sealed into the pressure cylinder and that with a detachable paint receptacle and disposable pressure cylinder. With the former, one is not able to mix his own paint. Despite this, many design offices and quite a few professional modelmakers use sealed paint bombs almost exclusively. Both types of paint bombs have additional drawbacks: no control over the amount of air pressure or the shape and size of the spray cone, and a sometimes excessive air pressure. Too much air pressure will create a spray mist and produce a dry grainy paint finish. Paint bombs spray large quantities of paint, making extremely fine painting difficult. Their nozzles should be held about 12" from the work. Some small disposable pressure cylinders can be used with artist's air brushes. Ambroid's Jet-pak consists of a compressed air cylinder, a pint paint jar and a nozzle. The entire unit costs about $3. Air cylinder replacements cost $1.80. The Badger Airbrush Company's Model 250 works with a can pressurized at 80 pounds per square inch, providing $\frac{1}{2}$ hour of power. The air brush costs $6.00, and each can costs $1.80. Another manufacturer of this type of unit is Wren Pak.

ARTIST'S AIR BRUSHES

These can be powered by: air compressors made especially for them, improvised compressors (vacuum cleaners, etc.), compressed gas cylinders and even (though not recommended) spare tires and tire pumps. Most air brushes are meant to be used with the steady 20 to 40 pound per square inch pressure that only an air compressor or gas cylinder can provide.

Garden Type Hand Pumps

These cost about $10, and may be purchased from large hardware stores. When attached to an air pressure regulator and gauge (obtainable from the same source and costing a bit over $5), they may be used with an air brush. The pressurized air is stored in a tank which dispenses a brief supply of nonpulsating air to the brush.

Compressed Gas Cylinders

These can be rented or purchased. Refills are inexpensive if only sporadic painting is done. For constant painting, it is more economical to purchase an air compressor.

Compressor Systems

These come in two types:

1—The compressor pumps air through a pressure regulator; and this system supplies a constant flow of air through the sprayer (which must be a bleeder type).

2—The compressor pumps air into a storage tank; an automatic valve idles the compressor when the pressure in the tank builds above the desired level and starts the compressor when the tank pressure drops.

Compressors are manufactured by such companies as Spray-It, Gamco, Binks, De Vilbiss, etc. Those from Spray-It cost from $10 up, the others from $60 up to $400 (for $\frac{1}{6}$ to $\frac{3}{4}$ hp machines).

Air brushes are manufactured by Wold, Thayer and Chandler, Paasche, etc. Prices start at over $30, and can approach $100 for instruments capable of very fine lines.

Paasche Air Brush Company sells a very handy $25 "traveler's spray unit" that contains a small tank of compressed gas (1 to 3 hour supply) and an air brush.

Stewart-Lundahl makes a $4 air brush that can be run with a vacuum cleaner.

Gamco sells a $6 snap-on attachment that permits the using of fixative, oil paints, lacquer, India ink, glue, plastic sprays, etc. in most fine air brushes without endangering them. The air brush serves only as the source of air; the attachment does not allow possibly injurious material to circulate through it.

To operate an air brush, fill its small reservoir, using a long-haired paint brush to transport the paint. Press down on the trigger to start air flowing through the brush, press down and back to start the paint spray. The farther the trigger is pulled back, the greater will be the amount of paint that will be sprayed. If the air brush can be adjusted to blow a lot of air but little paint, it can be held nearer to the work. This is useful when painting small multifaceted objects.

SPRAY GUNS

These are larger versions of the air brush. They are used for applying the heavier lacquers used to paint acrylic models and for painting large areas. Paint is held in glass jars, not in the open reservoirs used by air brushes.

Atlas sells a compressor and spray gun for $30.

Johnson sells a $23, "400" model Spray-It set which contains a $\frac{1}{4}$ hp compressor and a spray gun. The company's Spray-It guns alone cost from a bit over $10 to over $15.

Speedy Sprayer sells several guns for $9. Binks, Eclipse and De Vilbiss make heavy spray guns that range in cost from $20 to $130. Some of these companies also make flock spray guns.

VISCOSIMETERS

These may be used to check the correct viscosity of the paint mix. Johnson sells one for $1.

AIR DUSTING GUNS

These are for cleaning dust and shavings from the work; they may be run off of a compressed air system.

Speedy Sprayer makes one for $2.50; De Vilbiss makes several for from $3 to $5.

THICKNESS GAUGES

These are for measuring all types of adhesives and paints and are made by Nordson. Some measure wet films, others dry. These gauges are accurate down to $\frac{1}{2}$ mil.

General Spray Techniques

The following techniques should be used when painting with any sprayer; however, it is more important to use them with air brushes, spray guns and paint bombs, since the results obtained with other types of sprayers are, at best, too crude to be improved by even the strictest adherence to technique.

Paint used for spraying must be of a thinner consistency than paint applied by brush. The former should be of a milk or water-like thickness. In general: Enamels require little thinning because they usually come from the container with enough oil. Lacquers, because of their fast evaporation, must be well thinned. Using paint that is too thick may clog the sprayer or cause it to spatter or may not feed through the system. If the paint is too thin, it will run on the object being painted or require several coats to cover.

Textures may be worked into finishes by varying the distance of the sprayer to the object being painted. As the sprayer is moved beyond its optimum distance from the work, the finish first becomes mat, then rough and sandy looking. Thus, a rough finish rather than a smooth one, could mean the sprayer is being held too far from the work.

The optimum distance of the sprayer from the work will depend on the characteristics of the paint and on the sprayer. The proper distance between the spray and the surface also depends on the color being used. Light colors usually require more thinning than dark ones. In general, the paint should reach the object just before it dries. Small objects may be secured in place with 2-faced masking tape while they are being sprayed.

Since the sprayer may spatter on starting, aim it at a piece of scrap until its spray becomes uniform. Spray with overlapping strokes. Successive passes should overlap about $\frac{1}{2}$ the width of the preceding stroke. The previous stroke should still be wet when it is overlapped; otherwise, the paint will not flow together, and may dry in streaks. If attempting to spray a glossy finish, carry the paint strokes beyond the edges of the work before circling back for the next pass. If this is not done, the edges of the work will be less glossy than the center. This phenomenon occurs because the paint along the edges travels farther from the sprayer than the paint deposited at the center of the work, and so strikes the object when it is in a drier state. By finishing the stroke beyond the edge, the mat paint will not come in contact with the work. Another way to prevent this difference in degree of gloss is to hold the sprayer perpendicular to the work.

Paint sags when too much is sprayed in 1 place; it forms ridges, puddles and, possibly, drips. To prevent sagging: hold the sprayer farther from the work, don't spray as much paint, modify the spray pattern so as to leave less overlap on each pass or speed the movement of the sprayer across the work. Once sag has formed in enamel paint, it may be removed by leveling the ridges with a soft brush; runs may be removed with a lintless cloth dipped in turpentine or enamel thinner. To remove sag from lacquer, let the paint harden and, then, with fine, wet abrasive paper, sand the ridges off. Or, while the paint is still wet, try to brush the ridges out with a soft brush dipped in thinner. When the paint has dried, brush strokes may be sanded off and the surface repainted.

If the correct amount of paint is being sprayed, but dribbles start to form as the paint dries, try changing the position of the object several times during the drying period, and let gravity level the paint.

As in brush painting, it is better to build up a thick coat with several thin ones than to try covering with 1 coat. Allow each layer to dry thoroughly before applying the next.

To clean a sprayer, fill its reservoir with paint solvent and let some of it spray through the system. If using an air brush or spray gun, also place a finger over the nozzle while the spray is still coming out. This will reverse the flow of the thinner back through the sprayer. Next, remove the finger from the nozzle and let the spray continue in the regular way until there are no traces of paint in the spray. Clear the nozzle of an aerosol can by inverting it and spraying for a second or 2.

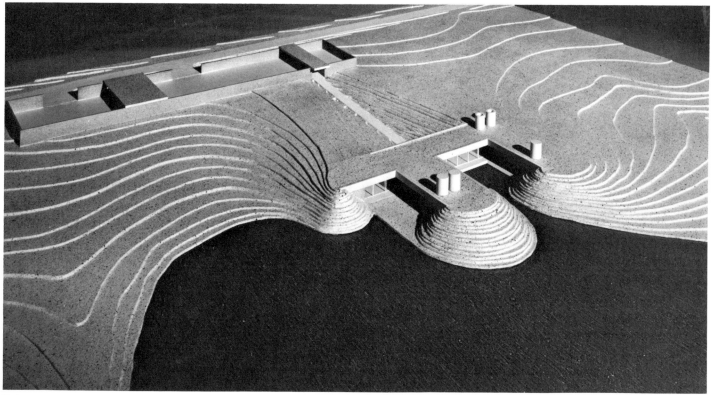

11-4

Project: GEIER HOUSE, CINCINNATI, OHIO.

DESIGNED BY: Philip Johnson Associates.
MODELBUILDER: Joseph Santeramo of the architect's captive model shop.
PHOTOGRAPHER: Louis Checkman.
SCALE: 1/32″ = 1′.
Contours of this presentation model were constructed of spackle painted cardboard. The rest of the model was made from acrylic. The texture of the water was formed by streaking solvent across the plastic.
The photograph was taken with a 4″ × 5″ Sinar view camera, 6⅜″ lens and Super Panchro Press "B" film. 1 750-watt spot was used.
CONSTRUCTION TIME: about 125 hours.

Safety Considerations

Spray only in a thoroughly ventilated room. Wear a respirator when using toxic paints. Be careful not to allow fire or electrical sparks to come in contact with the mist caused by quick drying paints the solvents of which are usually highly flammable. Your insurance company may require a spray booth or, if one is lacking, they may greatly increase the fire insurance premium.

PREFABRICATED PAINT SPRAY BOOTHS

These may be obtained from De Vilbiss; they are constructed from 7′ high metal partitions. Booths come equipped with lights and a fan. A 6 × 5′ booth costs $500; small (3 × 2½′ high) booths that are mounted on legs cost a little under $200. Small (2 × 1½ × 1½′) paint booths containing a turntable are obtainable for $3 from Practra; they make a good enclosure for light air brush spraying.

DIP AND SMEAR PAINTING

Besides applying paint by brush or sprayer, it is possible sometimes to sponge on paint to create a rough finish. This technique is especially useful when trying to paint ground or rocks realistically. Paint may also be applied by dipping the object into a thinned paint mixture. This is a time saver when painting complex 1-color objects such as trees, cars, etc. The object being dipped can be held on a pin or wire frame. After dipping, set it on a sheet of glass to dry. Stand the object so that the paint will drip toward the base.

SIMULATED WOOD

By applying paint with a very stiff brush and intentionally streaking it, many types of wood grains may be simulated. Aero Gloss has a line of over 10 spray wood colors. Floquil's Flo-Stains can be used to stain wood or any light colored surface. Use their light buff Flo-Paque paint as an undercoat on nonwood surfaces or when staining wood a lighter color. Their stains come in cherry, driftwood, mahogany, maple, natural pine, oak, walnut, scotch pine green, silver spruce and blue and yellow poplar.

WEATHERING

Sometimes the modeler will desire to give some part of a model a weathered appearance. This is done to contrast old and new construction or to mute the colors of ready-painted automobiles, people, etc. A simple way to achieve a weathered finish is to dust the object with powdered charcoal or talcum powder (depending on the desired effect) and then to blow off the excess dust. Floquil makes special paints in the following whimsical colors: dust, rust, mud and grime.

FLOCKING

Flock (a soft, woolly fiber) is widely employed to give the impression of grass or moss to baseboards or to simulate certain types of upholstery fabric. Professionals apply flock with a special spray gun, but good results can also be achieved by first painting the surface with a coat of slow drying paint the same color as the flock. Then sift the flock fiber on the paint and blow off the excess when the paint has dried. Flock is available at many artist's supply stores. Inexpensive pump action flock sprayers are obtainable at many model train stores. Small Sales Company sells 1 color of flock and an applicator as part of a 50¢ set. The flock comes in white, black, rose, scarlet, silver, maroon, pink, yellow, gold or 2 shades each of brown, green and blue. For extremely even flocked surfaces, use a ready-made flocked paper, which is also available at artist's supply stores.

TYPES OF PAINTS

In earlier sections of this book will be found painting instructions for balsa, building paper, metal, paper and cardboard, plaster, plastic and wood. Many characteristics of the various general types of paints are enumerated there.

Oil Paints

Oil paints are very easy to apply by brush, but their long drying time limits their usefulness to the modelmaker. Artist's oil paints come in about the largest color range of any paints, but their thickness hides model detail and their finish is not abrasion resistant.

The vehicle of oil paint can be linseed, soybean or tung oil. Oil paints are thinned with turpentine or mineral spirits. They come with high gloss or flat finishes. The high gloss can be flattened if a great quantity of turpentine is mixed into it, but it will not be so affected if mineral spirits are used. Thinners will not rejuvenate dried out paint. Turpentine also hastens drying; oil retards it. If a paint skin has formed in the paint container, remove it whole. If parts of the skin get mixed into the paint, strain the paint through 2 thicknesses of gauze. Interesting rough finishes useful in the representation of stone, earth, etc., can be modeled with oil paint.

Both varnish-based and oil-based enamels are oil paints. Enamels are useful because, among their other attributes, they produce a higher gloss than lacquers. Quick drying enamels are self-leveling and dry in 4 hours. Enamels may be used over oil, lacquer, shellac, casein, rubber-based and vinyl-plastic water paints. A sealer should, however, be used between water paints (except vinyl-plastic water paints) and enamels.

Japan colors, quick drying oil paints, can be obtained in 10 colors from Model Shipways. They dry in 2 hours to a really fine, flat finish. Mix them with quick drying varnish for a satin finish.

Water Paints

Watercolors, because of their transparency, lack covering power. To improve this condition, mix them with flake or Chinese white. In general, water paints have limited usefulness in model making.

Poster colors are of more use to the modeler. One of their biggest drawbacks, the ease with which they can be marred, can be eliminated by giving them a finishing coat of crystal or spirit varnish. This will also increase their richness and depth of color and give them a gloss.

Texture paints are useful in coloring plaster ground constructions. They come in powdered form, and may be applied by brush or spatula, depending on how thick they are mixed.

Plastic watercolors, also called polymer, vinyl or acrylic colors, are a new type of water paint. They are available at art supply stores, and can be used in a thin wash, thick, or mixed with gesso. They dry to a semi-mat finish, but may be mixed with a medium that produces a glossy finish. Dried paint is waterproof, and must be removed with paint remover.

Lacquers

Lacquer is a term frequently applied to any quick drying paint. True lacquer used to have a nitrocellulose base (now some are being made with acrylic, vinyl or other bases). These paints are quick drying; thinners vary with different brands, though either acetone, glycol ether or amyl acetate can be used with most. Do not use more than 1 part thinner to 1 part paint. The same, or cheaper, thinner may be used as a paint remover. Cellulose paints are opaque and inflammable; they can be used on wood, composition board, metal, paper and many plastics (including acrylic). Their rapid drying is ideal for spray application but difficult for brush application. For extensive brush painting, use special brushing (slower drying) cellulose paints or the regular paint mixed with a retarder. Apply by brushing in 1 direction. Allow the previous coat to dry, 1 or more hours, before applying the next. Use No. 400 wet paper between coats. Most top coat lacquers dry to a mellow luster. For a high-gloss polish, apply a silicone car polish or furniture polish, or apply a coat of high-gloss clear lacquer. To reduce the normal luster, add a flattening agent to the paint. During warm and humid weather, moisture may retard drying time. A fan can help to rectify this. Extreme moisture may cause the lacquer to turn a whitish color; painting under these conditions should be avoided, or use a special summer lacquer thinner or add retarder mix to the regular thinner. Lacquers cannot be applied over oil paints; they would dissolve them. Although lacquer dries rapidly, avoid handling painted objects for several hours.

Industrial and automotive lacquers are used by many professional modelmakers on acrylic and other materials. These lacquers must be spray painted; they provide a flat finish, and do not ruin detail. Some of the heavier lacquers of this type require between 60 and 70 pounds of spraying pressure.

Behlen and Brother Spray Lacquer line, which can be obtained in semigloss and flat finishes, includes 30 colors, 3 whites (including flat), 2 grays, 2 blacks (including flat), and clear gloss, semigloss and flat.

Behlen and Brother Brush Lacquer line includes 13 colors, white, gray, black and clear.

Practra Lacquers come in about 20 colors. They dry in 5 minutes to a smooth, hard, glossy finish, and can be used on metal, wood, paper, plastic, etc.

Synthetic Enamels

Enamels have a high-gloss finish, and may be used on wood, plaster, metal, paper, etc. Strain enamels to insure that they will form an absolutely smooth coat. Synthetic enamels are best applied by brush, and should be as thin as possible. Use a soft brush, and apply in one direction using even strokes. Since they dry rapidly, work fast. Do not run the brush over an area that has just been painted. Objects to be painted must be completely grease free. Wood must be perfectly dry or the enamel will soon crack and peel. Use synthetic filler as an undercoat, and to fill wood. Sand with wet paper. Synthetic enamels dry in about 4 hours, but allow twice this time before again working on the surface. Sand smooth with extremely fine, wet, abrasive paper, and, if a high-gloss coat is desired, polish with metal polish.

Behlen and Brother sells fast drying alkyd enamels in jet-spray cans. Their line includes 5 metallic colors, gloss and flat white and black, 11 glossy colors and clear.

Krylon Spray Enamels are universally available and come in 13 colors, 7 fluorescent colors, 4 metallic colors, 2 blacks, 2 whites and 3 grays.

Practra Namel can be obtained from hobby stores in small spray cans and in tiny bottles. The spray paint comes in 29 colors, 12 metallic colors, 2 blacks, 2 whites, gray and clear. Their brush-on line is almost as extensive.

Testor's Spray Pla Enamel comes in 15 colors, 3 metallic colors, 3 transparent colors, 2 whites and 2 blacks.

Testor's brush-on Champion-Pla enamels come in $\frac{1}{4}$ ounce bottles in 44 colors, 5 metallic colors, white, gray, and black.

Illinois Bronze Powder and Paint Company's Spray-O-Namel comes in 15 ounce spray cans and consists of 21 colors, 7 metallic colors, 7 whites, 2 grays, 4 blacks, and clear, gloss and satin top coats.

Illinois also sells Shining Armor Enamels, which come in 3 ounce spray cans or in 2 ounce and 1 pint containers. All 3 types of containers are available in 12 colors, 2 whites, black, and clear.

Floquil Model Paints

These are exceptionally versatile, waterproof paints that may be applied without a primer to all materials. They dry quickly (in 2 to 5 minutes), and are self-leveling. Being especially engineered for model work, they can be applied in a coat that is unusually thin but which adequately covers the model, thus preventing even the smallest detail from becoming obliterated. The trade name of this line is either Floquil Model Railroad Colors or Flo-Paque Colors, depending on whether or not they are purchased in model shops or in arts and crafts centers. Both brands are identical except that the latter comes in more colors (over 50 as compared with over 30). Both use Dio-Sol as a solvent. Dio-Sol is also used to clean brushes and surfaces to be painted and to thin paints intended for spray application.

Floquil's line also includes retarder, glaze (which is either mixed with Floquil paints to create an eggshell or semi-gloss finish or applied over dried paint to produce a medium-gloss finish), Hi-Gloss (which is applied over regular paint), Crystal-Cote (an abrasion resisting, clear top coat), daylight fluorescent and night luminescent colors, and wood stains.

Metallic Finishes

PAINTS

Metallic finishes can be effected in several ways. Chrome and other metallic oil-based paints, lacquers, and enamels may be used. Some are obtainable in spray cans (see the synthetic enamel section). Various companies, Practra among them, also make metallic paints for styrene. Metallic paints show finger marks, and are not as brilliant as metal foils.

Behlen and Brother Jet-Spray Alkyd Enamel comes in aluminum, copper and gold leaf.

Illinois Bronze Powder and Paint Company Met-L-Namel Spray or Brush comes in brass, bright gold, antique gold, copper, platinum, silver and chrome plate.

Practra Spray Namel comes in copper, chrome silver, silver mist, gold mist, gold leaf, metallic blue, green and turquoise.

Practra Brushing Namel comes in chrome silver, gold leaf, copper, bronze, flat aluminum, metallic red, blue and green.

Testor's Spray Pla Enamel comes in gold, silver and copper.

Floquil Model Railroad Colors come in gun metal, antique bronze, copper, brass, bright gold and bright silver.

A.M.T. Corporation has 7 metallic lacquer paints that come in aerosol cans in brass, bright gold and bright silver.

Floquil Flo-gilt comes in old and bright silver and gold, brass, copper, antique bronze and gun metal.

POWDERED METAL

Aluminum, gold, brass, copper, etc. colors come in powder which is mixed, by the modeler, into lacquer thinner and clear lacquer, and is then spray applied. To prepare the powders for brush application, thin them with turpentine or enamel thinner, using quick drying varnish or bronzing liquid as the vehicle.

Behlen and Brother sells 1 ounce and 1 pound containers of bronze powders that come in almost 30 shades of gold, bronze, brass, aluminum, copper, metallic green and metallic red. These powders are mixed with their bronzing liquid (a quick drying varnish), and, when dry, may be burnished for greater luster.

WAX

The American Art Clay Company makes cylinders of wax that contain metallic powder. These can be rubbed into wood, metal, plaster, etc. and buffed to a luster. They are thinned with turpentine. This line, called Rub'n Buff Metallic Finishes, comes in gold, silver, copper, and antique gold.

METAL FOILS

Of all the metal finishes, none can surpass actual foil or leaf for realism. Household aluminum foil makes good polished chrome; it can be stretched over complex curves and held in place with rubber cement or shellac. Use a wood dowel to roll the foil flat and to burnish it into place. To represent anodized aluminum, spray translucent colored lacquer over aluminum foil (or, for that matter, over surfaces painted with aluminum paint).

Gold and silver leaf can be represented by Fasson adhesive papers which come in gold and silver. Lacking these, use aluminum foil sprayed with mat finish for silver leaf and aluminum foil sprayed with yellow translucent lacquer for gold foil.

The National Foil Company sells half-fine, shiny gold foil (No. S-2) and half-fine, shiny silver foil (No. S-1); both have a slightly dotted finish. Their emery shiny silver (No. S-1) has a stippled finish and their pebbly shiny silver (No. S-1) has a hammered texture.

Real metallic leaf can be obtained from shops carrying supplies for the sign painting and bookbinding trades. Thin sheets of leaf are held in place by size or burnishing clay. The latter is mixed with warm water until it is the consistency of heavy varnish; care must be taken to stir the mixture until it is smooth and free from bubbles. The mix is applied to the surface to be gilded and allowed to dry. Then it is sanded with 7/0 paper and dusted, and another application is made, allowed to dry, sanded and dusted. The surface is then wet, and made tacky with a 10% solution of alcohol. Metal leaf is applied and carefully pressed down with cotton batting. After being allowed to dry overnight, the leaf is burnished with agate burnishers. A coat of clear Leaf Lacquer, or French varnish may be applied to the leaf to protect it and to prevent discoloration.

SENDING OUT

To avoid the complications that a truly effective metallic finish entails, some professional model-makers send out wood, plaster and plastic parts to a metalizing shop for spraying, or send metal parts to an electroplating shop for plating. Illustration 8-10 shows brass that has been nickel-plated, by an outside shop, to represent stainless steel.

Shellac

Shellac is a natural gum that may be bought in flake form, or it may, more usually, be obtained already dissolved in denatured alcohol. 2 types are available: natural (which is orange in color) and bleached (which is white). White shellac makes a

good undercoat for objects that will be painted with translucent or transparent paints. Behlen and Brother sells shellac in a jet spray can.

Varnish

Varnish is a combination of resin, drying oil, drier and solvent (turpentine or mineral spirits). It usually comes in a clear state, and may be pigmented. It is best to spray varnish, since application with a brush often fills up detail.

Novelty Finishes
FLUORESCENT PAINTS

The Illinois Bronze Powder and Paint Company's Spray-On fluorescent paint line of 4 colors comes in aerosol cans. They can be applied to Styrofoam and to many other plastics, as well as to most other materials. This paint glows brightly in any light.

Flo-quil's Flo-Glo daylight fluorescent paint comes in 7 colors. Their Nite-Glo night luminescents appear off-white in daylight and glows in the dark.

TEXTURED PAINTS

Wrinkle Finish Spray-O-Namel made by the Illinois Bronze Powder and Paint company comes in aerosol cans in 6 colors, 1 metallic color, black and 2 grays.

Metallic hammer finishes can be achieved with Illinois Bronze Powder and Paint Company's Hamm-R-Spray. These come in aerosol cans in 2 colors, 3 metallic colors and gray.

High-Gloss and Flat Finishes

It is very useful to be able instantly to alter glossy or flat finishes at will. One use is to dull the shine of Zip-A-Tone overlays. Krylon has a mat finish spray in an aerosol can as does Testor's (their Dullcote spray). Testor's has a gloss finish called Glosscote which also comes in an aerosol can. Other ways of creating high-gloss and flat finishes are listed under the various types of paints. In general, a high-gloss finish may be achieved with liquid wax or metal polish.

Floquil's Aqua-Cote is a transparent coating that adds a wet look. Its drying time is 24 hours.

12 THE BASE

The base of a model, like the foundation of an actual structure, must be rigid. The fact that warpage must be avoided is obvious considering what it will do to the model resting on it. The base also must not rack and distort even if improperly lifted.

Small models may be safely constructed on $\frac{3}{8}''$ plywood or $\frac{1}{2}''$ cardboard, Celotex or Homosote. When the dimensions of the model are greater than $2 \times 3'$ or when the model weighs more than a few pounds, these minimal materials must be increased in thickness. When the base is as large as $3 \times 4'$, it is usually more practical to build a frame from 1×1 or $1 \times 2'$ lumber and to top it with a thin sheet of plywood, Celotex or cardboard than to use a massive slab of these materials. When using plywood, run its exterior grain parallel to the long edge of the baseboard.

Underframing, to stiffen the baseboard and keep it from warping, should be considered even for quick design models. If baseboards have been saved from previous models, it is possible to amortize, over several models, the time that their construction took. The small extra effort required to build a framed baseboard that can be used on 3 or 4 models is worthwhile, since it is unpleasant to work even briefly on a surface that is not warp-free.

Baseboards of small models should be rectangular or square. Those that follow an irregular outline are hard to construct and pack and may present damage-prone corners.

Life-Like Products, Incorporated, sells $2'' \times 4'' \times 2''$ deep foam plastic boards for $3.50, the flat tops of which are covered with green, grass-like particles. The boards are strengthened by a waffle pattern cast into their underside, and make a nice ready-made baseboard for models.

If the model is large enough to make handling and shipping a problem, construct it in several sections. These should be about $4 \times 8'$ or some other convenient-to-move size. Just as some homemade boats have been built too large for their removal from a cellar workshop, so have some models been built too large for their removal

from the shop. When building a 2 or more part baseboard, have the joint between the boards follow a naturally occurring line—the side of a building, wall or road—and not cut across the structure. Join the baseboard sections together with dowels or mortise and tenon attachments that can be easily taken apart. Screw or bolt the assembled baseboard together, locating the fasteners so that they are easily accessible for disassembly.

12-1

Project: SAUSALITO YACHT CLUB.

Designed by: Theodore T. Boutmy.
Modelbuilders: members of the architect's staff.
Scale: $1/8'' = 1'$.
The roof of this presentation model was made from a single piece of stiff paper. Walls were constructed from illustration board covered with colored paper. Decks, railings and structural members were made from balsa, baseboard from a plywood sheet stained blue. The shore: Homosote.
Construction time: about 75 hours.

95

FRAMING THE BASE-BOARD

Framing members may be simply nailed together or, for greater strength, rabbeted or dadoed (See the Appendix for these and other strong joining techniques). Triangular shaped plywood plates may also be used as reinforcements, as may metal angles.

Framing may be made from pine or Douglas fir. When selecting wood, make sure it is straight grained, free from knots and warps and completely dry. It is worth a visit to the lumberyard to select personally so-called uniform wood strips the actual dimensions of which are also similar; otherwise, one may find that the actual variations make neat carpentry difficult. Place framing members along or under the edges of the baseboard, and, to prevent sagging, across the center of the board. Run these members from the long edge of the board to long edge.

Bonding Lumber

The lumber used for framing or the internal bracing of large models or display stands may be bonded with casein, acrylic resin or aliphatic resin glues. The latter 2 are good gap fillers; aliphatic glue is the fastest drying of the 3. All 3 can be colored to match the wood so as to prevent any excess squeezed out of a joint from leaving too noticeable a stain. Color the casein glue with water-soluble dye or alkali-proof dry earth colors that have been dissolved in water. Color the resin glues with soluble acid-fast dye.

EDGING

If you intend to construct an attractive edge on a small baseboard, either make the base from plywood and dado in hardwood edging strips, or build the baseboard by the frame-and-cover sheet technique. The edging strips may then be nailed or cemented to the frame. Thus the cover sheet may be of thin or of soft material (cardboard, Homosote, Celotex, etc.). Edging may simply be a facia board, or it may be any of the trim moldings that are available at the local lumberyard. Rectangular "strips," "lattice strips" and "squares," available in white wood, white pine and occasionally in oak, come in the inch sizes shown in the table on this page.

For fancy edgings, the following molding styles may be used alone or in combination with one another : beads ; coves ; batterns ; door stops ; quarter-rounds ; back bands ; bases, glasse, O.G.'s ; panel, fillet, conge and floor moldings ; solid growns ; clam shell and sanitary trims. Since these strips come in minimum widths of $\frac{1}{4}''$, they are of greatest use on fairly large models.

Simple edgings can also be cut from sheet stock with a bench-mounted circular saw. A router can also be used to cut intricate molding shapes. Both tools enable one to work in mahogany and other attractive woods.

Edging for baseboards with irregular thicknesses due to a nonlevel ground line may be constructed after the contours are all in place. The edging may be made from $\frac{1}{4}''$ plywood or $\frac{1}{4}''$ pine trim. Place the uncut material along the side of the base and trace the uneven ground line on it. Cut the edging on a power or hand saw, allowing about $\frac{1}{8}''$ excess material. This will later be sanded down to the tops of the contours. For good results, miter the intersections of the edging. Screw or brad-nail the edging in place. The heads of these fasteners should be driven below the wood surface; the resulting holes can be plugged with dowels when using screws, or filled with plastic wood if brads are being employed. The edging may then be stained or painted; if reasonable care has been taken in its fabrication, the edging should be of the same quality as fine picture frames or furniture detail.

AVAILABLE RECTANGULAR TRIM MOLDING

Inches	1/4	3/8	7/16	1/2	5/8	3/4	25/32	1 1/8	1 3/8	1 3/4
1/2	X	X		X						
5/8					X					
3/4				X		X				
7/8	X	X			X					
1 1/8			X				X	X		
1 3/8	X	X	X				X		X	
1 5/8	X		X							
1 3/4		X					X	X	X	X
2 1/4							X			
2 5/8	X		X							
2 3/4		X					X	X	X	X
3 5/8	X		X				X			
3 3/4							X	X	X	X

FINISHING THE BASE-BOARD

If the model is on a level site or if there are extensive bodies of water around it, one may choose to have a baseboard that, uncovered or only stained, can abstractly represent the ground or water. Stained wood, Upson panels, Sheetrock, Masonite, Celotex, and flake board have all been effectively used in this way.

The base edging may be painted, or if a natural wood finish is desired, stained, shellacked or covered with Flexwood, or Weldwood Flexible Wood Trim. The latter 2 are cemented in place and rolled flat. Plywood edging tape, a wood veneer with pressure-sensitive tape backing, also may be used. To apply, simply strip off the protective backing paper, press the tape into place and run a warm iron over it. All these veneers may be lightly sanded and stained.

Painting the Baseboard and Its Framing

A great difficulty in painting wood is to achieve a grain-free finish. Some paints can even raise the grain of the wood and thus add to the problem. If the paint being used does this, despite one's having properly sealed and sanded the work, use Firzite wood sealer obtainable at lumberyards.

The procedure for obtaining a smooth finish is to fill in cracks and nicks with plastic wood. Sand smooth and apply 2 or more coats of sanding sealer. Sand between these coats, starting with No. 300 paper and then changing to No. 400. Sand with the grain, frequently blowing the sanding dust from the work. Sanding sealers that can be used are : various commercial sealers, shellac, thinned dope, dope or clear lacquer mixed with talcum powder. Good for finishing end grain wood is Ditzler's Rip Rap primer, which is purchasable in automobile supply stores, and which must be spray applied. Sealers can also serve as the primer coat. When the sealed surface is velvety smooth, it may be, if so desired, polished with a very fine steel wool. Paint the wood with dope, poster color, oil paint or any other finish. Apply the paint with the grain.

To prevent pitch or sap from coming through the finish, shellac knots or other areas that could produce sap.

For natural finishes, use furniture polish (which comes in various wood colors) or wood stain directly on the sanded wood.

SIMPLEST PLOT PLANS

The simplest way to represent the ground and its contours is to cement on the baseboard an aerial photo or a black-on-white print of the plot. Photographs are used mostly with very small scale town planning models. Plot plans may be used with models in all scales. Roads and existing buildings can be colored in on the print, and models of important buildings and trees cemented in place.

LAMINATED CONTOURS

The simplest way to construct ground contours is to laminate them from sheet material. Laminated contours can be very attractive ; in fact, more than a few models have few aesthetic virtues other than a fascinating lamination pattern.

Lamination thickness should represent a significant increment of grade elevation. If the model is to aid in design, use a lamination thickness equal to the increment that is drawn on the plot plans. While laminated construction is usually associated with less elaborate models, it has often been used on highly detailed, professionally constructed models. Laminations may be made from such interesting looking materials as cork sheet (for a rough earth look), or corrugated cardboard (on very rough models). More standard laminations can be finished by being painted, covered with flock, covered with green cloth (whose texture represents grass in a very interesting way), or even covered with a plaster coat to create a continuous contour.

Use a material for lamination that is homogeneous, not one constructed out of plys of various compositions. This excludes such materials as illustration and mat board the finished edges of which would always show the plys.

To construct laminated contours: (1) Make a map of the site with the contours represented by continuous lines. Have this map reproduced to the scale of the model. (2) Transfer each contour line to a sheet of the material being used. To transfer the lines, cover the bottom of the map with powdered graphite, place the map over the sheet material and trace along the desired contour. If intending to lighten the assembly, decide at this point what material will be cut away. The best system to use is to leave about a 1" wide surface for the next (higher) lamination to rest on. (3) Cement the plys together. If the assembly is in danger of sagging where the lighting hole has been cut, make support piers from sufficient plys of cemented together material. These may be temporarily wedged in place or permanently cemented into the model. Nails, pins or brads may be used to strengthen the assembled laminations. They will also serve to hold the assembly together while the cement is drying.

Place buildings on laminated contours by excavating the shape of the building into the contours so that the building rests on the lowest elevation that intersects the building. If only a few plys need be excavated, do this with a mat knife after the laminations have dried. If many plys must be cut or if laminating with tough material, lay out and cut the excavations at the same time as the contours.

An interesting way to make contours is to place the contour plan on a thick board of wood and to cut the board along each contour line. Reassemble the wood with adjacent boards depressed or raised so as to describe properly the contour heights (14-6).

PLASTER CONTOURS

Continuous contours are most easily constructed from plaster, wire mesh and wood formwork. The construction procedure is as follows:

1—Tack a plot plan, the same scale as the model, on the baseboard. On it draw a 4″ or larger grid. (4″ represents a very conservative spacing of supports for the plaster and may, on some models, be increased.)

2—Cut 1″ dowels or 1 × 1″ pine strips to lengths that correspond to the various heights that the wire mesh must be held above the baseboard at the intersections of the grid. Cut these posts carefully so that they will stand squarely at 90° angles to the baseboard.

3—Cut holes into the site plan where the posts will be mounted. Attach the posts to the baseboard by cement, screws or nails.

Another technique that may be used to build the under support of the mesh is shown in illustration 12-2A, B and C. Plywood or heavy cardboard formers are cut to the proper contour and are mounted on the baseboard. If the elevations vary greatly, it may be wise to build an egg crate of formers (12-2E).

4—Cut rough edging strips of plywood to go around the baseboard. These strips will support the wire mesh along the edges of the model.

5—Remove the plot plan.

6—Place galvanized iron wire mesh (chicken wire) or No. 12 Japan iron wire screening over the posts. Hold the mesh in place with broad-head galvanized nails, carpet tacks or staples; or notch the sides of the posts and wind wire through the mesh and around the notches. If, despite precautions, the plaster should rust the fasteners,

producing a stain on the surface of the plaster, cover the stain with paint.

Contours may be formed in the mesh by hand pressure. Abrupt changes in level may require occasional cuts in the mesh; the material is then either overlapped or spread apart and a piece of scrap mesh is wired in place over the resulting void.

7—Trim any mesh hanging over the plywood edging strips. Hammer the edge of the mesh into the edge of the edging strips, being careful not to shatter the wood.

Instead of using mesh, it may be better to pile crumpled paper and/or rock wool insulation around the dowels or blocks, up to within $\frac{1}{2}$″ of the height of the desired elevations. Plaster or wood putty is then applied directly to the top of the paper and insulation.

8—Mix a sufficient quantity of plaster to a heavy cream texture.

9—Soak wide strips of surgical bandage, muslin, scrim or buckram in the plaster. Cover the mesh with several layers of this. If the mesh still shows through, the plaster mix is too thin.

As alternatives to these materials, use strips of newspaper dipped in wallpaper paste or Casco glue. These should be laid in a crisscross pattern on the mesh in a depth of about 10 layers. Speed the drying of the paste with infrared bulbs. Once dry, give the assembly a surface coat of texture paint, which leaves it ready for color painting.

A third alternate choice is the use of $\frac{1}{4}$″ mesh screen (hardware cloth) for the mesh and the application of a stiff mix of plaster directly on it.

Still another possibility is to place posts as far apart as 1′ o.c. and to join them with a webbing of masking tape. Place crumpled-up newspaper between the posts, building up to the desired height. Apply strips of paper towels, plastic window screen, craft paper or gauze dipped in Hydrocal plaster. Build up 2 or more plys of the impregnated material, making sure that adjacent strips overlap. When the plaster has dried, remove the crumpled newspaper and apply a top coat of textured plaster.

10—Add more plaster to the mix, increasing it to a stiffer consistency. With a palette knife, smooth on blobs of this new plaster to the gauze that is already in place. Work the plaster with tools that have been dipped in water. The total plaster thickness should be $\frac{1}{4}$″; its top should be about $\frac{1}{8}$″ lower or on a level with the top of the edging of the baseboard. Each $\frac{1}{8}$″ thickness that can be

eliminated from the plaster will mean a 10 pound reduction in the weight of a 2 × 4′ model, so try to hold to the $\frac{1}{4}$″ thickness.

11—Prior to drying, the plaster may be textured by being studded with rocks, pebbles, landscaping granules, sand, sawdust or flock; or with brush strokes or tool working. Be careful not to leave trowel or finger marks in the plaster. These marks may be removed by stippling the wet plaster with a brush. The texture imparted to the plaster and the materials placed in it should not be grossly out of scale. Often a mat colored finish is all the texture needed to represent grass, sand or earth on a small-scale model. It is equally important that the earth or rocks are not shiny or smooth; this lack of texture will impart an unrealistic, waxy look.

Nails may be inserted into the wet plaster at points where one wants to have trees. When the plaster has dried, remove the nails and place tree trunks in the resulting holes.

12—If the base of the building, its areaways or other subground construction are to be sunk into the plaster, they must first be boxed out with plywood or cardboard. Cut an opening into the wire mesh before applying the plaster covered gauze, place the box, and shim it up with balsa strips (12-2D). Posts that would thrust through these areas must naturally be relocated, preferably so that they abut and help square up the boxed out construction.

Fast contoured bases for study models can be made by cutting formers from corrugated paper. Place wrinkled up newspaper between the formers to help support the plaster applied on strips of newspaper. A troweled-on plaster coat gives the top of the assembly its final form.

Plasters and Cements That May Be Used

Unlike casting plasters, plasters used to build contours need not be extremely dense or strong. The most important characteristics that should be considered are: texture, which should be compatible with the scale of the model; and the drying time, which for the top coat should be sufficient to allow working with it. When building the assembly with 2 or more coats of plaster, thoroughly wet the previous plaster layer before applying a new coat.

12-2

GROUND CONTOUR CONSTRUCTION

(A) FORMER CONSTRUCTION

(D) POST CONSTRUCTION

(A) PLAN OF SITE

(B) SECTION THROUGH F-F

(C) PLAN OF MODELS FRAMING

(E) EGGCRATE CONSTRUCTION

Some of the plasters that may be used are as follows:

Rough Coat Wall Plaster provides a subtle, textured finish. (Red Top Structo Lite and other brands.)

Patching Plasters give a smooth finish.

Scenic Plasters are obtainable from model train supply stores. One such plaster is Perma-Scene. It is earth colored and made by Permacraft Products.

One's Own Concoction of Scenic Plaster might include the following formulas: (1) 4 parts sawdust, 4 parts plaster, 1 part library paste. Dissolve the paste in water, then add the plaster and sawdust. This mix sets in about 15 minutes. (2) By using the previous formula but increasing the library paste to 2 parts and adding a drop of LePages glue for each pint of dry plaster and sawdust, the setting time of the mix will be extended to 8 hours. Mix the glue into the water prior to dissolving the paste in it.

High-Temperature Insulating Cement is manufactured by the Asbestos Supply Company of Washington. It has an extremely rough texture that may be used to create interesting effects. By straining out some of its coarser fibers, its texture can be modified. Casco powdered casein glue should be added to the dry cement to increase its binding ability.

Joint Cement is used in construction to fill the joints between dry wall panels. It is slow drying, and quite good for rock carving.

Texture Paint is made by U.S. Gypsum Company, Wasco Calcimine Company, etc. and produces a grainless imitation plaster surface. This paint, used by builders to finish gypsum wallboard, takes about 2 days to harden (fast drying texture paint hardens in less time), providing a long time in which to texture its surface.

Plaster may be colored with water paints and flat oil colors; the latter unevenly soak into the plaster in a very realistic way. Apply paints with an inexpensive brush. Dry colors, such as powdered tempera, mixed into the wet plaster give a dull, integral color.

Asbestos fibers mixed equally with plaster will add a great deal of resilient strength. Mix the fibers into the powdered plaster and then add water. LePages glue added to the mix will delay its setting time. Sawdust is sometimes mixed into plaster to change the texture. The mix should contain between 1/3 to 2/3 sawdust. Adding sawdust will also increase the drying time of the plaster.

SKIN CONTOURS

If a contour is desired that is very light or if the contour must be duplicated, the complicated skin-over-egg-crate construction technique may be used.

1—Obtain a contour map of the site and convert it to the scale of the model.

2—Draw a 2″ o.c. grid on the plan.

3—At each intersection of the grid, record how high the finished elevation will have to be. Start at the lowest grade with the minimum ground thickness that is desired, and work through the other grades.

4—Cut a strip from $\frac{1}{8}$″ thick wood or plywood for every line on the grid. Since the strip will be cut into a former for the grades that appear along that grid line, make it sufficiently wide to form the highest grade that will be encountered.

5—On each strip, draft the contour of the grid line that it represents. Also draw 2″ o.c. lines representing the intersections of the strip with all the strips perpendicular to it.

6—Using a jig saw, cut the contour line in each strip.

7—On a bench-mounted circular saw, cut $\frac{1}{8}$″ wide slots halfway into each strip along the 2″ o.c. lines. The slots should run from the top (finished grade side) halfway to the bottom on all the strips that run in 1 direction and from the bottom halfway to the top on the set of strips that run perpendicular to the first set of strips.

8—Cement the strips together into an egg crate.

9—From balsa, cut $1\frac{7}{8} \times 1\frac{7}{8} \times \frac{1}{2}$″ or thicker blocks. Cement 1 of these into each cell of the egg crate.

10—Carve the balsa to follow the contours of the egg crate.

11—The skin contour can be made from Samcoforma, a material used in the shoe industry to stiffen shoes, or from Celastic. See page 77 for instructions on working with Celastic. Sheets of Samcoforma are placed into a shallow enameled metal tray to be made pliable with liquid softener.

12—Take the material out of the liquid and allow any excess to run off. Lay the limp sheet on the wood contour form. Slightly overlap adjacent sheets. The softener will cement the strips together. Additional layers may be added for greater strength.

13—Remove the Samcoforma skin from the form and finish its edges.

14—Cutouts for buildings and areaways may be sawed into the hardened material and boxed out with wood or cardboard.

SHEET MATERIAL CONTOURS

Continuous contours may be made of "dry" materials if the site is fairly level. (1) Build up the form of the contours from parallel plywood or heavy cardboard formers or from an egg crate made of these materials. (2) Cement sheets of $\frac{1}{16}$″

12-3

COURTESY OF THE UNIVERSAL ATLAS CEMENT DIVISION, U.S. STEEL CORP.

***Project:* GIANT CONCRETE BOWL.**

DESIGNED BY: Raymond and Rapo.
MODELBUILDER: Theodore Conrad (a professional modelbuilder).
PHOTOGRAPHER: Robert Damora.
SCALE: 1/8″ = 1′.
Only 1/4 of this presentation model was constructed. Its shell concrete roof was vacuum-formed from acrylic. Columns, beams, setas and ramps were also made from acrylic; Railings from scribed acrylic. Cars were stretch formed from acetate that had been softened in acetone.
The photograph was taken with an 8″ × 10″ Deardorff view camera and Schneider Angulon wide-angle lens.

cardboard, plywood, sheetrock or balsa on the form. (3) Directly finish, paint and landscape the surface, or waterproof it by cementing on muslin and then covering it with a thin coat of plaster.

STYROFOAM CONTOURS

Contours may be quickly carved from lightweight Styrofoam planks. Cut the plastic to its approximate shape with a sharpened putty knife or a serrated bread knife. Check the thickness of the remaining material by pushing a stiff wire through to the baseboard and measuring the height of the wire. The last $\frac{1}{8}$ to $\frac{1}{4}$" of material can be eliminated by compressing it with blows from a hammer delivered through a block of wood. Individual rock outcrops may also be carved from Styrofoam. Carved plastic may be: (1) left uncovered or "landscaped" with a mixture of sawdust, flock or granules and glue; (2) covered with a thin layer of plaster; or (3) covered with a skin layer of plaster, impregnated fabric or Celastic. A plaster or skin layer, usually incorporated on presentation models, will protect the Styrofoam from abrasion. Celastic, to be molded on Styrofoam, must be softened with a special activator, since the regular one will melt the foam.

Contours can also be milled from Styrofoam. They resemble the stepped contours made by the laminating technique. Topo Foam of New York City will mill Styrofoam contours to specification. They work with 1/64", and larger, steps, producing a contour model so beautiful that even the most elaborate presentation model may be left unfinished or only painted.

TITLE PLATES

The title plate of a model can be as simple as hand lettering applied to a strip of illustration board, or it may be an engraved bronze plate.

Some of the almost unlimited possibilities are as follows:

Obtain letters made from plastic, wood or plaster and set them directly on the baseboard or on plates made from wood, plastic, illustration board, etc. Transfer or pressure-sensitive overlay letters may also be used in the same way. If an error is made, transfer letters may be removed with a piece of cellophane tape.

Interesting effects can be achieved by: (1) placing transfer letters on an acrylic sheet and spray painting the sheet; then carefully removing the letters and backlighting the sheet; (2) backlighting transparent or translucent plastic letters.

Avoid the dirt that eventually collects along the borders of pressure-sensitive letters (those that must be cut out and burnished in place) by using transfer letters (those that, when burnished, come away from their carrying sheet). Dirt may also be avoided by applying cutout pressure-sensitive letters to a mock-up board, then photocopying and using the resulting prints or photostats on the model.

Attach title plates with cement, brass escutcheon pins, fancy head nails, screws, etc.

LETTERS AND NUMBERS (UNDER 1″ HIGH) MADE BY PROFESSIONAL SIGN AND ART SUPPLY COMPANIES

Name	Thickness (inch)	Height[1]	Styles	Colors	Supplier and price
PLASTIC LETTERS					
Polystyrene molded letters	1/8	1/4″ (most styles)	5	Translucent white, black, blue, red, ivory, green, yellow	Spencer Industries; 10¢–16¢ each with plain backs, 16¢–24¢ with pressure-sensitive or magnetized backs; minimum order $10
Ready-cut Plexiglas letters	1/16, 1/8, 3/16, 1/4 (B & W only)	up to 1″	8	Black, white, 5 colors	Spencer Industries; 10¢–66¢ per letter, plus an extra 24¢ per letter for adhesive backing; minimum order $10
Cast Polyester letters	3/8	7/8″ and 1″	2	White	Spencer Industries; 34¢ per letter, plus 50¢ per letter to paint them (minimum charge for painting $12), plus 50¢ per letter to cement them or $1 to screw onto a backing, or $1.20 per letter to furnish threaded prongs with letters
Mitten Designer letters—cast	1/4 to 1/2	5/16″, 3/8″, 1/2″, 5/8″, 3/4″, 7/8″, 1″	7	White	Mitten Designer Letters; 9 1/2¢–23¢ per letter
Molded polystyrene letters	1/8	1/2″, 5/8″, 3/4″, 1″	5	4 colors; letters are translucent	Spencer Industries; 12¢–16¢ per letter; 20¢–24¢ with pressure-sensitive backs; minimum order $10
Hernard three-dimensional display letters of plastic-ceramic composition	1/4 or 3/8	3/8″, 3/4″, 7/8″, 1 1/4″	10	White	Hernard Mfg. Co.; 8¢–14¢ per letter; comes with flat back or with projecting pins
Planotype Re-usable plastic letters	Nil	5/16″, 3/8″, 7/16″, 1/2″, 5/8″, 3/4″, 1″	3	Black, white, red are opaque; 4 colors are transparent	Plano Scope Corp.; 1/3¢–3¢ per letter
BOARD LETTERS					
Hallcraft Die-Cut Board Letters	9/100	3/4″ & 1″	2	White	Art supply stores; about 1¢ per letter
TRANSFER LETTERS					
Prestyle Instant Letters	Transfers from carrying sheet by light pressure	8 to 160 points (but not in all styles)	70	Black, white, some in red, yellow, blue, or gold	Art supply stores; $1.50 per 10″ × 15″ sheet
Cello Tak	Transfers from carrying sheet by light pressure	10 to 188 points (but not in all styles)	Approx. 150	Black, white, red (opaque)	Art supply stores; $1.00 per 10″ × 15″ sheet
Decca-Dry line of Chart-Pak Inc.	Transfers from carrying sheet by light pressure	8 to 180 points (but not in all styles)	Approx. 35	White, black, some in blue, red	Art supply stores; $2.25 per 13 1/4″ × 16 1/2″ sheet
Prestyle	Transfers from carrying sheet by light pressure	8 points to 3″ high (but not in all styles)	Approx. 60	Black, white, red, blue, yellow, gold	Art supply stores; comes in 12″ × 16″ sheets
Instantype Inc.	Transfers from carrying sheet by light pressure	6 to 180 points (but not in all styles)	Approx. 35	Black, white, red, blue, green, orange, yellow	Art supply stores; $1.50 for most 10″ × 15″ sheets
PRESSURE-SENSITIVE OVERLAYS					
Artype	Cut out and burnish in place	6 to 120 points (but not in all styles)	107	Black, white	Art supply stores; $1.00 per 10″ × 14″ sheet
Craf-Type letters by Craftint	Cut out and burnish in place	8 to 120 points (but not in all styles)	Approx. 100	35 colors	Art supply stores; 85¢ per black or white sheet, $1.35 per colored sheet
Graphic Products Corp.'s "Format"	Cut out and burnish in place	6 to 144 points (but not in all sizes)	Approx. 100	Black	Art supply stores; $1.40 per 10″ × 14″ sheet
Cello Tak	Cut out and burnish in place	5/32″ to 1 9/16″	Over 50	Black	Art supply stores; $1.00 per sheet

[1] Lettering of 8 points is about 3/32″ high, and 72 points is about 3/4″ high. Several makers of pressure-sensitive overlays will make up sheets in custom styles, colors and sizes.

TITLE PLATES (WITH LETTERS UNDER 1″ HIGH) MADE BY PROFESSIONAL SIGN COMPANIES
(All may be purchased from Spencer Industries)

Name	Background plates				Letters			Price
	Material	Thickness	Size (inches)	Construction	Styles	Height¹ (inches)	Colors¹	
PLASTIC								
Filing cabinet label plates	Black Bakelite	3/64″	3 × 1 7/8 & special sizes	Engraved	1	Various (whatever will fit)	White	$4 (including 3 lines of lettering) for 3″ × 1 7/8″ sign
Engraved Bakelite signs	Black or colored Bakelite	1/16″ (some); 1/8″ or 3/16″ (black)	Any	Engraved	6	Various (whatever will fit)	White or black	6¢–10¢ per square inch of Bakelite plus 18¢–60¢ per letter; minimum charge $5
Engraved Bakelite desk signs	Black, white, or mahogany Bakelite	Has desk stand	2 × 8	Engraved	1	Various (whatever will fit)	White or black	$8 (including 1 line of lettering); extra lines $2 each
Engraved Plexiglas signs	Colored Plexiglas	3/16″	Any	Engraved (from the back of the plate)	6	1/2 & 1	Various	6¢ per square inch of Plexiglas plus 30¢ to $1.10 per letter
Engraved white Plexiglas signs	White translucent Plexiglas	1/8″	Any	Engraved	1	Various (whatever will fit)	Black	6¢ per square inch of Plexiglas, plus 22¢–28¢ per letter
"Howdy" pins	White or black Plexiglas	3/16″	2 3/8 × 3/4 or 3/8	Engraved from front	1	Various (whatever will fit)	Various	$3.60 (including 2 lines of lettering)
Raised letter Plexiglas signs	Plexiglas	1/16″, 1/8″, 3/16″, 1/4″	Any	Cut Plexiglas	7	Various	White, black, 5 colors	5¢–12¢ per square inch of Plexiglas background, plus 30¢–66¢ per letter, plus 1/3 the cost of the letters to cement to background
Formica on solid wood plaques	Wood covered by Formica (colored or simulated wood finish)	1 1/4″	Any	Engraved	5	1/4 to 1	Various	6¢ per square inch of wood, plus 18¢–60¢ per letter; minimum charge $25
WOOD								
Solid or veneer wood plaques	Walnut, oak, mahogany, or maple	3/4″	Any	The wood plaque may be used as a background for plaques of other materials, or letters may be mounted directly on it. Edge of plaque can be square, beveled, o.g., etc.				6¢ per square inch of wood (dull lacquered finish); 8¢ per square inch (hand rubbed finish); minimum charge $16
METAL								
Bronze signs	Bronze	1/8″	Any	Engraved and filled with enamel	11	1/2 & 1	Ivory	30¢ per square inch of bronze, plus $2–$2.50 per letter
Cast Porcel bronze signs	Dark-brown stippled bronze	1/8″	Any	Raised and inlaid with vitreous enamel	1	1/2, 3/4 & 1	Any color	$1.25 per square inch of bronze, plus $2.00–$2.50 per letter; minimum charge $25
Die-stamped bronze signs	Die-stamped bronze with an architectural bronze finish	22 gauge	1 1/2 × 8, 1 1/2 × 10, 2 1/2 × 10, 2 1/2 × 12, 3 1/2 × 12	Die embossed (raised)	1	Various (whatever will fit)	Bronze	1 1/2″ × 8″—$9; 1 1/2″ × 10″—$11; 2 1/2″ × 10″—$12; 2 1/2″ × 12″—$14; 3 1/2″ × 12″—$20 (the price of the latter size includes 2 lines of lettering; the prices of all others include 1 line of lettering)
Cast bronze or alumilited aluminum deck signs	Cast bronze or alumilited aluminum on an easel	Easel can be cut down to various thicknesses	8 1/2 × 1 5/8 or 10 × 2 1/2	Raised	10	Various 1/4 & larger	Bronze	$10 for small size, $14.50 for larger, including 2 lines of lettering
Cast bronze or alumilited aluminum	Cast bronze, alumilited aluminum, or satin aluminum	1/8″–1/4″	Any	Raised	10	Some styles come in 1/4, 5/16, 3/8, 7/16, 1/2, 5/8, 3/4, 7/8, 1	The metal is satin finish	60¢ per square inch for bronze, 50¢ per square inch for alumilited aluminum, 45¢ per square inch for satin aluminum (including less than 1 letter per square inch of plate); additional lettering 25¢ per letter; minimum charge $10
"Desk-N-Door" markers	Aluminum, yellow, brass, bronze, solid walnut with rubbed oil finish; metal plates are mounted on walnut, birch, or ebony	20 gauge	7 × 1 metal plate on 8 1/2 × 2 wood plate	Engraved	1	Various	Gold or silver on walnut plaque or black on metal plaques	Aluminum $4.50, brass $6, bronze $7.50, walnut $4.75 (including up to 2 lines of lettering with up to 20 numbers or letters per line)
Die-embossed alumilited aluminum signs	Alumilited aluminum finished in 5 colors or black; plate has a gold or aluminum borderline	3/32″ and up	Any	Raised	3	5/8 & 7/8	Gold or aluminum	20¢ per square inch of aluminum, plus 60¢ per letter
Engraved brass & aluminum plates	Brass, silver, anodized aluminum, or gold anodized aluminum; all finishes are bright satin	1/16″ & 1/8″	Any	Engraved and filled with enamel	2	Various	Black or colored	10¢–15¢ per square inch of plate, 17¢–$1.40 per letter; minimum order $10
Engraved stainless-steel signs	Stainless steel	18 or 20 gauge	Any	Engraved	2	Various	Black or colored	12¢ per square inch of steel plus 25¢–$1 per letter; minimum order $10

¹ "Various" indicates that manufacturer can supply a fairly large selection of sizes or colors.

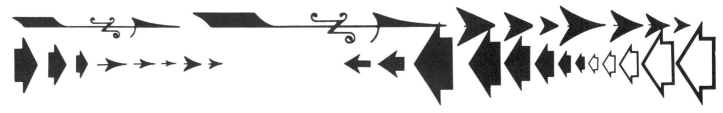

12-4

SOME AVAILABLE PRESSURE-SENSITIVE OVERLAY ARROWS (shown at full size):

Top row (left to right):
Craftype: "north arrows" (2, they come 16 per sheet), "arrow heads" (7, they come with about 250 on a sheet).
2nd row:
Craftype: "arrow heads" (8). Artype: No. 3000 (13, about 300 come on a sheet).

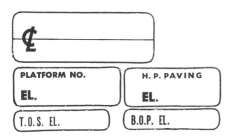

12-5

SOME ELEVATION AND CENTER LINE MARKERS SOLD BY ENGINEERING MODEL ASSOCIATES:

Labels are shown at full size; they come with a tape backing.

North Signs and Other Captions

Graphics in the form of keys (that explain symbolism), north signs, arrows to indicate flow of traffic, and nameplates for individual rooms and buildings can greatly enhance the appearance of a model and aid in communicating desired facts about the project.

North signs may be cut from acrylic, illustration board or paper, or salvaged from compasses and inexpensive maps. Artype makes pressure-sensitive overlay north signs (12-4) that are up to $1\frac{1}{4} \times 1\frac{1}{4}$" in size (see their sheet No. 3,044). Their sheets No. 3,000 and No. 3,004 contain smaller arrows. Craftint also has arrows that are suitable for small north signs and flow-direction indicators (12-4), as does Graphic Products Corporation. Cello Tak makes 2 sheets of transfer arrows. Prestype also makes transfer arrows, as does Instantype, Inc. Presstamp sells 3 sheets of transfer arrows. Sheet No. 70,504 contains 13 styles of directional arrows, sheet No. 70,505 has 4 styles; sheet No. 70,500 has 7 styles of north arrows.

Chart-Pak's Trans-Pak line of die cut pressure-sensitive arrows comes in roll form. Peel the arrow and a section of its carrier tape from the backing paper. Position it on the model. Press it in place and remove the tape. 15 styles of arrows are available, costing between $1 and $3 per roll.

Design Specialties sells 21 rubber stamps which contain north or flow arrows. Costs range from $1 to $1.25 per stamp. Instant Landscape sells 20 stamps that contain north arrows. Cost runs from $1.25 to $3 per stamp.

Engineering Model Associates, Inc. sells adhesive-backed small labels that are useful in identifying parts of study models (12-5). The labels are round, with $\frac{1}{4}$ to $\frac{5}{8}$" diameters, or oblong, measuring $\frac{3}{8} \times 1\frac{1}{4}$" to $\frac{3}{4} \times 2$". They also have labels with "H.P. paving" and "el." printed on them.

Presstamp sells dry-transfer overlays of scale, indicating keys for the following scales: 1/400, 1/200, 1/100, 1/50, 1/40, 1/32, 1/30, 1/20, 1/16, 1/10, 1/8, and 1/4" = 1'.

For greatest protection against abrasion and dust, place north signs, long verbal descriptions and symbol keys under a sheet of acrylic.

13 VARIOUS SHAPES AND HOW TO MODEL THEM

Opaque or transparent	Roughly constructed or precise	One (or a few) of a kind or mass-produced	Construction techniques
Simple, solid blocks, all sides flat			
Opaque	Rough	One	Rough cut, clay or plasticine, foam plastic, acrylic or wood; several plys of board
		Mass-produced	Cast plaster; clay or plasticine pressed into molds; any of the above; if blocks are small, cast polyester, epoxy or metal
	Precise	One	Wood, acrylic, plaster, ren wood
		Mass-produced	Cast plaster; any of those in the above box; if blocks are small, cast metal, polyester or epoxy
Transparent	Rough or precise	One	Acrylic
		Mass-produced	Cast polyester resin, acrylic
Solid blocks curved in one direction (columns, drum shapes, etc.)			
Opaque	Rough	One	Carved or turned: wood, acrylic, foam plastic, clay or plasticine; acrylic tubing and rod, wood dowel, metal rod or tubing; former and plank construction (for larger shapes)
		Mass-produced	Clay or plasticine pressed into molds; cast plaster; any of those in the above box
	Precise	One	Turned: acrylic, wood, plaster, ren wood; acrylic tubing and rod, wood dowel, metal rod or tubing; former and plank construction (for larger shapes)
		Mass-produced	Cast plaster; any of those in the above box; if shapes are small, cast metal, polyester, or epoxy may also be used
Transparent	Rough or precise	One	Acrylic rod or tubing
		Mass-produced	Acrylic rod or tubing; cast polyester resin

(continued on next page)

	Opaque or transparent	Roughly constructed or precise	One (or a few) of a kind or mass-produced	Construction techniques

Solid blocks curved in one direction and scalloped (fluted columns, decorations, etc.)

	Opaque	Rough or precise	One	Clay, plasticine, or foam plastic fluted with a tool; carved: wood or acrylic; embossed Bristolboard or polystyrene bent to shape on a frame; fluted detail may also be drawn if a 2-dimensional representation is acceptable, acrylic tubing or rod wood dowel or metal rod or tubing with flutings cut in
			Mass-produced	Cast: plaster, metal, polyester or epoxy; clay or plasticine pressed into a mold; any of those in the above box
	Transparent	Rough or precise	One	Acrylic
			Mass-produced	Cast: polyester resin, acryiic

Solid blocks curved in two directions (domes, etc.)

	Opaque	Rough or precise	One	Carved or turned · wood, acrylic, foam plastic; carved clay or plasticine; former and plank construction
			Mass-produced	Cast plaster; clay or plasticine pressed into a mold; any of those in the above box; domes may also be cut from balls or located ready-made
	Transparent	Rough or precise	One	Acrylic
			Mass-produced	Cast polyester resin, acrylic

Solid, highly detailed objects (column capitals, moldings, small furniture, etc.)

	Opaque	Rough or precise	One	Carved: acrylic, plaster or wood
			Mass-produced	Cast: polyester, plaster, epoxy or metal

Punctured, highly detailed objects (grills, etc.)

	Opaque	Rough or precise	One	Carved or machined: sheet acrylic, polystyrene, metal; etched metal; detail may also be drawn if a 2-dimensional representation is acceptable
			Mass-produced	Cast: polyester, epoxy or metal; detail may also be drawn if a 2-dimensional representation is acceptable

Simple slabs

	Opaque	Rough or precise	One	Illustration and other boards, sheet, wood, plywood, composition board, acrylic, acetate
			Mass-produced	Cast: metal, polyester, epoxy; any of those in the above box
	Transparent	Rough or precise	One or mass-produced	Sheet acrylic, acetate

Punctured slabs or slabs with recessed or projected details (facades, furniture fronts, etc.)

	Opaque	Rough or precise	One	Build from plys of: illustration or other boards, sheet wood, acrylic, polystyrene, acetate; milled acrylic, etched metal; detail may also be drawn if a 2-dimensional representation is acceptable
			Mass-produced	Cast: plaster, metal, polyester or epoxy; reproduced drawings; any of those in the above box
	Transparent	Rough or precise	One	Build from plys of: sheet acrylic, acetate; milled acrylic
			Mass-produced	Cast polyester resin; any of those in the above box

Opaque or transparent	Roughly constructed or precise	One (or a few) of a kind or mass-produced	Construction techniques
Complex slabs (folded plate construction, complex skylights, etc.)			
Opaque	Rough or precise	One	Illustration and other boards, sheet wood, acrylic supported on a stripwood skeleton or on a balsa or foam plastic core
		Mass-produced	Cast: metal, polyester or epoxy; any of those in the above box
Transparent	Rough or precise	One	Sheet acrylic, acetate
		Mass-produced	Cast polyester resin; any of those in the above box

Slabs curved in one direction (vaults, curved walls, etc.)			
Opaque	Rough or precise	One	Bent illustration and other board; laminations of several plys of Bristolboard; card and other board wet-formed against a mold; bent sheet wood; hammered or bent metal formed against a mold; gum strip or Fiberglas lamination; acetate softened with solvent and bent on a mold; vacuum or drape-formed sheet acetate or acrylic; Sculpt-O-Glas
		Mass-produced	Cast: plaster, metal, polyester or epoxy; vacuum or drape-formed: sheet acetate, acrylic or polystyrene; run plaster; any of those in the above box
Transparent	Rough or precise	One	Vacuum or drape-formed sheet acetate or acrylic; Sculpt-O-Glas; acetate softened with solvent and bent on a mold
		Mass-produced	Cast polyester; any of those in the above box

Slabs curved in two directions (concrete shells, domes, molded furniture, etc.)			
Opaque	Rough or precise	One	Cardboard and other boards wet-formed against a mold; hammered metal; gum strip or Fiberglas lamination; sheet acetate softened with solvent and bent on a mold; vacuum or drape-formed sheet acetate or acrylic; Sculpt-O-Glas
		Mass-produced	Cast metal, polyester, or epoxy; vacuum or drape-formed sheet acetate acrylic or polystyrene; any of those in the above box
Transparent	Rough or precise	One	Vacuum or drape-formed sheet acetate or acrylic; Sculpt-O-Glas
		Mass-produced	Cast polyester resin; any of those in the above box

Thick-walled structures curved in several directions, walls have varying thicknesses			
Opaque	Rough or precise	One or mass-produced	Carved: wood, ren wood, acrylic, plaster, air drying clay, sculpt stone; former and plank construction; Celastic, plaster or plaster-impregnated cloth; or mesh or buckram mounted on a wood skeleton

(continued on next page)

Opaque or transparent	Roughly constructed or precise	One (or a few) of a kind or mass-produced	Construction techniques

Frames whose members have square and rectangular cross sections (framing models, sun shades, etc.)

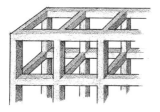

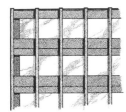

Opaque or transparent	Roughly constructed or precise	One (or a few) of a kind or mass-produced	Construction techniques
Opaque	Rough or precise	One	Stripwood, strip illustration and other boards, strip acrylic, strip polystyrene, soldered metal strip
		Mass-produced	Cast: metal, polyester, epoxy; any of those in the above box

Frames set against glass (exterior wall construction)

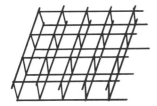

Opaque	Rough or precise	One	Stripwood, strip illustration and other board, strip acrylic, strip polystyrene, metal strip, cemented to the glazing or inlaid into it; detail scribed into acrylic, or drawn, if a 2-dimensional representation is acceptable
		Mass-produced	Cast: metal, polyester, epoxy; any of those in the above box

Frames whose members have thin, round cross sections (space frames, geodesic domes, etc.)

Opaque	Rough or precise	One or mass-produced	Metal or acrylic rod or tubing, wood dowel; an egg crate may be constructed from acrylic and lines scribed or painted onto it in the appropriate places

Frames whose members are tapered or curved in 1 direction (cast concrete frames, furniture parts, etc.)

Opaque	Rough or precise	One	Sheet wood, illustration and other boards, acrylic, polystyrene; detail may also be drawn if a 2-dimensional representation is acceptable
		Mass-produced	Cast: metal, polyester, epoxy; any of those in the above box
Transparent	Rough or precise	One	Sheet acrylic
		Mass-produced	Cast polyester resin; sheet acrylic

Opaque or transparent	Roughly constructed or precise	One (or a few) of a kind or mass-produced	Construction techniques
Frames whose members are curved or tapered in 2 directions (vaulting, decorative designs, cast concrete frames, etc.)			
Opaque	Rough or precise	One	Carved : acrylic, stripwood ; detail may also be drawn if a 2-dimensional representation is acceptable
		Mass-produced	Vacuum-formed sheet polystyrene or acrylic ; cast ; metal, polyester, epoxy or plaster ; any of those in the above box

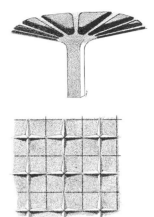

14 MASSING MODELS

Models may be arbitrarily divided into 5 over-lapping categories :
1. rough massing solid models used mostly for study
2. solid models with selective details
3. roughly detailed hollow models
4. fully detailed hollow models
5. engineering test models.

The photographs in this chapter are arranged in approximate order of the complexity of models—from the simplest solid models through the most complex solid models with extensive detail.

Converting a Study Model into a Presentation Model

Often, late in the design of a project, it becomes evident that a model is needed for some minor presentation use. Since the cost of a new model is not usually warranted, it becomes necessary to refurbish the rough design model. If such a situation could be foreseen, it would be possible to plan ahead and, at the start, build a more solid baseboard and a better constructed model of an existing building, as well as lay in a supply of model cars, trees, etc. Later stages of the design model could also be built with a thought to permanency. Once the design had been com-pleted, the model could be inspected, and shabby looking or underdetailed parts rebuilt. This would achieve an overall savings in time, and allow one to design on a more detailed structure.

ROUGH MASSING SOLID CONSTRUCTION MODELS

Massing models are most often used as a pre-liminary design aid ; this need not, however, pre-clude their use for presentation. Those that are a

14-1

AN EXTREMELY SIMPLE TOWN PLANNING STUDY MODEL.

PROJECT: Gehag Housing Redevelopment, West Berlin, Germany.
DESIGNED BY: The Architect's Collaborative.
MODELBUILDERS: members of the architect's staff. under Benjamin Thompson.
PHOTOGRAPHER: Robert D. Harvey.
SCALE: 1 : 500.

The buildings in this utilitarian model were cut from pine. They were placed on a roughly drawn plane of the site. Existing buildings, park areas and the boundaries of the project were colored in for emphasis. Trees were made from map pins.
The photograph was taken with a 5″ × 7″ view camera, 10″ lens and Super Panchro Press type B film.
CONSTRUCTION TIME: about 40 hours.

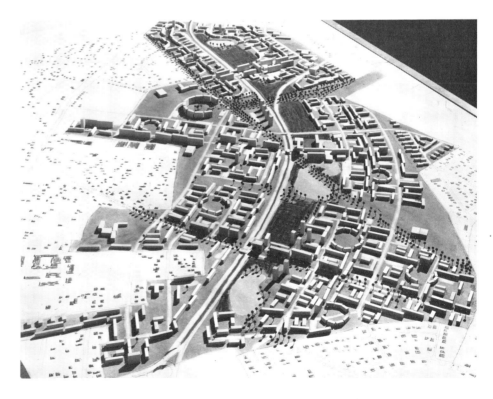

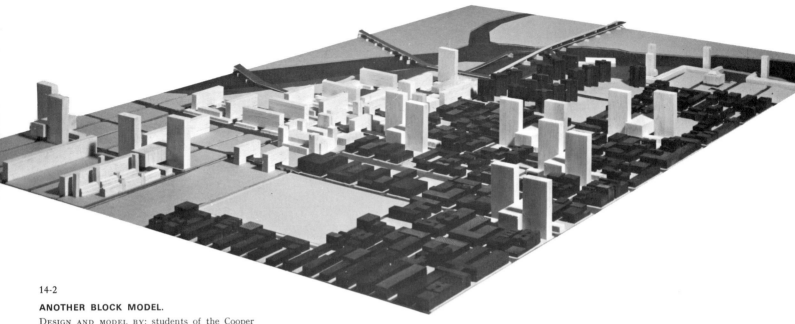

14-2

ANOTHER BLOCK MODEL.

DESIGN AND MODEL BY: students of the Cooper Union School of Art and Architecture, New York City.

SCALE: 1″ = 100′.

The baseboard of this presentation model was made from Homosote board set into a pine frame. Buildings were constructed from pine blocks. Existing buildings were painted black; proposed building left unpainted. Sidewalks were formed from cardboard.

14-3/14-4/14-5/14-6/14-15

5 BLOCK MODELS.

DESIGNED BY: Students at the Eth-Zurich, Switzerland.

PHOTOGRAPHER: Peter Grünert, Zurich, Switzerland.

14-3

Model of a town for 3,000 people. Scale: 1:1000. Buildings were rough cut from wood. Trees were made from plaster slabs into which stones were embedded. Roads and contours were constructed from cardboard.

14-4

Baseboard was made of Masonite; roads cut from cardboard sheet. Buildings were constructed from balsa sheet.

14-5

SCALE: 1:500. The baseboard was stained wood; roads were made from cardboard; high rise buildings from milled wood sections; trees from a bizarre, but charming, assortment of toy wood beads.

14-6

SCALE: 1:500. Blocks were used to represent each dwelling unit of the project. In this way, setbacks and staggered facades could easily be experimented with. The rich appearance of these stained wood blocks allows them to be used for presentation as well as for study. Note how the contours have been cut from a single sheet of wood and reassembled to form the correct slope.

14-15 (on page 110)

Model of a town center. Scale: 1:500. Contours were made from strawboard; buildings, from cardboard and balsa; trees from pipe cleaners.

study tool should be fabricated in a minimum of time with simple tools. Only by developing the most expeditious techniques will one be likely to use this type of model as often as good design requires. Only when one has built and studied enough designs, and reached a final concept, should one wish to refurbish the final sketch model or build one of more durable materials for presentation use.

A solid massing model with detail, selectively chosen and ingeniously built, can look completely professional despite the speed at which it was constructed. Many such sensitive models are more impressive to behold than professionally made, highly detailed expensive models. The important things to remember are: (1) Choose modeling materials with which the prototype can be best presented; (2) try to select materials the natural colors and textures of which require no finishing steps; (3) show only those details that are important to the fundamental design concept.

The more adroitly constructed the model, the greater its use as a design aid. Additional value will be obtained if existing adjacent buildings are modeled also, if it is studied at eye level with a small mirror, and if it is transported to the site so that factors not conceived in the drafting room become evident.

The site may be represented by laminated contours, or a plot plan may be dry mounted onto the baseboard and effectively colored with pastels or pencils (14-1).

14-3

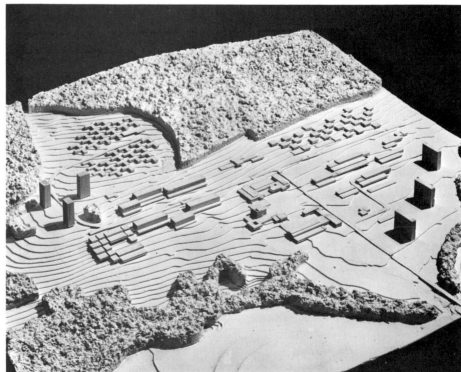

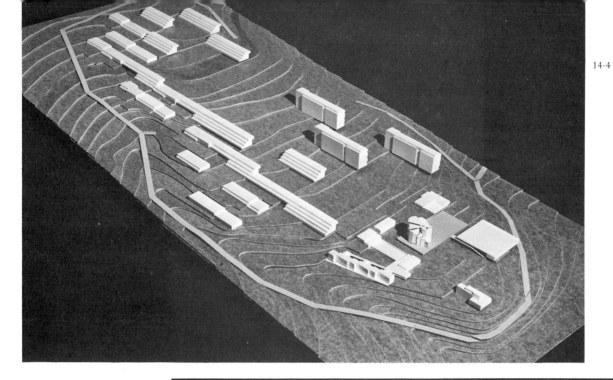

14-4

14-6

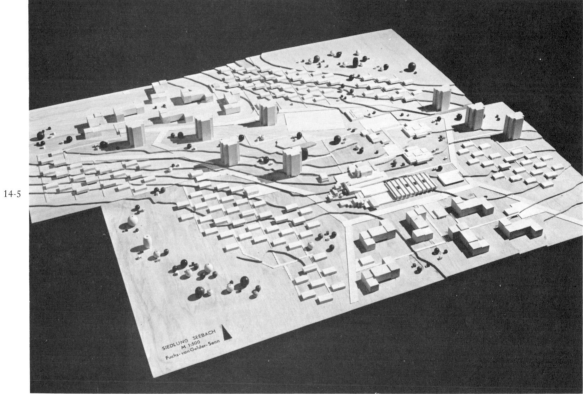

14-5

SIEDLUNG SEEBACH
M 1:600
Fuchs- von Gelder- Senn

14-6

Fast massing models of buildings and town planning solutions may be made from any material that can be added to and easily cut. Thus, such pliable materials as clay and plasticine may be used, as may Styrofoam. Small, preformed, modular blocks of wood (14-6) or miniature magnets (for very small studies) may be kept on hand for repeated use. All these materials allow one to eliminate a part or decrease a dimension with one chop of a knife or by taking away some of the blocks. Adding material is almost as simple, except that with Styrofoam the new material must be glued in place. Naturally, clay is best when modeling buildings with extensive curved shapes.

Incidentally, a lifetime supply of various sizes of pine or balsa block can be cut on a band or circular saw in an hour or 2, or several hundred magnets with $\frac{1}{4}$ to 1″ dimensions may be purchased for a few dollars from such mail-order houses as Spencer Gifts.

Sometimes rough massing models may be constructed from cardboard, scored and bent into boxes (14-20). To save time, each wall may be provided with a tab for stapling it to adjacent walls. Gussets or stripwood may be used to square-up surfaces. Such cardboard boxes may be made in the forms shown in 14-7.

For the presentation block model, clay, plasticine, Styrofoam, cardboard or cutout wood may be used, or even acrylic blocks in the desired shape. If lacking the power tools to do a neat job, substitute a cutting jig or miter box and handsaws. The varieties of wood that may be used are limitless, though balsa, naturally, is the easiest to cut. See page 75 for solid block construction and page 76 for the bread-and-butter construction technique. Large clay or plasticine masses may be built on a cardboard or wood undershape to save material. Board may also be used to represent free standing walls and other structures that would be difficult to model with the plastic material.

If modeling a multifloor building on a small scale, construct it from laminations of illustration board, each floor represented by 1 layer. The plys of material in the board will very realistically represent the spandrels and glass area of each floor. Every other layer may be indented to represent window strips, the unindented layers representing the spandrels (14-23).

If the building has extensive glass areas, and the effect of glass is to be incorporated into the model, cut the buildings from acrylic. Opaque roofs and end walls can be created by sanding those surfaces, by painting them or by covering them with Bristolboard.

If the project contains many buildings of the same general plan (such as a housing project), have a local carpentry shop mill a prototype shape in hardwood strips. Then cut the individual buildings from the strips. The walls of wood models may be stained or spray painted; roofs may have paint stippled on to create a contrasting effect or the feeling of roofing. Roughly carved blocks may be covered with Bristolboard if other ways of finishing loom too large, or they may even be left rough (14-8).

SOLID MODELS WITH SELECTIVE DETAIL

When the design problems of basic massing have been solved, it may be wise to study the influence of windows, penthouses, setback floors, overhangs and major textures on the design. Such minor forms as stair bulkheads, parapet walls and recessed parts of a facade may also be introduced.

↑14-8

↓14-9

14-8

A WOOD BLOCK MASSING MODEL WITH DETAIL CUT ON BAND SAW.

DESIGN AND MODEL BY: students of the Cooper Union School of Art and Architecture, New York City.

SCALE: 1″ = 20′.

Pine was used for this design model. Model was photographed on a polished table.

14-9

A PRECISELY CONSTRUCTED BLOCK MODEL.

PROJECT: the Ford Motor Company glass plant, Nashville, Tennessee.

DESIGNED BY: Giffels and Vallet, Inc., L. Rossetti.

MODELBUILDER: the architect's captive model shop.

PHOTOGRAPHER: Lens-Art.

SCALE: 1″ = 100′.

The buildings of this presentation model were made of acrylic. Ground contours were constructed of flocked mounting board, roads of Bristolboard.

↑14-10

14-10

SMALL-SCALE BLOCK STUDY MODEL WITH SOME DETAIL.

PROJECT: Rockland Garden Apartments, New York State.

DESIGNED BY: Oppenheimer, Brady and Lehreke.

MODELBUILDERS: members of the architect's staff.

PHOTOGRAPHER: Gerard Vitale.

SCALE: 1/32″ = 1′.

Buildings were made from balsa blocks. Walls and roofs were of cardboard sheet composed of 2 differently colored plys. Varying colors were used to represent roofing and ajacent fascia, or exterior wall material and window trim.

Trees were made of lichen, contours cut from sheet Masonite.

CONSTRUCTION TIME: about 40 hours.

14-11

A BLOCK MODEL MADE FROM ACRYLIC AND WOOD BLOCKS.

DESIGN AND MODEL BY: students of Pratt Institute School of Architecture, Brooklyn, New York.

SCALE: about 1/64″ = 1′.

This clean-looking town planning model for presentation combines new building made from acrylic with existing buildings cut roughly from wood block and illustration board. Sidewalks were made from paper laid upon the cardboard contours of the model. Stone walls were represented by cork board; plaza paving by Zip-a-Tone overlay. Trees were made of synthetic sponge.

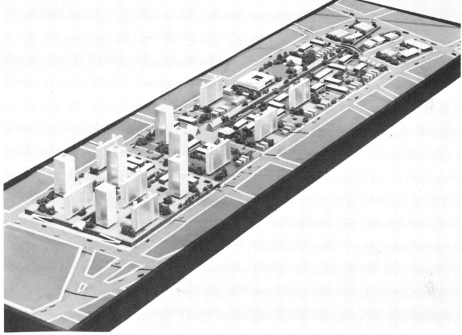

↑14-11   ↓14-12

14-12

AN ILLUMINATED TOWN PLANNING MODEL.

PROJECT: First Prize winning entry for Carson, Pirie, Scott & Company, Chicago Centennial Competition.

DESIGNERS: William N. Breger, Joseph D'Amelio, William H. Liskamm, Leon Moed and Herbert Tessler.

MODELBUILDER: Herbert Tessler.

PHOTOGRAPHER: William Liscamm.

SCALE: 1″ = 100′.

Buildings were made of scribed acrylic, carved wood or illustration board. They were illuminated by a battery of lights located under the baseboard; light penetrated the board through carefully placed holes and slits. Street lights were simulated by pin heads dipped into fluorescent paint. Cars were made of rice grains.

CONSTRUCTION TIME OF THIS 7′ BY 7′ MODEL: about 650 hours.

14-13

14-14

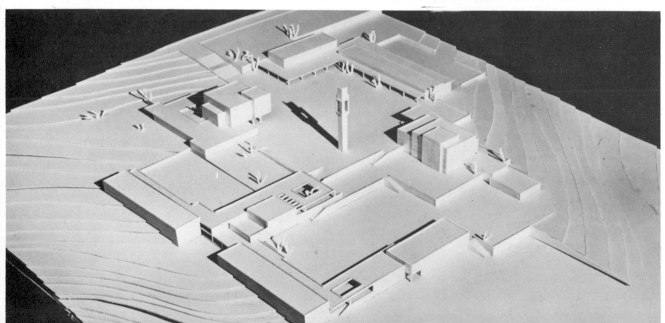

14-15(see page 106)

14-13

A SIMPLE ACRYLIC AND BRISTOLBOARD MODEL.

PROJECT: design for a hospital.
DESIGNER, MODELBUILDER AND PHOTOGRAPHER: Sanford Hohauser.
SCALE: $1'' = 40'$.
Buildings were cut from acrylic sheet, window walls lightly sanded, and mullions were scribed in. Masonry wall areas were represented by unpainted 2-ply Bristolboard, as were roofs. Contours were made of chipboard on a Homosote base; roads and paths were painted on. Trees were constructed from cellulose sponge, cars from stripwood. The pond was made of a sheet of mat acetate. The model was used for presentation and to study the relationship of buildings on various levels of the site.
The photograph was taken with a $4'' \times 5''$ view camera, 90 mm Wollensak Raptar wide-angle lens, and Super XX film.
CONSTRUCTION TIME: about 45 hours.

14-14

AN INGENIOUS BLOCK MODEL.

DESIGN AND MODEL BY: students of Pratt Institute School of Architecture, Brooklyn, New York. The design is of a low income housing project for Hoboken, New Jersey.

SCALE: about $1/30'' = 1'$.
The 4 tower buildings were very precisely constructed of illustration board. Columns were made of stripwood; low, white buildings of cardboard. Existing buildings were quite effectively made from toy Lego pieces spray painted to show age and grime. Trees were made from baby's-breath.

14-16

CARDBOARD BLOCK MODEL WITH SELECTIVE DETAILS.

PROJECT: Junior High School No. 292, Brooklyn, New York.
DESIGNED BY: Charles Luckman Associates.
MODELBUILDERS: members of the architect's staff.
PHOTOGRAPHER: Dick Evans.
SCALE: $1/32'' = 1'$.
The entire model was made from board. Baseboard comprised 2 illustration boards wrapped around a core of board formers, which created contour levels. The building was constructed in box form from single-ply illustration board. Walls were then painted black. Spandrels and columns were cut from 3-ply Bristolboard and mounted on the box. This simple technique was used to create an impressive degree of realism. Brick walls and roofing were simulated with texture paper. The building lifts out of the base to allow insertion of other study schemes.

Care must be taken to keep all detail on a consistent level (14-10 and 14-15).
Clay may be conveniently embossed with window shapes with an acrylic or wood stamp. Textures may also be embossed or tooled into the clay. Embossed plastic building paper may be pressed against clay, leaving the desired detail in it.
Entire facades may be detailed by affixing black on white reproductions of the elevations of the building on cardboard or wood block (14-19, 14-20 and 14-21).
Individual windows may be stenciled onto the model. Cut the stencil from acetate, then spray paint, or draw the openings. By spraying more paint on 1 or 2 corners of the windows, a shadow effect can be achieved. Strip windows may be indicated by tape. These techniques allow windows to be represented at scales as small as $1'' = 100'$.
Mullions and pilasters may be quickly constructed from stripwood or thread pasted onto the block. Parapets can be made by sheathing the walls of the block with thin Bristolboard and running it past the roof level. Balconies can also be made from Bristolboard. Plaza and paving textures can be represented by pressure-sensitive overlays or photostats of the design.

14-16

14-16A

READY-MADE HOUSES.

Rear and Middle Row:
Selley: cast metal, 1/64″ = 1′.
Front Row (Left to Right):
Selley: 1 house. Devpro: 2 cast metal houses,
1/50″ = 1′. Model Makers: 4 cast plastic houses
(No. B-1), 1/100″ = 1′.

14-17

A SIMPLIFIED MASSING MODEL.

DESIGN AND MODEL BY: students of the Cooper
Union School of Art and Architecture, New York
City.
PHOTOGRAPHER: David Hirsch.
This roughly constructed but effective model was
made from various types of board. Some of the
vertical shapes were made of milled wood.

Acrylic blocks may have spandrels and mullions
scribed into them (14-12), or the spandrels may
be represented by first spray painting the protective paper and then cutting away the paper where
the windows are to·be.

Additional detail can be added to a block model
by the technique used in 14-16. The block sub-
structure is covered with 1 or more plys of cardboard or paper cut out to represent doors,
windows and moldings. Windows can be of
acetate with black paper behind them (to give
the effect seen on a prototype building on a sunny
day) or more simply made, as was done in the
model illustrated, by painting the block black.

The scale of the model can be quickly indicated
by roughly constructed cars, people and trees or
by using accouterments that have been stripped
from another model.

Solid Town Planning Models

Models are indispensable to the study and
planning of urban areas, especially hilly sites where
not only the plan layout but the relationship of
buildings on different levels must be analyzed.
Models are also used to present future planning
schemes to the public. Some cities maintain up-
to-date small scale planning models that show all
the buildings in the entire metropolis.

Besides the usual construction techniques,
town planning models of subdivisions may be
made with small cast houses offered by various
companies (14-16A). Model Makers can supply
1″ = 100′ scale houses with pitched roofs in 3
colors for about 12¢ each. Both Devpro and Selley
make many styles of cast metal house models in
a 1″ = 50′ scale.

Solid Interior Models

A reusable adjustable rack may be fabricated to
hold drawings of all 4 walls of interiors. These
drawings are mounted on board, and slip into the
rack. Into this boxed out area, rough mock-up,
solid block facsimiles of furniture may be set.
Curved objects such as chairs can quickly be
modeled from clay ; swatches of material intended
for use can be pressed into the clay. Angular
furniture can be cut from the same materials that
are used to make block models of buildings, and
set on pin legs. Since furniture is often repetitively
used, it is sometimes practical to draw its elevations, reproduce the drawings in the desired quantity, color the reproductions and mount them on
rectangular wood blocks. Pieces of Flexwood,
colored paper and fabric samples liberally employed, will create quite realistic, quickly made

14-18

A BLOCK MODEL WITH SOME DETAIL.

PROJECT: George Washington Carver Junior-
Senior High School.

DESIGNED BY: Curtis and Davis.

MODELBUILDERS: members of the architect's staff.

PHOTOGRAPHER: Frank Lotz Miller.

The model was built entirely of unpainted balsa
wood. Baseboard was made of stained plywood;
trees of twisted copper wire.

The photograph was taken with a 5″ × 7″ Nova
wide-angle camera, 120 mm lens and Super
Panchro Press B film.

14-19

**A SIMPLE MODEL WITH EXTENSIVE DRAFTED
ON DETAIL.**

PROJECT: Concordia Senior College, Fort Wayne,
Indiana.

DESIGNED BY: Eero Saarinen and Associates.

MODELBUILDERS: members of the architect's staff.

PHOTOGRAPHER: Richard Shirk.

SCALE: 1/32″ = 1′.

Roofs and walls of this presentation model were
made of cardboard. Wall textures and window
details were drawn on. Contours made of flocked
cardboard; water from an acrylic sheet; and trees
from rubberized horsehair.

←14-22

↓14-23

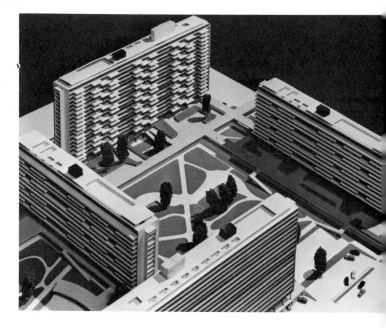

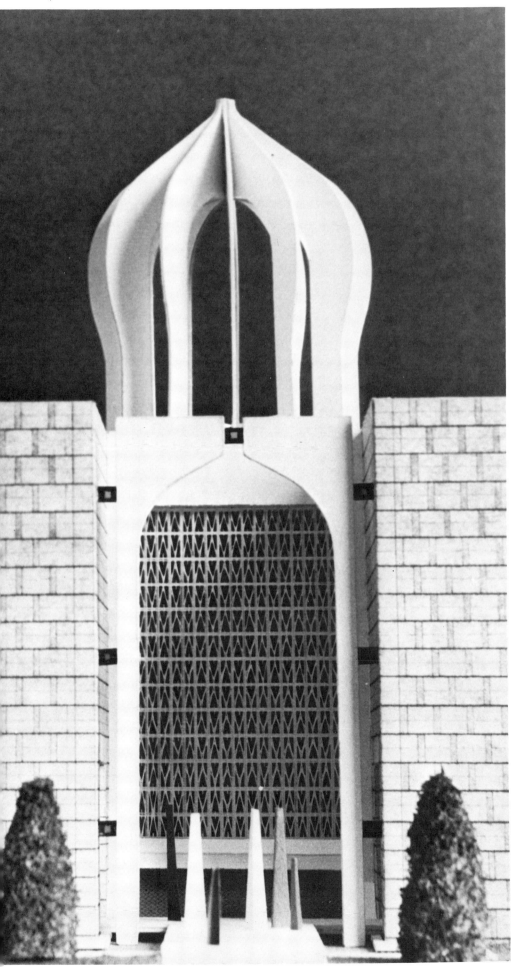

14-20
A BLOCK MODEL WITH SELECTIVE DETAILS ADDED.

PROJECT: Brooklyn Bridge Southwest Development, New York City.
ARCHITECT: Kelley and Gruzen. Project designers: Robert Genchek and Robert Greenstein.
MODELBUILDERS: members of the architect's staff.
PHOTOGRAPHER: Robert Genchek.
SCALE: 1″ = 40′.
Baseboard and building shapes and ramps and fences (between yards) were made from cardboard. Wall details were constructed from black and white prints pasted to the basic cardboard form. Trees were formed from loofa, grass areas from sprayed paper. Note how the water tank enclosures of the high building were simplified on this study model.

14-21
SOME ELABORATE, DRAWN DETAIL.

PROJECT: The Pakistan Pavilion at the New York 1964–65 World's Fair.
DESIGNER: Oppenheimer, Brady and Lehrecke.
MODELBUILDERS: members of the architect's staff.
PHOTOGRAPHER: Gerard Vitale.
SCALE: 1/4″ = 1′.
Walls, roof and cupola were made from cardboard. Concrete blocks and grill patterns were created from a black-on-white reproduction of a tracing.

14-22
A HUGE, SMALL-SCALE MODEL.

PROJECT: Model of New York City displayed in the New York City Pavilion at the New York, 1964–65, World's Fair.
MODELBUILDER AND PHOTOGRAPHER: Lester Associates, Thornwood, New York.
SCALE: 1″ = 100′.
This model, one of the largest town planning models ever constructed, served 2 purposes: after being on display at the World's Fair, it was used as a town planning aid. The model, which measures 100′ by 200′, was built on 270 4′ × 10′ baseboard sections. Joints between boards were filled and carefully painted.
The 725,000 small buildings (typical apartment houses, brownstones and churches) were stereotyped in form and cast in Epoxy. The 125,000 major buildings were individually made of acrylic. Bridges were made from milled brass sections.
Water areas were painted. Cars were cut from acrylic strip; trees from foam plastic.
At the fair, the model was viewed by spectators riding in a 4-seat abbreviation of a subway car at a scale elevation of about 20,000′.
CONSTRUCTION TIME: about 60,000 hours. Total cost: $625,000.

14-23
A SIMPLIFIED CARDBOARD MODEL.

DESIGN AND MODEL BY: students of Pratt Institute School of Architecture, Brooklyn, New York.
SCALE: about 1″ = 30′.
This cardboard presentation should be contrasted with that shown in illustration No. 15–16. In that model, punctured windows dictated constructing the buildings as boxes. In this design with its strip windows, the model could only be simplified (in cardboard) by constructing the buildings as a series of slabs. Several textures of card and mat illustration board were used. Elevator and star penthouses were made from wood blocks.
Planted areas were painted. Autos were carved from wood; trees made of synthetic sponge.

furniture. Such techniques may be used in all planning situations where objects that are predetermined in shape must be juxtaposed within the designed area. This includes models of interiors, stage sets, factory and office layouts and displays; also, gardens, parks and other landscaped areas where a supply of store-bought model train trees may be reused from study model to study model.

If the rack mock-up will not suffice, walls can be quickly fabricated from corrugated and other types of cardboard pinned to the baseboard.

15 HOLLOW MODELS

15-1
AN EFFECTIVE SEMIDETAILED MODEL RAPIDLY CONSTRUCTED FROM ROUGH CHIPBOARD.

Project: Reston.
Designed by: Whittlesey and Conklin.
Modelbuilders: members of the architect's staff.
Photographer: Louis Checkman.
Scale: $1'' = 20'$.
Walls and floors of this study and presentation model were cut from chipboard and, in the tower building, were assembled around balsa cores and columns.

Trees were made from natural twigs; people cut from cardboard and cast; water made of thin, opaque plastic cemented to the baseboard.
The photograph was taken with a $4'' \times 5''$ Sinar view camera, 90 mm Angulon lens and Super Panchro Press type B film. 1 750-watt spot and 1 lesser floodlight were used for illumination. The floodlight was bounced into the shadow, created by the spot, to pick up details in this area. 2 other floods were used to light the blue backdrop with its airbrushed cloud formations.

Hollow models differ from solid block models by being usually more complicated to construct, by containing more detail and, of course, by being hollow.

ROUGHLY DETAILED HOLLOW MODELS

A judicious evaluation of the degree of detail to be shown can result in huge savings of construction time without lessening the effectiveness of a model. Often a roughly detailed model can prove as effective a study and presentation tool as a superdetailed, professionally made, acrylic one. Savings can also be achieved by using easy-to-work-with materials that resemble the prototype and require little or no finishing. Illustrations 15-1 and 15-2 show unfinished materials that have been successfully used. Illustrations 15-3, 15-4 and 15-5 show the effectiveness that can be achieved despite simplification of detail. When constructing a built-up model, additional problems, such as internal bracing and the treating of internal detail, must be solved.

INTERNAL BRACING

Internal bracing is needed by all hollow models so that they can resist warpage caused by (1) room temperature changes, (2) exposure of parts to artificial light or sunlight, and (3) the painting and applying of other parts to the model. Models can be braced with an internal framework, or carcass, as it is sometimes called. This frame can be in an arbitrary form if the inside of the model will not be seen, or, on models where it will show, it can be disguised in the form of floors or interior partitions.

A good rule to follow if lacking an aircraft designer's knowledge of internal bracing is to put as much bracing as time permits into the model.

I have seen 50 year old models built entirely from thin Bristolboard that, because of elaborate and well placed internal buttressing, have resisted countless climatic changes, and are as plumb as the day they were built.

The backs of walls or floors can be braced with strip material that is: (1) run parallel to the long dimensions of the surfaces, or (2) behind all 4 edges of the surface. Use plenty of cross braces with both systems. For plywood or cardboard with a discernible grain, a good number of the strips should run at right angles to the grain of the outside plys. The grain of board can be determined by flexing it in both directions: The grain runs in the most easily bent direction. A better way to prevent flat surfaces from warping is to apply a backing sheet over the strips. This sheet should be made from the same material as the exterior or viewed face of the object. One may also build one's own multi-ply material, as shown in 15-6.

Walls and floors can be simultaneously braced together and set into true 90° relationship by any of the methods shown in 15-7 or, in very large scale models, by metal angles screwed in place. Technique A and B should be used on small and medium-size models, and can also be used to true up wall intersections. Technique C and D can be used on larger models or where walls must be removable. If demountability is required and the

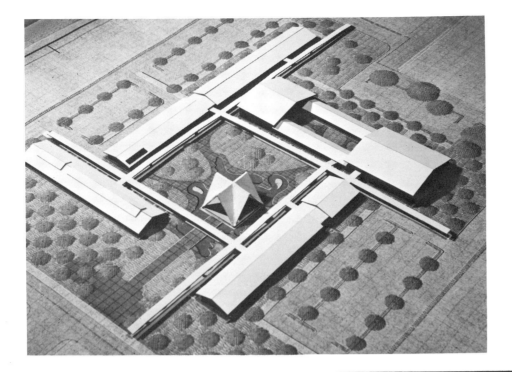

15-2

A VERY SIMPLE CARDBOARD MODEL WITH SELECTIVE DETAIL.

PROJECT: Los Altos Civic Center, Los Altos, California.
DESIGNED BY: Ernest J. Kump.
PHOTOGRAPHERS: Elsie and Roland Wolfe.
Simple cardboard construction combined with a fairly detailed, though rapidly executed, plot plan resulted in this highly effective massing study model. A good professional set of photographs enhanced the usefulness of the model, permitting it to be extensively published. Plot plan was black-on-white; internal bracing, stripwood.

15-3/15-4

A DETAILED MODEL MADE FROM "ROUGH" MATERIALS.

PROJECT: Science building No. 2 at the New Paltz, New York College of the State University of New York.
DESIGNED BY: Davis, Brody and Associates.
MODELBUILDERS: members of the architect's staff.
PHOTOGRAPHER: presentation model: Louis Checkman; study model: a member of the architect's staff.
SCALE: 1/4″ = 1′ (both models).
The presentation model was built from heavy cardboard, balsa and pine, and was not painted. The effect emphasized the viewers' conception of the framing system of the building. The baseboard was plywood upon which cardboard formers creating the ground level were set. These were covered with a layer of cardboard. People were bent from thin cardboard.
The study model was built to aid in the design of the structure. It was made from the same materials as the final model.
CONSTRUCTION TIME (for the presentation model): about 200 hours.

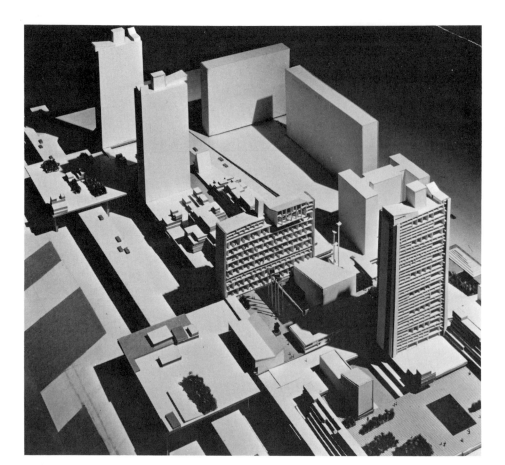

15-5

A CARDBOARD STUDY MODEL BUILT IN EGG-CRATE FASHION.

PROJECT: Litho City, New York City.
ARCHITECT: Kelley and Gruzen. Project designers: Jordan Gruzen, Richard Rosenthal and Mel Smith.
MODELBUILDER: members of the architect's staff.
PHOTOGRAPHER: Louis Checkman.
SCALE: 1″ = 50′.

The entire model was built from paper and illustration board. 6 or 7 different thicknesses were used, from 3-ply Bristolboard up through double weight illustration board. Detailed, high rise buildings were an exercise in precision cutting and tweezer holding.

Water was represented by blue Zip-a-Tone; the plaza by patterned Zip-A-Tone. Trees were tufts pulled from a carpet sample. Cars were cut from illustration board. People were represented by triangular pieces of black paper.

The photograph was taken with a 4″ × 5″ Sinar view camera, 6⅜″ lens and Super Panchro Press type B film. Lighting was achieved by one 1 750-watt spot. This provided dramatic contrast for the photograph. No second light was used to bring out detail in the shadowed areas, since this would have shown the crudity of the model and would have lessened much of the contrast of the photo.

15-6

WOOD WALLS.

Grain arrangement that obviates the need for internal bracing.

(15-6)

ATTACHING WALL TO FLOOR OR BASEBOARD

15-7

Removable construction

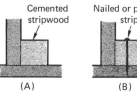

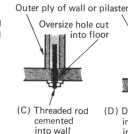
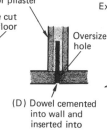
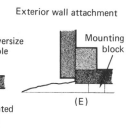

(A) Cemented stripwood

(B) Nailed or pinned stripwood

Outer ply of wall or pilaster
Oversize hole cut into floor

(C) Threaded rod cemented into wall

Oversize hole

(D) Dowel cemented into wall and inserted into oversize hole cut into floor

Exterior wall attachment

Mounting block

(E)

WOOD WALLS—GRAIN ARRANGEMENT THAT OBVIATES THE NEED FOR INTERNAL BRACING

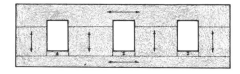
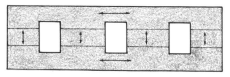

15-8

WALL CONSTRUCTION

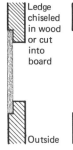

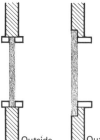
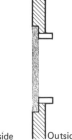

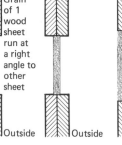
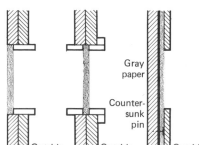

Wood board or acrylic

Acrylic mullions are scribed on

Outside of building

Ledge chiseled in wood or cut into board

Outside

Grain of 1 wood sheet run at a right angle to other sheet

Outside

Outside

Stripwood

Outside

Outside

Outside

Outside

Gray paper

Countersunk pin

Outside

Outside

model scale is small, the rods or dowels may be built into pilasters hidden inside the model.

If the back of the wall will be seen, it may still be attached at a true 90° angle to the floor by temporarily pinning or tack cementing the strips in place until the wall-floor joint has dried.

Professionally made acrylic models are braced with: large pine blocks placed inside unseen parts of the building, thinner pine strips that are used where bulky blocks would be visible and plywood

sheeting behind thin acrylic walling that might buckle without this additional stiffness.

ATTACHING THE BUILDING TO THE BASE

If the ground is constructed of laminations, cut out a depression to secure the building. To bring

the building up to the proper level, mounting blocks may have to be employed (15-7E). If the model must be removable, do not cement the walls or the perimeter strip to the floor.

INTERNAL DETAIL

The problem of having to show interior detail and to construct the inside of the model neatly can be eliminated, to a large degree, by employing

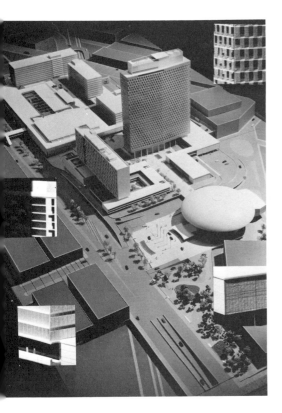

15-9

A CLASSIC STUDY IN HOW DIFFERENT FACADES CAN BE SIMPLY REPRESENTED.

PROJECT: Back Bay Center, Boston, Massachusetts.
DESIGNED BY: Hugh Stubbins and Associates, Inc.
MODELBUILDERS: members of the architect's staff.
PHOTOGRAPHER: Robert D. Harvey.
SCALE: $1'' = 30'$.

This simply constructed, highly effective model was achieved by combining acrylic and cardboard construction. The model was so effective that it was possible to take dozens of first-rate photos (over-all and close-up). This number is impressive even when the complexity of the project and the high quality of the architecture are taken into consideration.

High buildings were made from plastic sheet. They were stiffened by the floor construction. Fenestration was formed with Scotch Drafting Tape cut to shape (upper right-hand corner and lower left-hand corner). Balconies were made of strathmore board (insert middle of left side of photo.).

The convention hall (circular building) was turned from wood by a wood-turning shop.

Extensive nonfenestrated walls were made from Strathmore board as were stone walls, roofs and ramps. Details were drafted onto these surfaces (lower right-hand insert). Trees were made of lichen. Cars were made from wood, and people from stripwood.

The model was used for presentation.

The photographs were taken with a $5'' \times 7''$ view camera, $10''$ lens and on Super Panchro Press type B film. Some low level shots (not shown) were made with a Schneider Angulon 120 mm wide-angle lens.

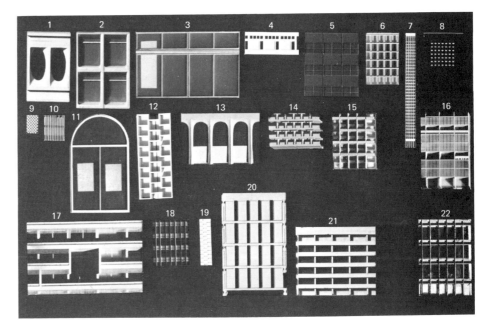

windows glazed with dark transparent plastic (10-1) or of backing up clear glazing with dark, opaque sheets (15-8J). If the sheets are kept a fraction of an inch behind the plastic, the effect will be more realistic. When handled correctly and if the windows are not too large, the effect is much like that of an actual building viewed on a very bright day.

WALL CONSTRUCTION

Any of the wall systems shown in 15-8 can be used: the first, A, is the easiest to construct, the strongest and the one requiring the least number of precision cuts. It may be used on models as small as $\frac{1}{32}'' = 1'$. The other styles require individual cutting of the glazing of each window or window strip and extensive bracing of the wall material. Styles D, F and I are the ones which appear best when viewed from the rear.

Illustration 15-8J shows alternate ways of fastening the various plys which make up the wall. Pins can be used to fasten all but the outer ply. This layer can be cemented to small pieces of paper which are speared by the pins. Simulated building material may be applied where needed. Illustration 15-9 shows an acrylic model that combines scribing and overlays.

Illustration 15-10 shows many of the more sophisticated construction techniques used by a single professional modelbuilder in his acrylic, or acrylic and metal, models.

It is very helpful to be able to lay out wall materials directly from an elevation drawing of the building. The drawing can be laid over materials and window corners; other key points can be transferred with a series of pinholes. This technique is superior to the use of carbon paper because it does not deface the material so badly.

WINDOWS

Windows on Acrylic Buildings

Small-scale acrylic models usually have window mullion detail scribed into the plastic walls. The

15-10

SOME HIGHLY DETAILED WALL AND WINDOW ASSEMBLIES:

Above are pictured problems and how they were solved by Eastern Architectural Models, a leading New York City professional model shop. They have rebuilt their power tools to achieve a machining tolerance of 1/10,000''. They can make acrylic mullions as narrow as 1/100''.

Top Row, Left to Right:
1—Acrylic was cut out then filed to shape.
2—Window frame was made from extruded polystyrene. Extrusion was done by an outside shop, then cut into required thickness and other details carved into it. Window was constructed of acrylic into which rails were machined.
3—Metal inlaid into acrylic sheet.
4—Made from small pieces of acrylic butt- and dado-jointed together and cemented.
5—Acrylic with grooves cut into it. The spandrel panels were made from second plys of acrylic.
6—Acrylic. Verticals are represented by grooves cut into the backing sheet, horizontals by strips set into grooves in the backing.
7—Acrylic, with white paint rubbed into scored lines.
Middle Row, Left to Right:
8—Acrylic strips joined in an egg-crate fashion.
9—Milled acrylic. Grooves were cut along a length of strip stock. The strip was then cut perpendicular to its long axis and the pieces joined together in a staggered fashion to form a checkerboard effect.
10—Milled acrylic. Equidistant grooves were cut into 1 side of sheet stock. The other side was then milled through in places to create the openings.
11—Acrylic with the frame painted on.
12—Individual pieces of acrylic strip butted together and cemented.

13—Cast metal.
14—Acrylic. Back sheet was channeled to receive strip acrylic balconies.
15—Acrylic. Back was made from square strips joined side to side. Some horizontal lines were painted; others were made from acrylic strips set into grooves in the back sheet as were the vertical lines.
16—Acrylic sheet for backing. A grid of strip material was mounted onto it and some of the voids were plugged with blocks. Fine horizontal lines were obtained by painting the entire surface of the block and then scratching away some of the paint to form lines.
Bottom Row, Left to Right
17—Acrylic. Horizontals, columns and sunshades were set into grooves cut into the backing sheet. Some of the fine vertical lines were painted on spandrel strips (see description for No. 16). Other fine vertical lines (see second row of lines from top, left side of facade) were made by painting milled grooves.
18—Acrylic. Horizontals are painted; verticals are strips which were set into grooves cut into the backing sheet.
19—Milled acrylic sheet was then cut into the desired width. The resulting strips were cemented together in a staggered fashion.
20—Acrylic. Beams (running perpendicular to the facade) are milled strips which were set into grooves in the spandrel. Panels between the windows were set between the spandrels.
21—Acrylic. Horizontals and verticals were butt joined to the backing sheet.
22—Acrylic. Horizontal lines were milled into the backing sheet. Verticals are strips which were set into grooves.
NOTE: The white rectangles that appear under Nos. 3, 8, 11, 13, 15, 16 and 17 are strips of tape used to mount the assemblies to their display board.

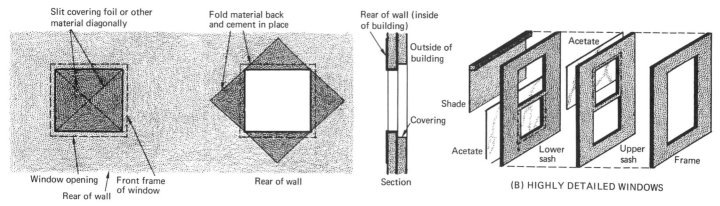

Slit covering foil or other material diagonally

Fold material back and cement in place

Rear of wall (inside of building)

Outside of building

Shade

Acetate

Covering

Window opening

Rear of wall

Front frame of window

Rear of wall

Section

Acetate

Lower sash

Upper sash

Frame

(A) APPLYING WALL COVERING MATERIAL TO WINDOW OPENINGS

(B) HIGHLY DETAILED WINDOWS

lines are then filled with paint. Any excess that spills over onto the glass area may be removed with a swab stick dipped in paint remover or thinner. Thicker mullions may be represented by thin tape. The protective paper of the plastic can be left in place over fairly broad areas which must be both opaque and slightly raised and which must have paint applied directly on them.

Etched metal has also been used to represent window walls (8-13). Larger scale models have mullions and window sills built up from metal, acrylic or wood strip material. These strips are set into grooves milled into the side of the building. A hypodermic-like applicator should be used to place cement in the grooves. Since metal and wood expand at different rates from that of acrylic, the mullions will buckle if the model is subjected to wide temperature changes. Thus, this type of model should be protected from temperature changes. Illustration 15-10 shows various techniques used to construct complex windows and window walls.

Roughly Represented Windows

If there are many hundreds of windows to represent, it may be practical to have a rubber stamp or metal embossing die made, or one might: (1) draft several windows, or (2) photograph the original and have a series of copy prints made from the first negative. These can be cut up and mounted on the model.

Ready-Made Windows (Cast or Printed)

See illustration 15-12 for many of the ready-made windows that can be purchased. Their use-

15-12

AVAILABLE READY-MADE DOORS AND WINDOWS SHOWN AT FULL SIZE.

DOORS:
Top row (left to right): Dyna Models Products (5 cast metal doors, painted white; cost 35¢ to 50¢ for 2 of a kind). Walthers (4 doors printed on white paper). Selley (1 cast metal door. This door is also sold by Model Hobbies.) Model Hobbies (cast metal door).
2nd row: Model Hobbies (2 doors and a frame, cast metal. 4 embossed wood doors.) Christoph Products Company (2 cast metal doors and a frame No. 1882, 1883, 1881). Suydam and Com-

pany (2 green cast plastic doors from set HO S-119G and red doors No. 500-15, No. 500-16 and No. 500-4).
3rd row: Selley (6 cast metal windows). James Bliss (printed on white paper, 2 from set No. 860, 2 from set No. 861—these can also be purchased at 3/4 of this size—and 3 from an unnumbered set—which can also be purchased at 1½ and 2 times this size. Sets comprise many doors printed on a sheet)

WINDOWS:
4th row: Selley (7 cast metal windows).
5th row: Selley (15 cast metal windows).
6th row: Selley (1 cast metal window). Christoph Products (3 cast metal windows No. 1891, No. 1892, No. 1893). James Bliss (1 window printed on white paper, from set No. 860). Model Hobbies (4

cast metal windows). Dyna Models (5 cast metal windows painted white). Suydam and Company (1 green cast plastic window from set HO S119G).
7th row: Suydam and Company (cast plastic, 4 from green set HO S119G and the following in red: (500-13, 500-18, 500-19, 500-17). Walthers (printed on acetate with white ink, 4 windows from their white ranch and colonial window set).
8th row: Walthers (printed on acetate, 4 windows from their white ranch and colonial window set, and 1 from set HO V340. Printed on white paper, 4 windows and a grill.).
9th row: Walthers (printed on acetate with black ink, 3 windows from set HO V340, 9 windows printed on white paper).
10th row: Walthers (3 windows and a shutter printed on white paper).

fulness can be increased many times by modifying their shape. Ready-made windows and windows built up from small parts should be attached to walls before the walls are set into the model. The walls should be clamped under books until the cement holding the windows has dried.

Window Screens and Blinds

Venetian blinds can be simulated by a pressure-sensitive overlay with a parallel line pattern. Window screens can be made from a pair of women's nylon hose. Carefully stretch and pin the nylon on the work surface and coat the window or window wall with cement. Place the window or window wall on the nylon and clamp it in place. The excess material can be trimmed off when dry.

Tinted and Stained Glass

Tinted glass may be simulated with colored acetate or acrylic or by spraying the back of clear acrylic with translucent lacquer. Stained glass may be created by hand painting acrylic with translucent lacquer; if the scene represented does not have to be completely true to the prototype, a fairly wide selection of translucent stained glass designs printed on acetate may be obtained from stores that carry quality Christmas cards. Kemtron will custom etch metal sheets to specifications. These can be used to represent stained or etched glass (16-3).

DOORS

Most of the techniques used to make windows may also be employed in door construction.

Operating Doors

Functional doors may be made by inserting 2 pins, the heads of which have been removed, into the top and bottom of the door. The pinpoints protruding from the door act as its pivot. Hinges may also be made from strips of linen or other thin fabric.

Ready-Made Doors (Cast or Printed)

Several lines of cast or printed windows and doors are commercially available (15-12). Due to the small number of scales in which they are made and their often outdated style, they are of limited value to the modelmaker. He can, however, sometimes make modifications by filling or cutting off parts. Other ready-made lines, not depicted, are made by Small Sales Company (3 plastic doors with frames and 2 garage doors in a $\frac{1}{4}'' = 1'$ scale) and Alexander (2 cast metal doors in a $\frac{1}{8}'' = 1'$ scale).

FLOOR AND ROOF CONSTRUCTION

Floors and roofs should be braced in the ways described on page 116. Care must be taken to construct an absolutely flat roof, otherwise its corners will lift from the walls or, worse yet, warp the entire model. To prevent this, roofs and floors should be mounted to the walls by being rested (not cemented) on strips (wood or acrylic) cemented to the outside walls.

Try to cut out all floors simultaneously to insure uniformity of shape. Complexly shaped roofs (mansards, folded plate, etc.) may in some cases

15-13

METAL AND ACRYLIC FACADES.

PROJECT: Time-Life office building, New York City.
DESIGNED BY: Harrison and Abramovitz.
MODELBUILDER: Thomas W. Salmon and Associates (a professional modelbuilder).
PHOTOGRAPHER: Louis Checkman.
SCALE: 1/16″ = 1′.
Facades of this presentation model were made from acrylic sheet with inlaid mullions of aluminum. The plaza and roof designs were painted on acrylic. Cars and people were cast in metal.
The photograph was taken with a 4″ × 5″ Sinar view camera, 90 mm Angulon lens and Super Panchro Press B film. One of the reasons that a wide-angle lens was used was to increase the convergence of the vertical lines of the tower. 1 750-watt spot was used to illuminate the model. Bounced light from 1 flood illuminated detail in the areas put into shadow by the spot.
Model cost the client about $5,000.

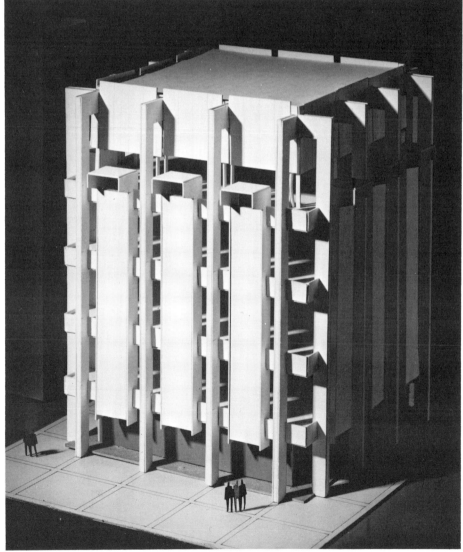

15-14

A FAIRLY COMPLEX CARDBOARD MODEL.

PROJECT: Chemistry Research Building, Tufts University, Medford, Massachusetts.
DESIGNED BY: The architect's Collaborative, Inc., Alex Cvijanovic in charge of project.
MODELBUILDER: the architect's model shop.

PHOTOGRAPHER: Phokian Karas.
SCALE: 1/8″ = 1′.
This example of a neat, but rapidly constructed, cardboard model was made entirely from 1/32″ Strathmore board. People were made from painted board. The model started as a study model but was later used for presentation.
CONSTRUCTION TIME: about 60 hours.

ANOTHER RAPIDLY CONSTRUCTED CHIP-BOARD MODEL.

PROJECT: Charles Tower Housing.
DESIGNED BY: Whittlesey and Conklin.
MODELBUILDERS: members of the architect's staff.
PHOTOGRAPHER: Louis Checkman.
SCALE: 1″ = 20′.

Walls, balconies and stadium of this design and presentation model were all made of chipboard; note the brick-like effect, at this scale, of its surface. Trees were made of lichen.

The photograph was taken with a 4″ × 5′ Sivas view camera, 90 mm Angulon lens and Tri-X Pan film. 2 floodlights were used to illuminate the blue paper backdrop. The model was illuminated with a 750-watt spot, and bounced light from a flood picked up detail in the shadow caused by the spot.

15-16

A DETAILED CARDBOARD PRESENTATION MODEL.

PROJECT: Head House Square Redevelopment.
DESIGNED BY: Frank Weise.
MODELBUILDERS: members of the architect's staff.
PHOTOGRAPHER: William Watkins.
SCALE: 1″ = 20′.

This is a good example of what can be done with board. All parts of this model except dormers and cupolas, which are of wood, were made from illustration board. Windows were punched out with an X-Acto chisel blade. Rounded windows were cut with a paper punch. The board was assembled with Elmer's glue; joints were filled with spachtling compound, and sanded. Model was painted with casein paints. Trees were made from natural weeds.

CONSTRUCTION TIME: about 700 hours.

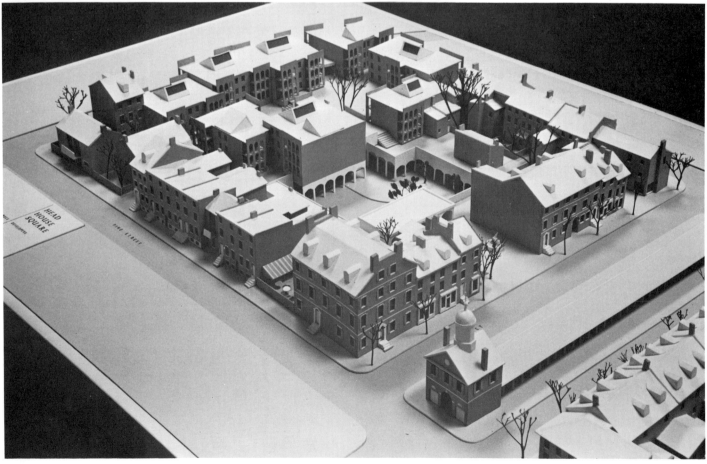

15-17/15-18

A FAIRLY DETAILED TOWN PLANNING MODEL USED FOR STUDY AND PRESENTATION.

PROJECT: Litho City, New York City.
ARCHITECT: Kelley and Gruzen. Project designers: John Gruzen and Peter Samton.
MODELBUILDERS: the architect's staff.
PHOTOGRAPHER: the architect's staff photographer
SCALE: 1″ = 50′.

The major buildings of the model were constructed in the following way: 1) pine blocks were cut (on a band saw) to the plan shape of the building; 2) the blocks were then sawed into floors; 3) the resulting sheets were stacked on wood cores. Some buildings were made opaque by having basswood strips placed between each slab. Existing buildings were made from reddish brown mahogany, new buildings from white pine. Buildings were left unsanded.

The baseboard, which measures 9′ × 7′, was built in sections from 3-1 3/4″ solid core birch doors. Contours were built up by: 1) cutting streets from mahogany strips. Each strip has the contour of the street cut into it. 2) Strips were cemented in place and the areas between them were brought to grade by fitting wood blocks into them. Roadbeds were stained; sidewalks left unstained.

Water was represented by staining and waxing the exposed door material. People were made from headless pins; cars were bought ready-made. Trees were made of loofa applied to bronze wire trunks. Boats were carved from balsa.

have to be first mocked-up out of $\frac{1}{8}$ or $\frac{1}{4}$″ square balsa strip. Measurements for the final model may then be taken directly from the mock-up. See illustration 9-3 for ways to frame a complexly folded plate system. Sloping roofs can be built on acrylic or stripwood framing that is a simplification of the prototype.

DOMES AND VAULTS

They may be made in any of the ways shown in the table on page 103. Professional modelmakers sometimes make large forms by draw forming hot acrylic sheets over a plaster mold. Smaller ones may be vacuum-formed or hot-drawn from acetate or styrene, and built-up from several plys of Bristolboard or brown adhesive paper. Town planning models may have these structures molded in plasticine on carved wood molds. Often, ready-made acrylic or acetate hemispheres can be purchased (see page 63 for some sources), or cut from toy balls.

COLUMNS AND RIB VAULTS

Columns with capitals can be carved from wood or plastic, vacuum-formed from polystyrene (19-7) or cast. Other types of columns can be made in the ways shown in the table on page 102. Vaulting can be formed from stripwood, plastic or in any of the ways noted in the table.

There are 2 ways of affixing columns to the model: (1) The columns can be attached to the adjacent floor slab and then all the slab-column assemblies fixed 1 over the other; or (2) all the floors can be clamped together, holes drilled to take the columns, the slabs blocked at appropriate

distances apart and dowels inserted that run continuously from the roof to the ground. Any columns with complex shapes or with capitals can fit right over the dowels. If square columns are needed, use strip material in place of the dowels. In many instances, spaces between square strips and round holes will not be seen on the finished model. If, however, these gaps prove to be objectionable, they can be plugged with a filler material. To prevent the filler from falling through the holes, construct a temporary jig that slips around the top of the column. This will also provide a surface against which the filler can be compacted. A coat of release agent will keep the jig from sticking.

SKYLIGHTS

Saw-toothed factory skylights, and other large skylights, may be made by scoring and coloring thin acrylic sheet. Large-scale versions of these may have their mullions represented by tape. Small-scale skylights can be cut from acrylic block with scored and painted mullion lines. Bubble domes may be blown or sheet formed from clear acetate; if the scale allows, they can be cut from transparent pill casings (purchasable empty and in several sizes from pharmacies). Other skylight producing techniques that may be used are shown in the table on page 103.

15-19

HIGHLY DETAILED MODELS OF WOOD FRAME CONSTRUCTION.

DESIGN AND MODEL BY: students of the Cooper Union School of Art and Architecture, New York City.

SCALE: $3/4'' = 1'$.

These models, which accurately depict each facet of typical wood construction, were made from stained balsa and basswood. Through the construction of models such as these, students learn how a structure fits together and the purpose of each of its parts.

15-20

A FULLY DETAILED, THOUGH SIMPLY CONSTRUCTED, MODEL.

PROJECT: the Goldman Schwartz Art Studios, Brandeis University, Waltham, Massachusetts.

DESIGNED BY: Harrison and Abramovitz.

MODELBUILDER: the architect's captive model shop.

PHOTOGRAPHER: Louis Checkman.

SCALE: $1/8'' = 1'$.

Walls, roofs and steps of this design and presentation model were made from illustration board. Windows were made from acrylic; mullions from tape; trees from dried weeds cemented on natural twigs; and plants were made from lichen.

The photograph was taken with a Sinar $4'' \times 5''$ view camera, 90 mm Angulon lens and Super Panchro Press "B" film. The large spray painted backdrop was illuminated by 3 floodlights. 1 750-watt spot was used on the model and 1 bounced flood was employed to lighten detail in the shadow caused by the spot. Note that the spot comes from behind the model, emulating the northern light that the prototype building will encounter.

CONSTRUCTION TIME: about 100 hours, including time spent fully detailing the interior of the model.

15/21

CONSTRUCTING AN ACRYLIC MODEL.

PROJECT: competition for the design of city government offices for Fürth.

DESIGNED BY: Joseph Alfred Frank. Associate Architects: Rolf Janke and Heinz Musil.

PHOTOGRAPHER: Photo 15-21F, Heinz Musil. All others, Rolf Janke.

SCALE: $1/16'' = 1'$.

Photograph A shows the cores (which were each made from several blocks of acrylic) of the building being assembled to the acrylic floors. The wood-positioning jig was used to hold the parts in place as the cement set. In actual practice, the jig was placed in a vertical position to the work surface and parts of the building were stacked alongside it. The cores could also have been made of 2 pieces of plastic inserted through holes cut into the floor slabs. This would have necessitated the making of position-blocks to keep each floor the proper distance from the next.

Photograph B shows the columns of the building cemented in place.

Photograph C shows the 2-floor building in place. Its columns were cemented against the floor and roof slabs were set into grooves. Walls were made from acrylic sheet to provide internal bracing. The entire model was painted the same color as the interior.

Photograph D shows the steps required to model the facades. The sheet second from left was scribed with all the required horizontal lines. Opaque areas were made with tape, spray painting, overlays of various types or by leaving the protective paper of the plastic in place and then painting it. The sheet second from right has had the dark spandrel covers applied. These were made from tape, spray paint or strip material. The right-hand sheet is shown with the roof grill in place. This was constructed with a series of tapes. The facades were given beveled corners for a neater joint.

Picture E shows vertical mullions being applied. These were made from strip material which was cemented in place with the aid of the hypodermic solvent applier. Grooves had to be cut through the overlay material to receive the mullions.

Picture F is of the completed model.

↑15-19 ↓15-20

←A

B→

←C

D→

←E

F→

125

16 FINISHES (SIMULATED BUILDING MATERIALS)

Wall, floor and roof finishes may be simulated in many ways with a high degree of detail. They may be drafted on a multitude of materials; embossed on paper, board or polystyrene with a custom-made die; scribed in. paper, board, or styrene; or vacuum-formed in plastic. See Chapter 8 for further discussions of these processes and page 50 for data on applying and painting simulated building materials.

In this chapter I have listed most of the simulated building materials that are manufactured and some of the full size architectural products that can be converted into model use. The stock of samples from an ordinary office will provide additional materials that can be used directly or modified for finishing purposes.

STONE

Stone embossing is achieved in a slightly different way from the embossing of regularly shaped materials: (1) Let a can of enamel of the desired color stand until much of its oil comes to the surface; (2) pour off the oil and trowel the remaining pigment onto illustration board or other sheet material; (3) after the paint begins to set, emboss the stone with a wood scribe. Gesso may be used in place of the enamel in this technique.

Large stone work can be cast in plastic of plaster on a homemade pattern.

MARBLE

Hand painting is the technique many professional modelbuilders use to create marble, granite and other patterned stones.

Marble may be represented by marbleized paper. White marble may be represented by white, opaque acrylic; alabaster by U.S. Products Corporation's Lustrelite, or it may be hand painted. To paint a marble texture, first apply the basic color of the stone. While the paint is wet, dab or sprinkle on the other colors. A feather may be used to smear the paint into realistic swirls and striations.

Complex plaza or floor patterns may also be masked and sprayed (24-3), made from tape, scribed, penciled or inked in. To protect the more delicate of these effects, a coat of clear lacquer or varnish may be applied, or cover them with a thin sheet of acrylic.

SHINGLES

Besides the usual drafting and scribing techniques, shingles and roof tiles may be constructed in the following ways: (1) On thin illustration board or thick Bristolboard, score the vertical lines lightly. (2) With a blade, heavily score the horizontal lines, making the cut at an angle to the surface of the board. (3) Lift the edge of each shingle with the blade. (4) Impart color to the shingles in the form of a thin poster color wash and warp them slightly for a realistic effect.

Large-scale shingles can be cut in strips from 2-ply Bristolboard. Cut the strips twice as wide as the exposed part of the shingles. Tape graph paper to the cutting board as a guide in dimensioning the shingles. Then mount the strips one over another to provide a highly realistic effect.

SPANISH TILES OR PANTILES

They may be pressed out of 2-ply Bristolboard. Use carved hardwood or extruded plaster, male and female dies. Dampen the board and place it between the dies; then clamp them together. Spanish tiles may also be made from soda straws cut lengthwise in the proper dimensions.

UNTEXTURED METALLIC FINISHES

These may be achieved through the use of the paints and other materials described on page 94 .

CORRUGATED METAL

Scribe a corrugated metal pattern into a sheet of heavy metal foil. Use a sharpened wood dowel or hair comb as the scriber and coat the back of the scribed sheet with cement to stiffen it.

STRUCTURAL GLASS

It can be simulated with colored, opaque acrylic or acetate.

GLASS BLOCKS

Their pattern can be scribed into acrylic.

WOOD FINISHES

Wood may be approximately modeled at $\frac{1}{4}''$, and larger, scales with Flexwood veneers. Use mahogany, sapeli, makori or other fine grained tropical wood. The grains of quartered walnut, ribbon or quartered fiddleback mahogany, red Philippine mahogany, lacewood, white gum, redwood burl, or elm Flexwood will reasonably conform to $1''=1'$ and larger scaled models. Other species or scales of wood must be custom painted, or, in some instances, a fine grain veneer may be stained another color to approximate the wood needed.

Besides fabric-backed Flexwood, there are thin (1/200" or less) veneers mounted on paper. They are imported by the Microwood Corporation, and cost $1.60 for a 25 × 25" sheet. Also 1/28 and 1/16" thick wood veneers can be obtained in 4 to 12" wide sheets from Craftsman Wood Service Company.

GRILLS

Professional modelmakers often cast grills in metal by using flexible molds. The original patterns are machined from bronze.

Sometimes a perforated metal sheet or embossed, plastic, louvered, ceiling lighting fixture cover can be located that comes close to the requirements. Plastic waffle patterns are made by companies such as Benjamin Electric Company (No. L-120) and Rotuba Extruders Incorporated (Nos. R-1, R-7 or R-9).

Many styles of perforated metal can be obtained from Charles Mundt and Sons. Among these are sheets with round holes as fine as 950 holes per inch and slot perforations that measure $0.018 \times \frac{1}{8}''$ and up, and many other styles.

16-1

READY-MADE WALL, FLOOR AND ROOF FINISHES.

Line 1:
BRICK: A-1 (Suydam S115), B-1 (Holgate and Reynolds HO-101, embossed), C-1 (Holgate and Reynolds, HO red brick), D-1 (All Nations line, brick, embossed), E-1 (Real Like, old brick), F-1 (Model Hobbies, red brick), G-1 (Aristo Craft-Herpa paper), H-1 (Superquick, D-2 yellow), I-1 (Superquick, D-1 red), J-1 (Walthers V162), K-1 (Vollmer, brick embossed), L-1 (Real Like, new brick), M-1 (Blue-Zip, BP-67, B462), N-1 (Holgate and Reynolds—O gauge red brick), O-1 and P-1 (Holgate and Reynolds, 2-121 brick, embossed).
Line 2:
BLOCK: A-2 (Suydam S116, concrete block), B-2 (Model Hobbies or Aristo Craft, concrete block), C-2 (Blue-Zip, B466, BP13), D-2 (Northeastern), E-2 (Walthers).
STONE-REGULAR COURSING: F-2 (Aristo Craft-Rivarossi), G-2 (Walthers V160), H-2 (Walthers V169, cobblestone patio), I-2 (Vollmer, embossed), J-2 and K-2 (Holgate and Reynolds, O stone, embossed), L-2 (Holgate and Reynolds, HO-122 field stone, embossed), M-2 and N-2 (Superquick, gray sandstone walling coarser style, D-10), O-2 and P-2 (Superquick, gray sandstone walling ashlar style, D-8).
Line 3:
A-3 and B-3 (Walthers, V165), STONE-IRREGULAR COURSING, C-3 and D-3 (Vollmer embossed), E-3 and F-3 (Real Like stone), G-3 and H-3 (Superquick, HO-00 gray rubble walling, D-12), I-3 and J-3 (Faller 5520/4, embossed), K-3 and L-3 (Holgate and Reynolds, O-112 stone, embossed), M-3 and N-3 (Aristo Craft-Herpa, embossed), O-3 and P-3 (Walthers).
Line 4:
A-4 (Walthers), B-4 (Holgate and Reynolds, HO stone), C-4 and D-4 (Holgate and Reynolds, H-102 stone, embossed), E-4 and F-4 (Holgate and Reynolds, HO-107 lannon stone, embossed), G-4 (Model Makers), H-4 (Model Makers), I-4 (Model Hobbics, brown-stone), J-4 (Walthers, V169 flagstone walk), K-4 (Northeastern), L-4 (Holgate and Reynolds, HO patio stone), M-4, N-4, M-5 and N-5 (Faller 5520/5, embossed), O-4, P-4, O-5 and P-5 (Superquick, HO-00 pink paving stone and curb, D-7).
Line 5:
SIDING: A-5 (Blue-Zip, B328, BP159), B-5 (Rupaco Paper Co., embossed), C-5 (Ross Board No. 18, embossed), D-5 (Blue-Zip, BP125, B324), E-5 (Rupaco Paper Company, embossed), F-5 (Blue-Zip, BP162, B348), G-5 (Northeastern 1/32″ o.c., milled), H-5 (Kemtron X1153, scribed board, etched), I-5 (Blue-Zip, BP158, B323), J-5 (Blue-Zip, BP25, B325), K-5 (Louis Jacobs Paper Company, 953-530, rib, embossed), L-5 (Blue-Zip, BP119, B335).
Line 6:
A-6 (Northeastern 1/16″ o.c., milled), B-6 (Blue-Zip, BP-33, B334), C-6 and D-6 (Kemtron, X-1152, HO grained wood, etched), E-6 (Walthers), F-6 (Blue-Zip, BP47, B333), G-6 (Northeastern 1/8″ milled). BOARD AND BATTEN: H-6 (Blue-Zip, BP48, B436), I-6 (Holgate and Reynolds, HO clapboard), J-6 (Real Like), K-6 (Walthers V508), L-6 (Northeastern 3/32″ o.c., milled), M-6 and N-6 (Northeastern 3/4″ o.c., milled). FORM WORK IMPRINT ON CONCRETE: O-6 and P-6 (Northeastern 1/16″ wide, milled).
Line 7:
A-7 and B-7 (Northeastern 3/16″ wide, milled). RANDOM SCRIBED SHEATHING: C-7 and D-7 (Northeastern, milled). SCRIBED SHEATHING: E-7 (Northeastern 1/32″ o.c., milled). CLAP-

A B C D E F G H I J K L M N O P

1
2
3
4
5
6
7
8
9
10
11
12

BOARD: F-7 (Northeastern 1/8″ o.c., milled), G-7 (All Nations, embossed), H-7 and I-7 (Northeastern 1/2″ o.c., milled. CORRUGATED: J-7 (Northeastern .040″ o.c., milled), K-7 (Real Like, embossed), L-7 (Suydam S-100, embossed), M-7 (Aristo Craft, embossed), N-7 (Northeastern 1/8″ o.c., milled), (Rupaco Paper, embossed). ROOF TILE: P-7 (Aristo Craft–Rivarossi).
Line 8:
SLATE ROOFING: A-8 (Louis Jacobs, blockette, 960–572, embossed), B-8 (Walthers, V172), C-8 (Vollmer, embossed), D-8 (Louis Jacobs, wading, 985–539, embossed), E-8 and F-8 (Faller 5520/D3, embossed. HEXAGONAL: G-8 (Walthers, V169, patio tile), H-8 (Louis Jacobs, hammered, 952–591, embossed), I-8 (Walthers). SHINGLES: J-8 (Holgate and Reynolds, HO-130, asphalt roofing, embossed), K-8 (Model Hobbies, blue shingles), L-8 (Walthers V173), M-8 (Holgate and Reynolds, HO-104, shake roofing), N-8 (Vollmer, embossed), O-8 (Holgate and Reynolds, HO-104, shake roofing, embossed), P-8 (All Nations, embossed).
Line 9:

A-9 (All Nations, embossed), B-9 (Holgate and Reynolds, O-113, roof shingles, embossed). MISCELLANEOUS ROOFING: C-9 (Superquick) HO-00 red tile, D-4), D-9 (Superquick HO-00 gray slate, D-5), E-9 (Aristo Craft–Herpa), F-9 (Aristo Craft–Rivarossi), G-9 (Vollmer, embossed), H-9 (Aristo Craft–Herpa), I-9 (Faller 5520/01, embossed), J-9 and K-9 (Vollmer, embossed), L-9 and M-9 (Vollmer, embossed). MISCELLANEOUS: N-9 (Suydam, S110, milled), O-9 (Timbertone TG-804, embossed), P-9 (Queen's Guard "Camino," embossed).

Line 10:
PAVING: A-10, B-10, A-11, and B-11 (Blue-Zip, B304, BP102), C-10, D-10 and E-10 (Aristo Craft–Herpa). TILE: F-10 (Blue-Zip, B439, BP21), G-10 (Blue-Zip, B438, BP12), H-10 (Blue-Zip, B430, BP39). SQUARES: I-10 (Blue-Zip, NH-3RE, B553), J-10 (Blue-Zip, BP114, B410), K-10 (Blue-Zip, B409, BP22). DIAMONDS: L-10 (Rupaco Paper, embossed), M-10 (Rupaco Paper, embossed), N-10 (Revere Foil, diamond G, embossed), O-10 (Mirro-Brite Mylar No. 2001,

embossed). CHEVRONS: P-10 (Blue-Zip BP37, B423).
Line 11:
WATER: C-11 (Blue-Zip, BP195, B448), D-11 (Blue-Zip, BP79, B446). DOTTS: E-11 (Ross-board No. 2, embossed), F-11 (Ross-board No. 27, embossed), G-11 (Blue-Zip BP99, B15), H-11 (Blue-Zip, B16, BP154). MISCELLANEOUS: I-11 (Blue-Zip, B342, BP167), J-11 (Ross Board No. 18, embossed), K-11 (Mirro-Brite Mylar No. 2003, embossed), L-11 (Rupaco Paper, embossed), M-11 (Louis Jacobs, No. 938–602 thimble, embossed), N-11 (Mirro-Brite Mylar, embossed), O-11 (Mirro-Brite Mylar No. 2002, embossed), P-11 (Louis Jacobs, No. 984–505 book cloth, embossed).
Line 12:
A-12 (Kemtron, X-1141 HO diamond tread, etched), B-12 (Fulford No. 2, embossed), C-12 (Louis Jacobs, No. 939–569, kid, embossed), D-12 (Gilford Leather Pearltone, embossed), E-12 (Rupaco Paper, embossed), F-12 (Fabric Leather Corp., Elastic Plyhide), G-12 (Kalflex, SE-190), H-12 (cork). I-12 (Dyna-Model Products, Shingles).

Harrington and King has perforated metal sheets with round holes as small as 1,479 per square inch. They come staggered, in rows and with various hole diameters and hole proximations. Other patterns from this company include: rectangular slots, $0.018 \times \frac{1.1}{32}''$ and larger, arranged in rows or staggered; oblongs (slots with rounded ends), $3/64 \times 1/8''$ and larger, arranged in rows or staggered; square holes, $1/16''$ and larger; triangular perforations and many more.

Common copper mesh can also be used at small scales to indicate grills.

The Ozachrome process can be employed to print a grill pattern on acetate, which then may be mounted on acrylic for additional stiffness.

Sandblasted glass screens can be represented by single ply Strathmore Patent Office Board. It is a slightly translucent material and stiff enough to be self-supporting.

WROUGHT IRON ORNAMENTATION

Wrought iron ornaments may be cut from thin shimmed brass that is sliced into very narrow strips and then burnished into curlicues. If it is not important that the exact pattern be represented—only some indication of a filigree effect—glue lace to a thin sheet of acetate and, when dry, cut out panels of the desired shape.

MOLDINGS AND CORNICES

All sorts of moldings may be built up from strips of thin Bristolboard. Half-rounds may be molded from wet paper over a dowel. Larger moldings can be extruded from basswood or polystyrene if a reground X-Acto blade is used as a scraper. A scraper may also be made out of a small, old file or hack saw blade; it should be cut as per illustration 8-20. When using a saw blade, first remove its temper, file the desired cutting edge and then retemper. The scraper may be hand held and drawn along a straightedge, or set into a hardwood guide (8-20) and drawn along a workbench edge. It is best to cut the molding with a series of light cuts rather than trying to do it all at once.

In past years, quite intricate moldings in scales as small as $\frac{1}{16}'' = 1'$ were run in plaster. There is no reason to hesitate about modeling moldings with the above techniques in any visible scale. Other catch-as-catch-can materials with which to represent moldings approximately are as follows:

Tapes

The Applied Graphics Company sells $\frac{1}{4}''$ wide decorative tapes that have interesting patterns, and may be of some use in the representation of moldings.

Custom-made tapes in any pattern can be ordered from Chart-Pak, Inc. Their minimal order is 3,000″ of tape. This costs from about $40 to $60.

Wires

Sometimes it is possible to locate moldings from among the hundreds of decorative wires that are sold by Samuel Moore and Company, Inc.

Pressure-Sensitive Overlays

Several lines of pressure-sensitive overlays carry patterns that may be used as moldings (16-3). These include those made by Craftint and Graphic Products Corporation.

GUTTER OR DRAIN PIPES

They can be made from aluminum or brass tubing. Gutters are made by sanding half of the tubing away.

128

16-2

WINDOW WALLS MADE FROM ETCHED METAL.

PROJECT: Society Hill Redevelopment, Philadelphia, Pennsylvannia.
DESIGNED BY: I. M. Pei and Associates.

MODELBUILDER: the architect's captive model shop.
PHOTOGRAPHER: Pei's model shop.
SCALE: $1'' = 50'$.
This presentation model employed the unusual technique of etching to gain most of its detail. Buildings were roughed out in solid wood blocks. The etched metal facades were then glued in place and corners were miter joined.

16-3

READY-MADE MOLDING.

Top line and top 4 in vertical column are from Craft—Type sheet No. 1051 (pressure-sensitive overlay). Next 6 in vertical column are from Craft—Type sheet No. 1052 (pressure-sensitive overlay). Lowest shape in vertical row and 2 shapes in bottom line are custom-made brass sheet from Kemtron.

RIVETS, NUTS AND BOLTS, LIFT RINGS, VALVES

Sometimes it is necessary to represent these small objects on $\frac{1}{8}''$ or $\frac{1}{4}''=1'$ models. Rivet or boltheads may be embossed into Bristolboard, metal foil, or 0.015" polystyrene sheet. Pour cement, glue or shellac over the back of the sheet to make it better able to withstand handling. Indentations can be made in sheet metal with an automatic, adjustable center punch delivering to rivets uniform blows of any strength. Lacking an automatic punch, fairly even embossing can be accomplished by (1) drafting a line onto a sheet of brass; (2) laying out the intended spacing of the rivets along the line; (3) drilling and then countersinking holes at each rivet location; (4) laying Bristolboard, foil or plastic sheet on the brass, using the drafted line as a guide and, with a blunt pencil point or other scribe, embossing the rivets. If the embossing is done on a light table, it will be possible to see the holes in the brass sheet.

Ready-Made Products

Lift Rings on Shanks are sold by Kemtron in 4 diameters from $\frac{1}{32}$ to $\frac{1}{16}''$.

Nuts and Washers on Bolt Ends are sold by Kemtron in $\frac{1}{16}$, $\frac{3}{32}$ and $\frac{1}{8}''$ diameters. Walther's has them in 4 sizes, made of brass or plastic, with square or hex nuts, a total of 16 products.

Nuts and Washers are sold by Kemtron in $\frac{1}{16}''$ diameter.

Valves are sold by Selley in the following forms: angle, globe, stick and straight. They range from $\frac{1}{8}$ to $\frac{9}{16}''$ heights.

16-4

READY-MADE STAIRS.

Top:
Bliss ladder.
Middle:
Model Makers plastic bulk stair material. (No. D-12), $1/32'' = 1'$ scale.
Bottom:
Suydam milled wood bulk stair material (No. 106).

STAIRS AND STEPS

Stairs require great accuracy in their fabrication since the slightest imperfection can be readily seen against the regular pattern of steps. To know the exact floor to floor dimensions of the stair run, measure the model, not the plan of the building. Small scale stairs may be made by cutting to the correct length stripwood or acrylic whose cross section equals the height and slightly more than the depth of the stair. Each strip will represent a step. The strips are than cemented one over another in a setback arrangement, each setback having the dimension of a step. When dry, the assembly is turned over and the bottom is sanded smooth. Bristolboard or stripwood stringers can then be added, followed by wire or stripwood balusters and newels and then handrails.

Stairs may also be cut from an acrylic or hardwood block with a power jig saw. Lacking this, cut them with a knife from a hard balsa block and face the treads and risers with Bristolboard.

Larger stairs and those with open risers may be constructed from cardboard, acrylic or wood sheet. Pin the carriage of the stair to an elevation of the stair and add the treads and risers, using blocks of wood to support them at perfect 90° angles to the carriage while the cement is drying. If many similar stairs must be constructed, a metal jig will aid in the notching of the carriage and the outer stringers.

Ready-Made Stairs (16-4)

Ladders, $\frac{1}{8}$ to $\frac{1}{2}''$ wide by about $1\frac{1}{2}''$ long, of cast metal, are available from Marine Model Company.

Stairs, in a $\frac{1}{8}=''1'$ scale, in cast metal and with open risers, are available from Alexander. In $\frac{1}{4}$, $\frac{3}{8}$, $\frac{1}{2}$ and $\frac{3}{4}''=1'$ scales and, in 30 to 36" widths, plastic stairs with open risers are available from Industrial Model Supplies.

17 LANDSCAPING ELEMENTS

Often the modelmaker will hurry the fabrications of his landscape, considering it a bothersome and unimportant last step. This is unfortunate since proper care taken in the construction of the landscape will not only enhance the model but be a design aid for the architect. This is true even with models that are originally intended strictly for presentation. Many last minute landscaping problems become evident only with the construction of a display model. Techniques must be found by each modelmaker whereby he can rapidly

17-1

A HIGHLY DETAILED LANDSCAPE MODEL.

PROJECT: The Joāo Arnstein House, Sâo Paulo, Brazil.
DESIGNED BY: Bernard Rudofsky.
MODELBUILDER: Theodore Conrad (a professional modelbuilder).
PHOTOGRAPHER: Soichi Sunami.
SCALE: 3/16" = 1'.
Walls of this model built in the days prior to the widespread use of plastic, were made of wood and finished with a layer of illustration board. Spanish tiles were made from dowels; the flagstone paving was formed from individually cut Bristolboard pieces, cemented to a cardboard backing. Trees were made of sawdust on wire armatures; plants were made of lichen; and some of the large leaf varieties were cut from paper.

REPRODUCED THROUGH THE COURTESY OF THE MUSEUM OF MODERN ART, N.Y.C.

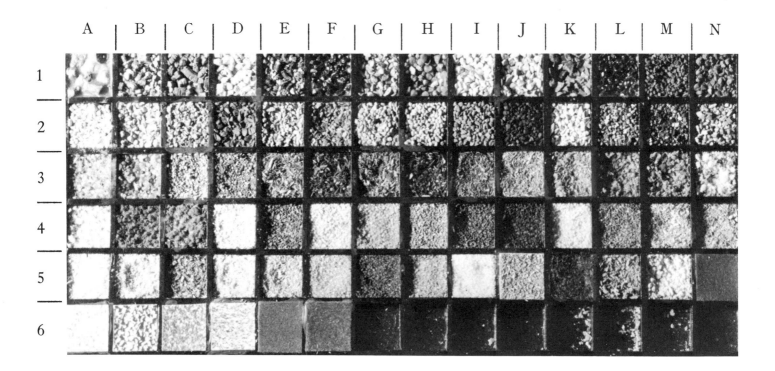

A | B | C | D | E | F | G | H | I | J | K | L | M | N

1 2 3 4 5 6

17-1A

READY-MADE GROUND COVERS

All colors are matt unless otherwise specified. Granules are shown at full size.

	A	B	C	D	E	F	G	H	I	J	K	L	M	N
1	B & H scenic stone H107 (gray tan)	Permacraft brown sceni rock (light brown)	Permacraft red sceni rock (rust)	Permacraft white sceni rock (light gray)	Perma-craft black sceni rock (charcoal gray)	B & H O coal H 126 (shiny black)	B & H O gray ballast H 123 (medium gray)	B & H O ballast H 103 (tan)	O gravel H 104 (light gray)	B & H O yellow ballast H 125 (yellow-ish tan)	B & H O cinder ballast H 110 (brown-ish gray)	B & H HO coal H 108 also UPC coal No. 607 (shiny black)	UPC blue stone No. 609 and Tru-scale blue stone T-18 (royal blue)	UPC red stone No. 608 (burnt sienna)
2	UPC ballast and Permacraft gray ballast (greenish gray)	UPC sandstone and B & H HO yellow ballast H 124 (yellowish tan)	UPC earth No. 603 (light brown)	B & H iron ore H 115 (burnt sienna)	B & H HO gray ballast H 122 and True-scale gray ballast T-15 (greenish gray)	B & H HO cinder ballast No. 109 (Green-ish gray and brown)	Tru-scale gravel T-20 (light greenish gray and tan)	Tru-scale sand-stone T-19 (lighter greenish gray and tan)	Tru-scale red stone T-17 (red)	Tru-scale coal T-16 (black)	B & H HO gravel H-102 (light gray)	Perma-craft brown sceni stone (tan)	Perma-craft black cinder ballast (dark gray)	Perma-craft red sceni stone (light brown)
3	B & H scenic sand H 106 (gray tan)	B & H HO ballast H 101 (gray tan)	Permacraft red sceni soil (light brown)	Permacraft brown sceni soil (grayish tan)	Tru-scale light grass 0410 and UPC grass No. 601 (bright green)	Tru-scale dark grass 0410 (dark (bright green)	Tru-scale light earth 0411 (light brown)	Tru-scale dark earth 0411 (dark brown)	Life-Like grass S107S (bright green)	Perma-craft grass (light bright green)	Tru-scale imitation earth (old) (tan)	Tru-scale orna-mental flowers red and green O507 (bright green with red spots)	Tru-scale orna-mental flowers green O507 (bright green)	Tru-scale orna-mental flowers yellow and green O 507 (bright yellow with green spots)
4	Tru-scale ornamental flowers yellow 0507 (bright yellow)	Tru-scale ornamental flowers blue 0507 (dark blue)	Tru-scale ornamental flowers red 0507 (bright red)	B & H exac-scale HO lime-stone ballast H 145 (light gray)	B & H exac-scale HO iron ore H 155 (rust)	B & H exac-scale HO lt. gray ballast H 156 (light gray)	B & H exac-scale HO brown ballast H 157 (yellow-ish tan)	B & H exac-scale HO gray ballast H 150 (medium gray)	B & H exac-scale HO brown ballast H 151 (dark brown)	B & H exac-scale HO nut coal H 153 (black)	B & H exac-scale HO yellow ballast H 158 (very light tan)	B & H exac-scale HO cinder ballast H 152 (tanish gray)	B & H grass H 111 (very light green)	B & H earth H 112 (tan)
5	B & H natural sawdust H 127 (very light tan)	B & H leaves H 116 (light tan with red particles)	B & H black earth H 119 (charcoal gray)	B & H Ripe grain H 117 (light yellow)	B & H red earth H 118 (light rust)	Anderson gray ballast (medium gray)	Anderson cinder fill (charcoal gray)	Anderson iron ore (grayish brown)	Ander-son lime-stone (light gray)	Tru-Scale earth mat ME-100 (light green)	Walthers tex-kote brown earth (dark brown)	Real like ground cover (light green)	UPC sand spray No. 625 (yellow-ish tan)	Tru-Scale grass mat MG-100 (brown)
6	Photo of a Life Like path mat	Photo of a Life Like ballast mat	Photo of a Life Like grass mat	Photo of a Life Like earth mat	UPC special grass mat	UPC regular grass mat								

present reasonably accurate facsimiles of each element of landscaping that he is called upon to model. Landscaping is one area in modelmaking wherein success usually comes from the use of a combination of a great number of materials rather than from minimalization. A good supply of many of the products named in this chapter should be kept on hand. With bits and dashes of various of these materials, the modelbuilder can achieve an interesting, accurate and authentic looking landscape.

MODELS OF LANDSCAPE ARCHITECTURE

Exact model replicas of gardens and landscaping schemes are seldom made due to the complexity of making exact models of trees and bushes, the relative smallness of budget for such commissions and the need to represent only the volume of each unit of vegetation, since its detail and color are widely known. Sketchy representations of trees and bushes, for use on design models, may be made from balls of plasticine, Styrofoam or rolled-up paper.

GROUND COVER

Earth, grass and other items of ground cover should be planned from a color photograph of the existing site conditions or, if these will change, from photos of other landscapes. In general, try to emulate the mottled texture and color of natural ground cover; slick looking cover is not realistic. Mottling can be done by using granules or sawdust in different sizes or colors.

Paint

Plaster and other ground simulating materials may be painted with oil paints. Oil is best because of its dull finish, the large range of available colors also simplifies the problem of mixing. The following colors may be used directly from the tube: raw and burnt umber, Vandyke brown or raw and burnt sienna. Exact ground colors may be blended by combining several of these colors. Colors should be built up carefully from several coats of thinned paint. If too dark a color is created, it may prove impossible to lighten with the thin translucent paint that should be employed.

For grass colors: pale green may be mixed from light chrome green and white; medium chrome green, light yellow and white; or by adding black or Vandyke brown to either of these mixtures. Medium green may be mixed from various combinations of green, yellow, red, white and black. Dark green (the color of lush grass) is mixed from light chrome green, ultramarine and white.

Integral Texturing and Coloring of Plaster

If the ground contours are made from plaster, they may be integrally colored and textured. Texturing is achieved by stippling the wet plaster with a stiff brush to produce a rough, eroded, earth effect. Integral coloring can be done in many ways.

PLASTER DYES AND PAINTS

Dry Pigments

Dry powdered pigments, or plaster coloring powder pigments, as they are sometimes called, contain their own adhesive. They may be obtained in hardware stores. To apply, spray the set plaster with water and sift on the pigment. It may also be applied to setting plaster or to powdered plaster before water is added. Several applications of pigments may be used to create the effect of grass on soil. Certain of these pigments, calcimine and casein dry paint among them, will slow the setting of the plaster. Inert dry colors will not do this. Use about $\frac{1}{2}$ cup of the latter with each gallon of dry plaster. Wet dye mixed into the water and used with pigment can create additional effects. Sawdust or flock may be mixed with dry pigment to represent coarse grass; small bits of lichen may

also be added. If these large admixtures do not readily stick, spray the ground with gum arabic and water, Krylon Mat spray, varnish or clear lacquer. The pigment mixing formulas used to obtain various colors are:

Gray is achieved by mixing burnt umber into the plaster. The proportion of pigment to plaster should be 1 : 20 to 1 : 10, depending on the shade required.

Reddish rock is medium chrome yellow (3 parts), burnt sienna (1) and plaster (15).

Yellowish grass is medium chrome yellow (3), raw umber (1), medium chrome green (2) and plaster (4).

Bluegrass is medium chrome yellow (3), raw umber (1), medium chrome green (2) and plaster (4).

If pigments are not mixed together too evenly, the resulting color will be more realistic.

Liquid Dye

Plaster may be colored with a poured or dabbed on application of fluid dye or diluted India ink. Rough surfaces absorb more color than smooth areas, and dye is absorbed by dried plaster much faster than by plaster that has been wetted down. These variable factors can be most useful.

If an area has been overcolored with fluid dye, bleach out the dye with a mixture of 1 or 2 drops of perchlorate bleach (Clorox, etc.) in 2 ounces of water.

Flock

Flock may be mixed into ground-representing plaster. The plaster will whiten the color of the flock. Thus, dry pigments must often be used in conjunction with flock. If applying flock on top of plaster or other dry ground materials, use the adhesives recommended for use with dry pigments that have been mixed with granules. The flock should be sprinkled on the adhesive with a sieve. Spray shiny flock with Krylon Mat fixative to dull it. Flock as well as granules should be applied only to ground that has already been painted; no matter how carefully flock is applied, small areas of bare ground will show through.

Scatter Granules (17-1A)

Many sizes, colors and shapes of granules are packaged for sale to the model railroad hobbyist. They are used to simulate almost all loose ground covering materials, from grass to boulders. Granules may be combined with dry pigments, flock, real earth, sand or colored sawdust to form additional textures and colors. A drawback of commercial granules is its often unrealistically bright color.

Cementing

Since adhesives will inevitably be visible, they must be transparent, and have a mat finish. Among those that can be mixed into the granules is Dyers' powdered cement. The conglomeration is placed on the model and sprayed with water, or the cement may be mixed with water and painted on, with the granules sifted onto the model last.

Casein glue (Weldwood, etc.) may also be used. Paint the model with it; allow it to dry partially; go over it with water to thin it out, and then sift on the granules.

Other usable adhesives are: Perma-Stick made by Permacraft Products, Casco, Life-Like adhesive, Natural Scale Scenics adhesive, Le pages glue or white glue.

Granules should be applied by shaking them out of a jar that has holes cut into the lid; A 2-piece, screw-on cover may be modified by removing the center disc and replacing it with a section of wire mesh. Press the granules on the model, making sure they are in contact with the adhesive; allow the adhesive to dry and then blow the unstuck granules from the model.

ADDITIONAL COMMERCIALLY MADE GRANULES, TEXTURE SPRAYS, AND PAINTS

Color	Name of product (and its form)	Manufacturer or supplier
White	Snow (spray)	Life-Like Products
	Snow (granules)	Life-Like Products
	White sand (granules)	Life-Like Products
	White Tex-Kote (flock)	Walthers
Gray	Ballast gray (granules)	Faller
	Gray ground cork (granules)	Faller
	Gravel (granules)	Life-Like Products
	Gray (spray)	Natural Scale Scenics
	Ballast (granules)	Andersons
	Rocks (granules)	Real-Like
Black	Coal (granules)	Faller
Blue	Light blue (granules)	Faller
	Bluestone (granules)	Natural Scale Scenics
Yellow	Blossom yellow (granules)	Faller
Red	Flower red (granules)	Faller
Brown or soil color	Plowed field (granules)	Faller
	Rocky soil (coarse cork granules)	Faller
	Earth (granules)	Life-Like Products
	Earth (colored paint)	Floquil
	Earth (spray)	Life-Like Products
	Earth (spray)	Natural Scale Scenics
Green	Forest (light-green granules)	Faller
	Grass (granules)	Real-Like
	Grass (spray)	Life-Like Products
	Grass (granules)	Life-Like Products
	Green Tex-Kote (flock)	Walthers
	Grass (granules)	Natural Scale Scenics
Sand color	Sand (granules)	Faller
	Sand (spray)	Natural Scale Scenics
	Sandstone (granules)	Natural Scale Scenics
Miscellaneous	Flower-strewn meadow (granules)	Faller
	Wood fiber (granules)	Tru-Scale

17-2/17-3

Project: **THE PONCE MUSEUM OF ART, PONCE, PUERTO RICO.**

DESIGNED BY: Edward Durell Stone.
MODELBUILDER: Theodore Conrad (a professional modelbuilder).
PHOTOGRAPHER: Louis Checkman.
SCALE: 1/8″ = 1′.

Most of this presentation model was made from acrylic. Grills were cast from metal. The skylight and roof soffit pattern was milled from acrylic. Stone walls were effected by painting the acrylic with thick paint and then scribing. Palm trees were made of paper leaves on wire stems; other trees were made of sawdust on wire armatures; people were cast in metal.

The photographs were taken with a 4″ × 5″ Sinar view camera, 6⅜″ lens and Trix-X film. Only 1 750-watt flood was used on the bird's-eye view (17-3). This was used to simulate the harsh tropical sunlight of Puerto Rico. The other photograph had light from a flood illuminating areas put in shadow by the spot.

Spray Textures

A few of the companies that sell granules also have lines of aerosol spray finishes in earth, sand and other textures. While some of these will create a satisfactory ground finish rapidly, others have a tendency to flow erratically from the can. Some come out dry and in short ribbons, others will not spray at all. Before purchasing this product, test individual cans at the store.

Other Materials

Sawdust or small wood chips may also be used; they may be stained with thinned oil paint. Apply them to the model with the same cements used with granules.

Ground-up foam rubber obtained in scrap pieces from upholstery shops is also a possibility. Use latex or synthetic latex foam, not polyurethane, which yellows with age. Cut the scraps into grape-size lumps, color with thinned oil paint or fabric dye; grind the dried pieces in a meat grinder. Several textures can be produced: the finest can be used as grass or leaves, the coarsest as clumps of small plants or even, on small-scale models, as shrubs.

Landscaping Mats

Several companies sell paper sheets on which granules have already been attached. These sheets measure roughly 3 by 4′, and cost about $1 each. Faller's mats have a foam rubber backing. Mats may only be used to cover relatively flat surfaces.

Earth mats are sold by: Life-Like Products, Inc. (17-1A, 6D), Faller, and Tru-Scale.

Grass mats are sold by: U.P.C. Natural Scale Scenics (in both regular (17-1A, 6F) and heavy pile (17-1A, 6E)), Tru-Scale (17-1A, 5N), Faller, and Life-Like Products, Inc. (17-1A, 6C). Green flocked paper may also be used; its fine texture is in scale on models as small as 1″ = 40′ (14-9).

Cement landscaping mats with the same adhesives used with loose granules. Apply the adhesives to the ground and to the back of the mat with a 3″ brush or paddle, being careful not to let the excess squeeze out on the top of the mat. Press the mat down with a roller.

Sand and Pebbles

Sand and pebbles may be represented by any 1 of the several white or gray commercial granules that are available, especially: Life-Like's white sand or gray scenic stone; Anderson's or B. and H. Products' ballast; and Natural Scale Scenics' sand spray. White aquarium sand may also be used.

Stones, Rocks and Boulders

Several of the commercially obtainable granules may be used to represent smaller stones. These include Permacraft Products' red and brown Sceni-Stones and red, brown, black and gray Sceni-Rock; Real-Like's rocks.

Larger rocks and boulders may be cast or built up from plaster. If the latter technique is employed, mix retarder into the plaster to extend its working time. Roughly form the rocks with a knife blade. Detail imparted while the plaster is still plastic will lose sharpness before the plaster dries and give the rock an eroded appearance. After the plaster has hardened, cracks and rugged details can be sculptured with a knife or scribe. To increase the depth of an outcropping, build it up with soft wood pieces or Celotex.

Boulders may also be made from natural stones, pieces of rough bark, foaming plastic, Celotex, Vermiculite, hardened plaster, balsa or hadite that has been crushed in a meat grinder. Hadite may be obtained from lumberyards. Cliffs may also be represented by thin striated pieces of sandstone, other natural rocks or by cork bark. Boulders may also be made by placing wet clay in a burlap bag and kneading it. When the clay is dry, remove it from the bag and break it apart into realistic shapes (8-25). If extensive boulders and cliffs must be modeled, pre-estimate their weight and use one of the lighter materials if there is a possibility that this weight may become excessive.

If the ground is made from plaster, all the above-mentioned materials may be embedded in it while the plaster is still wet. If the ground is made from a dry material, cement the rocks to it with household cement applied in double coats to both the rocks and the ground. Rocks made from most of these materials may be improved in appearance if, after they have been cemented in place, they are touched up with wet plaster. If Styrofoam or other foaming plastics are used, plaster must be applied to close up the pores of the material, unless a stylized effect is desired.

REPRESENTING SPECIFIC ROCKS

Shale is best simulated with Celotex that is not touched up with plaster.

Conglomerate rock formations (which in nature are boulders mixed with clay or silica) can be modeled by combining large and small granules or sand with real rocks.

Cliffs and other areas of extensive rock outcropping should be shown with sufficient detail to look convincing. Usually there is a scattering of boulders and pebbles at the foot of such a rock formation.

Various types of rocks may be represented by the following oil colors:

Basalt is dark gray to blue black.

Brownstone is Vandyke brown plus a touch (5%) of orange.

Granite is medium gray with small highlights of lighter gray blended into the darker areas.

Blue Granite is ultramarine and black.

Gray Granite is black with a translucent ultramarine overwash.

Red Granite is claret.

Limestone is pale gray with areas of burnt sienna and ultramarine.

Red Sandstone is Indian red plus burnt sienna or Vandyke brown.

Yellow Sandstone is light chrome yellow and Vandyke brown or raw umber.

Schist is pale olive.

Shale is burnt sienna with bands of Vandyke brown.

Paths and Roads

Paths and roads may be painted on earth contours or may be represented by flocking, granules, landscaping mats (17-1A, 6A and 6B), colored paper or painted sandpaper. All these techniques can also be used on stepped contours.

Commercial mats made by Life-Like Products, Inc. may be used to represent paths or parking lot paving. Gravel paths may be simulated by ballast mats, which can be found in model railroad hobby shops.

Paints used to represent paths and roads should be mixed with sand or talcum powder to effect a mat, textured finish.

Sidewalks and Paving

Sidewalks should have their top elevations above those of roads or gutters. This even helps the realistic look of models the scales of which are as small as 1″ = 40′. Sidewalks can be made from Bristolboard or they can be spray painted on the ground contour. Very small scale models may have concrete sidewalk slabs represented by cross-hatched pressure-sensitive overlays. Large-scale models may have curbs made from stripwood. Traffic division lines may be ruled in white ink or may, in large-scale models, be represented by white tape.

Various of the flat finishes shown on page 127 can also be used to represent the following types of paving: hexagonal and square paving blocks, cobblestones, radiating stone blocks, stone slabs and patio stones.

HIGHWAY MODELS

Complex highway interchanges and road systems are most easily presented and studied through the use of models. Models allow the civil engineer to study sight lines and plan signal and sign locations, sometimes difficult to do on drawings. Models aid the construction engineer in planning construction staging. They also show the owners of abutting property how their property will be affected by the road, and are used to generate public interest in projects and to aid legislative approval.

A highway model is often constructed to a 1″ = 50′ scale. The baseboard may be built from $\frac{1}{2}$″ plywood in 3 × 4′ sections for shipping convenience. Transportation cases often are built for each section. Grades are built up by dowels or wood strips. Crumpled paper and rock wool insulation are piled around the dowels to within $\frac{1}{2}$″ of the final ground elevation. These rough materials are then covered with 2 layers of wood putty. The road is represented by $\frac{1}{32}$″ balsa sheet. Curbs, traffic islands, handrails, etc. are also made from balsa. Guardrail is usually made of wire mesh. The entire model is given a coat of shellac; then vegetation and houses are added.

ATHLETIC FIELDS AND PARKING LOTS

Athletic and parking fields may be carefully masked and flocked, or made from green flock paper. White lines may be ruled in. Rough study models may have the fields represented by a black-on-white print made from the plot plan.

FARM FIELDS

Farm fields may be represented on small-scale models by forming a patchwork of green, yellow and brown fields out of cemented-on granules, or flock; pieces of different colored, flocked paper may also be used.

Plowed fields may be made by drawing a coarse comb over the ground-representing plaster while it is still wet. Paint it with oil paints that have a high oil content to impart a wet look. If the ground

17-4

Project: **WEST SIDE HIGH SCHOOL, NEW YORK CITY.**

Designed by: Charles Luckman Associates.
Modelbuilder: Alexander and Jones.
Scale: 1/16″ = 1′.
This small-scale, highly detailed presentation model of a courtyard was made entirely of acrylic painted with automotive lacquer. Pencil lines account for the paving pattern. The pedestal (lower left center) was turned from acrylic.

17-5

LARGE-SCALE MODEL OF A PLAYGROUND.

Designed by: The Playground Corporation of America, which also manufactures the equipment that was used.
modelbuilder and photographer: A member of the designer's staff.
Scale: 1″ = 1′. This large scale was used because more acceptable materials were available at this size; the scale also aided in the taking of realistic photographs.
Children's figures were cast in Epoxy and reused in many other playground setups. Curbing was cut from Homosote. Pipe structures were made from soldered rod. " Polyblocks " and climbing " trees " were cast from metal. Dome-like shapes were cast out of low melting point metal in rubber or plaster molds. Ground cover was made of colored sand. Trees were made of natural boxwood branches with babies'-breath for foliage.
The Playground Corporation makes models of all their large playground setups. The castings of their standard play equipment are thus reused.
Time required to set up this playground and to cut curbs (but not to cast figures and equipment) was about 75 hours.

133

is not made of plaster, cover it with a thin sheet of colored wax or clay or with a heavy application of oil paint and emboss these materials with the comb.

Wheat and other similar long stem crops may be represented with binder twine, obtainable in lumberyards. Cut the twine to appropriate lengths, untwist the fibers and paste their ends to the ground or set them into the wet plaster ground.

SMALL SCALE BRIDGES, ELECTRICAL WIRE PYLONS AND PLAYGROUND EQUIPMENT

These small, spindly objects may be made from soldered (hot or cold) brass strips and wires. Large-scale models may be made from Bristol-board. Bridges and pylons may also have sides made of thin sheet acrylic. Score the plastic to represent the struts of the prototype. Rub paint into the scored lines and assemble the structure. Another technique requires carving the outline of the object into a block of clear acrylic. Polish the plastic and scribe the detail into its sides, then paint the scored lines. If the plastic is finished correctly, it will be almost invisible, only the scribing will be noticeable. If several objects are to be modeled, bending and gluing jigs will save time.

WATER

Water is potentially the most charming bit of entourage found on model. It may be simple, represented with single-ply materials, or, for greater realism, it may be build up of several layers. For an illusion of depth, use 2 levels of material: 1, representing the surface of the water, should be clear plastic; the other, representing the bed of the water course, can be the material of the contours with an overlay of scale pebbles and stones.

The color of real water is influenced by 3 factors: (1) the actual color of the water modified by mud, algae and other material in the water; (2) the color of the bottom, which is also dependent on the clearness of the water and its depth; (3) the light reflected from the surface of the water. The latter 2 factors should be represented by transparent colors.

Deep water under a clear sky is usually blue; deep water that is not reflecting the sun is green; water close to shore is greenish-blue or greenish-black; muddy water is brown. Other influencing factors are shallowness and whether or not the bottom is sandy or strewn with rocks. Banks of streams and other muddy spots should be painted Vandyke brown; a top coat of varnish or shellac will give it a wet look.

Ripples caused by the wind are usually more pronounced in the center of a body of water. Other ripples may be formed by floating objects or by water dripping. Wave formation and size should also change, theoretically, as the waves get closer to shore. A collection of color photographs of various bodies of water is a useful reference.

Build the shoreline by overlapping the water representing material with the simulated ground material rather than trying to cut the water material to the exact shape of its bank.

Reflecting Pools and Other Smooth Water

To show reflections, the underside of transparent plastic may be painted a dark color (4-14). Black acrylic has a good reflecting surface that represents still water at night or under a dark sky.

If the ground contours are laminated, water may be represented by inserting a blue ply made

17-6/17-7

Project: **THE FESTIVAL OF GAS PAVILION AT THE 1964–65 NEW YORK WORLD'S FAIR.**

DESIGNED BY: Walter Dorwin Teague Associates.
MODELBUILDER: Form and Function, Inc. (a professional modelbuilder).
PHOTOGRAPHER: John Bradley.
SCALE: $1/8'' = 1'$.

This presentation model was built almost entirely of acrylic. Internal bracing was achieved by 1/16" acrylic strips cemented inside of the wall to ceiling intersections. Water was made of a 1/8" sheet of textured acrylic, mounted with the texture up and the underside painted aqua. Pavement lines were made by pantograph, using a plan as the guide. The ring-shaped rail on the second floor was turned on a lathe from acrylic. Railing was constructed of 1/32" acrylic with banister painted and lower rails scribed. People, chairs and table were cast from white metal in rubber molds. Patterns were carved from brass. Pine trees were made of green sawdust glued to cast metal armatures.

The model, only about 3/4 of which is pictured, cost the clients between $12,000 and $15,000.

from the typical lamination material or from blue acrylic. Blue Bourges or other pressure-sensitive overlays may also be used. These are the simplest-to-apply materials that show reflection (14-19).

Frozen water may be represented by paraffin stained a pale blue-green or by spraying Spray-O-Namel glass frosting (made by the Illinois Bronze Powder and Paint Company) on an acrylic sheet.

Rough Water

Rippled acrylic or cathedral glass are available in textures that represent water of various turbulences (25-3). Acrylic is preferable because of the ease with which it can be cut and the safety with which it can be used.

Very small scale models may have fairly rough water represented by mounting smooth sheet acrylic over a layer of embossed paper or rough board.

17-8

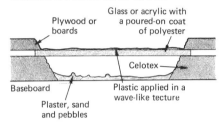

CONSTRUCTING BODIES OF WATER

Acrylic may also be carefully etched with solvent to form beautiful wave formations (11-4).

Also, sheet acetate can be soaked in acetone until it is almost dissolved, then it can be removed from the bath with a spatula and put into place. Then stipple and work the surface into the desired finish. In another technique, slightly soften the plastic and form it on a rough, partial wood form. When it is dry, remove it and place it on the model (15-1).

LIQUID PLASTIC MATERIAL

Casting plastic, water glass (sodium silicate), or Stewart-Lundal's Plasticate glue may be applied to the model in either of 2 ways:

By Applying It Directly to a Bed Cut into the Ground

This is best done when the ground is made out of plaster. (1) Model or stipple the wet plaster to create the approximate texture wished as the top of the water. Ripples may be gouged into the plaster with a pointed tool. The wet plaster will partially level itself, creating realistic waves. If the plaster does not level fast enough, hold the side of a revolving power tool under the baseboard and vibrate the plaster to a more level finish. (2) Paint the plaster. (3) Apply the liquid plastic material.

By Applying the Liquid Plastic to a Sheet of Clear Acrylic That Is Held above the Bed

(1) Place pebbles, stones and vegetation on the painted bed. (2) Fix the acrylic sheet into the bank. (3) Coat it with plastic or water glass. (4) Allow it to set partially, then stipple and model it to shape.

Several layers of the liquid plastic will increase the illusion of depth as will coloring it with dye. If applying several layers, the first and second layers should be about $\frac{1}{16}$" thick, and dyed. Have the color of 1 layer represent the color of the bottom, and the other represent the color of the water and the reflected sky. The top layer should be clear; with water flowers, boats or other floating objects embedded in it. Mixing instructions for casting plastic appear on page 87.

17-9

Project: HOUSE ON LONG LAKE, NEW YORK.

Design, model and photograph by: Sanford Hohauser.
Scale: $1/4" = 1'$.
The 4' × 5' baseboard of this design and presentation model was reusable. Its bottom was a 3/4" plywood sheet onto which was screwed removable pine formers that ran 6" on center from the front to the rear of the board. To be able to vary the contours of the site quickly, so that the base could be used with other design models, the formers were either shimmed up or replaced with new formers. Stapled to the top of the formers was a sheet of wire mesh that was covered with a 1/8" layer of plastilene. The walls, roof and floor of the building were made from 2 layers of single weight illustration board separated by a balsa strip core. Real water was used.
The photograph was taken with a 4" × 5" press camera, Wollensak Raptar 90 mm wide-angle lens and Super XX film.
Construction time (not including base): about 25 hours.

Waterfalls

The white water of rapids and waterfalls may be represented by frosted cellophane. Foam can be simulated by cotton that has been fluffed and pulled apart or with fine steel wool painted white.

Use of Real Water

Real water, while it can be extremely realistic for forming, for example, concentric ripples for photographic purposes, is very difficult to work with. It should be used only if it will aid photography, and then only if extreme pains have been taken to waterproof the bed and banks of the water body. Because of surface tension and other factors, water will appear to be out of scale. Mineral oil, on the other hand, forms ripples that are more realistic than those that can be made with water.

To provide a feeling of depth, real water must be applied over a painted bed or it must be tinted. $\frac{1}{2}$ teaspoon of copper sulfate (obtainable in garden shops) added to each 2 gallons of water is a good tint. Miniature pumps may be employed to agitate the water. Faller sells a miniature 12 to 16 volt a.c. pump. 2 examples of the use of real water may be seen in 9-3 and 17-9.

Stylized Water

An interesting artificial product that resembles a rapidly running river, and has the feeling of a Japanese print can be obtained by using Salubra Sales Corporation's Tekko No. 819-700-22 wall covering fabric. The fabric should be mounted under a thin sheet of acrylic.

Zip-a-Tone patterns 447, 448 (16-1A, C-11) and 449 mounted under blue acetate or acrylic make other usable stylized patterns.

If the baseboard is made out of wood, it may be stained or polished to represent water. See 12-1 and 15-8.

Animation

Animation may be achieved by mounting one or more rotating, internally lighted drums under a translucent water-representing material. The drums, covered with acetate on which a ripple pattern has been painted, will simulate running water. Lights mounted behind rotating discs into which windows covered with colored cellophane have been cut may be used instead of the drums.

Fountains

Fine water sprays may be represented by shiny steel or silver wire. If the fountain has a series of fine sprays, these may be made from silver colored mesh from which the wires running in one direction have been removed. Remove all but the last few wires on one end of the sheet. That end, which holds the assembly together, is set deep into the model. Fountains with a greater density of sprayed water may be built out of cellulose cement dripped over an acrylic core.

Snow and Ice

Snow may be represented by any of the commercially available white granules (see page 131), especially Walther's white Tex-Kote or Life-Like snow granules. Life-Like spray snow, and many

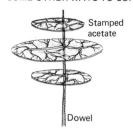 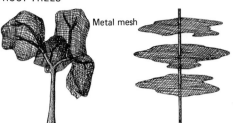 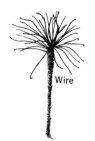 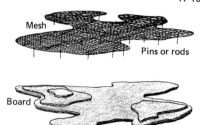

of the sprays found in stores around Christmas time, may be used on larger scale models. Before purchasing a spray, test it. Some products come out of the can too wet or in too rough a texture. 2 makes that have worked well for me in the past are Make It Snow and Aero Snow.

Icicles may be represented in larger scales by bits of twisted cellophane that have been dipped in a solution of sodium silicate (water glass).

TREES

Trees are among the elements of the model that one, most properly, will want to construct as fast as possible. The most expeditious solution is the purchase of ready-made trees in the middle scales $\frac{1}{16}'' = 1'$ to $\frac{1}{4}'' = 1'$) or the purchase of armatures (on which to place foliage) in all scales.

Have available a book of tree photographs in color; it will be a handy reference. The proportion, color and density of foliage of the prototype should be copied. Even hypothetical trees should be modeled with some species in mind. Basic tree colors are dark green and yellow for deciduous trees and dark green for evergreen trees. Wads of plasticine may be used to hold trees upright on the workbench while working on them.

Trunks and Twigs

The skeletal structure of trees may be constructed from many materials. In all cases, the tree should be set into holes drilled in the model base.

CAST LIMBS

Trunk and branch systems may be cast from metal in 2-part molds. Surprisingly delicate limbs may be achieved if the molds are accurately made. Several companies listed on page 139 sell these parts ready-made.

The Microform Corporation has an extensive line consisting of about 40 tree armatures (17-14). These include many species and sizes ranging from 1 to 7" in height.

Amron Products sells sticks formed to resemble evergreen tree trunks. Diameters range grom $\frac{1}{16}$ to $\frac{3}{16}''$ and lengths from 13 to 14". Cost is about $1 for 2 dozen.

WOUND WIRE

Wound thin copper, or soft iron, florist or picture frame wire can be used to produce the trunk and branches of trees that are in $\frac{1}{32}'' = 1'$ scales and larger.

Some experimenting will be necessary to determine how many strands will be needed to produce specific tree species. Some trees with many branches require as many as 50 or more strands to reproduce them in a $\frac{1}{4}'' = 1'$ scale. Start this way: (1) Cut the wires to lengths that run from $\frac{1}{2}$ to $1\frac{1}{2}$ times the intended height of the model tree. (2) Place the wires together so that all the lengths are even at 1 end. (3) Use 2 pairs of pliers or a vise and a pair of pliers and twist the wires to form the trunk of the tree below the first branch. (4) Separate the strands above the twisted area into groups that represent major branches. Each group should have both long and short strands. (5) Twist each branch into shape, leaving the last fraction of an inch of each strand to stand alone. Additional short strands of wire may be added where needed to increase the number of branches. (6) The trunk may be finished with a coat of clay, plastic wood or plaster. Clay, if applied wet, will create the effect of smooth bark. Plastic wood will be slightly rougher. If desired, paint it with cellulose thinner to smooth it. Sand rubbed into any of the covering materials will give a rough bark effect. Patterned bark may be formed by scratching the cover of the trunk with a scribe. Knots, stumps and other irregularities may be modeled in the covering material. (7) Paint the trunk with mat oil or cellulose paint if it is covered with clay or plastic wood, or with mat cellulose paint if it is covered with cellulose putty. If the tree is in a small scale, step 6 may be omitted and the trunk dipped into thick, mat, latex house paint.

Multistrand copper electrical wire can also be used: (1) Strip away insulation above the place where the trunk divides into branches. (2) Twist the thin wire strands into a realistic number of main branches. (3) Divide the main branches into smaller branches. (4) Cover the trunk and main branches with plaster of Paris, putty, plastic wood or clay.

Less pliable wire may also be used. Cut it into strands of the appropriate length. Lash these together with fine florist's "hair" wire to form branches. Hair wire may also be used to hold together the strands that make up thicker branches and to create fine twig ends.

Conifers should be constructed in the same manner as a bottle brush. Continue the trunk to the top of the tree, thinning down the number of wire strands the higher it goes. Form the foliage by introducing sisal bristles into the twisted wire, trimming them with scissors. Dip paint the finished tree in dark green paint and sprinkle fine sawdust onto it while it is still wet.

NATURAL TWIGS

Many natural bushes have twigs of the correct size and articulation to be used on models (3-3 and 15-20). Twigs should be shellacked or varnished prior to use. Privet twigs are about right for $\frac{1}{8}''$ and larger scale trees. Babys'-breath stripped of its buds makes good branches, as do the twigs of many other bushes and trees. A twig from a tree can be used as the trunk of the model and babys'-breath can be cemented onto it, or several sprigs of babys'-breath can have their stems bound together with thread. A coating of plastic wood can be used to cover the thread and to form a trunk of correct diameter. Pine trees can be effectively represented by long straight twigs on which babys'-breath branches are cemented. The foliage can be made from cellulose sponge torn into realistic clumps.

Other Trunk Materials

Small-scale tree trunks can be made from brads, pins or lengths of metal rod.

EVERGREENS

Cement asparagus fern into holes that have been cut in tapered splinters broken off of cedar or ash stakes or made from balsa. Turn the wood on a drill to create its shape; a bark-like texture can be achieved by sanding with rough sandpaper.

The trunks of very small pine trees can be made from wound wire; their foliage can be represented by a great number of thin wires inserted into their trunk much in the same fashion that bottle brushes are constructed.

PALM TREES

These are difficult to model accurately. Small ($\frac{1}{6}''$ scale and under) palm trees can be made from wire. Several strands can be wound to represent the trunks. Their ends can then be left loose to create somewhat stylized leaves. Loosely twisted, fine wire can be added below the leaves to represent the fronds.

Larger scale palm trees may have their trunks made from thin straw or dowels wired together along the length of the trunk. One end of the material can be unwired and spread in a natural leaf arrangement. Leaves can also be cut from wire mesh and mounted on a rod or dowel trunk, or they may be cut from paper (17-3).

Foliage Material

Foliage may be fabricated from 1 or a combination of several of the materials mentioned later in this section. All should be torn, not cut, to shape. Flat or regular surfaces should be pulled apart to form the irregularities that are found in nature. Some types of foliage material (most notably sawdust and other small granules) should be applied to a bulk-creating underlayer of steel wool or lichen. Foliage may be affixed to model twigs by dipping the latter in shellac or (better yet) in a rubber-base adhesive such as Pliobond or Walthers' Goo and then sifting on the foliage. If an underlayer of steel wool or lichen is used, attach the top foliage layer with thinned liquid latex. When 2 different types of foliage materials are to be used in 1 tree, place spots of glue on the first material and sprinkle the second onto it.

PAINTING

Spray painting or dip dyeing is recommended since it is impossible to reach all of the recesses of the foliage with a paintbrush. Spray painting produces a more realistic, uneven effect. Highlights can be brushed on, or foliage of different colors may be combined on each tree. Always use mat colors. Foliage material may be dyed by: (1) placing it into a bag folded from a piece of loosely woven fabric; (2) dipping the bag into a can of water dye; and (3) allowing it to dry on a newspaper.

Here are the oil colors used to represent various species of foliage:

Autumn leaves are ochre (4 parts), red (2 parts).

Elm leaves are green (5), light yellow (1).

Maple leaves are red (8), ochre (1).

Oak leaves are ochre (4), burnt umber (2), red (1).

Pine needles are light green (6), burnt umber (1), light yellow (a touch).

Other paints that may be used are latex paints or Floquil flat lacquers.

17-11

Project: **ONE OF THE MODELS ON DISPLAY IN THE FORD PAVILION AT THE 1964–65 NEW YORK WORLD'S FAIR.**

MODELBUILDER: Display and Exhibit Company (a professional modelbuilder).

SCALE: $1/2'' = 1'$.

Thatching was made of cord; wood members of stripwood; bricks were individually cut from vinyl and then assembled on the wall of the model. Cobblestones were cut into alabaster slabs. Shingles were cast in polyester resin. Metal grills and filigree were etched into brass. Tree trunks and branches were constructed of wire; hedges cut from rubber upholstery padding; grass made of velour cloth brushed with green paint and glue. People were carved from white oak.

17-12

READY-MADE TREES:

These trees, from the plastic Make-Up line sold by Britains Ltd., must be assembled, a procedure which takes a few minutes per tree. Trees range from 5″ to 12″ high.

Front row (righthand side): Apple (No. 1801).

2nd row (left to right): cedar (No. 1824), oak (No. 1822), poplar (No. 1820).

3rd row (left to right): silver birch (No. 1806), fir (No. 1809), Scots pine (No. 1810).

17-13

READY-MADE TREES:

Front row (left to right):

Faller (3 trees from set No. 317, which contains 8 trees or so per set), (3 trees from set No. 320, 5 trees or so per set). Roco HO Model Miniatures, from A.H.M. (2 trees from set No. Z-185 that contains 6 trees per set). Bachmann Brothers (6 trees from set No. 1404 which contains 7 trees; some are blue).

2nd row:

Life-Like green shade tree (S00 1 R); autumn (S002R). This is red-brown. It also comes in orange-green); spring tree (S006R)). This is yellow-green. It also comes in white-red and red-white-green); assorted fruit trees (S004R)). This is green with red fruit. It also comes with green and orange fruit); green shade tree, small (S020R). U.P.C. green shade trees (No. 642) (2—one is red). Fruit tree (No. 643).

Rear row:

3 trees from Bachmann Brothers autumn tree assortment. Britains Ltd. young beech (No. 1807). Life-Like evergreen tree (S003R). Life-Like poplar tree (S005R). Life-Like small evergreen tree (S022R). U.P.C. Natural Scale Scenics evergreen (No. 641).

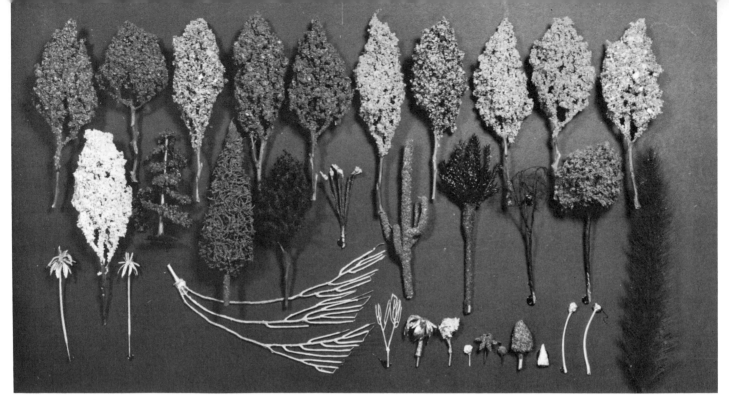

17-14

MATERIALS THAT MAY BE USED

Norwegian Lichen (6-1) (sometimes known by the trade name of Lychen)

Coarse lichen can be used as a filler material on the insides of large-scale trees. Fine ends should be saved for the outside, visible foliage of these trees and for small-scale trees.

The mixed package lichen, sold by companies such as Life-Like and Walthers, comes in red, green and orange shades. Tru-Scale's comes in natural color, rust or green.

Dixie cup lichen, a plant similar to Norwegian lichen but finer, is sold by Amron. It comes in light green and has occasional yellow buds.

Cement with Life-Like ballast cement: apply by dipping the lichen into a shallow plateful of the adhesive.

Raw lichen, and for that matter any natural plant, must be processed to prevent its drying, becoming brittle and dropping from the trees. Packaged lichen that is commercially available has already been processed and much of it will remain pliable for over a decade. Raw lichen is much less expensive than the packaged product. To process lichen: (1) Soak it in warm water for several minutes; knead it to aid in the penetration of the water. (2) Remove it from the water and squeeze out all excess moisture. (3) Place it in pickling solution for 24 hours or more. The solution can be made from 1 quart of glycerin, 1 quart of acetone and 2 quarts of denatured alcohol. This will produce 1 gallon of solution, enough to pickle 1 to 2 bales of lichen. The glycerin and alcohol are purchasable at drugstores; acetone may be obtained at paint stores. (4) Remove the lichen, spread it on newspaper until it has dried. (5) It then may be dip or spray painted with Tintex, Aniline dye or artist's oil colors diluted to a soup-like consistency. Lichen may also be dyed while it is being pickled. Add 1 ounce of aerosol or Unox penetrant (both are available from drug-stores) to each quart of pickling solution.

Dried out lichen may be rejuvenated by soaking it in water and then dipping it into a mixture of 1 part glycerin and 4 parts water.

Loofa

This is a dried fiber sponge imported from Japan. It is coarser and drier looking than lichen, which it roughly resembles. It is sometimes used plain or it is covered with a cemented-on mixture of saw-dust, very small wood chips and plastic wood.

Other Foliage Materials

Cellulose sponge, natural sponge, foam rubber, wire wool (6-2), underlying felt, wire mesh, or looped thin wire (14-18) may be arranged realis-tically on trunks to form interesting middle and large-scale trees. Rubberized horsehair (14-19), dried tea leaves or short lengths of wool yarn may also be used as foliage.

Amron Products sells 4 types of foliage material for the making of evergreens: Minipine, Minifern, Minifir and Minispruce. These cost $1 for each packet.

Small wood chips, coarse sawdust and plaster may be mixed to form a realistic foliage for small $\frac{1}{32}″=1'$) scale trees (11-2). The wet mix can be placed on trunks made from nails.

Many of these materials may be combined to create a greater articulation of form.

Entire Trees (Trunks and Foliage)

NATURAL PLANTS

There are several natural plants the small buds and leaves of which allow them to be used as stylized model trees in $\frac{1}{32}″$ and larger scale models.

A few of these plants may be bought in some large florist shops, but most may be obtained from the great outdoors. These are best picked in autumn when they have dried out. Soaking $\frac{1}{2}$ day in glycerin will preserve them, or they may be sprayed with Krylon mat spray. Natural plants can be colored with fabric dyes or sprinkled with flock or sawdust for extra detail.

Babys'-Breath (Gypsophila) has many small blossoms and a detailed twig system which make realistic fruit trees and birch foliage (15-20). It may also be used to represent other species stylistically. Its delicate stem may be reinforced with plaster-coated twisted wire. Some florist shops sell it in assorted colors.

Yarrow (Achillea Millefolium or Milfoil) has dense $\frac{1}{4}″$ diameter buds and a detailed twig system which make it a good material to represent underbrush or pine needle clumps.

Spiraea has a shape resembling poplar trees.

Asparagus Fern resembles the boughs of cedar and fir trees.

Gorse has very small leaves which make a good representation of pine.

Millet Seed Sprays (used as bird food) may be threshed to remove the seeds, which then may be used as foliage.

Other Usable Natural Plants are celux, straw flowers, sumac weed, kochia (burning bush), fine leaf cedar and sprigs of small evergreen needles.

Amron Products sells small, green dried plants that resemble pine boughs. They charge $1 for material sufficient to make six 8″ high pine trees.

Trackside Specialties sells a kit containing 10 different types of plant life. The material comes in natural colors, and it may be used as is or dyed with textile colors. A bag costs $1.80.

READY-MADE TREES

Several companies sell ready-made trees to the model railroad hobbyist.

AVAILABLE MODELS OF TREES, TREE TRUNKS, AND BUSHES

Height (inches)	Manufacturer's name for tree (and where illustrated)	Price	Material and stand	Manufacturer or supplier
CONIFER TREES				
Under 2 1/2	Small pine (17–13, front row)	65¢ for set	Plastic sections that lock together, with stand	Faller
3	Small evergreen (17–13, rear row)	6 for $1.00	Granules on thread branches, with plastic trunk and stand	Life-Like
3 1/2	Evergreen (17–13, rear row)	5 for $1.00	Granules on thread branches, with plastic stand	U.P.C.
3–5	Pine	6 for $1.00	Granules on real twigs, no stand	Tru-Scale
Under 4	Pine (17–13, front row)	8 for 80¢	Plastic sections that lock together, with stand	Aurora and Bachmann Plasticville
Under 4	Pine (17–13, front row)	6 for 25¢	Plastic sections that lock together, with stand	A.H.M.
About 4	Large pine (17–13, front row)	$1.20 for set	Plastic sections that lock together, with stand	Faller
5	Evergreen (17–13, rear row)	5 for $1.00	Granules on thread branches, with plastic stand	U.P.C. and Life-Like
5	Pine—also available partly covered with snow (17–14, second row)	5 for $1.00	Granules on wire branches, no stand	Real-Like
Up to 6 (to trim to size)	Evergreen (17–14, second row)	Box for $2.00	Natural plant, no stand	Selley Tom Thumb Trees
5–6 1/2	Pine (17–14, second row)	4 for $1.00	Granules on real twigs, no stand	Tru-Scale
8	Fir and scots pine (17–12)	35¢ each	Plastic, in kit form, with stand	Britains Ltd.
8	Cedar (17–12)	65¢ each	Plastic, in kit form, with stand	Britains Ltd.
FRUIT				
1 1/2–2	Orange, apple	4 for $1.00	Natural foliage, no stand	Wm. Walthers
2 1/2	Orange, apple, lemon (17–13, middle row)	5 for $1.00	Granules on thread branches, with plastic stand	U.P.C.
3	Orange, apple (17–13, middle row)	6 for $1.00	Granules on thread branches, with plastic stand	Life-Like
3–5	Orange, apple	4 for $1.60	Natural foliage, no stand	Wm. Walthers
3–5	Orange, apple (17–14, top row)	6 for $1.00	Granules on real twigs, no stand	Tru-Scale
5	Apple (17–12)	35¢ each	Plastic, in kit form, with stand	Britains Ltd.
5–6 1/2	Orange, apple	4 for $1.00	Plastic, in kit form, with stand	Tru-Scale
SPRING TREES				
3	Red, red–white–yellow, green–white–yellow, white–red, and white–blue (17–13, middle row)	5 for $1.00	Granules on thread branches, plastic stand	Life-Like and U.P.C.
3–5	Spring (17–14, top row)	5 for $1.00	Granules on real twigs, no stand	Tru-Scale
5–6 1/2	Spring	4 for $1.00	Granules on real twigs, no stand	Tru-Scale
AUTUMN TREES				
3	Autumn	5 for $1.00	Granules on thread branches, with plastic stand	U.P.C.
3–5	Autumn (17–14, top row)	6 for $1.00	Granules on real twigs, no stand	Tru-Scale
4	Autumn (17–13, middle row)	5 for $1.00	Granules on thread branches, with plastic stand	Life-Like
4–7	Autumn tree assortment (17–13, rear row)	18 for $3.50	Plastic sections that lock together, with stand	Bachmann Plasticville
5–6 1/2	Autumn	4 for $1.00	Granules on real twigs, no stand	Tru-Scale
SHADE TREES				
2 1/2	Green shade (17–13, middle row)	5 for $1.00	Granules on thread branches, with plastic base	U.P.C.
3 1/2	Small shade (17–13, middle row)	6 for $1.00	Lichen on plastic trunk and stand	Life-Like
3–5	Green shade (17–14, top row)	6 for $1.00	Granules on real twigs, no stand	Tru-Scale
4	Green shade	5 for $1.00	Granules on thread branches, with plastic base	U.P.C.
4	Shade trees (come in 2 colors and also partly covered with snow) (17–14, second row)	5 for $1.00	Flock on natural branch, no stand	Real-Like
5	Large shade (17–13, middle row)	5 for $1.00	Lichen on plastic trunk and stand	Life-Like
5–6 1/2	Green shade	4 for $1.00	Granules on real twigs, no stand	Tru-Scale
OTHER DECIDUOUS TREES				
1/4 and 1/2	Deciduous	3¢ each	Sponge rubber foliage	Model Makers
Under 1–7	34 sizes and styles of deciduous trees and bushes (17–14, third row)	11¢–78¢ each	Cast metal armature, no foliage or stand	Microform Corp.
1	Deciduous	30¢ without and 40¢ with foliage	Metal armature, with or without sponge foliage, no stand	Model Makers

(continued on next page)

Height (inches)	Manufacturer's name for tree (and where illustrated)	Price	Material and stand	Manufacturer or supplier
1	Deciduous	10¢ each	Cast metal armature, no foliage or stand	William Mattison
1 1/2	Deciduous	15¢ each	Cast metal armature, no foliage or stand	William Mattison
1 3/4–4	8 sizes of deciduous trees (17–14, third row)	8¢–17¢ each	Cast metal armature with foliage, no stand	Devpro
2	Deciduous	45¢ without and 55¢ with foliage, each	Metal armature, with or without sponge foliage, no stand	Model Makers
2	Deciduous	20¢ each	Cast metal armature, no foliage or stand	William Mattison
2–4	Oak, maple, elm	15 for $1.50	Natural foliage, no stand	Wm. Walthers
3	Deciduous	70¢ without and 85¢ with foliage, each	Metal armature, with or without sponge foliage, no stand	Model Makers
3	Deciduous	30¢ each	Cast metal armature, no foliage or stand	William Mattison
4	Deciduous	40¢ each	Cast metal armature, no foliage or stand	William Mattison
4	Deciduous (17–14, second row)	$1.00 without and $1.20 with foliage, each	Metal armature, with or without sponge foliage, no stand	Model Makers
4–6	Oak, elm, maple	10 for $1.50	Natural foliage, no stand	Wm. Walthers
4 1/2	Foliage trees	4 for $1.35	Sponge rubber foliage, with stand	Faller
4 1/2	Flowering trees	4 for $1.25	Sponge rubber foliage, with stand	Faller
5	Poplar	5 for $1.00	Granules on thread branches, plastic trunk and stand	Life-Like
6–10	Oak, elm, maple	5 for $2.50	Natural foliage, no stand	Wm. Walthers
8	Silver birch, (17–12) copper beech, (17–13, rear row)	35¢ each	Plastic, in kit form, with stand	Britains Ltd.
8	Deciduous	80¢ each	Cast metal armature, no foliage or stand	William Mattison
8 1/2	Oak (17–12)	65¢ each	Plastic, in kit form, with stand	Britains Ltd.
9	Birch	3 for $1.35	Sponge rubber foliage, with stand	Faller
9	Poplar	3 for $1.00	Sponge rubber foliage, with stand	Faller
11 1/2	Poplar (17–12)	65¢ each	Plastic, in kit form, with stand	Britains Ltd.

PALM TREES

Height (inches)	Manufacturer's name for tree (and where illustrated)	Price	Material and stand	Manufacturer or supplier
2 and 2 1/2	Palm (17–14, third row)	52¢ and 56¢ each	Cast metal trunk and foliage, no stand	Microform Corp.
4 1/2	Palm (17–14, second row)	3 for $1.00	Natural plant on a stem, no stand	Real-Like

CACTI

Height (inches)	Manufacturer's name for tree (and where illustrated)	Price	Material and stand	Manufacturer or supplier
2 1/2 and 4	Octillo and saguaro (17–14, second row)	5 for $1.00 (mixed)	Granules on stem, no stand	Real-Like

BUSHES AND SHRUBS[1]

Height (inches)	Manufacturer's name for tree (and where illustrated)	Price	Material and stand	Manufacturer or supplier
3/4	Hedge rows (17–15, top row)	4 for 75¢	Sponge rubber foliage, with stand	Faller
1	Flowering bushes (17–15, top and bottom rows)	7 for $1.00	Granules on real twigs, no stand	Tru-Scale
1	Flowering plants (17–15, bottom row)	10 for $1.00	Granules on real twigs, no stand	Tru-Scale
1	Flowering bushes	6 for $1.00	Granules on wire, no stand	Real-Like
1	Hedges	32″ for 50¢	Granules on wire, no stand	Real-Like
1–2	Shrubs	50 for $1.00	Natural foliage, no stand	Wm Walther
1 1/2	Flowering shrubs (17–15, top row)	4 tor $1.00	Sponge-rubber foliage, with stand	Faller
1 1/2	Bushes (17–15, top row)	4 for $1.00	Sponge-rubber foliage, with stand	Faller

[1] See also short armatures under "Other deciduous trees."

MISCELLANEOUS TECHNIQUES

Balls of natural cork or wood, spherical or oval buttons (14-5), obtainable in $\frac{1}{2}$ to 2″ diameters from beadcraft, knitting and accessory stores, make interesting stylized trees. Also interesting are map pins or balls of foamed plastic.

Rubber Stamps

Cut in the pattern of tree elevations, these can be obtained from 2 companies. With them, images of trees can be stamped onto prefixed acetate sheet. These are cut to outline and then mounted on the model. Stamps of trees in plan view can also be used: acetate discs stamped with these may be mounted one above the other (with some space in between) on a dowel.

Design Specialties sells stamps of elevation views of trees in the following scales and quantities: $\frac{1}{16}″ = 1′$ (4 different styles), $\frac{1}{8}″$ to $\frac{1}{16}″$ scales (12) and a $\frac{1}{8}″$ scale (3). Cost runs from $1.00 to $3.50 per stamp. The company also sells 19 different leaf patterns in a $\frac{1}{8}″$ scale for $1 per stamp; and elevation views of plants in a $\frac{1}{8}″$ scale (1 style) and a $\frac{1}{4}″$ scale (3 styles), with a cost of $1 to $1.60 per stamp. They sell elevation views of shrubs or small trees in a $\frac{1}{8}″$ scale (12 styles) and a $\frac{1}{4}″$ scale (19 styles) with the cost running from $1.25 to $2.00 per stamp.

Instant Landscape sells stamps of elevation views of trees in the following sizes and styles: $1\frac{1}{2}$ to 2″ high (45 different styles costing $2.00 to $2.40 per stamp), $2\frac{1}{2}$ to 3″ high (52 styles costing $3.00 to $4.60 per stamp). They also sell 46 elevation views of shrubs and plants in heights ranging from $\frac{1}{4}$ to 2 inches. Cost runs from $1.25 to $3.40 per stamp.

Design Specialties sells plan view stamps of trees in the following scales and quantities: $1/200″ = 1′$ scale (12 different styles), $1/100$ to $1/32″$ scale (105 styles), $1/16$ to $1/50″$ scale (50 styles), $1/32″$ and larger scale (99 styles), $1/8″$ and larger scale (50 styles). Costs run from $1 to $2 for each stamp.

Instant Landscape sells stamps of plan views of trees in the following sizes and quantities: $\frac{1}{2}″$ diameters (39 different styles, for $1.25 each); $\frac{3}{4}″$ diameters (15 styles, $1.35 each); 1″ diameters (39 styles, $1.50 each); 2″ diameters (39 styles, $2.40 each); and 3″ diameters (39 styles, $3.40 each). They also have the following stamps of plan views of shrubs: $\frac{1}{2}″$ diameters (10 styles for $1.25 each); 1″ diameters (10 styles, $1.50 each); and $1\frac{1}{2}″$ diameters (10 styles, $2.00 each).

Transfers

The dry transfer Lettraset line of Chart-Pak, Inc. has 7 styles of plan views of trees (sheet Nos. AS622 and AS623) and 29 styles of elevation views of trees (sheet Nos. AS620 and AS621). These $\frac{1}{16}$ and $\frac{1}{8}″ = 1′$ scale images may also be applied to acetate, and mounted on the model.

17-15

READY-MADE BUSHES AND SHRUBS:

Top row from left to right:
Tru-Scale: flowering climber (part of set No. 412), flowered bushes (part of set No. 413, 2 pieces), bush (No. 383), blooming bush (No. 367), hedge (No. 384).

Bottom row:
Tru-Scale: flowered plants (No. 407, 8 pieces), flowered bushes (No. 413, 2 pieces), flowering climber (No. 412).

Presstamp sells transfers of elevation views of 21 styles of trees in a $\frac{1}{16}$ to $\frac{1}{8}''=1'$ scale. They also sell elevation views of 9 kinds of shrubs in both $\frac{1}{8}$ and $\frac{1}{4}''$ scales. They sell transfers of plan views of trees in the following scales and quantities: 1/100 to 1/32''=1' (26 different styles), 1/50 to 1/16'' scales (26 styles), 1/32'' scale and larger (52 styles), $\frac{1}{8}''$ scale and larger (26 styles). They also sell plan views of 3 kinds of shrubs and hedges in each of $\frac{1}{16}, \frac{1}{8}$ and $\frac{1}{4}''$ scales.

Extensive Tree Stands in Small Scales

When the model has a scale so small that the inclusion of tree trunks and limbs is unnecessary, large groups of trees may be represented by clumps of lichen, cellulose or natural sponge (14-13) or fine wire wool. The grouping may also be cut out of a rough acoustical tile, foamed plastic, wire mesh, several plys of cardboard or plaster (14-3).

Hedges and Bushes

Almost all the techniques suggested for making trees can be employed in the simulation of hedges and bushes. Very small scale models may have granulated cork, colored sawdust or fine wood chips sprinkled on cement-covered areas of the ground.

Flowers

In large scales, flowers may be represented by small dip painted pieces of cellulose sponge, or small bits of lichen may be sprinkled with commercially made granules or with small drops of enamel paint. In addition, flowering bushes or hedges are sold by Faller, Tru-Scale and Real Like. See the chart above.

Smaller scale flowers may be represented by the commercially made granules that are available. These are sold by Walthers (their line has 4 colors) and Tru-Scale (whose line comes in 6 colors). Flower beds may be represented by areas of Casco glue or cellulose cement on which green, coarse sawdust (to represent leaves) and multicolored bird seed, commercial granules and flock have been placed.

Plants

Ivy may be represented by coarse, green sawdust or granules cemented to the walls of the model.

Vines can be made out of steel wool that has been spread out, painted green and cemented in place; or they can be made of small bits of lichen attached to strands of thin, flexible wire.

Fallen leaves are made out of appropriate granules or out of brightly colored lichen cut into very small pieces and cemented on the ground.

House Plants

Plants in larger scales (1 and $1\frac{1}{2}''=1'$) are often used in detailed models of interiors. As with other forms of vegetation, each plant should conform to a recognizable prototype. Sometimes reasonable facsimiles may be obtained from real plants and bushes (19-1). More often it will be necessary to make the model leaf by leaf from colored paper, applying this to wire stems. Some of the ways to make large-scale plant models are as follows:

Make Sansevierias by cutting individual spikes from paper. Then paint in the tiger stripes with green and yellow paint.

Make Aloes by tightly rolling paper into a cylinder. Slice it vertically and peel it back into an authentic looking configuration.

Make Grass-Like Plants by rolling paper tightly into a cylinder. Slice it down from its top into a spray of narrow leaves.

Make Ivy and Other Trailing Plants by gluing dried tea leaves on stems made from thin wire. Spray paint them green.

Make Large Leaf Plants by cutting leaves individually and gluing them to stems made from multistrand wire.

18 SCALE-IMPARTING ELEMENTS

Miniature people and cars should not be considered elements of decoration on models. If properly used, they can aid in the visualization of a prototype—the prime purpose of the model. These elements should impart an over-all feeling of scale to the model. They may also be used to give some idea of the actual crowd of people and vehicles that will surround the completed design or travel through it. Perhaps an inclusion of a realistic number of people and vehicles will aid the designer in recognizing how basic a role these elements will play in the aesthetics of the prototype.

PEOPLE

As with other articles of entourage, miniature people must complement, not compete with, the architectural portion of the model. They should not be painted so garishly or improvised in such a bizarre fashion as to create a greater impression than the building. Extra care must be taken in the case of rough models where ill-chosen manikins can compete for the viewer's attention. The main uses of model people are to establish the scale of the building and to add realism to the model. Whenever it is possible, buy ready-made figurines. There are so many on the market in the 1/50 to 1/4″=1′ scale range that it makes little sense to attempt to make one's own. When it is necessary to fabricate these models, try to select a simple technique; time spent on making people does not benefit the modelbuilding—the actual goal. About the only time it would be wise to spend time on figure construction is when the figures are to be reused on several models or when constructing casting dies that are to be used on many models. Abstract people, easier to make than accurately detailed ones, cannot easily establish scale or add realism to the model.

People should be naturally grouped on the model. They should stand, walk or sit in groups of 2's and 3's, and the group should congregate around entrances and other places of naturally high traffic: they should not be evenly distributed along all sidewalks and paths, unless this will be the prototype condition.

Ready-Made Figures

In many scales, unpainted, ready-made figures can be obtained for as little as 5¢ each and beautiful hand painted figures for around 50¢. It is not possible to cast or carve a figure that economically compares with ready-made ones, but it is possible, by using short cuts and mass production techniques, to paint ready-made figures at a cost that is substantially less than the cost of those that are ready painted. Many professional modelmakers cast figures and vehicles in metal, and will sell these castings to designers. A short search should unearth the name of a local modelmaker who could supply one's needs at most scales up to $\frac{1}{4}″=1′$ for figures and up to $\frac{1}{8}″=1′$ for vehicles.

When working with commercial figures, the production procedure should be as follows:

1—Clean all casting flash from the plastic or metal figures. Scrape off major irregularities from plastic figures with a single-edge razor and smooth off the casting lines with a small jeweler's file.

2—Cut off the standing pedestal.

3—Paint all flesh areas.

4—Mix and paint all other colors, singly, proceeding from one figurine to the next, spotting in the color where it is needed.

5—Paint all figures with flat finish. If it is acceptable, the figures may also be spray painted 1 color. This saves time and does not detract, at a $\frac{1}{16}″=1′$ scale and smaller, too badly from realism, especially when several colors are used and the differently colored figures are mixed together when mounted on the model.

6—Mount the figures on the model by pasting them to the ground, using drops of Epoxy glue or acetate cement. Or, if there is trouble making them stand while the cement is drying, paste them on small pieces of clear, thin acetate and then paste the plastic pedestal to the model. Wood blocks with holes cut into them can be used as positioning jigs for holding the figures upright while the cement is drying.

Care must be taken to select ready-made figures that are accurately scaled. Some manufacturers are not too careful about the height of their figures, and many have the tendency to cast heads that are out of proportion (an adult's head should be 1/7 to 1/8 of his total height).

Forming Each Figure Individually

Because of the large number of people that must be fabricated, a production system should be selected with the fewest possible steps. Following are some techniques that can produce adequate figures:

FIGURES CUT OUT OF BRISTOL OR ILLUSTRATION BOARD AND FINISHED ON BOTH SIDES

Perhaps the simplest way to make figures is to cut them out of board. Fold the arms, legs and torsos into a natural standing, sitting or striding pose. If the figures are not folded, they tend, when viewed from their side, to look like random pipes or rods protruding from the sidewalk. Make figures out of colored paper, paint them or leave them white (15-1 and 19-8).

FIGURES STAMPED ON BOARD AND THEN CUT OUT

2-dimensional figures, suitable for use on diorama models, may be made by using the rubber stamps manufactured by Design Specialties, Inc. This company makes stamps for 10 different styles of people in a $\frac{1}{16}″=1′$ scale; 14 different styles of people in a $\frac{1}{8}″$ scale and 14 in a $\frac{1}{4}″$ scale. Stamps cost $1.00 to $1.40 each. Instant Landscape, Inc. makes stamps for 59 different styles of people in a $\frac{1}{16}″=1′$ scale; 59 in a $\frac{1}{8}″$ scale; 59 in a $\frac{1}{4}″$ scale and 59 in a $\frac{1}{2}″$ scale. Their stamps cost $1.25 to $3.40 each. Stamp the appropriate scale figure onto Bristol or double-faced illustration board, cut them out and mount them on the model. Photographs of people may also be dry-mounted on board (1-1). A semi-abstract 3-dimensional figure may be made by using rubber stamps on prefixed acetate (or other transparent bendable plastic that will take ink); cut out the figure, bend it into a natural pose and mount it on the model.

TRANSFER FIGURES APPLIED TO BOARD AND THEN CUT OUT

Presstamp, Inc. makes burnish on transfers of people. They have 14 different styles in a $\frac{1}{16}″=1′$ scale, 14 in a $\frac{1}{8}″$ scale and 13 in a $\frac{1}{4}″$ scale.

FIGURES CARVED FROM WOOD STRIP OR DOWEL

A simple carving sequence should be devised so as to result in a reasonably convincing figure with a minimum number of cuts. Arms and legs should be splintered away from the torso and reglued in a natural position. Paint the figures following the procedure outlined for ready-made figures. See illustration 5-1 for 1 interesting style and 18-3, row 7, for another.

The next 2 techniques are rather tedious, but can result in superb figures. It is perhaps best to use these systems for larger (over $\frac{1}{4}″=1′$) scales and for instances when relatively few need be made:

WAX FIGURES

1—Bend a soft wire armature into a natural pose.

2—Heat the wax (candle wax, beeswax or the hard wax used in electroplating) to a temperature a bit higher than its melting point (too high a temperature will delay the hardening of the wax).

3—Use a cheap brush to apply the wax to the armature, and build up the figure in successive layers. The wax must be allowed to dry between coats. Water applied by finger will hasten its drying. Fine detail may be carved into the wax.

4—Prime the finished figure with white liquid shoe polish, then paint with poster or model railroad oil colors, and apply a coat of flat finish.

FIGURES BUILT UP OF PLASTER

1—Make a soft wire armature; bend it into a natural pose.

2—Mix plaster of Paris to the consistency of cream cheese and apply it to the armature. Hasten setting by baking under a 100 watt bulb.

3—Build up the final shape and details with thinly mixed plaster applied by brush.

4—Paint the finished figure with model railroad oil paints or poster colors.

FIGURES BUILT UP OF CLAY OR SCULPT-METAL

Crude figures done at a $\frac{1}{8}″=1′$ and larger scale may be modeled out of these materials.

FIGURES MADE OUT OF A NAKED ARMATURE OF WIRE

Make an armature of thin, easily bent wire. Figures at a $\frac{1}{8}″$ or larger scale should have torsos and heads built up with plastic wood.

Casting Figures

Before undertaking the complications of casting, determine whether or not the number of figures needed warrants this technique. See page 81 for a review of some of the considerations.

MAKING FIGURES FROM CAST METAL

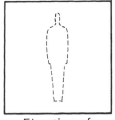

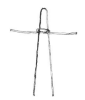

Elevation of
plaster mold

Slits made
in figure

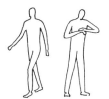

Some final positions
of the limbs

MAKING FIGURES FROM WIRE

CASTING ROUGH FIGURES IN METAL

Because of the flexibility of lead, it is possible to cast a basic figure that can then be bent into various postures and filed into modified shapes.

1—Carve the front of the figure in a hardwood female mold. Use a gouge to hollow the wood and finish with sandpaper. Place a second block of wood on top of the first. Drill 2 or 4 holes for the keys (which can be nails or dowels). The style of the figure should be one that lends itself to modifications of many poses and physiques. Make the figure at about a scale of 6′ 3″ tall, since some leg length will be bent under to make feet. Also, make the head oversized so that some of the material can be made into a hat. Making several dies will expedite casting.

2—Remove the second block, spread graphite powder on the carved first block. Press the blocks together, transferring the outline of the cut to the second block. Hollow out the second block. Gouge out the air vents and filling channel.

3—Clamp both finished mold halves together in a vise, or with clamps.

4—Melt some lead in a ladle and pour it into the filling channel.

5—Remove the casting from the mold. Cut off the metal that has been cast in the filling channel and air vents and any flash that has formed along the mold intersection.

6—Using pliers, bend the ends of the legs to form feet. With a fine file, shape the shoes with a few strokes. Illustration 10-3 shows a figure with feet cast in their final position.

7—With pliers, pinch the head, forming a hat brim. If the figure is to be hatless, then file the excess metal from its head.

8—With a square jeweler's file, flatten out the face on both sides of the nose, and shape the chin.

9—Flatten out the ends of the arms to form hands.

10—File the figure in appropriate places to give it a natural form.

11—Bend the figure into a walking, sitting or standing position.

12—Paint and flat finish.

Note: This technique is acceptable for people above a $\frac{1}{16}$″ scale. At $\frac{1}{16}$″=1′, hat brims, noses and other small details are impossible. At a $\frac{1}{4}$″=1′ and larger scale, it is possible to cast cuffs, belts, ties, etc. In larger scales, make separate dies for men and women and perhaps for fat figures.

CASTING FINE FIGURES IN WAX, METAL OR EPOXY
(17-5, 17-6 and 24-3)

1—Carve the figure out of Plexiglas, using fine burrs mounted on a light electric powered hand drill. The figure must be formed so that it can be easily removed from the female mold—legs must be together and arms must lie close to the torso to prevent undercuts.

2—Cast a mold in plaster of Paris or rubber.

3—Remove the Plexiglas original from the female mold.

4—Cast the final figures in wax, Epoxy or lead. For better detail or when cutting extremely small figures, cast in Zamac metal.

5—Once removed from the mold, the legs and arms of the figures may be cut apart and bent to simulate posture.

Abstract Figures

Abstract figures should not violate the human figure relationship between height and width, nor should they be far from correct height. There have been many unfortunate models wherein the figures have been so abstract as to be unrecognizable. Some abstract techniques that may be used are:

PINS WITHOUT HEADS

These make very realistic figures at a small (under $\frac{1}{32}$″=1′) scale. The pins should be held with pliers as they are driven into the baseboard. Small wood strips or dowels may also be used (14-17).

MAP TACKS

These are sometimes effective at a $\frac{1}{16}$″ scale.

NAILS WOUND IN WIRE
(18-3, row 7)

These can be used on rough models if this type of abstraction is desired.

TWISTED TIN FOIL

This may also be used (25-1) as may be fabric wound around a nail (5-9).

CARRAWAY SEEDS

These may be used, pasted on end, at scales around 1/64″=1′.

Photographic Composites

Photographs of people may be taken, printed at the proper scale and superimposed on photographs of the model. The composite may then be photocopied and prints made from the copy negative.

A rather whimsical technique that was used in the 1964-65 New York World's Fair was to project a motion picture of actual people into a model. This naturally would work only in a large-scale model displayed in a fairly dark room. The results, as can be imagined, were quite spectacular.

VEHICLES

As in the case of modeled figures, it is best to buy ready-made products whenever they are available.

TECHNIQUES FOR MODELING FIGURES, AND AVAILABLE READY-MADE FIGURES

	Ready-made figures					Forming each figure individually				Casting figures		Abstract figures		
Scale	Supplier and where illustrated (Note: Most lines include several figure styles)	Painted?	Approximate cost (each) (Note: Some must be bought in sets)	Cut from board or stamped on board and then cut out	Carved from wood	Built from wax	Built from plaster, clay, or sculpted metal	Made from a wire armature	Roughly cast in metal	Accurately cast in wax or metal	Pins or nails	Dowels or wood strips	Nails wound in wire or tin foil
1/80″ = 1′	Microform Corp. (18-3, Row 7)	No	5¢						X		X		
1/50″ = 1′	Devpro	No	5¢						X		X		
	Microform Corp.	No	3¢										

(continued on next page)

Scale	Supplier and where illustrated (Note: Most lines include several figure styles)	Painted?	Approximate cost (each) (Note: Some must be bought in sets)	Forming each figure individually				Casting figures			Abstract figures		
				Cut from board or stamped on board and then cut out	Carved from wood	Built from wax	Built from plaster, clay, or sculpted metal	Made from a wire armature	Roughly cast in metal	Accurately cast in wax or metal	Pins or nails	Dowels or wood strips	Nails wound in wire or tin foil
1/32 = 1'	Microform Corp. (18–3, Row 6)	No	8¢		X				X		X		
	Model Makers (18–3, Row 6)	No	4¢										
	Tolo Industries	Yes or no	10¢, 30¢ painted										
1/30" = 1'	William Mattison (18–3, Row 6)	No	10¢										
	Tolo Industries	Yes or no	11¢, 13¢; 32¢, 25¢ painted		X				X			X	
1/20" = 1'	Microform Corp.	No	9¢	X	X								
	Tolo Industries	Yes or no	25¢, 30¢; 45¢, 50¢ painted										
1/16" = 1'	Devpro (18–3, Row 6)	No	8¢	X	X	X		X	X	X	X	X	X
	Microform Corp. (18–3, Row 6)	No	10¢, 12¢										
	Model Makers (18–3, Row 7)	No	5¢										
	Tolo Industries	Yes or no	35¢, 40¢; 60¢ painted										
	William Mattison	No	10¢										
1:160	K. A. Clark (in clothing of 1900)	Yes	10¢	X	X	X		X	X	X	X	X	X
	Gulliver Country Series (18–3, Row 6)	No											
1:152	Treble-O-Lectric	No	3¢	X	X	X		X	X	X		X	X
3/32" = 1'	Devpro	No	10¢	X	X	X		X	X	X		X	X
	Microform Corp.	No	12¢										
	William Mattison	No	10¢, 12¢										
1:120	Aristo Craft (18–3, Row 6)	Yes	20¢	X	X	X		X	X	X		X	X
	Fetyk	No	17¢										
	Merten	Yes	4¢										
	Model Makers (18–3, Row 6)	No											
	Slater's	Yes	6¢										
	Aristo Craft (includes laborers, bicyclists, athletes, Salvation Army band) (18–3, Row 5)	Yes	50e; 75¢ for cycles	X	X	X		X	X	X		X	X
	Atlas (18–3, Row 3)	No	3¢										
	Microform Corp.	No	15¢										
	Model Makers (18–3, Row 5)	No											
	Plasticville (18–3, Row 3)	No	4¢										
	(Preiser)	Yes or no	4¢, 5¢; 15¢ painted										
	Ralph Dillon	Yes	35¢										
	Revel	Yes	6 for 98¢										
	Selley Mfg. Co. (18–3, Row 3)	No	6¢										
	Slater's (18–3, Row 5)	No											
	Thomas Industries (includes Salvation Army band, sidewalk Santa) (18–3, Row 5)	Yes	65¢										
	Tolo Industries	Yes or no	10–20¢										
	Walthers (18–3, Row 5)	Yes or no	10¢										
	Walthers (Weston Line) (18–3, Row 3)	Yes	45–65¢										
	Walter Merten (includes bathers, equestrians, laborers) (18–3, Row 4 & 5)	Yes	About 15¢										
	William Mattison	No	12¢, 15¢										
	Airfix (18–3, Row 2 & 3)	No	1¢, 2¢										
3/16" = 1'	Devpro (18–3, Row 2)	No	16¢	X	X	X	X			X			X
	Microform Corp. (18–3, Row 2)	No	21¢										
1:52	Wrenn Ltd. (18–3, Row 1 & 2)	Yes	25¢	X	X	X	X			X			
1/4" = 1'	Bassett-Lowke	Yes	20¢	X	X	X	X			X			
	Microform Corp. (18–3, Row 1)	No	30¢, 33¢										
	Ralph Dillon (includes laborers)	Yes	65¢										
	Selley Mfg. Co. (includes laborers) (18–3, Row 1)	No	10¢										
	Tolo Industries (18–3, Row 1)	Yes or no	$1.10, $1.15; $1.50 painted										
3/8" = 1'	William Mattison (18–3, Row 1)	No	20¢, 40¢				X			X			
	Elden	Yes	40¢	X	X	X				X			
	Microform Corp.	No	32¢–54¢										
	Scalextrics	Yes	45¢										
	Ulrich (limbs are adjustable)	No	30¢										
	Toy stores[1]												
3/4" = 1'	Flagg (includes fabric clothing), obtainable in toy stores	Yes	$1.00		X	X				X			
1" = 1'	Caco Biege-Püppchen (18–2) (includes fabric clothing), obtainable in toy stores or at B. Shackman & Co.	Yes	About $1–$2.00		X	X				X			
	Flagg (includes fabric clothing)	Yes	$1.40										

[1] It is possible with some searching to obtain metal or plastic toy soldiers the stances and clothing of which can be modified by cutting them apart and rejoining them in the position desired, filing off their helmets, guns, etc., and repainting their clothing. This may be more bother than it is worth, but if a store or catalog can be found with a large enough selection, choosing ready-made figures will require less work than building up figures from scratch. Many model soldiers are scaled at 3/8" = 1'. Timpe Model Toys and Herald Models have plastic soldiers that cost 25¢–40¢ each.

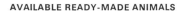

AVAILABLE READY-MADE ANIMALS

Scale (approx.)	Supplier	Some of the types of animals included	Painted?	Approximate cost (each)
1/10″ = 1′	Fetyk	Farm	No	10¢
1/8″ = 1′	Aristo Craft	Zoo and farm	Yes	15¢–20¢
	Associated Hobby Manufacturers	Farm	Yes	1¢
	Plasticville	Farm	Yes	4¢
	Preiser	Farm	Yes	5¢–20¢
	Ralph Dillon	Dogs; farm and zoo	Yes	25¢–$1
	Revel	Farm	Yes	15¢ (approx.)
	Selley	Dogs; farm and zoo	No	5¢–25¢
	Walter Merten	Farm and zoo	Yes	15¢–25¢
	Walther	Farm	Yes	45¢
	Weston	Dogs, pigeons	Yes	25¢–10¢
1/4″ = 1′	Plasticville	Farm	Yes	5¢
	Ralph Dillon	Dogs and farm	Yes	30¢–50¢
	Selley	Dogs (18–3, Row 1), farm, birds	No	5¢–25¢
	Walther	Farm	Yes	55¢
3/8″ = 1′	Britains Ltd.	Farm and zoo	Yes	

18-2

READY-MADE FIGURES:

A few representative figures from various manufactuers' lines.
Shown at 1/2 size:
Top row: Caco Biege—Püppchen (1″ = 1′). Doll family from Germany.
2nd row: The rest of the doll family (the first 5 figures are imported by B. Shackman and Company, New York City. They are in color and have fabric clothing). Teenettes (a bit under 3/4″ = 1′). Purchasable in variety stores. 6 for 59¢, unpainted plastic. They are made by the Multiple Products Corporation, New York City.

18-3

READY-MADE FIGURES:

Shown at full size.
Top Row:
William Mattison: (8 unpainted metal figures at 1/4″ = 1′. Microform: (figure No. 273, 1/4″ = 1′, unpainted metal). Selley: (3 dogs and 2 people at 1/4″ = 1′, unpainted metal). Tolo Industries: (1 figure at 1/4″ = 1′, unpainted metal). Wrenn: (4 painted plastic people from set No. A 10, 1:52 scale).
2nd Row:
Wrenn: (the rest of set No. A 10, 2 figures). Devpro: (1 unpainted metal figure at 3/16″ = 1′). The Microform: (1 figure, No. 276, at 3/16″ = 1′, unpainted metal). Airfix: (15 figures and a motor scooter, from set No. 56, unpainted rubber, scale is between HO and O gauge or about 3/16″ = 1′).
3rd Row: (1/8″ (or so) = 1′):
Airfix: (the remaining 1 type of figure from set No. 56). Atlas: (11 unpainted plastic figures of the 24 from set No. 1411–69). Revel: (6 painted plastic figures from their "townspeople" set). Weston: (2 painted metal figures). Plasticville U.S.A.: (2 unpainted plastic figures from their set of 24). Selley: (2 unpainted metal figures).
4th Row (1/8″ or so = 1′).
Merten: (6 painted figures and a dog from set No. 2180 and 6 painted figures from set No. 976).
5th Row (1/8″ or so = 1′):
Merten: (6 painted figures from set No. 867; 6 painted figures from set No. 818). Aristo Craft: (5 painted figures from set ST 1:100 and 5 painted figures from set ST 5:100. Aristo Craft figures are made by Preiser. Thomas: (1 painted metal figure, No. 64). Walthers: (1 painted metal figure, No. F115). Slater's: (3 unpainted plastic figures and a plastic base strip from set which includes paint and 50 figures). Model Makers: (No. H-2, 3 unpainted plastic 2-dimensional figures).
6th Row:
Merten: (6 painted figures from set No. T853, TT gauge). Aristo Craft: (5 painted figures from set No. TT2:119, TT gauge). Model Makers: (3 unpainted plastic 2-dimensional figures from set No. H-1, 3/32″ = 1′). Kemtron: (3 black custom etched 2-dimensional metal figures). Gulliver Country Series: (No. EL-167, 8 from the unpainted plastic set of 12, 000 gauge figures. These can be purchased from: International Models). The Microform: (No. 358, 1/16″ = 1′ unpainted metal figure). Devpro: (unpainted metal, 2 figures, 1/16′ = 1′). Kemtron: (3 custom black etched 2-dimensional metal figures).
7th Row:
Model Makers: (1 gray wire figure, 1/16″ = 1′), (1 yellow wire figure, 1/32″ = 1′). William Mattison: (1 figure 1/32″ = 1′, unpainted metal). Microform: (1 unpainted metal figure No. 473, 1/80″ = 1′). Figures made by the author: figure cut from balsa sheet that has been covered with paper. 2 roughly carved from wood; 1 has wire arms. A painted wood figure bought at a Japanese curio shop.

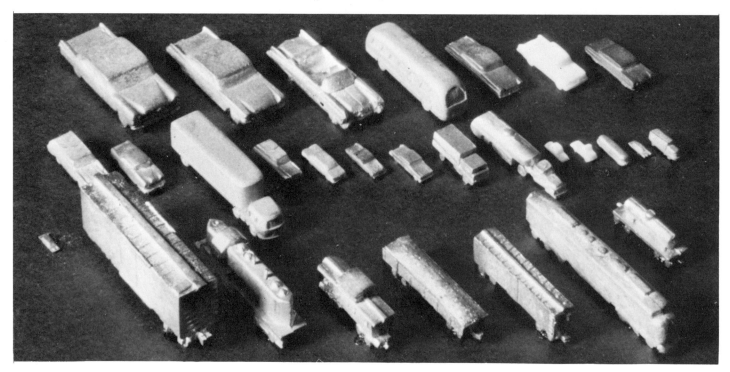

18-4

READY-MADE VEHICLES:

Rear Row (left to right):
William Mattison: 1/16″ = 1′ (2 cars). Devpro: 1/16″ = 1′. Microform: No. 438 (bus), 1/32″ = 1′. William Mattison: 1/20″ = 1′. Model Makers: No. A-4, 1/32″ = 1′. William Mattison: 1/40″ = 1′.

Middle Row:
Devpro: (station wagon), 1/32″ = 1′. Selley: 1/32″ = 1′. Microform: No. 395 (truck), 1/32″ = 1′.

Devpro: (station wagon), 1/50″ = 1′. Microform: No. 344, 1/50″ = 1′. William Mattison: 1/50″ = 1′. Tolo Industries: (car and truck), 1/50″ = 1′. Devpro: (tank truck), 1/50″ = 1′. Model Makers: No. A-1 (car and truck), 1/100″ = 1′. Microform: No. 431 (bus), No. 432 (car), No. 429 (truck), 1/100″ = 1′.

Front Row:
Selley. 1/10″ = 1′ (car). Devpro (boxcar), 1/32″ = 1′; (2 locomotives and 3 freight cars), 1/50″ = 1′; (tank car), 1/100″ = 1′.

18-5

READY-MADE VEHICLES:

Rear Row: (Left to right).
William Mattison: 3/32″ = 1′. Devpro: 3/32″ = 1′. Arnold Rapido: (2 cars and a micro bus), 1 : 152 scale.

Middle Row:
Arnold Rapido: 1 : 152. Lone Star Products Gulliver Country Series: car. Devpro: (station wagon) 5/64″ = 1′. Model Makers: (No. A-6), 3/32″ = 1′. William Mattison: 3/32″ = 1′.

Front Row:
Selley: 1/16″ = 1′. Lone Star Products Gulliver Country Series: (2 trucks and a bus).

18-6

READY-MADE VEHICLES:

All come painted and assembled except as noted.
5th row, left to right:
Lesney Match Box Series: Lincoln Continental, police car and Mercedes Benz No. 220 (5/32″ = 1′). Corgi toys: No. 241 Ghia L6.4 (about 1/4″ = 1′). Dinky Toys: Rolls Royce Silver Cloud III (1/4″ = 1′).

4th row (all about 5/32″ = 1′):
A.H.M.: U-308 road scraper. Ulrich: Fruehauf trailer truck (comes unpainted in kit form). A.H.M.: U-303 roadgrader.
3rd row (all are about 1/8″ = 1′ except as noted): Tolo Industries: trailer truck cab, and car (both are unpainted). Lesney Matchbox Series: Volkswagon pick-up truck. Viking-Models: Volkswagon, Lincoln Continental, and type "E" Jaguar (5/32″ = 1′).
2nd row:

Anguplas: Rolls Royce "Phantom" I and Ford Galaxie (1:86 scale). Microform Corporation: No. 339 (unpainted, 1/8″ — 1′). Schuco Piccollo: No. 724 Mercedes 220, No. 741 Mercedes delivery truck and No. 707 B.M.W. 507 (under 1/8″ = 1′ scale).
1st row:
Aristo Craft: 4 cycles and rack No. 43–59 (about 1/8″ = 1′ scale). Schuco: oil tank truck (about 5/64″ = 1′). Lesney Matchbox Series: crane and dump truck (5/64″ = 1′).

Ready-Made Vehicles

The same procedures that were listed for cleaning flash and painting ready-made figures should be followed with vehicles.

I have listed many of the commercially available vehicles and their scales. Some lines of cars, notably those sold as toys (as opposed to those sold to hobbyists or to architectural modelmakers), do not have their scales stamped on their box. When purchasing these brands, it is best to go to a store the staff of which is equipped with a rough knowledge of the length of several types of cars. It is then possible to measure the models to determine their scale before purchasing them. One drawback to casting vehicles (or to using vehicles cast by professional modelmakers) is that cast vehicles are not hollow and thus they (1) lack internal detail; (2) lack the advantage of having see-through windows; and (3) must be hand-painted. Thus, many modelers prefer to use ready-made vehicles that are sold in model railroad stores. These can be obtained in some numbers at 1 : 152 to $\frac{3}{32}$″ = 1′ scales and, in an unbelievable profusion, at $\frac{1}{8}$ to $\frac{1}{2}$″ = 1′ scales. Many are ready-made but occasionally it is necessary to assemble a kit to get a specific type of car at some of the larger scales.

READY-MADE CARS, TRUCKS, BUSES, AND BICYCLES

Scale	Supplier and where illustrated[1]	Types of vehicles included in line[2]	Approximate cost
1/100″ = 1′	Microform Corp. (18–4, middle row)	2 autos, bus, 3 trucks; unpainted; solid	Auto 3¢, bus 8¢, trucks 5¢, 6¢; 9¢
	Model Makers (18–4, middle row)	Auto; painted; solid	2¢
1/80″ = 1′	Microform Corp.	Auto; unpainted; solid	4¢
1/60″ = 1′	Microform Corp.	2 autos, truck; unpainted; solid	6¢
1/50″ = 1′	Devpro (18–4, middle row)	2 autos, 3 trucks; unpainted; solid	Auto 7¢, trucks 7¢, 9¢
	Microform Corp. (18–4, middle row)	6 autos, 2 buses, 2 trucks; unpainted; solid	Auto 9¢, bus 16¢, 18¢, truck 16¢, 21¢
	Model Makers (18–4, middle row)	Auto; painted; solid	4¢
	Tolo Industries (18–4, middle row)	2 autos, bus, 6 trucks; painted or unpainted; solid	Auto 18¢, 19¢; 26¢, 27¢ painted; bus and trucks·18¢–23¢; 26¢–31¢ painted
	William Mattison (18–4, middle row)	Auto; unpainted; solid	10¢
1/40″ = 1′	Microform Corp.	2 autos; unpainted; solid	14¢
	Tolo Industries	2 autos, bus, 7 trucks; painted or unpainted; solid	Autos 22¢–25¢; 31¢–34¢ painted; bus and trucks 25¢–37¢; 34¢–45¢ painted
	William Mattison (18–4, rear row)	Auto, 2 trucks; unpainted; solid	Auto 12¢, truck 25¢

(continued on next page)

Scale	Supplier and where illustrated[1]	Types of vehicles included in line[2]	Approximate cost
1/32″ = 1′	Devpro (18–4, middle row)	2 autos; unpainted; solid	12¢
	Microform Corp. (18–4, rear row and middle row)	4 autos, bus, 2 trucks; unpainted; solid	Auto 16¢, bus 23¢, truck 21¢ and 28¢
	Model Makers (18–4, rear row)	Auto; painted; solid	9¢
	Tolo Industries	3 autos, taxi, bus, 7 trucks; painted or unpainted; solid	Autos and taxi 25¢, 30¢; 40¢, 45¢ painted; trucks 30¢–42¢; 45¢–60¢ painted
	William Mattison (18–4, rear row)	Auto; unpainted; solid	15¢
1/30″ = 1′	Tolo Industries	3 autos, taxi, bus, 7 trucks; painted or unpainted; solid	Auto and taxi 27¢–32¢; 37¢–42¢ painted; bus and trucks 32¢–45¢; 42¢–55¢ painted
	William Mattison	Auto; unpainted; solid	15¢
1/20″ = 1′	Microform Corp.	4 autos; unpainted; solid	23¢
	Tolo Industries	4 autos, taxi, bus, 7 trucks; painted or unpainted; solid	Autos and taxi 35¢, 45¢; 55¢–65¢ painted; bus and trucks 45¢–70¢; 65¢–90¢ painted
	William Mattison (18–4, rear row)	Auto, 3 trucks; unpainted; solid	Auto 23¢, trucks 30¢–60¢
1/16″ = 1′	Devpro (18–4, rear row)	5 autos; unpainted; solid	20¢
	Microform Corp.	4 autos; unpainted; solid	25¢
	Model Makers	Auto; painted; solid	20¢
	Tolo Industries	4 autos, taxi, bus, 7 trucks; painted or unpainted; solid	Autos and taxi 40¢, 55¢; 65¢–80¢ painted; bus and trucks 55¢–$1.00; 80¢–$1.20 painted
	William Mattison (18–4, rear row)	2 autos; unpainted; solid	25¢
1:152	Arnold Rapido (18–5, rear and middle rows)	2 autos, bus; painted; solid	10 for $1.30
3/32″ = 1′	Lone Star Railways (about 3/32″ scale) (18–5, middle and front rows)	6 autos, 6 trucks, tow, pump, delivery, fire engine; painted; hollow	10¢ and 15¢
	Microform Corp.	Auto; unpainted; solid	49¢
	Model Makers (18–5, middle row)	Auto; painted; solid	55¢
	William Mattison (18–5, rear and middle rows)	2 autos; unpainted; solid	40¢
About 1/8″ = 1′	Anguplas Minicars (get from Assoc. of Hobby Mfgs.) (18–6, Row 2)	Over 50 autos: U.S. economy and family, foreign economy, family, sports, and antique cars; 5 foreign buses (single- and double-decker); 30 trucks (delivery flat, gas, beverage, cement, auto transport, tank, trailer); all painted; solid	Autos 25¢–60¢, trucks 25¢ up
	Aristo Craft (motorized, except bike) (18–6, Row 1)	2 trolley buses, bike; painted; solid	Bus $7.50–$15
	Atlas Tool Co. (motorized)	15 U.S. family and sports cars, station wagon; painted; solid	$3
	Dinky Toys (Dublo line)	Taxi, trucks (delivery, tank, etc.); painted; solid	50¢–85¢
	Jordan Products (kits)	6 antique autos, carriages, trucks, (stake, dump, delivery, tank); unpainetd; solid	$1–$1.75
	Lesney Matchbox Series (some of this line is at about 1/8″ = 1′ scale) (18–6, Row 5 & 3)	Family and sports cars, trucks (dump, milk, pickup, lorry, fire engine); painted; solid	50¢
	Microform Corp. (18–6, Row 2)	5 autos; painted; hollow	49¢–69¢
	Ralph Dillon	Horse-drawn buggy, surrey, wagon; painted; solid	$1
	Revel (trucks are kits)	7 Chrysler Corp. 1961 family cars; auto transport and van; painted; solid	Autos 7 for $2; trucks $1–$1.30
	Rex (from Assoc. Rex Hobby Mfgs.)	Foreign family and sports cars; painted; solid	50¢
	Selley	Horse-drawn buggy, surries, wagon; unpainted; hollow	35¢
	Tolo Industries (18–6, Row 3)	5 autos, 2 taxis, bus, 11 trucks (panel, pickup, box, flat); painted or unpainted; solid	Autos and taxis 80¢–$1.50, $1.05–$1.75 painted; bus and trucks 90¢–$2, $1.12–$2.42 painted
	Tyco (motorized)	6 sports and family cars; painted; hollow	$3
	Ulrich (kits) (18–6, Row 4)	6 trucks (tank, flat, dump); painted; hollow	$3
	Viking-Models (Wiking Verkehrs Modelle) (18–6, Row 3)	55 U.S. and foreign compact, family, sports, and police cars, 69 U.S. and foreign trucks (trailer, dump, carboy, flat, tank, delivery, beverage, log, lorry, stake, cement, van, and auto transport); unpainted; hollow	Autos 50¢, trucks 60¢–$1.95
1:75	Aurora (Highways Model Motoring) (motorized)	30 family, sports, and police cars, trucks (dump, stake, gasoline, trailer); unpainted; hollow	Autos $2–$3, trucks $3–$3.50
	Faller (motorized except for bicycle)	6 sports and family cars, bicycle; unpainted; hollow	Autos $3
	Tri Ang Minic (motorized)	12 sports, family, and police cars, 2 buses, 6 trucks (tank, tow, flat, and fire); painted; hollow	Autos $6–$7, bus $9, trucks $9–$11

[1] Ready-made and not motorized unless otherwise indicated.
[2] The number of vehicles available in most lines is rapidly increasing.

Scale	Supplier and where illustrated[1]	Types of vehicles included in line[2]	Approximate cost
3/16″ = 1′	Hubley	Cars and trucks; painted; hollow	Autos under $1, trucks $1.50
	Winross (from Sinclair's)	20 trucks (trailer, tank, flat, crane, wrecker, fire); painted; hollow	$1.25–$3.50
1/4 = 1′ (1:48)	A.H.M.	Family and sports cars, ambulance, truck; painted; hollow	$2–$4
1:45	Marklin	11 family, sports, and police cars; 9 trucks (tank, van, delivery, and stake); painted; hollow	Autos $1–$1.35, trucks $1–$4
1:43	Dugu (from Sinclair's)	Foreign antique, family, and sports cars; painted; hollow	$3.50–$6
	Eko (from Sinclair's)	Antique foreign cars; painted; hollow	$2.50
	Mercury	Family and sports cars; painted; hollow	$2.25–$2.75
	Rimi	Foreign and U.S. antique cars; painted; hollow	$1.75
	Rio (from Sinclair's)	16 foreign and U.S. antique, sports, and family autos; painted; hollow	$4–$6
	Safir (from Sinclair's)	Foreign antique and family cars; painted; hollow	$3
	Solido (from Sinclair's)	Foreign and U.S. family and sports cars and foreign antique cars; painted; hollow	$2–$3; $6.50–$7 for antique cars
	Tekno (from Sinclair's)	U.S. and foreign sports and family cars; painted; hollow	$4.50–$3.50
1:40	Corgi (from Sinclair's)	40 U.S. and foreign family, compact antique, and sports cars; ambulance, bus; 34 foreign trucks (car transport, dump, tow, van, platform, trailer, horse trailer, milk, gas); painted; hollow	$1.50–$3
3/8″ = 1′ (1:30) & (1:32)[3]	Airfix (kit)	12 foreign family and antique cars; unpainted; hollow	50¢
	Aurora (kit)	13 U.S. and foreign family and sports cars; painted; hollow	50¢
	Elden (motorized)	5 sports and family cars; painted; hollow	$4
	Pyro Plastics (kit)	14 old U.S. family cars; unpainted; hollow	50¢
	Revel (kits)	16 U.S. and foreign family and antique cars; foreign sports cars; unpainted; hollow	80¢–$1.50
	Scalextrics (motorized)	2 antique cars, foreign sports cars; painted; hollow	$6–$10
	Strombecker (motorized)	5 sports and family cars; painted; hollow	$4–$6
	V.P.I. (motorized)	Foreign sports cars; painted; hollow	$9
1/2″ = 1′ (1:24 & 1:25)[3]	A.M.T. (motorized; some are kits)	Family and sports cars; painted; hollow	Kits $1–$2, ready-made ones $10–$14
	Hawk (kit, motorized)	Family cars; painted; hollow	50¢–$1
	Jo-Han (kit)	12 family and antique cars; unpainted; hollow	$1–$2
	Lindberg Line (kit, motorized)	8 sports cars; painted; hollow	50¢
	Monogram (kit)	2 antique cars; painted; hollow	$3
	Revel (kit)	33 U.S. and foreign sports and antique cars; U.S. economy and family cars; unpainted; hollow	$1.50
Not to a constant scale	Lesney Matchbox Series (scale ranges from 1:40 to 1:55)	20 U.S. and foreign sports, antique and family cars, 32 trucks (auto, transport, hopper, moving-van, gasoline, flat, van, pickup, dump, and beverage); painted	50¢

[3] Car bodies at this scale are sold by several firms.

READY-MADE MODELS OF CONSTRUCTION EQUIPMENT

Scale	Supplier and where illustrated	Types of equipment included in the line[1]
About 3/32″ = 1′	Lone Star Railways	Concrete mixer, dump truck, pitch digger
About 1/8″ = 1′	A.H.M. (18–6, Row 4)	Bulldozer, roller, scraper, tractor, crane, grader
	Anguplas (get from Assoc. of Hobby Mfgs.)	Crane, grader
	Schuce	Crane, steam shovel, bulldozer, lift truck
	Viking-Models (Wiking Verkehrs Modelle)	Crane, steam shovel, bulldozer, steam roller, grader
3/16″ = 1′	Hubley	Cement mixer, dump truck, etc.
1:40	Corgi	Tractor, bulldozer
1:45	Marklin	Crane
Not to a constant scale	Matchbox Series (18–6, Row 1)	Roller, cement mixer, back hoe, bulldozer, clam shovel, grader, dumper, tractor

[1] All are painted and hollow.

Forming Each Vehicle Individually

There are several degrees of simplification with which individually to form small (up to $\frac{1}{8}$") scale vehicles.

THE SIMPLEST

Cut good, hard, stripwood to proper length. By using wood of several different cross sections, enclosed cars, convertibles, buses and trucks can be represented fairly convincingly at $\frac{1}{32}$" and small scales.

If time permits and a more detailed representation is desired, cut the outline of the passenger compartment into the sides of the strips. Other, more detailed techniques involve cutting the silhouette of the wheels of the vehicle into the strip, or cutting a small bit of material away from both sides of the window parts of the passenger compartment, or sanding the corners of the strip. More complex shapes can also be built up from 2 or more pieces of attached stripwood.

CARS STAMPED ON BOARD AND THEN CUT OUT

2-dimensional automobiles may be made by using rubber stamps sold by Instant Landscape. They make 1 stamp of car elevations in each of the following scales: 1/40, 1/20, 1/16, 1/8 and 1/4" = 1'. These cost $1.25 to $5.25 each. They also make 1 stamp of front views of cars in scales of $\frac{1}{16}$, $\frac{1}{8}$ and $\frac{1}{4}$". They also have rear views of autos in $\frac{1}{16}$ and $\frac{1}{4}$" scales. Front and rear view stamps cost $1.25 to $3.00 apiece. Design Specialties, Inc. makes 2 elevation view stamps at $\frac{1}{16}$, and $\frac{1}{8}$" scales.

TRANSFER AUTOMOBILES APPLIED TO BOARD AND THEN CUT OUT

Presstamp, Inc. makes burnished on transfers of auto elevations, 2 styles, in $\frac{1}{16}$ and $\frac{1}{8}$" scales.

Casting Vehicles

Vehicles may be cast in most any of the casting materials listed in this book. Plaster and other porous materials should, however, be avoided when making smaller scale vehicles. Small-scale vehicles may also be vacuum-formed from polystyrene sheet.

Photographic Composites

Photographic composites are rather difficult to achieve with vehicles because of the difficulties encountered in cutting out windows without destroying the roof posts. Also, the available number of exquisitely detailed ready-made vehicles makes perfect realism possible without having to resort to composites.

Animation

Traffic animation is often used on certain types of models that are to be viewed by the general public. Motion greatly increases the crowd appeal of the exhibit. Illustration 18-7 shows 1 possible construction of an animated road. For an additional effect, cars may also have working headlights. Electricity is carried through the conveyer loop to individual vehicles.

On very small scale town planning models, animation has been effected by representing each road lane by fabric or plastic tape strung over widely placed supports. Vehicles are seen as oblongs painted on the tapes. Air circulating above or below the tapes causes them to move up and down, creating the illusion that the cars are moving horizontally.

150

READY-MADE MODELS OF FARM EQUIPMENT

Scale	Supplier	Types of equipment included in the line[1]
About 3/32" = 1'	Lone Star Railways	Tractor
About 1/8" = 1'	Anguplas (get from Assoc. of Hobby Mfg.)	Foreign tractors
	Matchbox Series	Combine, tractor
	Ralph Dillon	Tractor, harrow
	Schuce	Tractor, conveyer belt
	Selley	Tractor, harrow
	Viking-Models (Wiking Verkehrs Modelle)	Tractors
1:40	Corgi	Combine, tractor, plow, harvestor
1:45	Marklin	Tractor
3/8" = 1'	Britains Ltd.	Cart, timber, trailer, tractor, plow, cultivator

[1] All are painted and hollow except Selley tractor and harrow.

Working Headlights

Night photographs are sometimes enhanced if the vehicles on the model have working lights. To install lights in $\frac{1}{16}$" and larger scale models: (1) drill out the nonworking headlights of the vehicles; (2) cement small lamps in the holes, using Elmer's glue; (3) run the wires of this lamp through the road bed, hiding them behind a wheel; and (4) attach a set for each car to a transformer in a parallel hookup.

TRAINS FOR TOWN PLANNING AND FACTORY MODELS

Kits and ready-made model train cars and locomotives are available in great numbers at 1:152, 1/10" = 1'; 1:87, 1:76, $\frac{3}{16}$" = 1' and $\frac{1}{4}$" = 1' scales. These are known as 000 or N gauge, TT, HO, OO S, and O gauge. At smaller scales, simple model trains may be abstractly carved out of balsa strips. Devpro sells unpainted cast metal cars (18-4, front row) at a 1/50" = 1' scale (2 locomotives and 5 freight cars), and at a $\frac{1}{32}$" = 1' scale (1 freight car).

AIRPLANES FOR AIRPORT MODELS

Small-scale aircraft can be carved from balsa quickly. If greater detail is desired, airline kits can be purchased from the local hobby store. Other nonairline planes are also available in scales ranging from 1:144 to 1:48. Often the hobby shop can have these kits assembled at a price that is a fraction of what it would cost the modeler

if he were to do it himself. Kits of commercial airline planes are manufactured as follows:

$\frac{1}{16}$" = 1': Lindberg Line (6 transports).

1:144: Frog (2 transports), Airfix (4 U.S. and foreign transports).

$\frac{1}{8}$" = 1' (about): Lindberg Line (2 transports), Frog (8 transports), Airfix (3 foreign transports, 2 foreign helicopters), and there is a fairly extensive selection of airliner models in various scales around 1:100 made by Revel, Aurora and Hawk.

SHIPS FOR TOWN PLANNING AND HARBOR FACILITY MODELS

Small-scale ships (1:500 and smaller) may be built out of balsa and cardboard. The former material is used to construct the hull and funnel. The board is used to make the decks and bridge structures. Dowels may be used for round funnels and wires for masts and derricks. Ready-made ships and kits that are of use to the architectural modelbuilder may be found at the following scales:

STREET LIGHTS AND TRAFFIC SIGNALS

Lights and signals are most easily constructed from wire, dowels or copper tubing (if working lamps are intended). Lamps may be made from carved acrylic rod, variety store pearls or from miniature bulbs. Ready-made lights and signals are available in 1:152, 1/10, 1/8 and 1/4" = 1' scales, but only at the $\frac{1}{8}$" scale is there a wide selection of styles.

18-7

ANIMATED TRAFFIC

Roadway · Pulley · Wire loop · Car attaching wire · Small tension spring · Slot · Electric motor

Scale	Supplier	Number and types of ships in the line
1:1200	Anguplas (ready-made) Superior Models Inc. (ready-made) Tri-Ang Minic Models (ready-made)	11 : ocean liners, freighters, tankers, tug 5 : oiler, tanker, transport, cargo 36 : ocean liners, freighters, tankers, barges, tugs, yachts, lifeboats, floating dry docks; also lighthouses, cranes, docks, etc.
1:400 to 1:600	Kits; miscellaneous manufacturers; some make easy-to-construct plastic kits	Many passenger liners and freighters
1:200	Kits; miscellaneous manufacturers (most take a long time to assemble)	A few passenger liners and freighters
1/16″ = 1′	Boucher (kit; takes a long time to assemble)	5 : tankers and cargo ships
1/8″ = 1′	Kits; miscellaneous manufacturers (some are easy to construct)	A few small crafts—tugs, fireboats, sailboats
5/8″ to 3″ long	James Bliss & Co. (ready-made)	Lifeboats and dories
4″ to 5″ long	James Bliss & Co. (ready-made)	Lifeboats

READY-MADE TRAFFIC LIGHTS AND STREET LIGHTS SHOWN AT 1/2 THEIR ACTUAL SIZE.

Traffic lights:
Top row: Aristo Craft (12–15 V, automatic blinking pedestrian signal). West Hudson Hobbies: (2 working). Aristo Craft: (working). Selley: (7, nonworking). Christoph: (No. 1731, 3 for 25¢, TT gauge nonworking and another).
Street lights:
Top row (continued): West Hudson Hobbies: (2 working lights).
2nd row: West Hudson Hobbies: (4 working lights). Aristo Craft (3 working lights, the 2nd is No. 2C-100, the 3rd No. 3C).
3rd row: Aristo Craft (5 working lights). Tyco (working boulevard street light No. 101:98).
4th row: Tyco: (working fluorescent street light No. 103:98 and working mercury street light No. 102:98). International Models: (working fluorescent street lamp and working round globe street lamp). Vollmer: (working lamp No. 6004 and working fluorescent street lamp No. 6021). Selley: (2 nonworking lamps).
5th row: Faller: (4 nonworking lights that come from set No. 4091, which contains 56 lights). Christoph: (4 nonworking lights, the 1st is from set No. 1730).

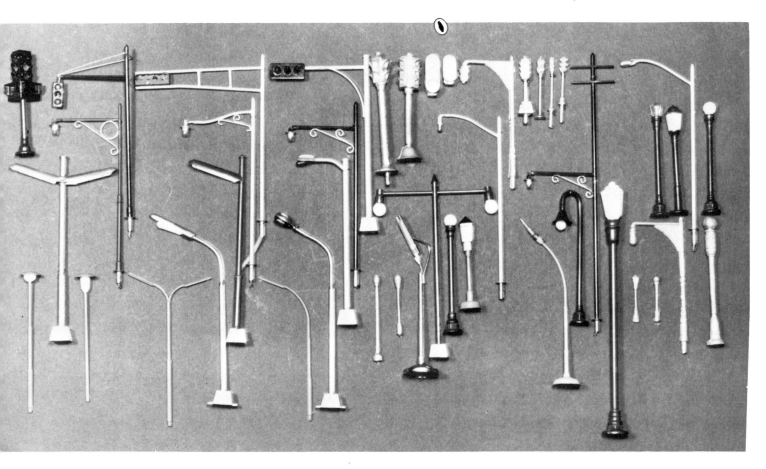

Scale; 1 : 152. Arnoldo Rapido working models: traffic signals—single ($2) and double ($3); street lights—2 types single-lamp on arm and 1 type double-lamp on arms ($3).

Scale 1/10″ = 1′. Christoph unpainted nonworking models: traffic signals (18-8, Row 1; about 8¢); street lights—several old-time and modern models (18-8, Row 5; about 8¢).

Scale approximately 1/8″ = 1′. Aristo Craft working models: traffic signals—3 lamps on arm (18-8, Row 1; $1.25), 3 lamps on stanchion with walk—don't walk sign (18-8, Row 1; $2); street lights—old-time gaslight on stanchion or lamp on stanchion (18-8, Row 2); 4 types with single lamps on arm and 2 types with lamps on 2 arms (18-8, Row 3; $1.25-$2.75). Atlas working models: street lights—old-time gaslight on stanchion, 2 types with lamp on stanchion, 3

types with single lamp on arm, telegraph pole with light (35¢ and 43¢). Busch working models: street lights—30 styles with single lamps on straight or gooseneck stanchion ($1). Ralph Dillon nonworking models: traffic signals—2 lamps on stanchion, 3 lamps on stanchion, 2 lamps on ornate arm (45¢-75¢); street lights—2 types with lamp on stanchion, lamp on arm (30¢ and 75¢). Faller nonworking models: many styles with lamps on stanchions and arms (18-8, Row 5). International Models, working: street lights—lamp on stanchion or lamp on arm (18-8, Row 4). Selley unpainted nonworking models: traffic signals (18-8, Row 1)—2 lamps on stanchion, 3 lamps on stanchion, 2 lamps on arm (10¢-25¢); street lights—lamp on stanchion, lamp on arm (6¢-25¢). Tri Ang Minic nonworking models: traffic signal—3 lamps on stanchion (8¢); street lights—1 lamp on arm or 2 lamps on arms (18-8,

Row 4; 12¢ and 20¢). Tyco working models: street lights—lamp on stanchion (18-8, Row 3), 2 types with lamp on arm 18-8, Row 4 (50¢). Vollmer working models: street lights—2 types with lamp on arm (18-8, Row 4; $1.75-$1.95 plus 60¢ for bulb). West Hudson Hobbies working models: traffic signals—2 types with 3 lamps on arm (18-8, Row 1; 75¢-$2.25); street lights—2 types with lamp on arm and 3 ornate types with lamp on arm (18-8, Rows 1 and 2; 75¢-$2.25).

Scale 1/4″ = 1′. Microform unpainted nonworking models: traffic signal—3 lamps on stanchion (65¢). Ralph Dillon nonworking models: traffic signal—3 lamps on stanchion ($1.50); street light—lamp on stanchion (85¢). Selley unpainted nonworking models: traffic signals—2 lamps on stanchion, 3 lamps on stanchion (25¢); street lights—lamp on stanchion (15¢), lamp on arm (35¢).

Scale	Supplier	Types of lights and signals and where illustrated	Approximate cost (each)
1 : 152	Arnold Rapido (painted ; working)	Traffic signal Street lights : 2 types of single-lamp on arm and 1 type of double-lamp on arms	Traffic signal $3; lights $2 single, $3 double
1/10″=1′	Christoph (unpainted ; nonworking)	Traffic signals (18-8, Row 1) Street lights : several old time and modern lights (18-8, Row 5).	About 8¢
About 1/8″=1′	Aristo Craft (painted ; working)	Traffic signals : 3 lamps on arm (18-8, Row 1), 3 lamps on stanchion with walk/don't walk sign (18-8, Row 1) Street lights : old-time gaslight on stanchion (18-8, Row 2), lamp on stanchion (18-8, Row 2), 4 types of fixtures with single lamp on arm (18-8, Row 3), 2 types of fixtures with lamps on 2 arms (18-8, Row 3)	Traffic signals $1.25 & $2 ; lights $1.25 to $2.75
	Atlas (painted ; working)	Street lights : old-time gaslight on stanchion, 2 fixtures with lamp on stanchion, 3 types of fixtures with single lamps on arm, telegraph pole with light	35¢ & 43¢
	Busch (painted ; working)	Street lights : 30 styles of fixtures with single lamps mounted on straight or gooseneck stanchion	$1
	Ralph Dillon (painted ; nonworking)	Traffic signals : 2 lamps on stanchion, 3 lamps on stanchion, 2 lamps on ornate arms Street lights : 2 types of fixtures with lamp on stanchion, lamp on arm	Traffic signals 45¢ to 75¢ ; lights 30¢ & 75¢
	Faller (painted ; nonworking)	Street lights : many styles lamps on stanchions and arms (18-8, Row 5)	
	International Models (painted ; working)	Street lights : lamp on stanchion (18-8, Row 4), lamp on arm (18-8, Row 4)	
	Selley (unpainted ; nonworking)	Traffic signals : 2 lamps on stanchion, 3 lamps on stanchion, 2 lamps on arm (18-8, Row 1) Street lights : lamp on stanchion, lamp on arm	Traffic signals 10¢ to 25¢ ; lights 6¢ to 25¢
	Tri-Ang Minic (painted ; nonworking)	Traffic signal : 3 lamps on stanchion Street lights : fixture with 1 lamp on arm, fixture with 2 lamps on arm (18-8, Row 4)	Traffic signal 8¢ ; lights 12¢ & 20¢
	Tyco (painted ; working)	Street lights : lamp on stanchion (18-8, Row 3), 2 types of fixtures with lamp on arm (18-8, Row 4)	50¢
	Vollmer (painted ; working)	Street lights : 2 types of fixtures with lamp on arm (18-8, Row 4)	$1.75 & $1.95, plus 60¢ for bulb
	West Hudson Hobbies (painted ; working)	Traffic signals : 2 types of fixtures with 3 lamps on arm (18-8, Row 1) Street lights : 2 types of fixtures with lamp on arm (18-8, Rows 1 & 2), 3 types of ornate fixtures with lamp on arm (18-8, Rows 1 & 2)	Both signals and lights 75¢ to $2.25
1/4″=7′	Microform (unpainted ; nonworking)	Traffic signal : 3 lamps on stanchion	65¢
	Ralph Dillon (painted ; nonworking)	Traffic signals : 3 lamps on stanchion Street light : lamp on stanchion	Traffic signal $1.50 ; light 85¢
	Selley (unpainted ; nonworking)	Traffic signals : fixture with 2 lamps on stanchion, fixture with 3 lamps on stanchion Street lights : lamp on stanchion, lamp on arm	Traffic signals 25¢ ; lights 15¢ & 35¢

18-8A/B/C

HOW SCALE-IMPARTING ELEMENTS CAN AID IN MODEL PHOTOGRAPHY.

PROJECT: a house with an atrium plan.
DESIGN AND PHOTOGRAPHS BY: Sanford Hohauser.
MODELBUILDER: William Gerbracht.
SCALE: ⅜″ = 1′.

The form for the earthwork podium, below which most of this underground house lies, was made from illustration board waterproofed with several coats of Liquitex acrylic polymer emulsion. The ground was illustration board, as were the house's partitions.

Earth texture was model railroad granules. The pool and the cup-shaped room, which rises on a column from the pool, were papier-mâché cast on plastic female molds. Water was a sheet of acrylic on which a sheet of wrinkled Mylar film was cemented. Fireplace and circular stair enclosure were acrylic tube. Chairs were styrene blown to shape on a toy vacuum-forming set. Ceiling rib vaulting was built up from ten layers of 3-ply Bristolboard. The model is illuminated by 35 small bulbs.

Due to the unconventional appearance of the exterior of this house it was necessary to use scale-establishing objects in many of the photographs. These included an auto, a set of oars, and an entire family of miniature cats.

The photographs were taken with a 4″ x 5″ press camera and Kodak Ektar lens, and a Honeywell Pentax 35 mm single-lens-reflex camera with a Super-Takumar lens.
CONSTRUCTION TIME: 350 hours.

SIGNS

Storefront signs, traffic signs, display graphics and other signs can be made in a number of ways. Those that are needed in limited numbers may be made from: (1) pressure-sensitive letters; (2) transfer letters the carrying sheet of which can be peeled away (provided the backing of the sign will not be adversely affected); (3) decals that are transferred by the application of water; (4) letters that are hand done with the aid of a lettering set stylus and guide; (5) letters cut from magazines and other similar sources.

Signs that must be duplicated a number of times can be made by: (1) rubber stamp; (2) being commercially printed on paper or being custom made as pressure-sensitive transfers; or (3) being photographically reproduced.

It is always advisable to form the sign on a sheet of Bristol or illustration board and then to apply it to the model, rather than trying to work directly.

Decals

Custom decals may be formed by using Simplex decal paper. This preparation, which comes in various colors, can be obtained from sign painters supply houses. Follow these directions:

1—Tape a sheet of it on a piece of glass and coat it with clear lacquer.

2—Trace the design on paper. The glass backing will prevent the pencil from breaking the decal.

3—Paint the design with oil paints.

4—Cut the design from the rest of the sheet.

5—Soak the design to release it from the backing paper. Apply it to the model, using blotting paper to smooth it down and push out air bubbles from beneath it.

The beauty of this system is that a sign containing art work can be applied directly to the model, and those areas of the sign that do not contain drawings and lettering are transparent.

Once in place, decals should be given a coat of dull varnish to anchor them. Old decals may be sprayed with Krylon No. 1,303 (crystal clear) to make them less brittle.

Rubber Stamps

These may be made into any pattern by the local stationery store. For crisp, dark stampings, use stamp, block printing or printer's ink. Sloppy stamping can be cleaned off some surfaces with benzine or Carbona and then another attempt made to get a clean image.

Commercially Printed Signs

Stationery printers can print most signs on paper or business cardboard. To save price, have the signs made by one of those companies which makes glue-backed address labels. Some are as inexpensive as $1 for 1,000, $2 \times \frac{1}{2}''$ stickers. But the dimensions and lettering style of the sign must conform to what the company is equipped to print; otherwise the price will increase.

Photographically Reproduced Signs

Signs can be laid out with pressure-sensitive or transfer letters (both can be bought as small as $\frac{1}{16}''$ high), the results photographed and positive prints made from the negatives. This process makes it easy to include original graphics on the sign; also, reproducing them does not entail too great a cost.

Photoengraved Metal Sign Plates

Designs to be made on zinc sheet may be sent out. A small sign costs a few dollars, and may contain lettering and any original art work desired.

18-9

READY-MADE SIGNS FROM SELLEY, shown at full size.

Top row: No. 0381, No. 0381, No. 0383, No. 0382. *2nd row:* No. HO 577, No. HO 577, No. HO 679. *3rd row:* No. HO 576, no number (2), No. HO 186 (6), No. HO 185.

AVAILABLE READY-MADE SIGNS

Scale	Supplier	Type of sign	Approximate price
1/10″ = 1′	Fetyk (painted)	Road traffic signs	Set for 10¢
1/8″ = 1′	Plasticville (painted)	Street and road traffic signs	24 for 80¢
	Ralph Dillon (painted)	Hypothetic business signs in 2 colors, 1 3/16″ × 1 3/16″ and 1 3/4″ × 5/8″, 45 styles; trademarks of 20 famous firms, 1″ × 1 1/2″ to 3/4″ × 1/2″; street and road traffic signs	Business signs and trademarks @ 50¢; street signs @ 25¢–35¢
	Selley (unpainted)	Street and road traffic signs (18–9)	@ 5¢
1/4″ = 1′	Plasticville (painted)	Street and road traffic signs	24 for 80¢
	Ralph Dillon (painted)	Street and road traffic signs	30¢–40¢
	Selley (unpainted)	Street and road traffic signs	@ 8¢

AVAILABLE READY-MADE STREET FURNITURE

Scale	Supplier	Item, price, and where illustrated
1/10″ = 1′	Christoph (unpainted)	Benches (19–7A; 8¢; fireplug (18–6A)
1/8″ = 1′ (about)	Ralph Dillon (painted)	Mailboxes (20¢–25¢), trash receptacles (20¢), hydrant (20¢), fire-alarm box (25¢), wood and concrete benches (30¢), street barricade (25¢)
	Selley (unpainted)	Mailboxes (18–6A; 4¢–10¢), trash receptacles (18–6A; 4¢); fire hydrants (18–6A; 4¢, 6¢), parking meter (8¢)
1/4″ = 1′	Ralph Dillon (painted)	Mailboxes (35¢–45¢), trash receptacle (50¢), hydrant (25¢), fire-alarm box (40¢), wood and concrete benches (50¢–60¢), street barricade (35¢)
	Selley (unpainted)	Mailboxes (10¢, 15¢), trash receptacle (18–6A; 15¢), wood and concrete benches (19–7A; 15¢–20¢)

18-9A

READY-MADE STREET FURNITURE:

Top Row:
Selley: 2 trash receptacles and 2 mailboxes, 1/4″ and 1/8″ = 1′ scale.
Bottom Row:
Selley: 2 fireplugs, 1/4″ and 1/8″ = 1′ scale.
Christoph: fireplug.

STREET FURNITURE

Objects can be made by casting, fabricating from balsa and dowels or, in the case of benches and trash receptacles, from Bristolboard. Trash receptacles can also be made by rolling fine wire mesh into shape on a dowel and pasting a paper disc at one end.

RAILINGS AND FENCES

Large-scale wire and stripwood railings and fences are best made with the aid of a hardwood assembling jig, or by being pinned over an elevation drawing. Illustration 8-9 shows a cutting guide that can be of great aid in helping to cut equal length stripwood stringers. The steel or hardwood bars should be drilled to take 2 screws each. The bars are individually clamped to the steel backplate and the holes extended into it. The holes are then threaded.

Small scale ($\frac{1}{32}'' = 1'$ and larger) railings and fences can be made by scoring acetate sheet and coloring in the lines.

Custom etched or cast metal railings can be made to specification by Kemtron.

18-10

READY-MADE FENCES, shown at full size.

Top row: Vollmer: (set No. 500 S contains 10 lengths of wire railing).
2nd row: Faller: (cast plastic, 2 types from set No. 525, set contains 48 lengths in 5 types, each in 6 different colors).
3rd row: Faller: (the other 3 types from set No. 525).
4th row: Plasticville: (cast plastic, 12 pieces cost 39¢). Kemtron (2 examples of their custom etched metalwork).

READY-MADE FENCES AND RAILING, AND MATERIALS FOR FABRICATION

Scale	Supplier	Style and price
1/16″ to 1/8″ = 1′	James Bliss	Stanchions only (use wires for rails) : for 1, 2, and 3 rails ; 3/16″ to 1/2″ high ; 5¢–7¢ each
1/10″ = 1′	Fetyk	Rail fence : 2 rails high ; 12 bars for 40¢
1/8″ = 1′ (about) most can be used at up to 1/4″ = 1′ scale	Artype (pressure-sensitive overlay)	Chain-link fence : use No. 4087, mounted on acetate
	Dyna Models	Split-rail fence : ready-made ; 18 1/2″ long for 50¢
	Faller[1]	Picket fence : assortment of 24 pieces of fence for 80¢
	Merit	Post and rail fence : 48″ for $1
	Model Hobbies	Board fence : kit, 6′ long for $1.50
		Post and rail fence : kit, 6′ long for $1.50
	Plasticville	Picket fence : 5/8″ high, 30″ long for 40¢
	Ralph Dillon	Rustic fence : 40¢ for 2 ready-made sections
	Real-Like	Rail fence : 3 rails high ; 50¢ for 24″ long, ready-made
	Semaphore Hobbies	Chain-link fence : comes in kits 3/4″ to 3″ high by up to 4′ long ; $2–$3.50
	Selley	Rustic fence : ready-made 25¢ for 2 sections
	Timbertone (wall covering)	Basket-weave fence : use Timberton No. TG–804 wall covering ; may be used in up to 1/4″ = 1′ scale
	Vollmer[1]	Metal railing : $2.25 for a 7 1/4″ length
	Zip-a-Tone (pressure-sensitive overlay)	Chain-link fence : use No. 599R, No. 433, No. 440 mounted on acetate
1/4″ = 1′	Plasticville[1]	Picket fence : 2 1/4″ high by 6″ long for 6¢
1/4″–1/2″ = 1′	Tropicraft	Rustic wood fence : use woven wood by Tropicraft-Kobe bamboo style
3/8″, 1/2″, & 3/4″ = 1′ (all 3)	Industrial Model Supplies	Rail and stair rail (both have 2 rails) ; $1 for 18″

[1] Illustrated 18–10.

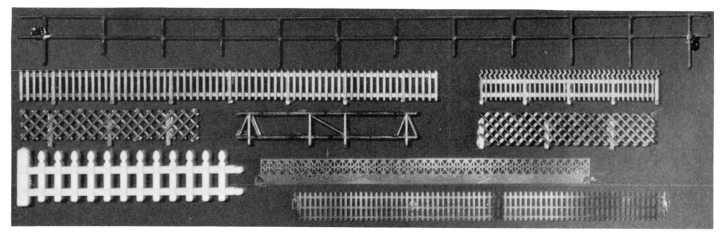

19 INTERIOR DESIGN MODELS

Models of interior spaces are of use not only to the architect and interior designer but to the office manager, householder, renting agent and others engaged in the arrangement of movable elements within habitable space. If a simple, nonpresentation, space planning model is desired, 2-dimensional cardboard cutouts can be made and manipulated on a floor plan. If the 3-dimensional aspects of furnishing must be studied, simple models may be constructed from wood blocks (19-5) or from cardboard (19-6). Walls and floors may be made from cardboard taped or cemented together. More complex models showing all or most of the details of each furnishing element are quite time consuming to construct and, in most instances,

superfluous since the appearance of various makes of furniture is well-known. Interior designers try to simplify construction by maintaining extensive collections of doll furniture, fabric samples and small shapes. It is also expedient to save furniture from past models for reuse with or without modification. To construct complicated pieces of furniture precisely, especially chairs, often costs as much as the purchase price of the full-size object. Therefore, highly detailed models of interiors are a rarity, especially if they are to be used solely for planning and client preparation. Detailed interior models are usually used as museum displays (and these are primarily period rooms), or in publications of highly original designs. To be feasible

economically, the latter must be sponsored by a manufacturer, an association or the publications ; or it must be a labor of love by the designer.

Models are especially helpful in presenting the true volume of an interior area—especially, the relation of ceiling height to other dimensions. Since perspectives of interiors very often take a spot outside of the room as their viewing point (in order to show a majority of the area), they often do not represent the true dimensions of the room to the viewer. To be able to see into the interior, it may be necessary to construct the model with one or more movable walls or in such a way that it can be pulled apart into sections. Larger scale models sometimes have a hole cut

19-1/19-2/19-3/19-4

FULLY DETAILED INTERIOR MODELS.

Designs and models are part of a collaborative project done by students of the interior design department of Pratt Institute in New York City for the Chemstrand Corporation.

SCALE: $1'' = 1'$.

All rooms: Wood tables and desks were made from wood veneer. Plant leaves were individually cut from paper and cemented on wire stems. Paintings were handpainted and mounted in stripwood frames. Ashtrays and bowls were modeled from clay. Upholstered furniture and pillows were carved from balsa, then covered with fabric. Venetian blinds were vacuum-formed from polystyrene.

Living room: (19–1.) The screen was made from wood which was first milled, then cut into small pieces and assembled. Turned brass planter tubes were purchased. The bench was made from basswood, the floor covering from illustration board, hanging chair of soldered wire. The tree bough was represented by a natural plant.

Reception hall: (19–2.) The small chair was vacuum-formed from polystyrene; other chairs were covered with thin vinyl plastic held in place with cement and pins. Metal chair and table legs were made from soldered brass strip and wire which was then plated. Glass table top was cut from acrylic sheet. Luminous ceiling was backlighted polystyrene.

Dining room: (19-3.) Planter was made from stained strip-wood; carpeting was constructed of veloured paper, upholstery of cotton fabric.

Bedroom-study: (19-4.) Stool and drafting table were made from basswood strip. Books were cut from balsa then covered with paper. Flooring was made of cardboard scored with a hard pencil to simulate cork tile. Rug was of felt and the bed was upholstered with dress fabric.

The realism of these model photos was enhanced by illuminating the model through its windows.

into the baseboard into which one may insert one's head.

Interior models are also extremely useful in designing tight areas such as display booths, bathrooms and kitchens.

SIMPLE RESIDENTIAL AND OTHER INTERIOR LAYOUT PLANNING MODELS

While most interior design commissions will not warrant the expense of making a 3-dimensional model, it is always useful to use 2-dimensional furniture templates when designing. These can be made from acetate or cardboard, or stock planning aids, such as the following, may be purchased:

Plan-It-Kit contains enough walls, windows, doors and 3-dimensional white styrene furniture to plan a house. Scale is $\frac{1}{2}'' = 1'$ and its cost is $8.

Plan-A-Room costs $15. This $\frac{1}{2}'' = 1'$ scale kit includes a gridded, clear plastic baseboard (that can be laid over a floor plan) and models of 89 pieces of furniture carved from wood.

Leslie Creations, Inc. Home-A-Minute Kit comes in a $\frac{1}{4}''$ scale. It contains a gridded baseboard, fiber partitions, doors, windows and kitchen cabinets, and costs $4.

Design Aid sells $\frac{1}{4}''$ scale home or office planning kits that include graph paper (for the base), color key, and over 250 2-dimensional, plastic templates. Prices run from $5 to $7 for each kit.

Presstamp makes burnish on transfers of the plan views of several types of furniture in $\frac{1}{8}$ and $\frac{1}{4}'' = 1'$ scales.

TOILET PLANNING

For toilet and washroom planning models, ready-made $\frac{1}{4}'' = 1'$ fixtures may be obtained from the following sources: Model Planning Company sells 2 sinks, 2 urinals, and 1 lavatory, w.c., shower and gang wash fountain (19-7A). Microform Corporation and Selley sell w.c.'s, urinals and basins.

HOME KITCHEN PLANNING

Several interior planners maintain a stock of modeled kitchen fixtures. These are arranged on a gridded baseboard upon which the floor plan of the kitchen has been sketched. The equipment is set into various arrangements, usually in the presence of the client (or his wife), until agreement is reached.

STUDYING THE RELATIONSHIP OF COLORS AND TEXTURES

The colors and textures of fabrics, paints, carpeting and wood finishes used in an area may be studied on simplified models that contain template representations of furniture set on simply constructed cardboard floors. Sample swatches of the contemplated finishes can be mounted on the templates and walls to give a rough idea of how the color combination will appear.

OFFICE LAYOUT PLANNING MODELS

Efficient office planning can be effected through the use of ready-made cast furniture available from several companies. Exact clearances may be studied with this furniture and the layout tightened into a design that balances space saving ideas with comfortable working conditions. Following

19-5

A FURNITURE LAYOUT PLANNING MODEL.

PROJECT: The Connecticut General Life Insurance Company Offices.
INTERIOR DESIGNED BY: Knoll Planning Unit.
MODELBUILDER: Ten Conrad (a professional modelbuilder).
PHOTOGRAPHER: George Cserna.
SCALE: $1/4 = 1'$.
All the simple volumetric pieces of furniture were cut from wood. The floor was constructed of scribed acrylic; mullions and partitions were made of painted acrylic.

19-6

FAIRLY DETAILED FURNITURE MADE FROM ILLUSTRATION BOARD.

PROJECT: United States Travel Office in Frankfurt, Germany.
DESIGNED BY: George Nelson.
MODELBUILDERS AND PHOTOGRAPHERS: members of the architect's staff.
SCALE: $1/2'' = 1'$.
Columns, walls, floor, stairs and furniture were almost entirely made from various types of board. Rugs were represented by upholstery fabric. The map of the United States was photostated from a larger map. The legs of the table near the map were made from wire. Sofas were made from balsa sheet covered with fabric.

This model was used to study both the spatial arrangement and the color scheme of the room. The model would, however, be eminently acceptable for presentation use.

are some of the companies supplying office planning models.

2-Dimensional Templates

Prestape sells pressure-sensitive office furniture templates in $\frac{1}{8}$ and $\frac{1}{4}'' = 1'$ scales.

3-Dimensional Models

"*Visual" Industrial Products, Inc.* sells a $\frac{1}{4}''$ scale, gridded baseboard made from clear acrylic; in cast metal there are: desks (60¢ to $1 each); tables (40¢ to $2.50 each); drafting tables; chairs; filing cabinets (35¢ to 75¢ each); coat trees; baskets; safes; office machines (over 90 models of all major manufacturers, $3 each); sofas; office workers (60¢ each); columns; walls and partitions. This company also can supply adhesive-backed sheet acetate plan templates of this furniture at 25% of the price of the casting. They also supply a package office planning kit with which offices of up to 3,000 square feet can be planned. This kit includes an acrylic baseboard, 112 castings of miscellaneous furniture and acetate templates of each casting.

Model Planning Company (20-4 and 20-6) sells $\frac{1}{4}''$ scale metal castings of office furniture, office machines, filing cabinets, drafting tables, vending machines and office workers. They also supply gridded baseboards and columns.

Microform Corporation sells $\frac{1}{4}''$ scale metal castings of desks, chairs, tables, filing cabinets, sofas, vending machines and safes.

Applied Research Corporation sells $\frac{1}{2}''$ scale polystyrene castings of chairs, desks, tables, filing cabinets and bookcases. They can also supply gridded baseboards and partitions in 9 lengths.

READY-MADE RESIDENTIAL FURNITURE

Doll house furniture obtainable at variety and toy stores is a marginal source of parts for the modelmaker. With luck, he may be able to cut apart, modify and reassemble some of the dated and styleless samples and create near facsimiles of the furniture intended for inclusion in his design. To avoid long, last minute searches for out-of-production models, the designer should, despite the cost, maintain a good supply of such furniture; over the years, he must add each interesting looking specimen that he encounters. Examples of doll house furniture (unusual because they were able to be incorporated without modification) can be seen in 19-7.

Another source of detailed furniture is the dealer in model period furniture, who supplies those whose hobby it is to collect miniatures. Many of these companies advertise in *Hobbies Magazine*. One such company is Chestnut Hill Studio Miniatures, whose line, like that of many other companies, is in a $1'' = 1'$ scale and includes over 500 handmade reproductions of period furniture, furnishings, paintings, silverware, china, glassware, rugs, etc. Many of these reproductions are in early American and 19th century American styles. Typical prices, for each item, are: chairs, $2 to $30; beds, $6 to $20; desks, $6 to $22; plates, $1 to $2.

B. Shackman and Company imports an extensive line of furniture and furnishings. Among these, are some examples of early American furniture (chairs and benches costing $13.80 to $16.20 per dozen) as well as of other period styles. The company also sells mattresses, pillows and bedspreads)a 6-piece set, composed of 2 of each item, costs $12 per dozen sets). They also have miniatures of kitchenware and dinnerware, including: 1 to 2" plates and bowls ($4.20 per dozen); 1 to $1\frac{1}{4}''$ high porcelain vases ($4.80 per dozen); 1 to $1\frac{1}{2}''$ high glass vases and pitchers ($1.50 per dozen); glass fruit on 1" glass platters ($2.60 per dozen); various types of food on 3"

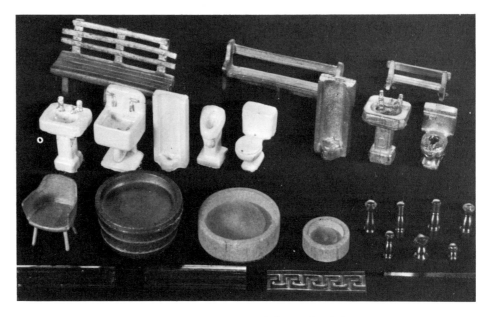

19-7A

READY-MADE FURNITURE.

$1/4'' = 1'$ scale.
Rear row: Selley: 2 park benches.
$1/8'' = 1'$ scale.
Rear Row: Christoph: park bench
$1/4'' = 1'$ scale.

2nd row: Model Planning Company: 5 painted toilet fixtures. Selley: 3 unpainted toilet fixtures. $1/4'' = 1'$ scale.
3rd row: Devpro bucket chair.
Miscellaneous scales:
3rd row: Bliss: 2 wood and 1 cast metal tubs, 7 brass stanchions.
Front row: Samuel Moore and Company: bead and fancy wires Nos. 1559, 1560, 1313 and 1811.

19-7

A VERY REALISTIC MODEL OF A DISPLAY.

PROJECT: the American National Exhibition, Moscow, Russia.
DESIGNED BY: George Nelson.
MODELBUILDERS AND PHOTOGRAPHERS: members of the architect's staff.
SCALE: $1'' = 1'$.
The columns and vaults of this presentation model were vacuum-formed from polystyrene. Each column was made in 2 pieces, its capital in 1. Ground cover was represented by sand. The figure of the man was created with a photograph. Chairs were represented by doll furniture. The model was also used to study the effects created by lighting the vaults from above.

platters ($4.80 to $6 per dozen); a salad set including a $3\frac{1}{4}''$ bowl ($6.90 per dozen sets); China tea sets, glass pitcher sets, and stoneware jug sets ($3.20 to $8.40 per dozen sets); pewter tea and coffee sets including $2\frac{1}{2}''$ trays ($16.20 to $18.60 per dozen sets); 15-piece sets of copper kitchen utensils ($16.80 per dozen sets); $2\frac{1}{4}''$ diameter and smaller pots and pans, 3 to the set ($6 per dozen sets); miniature packaged food cans, boxes and bottles, $\frac{1}{4}$ to $\frac{3}{4}''$ high, 12 per set ($3.20 per dozen sets). They also have some interesting candleholders, grandfather clocks and wall telephones.

A source of up-to-date furniture is The Microform Corporation. They sell a $\frac{1}{4}'' = 1'$ cast metal, modern furniture line which consists of sofa, chair, bucket chair and round table. In the next few years, other companies will probably start to stock cast modern furniture models, since the need for this type of product is great.

CUSTOM-MADE MODELS

Rough models may be constructed to most any scale larger than $\frac{1}{4}'' = 1'$. Fully detailed presen-

157

tation models most often are built to 1 or 1½"
scales; if using materials that take a fine finish,
however, there should be no trouble constructing
neat, photogenic models at somewhat smaller
scales.

Furniture Legs and Pedestals

Legs of small-scale models are best made from
pins and wire. In larger scales, they may be carved
from stripwood or acrylic. Fancy, carved legs and
pedestals can sometimes be improvised from
stamped brass eyelets, collars, grommets and
bushings or from the $\frac{1}{8}$ to $\frac{7}{16}$" highly decorative
brass stanchions that are available from model
boat supply houses, such as James Bliss and
Company (19-7A).

19-9

PRESENTATION MODELS OF FURNITURE.

DESIGNED, MODELED AND PHOTOGRAPHED BY:
William, Mattison.
SCALE: 1/2" = 1'.
The chair seat was bent from 3-ply Bristolboard;
the cushion was cut from foam plastic. Chair and
table legs were represented by brass rods notched
to receive the stripwood cross braces. Table
drawers were vacuum-formed of polystyrene.
Table top was made of walnut. Ashtray and small
pot were carved from plaster. The plant was
natural.

Chairs

Bucket chairs, and other chairs with curved
forms, may be cast (most often in several parts),
vacuum-formed out of polystyrene (19-9) or built
from formed flat material (Bristolboard: 19-6;
acetate: 24-5, etc.).

Thin Bristolboard should be bent over a balsa
or hardwood mold that has been covered with
wax paper. The chair should then be laminated
with several layers of board cemented together.

Wire chair frames should be made with the aid
of a hardwood bending jig.

Chairs and couches that do not have concave
shapes may have their seats and backs carved
from sheet balsa or cardboard.

Small-scale theater and church seats may be
constructed, in simplified form, from Bristolboard
bent to an "L" cross section. Each row of seats
can be made as 1 unit, omitting rests. For added
detail, the back of the row may be notched to
represent individual seats. The entire unit can then
be easily cemented to the floor in 1 piece. If the
row must curve, another series of slits can be
notched into the seat and the row carefully
curved to the desired shape.

19-8

A DETAILED MODEL OF AN ART GALLERY AND CAFE.

DESIGNER, MODELMAKER AND PHOTOGRAPHER:
William Mattison.
SCALE: 1/4" = 1'.
Chair seats were vacuum-formed from polystyrene
sheet on a toy vacuum-forming set. Chair legs
were made of pins that were heated and inserted
into the plastic seats. Bas relief was carved in
plaster. Pictures were miniature reproductions
purchased from a museum. Letters (over the door)
were created from a pressure-sensitive overlay.
Sculptures were formed in wire and built up with
layers of Duco cement and then sprayed with
aluminum paint. Floors and walls were made from
illustration board.
The photograph was taken with a 4" × 5" Speed
Graphic camera and Plus-X film.

19-10

MORE DETAILED MODELS OF FUNRITURE.

MODELMAKER: Form and Function, Inc. (a professional modelbuilder).
PHOTOGRAPHER: John Takeraas of Form and
Function, Inc.
SCALE: 3/4" = 1'.
The frame of the room divider was made from
square brass strips which were soft soldered together and then nickel-plated; shelves were constructed of acrylic.
Small glass bottles were made from Pyrex rods
that were heated and pulled to shape. The large
bottle was bought, ready-made, from a toy store.
Fiberglas chairs were simulated with vacuum-
formed 5/100" thick polystyrene shaped on a
plaster mold. Chair bases were made of nails that
were glued to the plastic. Crosspieces were filed
from wire and soldered to the nails.
Leather chairs were made of real leather on a
frame fabricated from brass rods and strips. The
3 wood and wicker chairs had lathe turned brass
legs and brass frames; their seats were built by
weaving over the frames.
Cigarette box was made of wood covered with
paper.
Bowl was vacuum-formed from polystyrene.
Silver canister and coffee pot were formed from
tin can metal bent into shape and soldered.
Pillow was carved from foam plastic and covered
with velvet.

PILLOWS AND CUSHIONS

These are made from carved balsa on which fabric is cemented (19-2), or the balsa may be painted and, while the paint is still wet, flock may be applied to it. When cementing fabric to wood shapes, carry the material around to the side of the cushion, where it will not be visible, and cement it there.

Tufting and pleating may be created by covering furniture with a very thin (about $\frac{1}{8}''$) sheet of foam rubber (the type used to protect delicate electrical and mechanical parts during shipping), and by then covering the rubber with the upholstery cloth. Tufts are made by pushing small pins through the fabric and rubber. To form pleats, pins with wire heads constructed in the form of a "T" are used. These pins are inserted through the fabric and rubber in rows, their heads pointing in the direction of the intended pleat, one head touching the next.

Cabinets, Tables and Shelves

This type of furniture may be simply built from sheet wood, acrylic or cardboard. Adjacent cabinet sides are kept at 90° angles by cementing strip-wood inside joints. Aluminum and stainless steel frames can be simulated by being constructed from highly polished, unpainted, clear acrylic. If a more exact facsimile of bright metal is needed, the frame may be constructed from soldered brass rod and sent out to be plated.

Cabinets and breakfronts may also be cut from blocks of such woods as beech; they are then covered with Bristolboard, colored paper or Flexwood, on which such details as drawers have been scribed. Larger, more detailed models may require individual parts to be vacuum-formed from polystyrene (19-9 and 19-10). Marble tops can be made from the materials suggested on page 126 Drawer pulls may be constructed from pin or nail heads or from tiny glass beads.

Rugs and Carpeting

Many materials possessing a fine pile-like texture are available for use as rugs and carpets. Among these is blotting paper, obtainable in a wide range of colors; it may have patterns painted on with thick poster color applied with a dry brush. When cementing the paper in place, take care to prevent the adhesive from coming through the paper. Art Felt (19-4) may be used in models of larger scales. Flocked paper or velvet fabric may also be used. Glue these materials in place with rubber cement. Cover the backs of all fabric materials with adhesive tape so that they will not unravel when cut.

The office sample box may often provide fabric or wall coverings the texture of which is reasonably close to the rug or carpeting desired. Among those that have proven to be exceptionally useful in the past are: Gilford Leather Company's "Fawn" (which comes in 15 colors); Timbertone Wall Covering No. TG-760 (which comes in 4 colors); Colortron Urethane Foam Fabric (which also comes in 4 colors); Fabric Leather Corporation's "Elastic Plyhide" (which comes in 13 colors); and Lauralee Associates, Inc. "Plush." These 5 products can be used to model floor coverings accurately at a $\frac{1}{8}''=1'$ scale and larger. Patterns may be directly painted on most rug representing materials or may, if the pattern is repetitive, be printed on with the aid of a lino or wood-block cut.

Fluffy Bathroom Mats may be represented by a piece of powder puff.

Fur Animal Skin Rugs may be made from pieces of 100% wool blanket material.

Persian Rugs may be represented by museum color reproductions of actual rugs.

19-11

MORE HIGHLY DETAILED FURNITURE.

PROJECT: Experimental House.
DESIGNED BY: George Nelson and Company.
MODELBUILDERS AND PHOTOGRAPHERS: members of the architect's staff.
SCALE: $1'' = 1'$.
Columns of this presentation model were made from groupings of basswood T sections. The dome was vacuum-formed from polystyrene. The grill, below the dome, was made from expanded honeycomb material. Carpeting was cut from a towel. The stool (in right-hand corner) was illustrated by a drawer pull. Books, bottles and dishes were represented by doll furniture. Drawers, shelving and desk were made from stripwood. Drawer pulls were created from pinheads. The record player was made from wood and pins. Statuary on the central tables came from charm bracelets. The wall clock and lighting fixture were made from wood and paper.
The photograph was taken with a 35 mm candid camera.
CONSTRUCTION TIME: about 40 hours, not including time spent building the furniture that came from the modelmaker's supply of odds and ends saved from past models.

Sisal Matting may be made from pieces of raffia (a finely woven rush work). On small-scale models, colored buckram may be used.

Fabric

Modeling fabric presents 2 major problems: (1) Finding a material the weave of which is not too oversized; (2) And finding, when creating miniature drapes and other hanging fabrics, some way of approximating the folds and stiffness of the prototype.

WEAVE

Good silk generally has a weave that is fine enough to represent precisely very rough upholstery fabric at scales only of over $\frac{1}{2}''=1'$. Shirt broadcloth (having about 80 threads per inch) can represent the same rough fabric in models of over $1''=1'$. Thus, it is almost impossible to find fabrics that can be used to represent fine weaves at the common $1''=1'$ interior model scale.

FOLDS

Realistic folds in small-scale models can only be made with paper. Gift wrap paper or colored paper may be used to represent the fabric. On large scaled models, folds may be imparted by dipping the fabric in a bath of 1 part Elmer's glue and 1 part water. Once removed, the fabric is pulled, folded and otherwise fashioned into shape as it dries.

Fabrics used in modeling can often be selected from an office selection of fabric samples. Often, other sample materials can also be of use in representing certain types of fabrics; Timbertone

Wall Covering No. TG-760 can be bent to form realistic drapes. Fabroid Spandrel Water Proofing made by Weatherguard Products Corporation can be used to represent leatherette. Kravet Fabric's Saran and Decron (group No. C-84) can be used for striped fabrics. Fabron "Gallant" No. 1207-3B can simulate striped awning fabric. Timbertone Wall Covering No. TG-804 makes good woven wool and Elastic Plyhide can be used to represent wool. All of the above materials may be realistically used on models of a $\frac{1}{4}''$ scale and larger.

Other materials that may be used for modeled fabrics are colored paper (including tissue paper) and box cover papers with woven texture patterns (obtainable from paper wholesalers). A trip to a large local retail fabric store, especially one maintaining a large selection of remnants, can also provide much useful raw material.

Fabric can be painted with textile colors obtainable at large artist supply stores. These paints do not bleed, or stiffen the cloth.

Wallpaper and Paint

These may be simulated by dry mounting patterned or colored paper to the walls of the model. If a test shows that the walls have a tendency to warp, this may be compensated for by dry mounting paper on their opposite side. Occasionally, a wallpaper pattern may be nearly simulated by a transparent pressure-sensitive overlay; thus, Craftone style No. 704 may be used to simulate roughly a paper with a star pattern, and styles No. 520 or No. 516 (of the same line) may be used to represent floral patterns.

Wood Finishes may be simulated with Flexwood.

19-12
A HIGHLY REALISTIC, THOUGH SIMPLY CONSTRUCTED, INTERIOR MODEL.
PROJECT: The great hall of the the John F. Kennedy Cultural Center, Washington, D.C.
DESIGNED BY: Edward Durell Stone.
MODELBUILDERS: members of the architect's staff.
PHOTOGRAPHER: Louis Checkman.
SCALE: 1/8″ = 1′.
From this well-conceived study model, several highly effective photographs were taken, the realism of which belie the small scale of the model. Walls and balconies were constructed of cardboard. Carpet was made from flocked paper, trees from wool balls. Drapes were gold damask pasted to board, people were cast, and chandeliers made from acrylic rods on which spangles were applied. The photograph was taken with a 35 mm Nikon reflex camera, 35 mm PC (perspective control) lens, which was raised in its track to counteract the convergence that was encountered at this camera angle. Plus X film was used. The chandeliers were lighted by 6-watt bulbs; the rest of the light used in the photographs was provided by spotlights aimed into the model through the side windows.

19-13
STUDY MODELS OF ARCHITECTURAL SCULPTURE.
PROJECT: the tower at the state of Hawaii Exhibit at the 1964–65 New York World's Fair.
DESIGNED BY: Reino Aarnio.
MODELMAKERS AND PHOTOGRAPHERS: members of the architect's staff.
These 2 metal and clay models were executed to study in detail the scultural concept.
Photograph was taken with a Polaroid camera.

Fabric Wall Coverings can, in some cases, be simulated by box cover papers that have the appropriate, subtle textures.

All of these finishes can appropriately be used at only $\frac{1}{4}″=1′$ and larger scales (especially the box cover paper).

Venetian Blinds and Accordion Doors can be vacuum-formed from polystyrene (19-4).

Fancy Wall Moldings and Period Furniture Trim can sometimes be made from the fancy wire extrusions sold by such outfits as Samuel Moore & Company, Inc. (19-7A).

Paintings and Murals

Often it is not too important to model a painting or mural accurately. If such be the case, a facsimile of the correct size and approximate coloration will suffice. There are many such objects to be used: miniature color reproductions of pictures (obtainable in postage stamp size from some art museums), postage stamps (U.S. and foreign, obtainable in packs costing a few cents, or more, from stamp dealers), parts of colored postcards or prints that depict famous works of art (also obtainable at art museums), reproductions of paintings cut from art magazines or advertising copy taken from popular magazines, etc.

The office sample supply may also be of some aid in providing painting and relief simulating materials. The following have been of use to me: Armstrong Tile Marbelle Linoleum (to represent marbleized patterns at $\frac{1}{8}″=1′$ and larger scales); Wall-Tex Fragrance (a floral design); Timbertone No. AC-2101 (a tortoise shell pattern); Fabron Sunfast (a hieroglyphic-like design); B. F. Goodrich Koroseal Spatio (for a Nivola-like relief); Guard Architectural Wall Covering—Moderna Nos. 20B through 27B (3-dimensional truncated triangles) and Stria Nos. 60B through 67B (for a swirl and loop pattern in relief); Timbertone No. SA-1-4505 and No. SA-4507 (for a marbleized pattern). Vin-L-Fab Spanish Crush Grain (for a design that resembles a Jackson Pollock when used at a $\frac{1}{16}″=1′$ scale); Robbins Rubber Tile

No. 592 (a marbleized pattern); RCA Rubber Wall Covering No. 770 (a marbleized paint streak pattern). The above samples may, most convincingly, be used in $\frac{1}{4}''=1'$ and larger scale models except when otherwise noted.

RELIEFS

Small representational reliefs may be cut from inexpensive foreign coins.

If an exact representation of a painting or mural is needed, paint it yourself. Intricate multi-ply screens, which in the prototypes are made from colored transparent and translucent cast plastic, may be made from several plys of Bourges Colotone.

Sculpture

If only a rough idea of the prototype is required, the sculpture may be made from charms, model people (filed or bent into artistic poses), pieces of costume jewelry or whatever can be found in the scrap bins to represent the endless extant styles of art.

If an accurate reproduction is required, it may be carved with the aid of a small motor tool from any dense wood or plastic. Metal sculpture may be made from sculpt metal or any of the plastic metals mentioned in that section of the book.

It might be noted that models can be effectively used to test accurately the effect of art work within an interior or against a facade. Illustration 19-15 shows such a use of a model. Model studies are also often made of large works of art: 19-13 shows 2 of the several model studies made of the sculptured tower at the Hawaiian Pavilion at the New York 1964-65 World's Fair.

CUSTOM-MADE ACCESSORIES

Books

These may be cut from cardboard of the proper thickness and covered with colored paper or parts of magazine advertisements that contain bits of small printing or pictures.

Mirrors

Surfaces may be made from smoothed tin foil or, providing one has confidence in one's glass cutting ability, pieces of actual mirror. Antiqued glass can be represented by painting the foil or glass or by such material samples as Kentile No. L-102 covered with a thin sheet of acetate.

Metal Coffee Services, Pots and Pans

These and other similar objects may be hammered or pressed from sheet metal.

Dishware

Articles may be vacuum-formed from plastic or formed with thin Bristolboard. The latter method requires a mathematical or intuitive plotting of the correct shape of paper required to form the vessel. Seams can be removed by filling with plastic balsa and light sanding. Small, 1″ diameter dishes and pots can sometimes be found in toy stores or in Japanese shops.

Bottles and Glassware

These may be turned most easily from acrylic rods. A representation of colored contents may be made in bottles by internally carving them from their bottoms and then filling the cavities with paint. 1 to $1\frac{1}{2}''$ high bottles are sometimes obtainable at toy stores or from novelty supply houses.

Pottery and Planters

These objects may be made in the same ways as dishware or, if they have thick walls, they can be turned from wood or plastic. If a nonsymmetrical shape is desired, it can be carved or modeled in fine clay. If large numbers of planters are needed, casting in low melting point metal is the best procedure. Tubs with $\frac{3}{16}$ to $\frac{9}{16}''$ heights by up to $1\frac{1}{4}''$ diameters, turned from wood, may be obtained from James Bliss & Co. (19-7A).

←19-14

19-14, 15

USING A MODEL TO STUDY THE RELATIONSHIP OF ART WORK AND FURNISHINGS TO A BUILDING.
PROJECT: Coventry Cathedral.
DESIGNED BY: Sir Basil Spence.
MODELBUILDERS: preliminary model: members of the architect's staff. Final model: City Display Organization (a professional modelbuilder).
SCALE: 1/4″ = 1′.
The preliminary model was made from illustration board and wood. Into it were placed design models of tapestry, icons, furniture, the pulpit and altar. These objects, designed by collaborating artists, could then be co-ordinated with the interior.
The final (presentation) model was made from illustration board and wood. The screen was made from soldered brass strip and scribed acrylic.

19-15→

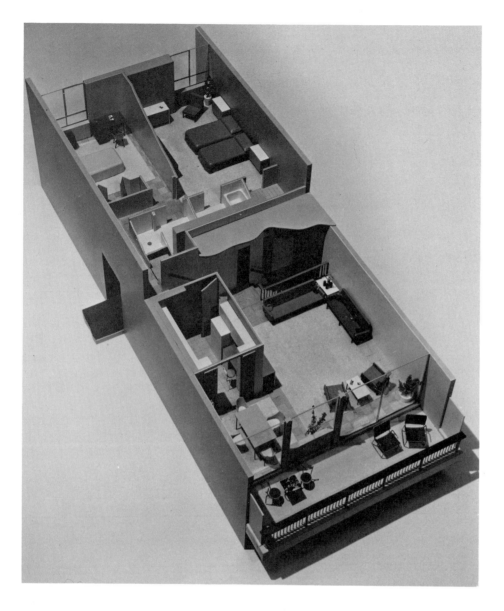

19-16

A RENTING MODEL.

PROJECT: Horizon House Apartments, Fort Lee, New Jersey.
DESIGNED BY: Kelley and Gruzen.
PHOTOGRAPHER: Louis Checkman.
SCALE: 3/8″ = 1′.

This fairly typical renting model was used to present the difficult-to-visualize concept of split level apartments to perspective tenants. Since models were made of several apartments, it was practical to carve much of the furniture, toilet, and kitchen fixtures; make female molds; and get the desired number of reproductions by casting in metal. Chair, table and desk legs and stair railings were made of brass rod. Table tops and doors were constructed in acrylic. Walls, windows and mullions were also made of acrylic. Flooring was drawn on colored paper. Plants were cut from paper or made from sponge.

The photograph was taken with a 4″ × 5″ Sinar view camera, 3⅜″ lens and Super Panchro Press "B" film. The model was illuminated by 1 spot and 1 bounced floodlight. The latter brought out detail in the areas placed in shadow by the spot.

19-17

CLAY STUDY MODEL OF A STAIR.

PROJECT: the grand staircase of the Metropolitan Opera House, Lincoln Center, New York City.
DESIGNER: Wallace K. Harrison. Consulting engineer: Ammann and Whitney.
MODELBUILDERS AND PHOTOGRAPHERS: members of the architect's staff.
SCALE: 1/2″ = 1′.

The construction techniques employed on this model may be used on most study models of curving ramps and staircases. Curved surfaces were made of plasticene on chicken wire; flat surfaces were wood; steps were constructed of plasticene. People were painted on board.
CONSTRUCTION TIME: about 50 hours.

19-18

STAGE-SET MODEL USED TO STUDY SILHOUETTE FORMATION.

Set for *The Lady's Not For Burning*, created for the Association of Producing Artists Repertory Group.

DESIGNED BY: Hugh Hardy.

MODELBUILDERS: the architect and Richard Casler.

PHOTOGRAPHER: Gil Amiaga, New York City.

SCALE: 1/4″ = 1′.

Columns, beams, steps, car, stool and table were made from cardboard as was the baseboard. Flags, figures and miscellaneous trim were made of paper. The window leading was simulated with string.

The photograph was taken with a 8″ × 10″ Deardorff view camera and Royal Pan film. Model was illuminated from its left side to simulate light coming through the window.

19-19

PRESENTATION MODEL OF A THEATER INTERIOR.

PROJECT: the space theater for Mark-I Enterprises.

DESIGNED BY: Hugh Hardy.

MODELBUILDERS: members of the architect's staff.

PHOTOGRAPHER: Gil Amiaga, New York City.

SCALE: 1/4″ = 1′.

Walls, scenery, seats and the people sitting on them were made from cardboard. The model was braced with stripwood. Roof truss was made of basswood strip. Standing people were bent from 3-ply Bristolboard.

The photograph was taken with an 8″ × 10″ Deardorff camera and Royal Pan film. Light shafts were created by blowing smoke into the spotlighted model.

Luggage

Unpainted, ready-made (cast) luggage is available at: a 1/10″=1′ scale (from Fetyk), a $\frac{1}{8}$″ scale (Faller and Selley) and in a $\frac{1}{4}$″ scale (Selley). Painted luggage is available from Dillon in $\frac{1}{8}$ and $\frac{1}{4}$″ scales. Unpainted luggage costs 1 to 5¢ each; painted luggage costs 15 to 25¢ each. Each manufacturer makes a handful of styles.

Packing Cases, Barrels, Milk Cans, Oil Drums

All may be obtained ready-made and unpainted in a 1/10″=1′ scale (from Fetyk), in a $\frac{1}{8}$″ scale (Selley); milk cans and oil drums are obtained in a $\frac{1}{4}$″ scale (Selley). All 4 objects may be obtained painted in a $\frac{1}{8}$″ scale (from Dillon) and the oil drums in a $\frac{1}{4}$″ scale (Dillon). The unpainted items cost about 2 to 4¢; painted ones cost 15 to 35¢.

STAGE-SET MODELS

Models are often used by stage-set designers as presentation devices and, despite certain problems, as design aids. Because it is impossible to represent lighting conditions and painted colors exactly (2 extremely important aspects of set design), models usually must be considered abstractions of the design. They may, however, be used to study the profile of various parts and the general lighting and color. The model is usually a simplification of the design, and colors are made more intense. The over-all mood derived from the model is more important than an accurate portrayal of the set.

Theater-in-the-round requires more extensive model study to investigate the juxtaposition of design parts when viewed from all sides. In the past, stage-set models were composed mainly of painted flats, and had few 3-dimensional model parts. The flats were often sent to the set constructor as a construction document.

USE OF MODELS IN EXHIBITIONS AND DISPLAYS

Models are extremely well received by the general public when they are used as parts of displays. They often become "show stoppers,"

19-20

A DISPLAY PLANNING MODEL.

Designed, modeled and photographed by: Sanford Hohauser.

Sale: 1/4″ = 1′.

This model was used in planning the exact design, content and position of each photograph that was to be displayed. Framework was made from cold soldered copper tubing; walls were made of mat board of various colors. Artwork was photographed with a $2\frac{1}{4}″ \times 2\frac{1}{4}″$ twin lens reflex camera positioned at such a distance from the original as to produce a negative that could be contact printed so as to produce a positive that would be in the scale of the model.

The photograph was taken with a $2\frac{1}{4}″ \times 2\frac{1}{4}″$ reflex camera and with Kodacolor film.

Construction time: about 25 hours.

especially when they are illuminated or animated. Fascination with models is such that not only window displays and corners of exhibition booths but entire world fair pavilions and tourist attractions, as well, have been successfully based on them. An example of the latter is Madurodam, a $\frac{1}{2}″$ scale model of a city, port and aerodrome which is a major attraction at The Hague, Holland.

Exhibition and store displays themselves are best represented by, and designed on, models. Actual graphics may be roughly drawn, photographically reproduced and mounted in the model. Clearances and visual juxtapositions between parts of the design may be studied with greater accuracy with models than with sketches. Occasionally, a model is used in place of plans and elevations to describe a display design to the contractor. The exhibit shown in 1-1 is an example of such a use. This display was built from the model and an accompanying set of details; no plans or elevations were supplied.

19-21

Project: ENTRY FOR THE FRANKLIN DELANO ROOSEVELT MEMORIAL COMPETITION.

Designed by: Joseph D'Amelio and Lloyd Glasson.

Modelbuilder: Lloyd Glasson.

Photographer: Sanford Hohauser.

Scale: 1/8″ = 1′.

This sculptural solution was designed and presented in a series of models. This final one was constructed of brass strip brazed together and polished. The photograph was taken with a 4″ × 5″ view camera, 90 mm Wollensak Raptar wide-angle lens and Panotomic X film. Illumination was 1 300-watt floodlight focused on the blue paper background for general illumination and a 100-watt spotlight, which created highlights on some of the rods.

Construction time: about 100 hours.

20 PIPING DESIGN AND FACTORY PLANNING MODELS

PIPING DESIGN MODELS

Piping design models (20-1) are extensively used in the design of chemical and petroleum producing plants; most major installations are designed on these models. The intricacies of pipe runs and intersections make it very difficult and inefficient, if not impossible, to rely exclusively on drawings for the countless references that

20-1

A PIPING DESIGN MODEL.

PROJECT: Power Island Plant.
MODELBUILDER Industrial Models, Inc. (a professional modelbuilder).
SCALE: 3/4″ = 1′.
The baseboard of this engineering design model was made of plywood stiffened with white pine. Most pipes were the standard plastic pipes that can be purchased from model builders. Large pipes were made of acrylic tube. Tanks, floors and columns were also constructed of acrylic.
The model cost the client about $30,000, including changes.

have to be made to each part of the design before it can be completed. It has been found that models can produce the following savings: reduction of over-all drafting and designing costs, minimization of the number of field changes to be made, expediting the training of operating personnel and saving of time for clients and consultants.

The Fluor Corporation, one of the nation's largest refinery and chemical plant designers, uses 3 types of design models:

1—"Plant Layout Model," a simple preliminary model which shows only the rough space requirements of the equipment and the general arrangement of the plant. When finalized, this model is photographed or drawn in plain view.

2—"Piping Layout Model," on which all piping runs are planned. They are represented by lengths of small diameter wire. Clearances can be checked by placing a washer with an outside diameter equal to that of the intended pipe over the wire. Wires are coupled with sleeves; plastic markers indicate the number of the line. This model is also photographed. Incidentally, center line piping models of this type are ideal for use with photographic drawing because pipes cannot be hidden behind other, larger lines.

3—"Piping Arrangement Model," which is the same as the second model except that the piping is represented by tubing of an exact scale diameter.

Model cost estimates run about $\frac{1}{2}$% of the construction costs of a $1,000,000 plant to 1/20% of the cost of a $30,000,000 project.

Often the model, along with dimensioned photographs, is sent in lieu of drawings to the construction site. The model is also used to aid in estimating; checking for errors made in the drawings; coordinating the design with the requirements of the safety, security, maintenance and production departments of the company; and facilitating personnel training.

Models made from color-coded pipe should preferably be photographed in color or, if black and white film is used, it should be of an orthochromatic variety to help differentiate the colors better.

Component parts for making piping design models may be ordered from several companies. Some of these are listed on the following pages. Architects and mechanical engineers can also use these parts in the planning of boiler rooms and other building areas containing extensive piping.

20-2

A PIPING LAYOUT MODEL.

PROJECT: Westinghouse Electric Corporation. Large Rotating Apparatus Department.
MODELBUILDER: Model Building Company, Inc. (a professional modelbuilder).
SCALE: $1/2'' = 1'$.
The design model was built entirely of acrylic, except for some valves and pipe fittings that were cast in metal.
The model cost the client about $1000.

20-3

A LARGE FACTORY LAYOUT MODEL.

PROJECT: The Westinghouse Electric Corporation, Switch Gear Department.
MODELBUILDER: Model Planning Company, Inc. (a professional modelbuilder).
SCALE: $1/4'' = 1'$.
A large (160,000 square feet of floor space) factory was planned from this model, which was constructed mainly of acrylic. Some of the machinery was cast from metal, and many of these pieces are standard castings that can be purchased from the Model Planning Company.
The model cost the client about **$35,000.**

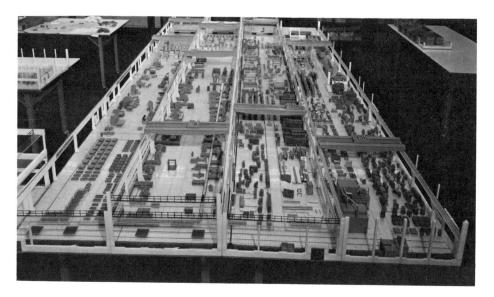

20-4

A DETAILED OFFICE AND FACTORY LAYOUT MODEL.

MODELBUILDER: Model Planning Company, Inc. (a professional modelbuilder).
SCALE: $1/4'' = 1'$.
Columns, stairs, floor and partitions of this design model were made in acrylic. Everything else was cast in metal, and can be purchased individually from the modelbuilder.

166

INDUSTRIAL MODEL SUPPLIES, INC.

This company supplies, in $\frac{1}{4}$, $\frac{3}{8}$, $\frac{1}{2}$ and $\frac{3}{4}'' = 1'$ scales, columns and beams (styrene), baseboards (Formica grids cemented to Novaply), such production equipment as: heat exchangers, pumps, manholes, ladders, stairs, platforms, machinery supports, flooring, people and pressure-sensitive title stickers. They also make complete models.

ENGINEERING MODEL ASSOCIATES

They supply the following equipment that can be used on models of $\frac{1}{4}$, $\frac{3}{8}$, $\frac{1}{2}$ and $\frac{3}{4}''$ scales: Piping made from various colors of butyrate plastic. (Sections friction fit into one another and into other equipment. Coupling pins or sleeves secure the connections.) They also supply plastic elbows, supporting T's, pipe bends, pipe reducers, pipe caps, insulation sleeves, instruments, flanges, valves, vessel heads, nozzles and saddles, railings, manholes, stairs and ladders. They supply metal castings of motors, pumps, turbines, platform brackets and lighting fixtures. For rough piping mock-up models, they supply $\frac{1}{16}''$ diameter plastic-coated wire used for the fast determination of pipe routing. This wire comes in 5 colors and uses sleeves to indicate the actual pipe diameter. They also make complete models.

FACTORY PLANNING MODELS

Study models that show the exact positioning of all production tools and equipment are of increasing importance in factory design. As the costs of construction, land and running an assembly line increase, so does the importance of designing the optimum utilization of space. Models are indispensable tools for the study of the complex interrelationships and clearances found among tools; they present the design easily to the many people who must check and work with it and who are unable to understand drawings fully. Not only will the designer and his client use the factory model, but so will the client's safety, security, maintenance and production departments, who must analyze and solve various work problems. Even after the factory has been completed, the models can still help to solve material handling and storage problems that invariably crop up.

Several model building companies specialize in factory and office layouts. Their service runs from building complete models of a prospective plant to supplying castings of furniture and tools for the designer's use in his own modelbuilding shop. Models are usually built with an acrylic sheet floor, scribed with a 1' grid on its reverse side to aid in the placement of tools and to show clearances at a glance. Columns and partitions are also made from acrylic. Upper floors, stiffened by beams, are supported by channels or acrylic strips that are affixed to the walls of the model; or each floor may be cemented to columns and to 1 story of exterior walls; the assembly is stacked upon the next floor.

Partitions may be constructed out of acrylic. Place the plastic sheet over a full-size elevation, scribe in all details and paint. Areas of frosted glass can be represented by sanded plastic.

Sometimes columns are made in 2 parts: a stubby socket and a full length column fitting into the socket. This allows the long column to be removed and work to proceed without the danger of breaking it. Roofs are often dispensed with, but sometimes they are constructed to serve as a dust cover and also as a device to keep unauthorized hands off the modeled equipment. Tools, equipment and people are cast from metal and are held in place with double-faced pressure-sensitive tape.

Factory models are sometimes photographed from the top down. The negative is dimensioned and processed through a blueprint machine to create final layout plans.

Some of the Companies That Supply Component Parts Are:

MODEL PLANNING COMPANY, INC.

They build $\frac{1}{4}''$ scale, simplified planning models for 1¢ per square foot. These include all partitions, walls, stairs, etc., but no equipment or roof. For an additional 4¢ per square foot, they supply models of equipment, workers and accessories. The square footage referred to is the floor area of the prototype building. The Model Planning Company also supplies component parts (20-4). They sell hundreds of metal castings of tools, processing equipment, storage racks, conveyers and workers; they also sell in Plexiglas: gridded floor material, stairs, many sizes of columns, $\frac{1}{16}$ to $\frac{3}{8}''$ thick walls and beams.

VISUAL PRODUCTION PLANNING, INC.

This company builds complete $\frac{1}{4}''$ scale models for $3\frac{1}{2}$¢ per square foot (for the equipment) plus 1¢ per square foot (for floors, walls, stairs, etc.). Roofs are not included. They can also supply component parts: gridded floors, stairs, many sizes of round and square columns, $\frac{1}{8}$ and $\frac{1}{4}''$ thick walls and castings of thousands of machine tools. The latter cost $1 to $6.50 (or more) each.

F. WARD HARMAN ASSOCIATES

They build complete $\frac{1}{4}''$ scale models and sell component parts, including: $\frac{1}{4}''$ thick floor grids; 1 and 2" high $\frac{1}{16}$, $\frac{1}{8}$ and $\frac{1}{4}''$ opaque white acrylic sheets for use as walls; 1 and 2" high $\frac{1}{8}$ and $\frac{1}{4}''$ square and round opaque white acrylic columns; $\frac{1}{2}$, $\frac{3}{4}$ and 1" wide stairs, sign posts, flow arrows; cast or built-up machine tools and nonproductive equipment and people.

"VISUAL" INDUSTRIAL PRODUCTS, INC.

This company builds complete $\frac{1}{4}''$ scale models for 3¢ to 7¢ per square foot; included are complete equipment, columns, partitions, outside walls, stairs and shafts, but no roofs. They also sell castings of all conceivable machines and equipment, numbering over 15,000 items. Equipment is color-coded. Each of the following categories of equipment is made in a separate hue: machine tools, incidental shop equipment (workbenches, cabinets, etc.), material handling equipment, moving equipment (trucks, cranes, etc.), office equipment and toilet equipment.

THE MICROFORM CORPORATION

They sell about 200 $\frac{1}{4}''$ scale castings of machine tools, conveyers, shelving and workbenches and 30 castings of workers.

ARISTO CRAFT

This company sells several types of bench-mounted machine tools.

20-5

READY-MADE VALVES FROM SELLEY, shown at full size.

20-6

READY-MADE OFFICE AND FACTORY EQUIPMENT AND FURNITURE.

SCALE: 1/4" = 1'.

Top row: 8 examples of Model Planning Company painted office equipment and people; the right-hand object is a column.

2nd row: 11 more examples of the same.

3rd row: 4 more examples of Model Planning office equipment and people. Microform: unpainted No. 61 (typist desk), No. 317 (office chair), and

No. 225 (filing cab.). Devpro: unpainted desk.

4th row: Devpro: unpainted typist chair, school chair and desk.

SCALE: 1/8" = 1'.

4th and lowest row: Devpro: unpainted desk and chair.

SCALE: TT.

4th row: Christoph: unpainted desk (from desk and chair set No. 1982), typist's desk and filing cab (from 8-piece office set No. 1841. Set includes 2 regular desks, 1 typist's desk, 3 chairs and 2 filing cabinets), and table and chair set No. 1982.

21 MECHANICAL ENGINEERING MODELS

21-1

A SMOKE BOX FOR THE TESTING OF THE DIFFUSION PROPERTIES OF VARIOUS TYPES OF PATTERNED GLASS.

Model used by Mississippi Glass Company to test its products.

SCALE: $1'' = 1'$.

The interior of the model was painted blackboard black. The glass sample to be tested was inserted into the window frame and lighted by a suitable source (in this instance a sealed beam headlight was used). Smoke was directed into the box and at the area around the outside of the window in order to define the light.

Test models similar to those used in architectural and interior design have found application in most of the mechanical engineering fields. Their use has been limited by the difficulty of finding the relationship between model and prototype characteristics and the cost of doing this. The majority of users up till now have been universities who seem to be the only group with enough capital to conduct research. When the basic formulas have been developed, individual engineering firms and smaller testing laboratories may be able to make greater use of models.

The following brief resume of some of the tests that may be performed on models is intended as a survey and not as an encouragement for the architect or interior designer to undertake this type of testing on his own. The complexity of the measuring apparatus involved, ratios of similitude and analysis make it too difficult for all but a relatively few specializing engineers to attempt model testing.

HEATING TEST MODELS

Studies in the temperature distribution of buildings have been performed on test models at the National Bureau of Standards. The complete validity of the use of models for this type of test has not been established. To be valid, a test must be conducted with a model the walls and ceilings of which are of scale thickness and proportional conductivity to the prototype. Heat input in the model must be proportionate to the square of the linear size reduction ratio. On some past tests, temperature was created by electric heating cables and was measured by copper thermocouples cemented to the walls of the model (to measure surface temperature or to measure air temperature) or attached to vertical posts. In the latter test, the thermocouple must be shielded from radiated heat by being housed in polished metal cylinders that are open at both ends.

VENTILATION TEST MODELS

Models have been used to predict the pattern of air flow through rooms and through fenestration of various shapes. The models are made in something close to a $1'' = 1'$ scale all windows, doors and other openings being faithfully represented. 1 side of the room is constructed in clear plastic to allow for visual observation of the test, which consists of mounting the model in a wind tunnel and blowing smoke into its windows, and then watching the smoke circulate through and out of the rooms.

Other ventilating tests employing smoke patterns have been made on models of landscaped areas to see how trees, other vegetation and ground contours influence the flow of prevailing winds over a building.

Tests to determine only the direction of air flow can be performed on small-scale block models on which short strands of thin string are fastened at 1 or 2″ intervals. The model is subjected in a wind tunnel to high winds applied in the direction of prevailing winds on the prototype. By studying the directions assumed by the strings, it is possible to locate areas of low or negative pressure and to design windows at these points to create a cooling air flow within the prototype.

The actual velocity of air moving through a building can be predicted by the wind tunnel testing of a model. Air pressure measuring gauges are mounted in the slip stream of the tunnel and at various locations in and around the accurately constructed, moderately large scale, model. Air velocity is related to pressure by the following *formula*:

$$\text{velocity at any point in the actual structure} = \text{prevailing wind velocity at the site} \times \sqrt{\dfrac{\text{air pressure at the same point on the model}}{\text{free wind pressure in the wind tunnel}}}$$

The accuracy of results achieved with ventilation model testing is very high. It is often more practical to test models than full-size mock-ups because finding natural breezes that correspond to optimum test conditions is relatively difficult. And to test a mock-up in a large enough wind tunnel would incur a large expense.

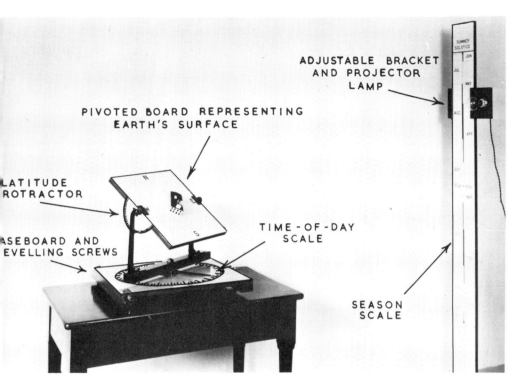

21-2

THE HELIODON.

The model was placed on a pivoted board which was adjusted to the correct latitude and time of day. The lamp on the vertical post was adjusted to the correct day of the year. The resulting shadows cast on the model were exactly what they should have been for that particular point in time and space.

This photograph was reproduced by permission of Her Majesty's Stationery Office, Crown copyright reserved.

21-3

THE PLEIJEL SUNDIAL.

This photograph was reproduced by permission of Her Majesty's Stationery Office, Crown copyright reserved.
The Pleijel Sundial was used to study the shadows cast by structures and landscaping. The sundial was north-oriented to the model; a lamp was maneuvered until the shadow of the post of the dial pointed to the desired day and time of day on the scale of the dial. The resulting model shadows now represent those that will be cast by the prototype at that day and time.

21-4

A MODEL USED TO STUDY THE NATURAL LIGHTING OF A CLASSROOM.

This photograph was taken at the Building Research Station, Watford, Herts, Great Britain, and is reproduced by permission of Her Majesty's Stationery Office, Crown copyright reserved.
SCALE: $1'' = 1'$.
To study the qualitative and quantitative light conditions in a room, a model, accurate in dimension, color and surface reflection, was constructed. It could be illuminated by a sky dome, a mirror sky or an out-of-doors overcast sky.

In this test, an overcast sky was used, and the model was studied visually through a small aperture on one side of the room; readings were made at several dozen points with a selenium rectifier photocell mounted at the end of a long probe. The photocell was attached to a micrometer from which the light rating was read. If the quality or quantity of the light was not adequate, or if glare was excessive, the window wall and skylight could be rebuilt and tested until proper lighting was achieved. In the model depicted, the ceiling was constructed so as to be adjustable up and down to facilitate reconstruction.

SUN ORIENTATION MODELS

Models may be accurately used to test the shadows cast by parts of buildings and by landscaping. Block or final presentation models may be used with a spotlight representing the sun. The spot should have a parabolic reflector and a Fresnel lens so that it will produce light with parallel rays. 2 interesting devices that simplify sun testing are the Heliodon (21-2) and the Pleijel sundial (21-3).

The Heliodon consists of a small table that can be rotated about its horizontal and vertical axis. Adjustment about the horizontal axis is to compensate for the latitude at which the prototype building will be constructed. The vertical axis is adjusted to relate to the time of day. A light representing the sun is mounted on the post. By adjusting it up or down, the time of the year can be counterpoised.

The Pleijel sundial is utilized by being placed on the model in correct north orientation. The light source is manipulated so as to make the shadow cast by the post of the sundial correspond to the desired day and time of day on the chart of the sundial. Light falling on the model will then correspond to this desired time.

Testing of Interiors

Special areas such as schoolrooms, laboratories and art galleries are especially dependent on the correct engineering of their orientation and fenestration. Illustration 21-4 shows a typical model experiment being conducted with a $\frac{3}{4}''$ scale model.

QUANTITATIVE ANALYSIS OF INTERIORS

Detailed models may be used for precise photometric measuring to determine: placement of windows and skylights that will avoid glare; color schemes; effect of light reflection from 1 colored surface to another; effect of light reflected from sky, grass and other elements outside the building; and loss of color due to shadow. The high degree of accuracy that may be achieved allows the model to more than compete with expensive full-size mock-ups in the solving of pilot problems.

Sun and sky may be presented in 1 of 2 ways:

1. A Hemispherical Sky Dome

This is often used by a leader in model testing: the Texas Engineering Experiment Station (21-5A). Its interior is finished with a white reflecting material such as texture paint, having an 85% coefficient of reflectivity. It is indirectly illuminated. The model is placed at the center of the dome with its floor below the horizon of the dome. This makes for a more naturally illuminated model ceiling, at the expense, however, of a less naturally illuminated rear wall. An artificial sky can only illuminate the ceiling of a model directly, and not indirectly, too, by bouncing its light from ground or floor· as does the real sky; hence the need to lower the test model.

To simulate an overcast sky, lighting of 100′ lamberts is created at the horizon and 250′ lamberts at the zenith of the dome.

To simulate a clear sky, intensities of 200 and 100′ lamberts are used. When testing under conditions of direct sunlight, the model is first tested in the dome and then removed from the dome and subjected, while in a darkened room, to the light from a spot. Readings obtained from these 2 types of tests are combined and the results tabulated. The reflection caused in the prototype by the ground is sometimes simulated on the model by back lighting a translucent baseboard. This allows the model to be mounted at the horizon line of the dome.

2. A Mirror Sky Setup (21-5B)

This is a more accurate way to represent a natural sky, especially when it is used to illuminate the model of a room that gets its light from a side window. The sky is a mirror-lined box from the top of which is hung a ceiling of white translucent diffuser material backed by rows of lights. This simulates a bright overcast sky (which is the minimum natural light condition to confront a building).

In general, since use of the real sky for model illumination is not considered consistently dependable, it is seldom used.

The modeled room, to be tested, is divided into an imaginary grid, and light measurements are taken at each of the intersecting points. If the room is an office or school, the measurements are taken on horizontal surfaces; if it is an art gallery, on vertical surfaces. Models may be as small as $\frac{1}{2}″ = 1′$ if limitations in the size of the artificial sky require this. More often, they are at a $\frac{3}{4}″ = 1′$ scale to allow more accurate light measurements. At the latter scale, error usually runs from 0 to 15% and averages under 5% if the reflectivity of the future landscape is known.

Interior surfaces should be exactly located, and they should all have the same reflectance as the prototype. This is accomplished by painting them an appropriate value of gray. All detail need not be shown, only that which affects reflectance is necessary. Windows must be glazed with glass or similar transmission factor material. For accurate testing, the windows must have mullions or a factor to compensate for the lack of mullions must be used. Terrain conditions also influence the amount of light reflected into the model. Thus a representation of about 100′ of ground is constructed with the model. Grass is often assumed to possess a 6% reflectance coefficient.

Photoelectric cells, some as small as 3″ in diameter by $\frac{1}{2}″$ in thickness, record the quantitative light intensity. They can be permanently mounted

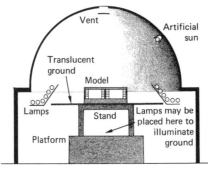

(A) THE ARTIFICIAL SKY

Vent
Artificial sun
Translucent ground
Model
Lamps
Stand
Lamps may be placed here to illuminate ground
Platform

(B) THE MIRROR SKY

Mirrors were placed around the entire perimeter of the box
Lamps
White diffuser material
Model
Window of model
Ground

21-6/21-7/21-8

Project: **DOBELL HOUSE, OTTAWA, CANADA.**

Designed by: Hugh Hardy, and Schoeler, Barkam and Heaton.
Modelbuilder: Hugh Hardy.
Photographer: Gil Amiaga, New York City.
Scale: over-all model, $1/4″ = 1′$.
The over-all model was made to study the massing of the building. The model of the summerhouse was made to study the light that was admitted by the windows and skylights. Model was built from cardboard. Ground contours were made of spackle-painted cardboard. Windows were painted on, with Zip-a-Tone stripping for mullions. Trees were represented by lengths of stripwood.
All photos were taken with a $8″ \times 10″$ Deardorff camera and Royal Pan film.

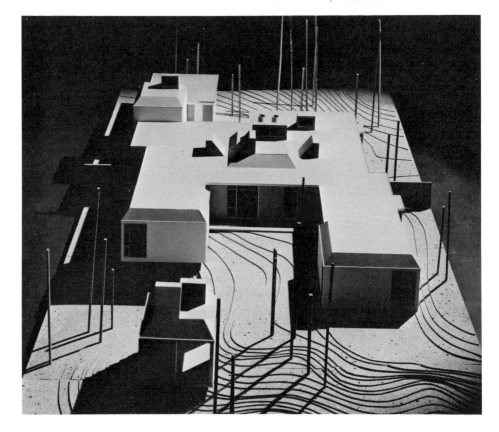

at specific locations in the model or on a movable probe. The walls and ceiling of the model may be movable to facilitate the testing of alternate solutions.

QUALITATIVE ANALYSIS

To be adequate for qualitative analysis, a model must be built at between $\frac{1}{4}$ and 1/20 of the size of the prototype. If it is too small, significant detail will be lost; too large and it will seem to be a small room and not a model. The model is best viewed from a hole cut in its floor; this permits one to stick one's head inside the model and to see the entire room by turning around. Viewing holes cut into walls or looking in through a window is less satisfactory. The interior of the model will appear more realistic if viewed with 1 eye closed through a weak (2 diopter) convex lens. Closing one eye will eliminate the normal stereopticon effect, created by both eyes, that contributes to the miniature look of a model. The lens aids the eye in adjusting to the short viewing distance.

Occasionally, a highly individualistic design may be studied in model form for the effects that will be achieved with skylights or atypical windows. Illustrations 21-6 and 21-7 show 2 partial models that were constructed to give a rough idea of the quality of the light admitted by skylights.

Artificial lighting is almost never accurately studied in model form. Bulbs are hard to duplicate at small scales, since, to be really accurate, both globe and filament size must be scaled down. Lighting fixtures are also rarely studied in miniature form because of the problems of duplication and because it is often less expensive to build them in full-size mock-up than to attempt to construct them as models.

ACOUSTICAL TEST MODELS

Rooms in which acoustics play an important role—auditoriums, theaters and conference rooms —may be tested in model form to determine their best shape, location, shape of necessary sound baffles, wall, ceiling and floor surfacing. Models are made to the scale of about 1:10 which allows for accurate measurements of the degree of sound absorption and reflection and of the time it takes for sound to reverberate. Tests have also been performed on models of streets to determine the noise level that will be encountered in the surrounding buildings.

To provide acoustical similitude between model and prototype, not only the linear dimensions of the model must be reduced but the wave length and time scale of the sound as well. Thus, if the model is at a 1:25 scale and it is necessary to test the reaction caused by a 500 cycle per second sound, a 12,000 cycle per second sound must be broadcast into the model. Sound produced by a white noise generator is filtered, amplified and broadcast into the model at the desired point. Sound readings are taken from a sound level meter connected to a microphone placed at desired points in the model.

FIRE PROPAGATION TEST MODELS

Several testing laboratories have tried to use models to aid in the formulation of theories about the growth of flames, fires and heat transfer, in connection with such influencing factors as wind, window areas, shape and size of structure and the amount of combustible material involved. Results have not been impressive because of the several, and often mutually contradictory, criteria of similarity that must be achieved between model and prototype.

Tests on models of small assemblies—walls, floors, etc.—to study their fire resistance are more successful because of an absence of contradictory similitude criteria.

21-9

SKYLIGHT DESIGN STUDIED ON A MODEL.

SCALE: $1'' = 1'$.
The model was used for a general study of the light conditions that would be encountered in the summer-house. The model was made of cardboard, with windows of acrylic and mullions of stripwood. Art work was cut from magazine illustrations. The sculpture was made from a Japanese puzzle.

DETAIL VISUALIZATION MODELS

Often it is worthwhile to build models of small portions of a design to aid in the visualization of important or complex detailing. The aircraft, automobile and appliance industries make extensive use of full-size mock-ups made from easy-to-work nonprototype materials. These mock-ups allow full-size equipment to be put into place, and clearances and details studied. Ships are often modeled at such large scales as 1:10 to allow for detailed investigation of all their parts.

Full-size mock-ups of window walls, windows, grills or custom-made wall textures are sometimes made by the modelbuilding shop from easy-to fabricate materials. The appearance of these assemblies, including the shadows which they cast, are studied, and any needed modifications made. Illustrations 21-10 and 21-11 show 2 typical window wall mock-ups. Illustration 21-12 shows a 1:10 scale study model of a window wall.

Structural engineers and, more infrequently, steel detailers also employ detailed models, in full or partial size, to visualize complex intersections. Illustrations 21-14 and 21-15 show several of the hundreds of cardboard and wood models that were made of the intersections of the steel work of the Sugar Grove radio telescope. Models of this type are quite frequently used to study intersections of geodesic structures and new fabricating systems.

Models may also be used to test the practicality of welding reinforcing bar intersections in shell concrete structures; these tests can determine

21-10

A FULL SIZE MOCK-UP.

PROJECT: Franklin Bank, Roosevelt Field Shopping Center.
DESIGNED BY: I. M. Pei and Associates.
MODELBUILDER: the architect's captive model shop.
PHOTOGRAPHER: Acker Photo Service.
This mock-up served as an aid in the study of the shadows cast by various parts of the facade and helped to explain the design to contractors.
Construction was made of wood, the section hung on a metal pipe scaffold.

21-11
FULL SIZE MOCK-UP OF A SPANDREL.

PROJECT: Place Ville Marie.
DESIGNED BY: I. M. Pei and Associates.
MODELBUILDER AND PHOTOGRAPHER: the architect's captive model shop.
The entire mock-up was constructed of wood except for the glazing. Window frame section detail was painted on.
The mock-up was used to study waterproofing problems and the general appearance of detail.

21-12
LARGE-SCALE MOCK-UP.

DESIGNED BY: Friedrich Wilhelm Kraemer.
SCALE: 1:10.
This mock-up was made to study the appearance of the window wall and its relation to columns, radiators and ceiling finishes. Walls, floors and mullions were made of wood; glass was represented by acrylic; brickwork pattern was drafted on paper.

21-13/21-14/21-15
GEOMETRIC VISUALIZATION MODELS USED BY STRUCTURAL ENGINEERS.

PROJECT: Radio telescope at Sugar Grove, West Virginia.
DESIGNED BY: Ammann and Whitney, consulting engineers.
Sometimes, when intersections are extremely complex, the structural engineer will resort to studying his design with the aid of geometric models. This radio telescope, due to its unprecedented size, created engineering problems that had never been faced by engineers.
The over-all model was used: 1) to present the design to Congress; 2) for publicity; 3) to aid visualization of the structure by engineer and contractor; and 4) for wind testing.
The pine, plywood, balsa and cardboard models of intersections that are illustrated are some of the more than 200 such models made by the engineer's staff to study the layout of intersections.

21-12

21-11

21-13

21-14

21-15

21-11
FULL SIZE MOCK-UP OF A SPANDREL.

PROJECT: Place Ville Marie.
DESIGNED BY: I. M. Pei and Associates.
MODELBUILDER AND PHOTOGRAPHER: the architect's captive model shop.
The entire mock-up was constructed of wood except for the glazing. Window frame section detail was painted on.
The mock-up was used to study waterproofing problems and the general appearance of detail.

21-12
LARGE-SCALE MOCK-UP.

DESIGNED BY: Friedrich Wilhelm Kraemer.
SCALE: 1:10.
This mock-up was made to study the appearance of the window wall and its relation to columns, radiators and ceiling finishes. Walls, floors and mullions were made of wood; glass was represented by acrylic; brickwork pattern was drafted on paper.

21-13/21-14/21-15
GEOMETRIC VISUALIZATION MODELS USED BY STRUCTURAL ENGINEERS.

PROJECT: Radio telescope at Sugar Grove, West Virginia.
DESIGNED BY: Ammann and Whitney, consulting engineers.
Sometimes, when intersections are extremely complex, the structural engineer will resort to studying his design with the aid of geometric models. This radio telescope, due to its unprecedented size, created engineering problems that had never been faced by engineers.
The over-all model was used: 1) to present the design to Congress; 2) for publicity; 3) to aid visualization of the structure by engineer and contractor; and 4) for wind testing.
The pine, plywood, balsa and cardboard models of intersections that are illustrated are some of the more than 200 such models made by the engineer's staff to study the layout of intersections.

21-11

21-12

21-13

21-14

21-15

at specific locations in the model or on a movable probe. The walls and ceiling of the model may be movable to facilitate the testing of alternate solutions.

QUALITATIVE ANALYSIS

To be adequate for qualitative analysis, a model must be built at between $\frac{1}{4}$ and 1/20 of the size of the prototype. If it is too small, significant detail will be lost; too large and it will seem to be a small room and not a model. The model is best viewed from a hole cut in its floor; this permits one to stick one's head inside the model and to see the entire room by turning around. Viewing holes cut into walls or looking in through a window is less satisfactory. The interior of the model will appear more realistic if viewed with 1 eye closed through a weak (2 diopter) convex lens. Closing one eye will eliminate the normal stereopticon effect, created by both eyes, that contributes to the miniature look of a model. The lens aids the eye in adjusting to the short viewing distance.

Occasionally, a highly individualistic design may be studied in model form for the effects that will be achieved with skylights or atypical windows. Illustrations 21-6 and 21-7 show 2 partial models that were constructed to give a rough idea of the quality of the light admitted by skylights.

Artificial lighting is almost never accurately studied in model form. Bulbs are hard to duplicate at small scales, since, to be really accurate, both globe and filament size must be scaled down. Lighting fixtures are also rarely studied in miniature form because of the problems of duplication and because it is often less expensive to build them in full-size mock-up than to attempt to construct them as models.

ACOUSTICAL TEST MODELS

Rooms in which acoustics play an important role—auditoriums, theaters and conference rooms —may be tested in model form to determine their best shape, location, shape of necessary sound baffles, wall, ceiling and floor surfacing. Models are made to the scale of about 1 : 10 which allows for accurate measurements of the degree of sound absorption and reflection and of the time it takes for sound to reverberate. Tests have also been performed on models of streets to determine the noise level that will be encountered in the surrounding buildings.

To provide acoustical similitude between model and prototype, not only the linear dimensions of the model must be reduced but the wave length and time scale of the sound as well. Thus, if the model is at a 1 : 25 scale and it is necessary to test the reaction caused by a 500 cycle per second sound, a 12,000 cycle per second sound must be broadcast into the model. Sound produced by a white noise generator is filtered, amplified and broadcast into the model at the desired point. Sound readings are taken from a sound level meter connected to a microphone placed at desired points in the model.

FIRE PROPAGATION TEST MODELS

Several testing laboratories have tried to use models to aid in the formulation of theories about the growth of flames, fires and heat transfer, in connection with such influencing factors as wind, window areas, shape and size of structure and the amount of combustible material involved. Results have not been impressive because of the several, and often mutually contradictory, criteria of similarity that must be achieved between model and prototype.

Tests on models of small assemblies—walls, floors, etc.—to study their fire resistance are more successful because of an absence of contradictory similitude criteria.

21-9

SKYLIGHT DESIGN STUDIED ON A MODEL.

SCALE: $1'' = 1'$.
The model was used for a general study of the light conditions that would be encountered in the summer-house. The model was made of cardboard, with windows of acrylic and mullions of stripwood. Art work was cut from magazine illustrations. The sculpture was made from a Japanese puzzle.

DETAIL VISUALIZA-TION MODELS

Often it is worthwhile to build models of small portions of a design to aid in the visualization of important or complex detailing. The aircraft, automobile and appliance industries make extensive use of full-size mock-ups made from easy-to-work nonprototype materials. These mock-ups allow full-size equipment to be put into place, and clearances and details studied. Ships are often modeled at such large scales as 1:10 to allow for detailed investigation of all their parts.

Full-size mock-ups of window walls, windows, grills or custom-made wall textures are sometimes made by the modelbuilding shop from easy-to-fabricate materials. The appearance of these assemblies, including the shadows which they cast, are studied, and any needed modifications made. Illustrations 21-10 and 21-11 show 2 typical window wall mock-ups. Illustration 21-12 shows a 1:10 scale study model of a window wall.

Structural engineers and, more infrequently, steel detailers also employ detailed models, in full or partial size, to visualize complex intersections. Illustrations 21-14 and 21-15 show several of the hundreds of cardboard and wood models that were made of the intersections of the steel work of the Sugar Grove radio telescope. Models of this type are quite frequently used to study intersections of geodesic structures and new fabricating systems.

Models may also be used to test the practicality of welding reinforcing bar intersections in shell concrete structures; these tests can determine

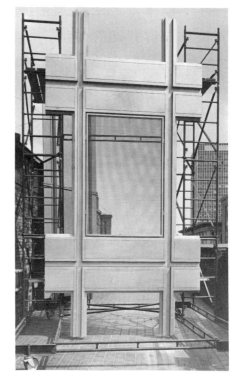

21-10

A FULL SIZE MOCK-UP.

PROJECT: Franklin Bank, Roosevelt Field Shopping Center.
DESIGNED BY: I. M. Pei and Associates.
MODELBUILDER: the architect's captive model shop.
PHOTOGRAPHER: Acker Photo Service.
This mock-up served as an aid in the study of the shadows cast by various parts of the facade and helped to explain the design to contractors.
Construction was made of wood, the section hung on a metal pipe scaffold.

whether or not the bars will interfere with the structure as it develops its intended curved shape.

Illustration 15-19 shows framing study models constructed by the architects of a school building to aid them in estimating the relationship of the building skeleton to its walls.

The complexities of mechanical equipment duct work and piping sometimes necessitate a model to aid the architect in determining relationships. Illustration 21-16 shows such a model of a fairly simple solution.

LOGISTICAL MODELS

While the use of models to show the placement of materials and equipment at a building site is not frequent, models are sometimes made of new erection systems to aid in briefing contractors and workers (21-17). Illustrations 21-18 and 21-19 show a 4-stage model used by a boiler manufacturer to demonstrate to potential customers the installation of his product.

Economic cutting and filling may be quickly planned if one: (1) constructs a box the outline of which is similar to that of the site; (2) erects stripwood posts (every few inches on center) the heights of which represent the existing grade; (3) fills the box to the top of the posts with sand; and (4) experiments with moving the sand around until a practical solution is reached.

21-16

21-16

A MECHANICAL EQUIPMENT STUDY MODEL.

PROJECT: Science building No. 2 at the New Paltz New York College of the State University of New York.

DESIGNED BY: Davis, Brody and Associates.

MODELBUILDER AND PHOTOGRAPHERS: members of the architect's staff.

SCALE: 1/4″ = 1′.

This partial model, which was used in conjunction with those shown in illustrations 15-3 and 15-4, was built to study the relationships of air conditioning ducts, gas and air lines and water pipes. Each was represented by bars or dowels. Colored tapes, on the floor, showed lines of pedestrian circulation.

21-17

MODEL USED TO STUDY AND DEMONSTRATE A NEW CONSTRUCTION TECHNIQUE.

PROJECT: prestressed beam erection method devised by Alfred A. Yee and Associates, Inc., Structural Engineers, Honolulu, Hawaii.

MODELBUILDER: scale models by Morse (a professional modelbuilder).

SCALE: about 1/4″ = 1′.

21-18/21-19

A DEMONSTRATION MODEL.

PROJECT: a series of demonstration models constructed for the Federal Boiler Company.

MODELBUILDER: William Tanguay Associates, Inc. (a professional modelbuilder).

PHOTOGRAPHER: William Tanguay.

SCALE: exterior scene: 1/4″ = 1′.
     interior scenes: 1/2″ = 1′.

This grouping of models demonstrates to prospective purchasers the installation of Federal's product. The model, consisting of 4 parts, was mounted on a plywood turntable. Walls were made of Masonite, the rough side facing out. People were cast from metal, the boiler was made from sheet metal, boiler tubes were soda straws.

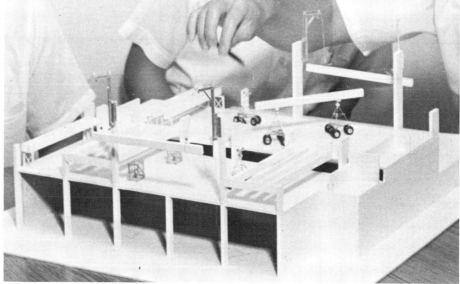

21-17

21-18   21-19

The following 2 pictures are of structural visualization models. These are used exclusively for the aesthetic study of the structure of a building, and should not be confused with the models depicted and described in Chapter 22, which are used for the physical testing of structural solutions.

Another type of visualization model is used in some architectual schools, notably Harvard, to teach basic structural and mechanical concepts. Lenox Industries manufactures several dozen of these models including ones that demonstrate: torsion, deflection, slenderness ratio, effects of end conditions on columns, bearing capacity, etc. These models give good graphic demonstrations of what happens within the members of a structure as it is loaded.

22-1

STRUCTURAL STUDY MODEL.

PROJECT: North Shore Congregation Israel, Glencoe, Illinois.

DESIGNED BY: Minoru Yamasaki and Associates.

MODELBUILDERS: members of the architect's staff.

SCALE: 3/8″ = 1′.

Model was built to study the placement of struts within vaults and the skylights between them. Vaults were made from basswood strips and Masonite.

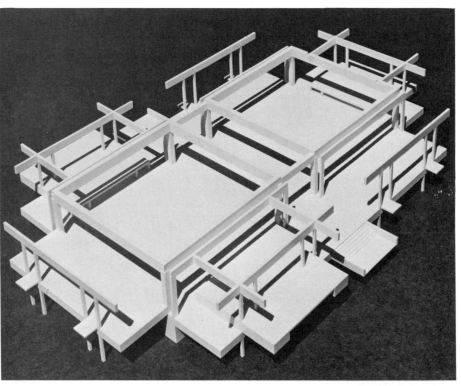

22-2

STRUCTURE STUDY MODEL.

PROJECT: Congregation Agudath Sholom, Stamford, Connecticut.

DESIGNED BY: Davis, Brody and Wisniewski.

MODELBUILDER AND PHOTOGRAPHER: Cyril Beveridge.

SCALE: 1/8″ = 1′.

This model was first used to study the structure and duct arrangement of the building. The outside walls, roof and other details were then added to make a presentation model. Acrylic was used throughout.

The photograph was taken out of doors with a reflex camera.

22 STRUCTURAL TEST MODELS

The use of models for structural testing is burgeoning. Engineers are being forced by the many new and highly complex structures to turn to models as a companion tool for the mathematical analysis of the strength and stiffness of their structures. The architectural student, of late, is being exposed more and more to laboratory work on model testing as many universities try to re-relate architectural design to structural engineering. The model serves this function well by presenting the visually oriented architectural student with a vivid picture, one which will, hopefully, develop his intuitive judgment regarding structural action.

Structural model testing can bridge some of the knowledge gap between the assumed and actual forces acting on a structure. It is especially useful in the study of forces acting in 3 dimension and in the study of the change in shape of a structure which results from its being loaded.

In the design of some types of structures, models and mathematics share the design burden with each other. With other structures, models must be used to obtain almost all the information; but even in these instances the engineer usually makes occasional spot mathematical checks. In some European countries, Portugal, for instance, construction codes accept designs created exclusively with models. Because models never provide more than a close approximation of the prototype, exact analogies may not be made. Inaccuracies may be due to errors in testing techniques or even to sloppiness expected from field construction of the prototype.

Much of the experimental work with models is being done in well-endowed universities in the attempt to solve new structural problems and to devise mathematical formulas for them. Knowledge gained of testing techniques will make widespread testing, by the individual engineer and testing laboratory, more feasible economically. Experimentation will also develop ways of replacing the testing of full-size or large-scale mock-ups with that of small-scale models. This will produce design cost savings that, in some cases, may encourage engineers to test several solutions for the price of just 1 large-scale test.

SHORTCOMINGS OF MATHEMATICAL ANALYSIS

The use of models is to a large extent necessitated by the present shortcomings of mathematical analysis:

1—Formulas are often based on an oversimplification of what is happening in the structure; minor forces are often ignored.

2—To compensate for the differences between actual conditions and mathematical assumptions of what the conditions are, various large safety factors must be used to achieve conservative analysis. Thus, for example, "lightness," which many designers strive to achieve through the use of minimal materials may well prove impossible.

3—Many complex structural problems cannot be solved with conventional, available formulas. Other structures require large amounts of time for the resolution of their parts into solvable units. Electronic computers have helped to solve these problems to a great degree; models, however, are sometimes used as a check on computers.

Structures with inherently difficult problems include: umbrella structures, complex shells, space frames, domes, inflated structures, hyperboloid shells, geodesic and lamella structures, folded plates and suspended roofs.

4—When solving a complete structure by resolving it into parts and analyzing these separately, the fact that other parts of the structure aid the part being tested is usually overlooked. Through the use of models, entire structures can be analyzed at once.

These 4 shortcomings of mathematical analysis can, in many cases, be overcome through the use of model testing in combination with mathematical computation.

RESISTANCE TO THE USE OF MODELS

1—Since it is more costly to use models than to rely on simplified calculations, with their inflated safety factors, engineers find that fees do not usually allow for model study. The architect should attempt to have the cost of model testing included in his fee on all commissions that result in unusual structures. The cost of the model can often be made up by eventual savings in construction costs.

2—Some engineers are reluctant to accept the results of model testing, since tests often suggest the use of lighter structures than those to which they have been accustomed.

This chapter is meant as a brief resume of what can be achieved through the use of models; it is not meant to encourage architects to construct test models, since this can be done successfully by only a relatively small number of engineers and testing laboratories.

22-3

STRUCTURAL TESTS BEING PERFORMED WITH THE AID OF STRAIN GAUGES.
PROJECT: The Kodak Pavilion at the 1964–65 New York World's Fair.
DESIGNED BY: Kahn and Jacobs and Will Burton, Inc.
ENGINEER: Lev Zetlin.
MODELBUILDER: Wiss, Janney Associates, structural engineers.
SCALE: 1:64.
Model testing was necessitated by the complexity of this shell concrete roof structure. The model was made from methyl mathacrilate. This material allows testing, performed within its elastic limits, to be accurately measured. Columns (not visible) were seated in plaster of Paris, and the entire assembly was mounted on a rigid base. The black line along the edge of the model was tape, which insured an airtight seal.
Loads were simulated by creating a vacuum below the model.
Rosettes of SR-4 strain gauges were applied to both top and bottom surfaces. Single or pairs of SR-4 gauges were attached to the supports of the structure to determine reactions the directions of which were known. A dial indicator gauge (with 1/1000" accuracy) was employed to measure deflection. The photograph shows it in place to measure horizontal deflection. It was also used to gauge vertical movement. Deflection ran from 1/25" to 1/50".

WHAT MODEL TESTS CAN SHOW

Models may be used for qualitative analysis—the appraisal of basic deformations, rotations and modes of failures. Some types of models may be used for quantitative analysis—the accurate measurement of these factors.

Testing can be used to determine force distribution, reaction to vibration, deflection, reaction to the application of prestressing, the existence of unusual boundary conditions, buckling, shrinkage and creep effects, compression, tension, shear, and, if micro materials are used, the ultimate strength and nature of failure may also be investigated.

TEST TECHNIQUES

Direct Testing Technique

Direct measurement testing of strain is used to study conditions within elastic or inelastic ranges or to determine ultimate strength. Models used with the direct testing method must be constructed to exact shape, or they may be slightly simplified.

STRAIN GAUGES AND MEASURING TOOLS

Strain may be measured with electrical resistance strain gauges that consist of fine wires cemented to the model. As the model is subjected to loading and its resulting strain, the wires are also strained. This changes the area of their cross section and, in turn, changes their electrical resistance; the latter is read on an instrument that translates electrical readings into strain readings. Single strain gauges applied in the direction of the stress are used to measure bending or axial load on the surface of beams, columns or truss members. Two gauges oriented in the direction of the stresses are used to measure the action of plate or shell structures when the direction of the prin-

cipal stresses is known. Three gauges coupled together are used to measure the action in a plate or shell subject to bending or axial load in several directions.

In addition to gauges, linear differential transformers or precision levels may be used to measure deflection. Illustration 22-3 shows 1 assembly of electrical resistance strain gauges and a dial gauge used to measure horizontal deflection.

BRITTLE LACQUER COATINGS

Certain lacquers may be applied to modeled and full-size structural components made from deformable material. When the member is loaded, the lacquer will crack. These fissures give good indications of the direction and magnitude of stresses and aid the engineer in determining where to put his strain gauges for quantitative analysis.

The magnitude of strain may also be measured directly from the amount of cracking. First, the number of cracks formed due to a given amount of deformation must be ascertained, then the cracks formed by succeeding tests can be counted. Comparing the number of cracks on the control test to the number in the latter tests can determine approximate stresses and their direction.

To test for tension, the model is painted with lacquer before it is loaded. To test for compression, the model is first loaded, then, while the load is still in place, painted with lacquer. Once it has dried, the load is removed and cracks representing compression will appear.

Indirect Testing Technique

A second way of obtaining information is to keep loading a model until a desired deformation occurs in 1 place. The resulting deformations in other parts of the structure are then measured to obtain the internal forces and moments and the external redundant forces and moments. The indirect method can only be used to study the behavior of a structure within its elastic range. Models built for this technique are distorted: different scales are used in their lateral and longitudinal measurements.

Dividing Complex Structures into Parts

Large repetitive structures may sometimes be modeled and tested in part and the results applied to the over-all structure. This requires preliminary investigation to determine whether or not the part selected is truly representative of the total assembly.

Accuracy

Accuracy of measurement of the reactions of the model may approach 1% in some quantitative tests, though many engineers are satisfied to achieve 5 to 10%. These results must then be translated into what may be expected of the prototype. This translation can also be highly accurate. Problems may be encountered in certain areas of each test which might negate the results of that part of the test without affecting the value of the over-all experiment.

Similitude

Models must be similar to the prototype in geometry, load distribution and response. If the model is being investigated within its elastic range, its Poisson ratio should be similar to that of the prototype. Each material, and its means of attachment to the model, must relate to the physics of the prototype. The engineer should design his model and its test with the same degree of intuition and judgment as he would use for the structure itself.

If the model is being investigated beyond its elastic range and up to its ultimate strength, as can be done with models made from micro materials, the deformation and strength characteristics of these materials must be similar to those of the prototype. Both materials must have stress/strain curves that can be related to one another by formula.

If the deformation produced by any test is large enough to influence the behavior of the structure, the strain scale of the 2 materials' stress/strain curves must be exactly equal.

Loading the Model

Uniform loads may be conveniently represented on the model by concentrated loads produced by weights, by vacuum pressure or by the pressure exerted through expanded air bags. Uniform loads caused by body forces may also be created by swinging the model in a centrifuge. Sometimes additional weights must be placed on a model to compensate for the lack of deadweight of the model material.

Types of Model Tests

As with many other human endeavors, model testing has been subject to fads. These are perhaps symptomatic of the newness of this evolving field. In the 30's, emphasis was placed on photoelastic testing; the next decade saw a shift of emphasis to strain gauge analysis. In the 50's, much use was made of brittle lacquer coatings of micro assemblies and brush-on photoelastic coatings placed on scaled down and full-size structural components. In the 60's, moiré fringe, 3-dimensional photoelastic and grid studies have been widely used.

ANALYSIS OF PLASTIC MODELS

The behavior of structures within their elastic limits may be quantitatively and qualitatively analyzed with the use of small-scale models made from nonprototype materials. Materials used, however, must be homogeneous and isotropic. The most popular of these materials are acrylic, polystyrene, vinyl, castable Epoxy resin and ethyl cellulose (aluminum, brass and steel are used infrequently for this type of elastic analysis). The response of plastics to tests is sufficiently accurate and their machining and forming sufficiently simple as to make them acceptable test subjects. Vacuum-forming, casting and machining are used to form the model. Sometimes these small-scale plastic models are preliminarily used to ascertain basic deflection in a structure. Subsequently, more elaborate models are constructed of micro materials or nonprototype plastic materials, and precisely tested.

ANALYSIS OF MODELS MADE FROM MICRO MATERIALS

A greater number of stresses and conditions can be analyzed on models that are made from scaled down prototype materials than on models made of plastic. These scale materials, referred to as "micro materials," must have characteristics that are quite similar to those of the prototype.

Micro materials must have a stress/strain curve similar to that of the prototype material. If the curves are similar in shape, they can be nearly equalized by applying a factor to the 2 axes of the curve obtained by the model test. This will convert the model test results into those that would be encountered on the prototype structure. Prototype materials and the model materials which may be used for duplication are:

Timber

This is extremely difficult to duplicate because of its cell and knot structure. Balsa has been used for small (1:30 to 1:20) scale models. The wood of the actual structure can be used on larger (1:5 scale or so) models. Scale pins are used to represent nails.

Reinforced Concrete

Cement mortar with scaled down aggregates is perhaps the most similar material that can be found, but its slow drying time makes its use inconvenient. Dental plaster, because of its very high tensile strength, may be used on ultimate load tests. Ultracal 30 gypsum plaster, with aggregates represented by crushed limestone and sand, is often used. Reinforcements may be made from wire mesh and threaded or deformed mild steel rods. Models have been constructed at a 1:5 to 1:15 scale with mock-ups of single beams and struts sometimes made at a larger scale. Future developments in testing may allow models as small as 1:50 to be employed.

Steel

Phosphor bronze is often used.

A difficulty that hampers the selection of any micro material is that the yield point of any material increases as the size of its parts decreases. This affects shear, compression, tension and other yield points. Sometimes the deflection that would result in a model is so slight that it is difficult to measure. This is one of the factors that encourages the use of models made of plastic. Plastics with their smaller moduli of elasticity (and greater deflection) are especially useful in the making of small-scale models.

PHOTOELASTIC ANALYSIS OF PLASTIC MODELS

Photoelastic analysis, unlike strain gauge analysis, allows one to view an optical pattern that is directly related to stress or strain acting along all parts of a structural member. It shows in their entirety, however, only those stresses which occur on the surface of the model. A model of the structure to be tested is constructed in a suitable transparent material such as gelatin, Epoxy resin or acrylic.

3-dimensional models are loaded and then heated to increase their deformation. Upon cooling, the stress is "frozen" into a still-loaded model. A section or slab is then cut from the model and viewed in a polariscope. Polarized light passing through the specimen will reveal a pattern of light and dark areas called fringes. This fringe pattern is caused by reorientation of the molecules of the model.

The relative magnitude of stress may be established by counting the fringe changes in each part of the model as it is slowly loaded; also, the magnitude may be vividly seen as colored patterns, if one uses a white light in the polariscope. The results of photoelastic tests may vary slightly between the prototype and the model because of the differences between the Poisson ratio of the model and that of the prototype material.

Illustration 22-4A shows a diagram of the components of a transmission polariscope; illustration 22-4B shows the components of a reflecting polariscope. The former is restricted for use with single plane models or sliced stress, frozen models; the latter can be used to study coatings on actual structures or models.

Illustration 22-6 shows the fringes formed on a loaded gelatin model of an earth trench. Illustrations 22-7, 22-8, 22-9A, and 22-10A are of photoelastically tested small-scale Epoxy models of a cylindrical shell and of a flat plate. Gelatin blocks are sometimes used to test simple shapes. The gelatin may be loaded, then frozen, and the loads removed and the object viewed while still frozen; or it may be viewed unfrozen while still loaded.

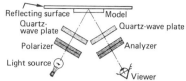

(A)THE TRANSMISSION POLARISCOPE   22-4

(B) THE REFLECTING POLARISCOPE

Reflecting surface   Model
Quartz-
wave plate   Quartz-wave plate

Polarizer   Analyzer

Light source

Viewer

22-5

THE TRANSMISSION POLARISCOPE OF PRINCETON UNIVERSITY'S ARCHITECTURAL LABORATORY.

The components of polariscope, designed by Dr. Robert Mark, are, from left to right, a view camera (that can be removed to permit direct observation), a Polaroid analyzer, a model table, a polarizer and a light source box.

22-6

POLARISCOPE ANALYSIS OF A GELATIN MODEL OF AN EARTH CUT.

The model was constructed and tested at the Princeton University Architectural Laboratory under the supervision of Professors Robert Mark and Roland Richards, Jr.
The photograph, which was taken through the polariscope, shows the fringes formed by stresses throughout the model. The cross grid was imbedded within the gelatin. Its distortion provides additional information about the forces at work in the cut. The 2 black strips in the cut were made by calibration tape.

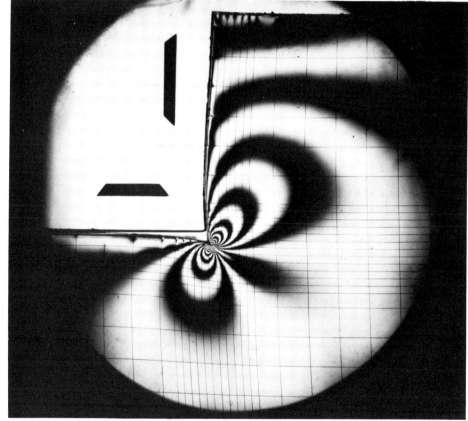

22-7/22-8

POLARISCOPE ANALYSIS OF A VAULT.

The model was constructed and tested at the Princeton University Architectural Laboratory under the supervision of Professor Robert Mark. The model of this end-supported thin cylindrical shell was machined from Epoxy. Construction and testing procedures were similar to those used with the flat plate floor system (see illustration 22-9). The second photograph was made of the fringe pattern observed through the surface of 1/2 the structure.

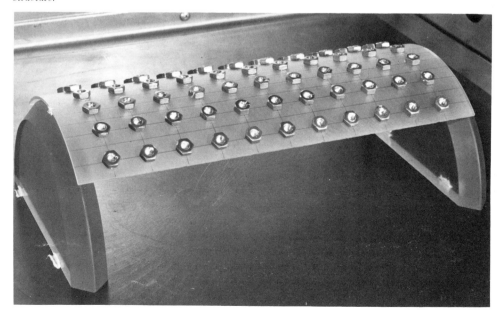

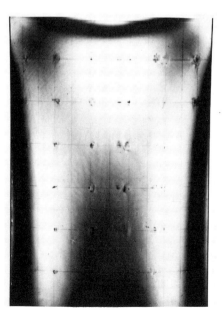

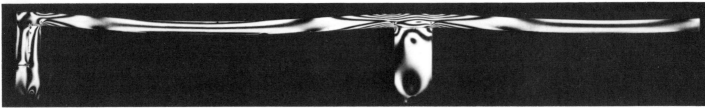

22-9A/22-10A

POLARISCOPE ANALYSIS OF A FLAT PLATE FLOOR SYSTEM.

The model was constructed and tested at the Princeton University Architectural Laboratory under the supervision of Professor Robert Mark. SCALE: 1:48.

The model was machined from Epoxy. Column stubs were supported on ball bearings to allow free end rotation. Loading was simulated by bolts; the model was then heated to 300°F and allowed to cool slowly with the loads still in place. This froze the stress into the plastic. Sections were then cut from the model; their edges were polished on a milling machine with care taken not to overheat the plastic and disturb the internal stresses. The sections were analyzed and photographed in a transmission polariscope. Illustration 22-10A is how one of the fringe patterns appears through the polariscope. The fringes relate to the internal stresses throughout the slice.

Photoelastic Coatings

Certain aluminum coatings can be painted or cemented on modeled or full-scale structural parts, or the part can be polished. This creates a reflective surface that is then coated with a bire-fringent material. The structure is then loaded and studied through a reflecting polariscope. The stressed birefringent material will reflect a colored fringe pattern. By comparing each color, quantitative stress measurements can be made.

MOIRÉ GRID ANALYSIS

If a simple grid pattern is viewed through a transparent sheet on which another grid pattern has been printed, a third pattern or fringe will be seen to form. This can be tested with 2 sheets of Zip-a-Tone. Fringe results from the interrelationship of the two grids. If one of the grids were to be rotated, new fringes would form. Moiré grid testing makes use of this phenomena. It may be used in the investigation of plates or sections of more complex structural components. 1 grid is photographically imprinted on the surface of the model, another grid printed on a transparent sheet and held against that surface. The moiré fringe, caused by the deformation of the model, forms when the model is loaded. Strains involved can be found from an analysis of the pattern. An alternate procedure is to use only the first grid and create a fringe by photographing the unloaded model, then loading the model and rephotographing it on the same film with the camera in the same position.

By visually observing and counting the fringes as they form, it is possible to analyze qualitatively how the surface of the model became deformed as it was loaded.

GRID ANALYSIS

A 2- or 3-dimensional grid is placed into a model made from a highly deforming material. The distortion of the grid is physically measured when the model is loaded. Often the grid is used in a gelatin block model. Illustration 22-6 shows a grid that has been inserted into a gelatin model of an earth trench. The loading superimposed on the model has caused distortion, which is visible.

WIND LOAD STUDY

Sometimes a high building of unorthodox shape must be model tested to determine the wind loads or oscillations to which it will be subjected. The model is loaded with weights that represent live and dead loads. To simulate wind, strings are attached to its walls and pulled taut, or the model is placed in a wind tunnel. Wind pressure is calculated in pounds per square foot which relates to wind velocity: wind pressure $= 0.0026$ (wind velocity)^2. To determine wind loads on the prototype requires the model to be subjected to wind speeds in excess of the winds that would be encountered by the prototype. The air flow pattern around the model must be similar at all altitudes, however to that which is expected around the prototype. Wind gusts must also be accurately duplicated. Wind loading is applied from each angle that might affect the prototype. Deflection or strain is measured from the model.

Models may also be used to test qualitatively any flutter to which unconventional roof shapes may be subjected.

Another use of test models is in ascertaining the pressure that will be caused on a high building by prevailing winds. The building and all surrounding structures and landscaping must be accurately modeled and tested in a wind tunnel. Such tests will determine the pressure put on the

22-9

A WIND TEST MODEL.

PROJECT: The Verrazano Narrows Bridge, New York.
DESIGNED BY: Ammann and Whitney, consulting engineers.
MODELBUILDERS: Marvin Wolff and the Celodyne Corporation, Valley Stream, Long Island.
A model of a short section of the bridge was constructed and tested for aerodynamic stability in the pictured low velocity wind tunnel. Test conditions were scaled to the model. For instance, if the model had been built at 1:100 scale, the velocity and duration of wind applied would be 1/10th the full scale wind. Tests were accurate to within 10%.

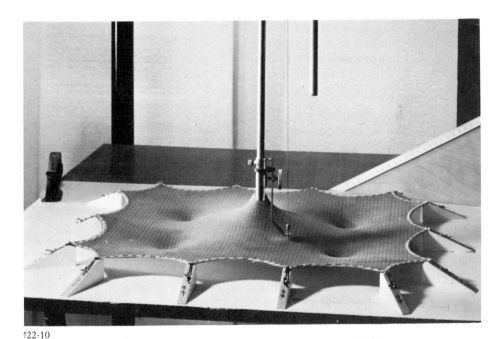

↑22-10

22-10/22-11/22-12

DESIGNING AND LAYING OUT A TENT STRUC-TURE WITH THE AID OF A MODEL, which, while not a true structural test model, is included in this chapter.

PROJECT: Orchestra Podium, Interban, Germany.
DESIGNED BY: Frei Otto and Ewald Bubner.
MODELBUILDERS: members of the architect's staff.
SCALE: 1/2″ = 1′.
The tent fabric was represented by a rubber sheet upon which a grid had been drawn. A hanging attachment held a gauge (see illustration 22-12) that measured the height of the tent as it stood unloaded or with weights on it that represented wind or water loads. The plumb line-like attachment (22-11) was connected to a pantograph machine which, when the plumb line was traced across the model, drew a contour map of the membrane. This drawing was used to aid the designer in laying out the canvas panels from which the final structure was built.

↓22-11

↓22-12

windows of the building. And this pressure must be taken into consideration when designing the window structure and its waterproofing.

MISCELLANEOUS USE

Models may also be used as starting points for some structural designs. Antonio Gaudi designed ceiling vaults on 1:10 models. He built these models upside down with cords to represent the struts of the vaults. The pull of gravity revealed the form that could best support the acting force vectors which were represented by hung weights. After establishing the best design on the model, the structure was mathematically checked.

MODELS OF RIVER SYSTEMS

Models are often employed by civil engineers in the planning of dams and bridges and in other situations where hydraulic design is an important factor. Huge models employing loose bed materials and water to are constructed of entire bay and harbor systems to study the causes of both currents and silting.

The shifting of land caused by flooding conditions is studied to see what effect it may have on bridge abutments. A model is made of a length of a river. Its horizontal scale, governed by cost considerations, may run between 1:100 to 1:300;

its vertical scale is exaggerated (being built in a 1:25 to 1:100 scale) to allow for a more rapid flow of water. Underlying earth contours are built from concrete; the final earth levels are built up of crushed anthracite or sand to simulate the movable river bed. Water is run over the bed at a controlled rate of flow to simulate various flood conditions. Currents are made visible by surface floating confetti or by injecting fluorescent dye below the surface of the water. After each experiment, a contour map is drawn to show changes in the river bed. A similitude must be maintained between model and prototype conditions. 1 test situation that comes to mind had a model of 1:120 horizontal and 1:36 vertical scale; the water velocity employed was 1:6; sand grain size was 1:3 and the time scale was 1:180.

23 SPECIAL MODELS

Various types of models usually found in museum and fair displays can be made by the designer to present certain aspects of his project. All of these types have a controlled viewpoint which makes them of use mostly in the depiction of interiors, gardens, building entrances and other parts of buildings.

PERSPECTIVE MODELS OR DIORAMAS

Dioramas are models that are meant to be viewed from 1 side. They are built in 1 or 2 point perspective; parts of the model closest to the viewing position are largest; other parts diminish in size up to the rear of the model, which is usually a painted backdrop on which the scene is also in perspective. The entire model is set into a box with 1 open side.

When planning a diorama, it is first necessary to decide which is the least important side of the room or area that is to be depicted; this will become the viewing opening. Next decide on the vanishing points. This can be done by making a series of sketches of the scene in the same manner in which a perspective would be planned. Once the best sketch has been chosen and the vanishing points located, the drawing must be transferred into the third dimension. This may be done (as suggested in 23-2) through the use of 3 or more sheets of cardboard. 1 sheet has the original sketch attached to it, and 1 sheet is set behind the first at a distance equal to the desired depth of the vanishing point of the diorama. The vanishing point is transferred through it as a pinhole; other cardboards are used to represent the major walls or facades that will be in the diorama. These cardboards should be taped to the first 2 and should intersect the rear board at the vanishing point. The front dimensions of walls or facades are transferred to the diagonal boards and diminish as they approach the vanishing point. A board representing the rear wall of the diorama may now be set into the mock-up. From this rough setup, working drawings can be made for the diorama. It should be noted that not only do the side walls of a diorama converge but so do its floor and ceiling. Usually the depth of the diorama and vanishing point is located by trial and error. The rear wall is often located in such a position that objects appearing on it will be about $\frac{1}{2}$ the size they would be if they were located at the front of the diorama. Once the depth at which the backdrop is placed is set, it can then be determined which objects will be modeled in the round

23-1

A DIORAMA.

This model, entitled "The Founding of the New York City Stock Exchange Buttonwood Agreement, May 17, 1792," is on display at the Museum of the City of New York.

SCALE: about 2" = 1' (at front of model).

Walls, windows, moldings and steps were made from wood. Brick pattern was scribed into gesso. Windows were glazed with real glass. Railings were brass; people were carved from plaster; curtains were made of paper.

The model was built 1' wider on the left side, 6" wider on the right side and 1' higher than its glazed viewing opening. The background, rear quarter of the right wall, and all of the left wall were painted. The ground sloped up to and joined the backdrop and the painted left side in a 4" curved, cove-like sweep. This was done to soften the visual transformation between modeled ground and painted surface.

The scene was lighted from above.

and which will be painted, either on vanishing side walls or on the backdrop. The diorama in 23-1 has painted flats for all of its left side and for the rear quarter of its right wall. Mock-ups of various objects may be quickly molded in clay to see whether or not their perspective is acceptable. If too many objects prove to look odd, it will probably be necessary to change the angle of the

perspective. Sometimes almost all modeling in the round is dispensed with: the side walls and many freestanding objects as well as the rear wall are made as 2-dimensional "flats" and only objects that can be seen into (past their front plane) such as chairs, tables, trees, etc., are made in 3 dimensions.

A drafting technique that may be used to find

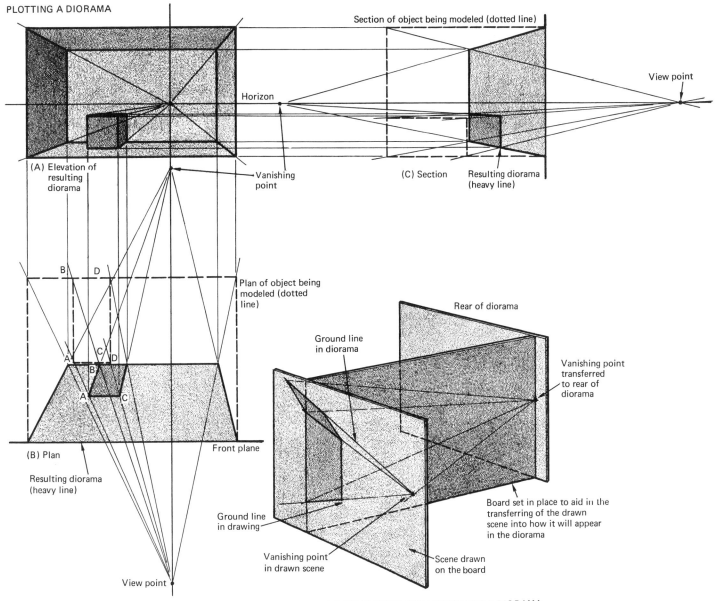

PLOTTING A DIORAMA

Section of object being modeled (dotted line)

View point

Horizon

(A) Elevation of resulting diorama

Vanishing point

(C) Section

Resulting diorama (heavy line)

Plan of object being modeled (dotted line)

Rear of diorama

Ground line in diorama

Vanishing point transferred to rear of diorama

B   D

A   C D
  B
  A   C

(B) Plan

Front plane

Resulting diorama (heavy line)

Board set in place to aid in the transferring of the drawn scene into how it will appear in the diorama

Ground line in drawing

Vanishing point in drawn scene

Scene drawn on the board

View point

A FAST METHOD FOR LAYING OUT A DIORAMA

the shape of various of the occupants of the diorama is shown in 23-2. By drawing lines from the viewpoint through various points on the superimposed plan and section (or elevation), and by seeing where these lines intersect lines drawn from the vanishing point, it is possible to tell where various points should fall when put into perspective on the model.

Dioramas are usually lit from the top down. To accomplish this, the box into which they are built should have a section left off for top-mounted lights. The front and top openings are often glazed to prevent infiltration of dust. The front glass may be sloped to prevent reflection. Exterior scenes must be painted with aerial perspective. Backdrops should be painted under the same lighting conditions by which they will be displayed.

Cycloramas

Cycloramas are the same as perspective models except that the sky background is painted on a curved wall which starts at the front of the model box and curves behind the entirely freestanding

model. Cycloramas are used to depict landscapes, freestanding buildings and anything that requires a curved sky backdrop. The location of the lighting makes the sky appear luminous and detached from other parts of the model. As with perspective models, various objects in the cyclorama may be drawn on 2-dimensional flats and placed in freestanding positions in front of the sky.

PEPPER'S GHOST

This intriguing name is given to a display device that automatically and instantaneously changes 1 modeled scene to another before the viewer's eyes. It can be used to show before and after, or stage 1 and stage 2 conditions, of a design project.

Illustration 23-3 shows a cross section of a Pepper's Ghost. The cycle runs like this: (1) cyclorama No. 1 is illuminated by the bulb; (2) the viewer is able to see this model through the polarized glass because of the high level of illumination behind the glass; (3) a timer revolves the drum-shaped shutter around the bulb, redirecting its light away from cyclorama No. 1 and

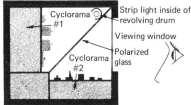

Cyclorama #1

Strip light inside of revolving drum

Viewing window

Polarized glass

Cyclorama #2

toward cyclorama No. 2; (4) since the rear of the polarized glass is now in darkness and its front illuminated, the polarized glass becomes a mirror, and projects the image of lighted cyclorama No. 2 to the viewer; (5) the drum shutter revolves again, starting a new cycle. The less important scene should be in the second position, since it is not as well illuminated, and often appears less distinct.

23-4/23-5

A TAKE APART PRESENTATION MODEL.

PROJECT: Madison Square Garden, sports and entertainment complex, New York City.
DESIGNED BY: Charles Luckman Associates.

MODELBUILDER: Alexander and Jones (a professional modelbuilder).
PHOTOGRAPHER: Louis Checkman.
SCALE: 1/16″ = 1′.
This model demonstrated the interrelationship of various facilities of the project. It was used to present the project to the client and to the public.

Walls, floors, roof and seats were made from acrylic sheet. The texture on the exterior wall was scribed into the plastic. The internal lighting system employed 1″ long, 4 to 5 amperes, General Electric Finger Line miniature fluorescent tubes, which have miniature starters and ballast and run on untransformed 110-volt current.

DISPLAY BOXES

Sometimes it is advisable to direct the viewer's attention toward 1 side of a model. This can be done by placing it into a viewing box. A few judiciously placed bulbs to represent natural lighting can make this a very effective model displaying technique.

TAKE APART MODELS

Occasionally, an architectural project will require an over-all model plus models of certain interior spaces. This may be necessary in order to show the interrelationship of areas in a complex structure (23-5), or to get a rough idea of interior decor. If these 2 types of models can be combined into 1 take apart model, considerable savings in cost and time can be achieved. Usually, with large buildings, a take apart model will require at least a $\frac{1}{8}″ = 1′$ scale, if interiors are to be shown in enough detail to be studied; a scale of around $\frac{1}{16}″ = 1′$ is required if a model merely illustrates the interrelationship of areas. Parts of the model should be pegged or splined together. To simplify making a neat parting line, the area immediately around the joint should be constructed first, put together, and the rest of the model then built. Removable roofs may also be constructed this way. The basic objective is to provide joining surfaces that are as massive and warp resistant as is practical.

Small-scale take apart models of multibuilding developments and town plans may have buildings attached to the baseboard by magnets or by having them doweled in place. These techniques may also be used to make a model demountable, and thus easier to pack and ship.

FLOW MODELS

When presenting or studying the designs of certain buildings, such as hospitals and factories in which the interrelationship of material, personnel or utility flow is important, it can be extremely effective to present this flow on a rough model. A model of this type may be made by cementing prints of the various floor plans of the building to cardboard or wood sheet. Flow arrows may be drafted onto the plans and areas of similar use may be color coded. Vertical utility and transportation cores are made from stripwood, and holes to receive them are cut through the various floors. The model may then be assembled and studied, with the floors separated from one another by small blocks or pegs. If floor sheets are made to the correct thickness, i.e. to represent the window sill to window head dimension of the building, it may also be possible to use the flow model as a massing model once roof structures and other details have been added to it.

MIRRORING A PARTIAL MODEL TO CREATE AN ILLUSION OF THE ENTIRE BUILDING

Models of symmetrical buildings, such as auditoriums, may be simplified by constructing only $\frac{1}{2}$ the structure. A large mirror may be placed against the center line and the effect of an entire building gained if viewed or photographed from the exterior. If the interior must be seen, a vision hole can be cut through the wall of the model that is opposite the mirror. Other holes may also be needed through which the model may be illuminated.

Long interior spaces such as corridors and halls may also be abbreviated by building a typical section and placing mirrors at either end. Both mirrors must have their surfaces parallel to one another. A peep hole is made in 1 mirror by scraping off a small circle of its silvering. The model segment is then illuminated. When viewed through the hole, the area will appear to be of great length, and the only distraction, caused by the reflection of the viewing hole, will be a dark spot reflected from the opposite mirror.

24 DISPLAYING THE MODEL

DISPLAY STANDS

The designer or his modelmaker should give some thought to the various ways in which a model can be displayed. Occasionally, a project is of such importance that it is wise to design a special transparent cover and display stand for the model. It must be decided which viewing angle will show off the model most advantageously. Models may be bracketed from walls so that they are viewed in elevation, plain view or with their ground plane at an angle to the wall. It is even possible to select a model-to-wall angle and a mounting height that permits the model to be viewed at pedestrian eye level or at almost plain view depending on how close the spectator stands. Display stands may be any available table or they may be custom constructed from wood or from tubular Sonotube. Tables may be cosmetically improved by having their legs encased in painted plywood skirts. All sorts of stand shapes may be custom constructed from wood: boxes, pedestals, cruciforms, intersecting vertical walls, etc.

Large landscape or town planning models should be mounted on very low stands or bracketed vertically from walls to allow them to be viewed from bird's-eye level. The importance of the display may justify placing the model with its ground elevation at eye level and building an elevated walkway around it to allow both pedestrian and bird's-eye level viewing.

Dioramas are most effective when their horizon line is at viewer eye level.

Models of individual buildings and interiors are best viewed when mounted on a 4' or higher stand. This allows the spectator to look into the model at pedestrian level.

The employment of mirrors may be necessary to show details that would otherwise be hidden from the viewer. They are especially useful when

24-1/24-2

Project: **THE ROY LARSEN HALL, HARVARD GRADUATE SCHOOL OF EDUCATION, CAMBRIDGE, MASSACHUSETTS.**

DESIGNED BY: Caudill, Rowlett and Scott.
MODELBUILDER: William M. Eichbaum (a professional modelbuilder).
PHOTOGRAPHER: Lawrence S. Williams (nighttime photo), Robert D. Harvey (daytime photo).
SCALE: 1/8″ = 1′.
This presentation model was mainly made from acrylic. Bay windows were built up from strips of the material. Model was internally braced with floors and partitions. Handrails were made from soldered brass wire. Internal lighting was achieved by 2 bulbs.
The nighttime photograph was taken with a 4″ × 5″ Sinar view camera, 121 mm lens and Royal Pan film. 1 small light illuminated the backdrop and 1 soft fill-in light was used on the model to bring out some of its detail.
The daytime photograph was taken with a 5″ × 7″ view camera, 120 mm wide-angle Schneider Angulon lens and Super Panchro Press type B film.
CONSTRUCTION TIME: about 230 hours.

space considerations keep spectators on only 1 side of the model. This problem may also be solved by placing the model on a continually rotating turntable. Such mechanisms are obtainable from local store-fixture supply houses. Motors and their gear trains should be enclosed in a box that is lined with sound deadening material. The Vue-More Corporation sells 2 to 3 rpm, 1' diameter turntables for under $15; and 2' models for about $30. The former has a 25 pound capacity; the latter can hold 10 times that weight.

VIEWING AND STUDY

To get the most use out of design models, it is important to view them under conditions that make them as realistic as possible. To focus on close elements of the model and to counteract the undesirable effects of binocular vision, use a low power reducing glass and close 1 eye. Black cloth may be draped around the model to eliminate undesirable light and distraction.

THE MODEL COVER

The transparent model cover performs 2 necessary functions: it keeps dust and spectators' fingers from the model. 1 piece acrylic domes made by the Building Products Division of the American Cyanamid Co. may be obtained from a local distributor. Hemispherical domes cost from $20 for a 24″ diameter dome to $175 for a 69″ dome. Their square base domes range in cost from $15 for a 17 × 27″ dome to $54 for a 33 × 74″ dome. Domes must be set on or in the model base to allow for expansion; otherwise they may crack. Covers may be constructed from acrylic. These may be built in the form of a flattened arch, a low hipped roof, a barrel vault or just a plain box shape. Provisions for periodically treating the cover with antistatic electricity spray should be made or the acrylic will be hard to dust. Display lights should not create reflections that will make viewing the model difficult. Sometimes this requires the construction of a cover the shape of which will be compatible with the expected lighting conditions.

DEHUMIDIFIERS

If humidity affects paper, cardboard or wood models, no matter how well they are waterproofed, it may be necessary to install a dehumidifier inside the cover. Small slabs of camphor ice will suffice if the model is small. If it is large, the electric dehumidifier sold by Empire may be required. It measures 9 × 3 × 3″, runs on house current and costs $8.

CLEANING THE MODEL

To begin with, all possible attempts should be made not to allow dirt to collect on models. A display model should be fully enclosed by a cover. If the model does not warrant the expense of an acrylic cover, it should be draped with a sheet of Mylar when not being viewed.

If the model does eventually collect a coating of dust, remove it by a careful brushing with a camel's-hair or static electricity brush. Both can be obtained from photographic supply stores.

Flocked areas of foliage may best be cleaned with a miniature vacuum cleaner. An ordinary home type cleaner may be modified by forming a wood plug to fit snugly into the end of the hose. A hole is drilled into the plug and rubber or neaprone tubing is inserted. An entire set of cleaning tools may be made by cutting the openings of several lengths of tubing into various shapes. The insertion of $\frac{1}{2}$″ lengths of flattened or crimped metal tubing into the flexible material will form additional opening shapes. Make sure that the metal is inserted far enough inside the flexible tubing to prevent it from scratching the model's surface.

The Industro-Motive Corporation makes a miniature vacuum cleaner attachment that may be plugged into any tank-type cleaner. This pencil-sized device, called a Nic-Nac Vac, has bristles on its nozzle.

See the acrylic and styrene sections of this book for ways to clean these materials.

SHIPPING

The safest local deliveries are made in person by the modelbuilder or members of his staff. They will then be able to stay and set up the model and its display stand. Very large or heavy models may be sent by a trusted moving company specializing in art or museum display moving. Deliveries of 100 or so miles can be made by the modelbuilder in a rented station wagon or truck. Intercity delivery should be made by air freight with delivery to the airport made by the modelbuilder or his moving company. The model should be picked up at its destination by the architect or owner.

Shipping Cases

The modelbuilder should take the responsibility for constructing or at least designing any shipping cases that will be needed for the model. Small and medium-size cases should be framed with 1 × 1 to 1 × 2″ pine and covered with plywood if the model is to be hand carried or shipped by air; or covered with wood boards if shipping is to be by truck, train or boat or if the case is larger than about 3 × 5 × 2'. When possible, consult a professional packing expert if the model is to be shipped long distances. Models that have 1 or more high buildings that cover a small portion of the baseboard area of the model should be constructed so that the high building can be detached from the base. This will diminish the total volume of the packing case. Blocks should be constructed inside the case to hold the model in place. All large model shapes should be individually braced with these blocks. The places where the blocks contact the model should be covered with felt or sponge rubber. The baseboard of the model should be screwed or belted into the case. Shock absorbing pads made from casting rubber or foaming plastic may also be cast to the contours of the model.

A new polyprophylene continuous hinge has proven its usefulness. It comes in coils, can be cut to any desired length, can be attached by nail or screw and does not need oiling. The Edmund Scientific Company sells 6' of $1\frac{1}{2}$″ wide by 1/10″ thick white hinge for $2.

Instructions about unpacking, setting up and cleaning the model as well as suggestions for lighting should be affixed to the inside of the case.

Small carrying cases may be constructed in the same manner as are packing cases. They should have handles to simplify handling.

INSURANCE

Models may be insured to cover most of the unpleasant eventualities that might overtake them while in transit or on display. Each model, its trip or exhibit, must be judgment rated by the underwriter, who will take into consideration the construction and packing of the model, how it is to be shipped, the fire rating of the building in which it is to be displayed and the safeguards taken. All-risk (including breakage) insurance can be taken out, but even this extensive form will exclude payments for damage caused to the model "due to its inherent weakness." To get rates for a specific model and situation, contact an insurance agent for information about inland marine type insurance.

INTERNAL LIGHTING FOR THE MODEL

Lighting can greatly increase the realism and attractiveness of a model, thereby enhancing its value as a display and study tool. Internal lighting can also be used to give a feeling of depth and, if located behind the model, can help kill reflections on transparent and translucent surfaces.

24-3

A COMPLEX INTERNALLY LIGHTED MODEL.
PROJECT: interior corridor in Place Ville Marie, Montreal, Canada.
DESIGNED BY: I. M. Pei and Associates.
MODELBUILDER AND PHOTOGRAPHER: the architect's captive model shop.
SCALE: 1/2″ = 1'.
Floors were made of painted acrylic, the ceiling of painted acrylic with a stippled finish. Mullions, door frames and store fronts were built of acrylic. Signs were laid out with pressure-sensitive transfer letters, photographed, and the negatives mounted in the model and lighted from behind. Other rear lights shone through holes in the ceiling to simulate the spotlights of the store. People were cast in plaster.

Miniature bulbs are obtainable from most model railroad and hobby stores; slightly larger bulbs are available from hardware stores. Small and miniature bulbs usually require less than 110 volts and will accept either a-c or d-c current; they can be operated by either a transformer or a battery. Model train transformers, with a variable voltage throttle control, and low voltage step-down transformers (new or surplus) are readily available, inexpensive and convenient to use. Model train transformers allow the dimming of lights at will or the use of various voltages. Bulb life, which is pitifully low in some brands, may be extended by running the bulb at a reduced voltage; this, however, will change the brightness of the light and alter the color of clear bulbs from white toward orange.

Computing the Number of Bulbs That Can Be Used with a Given Power Source

It is suggested that bulbs of a voltage rating equal to that of the transformer be employed. This allows the use of simple parallel circuitry. To estimate the maximum number of bulbs that can be used in a parallel hook-up with a transformer, first find the *output* wattage rating or current capacity of the latter. In addition, the wattage rating of the bulbs must be determined. The relationships can best be expressed as follows:

W_t (output wattage rating of the transformer $= E_t$ (voltage output employed) $\times I_t$ (rated current output in amperes)
W_b (wattage of each bulb) $= E_b$ (rated bulb voltage) $\times I_b$ (the measured current (ampere) drain of one bulb at the rated voltage)

Thus it follows that the maximum number of bulbs (N) that can be powered by a transformer is:

$$N = \frac{W_t \text{ (output wattage of transformer)}}{W_b \text{ (wattage of each bulb)}}$$

Remember that if the wattage is not known it can always be calculated by the rated or measured voltage and current if the formula $W = E \times I$ is used.

If for example: the transformer has an output of 6 volts at 10.5 amperes, and the bulbs in use are rated at 6 volts; by connecting an ammeter in series with 1 bulb and the 6-volt source, the current consumption can be measured and is observed to be 1 ampere. Therefore:

$$N = \frac{W_t}{W_b}$$
$$N = \frac{6 \text{ volts} \times 10.5 \text{ amperes}}{6 \text{ volts} \times 1.0 \text{ amperes}}$$
$$N = \frac{10.5}{1}$$
$$N = 10.5$$

Thus the maximum number of bulbs that can be employed is 10; if 11 or more are used, the maximum wattage rating of the transformer is overdrawn, and it may burn out.

The parallel circuit is the most commonly used; each bulb is located independently of the others in a separate parallel branch. Thus, if 1 bulb burns out, the others will continue to burn. Since the voltage received by each branch will be the same, all the bulbs must be of the same voltage as is the source.

An alternative hook-up method must be employed when a higher voltage transformer is used with lower voltage bulbs. In this circuit all of the bulbs are interconnected or hooked up in series. If 1 bulb burns out, then the entire circuit will go dead. In a series circuit, the voltages of the individual bulbs are cumulative, so different voltage bulbs can be employed as long as their total voltage equals the output voltage of the trans-

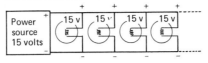
(A) THE PARALLEL CIRCUIT

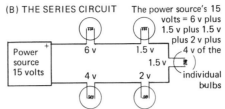
(B) THE SERIES CIRCUIT   The power source's 15 volts = 6 v plus 1.5 v plus 1.5 v plus 2 v plus 1.5 v plus 4 v of the individual bulbs

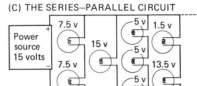
(C) THE SERIES—PARALLEL CIRCUIT

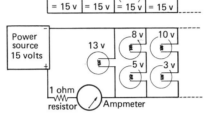
(D) SERIES—PARALLEL CIRCUIT TO USE IF POWER SOURCE'S VOLTAGE IS GREATER THAN THAT REQUIRED BY THE VARIOUS BRANCHES

former. The same transformer wattage considerations apply.

Combinations of parallel circuits, with branches made up of series circuits, can be used with a few bulbs of voltages other than those produced by the transformer. If 1 bulb in a series circuit of a parallel branch blows out, that entire branch, though not the whole parallel network, will be extinguished.

Another, but less preferable, method than matching bulb voltages to transformer voltages (or vice versa) is to use a dropping resistor to lower the transformer voltage to that of the bulbs. The resistor can be used in series and parallel circuits or in branches of parallel combination circuits. An ammeter must be used with the voltage dropping resistor method. If all the bulbs are of the same voltage but have a rating of less than that of the transformer, a parallel circuit, with the appropriate dropping resistor placed after the transformer output lead, can be used.

The ammeter (which, if one is working with an a-c transformer, must be designed for use with alternating current) is connected in series with the parallel branches after a resistor. Both the resistor and the ammeter are connected to either of the output leads of the transformer. The same procedure can be followed with a direct current hook-up, but a d-c meter must be used and polarity considerations adhered to. A temporary resistor (of about 5 ohms per desired volt drop) is used to simulate the current drain of the resistor that will be finally used. In the above diagram, a 2 volt drop is required. Let us assume that the ammeter reads 2 amperes; then by utilizing Ohm's Law we can compute the required resistance:

$$\text{resistance} = \frac{\text{voltage drop desired}}{\text{measured current}}$$
$$= \frac{2 \text{ volt}}{2 \text{ amperes}}$$
$$= 1 \text{ ohm}$$

The second criterion vital to the selection of the proper resistor is its heat dissipative power. Since

a resistor converts electricity to heat, the more heat dissipation is required the greater the voltage drop needed and the greater the current drain. Heat dissipation can also be measured in watts, and can be computed by the product of the voltage drop and the current drain of the resistor.

W (heat dissipation)
$= E$ (voltage drop) $\times I$ (current drain)

Be sure that the resistor selected has sufficient heat dissipation capacity; that is, be sure its wattage rating is high enough. Also be sure to have the resistor located in the model so that air can freely circulate around it, or wrap it with aluminum foil to increase its radiating area.

If it is desired to reduce the voltage to 1 bulb of a circuit, whether it be series or parallel, place the resistor into the circuit directly before that bulb and connect the ammeter at the same place to take the current measurement of just that bulb.

Flashing Bulbs and Wiring

Independently flashing bulbs can be used in place of regular bulbs in parallel circuits. If flashing bulbs are used in series circuits, all the bulbs in the circuit will flash simultaneously; only 1 flashing bulb is necessary to achieve this effect. Flashing bulbs are sold by Kemtron, International Models and Aristo Craft.

Bulbs may be wired with 15 ampere rated household wire, bell wire, or No. 22 or No. 24 wire obtainable in model train and hobby shops. When selecting wire, be sure to specify the braided variety as this type will reduce breakage and fatigue. Keep wiring neat by stapling it in place in the model, taking care not to penetrate the insulation. Painted circuitry may also be made use of to form electrical connections on any model surface.
1. Varnish the surface on which the circuit is to be run.
2. After the varnish has dried, paint the circuit lines with special silver conductive paint.
3. Insulate the lines with a second coat of varnish.

All hook-ups should be provided with an on-off switch.

Placing Bulbs in the Model

Make some provision to cool all bulbs that are rated at over 10 watts. Besides creating a fire hazard, the heat from large bulbs may warp the model. It may be possible simply to cut ventilation holes in installations or perhaps it may be necessary to add a small electric fan of the variety used in electrical appliances. Holes should provide a constant draft in the model. Small, air intake holes should be placed low on the model and larger outlet holes at the top of the model.

Models constructed from acrylic and other transparent or translucent materials must have black painted interiors to stop the passage of internal light. If this does not black out all light leakage, baffles should be placed around the bulbs, or the interior of the model should be lined with aluminum foil. If visible from the outside, the foil must be painted.

If the model is illuminated by a few high wattage, unbaffled lamps, rice or white tracing paper may have to be cemented inside the windows of the model to eliminate glare.

There is no need to illuminate the model in the same intensity as the prototype. Both the eyes of the viewer and long photograph exposures will compensate for the lower intensity and the illumination will seem to be "in scale." Illuminated models are most effectively displayed in a dark room.

Professional modelmakers often use full-size fluorescent or cold neon tubes in large models. These cut down the number of bulbs and amount of current needed, and also reduce the heat output of the lighting system. To prevent heat build-up, professional modelmakers sometimes wire a timer into the circuit which periodically cuts off the lights for a few minutes of cooling. Despite these precautions, there have been occasional fires started inside of models.

Bulbs may be colored with felt-tipped water-color marking pens or by dipping the bulb into special dyes obtained from radio stores or the model train sections of hobby stores.

Lighting Fixtures

WORKING FIXTURES

Light may be led from one place to another through a clear acrylic rod the ends of which have been polished. One end of the rod is aimed at the light source, the other is used to represent a lamp. In this way multibulb marquees and other fixtures may be created with only 1 or 2 bulbs mounted in the center of the marquee as a light source.

Scale spotlights may be constructed from Bristolboard or sheet metal and lined with aluminum foil for greater reflectance.

Fluorescent tubes may be represented by polished acrylic rods. These may be mounted behind slits in the ceiling of the model, with bulbs placed behind them. Parts of the rods that are visible through the slits can be lightly sanded.

NONWORKING FIXTURES

Globes

Nonworking lighting fixture globes may be improvised from empty gelatin pill casings (obtainable from most pharmacists), miniature light bulbs, or reshaped glass and plastic beads and buttons. Exact shapes may be carved from acrylic stock.

Covers for Large, Recessed Ceiling Fixtures

These may be made from vacuum-formed acetate. Large varieties of ready-made clear plastic shapes can often be obtained from local plastic fabricators (sometimes they may be prevailed upon to provide a good selection gratis). These shapes are used in packaging to cover the myriad small merchandise that is sold mounted on cards. From the resulting store of shapes, many needed covers can be cut.

Crystal Chandeliers

These may be roughly simulated by short lengths of acrylic rods cemented together. Sometimes the addition of spangles will give an added feeling of realism to the modeled fixture (19-12).

Lampshades

These are best made from colored paper; brackets and supports are best constructed from wire; bases from carved wood or acrylic.

In addition to the above, General Electric (24-7) has an extensive line of 3 to 60 volt Sub-Miniature Incandescent Lamps. These come in 13 bulb shapes and sizes; each obtainable in several voltages. Sizes range from $\frac{3}{16}$ by $\frac{1}{4}''$ and up. Bulbs can be obtained in 1 or more of the following base styles: screw, groove, flange or with pigtails.

General Electric's Miniature Incandescent Lamp Line comes in 24 shapes and sizes. Each is obtainable in several voltages ranging from 1.2 to 120 volts. Base styles that are obtainable include the 4 listed above plus bayonet, index and wedge.

They also make incandescent flasher lamps and 6″ (28 volt) and 12″ (53 volt) long fluorescent lamps.

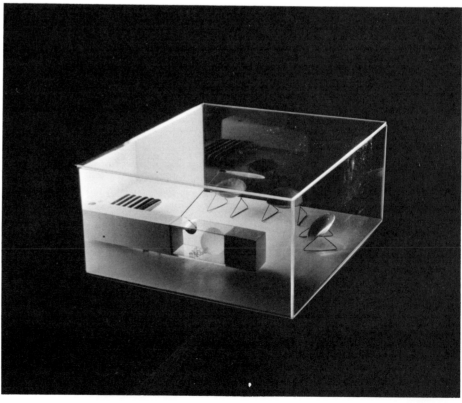

A HIGHLY DETAILED LARGE-SCALE MODEL.

PROJECT: the entrance of the New York City Playboy Club.

DESIGNED BY: Oppenheimer, Brady and Lehreke.

MODELBUILDER: Joseph Santeramo.

PHOTOGRAPHER: Louis Checkman.

This design and presentation model was built mostly of acrylic. The sidewalk was made from painted Masonite. Railing and mullions were built of brass strip. People were constructed from tin foil.

The photograph was taken with a Sinar 4″ × 5″ view camera, 90 mm Schneider Angulon lens and Super Panchro Press "B" film. The model was internally lighted from above the stair. Light from an additional small flood was bounced onto the right-hand wall to pick up some of its texture.

Project: **A ROOF-TOP OFFICE LOUNGE.**

DESIGNED BY: Sanford Hohauser and Joseph d'Amelio.

MODELBUILDER AND PHOTOGRAPHER: Sanford Hohauser.

SCALE: 3/8″ = 1′.

Walls of this design and presentation model were made from 2 layers of single weight illustration board separated by a balsa strip core. Glazing was done in acrylic. The cabinet was made of cardboard and acrylic. TV tubes were carved from acrylic. Chairs were formed on a wood male form from acetate that had been softened in an acetone solution.

The photograph was taken with a 4″ × 5″ press camera, 90 mm wide-angle Wollensak Raptar lens and Super XX film. This model was internally lighted temporarily by 2 pea size lamps.

CONSTRUCTION TIME FOR THE STRUCTURE AND A LANDSCAPED ROOF: about 50 hours.

AVAILABLE MINIATURE BULBS

Name[1]	Volts	Price (each)	Color	Type of connection	Manufacturer	Size (inches)
Micro-Miniature	1.2	30¢	Clear	Pigtails	Aristo Craft (No. 301)	1/16 diam. × 3/16
Pinlite	1.5	$5	Clear	Pigtails	Kay Electric Co.	1/64 diam. × 1/16
Lighthouse blinker bulb	1.5	50¢	Clear	Pigtails	Aristo Craft (No. 63)	
Micro-Miniature	3	60¢	Clear	Pigtails	Aristo Craft (No. 302)	1/16 diam. × 3/16
Grain of wheat	3	15¢	Clear, red, green	Pigtails	Aristo Craft (Nos. 10 to 12)	1/8 diam. × 5/16
Round (pea)	3	25¢ (inc. base)	Clear	Screw base with pigtails	International Models	
Round (pea)	3	27¢ (inc. base No. 41)	Clear	Screw base	Aristo Craft (No. 40)	1/4 diam. × 1/2
Button bulb	3	20¢	Clear, red, green, white	Pigtails	Aristo Craft (Nos. 181–184)	3/8 diam. × 1/4
Dome light	3	25¢	White	Pigtails	Aristo Craft (No. 70)	1/2 diam. × 3/8
Pea bulb (same as grain of wheat)	3.5	10¢	Clear, red, green	Pigtails	International Models	1/8 diam. × 5/16
Pointed	4	50¢	Clear, red, green	Pigtails	Aristo Craft (Nos. 51–53)	1/8 diam. × 5/8
Long, tubular bulb	3.5	27¢	Frosted	Clips	Aristo Craft (No. 81)	1/8 diam. × 1 1/4
Grain of wheat	8	20¢	Clear	Pigtails	Kemtron (X400)	1/8 diam. × 5/16
Round (pea)	8	29¢ (inc. socket)	Clear, red, green, amber	Pigtails	Kemtron (X401)	1/4 diam. × 7/16
Spotlight beam	6	17¢	Clear	Pigtails	International Models	
Caboose light (irregular cylindrical base)	8	50¢	Red, green, jewels	Pigtails	Kemtron (X444)	3/16 diam. × 5/8
Grain of wheat	12	15¢	Clear, red, green, amber, frosted blue (U.P.C. has first 3)	Pigtails	Aristo Craft (Nos. 1–6) Universal Powermaster (Nos. 81–83)	1/8 diam. × 5/16
Round (pea)	12	30¢ (inc. socket X402)	Clear, red, green, amber	Socket has pigtails	Kemtron (X401, X401–R, X401–G X401–A)	1/4 diam. × 7/16
Round (pea)	12	29¢ (inc. socket)	Clear, red, green, amber	Screw base has pigtails	International Models	
Round	12	15¢–20¢	Clear, frosted (U.P.C. also had red)	Pigtails	Universal Powermaster (12–15v), (75, 76 & 85), Aristo Craft (Nos. 20–21) or Kemtron (12v), (X403, X405)	1/4 diam.
Round (pea)	16	20¢	Clear	Screw base	Universal Powermaster (No. 84)	3/16 diam. × 9/16
Round cartridge bulb	12–15	30¢	Clear, red, green	Cartridge	Universal Powermaster (Nos. 87–89)	1/8 diam. × 7/16
Round	12	30¢ (inc. socket X407)	Clear	Holes to insert wires	Kemtron (X406)	7/16 diam. × 5/8
Pointed	16	54¢–57¢	Clear, red, green	Cartridge	Aristo Craft (Nos. 54–56)	
Pilot lamp, round bulb on cylindrical base	12	20¢	Clear, red, green	Pigtails	Aristo Craft (No. 50) or Kemtron (X404, X404–R, X404–G, X404–A)	3/16 diam.
Flat head (button bulb)	12	20¢	Clear	Pigtails	Universal Powermaster (No. 76)	3/8 diam. × 3/16
Flat-face bulb	12	20¢	Clear	Pigtails	Aristo Craft (No. 69R)	1/4 diam. × 3/8

[1] Some bulbs are shown in 24–7.

(continued on next page)

Name[1]	Volts	Price (each)	Color	Type of connection	Manufacturer	Size (inches)
Spotlight beam	12	17¢	Clear	Pigtails	International Models	1/8 diam. × 1/4
Radiant beam	12–15	15¢	Blue-green	Pigtails	International Models	1/8 diam. × 5/16
"Mini-Mag" magnifier tip	12	20¢	Clear, red, green, amber	Pigtails	International Models	1/8 diam. × 5/16
O Gauge old-time gas lamp	12	40¢	Frosted	Pigtails	Aristo Craft (No. 92)	
HO Gauge old-time gas lamp	12	30¢ 35¢	Clear, frosted	Pigtails	Aristo Craft (Nos. 93–94)	5/16 diam. × 1/2
Tubular	12	30¢	Clear	Pigtails	Kemtron (X414)	1/8 diam. × 7/16
Special tubular bulb	12–15	35¢	Clear		Universal Powermaster (No. 80)	3/16 diam. × 1/2
Short tubular	12–15	30¢	Clear	Screw base	Universal Powermaster (No. 79)	3/16 diam. × 1/2
Tubular bulb	16	30¢	Frosted	Clips	Aristo Craft (No. 80)	1/8 diam. × 1
Tubular	12	30¢	Clear	Pigtails	Kemtron (X415)	1/8 diam. × 1 1/8
Tubular	12	45¢ (inc. clips)	Red, green, amber, blue white	Clips	Kemtron (X420–W, X420–R, X420–G, X420–A, X420–B)	1/4 diam. × 1 1/2 long
Tubular (same as above)	12	35¢ (inc. clips)	Clear, frosted, red, green, amber, blue	Clips	Aristo Craft (Nos. 84–89)	1/4 diam. × 1 1/2 long
Tubular	12	30¢	Clear	Pigtails	Kemtron (X416)	1/4 diam. × 1 1/4
Tubular fluorettes	12–15	40¢ (inc. clips)	White, blue	Clips	International Models	2
Long tubular	12–15	40¢	Clear	Clips	Aristo Craft (No. 82)	1/4 diam. × 2
HO fluorescent lamp	12	25¢	Frosted	Pigtails	Aristo Craft (No. 83)	1/8 diam. × 7/8
O fluorescent lamp	12	30¢	Frosted	Pigtails	Aristo Craft (No. 90)	1/4 diam. × 1 1/2
Billboard light	12–15	40¢	Frosted	Bracket and pigtails	Aristo Craft (No. 115)	1/4 diam. × 1 3/8
Blinker bulb	12	45¢	Clear	Pigtails	Aristo Craft (No. 60)	
Blinker bulb	12	50¢	Clear	Pigtails	Kemtron (X421)	1/4 diam. × 7/8
Blinker bulb	12	25¢	Clear	Pigtails	International Models	9/16
Blinker bulb	12	35¢ (inc. base)	Clear	Screw base	International Models	9/16
Blinker bulb	12	43¢ (inc. base)	Clear	Screw base	International Models	1
Old-time headlights	12	65¢	Clear	Pigtails	International Models	1/2 high × 5/16 square
Bulb in brass case	12	25¢	Clear	Pigtails	Kemtron (X413)	3/16 diam. × 1/4
Grain of wheat	18	15¢	Clear, red, green	Pigtails	International Models	
Round (pea)	18	30¢ (inc. base)	Clear, red, green, amber	Base has pigtails	International Models	1/8 diam. × 5/16
Round (pea)	18	30¢ (inc. socket X402)	Clear, red, green, amber	Socket has pigtails	Kemtron (X401, X401–R, X401–G, X401–A)	1/4 diam. × 7/16
Round (pea)	19	29¢	Clear	Screw base	Aristo Craft (No. 42)	
Miniature tubular	19	29¢–32¢	Clear, red, green	Cartridge type	Aristo Craft (Nos. 57–59)	1/8 diam. × 7/16
Round (pea)	24	30¢ (inc. base)	Clear, red, green, amber	Screw base has pigtails	International Models	

[1] Some bulbs are shown in 24–7.

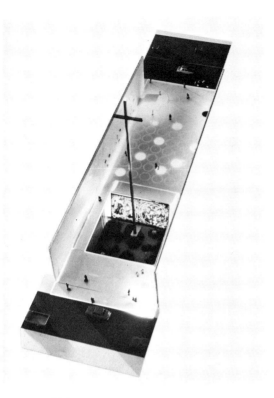

24-6

Project: ST. JOSEPH'S CHURCH.

DESIGN AND MODEL BY: Sanford Hohauser and Joseph D'Amelio.

PHOTOGRAPHER: Sanford Hohauser.

SCALE: 1/8″ = 1′.

The baseboard of this design and presentation model was made of plywood; sidewalks were done in illustration board. The building and its side walls were framed in balsa strip covered with illustration board. Side walls were painted with a rough coat of gesso to simulate stucco. The church was located below grade. Its roof, which was also the plaza, was made from 1/8″ acrylic sheet on illustration board into which circular skylights had been cut. The stair cover (upper left-hand corner) and the curved floor (above the stained glass window) were laminated from several thicknesses of 3-ply Bristolboard. The seats of the church were also bent from 3-ply Bristolboard. The stained glass was painted acetate. The cross was made of brass. People and cars were store bought. The model was illuminated by 6 15-volt miniature lamps.

The photograph was taken with a 4″ × 5″ press camera, 90 mm Wollensak Raptar wide-angle lens and Ektachrome film. Only internal illumination was used.

CONSTRUCTION TIME, INCLUDING A FULLY DETAILED INTERIOR: about 100 hours.

Fires

It may occasionally be necessary to represent fires, especially for photographic purposes. Fire may be represented with several small birthday cake candles burning among plaster of Paris logs. This is satisfactory in $\frac{1}{4}$″ scale and larger models the fireplaces of which have been constructed of nonflammable materials. A safer way to represent a fire is with a miniature bulb surrounded with tendrils of roughly cut red and yellow cellophane. Glowing coals can be represented by rear lighted, roughened fragments of red or orange acrylic.

Illuminated Signs

Illuminated signs may be constructed in many ways. Transfer letters·may be applied to sheet

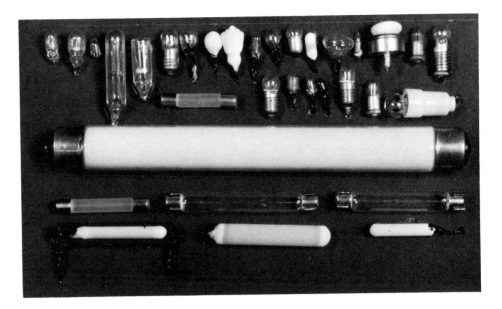

24-7

BULBS: shown at full size (their voltages and, in some instances, amperages and life expectancies are in parentheses).

Top row (from left to right): General Electric: No. 2139 (3 v, 0.19 amps, 350 hrs), No. 1784 (6 v, 0.2 amps, 1000 hrs), No. 680 (5 v, 0.06 amps, 100,000 hrs), No. 1757 (24 v, 0.025–0.035 amps, indefinite long life), No. 2138 (10 v, 0.035–0.045 amps, indefinite long life), No. 1767 (2.5 v, 0.2 amps, 500 hrs). Aristo Craft: No. 69R(12–15 v, yard floodlight), No. 20 (12 v, miniature round bulb), No. 94 (12 v, small frosted gas-type lamp), No. 1 (12 v, grain of wheat, No. 10, 3 v grain of wheat is similar), No. 21 (12 v, miniature round bulb), No. 50, No. 5 (12 v, frosted grain of wheat), No. M181 : 20 (3 v, clear button bulb), No. 51 : 40 (4 v, subminiature clear pointed bulb), No. 70 M171 (3 v, dome light). Aristo Craft: No. 57 : 29 (19 v miniature clear tubular lamp), No. 40 (3 v, miniature bulb with screw base shown inserted into a No. 41 miniature screw socket).

2nd row: Aristo Craft No. 80 (16 v, small frosted tubular lamp). Kemton: X-401 C (12 v clear), X-413 (12 v clear bulb in brass case). International Models (12–15 v, clear pea bulb; also obtainable in 12 v in amber, which is called a special shape spotlight bulb; 12–15 v radiant bulb). U.P.C. No. 80 (special tubular clear bulb with center lead, 12–15 v), No. 87 (cartridge bulb comes in red, green or clear, 12–15 v), No. 77 (covered socket with clear bulb and leads, 16 v).

3rd row: General Electric No. 5004 CW (cool white 28 v fluorescent).

4th row: Aristo Craft: No. 81 (3 v, small frosted tubular lamp), No. 82 (12–15 v, 2″ long clear tubular lamp with mounting clips), No. 84 (12 v, long clear tubular lamp with mounting clips).

5th row: Aristo Craft: No. 115 : 40 (15 v, universal billboard light), No. 90 (12 v, large fluorescent), No. 83 (12 v, frosted fluorescent).

acrylic. The sign may then be painted and the transfer letters removed to leave transparent illuminable letters on an opaque background. If opaque letters on a transparent background are desired, leave the transfers in place and do not paint the background. Transfer letters may also be applied to board. Photograph the layout and mount the photograph negative on the model.

SPECIAL EFFECTS

The use of special effects is sometimes appropriate on models that are to be extensively displayed.

Sound

Presentation models may warrant a recording that explains the project to the viewer. A tape recorder with a continuous tape can be used to provide a continuing commentary, or a system may be used whereby picking up an earphone or pushing a button will start a record. Cousino makes automatic continuous tape players costing from $100 to $230, including a tape cartridge. The lowest price model (R-7320) has a pre-amplifier but no speaker. It must be used with a telephone earphone or an accessory speaker or P.A. system. The least expensive model (AP-7328) that comes with a built-in speaker costs $125. Tape cartridges cost from $3 to $8 and deliver 3 to 40 minutes of playing time respectively. The tape can be activated by: (1) a $4.50 hand switch operated by the viewer; (2) a $23 footmat switch; or (3) a $30 timer that can be preset to

start the tape at any interval up to $8\frac{1}{2}$ minutes. Other, more theatrical effects have been achieved on occasion. Sounds associated with the project, such as organ music, waterfront sounds or aircraft engines have been used with church interiors, waterfront planning and airport models.

Smoke

Some museum and exposition display models of factory complexes have made use of smoke as an animation effect. Small amounts of smoke may be generated by the small units sold for use in model locomotives by such companies as A. C. Gilbert, Lionel and American Flyer. These units generate smoke by electrically heating a pellet or liquid oil. Cartridges generate smoke for about 1 hour and they run on 3 to 6 volts. These devices have a rather limited smoke making capacity; only enough for 1 smokestack. To produce a larger volume of smoke, it is necessary to construct a smoke machine from sheet metal. This can produce a sufficient quantity of smoke which is drawn to the electrical heating coil through a Fiberglas wick. If the model is of a low building and does not have enough interior space for the mounting of the smoke machine, the latter may be placed under the model and concealed with a wood skirt constructed around the baseboard.

If smoke is desired only for photographs, it may be blown through the chimney of the model by attaching a rubber hose and blowing cigarette smoke through it. Smoke may also be airbrushed on photographic prints.

189

25 PHOTOGRAPHING THE MODEL

The presentation model comprises only half of a presentation technique. To be of complete use to the designer and client, a model must be skillfully photographed to make 1 or more balanced presentations of the project. As a general routine, it may also be useful to photograph the design and test model for permanent records. For this form of photograph record, the skills of the ordinary professional or skilled amateur photographer are sufficient; but the creation of a first-rate presentation photograph requires extremely specialized skills and equipment, so much so that there are several commercial photographers whose entire livelihood comes from photographing architectural models. There are also several lens systems designed specifically for photographing the architectural and interior design model; and no doubt more remain to be created.

RULES FOR GOOD MODEL PHOTOGRAPHY

1—The picture must be taken from a viewpoint which makes the model look like an actual structure,

2—The resulting vanishing points should also be similar to what could be expected with a full-size building,

3—The foreground, midground and background of the picture must be reasonably in focus.

4—The model must have a compatible background.

These complications, together with those that are encountered in all photography (lighting, correct film selection and composition), make

25-1/25-2

PHOTOGRAPHS THAT DO JUSTICE TO A SUPERB MODEL.

PROJECT: The New York State Pavilion at the 1964–65 New York World's Fair.
DESIGNED BY: Philip Johnson Associates.
MODELBUILDER: Joseph Santeramo of the architect's captive model shop.
PHOTOGRAPHER: Louis Checkman.
SCALE: 1/8″ = 1′.
All circular structures (columns, and the exterior wall of the low building) were made from acrylic tubing. Floors, ramps and railing were also built of acrylic. The main ceiling was constructed of pieces of colored acrylic hung from a brass ring. The many prow shaped structures on the outside of the ring were also made from brass. The map on the floor was represented by a road map. The transparent sphere was blown from acrylic sheet. Figures were made from tin foil. The sculpture on the walls of the low building were made by dripping solder on wire mesh. The concrete-like finish was achieved by spattering lacquer on the acrylic. This model was used for design and presentation.
The photographs were taken with a 4″ × 5″ Sinar view camera, 90 mm Angulon lens and Super Panchro Press "B" film. 2 floodlights illuminated the airbrushed background. 1 750-watt spot placed low and to the right of the model provided its major illumination. A floodlight was used in the photograph of the exterior to bring out some of the detail in the shadow caused by the spot.
CONSTRUCTION TIME: about 250 hours.

model photography difficult. With the proper equipment and instruction, however, a fairly experienced amateur photographer should be able to produce professional results after practice that includes experimenting on several models. But the catch is that the proper equipment is expensive and the novice model photographer will have to take several (perhaps a dozen) photographs for each good one that he needs. An assistant to help with the lights and reflectors can ease the strain. Many offices have 1 or more employees who can turn out decent model photographs, but few can produce results that would be mistaken for the work done by a specializing professional.

Camera Viewpoint

Over-all bird's-eye photographs present only moderate focusing or background problems; it is with eye level and interior shots that serious complications arise. These shots must be selected and planned by determining the angles at which the actual building will be viewed and by determining which of these will make the best photographic presentations. Photographs should be composed similarly to renderings or paintings, with foreground objects framing the model, with a carefully planned, major center of interest and with perhaps 1 or more minor centers of interest.

Convergence

To appreciate convergence, study photographs of actual buildings and interiors and models. Note that photographs of buildings tend to have a more dramatic appearance. Their foreground elements seem closer to the viewer and their horizontal lines seem to converge more abruptly toward the horizon. Model photographs (especially those done by the unskilled) seem flat, the foreground too close to the background, etc. This is probably caused by their having been photographed from a distance that is greater (when scale is taken into consideration) than that in which a photographer would normally shoot a real building. To compensate for this it is necessary to: (1) photograph the model from a close camera position; and (2) use a wide-angle lens to make foreground elements appear to be closer to the viewer; this creates greater and more dramatic horizontal line convergence.

Focus

In photographing the front of an actual house, it would be necessary to stand perhaps a 100' from the building to get its entire facade in the picture. To add interest and artistic balance, try to maneuver a tree into the foreground of the picture; place the camera in such a position that the trunk of the tree would frame 1 side of the picture and its lower branches would frame the top. Thus the lens would be focused on the front facade of the house (100' away), on the farthest parts of the house that would be seen in the picture (perhaps 140' away) and on the tree (8' away). To reproduce this scene with great clarity, the lens would have to have a depth of field of from 8 to 140'. This capacity is not at all uncommon among even low price cameras as long as their focus and lens openings are adjustable. My moderately priced candid camera, for instance, will produce a sharp image of objects from 10' to infinity when its lens is stopped down to $f.8$ and it is focused at 20'. Depth of field, incidentally, is the distance between the closest and farthest objects that are in reasonably sharp focus.

In photographing this same scene on a $\frac{1}{4}'' = 1'$ model of the house, the following dimensions would be pertinent: lens to tree distance $= 2''$; lens to facade $= 25''$; lens to farthest part of house $= 35''$. Thus the lens must be capable of focusing sharply on objects that are from 2 to 35'' of its lens. No unmodified candid or reflex camera

can do this. My candid will produce a sharp image of objects 1' 11'' to 6' 10'' if it is focused at 3' (the closest that it can be focused) and if the lens is closed down to $f.32$ (the smallest stop for the lens). Notice that to increase the depth of field, the lens must be closed down. This is accomplished by setting it at a higher f. number. Incidentally, the f. number equals the focal length of the lens (the distance of the focal point of the lens to the film) over the opening of the diaphragm.

Taking this shot with a lens that could not give a sharp picture of both the foreground and the house would result in a technically poor picture and, perhaps worse, a picture with an unrealistic, model-like feeling. Some photographers try to solve the focus problem by moving the camera back until the increasing depth of field covers the entire model. Incidentally, this was done in about $\frac{1}{2}$ the low level shots of models that appear in this book. In the other $\frac{1}{2}$, the photographer either used special equipment to increase his depth of field or just overlooked the blurring of objects in the extreme foreground. For example, on the $\frac{1}{4}''$ scale model, I would have to position my candid camera about 2' from the tree. Thus I would be on a scale 100' from the tree and 200' from the house. This would result in a shot that would be sharp from the tree to far behind the house (the ground between the tree and the camera would be blurred, but it could be cropped from the print), however, (1) the tree would no longer frame the scene; and (2) the location of the vanishing points of the house would change, altering the dramatic perspective that a photograph of an actual building would have; and all this would make the shot look like that of a model.

To make the close-up focusing capabilities of candid and reflex cameras more like those of press-type cameras, it is possible to (1) use a portrait lens over the regular lens of the camera, (2) insert a lens extending tube or bellows between the camera and its normal lens in order to change its focal point. These 2 techniques will solve the problem of close-up focusing, but owners of candid and reflex cameras will still be faced with the limitation of a shallow depth of field.

Press cameras with double and triple extension bellows have lenses that can be moved out many inches (or even feet) from the film plate, thus providing the possibility of focusing on objects that are fractions of an inch away from the lens. This allows the camera to focus on anything, but does not improve its depth of field. In fact, the closer a lens is focused the shallower becomes its depth of field. To gain the depth of field needed when taking close-up model shots with a press camera or other camera that can be focused extremely close, it is possible to proceed in several ways: (1) by using a pinhole lens that has a huge f. rating or (2) by using a very expensive lens system with a large depth of field.

Usually only foreground blurring is disturbing. Often background blurring may permit the photographing of a model in front of a crude backdrop; also, a blurred background may at times minimize competition for the viewers' attention.

Backgrounds

A model, unlike many other photographic subjects, does not usually have a ready-made background. The background must be supplied by the photographer who has 3 basic choices: (1) He may set up a board, painting or photograph behind the model and photograph them together. The work of more than a few professional photographers can be identified by the cloud formations they invariably use. (2) He may photograph the model by itself, make a print, cut out the picture of the model and paste it onto a photo of a background; the resulting photocomposite may then be photographed and the new negative used to make all future prints. Or (3) he may photograph the model against a prototype background (25-3).

BACKDROPS FOR THE MODEL

Most professional photographers use either a large photograph of clouds (8-25) or white clouds airbrushed on a blue paper background (2-5).

It is also possible to use a wall, or sheets or rolls of plain white or colored paper or cardboard

25-3

THE MODEL PHOTOGRAPHED AGAINST A FOREGROUND AND BACKGROUND.

Competition entry by Paul Schneider-Esleben, Dusseldorf, Germany
PHOTOGRAPHER: Inge Goertz-Bauer.
SCALE: 1:500.
Buildings with fenestration were made from spray

painted acrylic. Other buildings were built of plaster. Water was represented by a sheet of cathedral glass.
This photo was used to illustrate the great sense of depth and realism that can be achieved by the use of foreground and background elements. In this photo the model was set up in front of a photo of the city. The mast of the ship was placed in front of the model.

as background; interesting effects can be created through the use of light. Use white or light gray material for black and white photos or blue material for color shots. Provide a halo or other model framing effects with spotlights. In addition to these simplest of backdrops, the following more complicated arrangements may be employed. A large sheet of opal glass may be used for a screen on which color or black and white slides can be rear projected. Substitute tracing paper sandwiched between 2 sheets of plain glass or a sheet of tracing paper mounted in a wood frame for the opal glass. Make color slides for projection by using slide producing color film. Black and white slides may be made directly if direct positive film is used, or favorite cloud shots may be sent to a processing lab and reproduced onto slides.

PHOTOGRAPHING THE BACKGROUND

Because the background is flat or, if it is projected, luminescent, and the model is 3-dimensional, a different and sometimes conflicting lighting problem arises. Most photographers evenly floodlight their photographs or painted-on sky backgrounds (1 300-watt bulb or so per 2 or 3 running feet of background). They then spotlight and floodlight their model, being careful to achieve model lighting that is of an intensity consistent with that of the background and also being careful not to cast model shadows on the background. This approach is the simplest, and should be used whenever possible.

Table top photographers, on the other hand, sometimes light and photograph their background separately, having placed a black cloth over the foreground. They then cover the background with a black board or cloth, remove the cloth from the foreground, light it and photograph it on the same negative. In this way they can achieve perfect exposure for both subjects. An alternative to this procedure is to illuminate and photograph the model, being careful that no light falls on the backdrop, and then illuminate and photograph only the backdrop. Both exposures are taken on the same piece of film.

SPLIT MATTING

When a press camera is being used, the model and its background may be viewed through the ground glass of the camera. Trace the silhouette of the model on a piece of tracing paper mounted on the glass. Cut 2 cardboard masks, 1 to obscure the foreground, the other to obscure the background. Put the background obscuring mask in front of the film holder and photograph the foreground at the exposure needed. Then repeat this procedure with the foreground obscuring mask.

It is also possible to (1) photograph the model in front of a black background, (2) print this picture in the darkroom with a cardboard mask covering the sky portion of the printing paper; and then (3) cover the part of the print that has the image of the model with a mask and print a sky negative on the print. This technique allows one to increase or decrease brightness and move cloud shots around in relation to the foreground.

Sky background may be obtained from photographic morgues (listed under "photographs-stock" in the yellow pages) or the modeler may take them himself. If the latter is decided upon, a more dramatic rendition may be achieved if the clouds are photographed through an infrared (A) filter (8-25). Sometimes stylized backgrounds representing a skyline or cityscape have been cut from black board and mounted on the backdrop or on flats in front of a sky backdrop. For aesthetic effects, it may sometimes be desirable to have the background out of focus.

PLANNING THE PHOTOGRAPHS

Photographic angles should be planned as carefully as the construction of the model. Sketches may have to be made to show the placement of lights and camera. Important photographs must be especially well planned. Take many different poses of the model even though these shots are not part of any foreseeable presentation. An extra hour or so spent taking a number of extraneous shots is not a waste; many of these photos have a way of becoming sleepers, and replace other photographs in the presentation. To decide on the angles to take, move the camera around the model, sighting it every 30° at 3 or more elevations.

Never assume that color shots can be copied in black and white. While occasionally the results will be satisfactory, most of the time the copy will have a rather odd looking tonal quality. If a Kodachrome 35 mm color slide is enlarged to an 8 × 10" black and white flat, it will lose sharpness. Because of these factors, only $\frac{1}{4}$ of the good color shots I have attempted to copy in black and white prints have turned out to be good. When taking color slides or photographs, also take a black and white shot from each viewpoint just for the records or for use in publications that cannot reproduce color.

LIGHTING

The purpose of lighting is to: (1) create shadows that emphasize the form and texture of parts of the subject; (2) articulate curved surfaces; (3) illuminate deep recesses of the model; and (4) bring the over-all illumination of the subject to a level that allows one to take the picture with a reasonably short exposure. All these uses should be kept in mind when arranging lights for each photograph. The arrangement of lights may be creatively thought through for each photograph; this procedure produces the best results. Or photographs may be mutually grouped into basic types and each of these types illuminated in an almost routine way. Surprisingly enough, this works well most of the time, and many successful photographers use a set order for placing their lamps; they use only slight modifications when they encounter an atypical model shape or texture that needs special treatment.

Basic light layouts usually are planned around: (1) a main light that is used to represent the sun and creates the major shadow; (2) 1 or more secondary or "high" lights to define important surfaces and textures and to create a separation between the model and its background; (3) "fill-in" lights to bring out sufficient detail in areas that are put into shadow by the primary and secondary lights; and (4) lights used to illuminate the background.

The Main Light

Since the main light emulates the sun, it is usually a spotlight placed high above the model. Try not to locate this light on the side of the model that represents north, since this can never happen in nature. If the primary light comes from over the camera, it will tend to flatten out the model. Illumination from the rear of the model silhouettes it and kills detail that is observable from the camera position. Side illumination usually gives the model an interesting shadowing of its mass but will reveal any crudity of detail or sloppiness of construction. Front illumination produces the most satisfactory color rendition on color shots.

The over-all illumination level of the photographic area may be raised by bouncing a large floodlight off the ceiling or walls of the room, or off sheets of white paper hung around the model or

25-4

CREATING A REALISTIC LOOKING SETTING.
PROJECT: The Davis Medical Foundation, Marion, Indiana.
DESIGNED BY: Harry Weese, Bruce Adams, John van der Meulen; Associate: John Dinkeloo.
MODELBUILDER: Callaghan and Seiler (a professional modelbuilder).
PHOTOGRAPHER: Hedrich-Blessing.
SCALE: 1/32" = 1'.
The entire presentation model including the water was made from acrylic. The stone wall, on the first floor of the building, was painted. The continuous slope of the ground contours was made from a plywood sheet on shaped wood formers. The photograph was taken with an 8" × 10" Deardorff view camera, 165 mm lens and Kodak Royal Pan film. The photograph was taken outdoors against the future surroundings of the building.

hung in front of the camera (with a hole cut out for the lens).

Secondary Lights

Floodlights are often used for secondary lights. These must be placed so that they do not cause secondary shadows, which are contrary to what can happen in nature.

The best position for secondary lights may be most easily established if the modeler (1) places the main light above the model; (2) walks around the model inspecting it for surfaces that need to be highlighted; (3) when he sees a surface that needs secondary lighting, places a lamp where he was standing and aims it at the surface to be illuminated. Does this wherever it is needed; (4) goes back to the camera and examines the lighting through the ground glass of the camera; (5) adjusts the intensity of the secondary lights by moving them closer or farther from the model until a good balance is achieved.

Different types of surfaces require different types of lights; mat surfaces generally require spotlights to bring out their detail, shiny objects require diffused spotlights for detail and to prevent glare. To emphasize texture, have the light glance across the surface at a low angle. Incidentally, textures, because of the play of light and shadow they create, often contribute more to the tonal values in a black and white photograph than does the color of the material.

Spotlights create shadows that have a sharp edge and give little illumination of the area within the shadow. Floodlights produce an indistinct shadow line and illuminate the area within the shadow to a greater degree. Back lighting adds to the 3-dimensionality of the subject. Test the effect of the lights by moving them around until the best composition is achieved. Try to imagine making a charcoal drawing of a group of forms, and use the lights to create the proper impression of mass on each form in the design.

Try to analyze the direction the light takes on good model photographs. I have listed the number of lights that were used to take some of the illustrations in this book. An analysis of this data can be very revealing.

If the model presents the problem of having both very dark and very light areas, the details of which it is necessary to see, try the procedure outlined on page 192, or keep illumination off the white areas by masking the lights with cardboard cut in the proper shape.

Early morning or late afternoon sun and shadows can be simulated by lamps placed at low levels. To produce shadows cast on the model by trees, hills and buildings outside of camera range (and that have not been modeled), cut masks out of cardboard and hold them in front of a lamp.

Fill-In Lights

Fill-in lights must not cast shadows. Prevent this by placing them at a low angle. If a mirror or white cardboard is used to bounce light from the main or from a secondary light, separate fill-in lights may be dispensed with. Diffused flood lamps or a flood with a reflector may also be used as fill-in lights. Small mirrors may be placed inside or on top of the model to bounce light into small hard-to-reach areas. The mirrors may be obscured from the camera by parts of the model. They may be held in place with plasticine or tape and may be partially masked with tape to provide any desired shape of reflecting surface. Small areas of the model may be illuminated if a mask is cut from cardboard and placed in front of a light.

If the illumination scheme does not throw enough light on the model to allow focusing through ground glass, use a hand held high wattage lamp to pan around the model as it is checked through the glass.

The Problem of Illuminating Shiny Surfaces

Some part of the model may have a shiny surface that causes unwanted reflections or light flares. To dispense with this annoyance, evenly light the shiny surface or spray it with matting spray. Very even illumination can be achieved by placing Fiberglas screens in front of the lamps or by constructing a "tent," around the model, made out of white paper hung from rollers or from the ceiling of the studio. Position lamps inside the tent and aim them at its walls. The tent can also be constructed from an acetate-like material called matte Kodacel. Lights are placed outside this tent and are aimed toward the model at about the same position in which they would be arranged to illuminate a nonshiny model. The Kodacel evenly spreads out the light. Both these setups should have the lamps throw their penumbrae above the view of the camera. Use floodlights; if an area is to be highlighted, use a spotlight. Once the over-all shine is under control, 1 or more controlled shiny highlights may be brought out by introducing a spotlight directly on the model. Controlled reflections may also be created on the shiny parts with strips of gray paper pinned to the interior of the walls of the tent. If the reflection produced has too sharp an outline, subdue it by using an unevenly sprayed piece of paper.

Full tenting, naturally, will produce a more even, pristine lighting on the model, not the natural lighting caused by the main, secondary, fill-in light arrangement. But tenting allows a starting arrangement from which one can experiment with the introduction of a main light to form the dramatic prime shadow.

The use of matting spray is less complicated than the use of a tent. With it any dramatic lighting scheme desired can be fully retained. Matting spray eliminates shine, replacing it with a luster. The spray broadens highlights and allows the camera to catch additional detail. Be careful that the spray used is compatible with all the plastic or painted surfaces to which it is applied. Photographers of still lifes often use a brush-on cosmetic liner such as Elizabeth Arden's Screen and Stage Make-Up No. 12. It is compatible with plastics, metals, etc.

Photographing the Model Out-of-Doors

While natural lighting produces a sharp shadow (if the sun is out) and eliminates the necessity of procuring and setting up artificial lights, its drawbacks make it of little use except for taking rush pictures when a lighting setup is not readily available. Besides the handicaps of wind, dust and possible audience, outdoor setups will not provide the secondary and fill-in lights that are needed for truly polished photographs.

Lighting Equipment

The basic lighting equipment for a simple studio should consist of a main spotlight of as high as 750 watts (if the models are extensive in size), and several lesser (200 to 300-watt) lamps. The smaller lamps may have built-in reflectors that produce a flood or a spot effect or they may be screwed into metal reflectors. The latter arrangement is cheapest in the long run. Sealed beam lights (650 watts) are useful for the illumination of large models. These bulbs and their holders sell for between $10 and $15. The life expectancy of the replaceable bulb is about 10 hours, which is considerably better than that of most photographic bulbs.

Some of the lamps should be set into sockets that have clamp ends. Others can be set into sockets that screw into inexpensive ($2 to $5) tripods. A 10-inch reflector, socket with clamp-on

swivel end, and cord can be purchased for as little as $2 for the set from many camera stores.

Also available are miniature spotlights which, at the turn of a lever, will give the effect of either a spotlight or a diffused floodlight. Pro Spot sells a 500-watt spot for $22. Fresnel lenses placed over spots will soften their outline.

Metal or wood hoops that hold Fiberglas light diffusing material are also available. These are mounted onto the reflectors by means of clips, and serve to spread the light more evenly.

Have available a supply of extension cords, white cardboard that can be cut into light masks or used as reflectors, tape to hold the cardboard masks to the metal reflectors, a few square feet of tin or aluminum foil from which to make multifaceted reflectors (this is pressed into a crinkled form and then cemented to cardboard) and mirrors; in addition, color compensating filters are essential when using outdoor color film with artificial lighting or when using a type of light that is not compatible with indoor color film.

PHOTOCOMPOSITES

Combining photographs of the model with other photographs can be used to: (1) add shots of existing buildings, backgrounds and other surroundings to the presentation of the model (8-13 and 10-5)—this may even eliminate model construction of existing buildings (1-7); (2) combine model photographs with rendered plans, elevations or perspectives for an original presentation technique; (3) add photos of cars, people, furniture, etc. to the model shot; or (4) combine all of the above in 1 presentation.

All shots to be in the photocomposite must be planned so that the objects depicted are photographed from the same angle above the horizon and illuminated from the same side. When photocompositing shots of automobiles and the modeled facades along which they are parked or the street facades of existing buildings and the street facade of the model, be sure that the facades are all at the same angle to the camera. Work with prints that are double or more the size of the intended reproduction. When reproduced to $\frac{1}{2}$ size, small miscuts and other blemishes will not be visible. Colored backgrounds may also be combined with black and white model photos and vice versa for unusual effects. Correct size photographs of people and cars may be pasted directly on prints of the photograph of the model. These may be especially shot for the composite or they may come from a stockpile of pictures.

Photocomposites are made more realistic by the casting of shadows from the objects shown in one photograph onto another. Shadows may be made with Bourges Solotone overlay sheets.

Foreground objects, such as cars, trees, etc., may be photographs pasted on cardboard and set up in the model; then the entire assembly (model and foreground entourage) is shot. This helps to reduce the depth of field that is needed to make a sharp composition.

When attempting to superimpose a photograph of the surroundings of the building onto the photograph of the model, the procedure to follow is this: (1) Before photographing the model, visit the site and note the desirability of the background, the best angles and elevations for taking background shots and determine whether or not a camera can be conveniently set up at these viewpoints. Make a sketch of the site which will include the elevations of the roofs of surrounding buildings and other locations at which the camera will be set up. Bring the camera on this trip and with its viewfinder determine the borders of shots to be taken from desirable viewpoints. (2) When photographing the model, attempt to take some shots from each horizontal and vertical angle that was impressive at the site. Also, use a lighting setup similar to natural conditions. (3) Select the

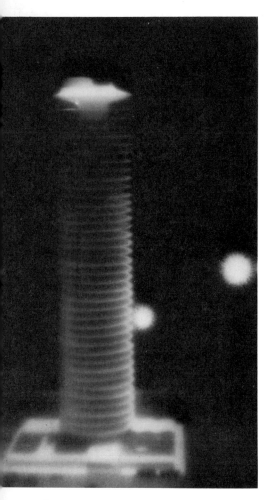

25-5

A PHOTOGRAPH TAKEN THROUGH A DIFFUSION DISC.

PROJECT: an office building.
DESIGNER, MODELBUILDER AND PHOTOGRAPHER: Sanford Hohauser.
SCALE: 1″ = 40′.
The tower of this quickly built presentation model was made from a paper tube on which floors made of mat board were attached. (On a later model the entire tower was encased in an acrylic tube upon which mullions were scribed.) The roof truss and water tank were carved from balsa.
The photo was taken with a 35 mm candid camera, 50 mm Wollensak Perfex Velostigmat lens and Kodachrome color film. A medium diffusion disc was used on the lens to create the foggy effect. The model was lighted with 3 grains of wheat miniature lamps (1 on the plaza and 2 on the roof). 2 pen-size flashlights aimed toward the camera created the effect of the light flairs.
CONSTRUCTION TIME: about 20 hours.

best photographs for the composite, noting the direction of their illumination. Plan the time to revisit the site to match this lighting. (4) At the site take several pictures, varying the exposures and filters, from each of the selected angles. If a camera with a ground glass viewer is available, insert the negative of the model shot (protected by a cellophane envelope) into it and precisely match the angle of the background.

MISCELLANEOUS TOUCHES

A small collection of props is used from time to time by most professional photographers. These consist of model trees and branches (usually sprigs of baby's-breath) propped up to frame an occasional photo. Illustration 25-3 shows an interesting use of a foreground prop.

Additional realism may be achieved if shadows from an intricate tree or adjacent building fall on the model. This may be achieved by cutting cardboard shapes to represent adjacent buildings, and mounting them and a spotlight in correct position to the model. Tree shadows may be cast by several boughs of baby's-breath mounted in a dense array of buds and stems.

BLACK AND WHITE PHOTOGRAPHS OF COLOURED MODELS

When photographing a colored model in black and white, see that its colors end up in a reasonably pleasant and contrasting assortment of gray tones. If a model painted in several harmonious colors turns out, when photographed in black and white, to have too many similar tones of gray to provide contrast, correct this problem with: (1) lighting that raises or lowers the tones of various surfaces, or (2) color filters which distort the brightness of certain colors. It is also possible to benefit by making a test exposure, with each type of black and white film used, of color charts of the paints, boards and other materials. By studying these tests, determine which colors must be especially illuminated or filtered in any photograph.

"NIGHT" PHOTOGRAPHS

Night photographs make interesting secondary shots of any model that is internally lit. The lights of the model must provide even lighting, or at least lighting that is as constant as is desired. Some bulbs may have to be shielded to prevent them from shining into the camera. Small reflectors the outside surfaces of which are painted black can be mounted in front of objectionable model lights to prevent glare from these bulbs from reaching the lens. Additional lights can be made by mounting miniature bulbs on 2 to 3′ long dowels held to illuminate those parts of the model that do not have enough light (24-5). The lights of the model may also be augmented by placing small flashlights inside the model or behind it. While it is usually best not to allow an unshielded miniature light to be photographed, sometimes doing just this can add the realistic touch of halation to the picture. Halation, making the picture look as though it were taken in the rain, is the spreading out of light coming from an unshielded bulb to form a sunburst-like radiance pattern. Halation may be created by taking the picture through a piece of insect screening. This forms 4-pointed stars, or, to create 8-pointed stars, take it through 2 pieces of screening held so that their threads cross one another diagonally. The halation in illustration 25-5 was made by taking the picture through a diffusion disc.

"FOG" PHOTOGRAPHS

Fog shots can be simulated by smearing vaseline on a sheet of clear glass and holding it about a foot in front of the camera lens, or by placing a diffusion disc over the lens (25-5).

"SUNSET" PHOTOGRAPHS

Dramatic sunset or sunrise photographs may be made by low lighting the model from its side or rear (see illustrations 8-4, 19-18 and 25-2). In dusk simulating photographs, the internal lights of the model may burn too strongly into the film if exposure is based on the internal plus the low level external illumination of the model. To rectify this, expose the photograph with the model illuminated only by the external lights. Then, without moving the camera and on the same film, take a shot that is exposed only by the internal lights of the model. This procedure may also be used when photographing interior shots that are illuminated by miniature lights as well as by auxiliary photo lamps.

PHOTOGRAPHING TIGHT PLACES

If it is necessary to take photographs from viewpoints that are inaccessible to the camera: (1) Shoot them off a mirror aimed at the desired view. The camera must be focused for the distance from lens to mirror plus the distance from the mirror to the image. (2) Secure a modelscope (see page 197).

DARKROOM TRICKS

There are several creative innovations that can be performed on negatives once out of the camera. Because of this and the fact that it is a generally good practice anyway, a processing laboratory should be selected that is geared and noted for high quality work. The premium price—and it may run an additional 100%—is very little considering that it has to be applied only against developing negatives, making contact sheets, master prints and 8 × 10″ negatives. The mass of photos may be made by a regular printer as contact prints from the 8 × 10″ negatives. Among the things that may be achieved in the darkroom are:

1—Manipulation of the enlarging processes to compensate for negatives or parts of negatives that are too dark or too light.

2—Burning an interesting horizon halo into the enlargement. This is done by cutting a cardboard template in the shape of the horizon and allowing the light of the enlarger to burn in the halo while the rest of the print is kept dark by the template.

3—Enlarging through a "homemade" or commercially obtainable screen (a texture printed on clear acetate), usually placed in contact with the printing paper. Obtainable textures resemble dry point etching strokes, charcoal paper, canvas, etc., and may be obtained at large photo stores. Other similar effects can be obtained through the use of various other commercial processes (25-6). Some of these techniques require many darkroom steps including special printing as well as solarization and the use of a texture screen. One may also simply make one's own screens with photographs of textures or through the reticulation of unexposed film.

4—Achieving a soft diffused focus by enlarging the negative through a diffusing filter.

5—By tipping the easel of the enlarger, printing pictures of models of high buildings with convergence similar to the distortion found in photographs of actual buildings.

6—Achieving photocomposites in the darkroom by printing parts of several negatives on 1 piece of enlarging paper. For this, the negatives must be masked and individually projected through the enlarger. Masks are made by (1) tracing parts of the negative on a sheet of tracing paper and then transferring this to a sheet of cardboard, or (2) projecting the image of the negative through the enlarger on a sheet of cardboard, then tracing and cutting out the intended lines of demarcation. The former mask must be used while sandwiched with the negative; the latter is placed on top of the enlarging paper. These techniques of achieving photocomposites have their drawbacks inasmuch as it can be fairly difficult to cut masks accurately.

what pictures are needed for the various presentations of the project. These presentations may include some or all of the following: photos for the client; for the office portfolio; for the basic press kit of the project; for an extended press kit for special publications; for the mortgagee, government agencies, etc. Certain shots must obviously be included: these are over-all bird's-eye views, ¾ or full front shots of the major facade. Beyond these staples, a combination of the importance of the view and the quality of the photo is important. Sometimes 1 or 2 great shots of the project will satisfy basic presentation requirements; but there are many instances when none of dozens of photos are acceptable; then, choose a handful of the best and analyze what steps to take, when reshooting, to improve them. Whether there are good results or bad, it is desirable to summarize what went wrong, concluding with a list of the major errors (underexposure, uneven lighting, etc.) so as to be aware of these problems in the future.

Have the photos that will be the backbone of the mass-produced presentations photocopied on $8 \times 10''$ negatives if more than 3 prints are needed; all the pictures subsequently ordered may then be contact prints rather than more expensive enlargements.

Coloring Enlargements

Enlargements may be colored with transparent oils or watercolors obtainable at photo supply stores. Since it is hard to apply color to glossy prints, and colored mat prints are often dull looking, best results occur when using paints with enlargements made on semimat, rough paper. Prints should not have too much contrast; they should have detail and not impenetrable black in shadow areas.

Submissions for Publication

Send as many prints as possible to each relevant publication. It is impossible to foresee which secondary shots will catch the eye of an editor. Each photo should have the name of the firm stamped on the back with the name of the project written in soft pencil, so as not to make an impression through the print. Prints should be glossy (they reproduce the best when they are rephotographed) and double-weight (less likely to crease under handling). Send all submissions packed between at least 2 sheets of corrugated cardboard. Do not rely on the legend "Photographs—Do Not Bend," to save the package from rough handling. Minor spots on the prints can be retouched with such products as Grumbacher Retouch Gamma Colors applied with a sable brush.

EQUIPMENT

The Camera

To qualify as a good camera for model photography, an instrument must have: (1) the ability to focus to within a few inches of the lens; (2) full negative size ground glass viewing (through the main lens to avoid parallax); (3) negative size that allows for making good $8 \times 10''$ enlargements; (4) an interchangeable lens system for wide-angle lens use.

Since color and black and white photos are often taken in the same photographing session, 2 cameras may be needed or, preferably, a camera with interchangeable film holders. The latter can be a press camera with cut film or, for black and white film, filmpack holders and, for cost conservation, an adapter to take roll color film.

25-6

AN INTERESTING PHOTOPRINTING PROCESS.

PROJECT: the Samuel F. B. Morse and Ezra Stiles Colleges, Yale University, New Haven, Connecticut.
DESIGNED BY: Eero Saarinen and Associates.
MODELBUILDERS: members of the architect's staff.
PHOTOGRAPHER: Joe Clark.
SCALE: $1/4'' = 1'$.

Walls and roofs, of this design and presentation model, were made from cardboard. Windows were constructed of acrylic, trees of stranded wire, people of cardboard. Stone work was simulated by sponging ink on the walls and ground.

The photoprint was made with a line reproduction process called "Impro," crafted by Joe Clark of Detroit, Michigan. Processes like this sometimes can be used to cover the crudity of a hastily built model or to transform a photograph into an exquiste, etching-like print.

Besides what can be accomplished in the lab, it may be desirable to alter the emphasis of certain parts of the finished photo. A background may be partially eliminated by putting a black or white Bourges Solotone acetate overlay sheet over it. These sheets are covered by a film that comes in various shades of gray. The shade may be removed to the desired outline by scraping with a stylus or by using a liquid remover. The acetate sheet is prepared, then mounted on top of the photo, and the assembly is sent to be photocopied.

The Dunning Process

This is a way to avoid the laborious cutting out of photographs to be used as overlays in a photocomposite. A brief resume of the technique is as follows: (1) photograph the intended background and make a slide of the shot; (2) tone the slide with transparent yellow dye and in the camera place it in front of unexposed film; (3) set up the model against a plain white board background, then illuminate the model with yellow light and the background with purple light. In the photograph, the yellow light coming from the model will pass through the yellow slide and record the image of the model on the film. The purple light of the background will illuminate the slide, and allow the detail on it to be transferred to the film. In the areas where no purple light comes from the setup, there will be no overlapping of background and model images since the background slide will not transfer to the film.

THE PRESENTATION

Making contact prints of all the photos taken provides much information about the composition, contrast and technical accuracy of each photo. Examine the prints under a magnifying glass that has the capacity of enlarging sections to the size they will be on an $8 \times 10''$ print. In this way it is possible to study the sharpness and grain that will appear on future enlargements. Also, note

Camera type	Sighted and focused through film-size ground glass?	Focusable within inches of the lens without supplementary lenses, tube, or bellows?	Parallax problem on close-up shots?[1]	Accepts interchangeable lenses?	Distorts perspective by tilts and swings?	Film size sufficient for prints larger than 8"×10"?	Film of same proportion as 8"×10" print?	Completely satisfactory, with modification (extension tube or bellows), for model photography?
35-mm candid	No	No	Yes	Yes (except for cheap models)	No	Only if care is taken	No	No, because of lack of ground-glass focusing and small film size
35-mm 1-lens reflex or 2 1/4" × 2 1/4" 1-lens reflex	Yes	No	No	Yes	No	With 35-mm film size, only if care is taken; with 2 1/4" × 2 1/4" size, yes	No	Yes, if small film size is no problem—get a magnifying lens (to aid in precise focusing) and a bellows
2 1/4" × 2 1/4" 2-lens reflex	Yes	No	Yes	Yes (except for cheap models)	No	Yes	No	Yes; get a magnifying lens and bellows
2 1/4" × 3 1/4", 4" × 5", 5" × 7", 8" × 10" or 11" × 14" press or studio camera	Yes	Yes (if bellows are of the double or triple extension variety)	No	Yes	Yes (with most makes)	Yes	Yes	Camera needs no modification; a 3 1/4" × 4 1/4" or 4" × 5" camera may prove the best all-around camera for model as well as full-size architectural and interior-design photography

[1] A parallax-correcting device is obtainable for twin-lens cameras. It comes in 3 models: one is used when the lens is 10"–13" from the subject; another when the distance is 13"–20"; the third for 20"–38" distances. Spiratone Inc. sells them for $4–$5 per set.

THE PRESS OR VIEW CAMERA

As is shown by the preceding table, the press camera is the best-suited commercially made device for taking model photos. The majority of the photographs in this book were taken with such a camera. The lens of a press camera is mounted at the end of an adjustable bellows, and may be extended or retracted to focus on close or distant objects respectively. On good press cameras, the lens may be swung and tilted in relation to the plane of the film. Tilting or revolving the lens forward or backward around its horizontal axis increases the depth of field of the camera. Swinging the lens or revolving it around its vertical axis can put a larger amount of vertical surface in focus. Most lenses may also be raised in relation to the film; this helps to eliminate convergence that is caused by aiming a camera up at high buildings. Lenses may also be slid from side to side in relation to the film to accentuate or eliminate the perspective of horizontal lines. A press camera would be an excellent choice for architectural and interior photography as well as for model photography. Prices range from a minimum of about $35 for a used $2\frac{1}{4}" \times 3\frac{1}{4}"$ Graflex Reflex to $75 for a used $4 \times 5"$ camera equipped with a wide-angle lens and 3 cut film holders (each holder has a capacity of 2 sheets of film). Additional lenses cost $20 or more. Film pack holders that accept packs containing 12 or 16 sheets of film and roll film holders that allow the camera to use certain types of roll film are also available. Polaroid makes an adapter for their instantly developed film that fits press cameras. It costs about $50. Each black and white photo costs 60¢ (this includes a negative and positive). This adapter aids in checking exposure, shadows and camera angle. It is conceivable that this might reduce the number of shots taken with regular film and thus effect an over-all savings. If nothing else, it would allow a clearer anticipation of results before the end of the photographic session. A new $4 \times 5"$ camera equipped with a wide-angle and a regular lens and all the film holders needed should cost no more than a good reflex camera, or in the neighborhood of $300.

When the lens of a press camera is extended far out of the camera, as in taking extreme close-ups, the f. number indicated by the lens is no longer accurate. The true number may be found by the following formula: actual (effective) f. number = lens to film distance times f. stop indicated on the lens over the focal length of lens; or look up the actual f. number on a Kodaguide No. 1225 effective lens aperture guide wheel. The more bulky the camera, the farther away from the model the centerline of its lens will be, no matter how close one tries to bring it. This is one of the few drawbacks of the press camera.

CUSTOM-MADE CAMERAS

An occasional model photographer will fabricate his own camera for close-up work. One that I have heard about embodies the following features: (1) It is extremely small ($2 \times 2 \times \frac{3}{4}"$ plus lens) so that it can be set right into the model. It has a lens center that can be placed on a scale 12 feet off the ground (when photographing $\frac{1}{8}"=1'$ scale models). (2) A pinhole (f. 74) lens gives the camera a depth of field of from $3\frac{1}{2}"$ to 2'. (3) A 25 mm focal length lens from a 16 mm motion picture camera is used to produce a wide-angle effect. (4) The camera uses 35 mm film and is focused through a nonpinhole lens substituted for the pinhole shooting lens. While cameras such as these work well, constructing them entails more trouble than most modelmakers are willing to endure.

Lens and Lens Extenders

The following lens systems may be employed, and will result in the following effects:

1—The regular lens of a camera with an inexpensive portrait lens attachment permits one to focus at closer objects but diminishes depth of field. This type of lens attachment is not needed on a camera such as a press camera that has its lens mounted on a bellows system. Nos. 2 to 4 are also unnecessary for this type of camera.

2—An extension tube inserted between the regular lens of the camera and the camera, as with the portrait lens, enables one to focus at closer objects but diminishes depth of field. Tubes tend to flatten out the perspective of the subject.

3—A bellows inserted between the lens and the camera tends to flatten out the perspective of the subject.

4—Using a telephoto lens and moving the camera further from the model increases depth of field but flattens the scene, making it look shallow.

5—Using a wide-angle lens improves depth of field of any given camera-to-subject distance and exaggerates depth of the scene, making it look deeper. The lens also makes the scene smaller and includes more in the picture. Most professionals use this type of lens for eye-level close-up model shots. In fact, the wide-angle lens used on a press-type view camera is the combination of equipment most often used.

6—Using a disc with a small (pinhole) opening inserted at the focal point of the lens works like a large f. opening, providing great depth of field. The scene is not foreshortened or exaggerated in depth. A pinhole lens can give a picture that has a depth of field of from 6" to 3'. The pinhole lens may be made out of thin metal (0.007" brass, etc.) sheet. Drill a hole (a No. 71 drill often works well) in the center of the disc and chamfer the hole from both sides so that in cross section its sides like look vees. Paint all of the disc flat black except the chamfered hole. Blacken the chamfer by holding it over a lighted candle. Now rate the lens for its f. number. In general, a pinhole lens with an opening smaller than f. 120 is impractical on a 50 mm lens. If the lens has a longer focal length, a smaller opening may be used. When a light meter is not calibrated to show the exposure required with an f. opening as small as the one above, the exposure may be found with the following formula:

$$\frac{\text{the square of the f. number} \times \text{the exposure recommended with any f. number shown on the meter}}{\text{the square of the above f. number (that is shown on the meter)}} = \text{the exposure to be used}$$

The disc must now be inserted in the lens at its exact focal point. It is advisable to have this operation done by a camera repair man. Some photographs taken with an f. 64 pinhole lens have had a depth of field from a few inches to 100'.

7—The regular lens is used by most professional photographers for taking long, bird's-eye model shots.

8—Using a regular lens, moving the camera far from the model, enlarging the resulting print and cropping off the unwanted border increases depth of field but also produces a flat looking picture similar to that obtained with a telephoto lens.

LENS EXTENSION TUBES

These are used to allow the lens to focus on close objects. They are sold by the manufacturers of a large number of quality cameras to fit these cameras; those that may be used on many cameras may be obtained from Spiratone, Inc. Most tube sets cost between $10 and $15. Tubes are inserted into the lens system of the camera which in turn must be focused through ground glass (if the camera is equipped with it) since the distance scale on the lens will no longer be applicable; if the camera has no ground glass, depth of field and point of focus must be established in the following way: (1) remove the back of the camera; (2) insert on the film rolls a strip of tracing paper held in the position that would be normally occupied by unexposed film; (3) use the paper as a substitute for ground glass. Open the lens aperture as wide as possible and experimentally move the camera forward and backward until the subject is in sharp focus on the paper; (4) measure the distance from the lens to the part of the subject which is in sharpest focus and the distances from the lens to the closest and farthest parts of the subject which are in acceptably good focus. This establishes the new depth of field and the distance from the subject at which the camera must be held. Also note the width of the field that is captured by the lens; (5) make a complete series of tests by placing the camera at various distances from the model. Each different tube naturally requires a new set of tests. Conversely, when constructing one's own tube for general use or even to take 1 specific shot, the length that will be needed may be ascertained in the following way: (1) locate the camera (with its back removed and tracing paper inserted into its rollers if the camera does not have ground glass focusing) at the distance from the subject at which the picture is to be taken; (2) unscrew the lens of the camera, and holding it by hand, move it back and forth between the camera and the test subject until the image is in focus. Record the distance that the tube must span; (3) construct the tube at that length. The homemade tube may be made from a mailing tube painted dull black inside. It may be wedged on the lens. Before attempting to produce a homemade tube, however, ask the camera store or the manufacturer of the camera whether or not a tube may be inserted into the lens system, and if so, at what point.

PORTRAIT LENSES

These may be obtained from the manufacturer of many quality cameras or from Kodak for $10 to $15 per set. The Kodak Portra Lens series consists of 3 lenses which are designated 1+, 2+ and 3+ to indicate their strength. Other companies make lenses up to 10+. Portra Lenses can be used 1 at a time or coupled to add up to a higher rating (This is done by simultaneously using a 3+ and a 1+ to equal 4+, etc.). The stronger lens should be closer to the camera. These lenses make depth of field rather unsubstantial. The following table explains what happens when a 35 mm candid camera is used with a 50 mm lens set at f. 22, or what happens when a $2\frac{1}{4} \times 2\frac{1}{4}$" reflex camera with a 75 to 80 mm lens is set at f. 32:

Portra lens(es) used	Camera focused at	Distance of lens to subject	Depth of field
1+	4'	22"	4 to $7\frac{1}{2}$" = $3\frac{1}{2}$"
3+ and 3+	4'	$5\frac{1}{2}$"	$\frac{3}{8}$ to $\frac{3}{8}$" = nil

The wider the lens is opened, the more the depth of field is diminished, and the center of clear focus moves in toward the lens. Naturally, the camera may be focused at over 4', the camera pushed back and a deeper depth of field enjoyed. Portrait lenses do not cut down the light that reaches the film, so their use does not require an additional exposure factor.

BELLOWS

These may be obtained from the manufacturers of several quality candid and reflex cameras for use with their own camera products. Spiratone, Inc. carries an extensive line of bellows that fit many cameras. Bellows cost about $20. They serve the same purpose as portrait lenses or extension tubes but have the additional feature of being able to be focused with greater versatility; some even have tilts, swings and other actions.

WIDE-ANGLE LENSES

The wider the angle of the lens (the shorter its focal length), the greater the depth of field it can achieve. Objects in the foreground seem closer and those in the background appear farther away than with a regular lens, thus dramatizing the perspective of the photo. The lens also covers a wide arc, one which is closer to what is seen by the unaided eye.

PERSPECTIVE CORRECTING LENSES

This type of lens is constructed so that its component optics can be shifted off axis. This performs the same basic correction as raising or shifting a press camera lens sideways. Thus a P.C. lens (as it is called) can be used to kill the convergence that will be photographed if one stands at the base of a tall building and takes a picture of it with the camera pointing up. Nikkor makes a $250 P.C. lens that fits its 35 mm camera. The lens has an f. 3.5 rating and is wide-angle (62°). It snaps a sharp picture down to $10\frac{1}{2}$" when taken at f. 32.

MODELSCOPE

An interesting, recent development in wide-angle lenses has been the Modelscope. This lens system, especially engineered for close-up and realistic, wide-angle photography of models, measures 12" by about a 15th of an inch in diameter (at its front end). These dimensions allow the lens to be placed at scale eye level inside the models, between buildings or into rooms so that prospective inhabitants can visualize how the finished edifice will look. Since the human eye cannot clearly discern detail that is closer than 10", the Modelscope allows an examination of the model in ways that were heretofore impossible. The instrument has an impressive depth of field

25-7

PHOTO TAKEN THROUGH A MODEL SCOPE.

PHOTOGRAPHER: the H.C.I. Sales Corporation (distributor of the instrument).

Note the unblurred foreground and realistic convergence toward 3 vanishing points.

(5 mm to infinity when viewing by eye). Its cost is about $350 for the viewer plus $100 for an adapter that will allow the viewer to be coupled to a camera. Lenses may be rented for between $10 and $20 per day. The photos obtained are of the quality of television pictures (25-7).

Tripods

Because it is always important to obtain the greatest possible depth of field, the lens will invariably have to be closed down as much as possible; this necessitates using long exposures. To make these extended exposures as well as to focus the camera and compose the picture requires a well-built tripod. To bring the camera close to the model, get a tripod the head and central shaft of which can be placed on the tripod legs in an inverted position. This will allow the camera to be mounted upside down. Carefully place the legs of the tripod on the base of the model and lower the camera until its top almost touches the model or its baseboard. This procedure will allow the camera to be brought in closer to the model than could be achieved by standing the tripod on the floor alongside the model and setting the camera upon it.

The tripod should allow the camera to be elevated to a height of at least 6'. Additional height may be obtained by mounting the tripod on a table. The tripod should have a head which can be swung 360°, precisely cranked up and down and tilted up or down a full 180°. The tripod should be picked for its sturdiness even if this means obtaining a somewhat bulky and heavy model. Many finely constructed tripods have legs that telescope out to their full length. The sections are then made secure by turning a knurled sleeve. It is often hard to turn these sleeves to release them, so a monkey wrench may be a needed accessory in your equipment bag. To meet all of the above requirements will result in a tripod cost of $25 or more.

Filters

Aside from color compensating filters that allow the use of outdoor color film with artificial illumination and vice versa, filters are seldom used on model photography. When taking black and white cloud shots for use as background, the various yellow filters may be used to accentuate the image of the cloud. The most dramatic cloud effects possible are obtained by using an infrared filter. The clouds in illustration 8-25 were taken through this type of filter; it both increases the whiteness of the clouds (and in many instances records clouds on the film which are not visible to the naked eye) and darkens the sky.

Since a filter of a given color allows the passage of light of only that color, it is possible, when taking black and white photos, to accentuate areas of the model by using a filter. For instance, in a model that is green and blue, a green filter will allow all the light coming from the green parts of the model to get to the film. At the same time, much of the light coming from the blue part of the model will not be transmitted. This will result in the green parts of the model appearing lighter, and more of their detail will be observable than without a filter; the blue parts will appear darker. A red filter will darken blues and greens almost to black, lighten reds and yellows almost to white, and only slightly darken browns. A yellow filter will darken blues, browns and greens and lighten reds. These effects can be achieved with panchromatic film only. Orthochromatic film produces different results.

Filters cut the total amount of light that reaches the film, therefore, a longer exposure is needed.

Film

Most of the photographs in this book were taken with panchromatic film such as: Plus-X, Super

XX, Tri-X, Royal Pan, Super Panchro Press B, etc. Choice of film seems to be one of personal preference, since most of these films work, in the hands of those who know them, with roughly the same excellence. If the shots must be greatly enlarged, use a fine grain film (such as Ansco Super Hypan, Kodak Panatomic-X or Plus-X, etc.) and fine grain developer. Always use a film that gives good contrast between the dark and light areas of the photographs. Since a tripod must be used, film speed is of little importance.

If the model has both very dark and very light areas, it will be necessary to solve the problem of how to illuminate the dark areas so that their detail will be observable and yet not overilluminate and "burn" out the neighboring light parts. In these instances, it is best to use a film of moderate contrast and to overexpose the photo slightly. The negative can then be slightly underdeveloped in a soft working developer. This procedure darkens the white areas and lightens the dark ones.

Photographs that are to be made into color prints will be of better quality if they are taken on film that produces a negative, not on film that makes a slide. The negative may also be used to make color slides. If both color and black and white prints of a shot are desired, the picture should be shot on both types of film rather than trying to make a black and white print from a color negative. The latter procedure more often than not produces inferior results.

Light Meters

Light meters are an absolute necessity. Some people may develop an "eye" for judging light intensity and relating it to exposure time and lens aperture, but this is extremely hard to achieve and is always a gamble. Use a meter that measures reflected light, preferably a meter that only picks up light from a narrow angle. Take readings of various parts of the model, making mental note of how the readings change from part to part. This change reflects the degree of brightness (or darkness) of each part of the model. If the range is too great for the picture contemplated, consider changing the lighting. If the readings are satisfactory, decide which reading to "favor" when selecting exposure time and aperture. Keep in mind what this selection will do to the other parts of the picture: will it cause overly dark or bright areas or loss of detail due to under- or overexposure?

Correct exposure is more vital and critical in color photography than in black and white. An underexposed color photograph will result in a loss of color as well as a dark print.

Some photographers take a test shot with a Polaroid camera; they immediately develop the shot, study and modify their lighting and exposure and then take the final photograph with their regular camera.

Motion Picture Sequence

Occasionally, a truly impressive presentation is needed to show the design of an important project to a large group of backers or to the voting public. Archetype Film, Inc. makes motion pictures of models on 16 mm color film or on black and white, silent or sound film. Their camera photographs the model through an original 2' long $\frac{7}{8}$" diameter lens system that may be placed inside the model, to traverse its streets or even its interior spaces. The results are truly unbelievable. The design shown by even rough, small-size models comes alive as the lens travels through the model at a scale eye level or takes a simulated helicopter trip above and around the building. The continuing changes of vista, evolving spaces and volumes, produces a presentation that can be obtained through no other media. The camera (25-8) is directed and

25-8/25-9

USE OF THE SNORKEL CAMERA TECHNIQUE FOR FILMING MODELS.

Illustration 25-8 shows the Snorkel and part of the motion picture and TV cameras.
Illustration 25-9 is a print made from the 16 mm motion picture taken of the model.

focused with the aid of a closed circuit television hook-up; the entire apparatus can be manipulated by a joy stick that raises, lowers, tilts and laterally moves the lens as the picture is being filmed. The result is great clarity, steady movement and a depth of field from 5" to infinity. Filming must be done at Archetype's studios at Princeton, New Jersey, since the camera, which incidentally was inspired by architect Vincent Kling, is quite unpor-

table. Cost runs from about $500 per minute for silent color film to about $1500 per minute for sound.

PHOTO DRAWING

Sometimes it is necessary to draw on a photo print. On presentation pictures, it may be desirable to combine techniques and render part of a project, while other parts are presented through the model photo; or it may be useful to add titles or dimension to the photograph. In some cases, working drawings have been made of refineries by taking photos of the detailed design model and adding dimensions and notes to the prints. It has been found that in the design of complex piping, this media is more easily understood than conventional drawings.

Lettering and simple drawing may be accomplished through the following techniques:
White lines may be made on a print by applying a bleach solution with a ruling or drawing pen. The solution may be concocted from potassium iodide (2 ounces), iodine (90 grams), gum arabic (90 grains) and water (8 ounces), or white ink may be used on mat prints. Black lines may be made on mat prints with black India ink.

If an entire part of a print must be obliterated, so that the area can be rendered completely, Bourges Cotocolor may be mounted on it and this area drawn on or rendered with pencil, ink or watercolor. The resulting modified print can then be photocopied and a supply of prints made from the resulting negative.

It is also possible to ink directly on the back of the negative, though this is not recommended because of the likelihood of failure. A safer procedure is to tape a sheet of acetate that is treated to take ink to the negative and to do pen work on that. Both negative and sheet may then be printed together in the enlarger.

Extensive photo drawing is done by some refinery designers via the following steps: (1) They photograph the model. (2) The image is projected through a magenta contact screen and is contact printed on a high contrast film (such as Kodak Kodalith ortho type 3 estar base, or Dupont C.O.S.). This results in halftone or a screen positive which is necessary if the model has been constructed of materials that have more than 2 colors, or if it is desirable to have its shadows show on the print. The screen brings about tone separation through its use of black dots on a white background or white dots on a black background. (3) The halftone is positioned over a positive showing the border lines and title block of the drawing and the sandwich is printed on a sheet of autopositive mat film. Other processes can also be used; the following one is simple and of use to the architect and designer: (1) Photograph the model (which should be painted with flat lacquers or paints to prevent undesirable highlights). Use Royal Pan film and illuminate the model from all sides by diffused light. Avoid overhead lights, since they cause deep shadows. (2) Develop the negative and make a Kodalith film at the desired scale. (3) Draw on the film with pencil or ink. Parts of the photo image may be removed with standard drafting room eradicators. (4) Make diazzo, blue-line or black-line prints of the results. The size of Kodalith film limits the drawing to a $24 \times 36''$ maximum.

APPENDIX A

TYPES OF CUTS AND JOINTS

TYPES OF CUTS

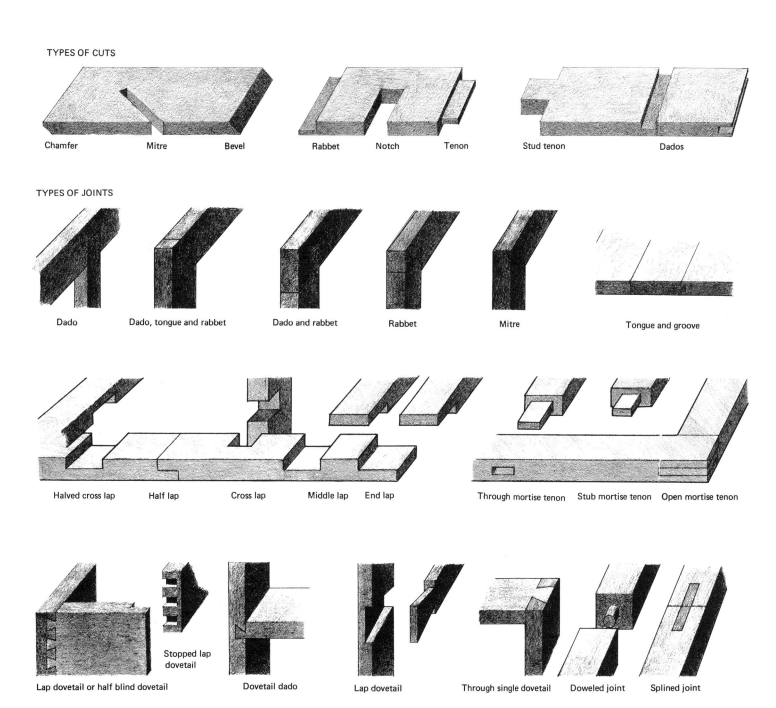

Chamfer   Mitre   Bevel

Rabbet   Notch   Tenon

Stud tenon   Dados

TYPES OF JOINTS

Dado   Dado, tongue and rabbet   Dado and rabbet   Rabbet   Mitre   Tongue and groove

Halved cross lap   Half lap   Cross lap   Middle lap   End lap   Through mortise tenon   Stub mortise tenon   Open mortise tenon

Lap dovetail or half blind dovetail   Stopped lap dovetail   Dovetail dado   Lap dovetail   Through single dovetail   Doweled joint   Splined joint

APPENDIX B: Suppliers

Below is a list of the suppliers of materials and tools which have been mentioned in the book. Most of them are listed with their addresses. Those that do not have addresses either cannot efficiently process small orders by mail, or manufacture items that are widely available in normal retail outlets. The page numbers refer to pages where the manufacturer's products are listed or described. Italicized numbers indicate mention within an illustration.

Since these companies experience normal business attrition, this list will become less useful as the years pass unless you keep it up to date. If, in the text, you read of a product that interests you and you desire to get additional information about it by sending for the manufacturer's catalog, send 25¢ in stamps with your request. Many companies charge this price for their brochure; those that do not will refund your money or ask for an additional quarter or so.

A. C. Gilbert. P. 189

Adco-Mold, 631 15th Street, Denver 2, Colorado. P. 85

Airfix Kits, purchasable from Associated Hobby Manufacturers, Inc. Pp. 144, *145*, 149, 150

Alexander Scale Models, 28 Ionia Avenue S.W., Grand Rapids, Michigan. Pp. 121, 129

All Nations, purchasable from Model Railroad Equipment Corporation. Pp. 50, *126*, *127*

Ambroid Company, Inc., 305 Franklin Street, Boston 10, Massachusetts. Pp. 36, 37, 67, 92

American Art Clay Company, 4717 West 16th Street, Indianapolis 24, Indiana. Pp. 70, 94

American Cyanamid Company, Building Products Division, 111 West 50th Street, New York, New York. P. 184

American Edelstaal, 350 Broadway, New York, New York. P. 33

American Flyer, P. 189

American Molding Powder and Chemical. P. 67

American Tool and Machine Company, Royersford 82, Pennsylvania. Pp. 29, 31, 32

American Viscose. P. 63

America's Hobby Center, 146 West 22nd Street, New York, N.Y. 10011. Pp. 53, 54, 55, 56, 58

Amron Products, P.O. Box 219, Ingleside, Texas 78362. Pp. 136, 138

A.M.T. Corporation, 1225 East Mable Road, Troy, Michigan. Pp. 67, 68, 94, 149

Angopias. Pp. *147*, 148, 149, 150, 151

Anderson, Arvid L., P.O. Box 392, Frederic, Wisconsin 54837. Pp. 67, *130*, 131, 133

Applied Graphics Corporation, Glenwood Landing, Long Island, New York. Pp. 46, 128

Applied Research Corporation, 2609 West 12th Street, P.O. Box 1316, Erie, Pennsylvania. P. 157

Archetype Film, Inc., 625 West 42nd Street, New York, New York. P. 198

Arco Tool, Inc., 421 West 203rd Street, New York, New York 10034. Pp. 23, 25, *28*, 28, 37, 75, 76

Aristo Craft Distinctive Miniatures, 184 Pennsylvania Avenue, Newark 2, New Jersey. Pp. 50, *126*, *127*, 144, 145, *145*, *147*, 148, *151*, 151, 152, 167, 185, 187, 188, *189*

Armstrong Tile. P. 160

Art Brown and Brothers Inc. P. 41

Artype, Inc., 345 East Terra Cotta Avenue, Crystal Lake, Illinois. Pp. 46, 50, 75, 99, *101*, 101, 154

Asbestos Supply Co. of Washington. P. 98

Associated Hobby Manufacturers, Inc., 3200 Boudinot Street, Philadelphia 34, Pennsylvania. Pp. 139, 145, *147*, 148, 149, 150

Atlas Tool Company, 378 Florence Avenue, Hillside, New Jersey. Pp. 92, 144, *145*, 148, 151, 152

Aurora Plastics Corporation, 44 Cherry Valley Road, West Hempstead, New York. Pp. 139, 148, 149, 150

Austin-Craft, P. 36

Austin, Weber, 416 Broad Street, Salamanca, New York

Babco, 60-10 Maurice Avenue, Maspeth, Long Island, New York. P. 28

Bachmann Brothers, Inc., 1400–1438 East Erie Avenue, Philadelphia 24, Pennsylvania. Pp. *137*, 139

Badger Airbrush Company, 9201 Gage Avenue, Franklin Park, Illinois 60131. P. 92

Bainbridge. P. 41

Barge. P. 37

Basset-Lowke Ltd., 18–25 Kingswell Street, Northampton, England. P. 144

Behlen, H. and Brother, Inc., 10 Christopher Street, New York, New York 10014. Pp. 94, 95

Benjamin Electric Co. P. 126

Bernz-O-Matic, Otto Bernz Company, Inc., Rochester, New York. P. 60

Best-Test. P. 37

Bestwall. P. 71, 86

B and H Products, 5710 1/2 West Diversey, Chicago, Illinois 60639. Pp. *130*, 133

Bienfang Paper Company, Inc., P.O. Box 408, Metuchen, New Jersey. Pp. 41, 66

Binks Manufacturing Company, 3114–44 Carroll Avenue, Chicago, Illinois 60612. P. 92

Birk Super Jet, manufactured by The Birk Manufacturing Company, Niantic 3, Connecticut. P. 60

The Black & Decker Manufacturing Company, Towson, Maryland 21204. P. 31

Bliss, James and Company Inc., 342 Atlantic Avenue, Boston, Massachusetts 02210. Pp. 56, 56

Blixt Soldering Iron, Imported by Roger-Crosbee Company, Dept. 52, 1810 Rowland Street, Riverton, New Jersey. P. 59

Blue-Zip. Pp. 46, 50, *126*, *127*

B. M. W., 329 Haydons Road, Wimbledon S.W.19, England

Boucher. P. 151

Bourges Color Corporation, 80 5th Avenue, New York, New York 10011. Pp. 46, 66, 135, 161, 193, 195, 199

Britain's Models, purchasable from Beatties of London. Britain's Models are made by Britain's Ltd., 186 King's Cross Road, London W.C.1, England. Pp. *137*, 139, 140, 145, 150

British Industries Corporation, 80 Shore Road, Port Washington, New York

Brouner, Fred, Corporation, 120 East 23rd Street, New York, New York 10010

Busch and Company Modelle, Luisen Strasse 10, Viernheim, West Germany. Pp. 151, 152

Butler. P. 41

Caco Biege-Püppchen. Pp. 144, 145

Camino Scale Models, Company, P.O. Box 155, Carmichael, California. Pp. 52, 54, 55, *127*

Carborundum Company, 300 Kuller Road, Clifton New Jersey. Pp. 17, 23, *28*, 28

Casco, manufactured by the Borden Chemical Company, Department T, 350 Madison Avenue, New York, New York. Pp. 37, 98, 131, 141

The Castolite Company, Woodstock, Illinois. Pp. 79, 81, 86

Celanese Corp. P. 66

Celastic, nationally distributed by Ben Walters, Inc. Pp. 77, 78, 80, 98, 99

Cello-Tak Manufacturing, Inc., 35 Alabama Avenue, Island Park, Long Island, New York 11558. Pp. 46, 99, 101

Cerro De Paso Corp. P. 88

Champion Decal Company, Box 1178, Minot, North Dakota

Channellock, Inc., Meadville, Pennsylvania. P. 18

Chart-Pak, Inc., 1 River Road, Leeds, Massachusetts. Pp. 46, 49, 99, 101, 128, 140

Chestnut Hill Studio, Box 38, Churchville, New York 14428. P. 157

Christoph Products Company, Guthrie & Hayes Circle, P.O. Box 306, Clarksville, Tennessee. Pp. *120*, *151*, 151, 152, 153, *153*, *157*, *167*

Clark, Joe, 30 Bartlett at Woodward, Detroit 3, Michigan

Clark, K. A., 5 Bryn Coed Road, Rhyl, Flints, North Wales, England. P. 144

Cloder Corporation, 49–51 Ann Street, New York, New York

Coating Products, 101 West Forest Avenue, Englewood, New Jersey

Colortron Urethane Foam, purchasable from S. Kagan Associates, Room 4405, Empire State Building, New York, New York 10001. P. 159

Columbia Vise and Manufacturing Company, Cleveland, Ohio. P. 17

Comet. Pp. 36, 68

Commercial Plastics and Supply Corp., 630 Broadway, New York, New York plus 8 other cities in the United States and Canada. Pp. 53, 56, 66, 67

Comp-Tool, Inc., 349 Prospect Road, Ashtabula, Ohio. P. 29

Con-Cor Models, 1254 No. Mayfield Avenue, Chicago, Illinois 60651. Pp. 54, 55

Contak, purchasable from Chart-Pak, Inc., Leeds, Massachusetts. Pp. 46, 50

Corgi Toys, purchasable from Reeves International, Inc., 1107 Broadway, New York, New York 10010. Pp. *147*, 149, 150

Cousino Audio Announcers, distributed by Audio Visual Services, 60 East 42nd Street, New York, New York. P. 189

The Craftint Manufacturing Company, 18501 Euclid Avenue, Cleveland 12, Ohio. Pp. 41, 46, 99, 101, 128

Craftone. Pp. 46, 159

Craftsman Wood Service Company, 2727 S. Mary Street, Chicago 8, Illinois. Pp. *17*, 17, 18, 126

Craftype. Pp. 101, 128

Creative Playthings, Princeton, New Jersey 08540. P. 18

Crescent, purchasable from Polks Hobby Store, New York City. P. 41

Crystal Craft, 4350 North Whipple, Chicago, Illinois. Pp. 79, 80, 81, 86

Magazines of interest to the Modelbuilder:
Professional Model Builder. Published bimonthly. Box 389, New Kingston, Pennsylvania 17072.
Model Railroader Magazine. Published monthly by the Kalmbach Publishing Company, 1027 North 7th Street, Milwaukee, Wisconsin 53233

Associations in the field:
Professional Model Builders' Association, Box 389, New Kingston, Pennsylvania 17072

Index

Note: Before actually beginning the construction of any object, it is suggested that the model-maker refer to all the relevant headings in the Index. For example, for information on constructing a plastic automobile, consult not only the pages listed for *vehicles* but also those for *plastics; models, solid;* and related topics such as *traffic*. The Index has been made as concise as possible so that the reader can skim it quickly when searching for relevant headings. Italicized references indicate illustrations.